ANOINT US IN YOUR COVENANT, ABBA-EMMANUEL

PHASE THREE FORMATION PROGRAM

by Michael Fonseca, D.Min.

© God's Embrace Renewal Centers, LTD. 2015
1601 High Hill Road
Schulenburg, TX 78956

No Claim to original U.S. Government words

Printed in the United States of America

International Standard Book Number 978-1514297490

Printed and bound by CreateSpace

Note on Websites: The publisher has used its best endeavors to insure that the URLs for external website referred to in this book are correct and active at the time is or will remain appropriate.

Cover: Basilica of St. Adalbert, Grand Rapids, MI

ANOINT US IN YOUR COVENANT, ABBA-EMMANUEL

PHASE THREE FORMATION PROGRAM

by Michael Fonseca, D.Min.

TABLE OF CONTENTS

PART ONE

PART TWO

ACKNOWLEDGEMENTS

It is with deep gratitude and appreciation that I acknowledge the gift of *God's Embrace Renewal Centers,* both as ministry and covenant community of Christian disciples.

I acknowledge as well, the Holy Spirit's transforming power and presence in our midst, as we seek to bring renewal to our beloved Catholic Church, especially at the parish and diocesan level.

I acknowledge with anticipation the participation of future Christian seekers in *God's Embrace Renewal Centers,* and pray that they will surrender wholeheartedly to the transforming action of the Holy Spirit in their lives!

I acknowledge with special gratitude Cherrie, my wife, whose constant encouragement and vision has put its stamp on the whole program, including this manual *Anoint Us in Your Covenant, Abba-Emmanuel.*

We have arrived at the end of a momentous milestone with the completion of this manual of the Third Phase. Over two years we have completed *'Lead Me into the Deep, Lord'* and *'Instruct Me in Your Ways, Lord'* of the First Phase, *'Mold Me as Your Disciple, Lord'* and *'Hallow Me as Your Disciple, Lord'* of the Second Phase, and *'Anoint Us in Your Covenant, Abba-Emmanuel'* of the Third Phase. Only the Holy Spirit could have made such an accomplishment possible. It has been a labor of much love and even greater trust in the Holy Spirit.

I have been greatly helped and encouraged by the covenant family of God's Embrace. I acknowledge the very significant role our Board of Directors has played in establishing God's Embrace on a firm foundation, and its continued commitment to the ministry. I acknowledge the important role the facilitators have played in strengthening the Program. I thank the staff of God's Embrace, especially Kristin Barnhill who has brought every manuscript into print. Once again I thank Cherrie, my wife, for her encouragement, support, and patience throughout this process which at times was arduous for her.

And in a very special way I wish to acknowledge my deepest gratitude to Ralph and Linda Schmidt for their encouragement, financial support, and unfailing commitment to us and our ministry. They have remained steadfast in their love and support from the very beginning. Cherrie and I are deeply grateful and ask the Lord to bestow His choicest blessings upon them and their family.

It is our hope that many others will come forward to support God's Embrace as we seek ardently the renewal of our beloved Catholic Church.

Finally, my prayer is for all our participants in our Three Phase Formation Program. At every stage of their formation, may they imbibe deeply the guidance and direction of the Holy Spirit in their lives, and experience the varied blessings of covenant living with our Triune God.

May *"Anoint Us in Your Covenant, Abba-Emmanuel"* stir many hearts toward a deeper commitment to our Lord and Savior, Jesus Christ! May our Triune God be praised now and forever!

INTRODUCTORY REMARKS

With *'Anoint Us in Your Covenant, Abba-Emmanuel,'* we begin the Third Phase of our Formation Program in God's Embrace Renewal Centers. So far we have covered much ground in our formation in Christian discipleship. We began with *'Lead Me into the Deep, Lord,'* which started us out on an amazing journey with the Holy Trinity over twelve weeks. Its purpose was to give you a good head start by making it easy to enter into a personal and intimate relationship with Jesus, who then would bring you to the Father through His Holy Spirit. We believed that if you gave the suggestions in the manual an honest effort, your discipleship would move into deeper waters, taking you away from the shore, and teaching you to trust the power and assurance of the Holy Spirit. He would then become the Keeper and Comforter of your soul. Hence, our first manual was titled *'Lead Me into the Deep, Lord.'* *'Instruct Me in Your Ways, Lord,'* was the sequel to *'Lead Me into the Deep, Lord.'* Through it we attempted to become familiar with the Old Testament, without which our understanding of Jesus and the New Testament would be jeopardized. Hence, most of the topics drew extensively, though not exclusively, from the Old Testament. The major focus throughout the first year was to get a proper understanding of who God really is from His revelation of Himself. An accompanying focus was to understand who we truly are in God's eyes, so that we will live our lives in the appropriate context of a covenant relationship with God. Through prayer and reflection, we trusted that the Holy Spirit would make right any skewed understanding we might have had of God and ourselves.

In the Second Phase of the Program, the overarching vision was Christian Discipleship. We began by making *'The Spiritual Exercises of St. Ignatius'* over twenty four weeks, using *'Mold Me as Your Disciple, Lord,'* as the accompanying manual to it. We saw that *'The Spiritual Exercises of St. Ignatius'* were undoubtedly an excellent tool of formation in discipleship. They have stood the test of time over five centuries and can be summed up in one sentence: *perfect freedom to serve God and His people selflessly.* No other vision or agenda can hold up against this world-view of discipleship. The disciple now makes sense of Christ's values and embraces them wholeheartedly. In such a joyous and wholehearted commitment lies perfect freedom.

'Hallow Me as Your Disciple, Lord,' was a follow-up to the Ignatian retreat. It built upon the participant's profound retreat experience by focusing on the discipleship of eight New Testament (Covenant) saints who lived out their discipleship in total obedience to the Father's will. Their example of wholehearted discipleship can be a source of much encouragement and strength as we seek to emulate them to enter more deeply into covenant union with our Lord Jesus Christ, our Way to the Father and the Holy Spirit.

The purpose of the First Two Phases was to build a solid foundation for our discipleship. The manuals built upon one another, leading the participant, slowly but surely, to surrender to the voluntary imposition of love that they placed upon their hearts: to make a complete offering of their lives to Jesus in response to His sacrificial love for them through His death on the cross. The titles of the manuals emphasized the development of this very personal and intimate covenant relationship between Jesus and His disciple, leading into covenant union with our Triune God. The development in discipleship was both progressive and intensive: from *Lead* to *Instruct* to *Mold* to *Hallow*. And the focus was always the participant's transformation. During this intensive spiritual journey the awareness began to dawn upon the participant that Jesus has become one with His covenant family. He is the Bridegroom and the Church is His bride. He is the Head and we are His body. While we can distinguish Jesus from us, we cannot separate ourselves from Him. This is what Jesus made clear to Saul: *"Saul, Saul, why are you persecuting me?"* (Acts 9:4) Jesus became sin so that we might become God's righteousness. (2 Corinthians 5:21) Hence, entering into covenant union with the Trinity through Jesus also means loving, serving, and laying down one's life for God's covenant family.

The focus then in the Third Phase of our Formation will be to explore this intimate and unbreakable bond between our Triune God and His covenant family. Our Triune God is quintessentially Emmanuel, God dwelling in the midst of and within His covenant family: *"I heard a loud voice from the throne saying, "Behold, God's dwelling is with the human race. He will dwell with them and they will be his people and God himself will always be with them [as their God]."* (Revelation 21:3) We celebrate God's Life and Presence within His covenant family: *"Do this in memory of me."* (Luke 22:19) We participate in God's divine life through the sacramental life of God's covenant family. There are amazing ramifications of this covenant bond between God and His covenant family that has been sealed through the blood of Jesus. During this year we will take to heart God's immense love for us as manifested in the way He has established His covenant family. And we will explore our identity as God's covenant family.

The manual for the Third Phase is *'Anoint Us in Your Covenant, Abba-Emmanuel.'* Every word of the title has special significance. The phrase *Anoint Us in Your Covenant* has special meaning as it relates very specifically to a covenant relationship with God. In the Old Testament, God set aside two categories of people to rule and serve His people as His worthy representatives. They were the kings and priests. When God established the monarchy in Israel, Samuel anointed Saul as the kingdom's first king: *"Then, from a flask he had with him, Samuel poured oil on Saul's head and kissed him, saying: "The LORD anoints you ruler over his people Israel. You are the one who will govern the LORD's people and save them from the power of their enemies all around them."* (1Samuel 10:1) Similarly the priests were set aside to serve God and His people in the covenant relationship established on Mount Sinai: *"Then take the anointing oil and pour it on his head, and anoint him. Bring forward his sons also and clothe them with the tunics, gird them with the sashes, and tie the skullcaps on them. Thus shall the priesthood be theirs by a perpetual statute, and thus shall you install Aaron and his sons."* (Exodus 29:7-9) There is one instance where God asks the prophet Elijah to anoint his successor: *"You shall also anoint Jehu, son of Nimshi, as king of*

Israel, and Elisha, son of Shaphat of Abel-meholah, as prophet to succeed you." (1 Kings 19:16)

In the New Testament three words are used, related to anointing: *"chrisma"* (ointment); *"Cristos"* (Christ or the Anointed One); and *"chrio"* (to anoint). Jesus was God's Anointed One or Messiah which means the Anointed One in Hebrew. Jesus was priest, prophet, and king, set apart to bring about the salvation of the world through His death on the cross. In Baptism, we are signed with the oil of the Catechumens on the chest, through which we are strengthened in preparation to be cleansed of original sin and to receive a share in God's divine life. The oil of Catechumens implies that we are still under the influence of the Evil One prior to baptism. After our baptism we were then anointed with the Chrism oil on the crown of our heads. Besides Baptism, Chrism (ointment scented with balsam) oil is used especially in the sacraments of Confirmation and Holy Orders through which the recipients share in the priesthood of Christ. Through our baptism we are already sharing in the priesthood of Christ. We have been set apart for God to be in covenant relationship with Him.

While we are anointed individually in the sacraments, the reality is that they make us members of God's covenant family. Undoubtedly, our discipleship will always be a personal acceptance of Jesus' invitation to come and follow Him. However, it will always be expressed and deepened within the context of God's covenant family. Jesus is the Head and we are His body. He is the Bridegroom, we are His bride. Hence the emphasis will always be on serving God in and through His covenant family. We are brought into covenant with our Triune God through Jesus, and have become His covenant family.

The names for God, *Abba* and *Emmanuel*, were deliberately chosen to convey the indescribable gift of covenant union that God has shared with us. Now that we participate in the divine nature (2 Peter 1:4), we have become sons and daughters of God. Jesus has shared with us all the blessings and privileges of His filial relationship with His Father. With Jesus we now call God, Our Father. God as *Abba* conveys this intimate covenant bond that has been established with us through His Son, Jesus. *Emmanuel* is another name for God that communicates God's passionate desire to dwell among and in us, to share His love and life with us, to celebrate His presence in our midst, to be the Father of His covenant family. As *Emmanuel*, God has expressed this unbreakable bond between Himself, the Original, and us, His image and likeness, by bringing us into covenant union with Him.

As in *'Hallow Me as Your Disciple, Lord,'* after your prayer sessions you will continue to answer the same three questions on a daily basis and a fourth question at the end of each week to help you express the grace or fruit of your prayer. You are already familiar with these four questions through your journaling. **Because of its bulk, we decided not to provide you with journal lines in the manual. You will have to come up with your own journal for the Third Phase.** Similarly, as with the other manuals, in *'Anoint Us in Your Covenant, Abba-Emmanuel,'* you will continue to do your set prayers at the beginning of each day, after which you will do your *MORNING*

FACE TO FACE WITH GOD from the manual. Each week you will also be offered Spiritual Reading as has been the practice in the program. Along with the material presented in the manual, you will read from the Old Testament, the New Testament, the Imitation of Christ, and the Catechism of the Catholic Church.

As for the structure of each week, on Day One you will ponder and pray on a reflection about the topic that is the focus of the session. On Day Seven, you will be offered topics on the Spiritual Life pertaining to advancing discipleship. These topics are spelled out in greater detail in Part II of the manual. You are encouraged to familiarize yourself with this valuable wisdom handed down to us by our saints. On Days Two through Five you will pray on Scripture passages pertinent to the theme of covenant life in question. On Day Six you will do a repetition of Days Two through Five. There will be exceptions, however, especially when you do the four Sessions on the Eucharist. As you have found out, Repetition is a simplified form of prayer that focuses on tasting and relishing the truth that has been pondered previously.

You will continue to have two sessions each month, every two weeks. If you cannot participate in a session, you will have the opportunity to do the session at home, via a video presentation or through our website. We will continue to use the same format for each program session, beginning with an Overview and brief instructions to help you proceed with Session One: Establishing God's Covenant Family, on your own. Two weeks later, at the second Program session you will watch a video presentation on Session One on which you have already prayed in the previous two weeks. After the presentation there will be a brief discussion on what God was saying to you as you watched the DVD. After the break, the participants will share from their journal notes that they kept during the previous two weeks. Designated facilitators will conduct the meeting and present the format to follow for the sharing. During each Program session, the facilitator will do a recap of each week of the session. The same procedure will be followed for all fifteen sessions.

All the Scripture passages have been taken from the New American Bible Revised Edition (NABRE). We continue to follow St. Ignatius of Loyola's suggestion that repetition is an important tool in the formation of disciples. Whenever appropriate, therefore, the author has used previously introduced material in the other manuals to enhance the participant's formation in discipleship.

PART ONE:

SESSION ONE
ESTABLISHING GOD'S COVENANT FAMILY

"A prophet like me will the LORD, your God, raise up for you from among your own kindred; that is the one to whom you shall listen. This is exactly what you requested of the LORD, your God, at Horeb on the day of the assembly, when you said, 'Let me not again hear the voice of the LORD, my God, nor see this great fire any more, or I will die.' And the LORD said to me, 'What they have said is good. I will raise up for them a prophet like you from among their kindred, and will put my words into the mouth of the prophet; the prophet shall tell them all that I command. Anyone who will not listen to my words which the prophet speaks in my name, I myself will hold accountable for it."

– Deuteronomy 18:15-19

JOURNEYING TOWARD THE AGE OF FULFILLMENT:

The Old Testament could be viewed as a period of waiting and preparation for the final age in which the Father would speak to us through His Son, Jesus Christ, as the Letter to the Hebrews 1:1-2 tells us: *"In times past, God spoke in partial and various ways to our ancestors through the prophets; in these last days, he spoke to us through a son, whom he made heir of all things and through whom he created the universe."* In times past, that is, in the Old Testament, God spoke through the prophets in varied and fragmentary ways. Through these varied and partial ways, God gave us hints of the age of Jesus, when the reign of God would be in our midst, when God would be Emmanuel, God-with-us, when the Father through His Son, would bring His plan of salvation to fulfillment. This inexorable process leading to Christ has been described by the Catholic Catechism as being in a state of journeying.

In Genesis 3, we see that God's glorious plan of salvation, envisaged for us as being created in God's image and likeness so that we might live in covenant relationship with our Creator, is interfered with through the sin of rebellion, resulting in covenant break-up. God takes immediate action, as the imminent and permanent break-up between the Original and His image is unbearable for God. In creating us in the divine image and likeness, God made this bond between Him and humans unbreakable. God, therefore, makes the first messianic prediction: *"I will put enmity between you and the woman, and between your offspring and hers; they will strike at your head, while you strike at their heel."* (Genesis 3:15) Christian tradition has seen in this passage more than unending hostility between the devil, identified as the serpent, and human beings. The devil's eventual defeat is implied in this verse, as 1 John 3:8 states that *"the Son of God was revealed to destroy the works of the devil."* In his letter to the Colossians, Paul frames it in more positive terms: *"For in him all the fullness was pleased to dwell, and through him to reconcile all things for him, making peace by the blood of his cross [through him], whether those on earth or those in heaven."* (Colossians 1:19-20) Genesis 3:15 has also been understood as the first promise of a redeemer for fallen humankind, the first Good News. Several Fathers of the Church interpreted the verse as referring to Christ and quoted Galatians 4:4: *"But when the fullness of time had come, God sent his Son, born of a woman, born under the law, to ransom those under the law, so that we might receive adoption."*

Some writers have described God's decision to create humans in the divine image and likeness as amounting to marriage through a covenant-bond, as through this indescribable act of Fatherly Love, God decided to establish a human covenant family for Himself. God's first covenant household was Noah and his family. Through Noah's descendant Abraham, God established a tribal covenant family through the twelve sons of his grandson, Jacob, whose name was changed to Israel. When God rescued His covenant family out of Egypt, a land of slavery and tribulation, He established His covenant family as a nation. In the Promised Land, this covenant family became a kingdom under the Davidic dynasty. Finally, through David's seed, Jesus, son of David and Son of God, established once and for all God's world-wide or Catholic covenant family comprising all peoples and all nations.

THE UNFOLDING POINTING TO JESUS:

In the Book of Exodus, the people are afraid of God's majesty and glory. God's presence, as manifested in the cloud over Mount Sinai, is too much for them. In their anxiety they plead with Moses to make sure that God does not speak to them directly but rather through him: *"Now as all the people witnessed the thunder and lightning, the blast of the shofar and the mountain smoking, they became afraid and trembled. So they took up a position farther away and said to Moses, "You speak to us, and we will listen; but do not let God speak to us, or we shall die."* (Exodus 20:19) And in Deuteronomy 18, as Moses is outlining the job description of the prophet when God's people enter the Promised Land, he makes an interesting prediction: *"A prophet like me will the LORD, your God, raise up for you from among your own kindred; that is the one to whom you shall listen. This is exactly what you requested of the LORD, your God, at Horeb on the day of the assembly, when you said, "Let me not hear again the voice of the LORD, my God, nor see this great fire any more, or I will die."* (Deuteronomy 18:15-16)

In the New Testament, this passage came to be understood in a Messianic sense. In John 6:14, after witnessing the multiplication of loaves and fishes by Jesus, the people exclaim, *"This is truly the Prophet, the one who is to come into the world,"* referring to Deuteronomy 18:15-16. In Acts 3:22-23, Peter explicitly identifies Jesus as the Messiah/prophet and cites this same passage from Deuteronomy. *"For Moses said: 'A prophet like me, will the Lord, your God, raise up for you from among your own kinsmen; to him you shall listen in all that he may say to you. Everyone who does not listen to that prophet will be cut off from the people."* It is not mere coincidence, then, that Moses and Elijah were present with Jesus at His Transfiguration to witness the fulfillment of the prediction that God had made through Moses many centuries ago in the desert. They did their witnessing by focusing on the forthcoming Exodus in Jerusalem that would institute the new and everlasting covenant (prophesied in Jeremiah 31:31-34) through Jesus' sacrifice on the cross.

In the prophets there is repeated reference to the Messiah who will redeem Israel. This longing for a Messiah got intensified during the reign of the kings when Israel forsook their covenant with God and inflicted upon themselves trials and tribulations that led to two prominent exiles. Isaiah 9:5-6 talks about the Messiah who will sit upon David's throne and bring much joy and jubilation to Israel: *"For a child is born to us, a son is given to us; upon his shoulder dominion rests. They name him Wonder-Counselor, God-Hero, Father-Forever, Prince of Peace. His dominion is vast and forever peaceful, upon David's throne, and over his kingdom, which he confirms and sustains by judgment and justice, both now and forever."* And the prophet Micah states that salvation will come through a "messiah," an anointed ruler. God will deliver Israel through a king in the line of David. *"But you, Bethlehem-Ephrathah* (home of the Davidic line), *least among the clans of Judah, from you shall come forth for me one who is to be ruler in Israel; whose origin is from of old, from ancient times. Therefore the Lord will give them up, until the time when she who is to give birth has borne, then the rest of his kindred shall return to the children of Israel."* (Micah 5:1-2) For us who have the advantage of knowing the New Testament, and can therefore appreciate the Old Testament in light of the New, these oracles from Isaiah and Micah clearly point to Jesus who will be the Messiah.

JESUS AS MESSIAH AND SON OF GOD:

Jesus referred to Himself as the Messiah. Mark begins his gospel account by describing Jesus Christ as the Son of God: *"The beginning of the gospel of Jesus Christ the Son of God."* (Mark 1:1) At His baptism, the Father in His encomium, proclaims Jesus as His beloved Son in whom He is well pleased: *"You are my beloved Son; with you I am well pleased."* (Mark 1:11) In Mark 1:15 Jesus begins His ministry by proclaiming that the kingdom of heaven is at hand, obviously through Him as Messiah. In Matthew 12:28, Jesus makes it very clear that the reign of God has already begun to be present through Him: *"But if it is by the Spirit of God that I drive out demons, then the kingdom of God has come upon you."*

John the Baptist was the last of the prophets. With John, the New Testament draws the curtain on the Old Testament prophets, thus beginning a new era in Jesus. The Synoptic Gospels tell us that Jesus began His ministry only after John the Baptist was arrested: *"After John had been arrested, Jesus came to Galilee proclaiming the gospel of God."* (Mark 1:14) The prophets were God's messengers, speaking in God's name, warning and exhorting God's covenant people to repentance and return to God. None of them ever pointed to themselves as the Messiah, especially John the Baptist. The people and the Jewish leadership were so impressed with John the Baptist that they were willing to believe that indeed he might be the Messiah. *"When the Jews from Jerusalem sent priests and Levites [to him] to ask him, "Who are you?" he admitted and did not deny it, but admitted, "I am not the Messiah."* (John 1:19-20)

The prophets also prophesied that the Messiah would come and redeem Israel. Micah's prophecy was mentioned a few paragraphs earlier. This is what Micah 5:3 says: *"He (the Messiah) shall take his place as shepherd by the strength of the LORD, by the majestic name of the LORD, his God; and they shall dwell securely, for now his greatness shall reach to the ends of the earth."* Jesus did have the majestic name of the LORD, as His name means, God is Salvation, or God saves. In fulfillment of these prophecies, Jesus points to Himself as being the Messiah. And His disciples, following upon His Resurrection, had no doubts that Jesus was both Messiah and the Son of God! They addressed Him as Lord!

On several occasions Jesus referred to Himself as fulfilling the Old Testament. In Matthew 5:17, Jesus says: *"Do not think that I have come to abolish the law or the prophets. I have come not to abolish but to fulfill."* Luke was writing for the educated Hellenists (Greek-speaking Jews) and Gentiles of his day. He singled out Second Isaiah (chapters 40 through 55) as his guide to the meaning of Christ's suffering and exaltation. In the two places (Luke 3:3-5 and 4:18-19) where he cites the Old Testament at any length, Luke 4:18-19, for instance, refers to the first Suffering Servant oracle in Isaiah 42, and refers specifically to verses 6-7: *"I, the LORD, have called you for justice, I have grasped you by the hand; I formed you, and set you as a covenant for the people, a light for the nations, to open the eyes of the blind, to bring out prisoners from confinement, and from the dungeon, those who live in darkness."*

Luke is no exception, therefore, to the general proposition that the evangelists, building upon the foundation of the earliest preaching in the primitive Church, have seen in the theme of the Suffering Servant an important key to unlocking the mystery of His redeeming death and resurrection. At all the great moments of His public life – baptism, transfiguration, three predictions of His passion, and the Last Supper – Jesus presented Himself as the Suffering Servant, obediently accepting His vocation to die for the salvation of all humans. It was true that this was a stumbling block at first to the apostles themselves, and later on, when they preached Jesus to the Jews; but it was a stumbling block which had been fashioned centuries before in their own sacred writings. *"He was spurned and avoided by men, a man of suffering, knowing pain, like one from whom you turn your face, spurned, and we held him in no esteem… Seized and condemned, he was taken away. Who would have thought any more of his destiny? For he was cut off from the land of the living, struck for the sins of his people. He was given a grave among the wicked, a burial place with evildoers, though he had done no wrong, nor was deceit found in his mouth."* (Isaiah 53:3; 8-9) To reject Him because He had suffered would mean that the Jews were renouncing their own history, as well as the testimony of one of their greatest prophets. It was this prophetic tone which echoes in Peter's second public discourse to the men of Israel after the Descent of the Holy Spirit: *"The God of Abraham, [the God] of Isaac, and [the God] of*

Jacob, the God of our ancestors, has glorified his servant Jesus whom you handed over and denied in Pilate's presence, when he had decided to release him. You denied the Holy and Righteous One and asked that a murderer be released to you. The author of life you put of death, but God raised him from the dead; of this we are witnesses." (Acts 3:13-15)

Through His miracles, Jesus made it clear that He had the power to forgive sins as only God can. Furthermore, in the first century the prevalent theological opinion saw a causal connection between sin and being diseased. If Jesus then were healing anybody of their disease, He did indeed have the power to forgive sin. In Mark 2:1-12, Jesus first forgives the sins of the Paralytic, and to demonstrate that He is God, and therefore has the power to forgive sins, He cures the man of his paralysis. *"But that you may know that the Son of Man has authority to forgive sins on earth – he said to the paralytic, "I say to you, rise, pick up your mat, and go home."* Jesus also made it clear that He had authority over the winds, sea, and storm, as only God has. In Mark 4:35-41, He silences the wind and the sea by simply saying, *"Quiet! Be still!"* The reaction of His disciples suggests that they are in the presence of the Divine: *"They were filled with great awe and said to one another, "Who then is this whom even wind and sea obey?"*

It is in the Transfiguration that Jesus makes it very clear as to what God's purposes are for His Son, on our behalf. The Transfiguration suggests that God's magnanimous plan of salvation, begun with the act of creating humans in His divine image and likeness, and then establishing His human covenant family through Noah, Abraham, Moses, and David, is now being brought to fulfillment in Jesus. Luke reports the Transfiguration immediately after Jesus' first prediction of His passion, death, and resurrection. The Transfiguration therefore, provides the heavenly confirmation to Jesus' declaration that His suffering will end in glory. In Luke 9:32, we are told that Peter and his companions were overcome by sleep, but becoming fully awake, they saw Jesus' glory, and Moses and Elijah standing with Him. The glory that is proper to God is here attributed to Jesus to make it clear that Jesus is indeed divine and the Son of God. Moses led his people out of the land of slavery through a mighty Exodus that led through the desert into the Promised Land. Jesus will now embark on an even mightier Exodus that will bring God's covenant family once and for all into God's Heavenly Sanctuary not made by hand: *"And behold, two men were conversing with him, Moses and Elijah, who appeared in glory and spoke of his exodus that he was going to accomplish in Jerusalem."* (Luke 9:30-31) The Father brings the event to a resounding finale when from the cloud came His voice, *"This is my chosen Son; listen to him."* (Luke 9:35) Luke identifies the subject of the conversation as the exodus of Jesus, a reference to the death, resurrection, and ascension of Jesus that will take place in Jerusalem, the city of destiny. Like the heavenly voice that identified Jesus at His baptism prior to His undertaking the Galilean ministry, so too here, before the journey to Jerusalem, the city of destiny, is begun, the heavenly voice again identifies Jesus as God's Son. The Father asks us to listen *to him (his Son)*: the two representatives of the Israel of old depart. They have fulfilled their mission of preparing for the establishment of the new and everlasting covenant in Jesus.

Jesus is left alone as the teacher whose words must be heeded now, as He establishes the New Israel, or God's Catholic (from *katholikos* in Greek, meaning world-wide) Covenant Family.

THE CELEBRATION OF THE EXODUS/COVENANT IN JESUS' TIME:

In the time of Jesus, the rabbis had the same understanding of the Exodus event as did Moses and his people. They saw each annual celebration of the Passover as a way of participating in the first Exodus. The Passover was not just a sacrifice; it was also a *"memorial"* or *"remembrance"* (Exodus 12:14) by which the Jewish people would both remember and somehow make present for themselves the deliverance that had been won for their ancestors in the Exodus from Egypt. This is how the Mishnah, Pesahim 10:5 interprets Exodus 13:8: *"In every generation a man must so regard himself as if he came forth himself out of Egypt, for it is written…"It is because of what the Lord did for me when I came forth out of Egypt."* The Mishnah refers in a general way to the full tradition of the Oral Torah. The Mishnah was composed entirely in the land of Israel and all the Rabbis quoted there were active in the Holy Land. The main body of the Mishnah consists of teachings attributed to authorities from about the middle of the first century A.D., through to the second decade of the third century A.D.

The father of the family would gather his household together around a large table. He would offer a prayer of blessing over the first cup, known as the *Cup of Sanctification*, or the *Kiddush Cup*: *"Blessed are you, O lord our God, King of the universe, who creates the fruit of the vine."* (Mishnah, Berakoth 6:1) During the Offertory at Mass, the priest makes a similar blessing over the bread and wine. After the blessing, the food would be brought to the table and laid out before the father. There were four key dishes: several cakes of unleavened bread, a dish of bitter herbs, a bowl of sauce, known as *haroseth*, and the roasted lamb, which interestingly enough the *Mishnah* refers to as *"the body."* At this point, the father and his household would dip some of the bitter herbs in the *haroseth* sauce and eat them. This brought the opening rites to an end even though the meal had not yet begun.

The Second Cup known as the *Cup of Proclamation* or the *Haggadah Cup* would then be mixed with water. Before they drank of this cup, the father of the family would tell them their story of salvation when God brought them out of the land of Egypt to the Promised Land. All the participants were *"bound to give thanks"* for what God had done for them. Then they would sing Psalms 113-114 which praised the Lord for His goodness and thanked Him for saving Israel from Egypt (Mishnah, Pesahim 10:6). These two Psalms, along with Psalms 115-118, were known as the *Hallel* Psalms, Psalms of "praise," which would be sung over the course of the whole meal.

The third cup was called the *Cup of Blessing* or the *Berakah Cup*. Then the father would pronounce a blessing and the actual meal would begin. This is when the Passover lamb and unleavened bread would finally be eaten. There were probably three steps: First, a blessing was said over the unleavened bread: *"Blessed are you, Lord God, who bring forth bread from the earth."* (Mishnah, Berakoth 6:1) Second, the meal probably began with an aperitif consisting of a small morsel dipped in the bowl of haroseth sauce. Judas was present at the Last Supper until this point when he dipped into the dish and then went out to betray the Lord (John 13:26-27). Thirdly, after the appetizer, the main meal was begun and consisted of eating the unleavened bread and the flesh of the Passover lamb. At the end of the meal, the father would say another blessing over the third cup. When this cup was drunk, the third stage of the Passover supper was complete. At the end of the meal, Jesus took the (third) cup, gave it to His disciples, and pronounced the words of institution.

Then the concluding rites of the meal would commence. The remaining portion of the Hallel Psalms would be sung, Psalms 115-118. *"I will offer a sacrifice of praise and call on the name of the LORD."* (Psalm 116:17) After the singing of Psalm 118, the fourth cup of wine would be drunk. According to the Mishnah, it was forbidden to drink any wine *"between the third and fourth cups."* (Pesahim 10:7) This fourth cup was known as the *Cup of Praise* or the *Hallel Cup*. When it was drunk, the Passover meal was complete.

JESUS AND THE NEW PASSOVER:

Jerusalem is the city of destiny. From his ninth chapter forward, Luke shows Jesus as resolutely making His way to Jerusalem to accomplish His Father's plan of salvation: *"When the days for his being taken up were fulfilled, he resolutely determined to journey to Jerusalem."* (Luke 9:51) 'The days for his being taken up,' is like the reference to His exodus in Luke 9:31 that Moses and Elijah make. It is probably a reference to all the events (suffering, death, resurrection, ascension) of His last days in Jerusalem. And Jesus resolutely determined to accomplish our salvation through His sacrifice on the cross. And He did this in the context of the Passover feast.

Jesus began His journey to Calvary in the Upper Room where He instituted the Eucharist: the meal of eating His body and drinking His blood in anticipation of His bloody sacrifice on the cross. Jesus followed all the traditions of the Passover. He offered to God the "sacrifice of thanksgiving," what Greek-speaking Christians would call the "thanksgiving" (eucharistia). Jesus celebrated the Last Supper on Passover night: *"And the disciples did as Jesus had directed them, and they prepared the Passover."* (Matthew 26:19) And when the hour came, He sat at table, and the apostles with Him. And He said to them, *"I have earnestly desired to eat this Passover with you before I suffer."* (Luke 22:14-15) Secondly, Jesus and His disciples ate the Passover meal in Jerusalem. Only in Jerusalem could the Passover meal be celebrated, because only the priests could slaughter the lambs in the temple precincts. Thirdly, they celebrated the Passover meal at night, and drank wine at the Last Supper, which was required for keeping the Jewish Passover (Mishnah, Pesahim 10:1). Perhaps, most important of all, Jesus' act of explaining the meaning of the bread unquestionably points to the Passover. The Last Supper also ended with the singing of a "hymn" (Matthew 26:30; Mark 14:26). The mention of the hymn refers to Psalm 118, known as the "Great Hallel" Psalm, which in Jewish Tradition was sung toward the end of the Passover meal.

There were differences between the Last Supper and the traditional Passover meal. The focus was on the "new covenant" prophesied by Jeremiah rather than on the old covenant. Secondly, Jesus shifted the focus away from the body and blood of the Passover Lamb, of which there is no mention, and turned it toward His own body and blood. *"And he took a cup, and when he had given thanks he gave it to them, saying, "Drink of it, all of you; for this is my blood of the covenant, which is poured out for many for the forgiveness of sins."* (Matthew 26:27-28) In no uncertain terms Jesus is saying, "I am the new Passover Lamb of the new Exodus. This is the Passover of the Messiah, and I am the new sacrifice." Another sign that the Last Supper was a new Passover is Jesus' command for His actions to be repeated: *"Do this in remembrance of me."* (1 Corinthians 11:25) He was commanding His disciples to perpetuate this new Passover sacrifice in the future. Echoes of the new Passover Meal were offered by Jesus in His Discourse on the Bread of Life in John 6. The Passover Meal was a covenant meal. And especially so was the new Passover Meal instituted by Jesus. This aspect is brought out very forcefully in the Discourse on the Bread of Life, and John 6:57 speaks to this very clearly: *"Just as the living Father sent me and I have life because of the Father, so also the one who feeds on me will have life because of me."*

The sacrifice of the Passover Lamb was not completed by its death. It was completed by a meal, by *eating the flesh of the lamb* that had been slain. Therefore, if Jesus saw Himself as the new lamb that would be slain, then it makes sense that He would speak of His blood being poured out, and command the disciples to eat His flesh. For the first century Jew, when it came to the Passover, you did not only have to slaughter the lamb; you had *to eat the lamb*, in order to fulfill God's law, in order to be saved from death! As with the old Passover of the first exodus, so it is with the new Passover of the Messiah's new exodus. The main difference is that in the new Passover the lamb is a person, and the blood of redemption is the blood of the Messiah. *"The cup of blessing which we bless, is it not a communion in the blood of Christ? The bread which we break, is it not a communion in the body of Christ?"* (1 Corinthians 10:16)

Jesus did not end the Passover Meal in the traditional way. Traditionally, the meal was over when everybody took a sip from the fourth cup and the father of the household declared the end by saying, "It is finished." According to the account in Luke we know that Jesus and His disciples drank from the cup for the second and third time. So they must have drunk from the cup for the first time as well, though there is no mention of this. This is what Luke 22:17-20 states: *"Then he took a cup, gave thanks, and said, "Take this and share it among yourselves; for I tell you [that] from this time on I shall not drink of the fruit of the vine until the kingdom of God comes* (this was the second cup)." *Then he took the bread, said the blessing, broke it, and gave it to them, saying, "This is my body, which will be given for you; do this in memory of me." And likewise the cup after they had eaten, saying, "This cup is the new covenant in my blood, which will be shed for you* (this is the third cup)."

In stating that He would not drink of the fruit of the vine until that day when He would drink it anew in His Father's kingdom, Jesus gives us a hint of the fourth cup. The fourth cup will be postponed till the kingdom is fully established through His sacrifice on the cross. It was the Jewish custom of giving wine to the dying criminals as a palliative, before they were nailed to the cross. Both Matthew and Mark tell us that Jesus was offered wine mixed with myrrh, a palliative or anesthetic, before He was nailed to the cross. But He refused to drink of it, because the Passover Meal tradition forbade any drinking between the third and fourth cups: *"They offered him wine mingled with myrrh; but he did not take it."* (Mark 15:23) Finally, the moment for Jesus to enter into His Father's kingdom has arrived, when He can drink from the fourth cup and end His Passover Meal and Sacrifice: *"After this, aware that everything was now finished, in order that the scripture might be fulfilled, Jesus said, "I thirst." There was a vessel filled with common wine. So they put a sponge soaked in wine on a sprig of hyssop and put it up to his mouth. When Jesus had taken the wine, he said, "It is finished." And bowing his head, he handed over the spirit."* (John 19:28-30) The Passover Meal was begun in the Upper Room and it ended on the Cross when Jesus indicated that His sacrifice on our behalf was completed with the proclamation, "It is finished."

Through His passion, death, and resurrection (new Passover), we are now God's universal covenant family, enabled to address God as Abba, Father, in the same way Jesus does. Through Jesus' resurrection, we too will rise from the dead. Through Jesus' resurrection, Satan, sin, and permanent death have been conquered. Through Jesus we have the power over them in our own lives. Through the Lamb that was slain we have been made sons and daughters of the Living God! It is our destiny to participate in God's divine nature as 2 Peter 1:4 tells us: *"Through these (knowledge of Jesus who called us by His own glory and power), he has bestowed on us the precious and very great promises, so that through them you may come to share in the divine nature, after escaping from the corruption that is in the world because of evil desire."*

PRAYER AND REFLECTION ON ESTABLISHING GOD'S COVENANT FAMILY

WEEK ONE: *"AND BEHOLD, TWO MEN WERE CONVERSING WITH HIM, MOSES AND ELIJAH, WHO APPEARED IN GLORY AND SPOKE OF HIS EXODUS THAT HE WAS GOING TO ACCOMPLISH IN JERUSALEM."* *(LUKE 9:30-31)*

SPIRITUAL READING FOR THE WEEK:

- **Anoint Us in Your Covenant, Abba-Emmanuel:** Session One
- **Old Testament:** Two or Three Chapters daily
- **New Testament:** Two or Three Chapters daily
- **Imitation of Christ:** One chapter daily

DAY ONE: MORNING SESSION

MORNING PRAYER: Acts of Faith, Hope, Charity; Daily Offering

Morning Face to Face with God:

Begin with Prayer to the Holy Spirit

REFLECTIONS ON ESTABLISHING GOD'S COVENANT FAMILY:

(After pondering each bullet point, express your sentiments in a short prayer)

- The Old Testament could be viewed as a period of waiting and preparation for the final age in which the Father would speak to us through His Son, Jesus Christ. In the Old Testament, God spoke through the prophets in varied and fragmentary ways.
- The prophets as God's messengers were in the unenviable position of doing God's bidding without knowing first-hand how God's oracles and promises would be fulfilled in the future. This inexorable process leading to Christ has been described by the Catholic Catechism as being in a state of journeying.
- In Genesis 3, we see that God's glorious plan of salvation, envisaged for us as being created in God's image and likeness so that we might live in covenant relationship with our Creator, is interfered with through the sin of rebellion, resulting in covenant break-up.

- God takes immediate action, as the imminent and permanent break-up between the Original and His image is unbearable for God. In creating us in the divine image and likeness, God made this bond between Him and humans unbreakable. God, therefore, makes the first messianic prediction, the first truly good news: *"I will put enmity between you and the woman, and between your offspring and hers; they will strike at your head, while you strike at their heel."* (Genesis 3:15)

- Christian tradition has seen in this passage more than unending hostility between the devil identified as the serpent, and human beings. The devil's eventual defeat is implied in this verse, as 1 John 3:8 states that *"the Son of God was revealed to destroy the works of the devil."*

- In his letter to the Colossians, Paul frames it in more positive terms: *"For in him all the fullness was pleased to dwell, and through him to reconcile all things for him, making peace by the blood of his cross [through him], whether those on earth or those in heaven."* (Colossians 1:19-20)

- Some writers have described God's decision to create humans in the divine image and likeness as amounting to marriage through a covenant-bond, as through this indescribable act of Fatherly Love, God decided to establish a human covenant family for Himself.

- God's first covenant household was Noah and his family. Through Noah's descendant Abraham, God established a tribal covenant family through the twelve sons of his grandson, Jacob whose name was changed to Israel.

- When God rescued His covenant family out of Egypt, a land of slavery and tribulation, He established His covenant family as a nation. In the Promised Land, this covenant family became a kingdom under the Davidic dynasty.

- Finally, through the seed of David, Jesus, son of David and Son of God, established once and for all God's world-wide or Catholic covenant family comprising all peoples and all nations.

- In the prophets there is repeated reference to the Messiah who will redeem Israel. This longing for a Messiah got intensified during the reign of the kings when Israel forsook their covenant with God and inflicted upon themselves trials and tribulations that led to two prominent exiles.

- Isaiah 9:5-6 talks about the Messiah who will sit upon David's throne and bring much joy and jubilation to Israel: *"For a child is born to us, a son is given to us; upon his shoulder dominion rests. They name him Wonder-Counselor, God-Hero, Father-Forever, Prince of Peace. His dominion is vast and forever peaceful, upon David's throne, and over his kingdom, which he confirms and sustains by judgment and justice, both now and forever."*

- For us who have the advantage of knowing the New Testament, and can therefore appreciate the Old Testament in light of the New, these oracles from Isaiah and Micah clearly point to Jesus who will be the Messiah.

What is God saying to you?

End with Prayer to the Holy Trinity

NIGHT SESSION: Examination of Conscience

For what are you grateful? For what are you contrite?

Please review briefly your Morning Prayer topic. Make it your last thought of the day

DAY TWO: MORNING SESSION

MORNING PRAYER: Act of Faith; Act of Hope; Act of Charity; Daily Offering

Morning Face to Face with God:

Begin with Prayer to the Holy Spirit

Prayer on Deuteronomy 18:17-19: Moses' quasi-messianic Prophecy of Jesus

"And the LORD said to me, What they have said is good. I will raise up for them a prophet like you from among their kindred, and will put my words into the mouth of the prophet; the prophet shall tell them all that I command. Anyone who will not listen to my words which the prophet speaks in my name, I myself will hold accountable for it."

Read the Reflection; ask our Triune God to fill you with deep gratitude and appreciation for being a member of God's covenant family:

Moses is addressing God's people on the topic of prophets. The Israelites are afraid of God speaking to them directly lest they die. They would prefer Moses speaking to them in God's name. It is in response to their wish that God then addresses Moses with the passage on which we are praying. Earlier in Deuteronomy 18:15, God had already revealed this prophecy to Moses: *"A prophet like me will the LORD, your God, raise up for you from among your own kindred; that is the one to whom you shall listen."* Jesus was this prophet about whom Moses was speaking in this passage. In John 6:14, the people identify Jesus as the prophet: *"When the people saw the sign he had done, they said, "This is truly the Prophet, the one who is to come into the world."* And in Acts 3:22, Peter identifies Jesus as the prophet about whom Moses had prophesied: *"For Moses said: 'A prophet like me will the Lord, your God, raise up for you from among your own kinsmen; to him you shall listen in all that he may say to you."* It is indeed amazing that God planned the establishment of His covenant family patiently, meticulously, and with amazing forethought into every divine action on our behalf!

What is God saying to you?

End with Prayer to the Holy Trinity

NIGHT SESSION: Examination of Conscience

For what are you grateful? For what are you contrite?

Please review briefly your Morning Prayer topic. Make it your last thought of the day

DAY THREE: MORNING SESSION

MORNING PRAYER: Act of Faith; Act of Hope; Act of Charity; Daily Offering

Morning Face to Face with God:

Begin with Prayer to the Holy Spirit
Prayer on Isaiah 9:1; 5-6: The Prince of Peace

> *"The people who walked in darkness have seen a great light; upon those who lived in a land of gloom a light has shone… For a child is born to us, a son is given to us; upon his shoulder dominion rests. They name him Wonder-Counselor, God-Hero, Father-Forever, Prince of Peace. His dominion is vast and forever peaceful, upon David's throne, and over his kingdom, which he confirms and sustains by judgment and justice, both now and forever!" [Please read Isaiah 9:1-6 for a better appreciation of the passage].*

Read the Reflection; ask our Triune God to fill you with deep gratitude and appreciation for being a member of God's covenant family:

We hear this passage read during the Christmas liturgy. God is offering His people a promise of salvation. We have seen the fulfillment of this prophecy in Jesus. Through Jesus, we have become children of the light: *"The people who walked in darkness have seen a great light; upon those who lived in a land of gloom a light has shone."* (verse 1) Reference is being made to the Assyrian exile which took place in 722 B.C. About 30 thousand Israelites were deported to Assyria from the northern regions of Galilee in the Northern Kingdom. Jesus began His ministry in the northern regions of Galilee. He is the great light that the people walking in darkness have seen. This transformation will be wrought, *"for a child is born to us, a son is given to us; upon his shoulder dominion rests."* (9:5) This verse speaks of a coronation as well, reminiscent of Jesus, the Risen Lord, on whose shoulder dominion rests. The theme of Jesus being the light of the world is especially highlighted in the gospel of John. The names given to the Messiah speak to the revelation of God as Trinity through Jesus: Wonder-Counselor (Holy Spirit), God-Hero (The Blessed Trinity's glorious plan of salvation), Father-Forever (knowing God as Abba the way Jesus knows), and Prince of Peace (Jesus who is Peace and gifts us with peace through His covenant oblation on the cross).

What is God saying to you?

End with Prayer to the Holy Trinity

NIGHT SESSION: Examination of Conscience

For what are you grateful? For what are you contrite?

Please review briefly your Morning Prayer topic. Make it your last thought of the day

DAY FOUR: MORNING SESSION

MORNING PRAYER: Act of Faith; Act of Hope; Act of Charity; Daily Offering

Morning Face to Face with God:

Begin with Prayer to the Holy Spirit
Prayer on Isaiah 49:5-6: The Second Servant-of-the-Lord Oracle
> *"For now the LORD has spoken who formed me as his servant from the womb, that Jacob may be brought back to him and Israel gathered to him; I am honored in the sight of the LORD, and my God is now my strength! It is too little, he says, for you to be my servant, to raise up the tribes of Jacob, and restore the survivors of Israel; I will make you a light to the nations, that my salvation may reach to the ends of the earth." [Please read Isaiah 49:1-7 for a better appreciation of the passage].*

Read the Reflection; ask our Triune God to fill you with deep gratitude and appreciation for being a member of God's covenant family:

The Second Suffering Servant Oracle speaks of a redeemer who from his conception has been designated by God for a special mission. In Luke 1:31 and 35, we are told that Mary will conceive in her womb and bear a son whose name will be Jesus. He will be great and will be called the Son of the Most High, and His conception will take place by the power of the Holy Spirit! In John 3:16, we are told about the special mission that God designated for Jesus: *"For God so loved the world that he gave his only Son, so that everyone who believes in him might not perish but might have eternal life."* However, what is most consoling in this oracle is the fact that salvation is universal, granted to Jew and non-Jew alike. This is clearly a paradigmatic shift in the understanding of covenant relationship with God: *"It is too light a thing that you should be my servant to raise up the tribes of Jacob and to restore the survivors of Israel; I will give you as a light to the nations, that my salvation may reach to the ends of the earth."* (Verse 6) Paul talks about this amazing gift or grace, given to Jews and Gentiles alike in Jesus: *"For I am not ashamed of the gospel. It is the power of God for the salvation of everyone who believes: for Jew first, and then Greek; as it is written, 'The one who is righteous by faith will live.'"* (Romans 1:16-17)

What is God saying to you?

End with Prayer to the Holy Trinity

NIGHT SESSION: Examination of Conscience

For what are you grateful? For what are you contrite?

Please review briefly your Morning Prayer topic. Make it your last thought of the day

DAY FIVE: MORNING SESSION

MORNING PRAYER: Act of Faith; Act of Hope; Act of Charity; Daily Offering

Morning Face to Face with God:

Begin with Prayer to the Holy Spirit
Prayer on Jeremiah 31:31-34: The New Covenant

> *"See, days are coming – oracle of the LORD – when I will make a new covenant with the house of Israel and the house of Judah. It will not be like the covenant I made with their ancestors the day I took them by the hand to lead them out of the land of Egypt. They broke my covenant, though I was their master – oracle of the LORD. But this is the covenant I will make with the house of Israel after those days – oracle of the LORD. I will place my law within them, and write it upon their hearts; I will be their God, and they shall be my people... Everyone, from least to greatest, shall know me – oracle of the LORD – for I will forgive their iniquity and no longer remember their sin."*

Read the Reflection; ask our Triune God to fill you with deep gratitude and appreciation for being a member of God's covenant family:

This theme of making a covenant with Israel is not a new one. In fact it is a common theme of the prophets, beginning with Hosea. According to Jeremiah, however, this covenant is different; it is new, and it has qualities that are different from the old one: One, it will not be broken as the old one was, and it will last forever; two, its law will be written in the heart, not merely on tablets of stone; three, the knowledge of God will be so generally shown forth in the life of the people that it will no longer be necessary to put it into words of instruction; four, all, from the least to the greatest, shall know God, for He will forgive their evildoing and remember their sin no more. This prophecy of the New Covenant was fulfilled through the life and work of Jesus Christ. Because of Jesus who is our High Priest, this covenant can never be broken. It will last forever, and it will be written in our hearts, because in Eucharist we receive the covenant personified in Jesus: *"This cup is the new covenant in my blood, which will be shed for you."* (Luke 22:20) Jesus is Emmanuel, God dwelling among us and within us! Through Him, forgiveness is universal, offered to all who accept Him as their Lord and Savior and repent of their sins.

What is God saying to you?

End with Prayer to the Holy Trinity

NIGHT SESSION: Examination of Conscience

For what are you grateful? For what are you contrite?

Please review briefly your Morning Prayer topic. Make it your last thought of the day

DAY SIX: MORNING SESSION

MORNING PRAYER: Act of Faith; Act of Hope; Act of Charity; Daily Offering

Morning Face to Face with God:

Begin with Prayer to the Holy Spirit
REPETITION OF DAYS TWO THROUGH FIVE:

Ask our Triune God to fill you with deep gratitude and appreciation for being a member of God's covenant family:

Today, you are doing a repetition of Days Two through Five of this week. In a repetition St. Ignatius says that *"we should pay attention to and dwell upon those points in which we have experienced greater consolation or desolation or greater spiritual appreciation."* (# 62) If you wish, you can do a triple colloquy: refer to #63 of the Spiritual Exercises.

What is God saying to you?

End with Prayer to the Holy Trinity

NIGHT SESSION: Examination of Conscience

For what are you grateful? For what are you contrite?

Please review briefly your Morning Prayer topic. Make it your last thought of the day

DAY SEVEN: MORNING SESSION

MORNING PRAYER: Act of Faith; Act of Hope; Act of Charity; Daily Offering

Morning Face to Face with God:

Begin with Prayer to the Holy Spirit

THE SPIRITUALITY OF THE DESERT:

(After pondering each bullet point, express your sentiments in a short prayer)   *one of the first crisis in the church*

- In the Fourth and Fifth Centuries, there was a mass movement into the deserts of the Middle East, especially Egypt, after the proclamation of the Edict of Milan in 313 A.D. by the Roman Emperors, Constantine and Licinius.

- After Christianity became the official religion of the Roman Empire through the Edict of Milan, it became acceptable and even respectable to be known as a Christian. The unfortunate consequence was a watering down of the practice of the faith. Consequently, a major transition began in the Church, leading to a blossoming of monasticism in the desert.

- The Spirituality of the Desert, especially in the Scetes desert of Egypt, emerged from an intense desire on the part of many Christians to live an authentic life of discipleship. In time they became known as the Desert Fathers and Mothers. The most well-known of these monks was St. Antony the Great who moved to the desert in AD 270-271. He is universally acknowledged as the father and founder of desert monasticism.

- St. Antony died in 356 AD. By then there were thousands of monks and nuns living in the desert. St. Athanasius of Alexandria, St. Antony's biographer, wrote that the "desert had become a city." The desert monasticism had a major influence on the development of Christian spirituality. And the informal gathering of hermits later on became the model for Christian monasticism.

- Three types of monasticism emerged in Egypt around the Desert Fathers and Mothers: The solitary hermit: St. Antony and his followers practiced this model in Lower Egypt. Then there were the cenobites: They were communities of monks and nuns in Upper Egypt, founded by St. Pachomius. The third model was a combination of the first two: They consisted of small groups of monks and nuns with a common spiritual elder, called an Abba or Amma. St. Amun was the founder of this model.

- Several such communities would come together in larger gatherings to worship on weekends. The Sayings of the Desert Fathers were compiled by these small communities of monks and nuns.

- In 270 AD, St. Antony heard a Sunday sermon stating that perfection could be achieved by selling one's possessions, distributing the proceeds to the poor, and following Christ (Matthew 19:21). St. Antony did just that, and took the step of moving deep into the desert to seek complete solitude.

- He soon realized that separating himself physically from material possessions did not necessarily ensure freedom from attachment to them. In the solitude of the desert,

St. Antony came to see that his mind and heart needed to be purified of inordinate tendencies. Indeed the mind was the chief battleground of the spiritual life.

- St. Antony viewed the solitude, austerity, and sacrifice of the desert as an alternative to martyrdom, considered as the highest form of perfection. This was especially true after the Edict of Milan, when dissipation and mediocrity had permeated the life of the Church.
- Life in the desert was a clear invitation to a life of simplicity, a separation from material goods, and focusing one's attention on refining and purifying the spirit.

What is God saying to you?

End with Prayer to the Holy Trinity

NIGHT SESSION: Examination of Conscience

For what are you grateful? For what are you contrite?

What prayer would you compose to express what God has said to you this week?

Please review briefly your Morning Prayer topic. Make it your last thought of the day

PRAYER AND REFLECTION ON ESTABLISHING GOD'S COVENANT FAMILY – CONTINUED

WEEK TWO: *"Then He took the bread, said the blessing, broke it, and gave it to them, saying, "This is my body, which will be given up for you; do this in memory of me." And likewise the cup after they had eaten, saying, "This cup is the new covenant in my blood, which will be shed for you." (Luke 22:19-20)*

SPIRITUAL READING FOR THE WEEK:

- **Anoint Us in Your Covenant, Abba-Emmanuel:** Session One
- **Old Testament:** Two or Three Chapters daily
- **New Testament:** Two or Three Chapters daily
- **Imitation of Christ:** One Chapter daily

DAY ONE: MORNING SESSION

MORNING PRAYER: Acts of Faith, Hope, Charity; Daily Offering

Morning Face to Face with God:

Begin with Prayer to the Holy Spirit

REFLECTIONS ON ESTABLISHING GOD'S COVENANT FAMILY:

(After pondering each bullet point, express your sentiments in a short prayer)

- Jesus referred to Himself as the Messiah. Mark begins his gospel account by describing Jesus Christ as the Son of God: *"The beginning of the gospel of Jesus Christ the Son of God."* (Mark 1:1)

- At His baptism, the Father in His encomium, proclaims Jesus as His beloved Son in whom He is well pleased: *"You are my beloved Son; with you I am well pleased."* (Mark 1:11)

- John the Baptist was the last of the prophets. The Synoptic Gospels tell us that Jesus began His ministry only after John the Baptist was arrested: *"After John had been arrested, Jesus came to Galilee proclaiming the gospel of God."* (Mark 1:14)

- The prophets were God's messengers, speaking in God's name, warning and exhorting God's covenant people to repentance and return to God. None of them ever pointed to themselves as the Messiah, especially John the Baptist: *"When the Jews from Jerusalem sent priests and Levites [to him] to ask him, "Who are you?" he admitted and did not deny it, but admitted, "I am not the Messiah."* (John 1:19-20)

- The prophets also prophesied that the Messiah would come and redeem Israel. This is what Micah 5:3 says: *"He (the Messiah) shall take his place as shepherd by the strength of the LORD, by the majestic name of the LORD, his God; and they shall dwell securely, for now his greatness shall reach to the ends of the earth."* Jesus did have the majestic name of the LORD, as His name means, God is Salvation, or Yahweh saves.

- In fulfillment of these prophecies, Jesus points to Himself as the Messiah. And His followers, following upon His Resurrection, had no doubts that Jesus was both Messiah and the Son of God! They addressed Him as Lord!

- At all the great moments of His public life – baptism, transfiguration, three predictions of His passion, and the Last Supper – Jesus presented Himself as the Suffering Servant, obediently accepting His vocation to die for the salvation of all men.

- Through His miracles, Jesus made it clear that He had the power to forgive sins as only God can. Furthermore, in the First Century the prevalent opinion saw a causal connection between sin and being diseased. If Jesus then were healing anybody of their disease, He did indeed have the power to forgive sin.

- Jesus also made it clear that He had authority over the winds, sea, and storm, as only God has. In Mark 4:35-41, He silences the wind and the sea by simply saying, *"Quiet! Be still!"* The reaction of His disciples suggests that they are in the presence of the Divine: *"They were filled with great awe and said to one another, "Who then is this whom even wind and sea obey?"*

- The Transfiguration suggests that God's magnanimous plan of salvation, begun with the act of creating humans in His divine image and likeness, and then establishing His human covenant family through Noah, Abraham, Moses, and David, is now being brought to fulfillment in Jesus.

- Luke reports the Transfiguration immediately after Jesus' first prediction of His passion, death, and resurrection. The Transfiguration therefore, provides the heavenly confirmation to Jesus' declaration that His suffering will end in glory.

- Moses led his people out of the land of slavery through a mighty Exodus that led through the desert into the Promised Land. Jesus will now embark on an even mightier Exodus that will bring God's covenant family once and for all into God's Heavenly Sanctuary not made by hand: *"And behold, two men were conversing with him, Moses and Elijah, who appeared in glory and spoke of his exodus that he was going to accomplish in Jerusalem."* (Luke 9:30-31) Indeed, Jesus' kingdom is not of this world!

- The Father brings the event to a resounding finale when from the cloud came His voice, *"This is my chosen Son; listen to him."* (Luke 9:35) Luke identifies the subject of the conversation as the exodus of Jesus, a reference to the death, resurrection, and ascension of Jesus that will take place in Jerusalem, the city of destiny.

- The Exodus from Egypt established the Mosaic Covenant. The New and Everlasting Covenant will be established by the Exodus of Jesus in Jerusalem. The Father asks us to listen *to him (His Son)*: the two representatives of the Israel of old depart. They have fulfilled their mission of preparing for the establishment of the new and everlasting covenant in Jesus.

- Jesus is left alone as the teacher whose words must be heeded now, as He establishes the New Israel, or God's Catholic (from *katholikos* in Greek, meaning world-wide) Covenant Family.

What is God saying to you?

End with Prayer to the Holy Trinity

NIGHT SESSION: Examination of Conscience

For what are you grateful? For what are you contrite?

Please review briefly your Morning Prayer topic. Make it your last thought of the day

DAY TWO: MORNING SESSION

MORNING PRAYER: Act of Faith; Act of Hope; Act of Charity; Daily Offering

Morning Face to Face with God:

Begin with Prayer to the Holy Spirit

Prayer on Micah 5:1-4: Restoration through the Messiah

"But you, Bethlehem-Ephrathah least among the clans of Judah, from you shall come forth for me one who is to be ruler in Israel; whose origin is from of old, from ancient times. Therefore the Lord will give them up, until the time when she who is to give birth has borne, then the rest of his kindred shall return to the children of Israel. He shall take his place as shepherd by the strength of the LORD, by the majestic name of the LORD, his God; and they shall dwell securely, for now his greatness shall reach to the ends of the earth: he shall be peace."

Read the Reflection; ask our Triune God to fill you with deep gratitude and appreciation for being a member of God's covenant family:

Like First Isaiah, chapters 1-39, the Book of Micah is focused on Jerusalem, Zion, and the Judean leadership. Like the other prophets, Micah is aware of the tradition that Zion or Jerusalem is the Lord's chosen place. Consequently, many thought that the city was impregnable. Micah is warning against that complacent view and is predicting the ruin of the city at the hands of the Babylonians (587 B.C.), and the exile of its people: *"Therefore the Lord will give them up, until the time when she who is to give birth has borne, then the rest of his kindred shall return to the children of Israel."* (Verse 2) Upon their return from exile, God will establish permanent peace through the messiah, *"whose origin is from old, from ancient times."* The gospel of John makes the same point about Jesus: *"In the beginning was the Word, and the Word was with God, and the Word was God."* (John 1:1) God will deliver Israel through a king in the line of David. Bethlehem-Ephrathah is the home of the Davidic line. The angel tells Mary that Jesus will be this king: *"You shall name him Jesus. He will be great and will be called Son of the Most High, and the Lord God will give him the throne of David his father, and he will rule over the house of Jacob forever, and of his kingdom there will be no end."* (Luke 1:31-33)

What is God saying to you?

End with Prayer to the Holy Trinity

NIGHT SESSION: Examination of Conscience

For what are you grateful? For what are you contrite?

Please review briefly your Morning Prayer topic. Make it your last thought of the day

DAY THREE: MORNING SESSION

MORNING PRAYER: Act of Faith; Act of Hope; Act of Charity; Daily Offering

Morning Face to Face with God:

Begin with Prayer to the Holy Spirit
Prayer on Isaiah 42:1-4: The First Servant-of-the-Lord-Oracle

> *"Here is my servant whom I uphold, my chosen one with whom I am pleased. Upon him I have put my spirit; he shall bring forth justice to the nations. He will not cry out, nor shout, nor make his voice heard in the street. A bruised reed he will not break, and a dimly burning wick he will not quench. He will faithfully bring forth justice. He will not grow dim or be bruised until he establishes justice on the earth; the coastlands will wait for his teaching." [Please read Isaiah 42:1-9 for a better appreciation of the passage].*

Read the Reflection; ask our Triune God to fill you with deep gratitude and appreciation for being a member of God's covenant family:

Only in Jesus Christ are the sweeping Servant-of-the-Lord oracles or prophecies fulfilled. The idea of saving the world through a humble, suffering servant rather than a glorious king is contrary to human thought. Based on the Davidic covenant found in 2 Samuel 7:1-29, religious Jews assumed that Israel would receive a political Messiah, a king who would deliver his people from their enemies and colonizers. The four oracles make it clear that the Messiah's strength would be shown in humility, suffering, and mercy. By His stripes we would be healed. He would suffer and die in our stead so that we could experience salvation from Him. In this First Oracle, Jesus is described as God's Chosen One who is filled with God's Spirit. God always initiates His mission. It is He who chooses the one He will send. The Father chose and sent His Son to bring forth justice to the nations through mercy and compassion: *"A bruised reed he will not break, and a dimly burning wick he will not quench; he will faithfully bring forth justice."* (Verses 3-4) While there is an extreme tenderness and gentleness in how the Suffering Servant will deal with His kinsfolk, He is also as durable and impregnable as flint: *"He will not grow dim or be bruised until he establishes justice on the earth."* (Verse 4)

What is God saying to you?

End with Prayer to the Holy Trinity

NIGHT SESSION: Examination of Conscience

For what are you grateful? For what are you contrite?

Please review briefly your Morning Prayer topic. Make it your last thought of the day

DAY FOUR: MORNING SESSION

MORNING PRAYER: Act of Faith; Act of Hope; Act of Charity; Daily Offering

Morning Face to Face with God:

Begin with Prayer to the Holy Spirit
Prayer on Luke 9:30-32: Jesus Transfigured

> *"And behold, two men were conversing with him, Moses and Elijah, who appeared in glory and spoke of his exodus that he was going to accomplish in Jerusalem. Peter and his companions had been overcome by sleep, but becoming fully awake, they saw his glory and the two men standing with him." [Please read Luke 9:28-36 for a better appreciation of the passage].*

Read the Reflection; ask our Triune God to fill you with deep gratitude and appreciation for being a member of God's covenant family:

The Transfiguration account follows on the first prediction of Jesus' death and resurrection, as if to give His disciples a preview of His victory over sin and Satan through His resurrection. The second and greater Exodus through Jesus will result in the establishment of the new and eternal covenant. The Transfiguration confirms that Jesus is the *Son of God* (Luke 9:35). It also points to the fulfillment of the prediction that *Jesus will come in his Father's glory* at the end of the age (Luke 9:26). Peter, James, and John are also taken apart from the others by Jesus, here and in Gethsemane as well (Matthew 26:37). Moses and Elijah are the two figures who represent the Old Testament Law and the Prophets. At the end of this episode, the heavenly voice identifies Jesus as the one to be listened to now. Jesus is the fulfillment of the Law and the Prophets. Moses and Elijah are in conversation with Jesus about His Exodus that He was going to accomplish in Jerusalem. This is a reference to the death, resurrection, and ascension of Jesus that will take place in Jerusalem, the city of destiny: *"When the days for his being taken up were fulfilled, he resolutely determined to journey to Jerusalem."* (Luke 9:51) The mention of exodus calls to mind the Israelite Exodus from Egypt to the Promised Land. What was begun in the first Exodus is brought to completion in the second Exodus! The Old Covenant is being replaced with the New and Eternal Covenant.

What is God saying to you?

End with Prayer to the Holy Trinity

NIGHT SESSION: Examination of Conscience

For what are you grateful? For what are you contrite?

Please review briefly your Morning Prayer topic. Make it your last thought of the day

DAY FIVE: MORNING SESSION

MORNING PRAYER: Act of Faith; Act of Hope; Act of Charity; Daily Offering

Morning Face to Face with God:

Begin with Prayer to the Holy Spirit

Prayer on Luke 22:15-16; 19-20: The Paschal Meal

> *"He said to them, "I have eagerly desired to eat this Passover with you before I suffer, for, I tell you, I shall not eat it [again] until there is fulfillment in the kingdom of God." ... Then he took the bread, said the blessing, broke it, and gave it to them, saying, "This is my body, which will be given for you; do this in memory of me." And likewise the cup after they had eaten, saying, "This cup is the new covenant in my blood, which will be shed for you." [Please read Luke 22:14-20 for a better appreciation of the passage].*

Read the Reflection; ask our Triune God to fill you with deep gratitude and appreciation for being a member of God's covenant family:

The Eucharist celebrates the Memorial of Jesus' sacrifice. The Memorial is the proclamation of the mighty works wrought by God for men. In the liturgical celebration of these events, they become present and real. This is how Israel understands its liberation from Egypt: Every time Passover is celebrated, the Exodus, which is an ever-living and salvific event, is made present and real among the believers. The participants experience in mystery this saving event in the same way as their ancestors did. In the New Testament, the *Memorial* takes on new meaning. In the Eucharist, the sacrifice Christ offered once for all on the cross remains everpresent and real in the Risen Lord. "As often as the sacrifice of the Cross by which 'Christ our Pasch has been sacrificed' is celebrated on the altar, the work of our redemption is carried out." (Lumen Gentium 3) The sacrificial character is revealed in the very words of institution: *"This is my body which is given for you"* and *"This cup which is poured out for you is the new covenant in my blood."* (Luke 22:19-20). The institution narrative is the only place where Jesus mentions the new covenant, from which the gospels and other books relating to Jesus are named the New Testament (Covenant).

What is God saying to you?

End with Prayer to the Holy Trinity

NIGHT SESSION: Examination of Conscience

For what are you grateful? For what are you contrite?

Please review briefly your Morning Prayer topic. Make it your last thought of the day

DAY SIX: MORNING SESSION

MORNING PRAYER: Act of Faith; Act of Hope; Act of Charity; Daily Offering

Morning Face to Face with God:

Begin with Prayer to the Holy Spirit
REPETITION OF DAYS TWO THROUGH FIVE:

Ask our Triune God to fill you with deep gratitude and appreciation for being a member of God's covenant family:

Today, you are doing a repetition of Days Two through Five of this week. In a repetition St. Ignatius says that "we should pay attention to and dwell upon those points in which we have experienced greater consolation or desolation or greater spiritual appreciation (# 62). If you wish, you can do a triple colloquy: refer to #63 of the Spiritual Exercises.

What is God saying to you?

End with Prayer to the Holy Trinity

NIGHT SESSION: Examination of Conscience

For what are you grateful? For what are you contrite?

Please review briefly your Morning Prayer topic. Make it your last thought of the day

DAY SEVEN: MORNING SESSION

MORNING PRAYER: Act of Faith; Act of Hope; Act of Charity; Daily Offering

Morning Face to Face with God:

Begin with Prayer to the Holy Spirit
THE SPIRITUALITY OF THE DESERT:

(After pondering each bullet point, express your sentiments in a short prayer)

- The life and example of St. Antony and the other hermits attracted many followers. They either lived alone or in small clusters. They were ascetics, renouncing a life of comfort and sense-pleasure. Instead they spent their days in prayer, singing psalms, fasting, giving alms to the needy, preserving love and harmony with one another, while keeping their thoughts and desires on God alone.

- They exerted an immense moral and spiritual influence on the Church. Many either joined them in the desert or sought their advice. By the time of St. Antony's death in 356 AD, there were about ten thousand Christians living in the desert.
- The first fully organized community of monks under St. Pachomius included men and women living in separate quarters. They supported themselves by weaving cloth and baskets, and doing other tasks.
- Each monk or nun had a three year probationary period, after which they gained full admittance into the community. All property was held in common, meals were eaten together and in silence. They fasted twice a week and wore simple peasant clothing with a hood. They spent time, together and alone, in prayer and spiritual reading, meditating on the scriptures.
- From the wisdom of the Desert Fathers and Mothers we learn that our souls too can be viewed as a desert: lonely, desolate, broken, and in need of water. The Desert Fathers and Mothers realized that their souls harbored the same distractions and turmoil that they had left behind in the towns and villages.
- They developed a different set of values in the desert: God is to be found in the silence of our hearts. Silence is arrived at through repentance, through the awareness that we are disordered and deceitful, and the realization that we can be saved only in surrender to Jesus.
- 'Desert' (eremos in the Greek) means 'abandonment.' 'Hermit' is derived from this Greek word. The spiritual life is about abandonment, surrender to God. In the physical desert out there, and in the desert of your soul, you face up to yourself, to your temptations and passions.
- You confront your heart as honestly and forthrightly as possible, without any preoccupation about what others will think and say about you. You reject all scapegoats, facing your demons squarely and honestly. Your sole objective is to know and do what God wants of you.
- While the desert is a place of quiet and silence, it is also the place where transformation is born and carried out. It is a place of confrontation, not withdrawal. It is a place of encounter where you will no longer be the same. The desert is where you move into repentance and stay in it permanently.
- In the desert, one does not withdraw from people. To live in the desert means to live for God.
- The hermit lived in a cell which symbolizes the soul. We can never escape from our soul, however much we might try to do so. We will find God first and foremost in our soul. Our spiritual progress will be reflective of the way we treat our soul. When we have become comfortable with God through repentance and forgiveness of sin, we will reflect God's goodness and joy.

- The desert teaches us that in the ultimate analysis, we have no control of much of life and our circumstances. What we do have is God's presence in our lives and His promise to be with us in all aspects of our lives. Through slow and arduous acceptance of self, we learn to be patient and loving, compassionate and forgiving, non-judgmental and humble.

What is God saying to you?

End with Prayer to the Holy Trinity

NIGHT SESSION: Examination of Conscience

For what are you grateful? For what are you contrite?

What prayer would you compose to express what God has said to you this week?

Please review briefly your Morning Prayer topic. Make it your last thought of the day

SESSION TWO
INCORPORATION INTO GOD'S TRINITARIAN LIFE

WHAT IS AT THE HEART OF SESSION TWO, WEEK THREE?

"I am a minister in accordance with God's stewardship given to me to bring to completion for you the word of God, the mystery hidden from ages and from generations past. But now it has been manifested to his holy ones, to whom God chose to make known the riches of the glory of this mystery among the Gentiles; it is Christ in you, the hope for glory. It is he whom we proclaim, admonishing everyone and teaching everyone with all wisdom, that we may present everyone perfect in Christ."

– Colossians 1:25-28

THAT MYSTERY NOW MANIFESTED TO HIS HOLY ONES:

The foundations of covenant union with God were laid from all eternity when our Triune God decided to create us in the divine image and likeness and be redeemed by Jesus, the Second Person of the Trinity and Incarnate Son of God the Father, so that we could share in the Triune God's divine nature. Paul talks about *"that mystery hidden from ages and generations past, but now manifested to his holy ones"* in Colossians 1:26. God has willed to make known to His holy ones the glory beyond price, the mystery of Christ in us, our hope of glory. The 'riches of the glory of this mystery,' has reverberations going as far back as God's glory being first revealed in the creation of the universe, especially in our creation as the Divinity's image and likeness. In the words of St. Gregory of Nyssa, our creation is a window into this 'riches of the glory of this mystery': "An image is not truly an image if it does not possess all the characteristics of its pattern… It is characteristic of divinity to be incomprehensible: this must also be true of the image. If the image could be essentially understood while the original remained incomprehensible, the image would not be an image at all. But our spiritual dimension, which is precisely that wherein we are the image of our Creator, is beyond our ability to explain… by this mystery within us we bear the imprint of the incomprehensible godhead." (On the Creation of Man, II (PG 44,155)

This 'riches of the glory of this mystery' is revealed in partial ways all through our history of salvation until it is revealed fully in Jesus Christ. God's glory was revealed at the Burning Bush, on Mount Sinai, on the face of Moses, to Isaiah in the Temple, in Jesus' teachings and miracles, in His Transfiguration, and most of all in His Resurrection. In His Resurrection, the Father glorified Jesus as the Son of God and Lord of the universe. The glory of the Resurrection was highlighted in the Risen Lord's repeated appearances to His disciples, and especially in the

Descent of His Holy Spirit upon His disciples! This 'riches of the glory of this mystery' is the visible manifestation of the holy and unsurpassable God in the person of Jesus Christ. In Jesus, the mystery of God has now been revealed. Jesus is Himself God, and the revelation both of the Father and the Holy Spirit. Jesus leads us into the Trinitarian Embrace, and He alone is our hope of glory and participation in the divine life.

GOD'S WISDOM REVEALED THROUGH THE HOLY SPIRIT:

In 1 Corinthians 2:6-16, Paul speaks to the Corinthians about this 'riches of the glory of this mystery' as 'God's wisdom' (1 Corinthians 2:7) which only the spiritually mature can understand. It is God's wisdom, mysterious and hidden, and planned before all ages for our glory. This wisdom can only be revealed to us through God's Holy Spirit. The Holy Spirit scrutinizes all matters, even the depths of God's being. No one knows what lies at the depths of God's being except the Holy Spirit. And the Holy Spirit reveals to us the depths of God's heart through the gifts He has given us. In Galatians 5:22-23, Paul tells us that the fruit or gifts of the Spirit are love, joy, peace, patience, kindness, generosity, faithfulness, gentleness, self-control. When we experience these gifts we receive an intimate appreciation of God's life, of the Trinitarian relationships and the meaning of being in a new and everlasting covenant with the Triune God who is Covenant itself.

Love being the first gift, 1 John 4:8-9 tells us that God is love: *"Whoever is without love does not know God, for God is love. In this way the love of God was revealed to us; God sent his only Son into the world so that we might have life through him."* We are heirs with Christ of God's eternal Life because of God's love for us. Joy and peace are innate gifts of the Risen Lord. They are the fruits of Jesus' victory over Satan, sin, and permanent death. They are offered to us as lasting signs of our insertion into God's divine life through Jesus: *"On the evening of that first day of the week, when the doors were locked, where the disciples were, for fear of the Jews, Jesus came and stood in this midst and said to them, "Peace be with you," When he had said this, he showed them his hands and his side. The disciples rejoiced when they saw the Lord. [Jesus] said to them again, "Peace be with you."* (John 20:19-21) The world does not know this peace and joy. Only Jesus can share His Peace and Joy with us who believe and have accepted Him as Lord and Savior. Jesus leads us to the Trinity who is the Source of divine life, and Jesus is both the Source and the Way to receive these Trinitarian gifts of peace and joy.

The Trinity shares with us their relational attributes that come so naturally to the Three Persons. As we enter more deeply into Trinitarian Life and put on the mind and heart of Jesus Christ, the Incarnate Son of God, we learn to become as the Trinity is in relationship to us. We learn to be patient and faithful as God throughout the history of human beings has been patient and faithful, both in His fidelity to the covenants and to us in our sin and rebellion.

Like God, under the tutelage of the Holy Spirit, we too learn to be kind and generous. Our gentleness (mildness in disposition) and self-control are a sharing in God's own transparency of spirit and fullness of light, brought about in us through our covenant relationship with the Triune God. It was always in God's plan of salvation that we would share in the divine nature as 2 Peter 1:4 tells us: *"Through these (God's own glory and power), he has bestowed on us the precious and very great promises, so that through them you may come to share in the divine nature, after escaping from the corruption that is in the world because of evil desire."*

JESUS, THE FULLNESS OF THE REVEALED MYSTERY:

In his Prologue, John 1:1 is at great pains to establish the believers' faith in Jesus as God: *"In the beginning was the Word; the Word was with God, and the Word was God."* John addresses Jesus as the Word of God who already existed at the beginning and therefore preceded time and creation. In the Old Testament the word of God is God's manifestation that is revealed in creation, in deeds of power and grace, and in prophecy, all of which could be summed up as Wisdom. John takes up all these strands when he addresses Jesus as the Word or Logos, and shows that Christ is the ultimate and total revelation of God.

Rabbinical Judaism glorified the Torah as divine wisdom and therefore as pre-existent with God before it was revealed. In John, Christ is the true Word of God existing with God. Through Jesus, the Word of God, and not through the Law or Torah, however, grace and truth originate. There is a similar thought in the Letter to the Hebrews 1:1-2: *"In times past, God spoke in partial and various ways to our ancestors through the prophets; in these last days, he spoke to us through a son, whom he made heir of all things and through whom he created the universe."* While the Word is divine, Jesus is not all of divinity. Jesus has been distinguished from another divine Person whom later on in the Gospel He calls His Father. The Letter to the Hebrews 1:3 continues in the same vein: *"Who (This Son) is the refulgence of his glory, the very imprint of his being, and who sustains all things by his mighty word."*

John continues to assert other dimensions of Jesus' divinity in the Prologue, 1:3-4: *"All things came to be through him, and without him nothing came to be. What came to be through him was life, and this life was the light of the human race."* Paul speaks in the same way in Colossians 1:16-17: *"For in him were created all things in heaven and on earth, the visible and the invisible, whether thrones or dominions or principalities or powers; all things were created through him and for him."* Neither John nor Paul calls Christ the Creator. 'Creator' is a title reserved in both the Old and New Testaments for the Father. Jesus, the Word, is the instrumental cause of creation. The Father mediates everything through the Son or the Word. This does not imply subordination but oneness in being. Similarly, throughout His life and ministry, Jesus did everything in the power of the Holy Spirit, beginning with the Holy Spirit coming upon Mary so that she would conceive Jesus in her womb, and being raised by the Father in the Spirit. Though they are distinct Persons in the Trinity, they always act in communion, in a movement of fellowship that is always Three in One and One in Three, based on having the same divine essence.

THE TRINITY ACTS IN COMMUNION IN DISTINCT ROLES:

We are all very familiar with John 3:16: *"For God so loved the world that he gave his only Son, so that everyone who believes in him might not perish but might have eternal life."* Jesus asserts categorically that the Father's love for us is so immeasurable and all-consuming that He gave us His only Son to be lifted up on the cross, that all who believe may have eternal life in Him. For this reason the Father willed that His Son would become one of us in John 1:14: *"And the Word became flesh and made his dwelling among us, and we saw his glory, the glory as of the Father's only Son, full of grace and truth."*

The ultimate manifestation of God's Word is to now become flesh. What an amazing paradox! Isaiah 40:6-8 says that *"All flesh is grass, and all their loyalty like the flower of the field. The grass withers, the flower wilts, when the breath of the LORD blows upon it." "Yes, the people is grass! The grass withers, the flower wilts, but the word of our God stands forever."* 'Flesh' is all that is passing, subject to death, imperfect, and at first glance, incompatible with God. This is the tremendous mystery of the incarnation, by which the eternal Word took on our exact human nature, becoming one with us in everything except sin as Hebrews 4:15 tells us; in everything, except what was incompatible with divinity. To express this mystery, John has deliberately chosen a word connoting man in his concrete, fallen state: sarx in the Greek, translated as flesh. And on several occasions the Father rejoices in His Son's identification with us in our sinfulness and brokenness (flesh), knowing fully well that in this identification lay our redemption and participation in the divine life! On the occasion of Jesus' baptism, on our behalf the Sinless One publicly identified Himself as sinner in need of repentance and forgiveness, *"A voice from heaven was heard to say: "You are my beloved Son; with you I am well pleased."* (Luke 3:22) There is the other intriguing passage found in Isaiah 53:10: *"But it was the LORD's will to crush him with pain."*

Just as the Father mediates everything through His Son, in the same way Jesus goes about fulfilling every step of His Father's plan of salvation in the power of the Holy Spirit. The angel Gabriel tells Mary in Luke 1:35: *"The holy Spirit will come upon you and the power of the Most High will overshadow you. Therefore the child to be born will be called holy, the Son of God."* At His Baptism, the Holy Spirit descended on Jesus in visible form like a dove. Luke 4:1-2 tells us that *"Filled with the holy Spirit, Jesus returned from the Jordan and was led by the Spirit into the desert for forty days to be tempted by the devil."* After His forty days in the desert, Jesus entered His public life and ministry in the power of the Spirit. Again and again in the gospels we are told that Jesus was moved by the Spirit when He worked miracles and did His teachings. Hebrews 9:14 tells us that Christ *"through the eternal spirit offered himself unblemished to God."*

His resurrection was the climax of His ministry and our entrance into God's life.

Just as Jesus acted in His Trinitarian relationships by carrying out His Father's wishes in every detail of the divine plan of salvation, and did everything in the power of His Holy Spirit, in the same way He made sure that we would live our lives in the power of the Holy Spirit who would re-create us in the image and likeness of Jesus, *"the image of the invisible God,"* so that like Him we too would be faithful to 'Our' common Father's will in every detail. Jesus made sure that we would receive the Holy Spirit from His Father: *"And I will ask the Father, and he will give you another Advocate to be with you always, the Spirit of truth, which the world cannot accept, because it neither sees nor knows it. But you know it, because it remains with you, and will be in you."* (John 14:16-17) And because the Holy Spirit acts in Trinitarian communion and harmony with the Father and Jesus, *"he will guide you to all truth. He will not speak on his own, but he will speak what he hears, and will declare to you the things that are coming. He will glorify me, because he will take from what is mine and declare it to you. Everything that the Father has is mine; for this reason I told you that he will take from what is mine and declare it to you."* (John 16:13-15)

INCORPORATION INTO TRINITARIAN LIFE:

Perhaps the two best passages in Paul's letters outlining our incorporation into Trinitarian Life are found in Ephesians 1:3-23 and Colossians 1:15-29. Let us begin our pondering of these eloquent and Spirit-revealed passages by taking to heart the prayerful advice Paul gives us in Ephesians 1:17-19: *"that the God of our Lord Jesus Christ, the Father of glory, may give you a spirit of wisdom and revelation resulting in knowledge of him. May the eyes of [your] hearts be enlightened, that you may know what is the hope that belongs to his call, what are the riches of glory in his inheritance among the holy ones, and what is the surpassing greatness of his power for us who believe, in accord with the exercise of his great might."* The profundity of this prayer is striking when we realize that our Mediator is Jesus. The Father of our Lord Jesus Christ is granting us a spirit of wisdom and insight to know Him clearly through the mediation of His Son. The reason for Jesus' death and resurrection was so that we could have *"a spirit of wisdom and revelation resulting in knowledge of him (the Father),"* as Jesus knows Him. We move towards this fuller knowledge of the Father every time we address Him as 'Father,' sharing in the filial relationship of Jesus toward His and now Our Father.

Paul makes it very clear that this knowledge of His Father is given to us by Jesus through the revelation of the Holy Spirit who scrutinizes all matters, even the depths of God (I Corinthians 2:10). The Father wishes us to share in the glorious heritage that is His in Trinitarian Life, and ours as members of the Church, God's covenant family. And the Father has absolutely no doubt in bringing this about, because *"[it is] in accord with the exercise of his great might, which he worked in Christ, raising him from the dead and seating him at his right hand in the heavens, far above every principality, authority, power, and dominion, and every name that is named not only in this age but also in the one to come."* (Ephesians 1:20-21) And now Paul makes a stunning assertion of the Father's power to transform, and His amazing love to share, when he describes us as the fullness of Christ because Jesus is the head and we are His body, incorporated into His divine life: *"He (the Father) has put all things beneath his feet and gave him as head over all things to the church, which is his body, the fullness of the one who fills all things in every way."* (Ephesians 1:22-23) Indeed, the Father will stop at nothing to incorporate us into His Trinitarian Life through His Son Jesus, and in the power of His Holy Spirit!

Jesus, then, is our Way, Truth, and Life! It is through Him that we are incorporated into the Life of the Trinity. Our discipleship is the witness to this explicit flowering of divine life in us as God's covenant family who are indwelt by the Father, Son, and Holy Spirit. We are now the branches, inextricably linked to the Vine and living abundantly the divine life which courses through Jesus who indwells us. Jesus has been raised from the dead and is seated at the right hand of the Father, as Son and Second Person of the Trinity, as well as Savior-Intercessor because He is the 'Lamb that was slain' for us.

Once again it behooves us to return to Paul's description of who Jesus is through His Resurrection: *"He is the image of the invisible God, the first-born of all creation… He is the head of the body, the church. He is the beginning, the firstborn from the dead, that in all things he himself might be preeminent. For in him all the fullness was pleased to dwell, and through him to reconcile all things for him, making peace by the blood of his cross [through him], whether those on earth or those in heaven."* (Colossians 1:15; 18-20) No wonder, then, that the Father proclaims uninterruptedly His sublime encomium of his Son: *"This is my beloved Son in whom I am well pleased!"*

Reflecting now on Ephesians 1:3-10, Paul tells us how we are incorporated into Trinitarian Life so that we now abide within the inner circle of the Trinity, participating in their Perichoresis or divine dance. As on other occasions, Paul singles out the Father's largesse and generosity toward us through His Son, Jesus Christ, and exclaims an ardent prayer of praise and indescribable gratitude: *"Blessed be the God and Father of our Lord Jesus Christ, who has blessed us in Christ with every spiritual blessing in the heavens!"* (Ephesians 1:3) At first glance, Paul seems to be indulging in gross hyperbole when he talks about God bestowing upon us every spiritual blessing in the heavens! But then he goes about outlining in great detail what these blessings are and it becomes clear that indeed he is not exaggerating but only emphasizing God's boundless generosity and largesse towards us! Here is Paul's list of blessings found in the text:

"God chose us in him before the foundation of the world." (Ephesians 1:4): God's plan to incorporate us into His divine Life was made from all eternity. It was deliberate, well thought out, and totally committed to, as opposed to being happenstance, accidental, and a mid-course correction.

"To be holy and without blemish before him." (Ephesians 1:4): To be holy is to be 'totally other than.' Only God is holy or 'totally other than' by nature and essence. Our holiness is the Holy Spirit's gift to us whereby we share in God's holiness. The Father's passionate desire is to transform us so that we will know ourselves as God's image and likeness, as God always intended for us to be. We will be made blameless through forgiveness of our sins and being washed white in the blood of Christ. Romans 5:8-9 tells us that *"God proves his love for us in that while we were still sinners Christ died for us. How much more then, since we are now justified by his blood, will we be saved through him from the wrath."* As a result of our holiness and blamelessness, we will be made like Christ, unblemished victims of sacrifice on behalf of the body of Christ (the people we serve) who is its head.

"In love he destined us for adoption to himself through Jesus Christ, in accord with the favor of his will, for the praise of the glory of his grace that he granted us in the beloved." (Ephesians 1:5): There is rare mention of God being addressed as Father in the Old Testament: *"For you are our Father. Were Abraham not to know us, nor Israel to acknowledge us, You, LORD, are our father, our redeemer you are named from of old."* (Isaiah 63:16) On some occasions God expressed the wish to be addressed as Father. However, had they addressed God by His name, they would have laid claim to having a personal and privileged relationship with God. The Hebrews had such a profound reverence for God that they would address Him only through pseudonyms. Even though God had revealed to Moses His name, God's people would never use it directly in addressing God, or even indirectly in making reference to Him. In the New Testament, however, Jesus asks us to address His Father as 'Our Father' when He taught His disciples how to pray. Jesus wanted us to share in the same filial relationship that He has with His Father, wanting us to claim His Father as our very own. And through His ultimate sacrifice on the cross for the forgiveness of sins, we are now adopted sons and daughters of the Living and Almighty God. Our adoption highlights the fact that God would not tolerate our permanent alienation from Him through sin, and would, instead, sweep us into His divine Embrace through His Son. We have been restored to our God-given dignity as sons and daughters of Jesus' Father in Heaven. With Jesus we now claim God as Our Father.

"In him (Christ) we have redemption by his blood, the forgiveness of transgressions, in accord with the riches of his grace that he lavished upon us." (Ephesians 1:7): Jesus redeemed or bought back our freedom from slavery to sin and alienation from God. He did this by swapping places with us, bearing the ignominy of Satan, sin, and death so that we might enjoy His freedom and salvation. The Letter to the Hebrews 10:10, 12, 14, sums it up well: *"By this "will," we have been consecrated through the offering of the body of Jesus Christ once for all…But this one offered one sacrifice for sins, and took his seat forever at the right hand of God… For by one offering he has made perfect forever those who are being consecrated."*

"In all wisdom and insight, he has made known to us the mystery of his will in accord with his favor that he set forth in him as a plan for the fullness of times, to sum up all things in Christ, in heaven

and on earth." (Ephesians 1:9-10): Jesus tells us in John 14:26, that this wisdom to understand fully the mystery, the plan that God was pleased to decree in Christ, will be given to us by the Holy Spirit: *"The Advocate, the holy Spirit that the Father will send in my name – he will teach you everything and remind you of all that [I] told you."* Only in acknowledging Jesus as Lord of heaven and earth, and Savior of the world, which grace is given to us by the Holy Spirit, can we participate in God's divine life!

PRAYER AND REFLECTION ON INCORPORATION INTO GOD'S TRINITARIAN LIFE

WEEK THREE: *"Blessed be the God and Father of our Lord Jesus Christ, who has blessed us in Christ with every spiritual blessing in the heavens, as He chose us in Him, before the foundation of the world, to be holy and without blemish before Him."* *(Ephesians 1:3-4)*

SPIRITUAL READING FOR THE WEEK:

- **Anoint Us in Your Covenant, Abba-Emmanuel:** Session Two
- **Old Testament:** Two or Three Chapters daily
- **New Testament:** Two or Three Chapters daily
- **Imitation of Christ:** One chapter daily

DAY ONE: MORNING SESSION

MORNING PRAYER: Acts of Faith, Hope, Charity; Daily Offering

Morning Face to Face with God:

Begin with Prayer to the Holy Spirit

REFLECTIONS ON INCORPORATION INTO GOD'S TRINITARIAN LIFE:

(After pondering each bullet point, express your sentiments in a short prayer)

- The foundations of covenant union with God were laid from all eternity when our Triune God decided to create us in the divine image and likeness and we were redeemed by Jesus, the Second Person of the Trinity and Incarnate Son of God the Father, so that we could share in the Triune God's divine nature.

- We are all very familiar with John 3:16: *"For God so loved the world that he gave his only Son, so that everyone who believes in him might not perish but might have eternal life."* Jesus asserts categorically that the Father's love for us is so immeasurable and all-consuming that He gave us His only Son to be lifted up on the cross, that all who believe may have eternal life in Him.

- For this reason the Father willed that His Son would become one of us in John 1:14: *"And the Word became flesh and made his dwelling among us, and we saw his glory, the glory as of the Father's only Son, full of grace and truth."*

- The ultimate manifestation of God's Word is to now become flesh. This is the tremendous mystery of the incarnation, by which the eternal Word took on our exact human nature, becoming one with us in everything except sin as Hebrews 4:15 tells us; in everything, except what was incompatible with divinity.

- On the occasion of Jesus' baptism, on our behalf the Sinless One publicly identified Himself as sinner in need of repentance and forgiveness, *"A voice from heaven was heard to say: "You are my beloved Son; with you I am well pleased."* (Luke 3:22) There is the other intriguing passage found in Isaiah 53:10: *"But it was the LORD's will to crush him with pain."*

- Just as Jesus acted in His Trinitarian relationships by carrying out His Father's wishes in every detail of the divine plan of salvation and did everything in the power of His Holy Spirit, in the same way He made sure that we would live our lives in the power of the Holy Spirit who would re-create us in the image and likeness of Jesus, *"the image of the invisible God,"* so that like Him we too would be faithful to 'Our' common Father's will in every detail.

- Jesus made sure that we would receive the Holy Spirit from His Father: *"And I will ask the Father, and he will give you another Advocate to be with you always, the Spirit of truth, which the world cannot accept, because it neither sees nor knows it. But you know it, because it remains with you, and will be in you."* (John 14:16-17)

- And because the Holy Spirit acts in Trinitarian communion and harmony with the Father and Jesus, *"he will guide you to all truth. He will not speak on his own, but he will speak what he hears, and will declare to you the things that are coming. He will glorify me, because he will take from what is mine and declare it to you. Everything that the Father has is mine; for this reason I told you that he will take from what is mine and declare it to you."* (John 16:13-15)

What is God saying to you?

End with Prayer to the Holy Trinity

NIGHT SESSION: Examination of Conscience

For what are you grateful? For what are you contrite?

Please review briefly your Morning Prayer topic. Make it your last thought of the day

DAY TWO: MORNING SESSION

MORNING PRAYER: Act of Faith; Act of Hope; Act of Charity; Daily Offering

Morning Face to Face with God:

Begin with Prayer to the Holy Spirit
Prayer on John 15:1-4; 5; 7-8: The Vine and the Branches

> *"I am the true vine, and my Father is the vine grower. He takes away every branch in me that does not bear fruit, and every one that does he prunes so that it bears more fruit. You are already pruned because of the word that I spoke to you. Remain in me, as I remain in you... Whoever remains in me and I in him will bear much fruit, because without me you can do nothing. ... If you remain in me and my words remain in you, ask for whatever you want and it will be done for you. By this is my Father glorified, that you bear much fruit and become my disciples." [Please read John 15:1-17 for a better appreciation of the passage].*

Read the Reflections; Ask for the grace to appreciate deeply God's gift of being able to share in the fullness of the divine life!

In John 15, Jesus tells us that He is the true Vine and we are His branches, and the Father is the vine-grower. The Father is actively involved in this process of our transformation as He prunes away every barren branch, and trims clean the fruitful ones to increase their yield. Further, through His incarnation, Jesus establishes an inextricable bond with us when He says that He is the Vine and we are the branches. If we live in Him and He live in us, we will produce abundantly. Apart from Him we will be withered, rejected branches. When Jesus thinks of Himself, He is at one and the same time the Second Person of the Holy Trinity and one of us, the son of man! We were called to be in covenant union with our Trinitarian God, and Jesus made that happen!

What is God saying to you?

End with Prayer to the Holy Trinity

NIGHT SESSION: Examination of Conscience

For what are you grateful? For what are you contrite?
Please review briefly your Morning Prayer topic. Make it your last thought of the day

DAY THREE: MORNING SESSION

MORNING PRAYER: Act of Faith; Act of Hope; Act of Charity; Daily Offering

Morning Face to Face with God:

Begin with Prayer to the Holy Spirit
Prayer on Ephesians 1:3-6; 13-14: The Father's Plan of Salvation
> *"Blessed be the God and Father of our Lord Jesus Christ, who has blessed us in Christ with every spiritual blessing in the heavens, as he chose us in him, before the foundation of the world, to be holy and without blemish before him. In love he destined us for adoption to himself through Jesus Christ, in accord with the favor of his will, for the praise of the glory of his grace that he granted us in the beloved… In him you also, who have heard the word of truth, the gospel of your salvation, and have believed in him, were sealed with the promised holy Spirit, which is the first installment of our inheritance toward redemption as God's possession, to the praise of his glory." [Please read Ephesians 1:3-14 for a better appreciation of the passage].*

Read the Reflections; Ask for the grace to appreciate deeply God's gift of being able to share in the fullness of the divine life!

Paul singles out the Father's largesse and generosity toward us through His Son, Jesus Christ, and exclaims an ardent prayer of praise and indescribable gratitude. At first glance Paul seems to be indulging in gross hyperbole when he talks about God bestowing upon us every spiritual blessing in the heavens! But then he goes about outlining in great detail what these blessings are and it becomes clear that indeed he is not exaggerating but only emphasizing God's boundless generosity and largesse toward us: God's plan to incorporate us into His divine Life was made from all eternity, was deliberate, well thought out, and totally committed to, as opposed to being happenstance, accidental, and a mid-course correction. Secondly, the Father's passionate desire is to transform us by forgiving us all our sins through being washed clean in the blood of Christ! Thirdly, we have been made adopted sons and daughters of God through Jesus. We have been sealed with the promised Holy Spirit who is the first installment of our inheritance, and is preparing us to receive our full inheritance, namely sharing in the fullness of God's love and life in heaven.

What is God saying to you?

End with Prayer to the Holy Trinity

NIGHT SESSION: Examination of Conscience

For what are you grateful? For what are you contrite?

Please review briefly your Morning Prayer topic. Make it your last thought of the day

DAY FOUR: MORNING SESSION

MORNING PRAYER: Act of Faith; Act of Hope; Act of Charity; Daily Offering

Morning Face to Face with God:

Begin with Prayer to the Holy Spirit
Prayer on Ephesians 2:4-7: The Generosity of God's Plan of Salvation
> *"But God, who is rich in mercy, because of the great love he had for us, even when we were dead in our transgressions, brought us to life with Christ (by grace you have been saved), raised us up with him, and seated us with him in the heavens in Christ Jesus, that in the ages to come he might show the immeasurable riches of his grace in his kindness to us in Christ Jesus."*

Read the Reflections; Ask for the grace to appreciate deeply God's gift of being able to share in the fullness of the divine life!

We are very unequal partners when it comes to our relationship with God. God is merciful and holy; we are recalcitrant and sinful. When we were dead in our transgressions, God chose to bring us to life through and with Christ. As a result we have been raised up with Jesus and are seated with Him at the right hand of the Father. The whole purpose of being seated with Jesus at the right hand of the Father is so that *"he (Father) might show the immeasurable riches of his grace in his kindness to us in Christ Jesus."* (Ephesians 2:7) The Sacred Writers emphasize the point that even while we live in space and time and belong to the Pilgrim Church making her way to the Heavenly Assembly, in a real sense, under the guidance and direction of the Holy Spirit, God has already seated us with Christ at His right hand, and we are already participating in God's life with the Heavenly Assembly. It is dimly now, then it will be in the full light of God's glory.

What is God saying to you?

End with Prayer to the Holy Trinity

NIGHT SESSION: Examination of Conscience

For what are you grateful? For what are you contrite?

Please review briefly your Morning Prayer topic. Make it your last thought of the day

DAY FIVE: MORNING SESSION

MORNING PRAYER: Acts of Faith; Act of Hope; Act of Charity; Daily Offering

Morning Face to Face with God:

Begin with Prayer to the Holy Spirit

Romans 8:14-17: Children of God through Adoption

His choice to adopt us

> *"For those who are led by the Spirit of God are children of God. For you did not receive a spirit of slavery to fall back into fear, but you received a spirit of adoption, through which we cry, "Abba, Father!" The Spirit itself bears witness with our spirit that we are children of God, and if children, then heirs, heirs of God and joint heirs with Christ, if only we suffer with him so that we may also be glorified with him."*

Read the Reflections; Ask for the grace to appreciate deeply God's gift of being able to share in the fullness of the divine life!

This passage is best understood within the context of a covenant relationship where both parties make an offering of themselves to each other, wholeheartedly and selflessly. Through Jesus, our Triune God has made a wholehearted and selfless offering of Himself to us. Paul tells us in what this has resulted: We are God's sons and daughters who are led by the Holy Spirit. This same Holy Spirit, who is present in the depths of the Father and Jesus, is also given to us to be present in our hearts, making us His holy temple, the place of His abode. Through the Holy Spirit we enjoy a new life, the very life of God. As a result, we have been made God's children through Jesus. With Jesus we now have the privilege of addressing God as 'Abba,' Father. We are free of the spirit of slavery to fear and sin. With Jesus we are heirs, heirs of God and joint heirs with Christ. According to Paul, we can only be joint heirs with Christ, if in this life we suffer with Him in His identification with His covenant family. In this way we will be glorified with Him in the heavenly assembly where the Lamb that was slain is surrounded by His victorious family washed white in His blood. Suffering with Christ who has identified Himself with His covenant family is our way of living in covenant with God, of wholeheartedly and generously making an offering of ourselves in humble and joyful service. He knocks on our door. It is for us to open our hearts and let Him in!

What is God saying to you?

End with Prayer to the Holy Trinity

NIGHT SESSION: Examination of Conscience

For what are you grateful? For what are you contrite?

Please review briefly your Morning Prayer topic. Make it your last thought of the day

DAY SIX: MORNING SESSION

MORNING PRAYER: Act of Faith; Act of Hope; Act of Charity; Daily Offering

Morning Face to Face with God:

Begin with Prayer to the Holy Spirit

REPETITION OF DAYS TWO THROUGH FIVE:

Ask for the grace to appreciate deeply God's gift of being able to share in the fullness of the divine life!

Today, you are doing a repetition of Days Two through Five of this week. In a repetition St. Ignatius says that *"we should pay attention to and dwell upon those points in which we have experienced greater consolation or desolation or greater spiritual appreciation."* (# 62) If you wish, you can do a triple colloquy: refer to #63 of the Spiritual Exercises.

What is God saying to you?

End with Prayer to the Holy Trinity

NIGHT SESSION: Examination of Conscience

For what are you grateful? For what are you contrite?

Please review briefly your Morning Prayer topic. Make it your last thought of the day

DAY SEVEN: MORNING SESSION

MORNING PRAYER: Act of Faith; Act of Hope; Act of Charity; Daily Offering

Morning Face to Face with God:

Begin with Prayer to the Holy Spirit

BENEDICTINE SPIRITUALITY:

(After pondering each bullet point, express your sentiments in a short prayer)

- St. Benedict was born in 480 AD in the Italian town of Norcia, and died between 543 and 547 AD. He founded twelve communities for monks at Subiaco, about 40 miles east of Rome. He then moved to Monte Cassino in the mountains of Southern Italy and founded a monastery where he died.

- St. Benedict is acknowledged as the Founder of Western Monasticism. His main contribution to the monastic and spiritual life is his 'Rule of Saint Benedict.' There are seventy three short chapters and it offers wisdom in two areas: spiritual or how to live a Christ-centered life in this world, and monastic governance, or how to run the monastery efficiently.

- For St. Benedict, prayer, study, work, and rest were all equally significant in God's eyes as we were doing all for the glory of God. They are all equally important for us, because balance and a rhythmic pattern of living are essential to a healthy spiritual life.

- Prayer is obviously of the utmost importance. However, it becomes an obstacle if it is done to the exclusion of other necessary tasks that are God's will for us. The same holds true for study where we immerse ourselves in the Word of God, and neglect our daily duties and need for rest and relaxation.

- The emphasis is always to maintain a proper balance between these four very important aspects of daily life. They are all equally holy because they are all God's will for us. When they are done in proper balance and rhythm, they provide excellent scaffolding for the building of a solid spiritual life.

- In the Rule, St. Benedict tells us to "hold nothing dearer than Christ," and to drop everything immediately when it is time for prayer. Every now and then we will be tempted to postpone or even neglect our daily prayer because we are in desolation, or tired and unbalanced. If we are to hold nothing dearer than Christ, then it follows that prayer should become our constant companion throughout the day.

- According to the Rule, prayer is also 'Opus Dei,' the work of God. Prayer is inseparable from the rest of the day. Hence it is to be used frequently and throughout the day to express our praise, adoration, thanksgiving, petition, and contrition in the midst of our daily activities and challenges.

- In times past, the church bells called us to pray the Angelus. We can create similar summons to prayer throughout the day: whenever our phone rings, to say a prayer for the person calling; every time the clock in our home chimes, to pray for our family members; after we have read an email, to pray for the sender; to say a prayer of adoration and praise every time we get into and come out of our vehicles, and so on.

- St. Benedict tells us to do everything for the glory of God, whether one is "in the garden, on a journey, in the field, or wherever he may be, sitting, walking, or standing."

At the end of the Rule of St. Benedict are the initials: U. I. O. G. D. They stand for the Latin, "Ut in omnibus glorificetur Deus! The translation is that in all things may God be glorified!

- In all things, would refer to every activity one is engaged in during the day. In other words, every task is holy because it has been ordained by God.

What is God saying to you?

End with Prayer to the Holy Trinity

NIGHT SESSION: Examination of Conscience

For what are you grateful? For what are you contrite?

What prayer would you compose to express what God has said to you this week?

Please review briefly your Morning Prayer topic. Make it your last thought of the day

PRAYER AND REFLECTION ON INCORPORATION INTO GOD'S TRINITARIAN LIFE- CONTINUED

WEEK FOUR: *"I AM THE GOOD SHEPHERD, AND I KNOW MINE AND MINE KNOW ME, JUST AS THE FATHER KNOWS ME AND I KNOW THE FATHER; AND I WILL LAY DOWN MY LIFE FOR THE SHEEP." (JOHN 10:14-15)*

SPIRITUAL READING FOR THE WEEK:

- Anoint us in your Covenant, Abba-Emmanuel: Session Two
- Old Testament: Two or Three Chapters daily
- New Testament: Two or Three Chapters daily
- Imitation of Christ: One chapter daily

DAY ONE: MORNING SESSION

MORNING PRAYER: Acts of Faith, Hope, Charity; Daily Offering

Morning Face to Face with God:

Begin with Prayer to the Holy Spirit

ON INCORPORATION INTO GOD'S TRINITARIAN LIFE:

(After pondering each bullet point, express your sentiments in a short prayer)

- Let us take to heart the prayerful wish Paul has for us in Ephesians 1:17-19: *"that the God of our Lord Jesus Christ, the Father of glory, may give you a spirit of wisdom and revelation resulting in knowledge of him. May the eyes of [your] hearts be enlightened, that you may know what is the hope that belongs to his call, what are the riches of glory in his inheritance among the holy ones, and what is the surpassing greatness of his power for us who believe, in accord with the exercise of his great might."*

- The profundity of this prayer is striking when we realize that our Mediator is Jesus. The Father of our Lord Jesus Christ is granting us a spirit of wisdom and insight to know Him clearly through the mediation of His Son. The reason for Jesus' death and resurrection was so that we could *"know Him (the Father) clearly"* as Jesus knows Him.

- The Father wishes us to share in the glorious heritage that is His in Trinitarian Life, and ours as members of the church, God's covenant family. And the Father has absolutely no doubt in bringing this about, because *"[it is] in accord with the exercise of his great might, which he worked in Christ, raising him from the dead and seating him at his right hand in the heavens, far above every principality, authority, power, and dominion, and every name that is named not only in this age but also in the one to come."* (Ephesians 1:20-21)

- Indeed, the Father will stop at nothing to incorporate us into His Trinitarian Life through His Son Jesus and in the power of His Holy Spirit!

- Jesus, then, is our Way, Truth, and Life! It is through Him that we are incorporated into the Life of the Trinity. Our discipleship is the witness to this explicit flowering of divine life in us as God's covenant family who are indwelt by the Father, Son, and Holy Spirit.

- Romans 5:8-9 tells us that *"God proves his love for us in that while we were still sinners Christ died for us. How much more then, since we are now justified by his blood, will we be saved through him from the wrath."* As a result of our holiness and blamelessness, we will be made like Christ, unblemished victims of sacrifice on behalf of the people we serve or the body of Christ who is its head.

- Our adoption highlights the fact that God would not tolerate our permanent alienation from Him through sin and would, instead, sweep us into His divine Embrace through His Son. We have been restored to our God-given dignity as sons and daughters of Jesus' Father in Heaven. With Jesus we now claim God as Our Father.

- Only in acknowledging Jesus as Lord of heaven and earth, and Savior of the world, which grace is given to us by the Holy Spirit, can we participate in God's divine life!

What is God saying to you?

End with Prayer to the Holy Trinity

NIGHT SESSION: Examination of Conscience

For what are you grateful? For what are you contrite?

Please review briefly your Morning Prayer topic. Make it your last thought of the day

DAY TWO: MORNING SESSION

MORNING PRAYER: Act of Faith; Act of Hope; Act of Charity; Daily Offering

Morning Face to Face with God:

Begin with Prayer to the Holy Spirit
Prayer on Romans 5:18-21: Grace and Life through Christ

"In conclusion, just as through one transgression condemnation came upon all, so through one righteous act acquittal and life came to all. For just as through the disobedience of one the many were made sinners, so through the obedience of one the many will be made righteous. The law entered in so that transgressions might increase but, where sin increased, grace overflowed all the more, so that, as sin reigned in death, grace also might reign through justification for eternal life through Jesus Christ our Lord." [Please read Romans 5:15-21 for a better appreciation of the passage].

Read the Reflection; Ask for the grace to appreciate deeply God's gift of being able to share in the fullness of the divine life!

Paul is reflecting on the world-views of sin as represented by Adam and his sinful progeny, and righteousness or justification as represented by Jesus. Sin made us incapable of entering into covenant union with God, of God's image and likeness becoming one with the Original! But God, in His infinite mercy and love for us, made sure that we would be snatched from the jaws of Satan, sin, and permanent death through His Son, Jesus: *"Where sin increased, grace overflowed all the more, so that, as sin reigned in death, grace also might reign through justification for eternal life through Jesus Christ our Lord."* (verses 20-21) You might want to repeat some of these verses over and over to taste and relish the immense love and mercy that God has for us in Jesus Christ!

What is God saying to you?
End with Prayer to the Holy Trinity

NIGHT SESSION: Examination of Conscience

For what are you grateful? For what are you contrite?
Please review briefly your Morning Prayer topic. Make it your last thought of the day

DAY THREE: MORNING SESSION

MORNING PRAYER: Act of Faith; Act of Hope; Act of Charity; Daily Offering

Morning Face to Face with God:

Begin with Prayer to the Holy Spirit

Prayer on Romans 8:31-35; 37: God's Indomitable Love in Christ

"If God is for us, who can be against us? He who did not spare his own Son but handed him over for us all, how will he not also give us everything else along with him? Who will bring a charge against God's chosen ones? It is God who acquits us. Who will condemn? It is Christ [Jesus] who died, rather, was raised, who also is at the right hand of God, who indeed intercedes for us. What then will separate us from the love of Christ? Will anguish, or distress, or persecution, or famine, or nakedness, or peril, or the sword? … No, in all these things we conquer overwhelmingly through him who loved us."

Read the Reflection; Ask for the grace to appreciate deeply God's gift of being able to share in the fullness of the divine life!

Paul is expressing some of his deepest convictions that he has arrived at in his relationship with Jesus, his Master and Lord! He is supremely confident that the Father will never be against us as He handed Jesus over for us all. Similarly, who can condemn us if God has acquitted us through Jesus? And Paul reminds us that Jesus is interceding for us at the right hand of the Father. The all-conquering power of God's love has overcome every obstacle to Christians' salvation, and every threat to separate them from God. That power manifested itself fully when Jesus was delivered up to death for our salvation. Through the Risen Lord, Christians can overcome all their afflictions and trials.

What is God saying to you?

End with Prayer to the Holy Trinity

NIGHT SESSION: Examination of Conscience

For what are you grateful? For what are you contrite?

Please review briefly your Morning Prayer topic. Make it your last thought of the day

DAY FOUR: MORNING SESSION

MORNING PRAYER: Act of Faith; Act of Hope; Act of Charity; Daily Offering

Morning Face to Face with God:

Begin with Prayer to the Holy Spirit

Prayer on Philippians 3:8-11: Righteousness from God

"For his sake I have accepted the loss of all things and I consider them so much rubbish, that I may gain Christ and be found in him, not having any righteousness of my own based on the law but that which comes through faith in Christ, the righteousness from God, depending on faith to know him and the power of his resurrection and [the] sharing of his sufferings by being conformed to his death, if somehow I may attain the resurrection from the dead."

Read the Reflection; Ask for the grace to appreciate deeply God's gift of being able to share in the fullness of the divine life!

As Christ's apostle, Paul has truly entered into a covenant relationship with His Master and Lord. He has also entered into a covenant relationship with God's covenant family. He has been transformed by the love and forgiveness of the Lord Jesus. He has been overwhelmed by God's love for us in Jesus. In Jesus, God and His covenant family have come together. This coming together and becoming one in covenant is the central purpose of the incarnation of Jesus. As a result, Paul has surrendered himself completely to Jesus, and Jesus is the only purpose of his life. Everything else is secondary: *"I have accepted the loss of all things and I consider them so much rubbish, that I may gain Christ and be found in him."* Furthermore, he understands ever so clearly, that his transformation or righteousness is due to Christ and not his own efforts. Paul is so enamored of Christ that he wants to be like his Master in all things, in his service of God's covenant family, even to the extent of sharing in Christ's sufferings so that he may attain the resurrection from the dead.

What is God saying to you?
End with Prayer to the Holy Trinity

NIGHT SESSION: Examination of Conscience

For what are you grateful? For what are you contrite?

Please review briefly your Morning Prayer topic. Make it your last thought of the day

DAY FIVE: MORNING SESSION

MORNING PRAYER: Act of Faith; Act of Hope; Act of Charity; Daily Offering

Morning Face to Face with God:

Begin with Prayer to the Holy Spirit
Prayer on Colossians 2:9-13: The Sovereign Role of Christ
    "For in him dwells the whole fullness of the deity bodily, and you share in this fullness in him, who is the head of every principality and power. In him you were also circumcised with a circumcision

not administered by hand, by stripping off the carnal body, with the circumcision of Christ. You were buried with him in baptism, in which you were also raised with him through faith in the power of God, who raised him from the dead. And even when you were dead [in] transgressions and the uncircumcision of your flesh, he brought you to life along with him, having forgiven us all our transgressions." [Please read Colossians 2:9-15 for a better appreciation of the passage].

Read the Reflections; Ask for the grace to appreciate deeply God's gift of being able to share in the fullness of the divine life!

Paul offers a paean exalting the sovereign role of Christ in our lives. Jesus is the image of the invisible God. Through Jesus, the Trinity is made manifest to us. Jesus is also the first-born of all creatures! Jesus is the son of man, the first-born of all creatures because through His death and resurrection, we now share in the divine fullness. Through our baptism we have been buried into the saving mystery of Christ's death. Consequently, we have been raised with Him through faith in the power of God who raised Him from the dead. By forgiving us all our sins, Jesus reconciled everything in His Person, both on earth and in the heavens, making peace through the blood of His cross! In His Person, Divinity and humanity have come together in covenant union! How very fortunate we are to be disciples of Jesus, and sons and daughters of the Living God whom we can address as our Father.

What is God saying to you?

End with Prayer to the Holy Trinity

NIGHT SESSION: Examination of Conscience

For what are you grateful? For what are you contrite?

Please review briefly your Morning Prayer topic. Make it your last thought of the day

DAY SIX: MORNING SESSION

MORNING PRAYER: Act of Faith; Act of Hope; Act of Charity; Daily Offering

Morning Face to Face with God:

Begin with Prayer to the Holy Spirit

REPETITION OF DAYS TWO THROUGH FIVE:

Ask for the grace to appreciate deeply God's gift of being able to share in the fullness of the divine life!

Today, you are doing a repetition of Days Two through Five of this week. In a repetition St. Ignatius says that *"we should pay attention to and dwell upon those points in which we have experienced greater consolation or desolation or greater spiritual appreciation."* (# 62) If you wish, you can do a triple colloquy: refer to #63 of the Spiritual Exercises.

What is God saying to you?

End with Prayer to the Holy Trinity

NIGHT SESSION: Examination of Conscience

For what are you grateful? For what are you contrite?

Please review briefly your Morning Prayer topic. Make it your last thought of the day

DAY SEVEN: MORNING SESSION

MORNING PRAYER: Act of Faith; Act of Hope; Act of Charity; Daily Offering

Morning Face to Face with God:

Begin with Prayer to the Holy Spirit

BENEDICTINE SPIRITUALITY:

(After pondering each bullet point, express your sentiments in a short prayer)

- The Benedictines take the vow of Stability. The monastery they enter becomes their abode for the rest of their lives. Stability is the antidote to boredom which creates the illusion that there is a more exciting and interesting opportunity out there.
- Stability advocates against a deep-seated tendency in us to give up what we are doing because it is boring or requires too much effort. And given the fact that our lives are characterized by great mobility and a plethora of gadgets, the mundane becomes quite boring and interminable.
- Stability calls for obedience to God as manifested in our daily responsibilities. And often times, in these responsibilities we are called to be obedient to humans who are our superiors. St. Benedict tells us that we are obeying God in obeying them, except when asked to do something unethical and sinful. In everyday life, our stability will manifest itself in our relationships and responsibilities, as consistent and dependable behavior.
- The Benedictine way of life calls for doing the ordinary things of daily life with loving attention and reverence because they are God's desire for us. It behooves us to do them carefully and with thought.

- A deep awareness of God's loving presence in our lives is at the heart of an attitude of simplicity. We feel secure and deeply loved by Him. We are the abode of the Blessed Trinity. Consequently, we live and act in a spirit of calmness and joy.

- Such a spirit creates a transparency in us which leads to being uncomplicated. Simplicity, therefore, is devoid of exaggeration, of a need to impress, of a desire to be better than others. Simplicity leads to making moderation a priority in our lives.

- St. Benedict desired that we live in a 'state of enough.' We need to keep this rule of conduct before us on a daily basis. We can mistakenly think that what we want is really what we need. When material excess has become part and parcel of our lives, our spirits get dimmed and become phlegmatic. ⌐ unemotional   fleg madik

- Moderation leads to balance in one's life. Balance is an attitude that does not come naturally to us. Unfortunately, there is too much rushing from one task to another, multi-tasking because we allot insufficient time for our duties. Consequently, we are in a frenzy, or depressed because we are feeling overwhelmed.

- Because of our sinful tendencies, we will tend towards doing too much or too little, towards having too much, towards placing ourselves before others. When one is in balance, one has time for one's duties because one takes the time to do every duty well. Accordingly, there is purposefulness in one's actions throughout the day.

- St. Benedict wanted his monks to treat everybody as 'the guest,' and that 'all guests should be welcomed as Christ.' Even the stranger should be welcomed as Christ the guest. At the heart of hospitality is our covenant relationship with Jesus. He has become one with us. We are His body, and He is the Head. We are the bride, and He is the bridegroom.

What is God saying to you?

End with Prayer to the Holy Trinity

NIGHT SESSION: Examination of Conscience

For what are you grateful? For what are you contrite?

What prayer would you compose to express what God has said to you this week?

Please review briefly your Morning Prayer topic. Make it your last thought of the day

SESSION THREE: THE DIVINE KENOSIS

"Though he was in the form of God, (he) did not regard equality with God something to be grasped. Rather, he emptied himself, taking the form of a slave coming in human likeness; and found human in appearance, he humbled himself, becoming obedient to death, even death on a cross."
– Philippians 2:6-8

THE DIVINE KENOSIS:

In order to incorporate us into God's divine life, Paul tells us in Philippians 2:7 that Jesus emptied Himself of His divinity and took the form of a slave. The Greek word for 'Emptying' is *Kenosis*. Jesus did not deem equality with God something to be grasped at, as Paul tells us. Out of unrestrained and compelling love for us, the Word of God emptied Himself of His glory so that He could become flesh and make His dwelling among us, as John 1:14, informs us. In this ancient hymn that Paul inserts into his letter, the early Christians sang that Jesus emptied Himself, and being born in the likeness of men took the form of a slave. We know that Satan tried to grasp at equality with God and continues to attract worshipers who proclaim him as God: *"The beast was given a mouth uttering proud boasts and blasphemies, and it was given authority to act for forty-two months. It opened its mouth to utter blasphemies against God, blaspheming his name and his dwelling and those who dwell in heaven. It was also allowed to wage war against the holy ones and conquer them, and it was granted authority over every tribe, people, tongue, and nation. All the inhabitants of the earth will worship it, all whose names were not written from the foundation of the world in the book of life, which belongs to the Lamb who was slain."* (Revelation 13:5-8) In Genesis 3:5, it is Satan in the form of the serpent who tempted Adam and Eve to do as he did: *"God knows well that when you eat of it your eyes will be opened and you will be like gods, who know good and evil."* But Jesus was God by nature, and unlike Satan, Adam and Eve, did not need to snatch at equality with God. Rather, Jesus did the very opposite and out of love for us, emptied Himself of His divinity so that we could become sharers in His divine nature! We share in this same illusion and desire to 'grasp at equality with God' like Satan and our first parents, and Jesus came to ransom us from our slavery to sin and pride.

TAKING THE FORM OF A SLAVE:

In order to liberate us from our sin and pride, Jesus emptied Himself and took the form of a slave, being born in the likeness of men. In the time of Jesus, slaves were divested of all rights. They were bought and sold as chattel because their masters had complete possession of their lives. Consequently, slaves did all the menial tasks that no one else cared to do but wanted done. They were looked down upon as subhuman, worthy of contempt and derision, and their progeny was passed on in slavery from generation to generation. Why then did Jesus become one of us and was willing to become a slave on our behalf?

The Old Testament offers us several hints into the amazing implications of God creating us in the divine image and likeness, and Jesus' willingness to become a slave on our behalf. In our creation, God established an inextricable bond between the image and the Original. And following the thinking of St. Gregory of Nyssa, can you truly have an image if it does not reflect the Original? It is Jesus who dies to our sin first and as our Savior and Lord helps us to die to sin in Him, so that we might live for God. Jesus took upon Himself our burden and slavery to sin so that we might enjoy His freedom as children of God. And so in Genesis 3:15, we have the first messianic promise made immediately after the Fall: *"I will put enmity between you and the woman, and between your offspring and hers; they will strike at your head, while you strike at their heel."*

Another amazing hint is offered in the Book of Leviticus 25:47-49, where Moses talks about the redemption of slaves: *"When your kindred, having been so reduced to poverty, sell themselves to a resident alien who has become wealthy or to descendants of a resident alien's family, even after having sold themselves, they still may be redeemed by one of their kindred, by an uncle or cousin, or by some other relative from their family..."* The word 'redeemer' originates from the Latin word 'redemptor,' meaning 'someone who buys back.' A redeemer buys back a slave's freedom by swapping places as the text tells us. The redeemer becomes the slave and the slave a free person. In Hebrew, the term *'Goel'* is used to translate 'redeemer,' and it means 'kinsperson.' The full implication of the text is that only a kinsperson could be redeemer to his enslaved family member, and the price would be his own exile into slavery!

In the Word becoming flesh, Jesus became our *'Goel.'* In Romans 5:8-10, Paul describes this grace-filled swap that Jesus embraced for our salvation: *"But God proves his love for us in that while we were still sinners Christ died for us. How much more then, since we are now justified by his blood, will we be saved through him from the wrath. Indeed, if, while we were enemies, we were reconciled to God through the death of his Son, how much more, once reconciled, will we be saved by his life."*

This theme of Jesus being our Goel or Suffering Servant is developed extensively in the Suffering Servant Oracles found in Isaiah 42:1-9; 49:1-7; 50:1-11; and 52:13-53:12 (Refer to *'Instruct Me in Your Ways Lord,'* Session 10). While all the oracles strike a hugely poignant and self-sacrificing note, it is fitting to ponder the following verses from the last oracle: *"But he was pierced for our sins, crushed for our iniquity. He bore the punishment that makes us whole, by his wounds we were healed. We had all gone astray like sheep, all following our own way; but the LORD laid upon him the guilt of us all."* (Isaiah 53:5-6) It was a Trinitarian decision that Jesus would take upon Himself our guilt so that we could savor and participate in God's love and life! Jesus was fulfilling God's demands for justice on our behalf so that we could enter into the Father's embrace and address Him in the same way Jesus does, as Abba, Father. In doing so we would come to know ourselves as God's image and likeness.

KENOSIS IN THE INCARNATION:

We shall now take a closer look at how Jesus emptied Himself in some of the key events of His earthly life and come to appreciate God's immeasurable love for us. In the genealogy of Jesus given to us in Matthew 1:1-17, three female ancestors are mentioned who clearly suggest that indeed, Jesus had very tainted blood lines. These three women are Tamar, Rahab, and Ruth. The story of Tamar is found in Genesis 38. She was the daughter-in-law of Judah, Jacob's fourth born son from Leah. She carried twins, Perez and Zerah, whose father was Judah, her father-in-law! Jesus descended from Perez and therefore had incest in his gene-pool. The story of Rahab, the prostitute, is found in the Book of Joshua, Chapters 2 and 6. Rahab's life was spared by Joshua because she hid the two Hebrew spies sent by him: *"Because Rahab the prostitute had hidden the messengers whom Joshua had sent to reconnoiter Jericho, Joshua let her live, along with her father's house and all her family, who dwell in the midst of Israel to this day."* (Joshua 6:25) Rahab was married to Salmon and they had Boaz who was Jesus' ancestor. Boaz married Ruth, a Gentile woman, and together they had Obed, Jesus' ancestor. The story of Ruth is found in the Book of Ruth, and her marriage to Boaz is narrated in Chapter 4, the last chapter of the book.

The birth of Jesus is rife with kenotic experiences as well. Luke 1 tells us about the announcement of the birth of Jesus. He was born to Mary, a virgin who conceived Jesus through the power of the Holy Spirit. While we don't have any specifics about how Mary and her family weathered this storm of her pregnancy outside of marriage, and why she was not stoned to death along with her son, we do have clear indications that Mary's pregnancy raised several suspicious questions. For one, Joseph was deeply disturbed when he first heard the news that his betrothed was with child, and knew for a fact that the child was not his. In the eyes of Jewish Law, Joseph had the power to expose Mary and have her stoned to death. Instead, *"Joseph her husband, since he was a righteous man, yet unwilling to expose her to shame, decided to divorce her quietly."* (Matthew 1:19) And had he chosen to divorce her quietly, Mary would still have had to contend with the disgrace that would accompany the fact of her pregnancy outside marriage. Once again, as in Mary's conception, it is the Holy Spirit who made the impossible happen and delivered her from the jaws of death. Joseph changed his mind after he was visited by an angel in a dream: *"Joseph, son of David, do not be afraid to take Mary your wife into your home. For it is through the holy Spirit that this child has been conceived in her. She will bear a son and you are to name him Jesus, because he will save his people from their sins."* (Matthew 1:20-21)

Another kenotic experience for the family is the unusual circumstances of Jesus' birth. In Luke 2:7, *"She (Mary) gave birth to her first-born son. She wrapped him in swaddling clothes and laid him in a manger, because there was no room for them in the inn."* Understandably, it was Census time and Bethlehem was crowded. The fact remains that the Lord of the Universe chose to be born in a stable that housed sheep and cattle. We are told as well that shepherds were sent by the angel of the Lord to visit the baby Jesus in the stable. Some of Israel's great heroes were shepherds like Abraham, Isaac, Jacob, Moses, and David. But in the first Century, shepherds, especially hirelings, had an unsavory reputation. The pious and devout were warned not to buy wool, milk, or kids from shepherds, on the assumption that their wares were stolen property. Shepherds, like tax collectors, were not allowed to fulfill a judicial office or be admitted in court as witnesses. In contrast to rabbinical contempt for shepherds, in John 10:11-13 Jesus distinguishes between the good shepherd and the hireling. In His kenotic birth, Jesus was seeking fellowship with the despised and sinful of humankind, symbolized by the shepherds. Jesus identified with them in calling Himself the good shepherd. They were the lost sheep and as Good Shepherd, He was there to find them.

The Presentation in the Temple and Flight into Egypt veil the divinity and sovereignty of the Son of God now become flesh as a human baby. The Presentation was supposed to be a joyful event for Mary and Joseph. They were there to fulfill their covenant obligation with God by offering Him their first-begotten son. To fulfill their religious obligations, they offered the sacrifice of *"a pair of turtledoves or two young pigeons,"* (Luke 2:24) in accordance with the dictate in the law of the Lord. On this holy and joyous occasion they even met two very holy persons in Anna, an 84 year old prophetess, and Simeon who *"was righteous and devout, awaiting the consolation of Israel, and the holy Spirit was upon him."* (Luke 2:25) Simeon had been told by the Holy Spirit that he would not experience death until he had seen the Anointed of the Lord. Accordingly he was led to Mary and Joseph and took the child in his arms and blessed God for displaying *"a light for revelation to the Gentiles, and glory for your people Israel."* (Luke 2:32) Then he changed the tone of his message: *"Behold, this child is destined for the fall and rise of many in Israel, and to be a sign that will be contradicted (and you yourself a sword will pierce) so that the thoughts of many hearts may be revealed."* (Luke 2:34-35) Once again, on behalf of their child, Mary and Joseph are invited into the kenotic experience of their son.

Similarly, the flight into Egypt leaves Mary and Joseph with much anxiety and uncertainty as they seek the safety of their child. In the dark of night they have to make a hasty and desperate retreat from the vicinity of Jerusalem into Egypt: *"When they had departed, behold, the angel of the Lord appeared to Joseph in a dream and said, 'Rise, take the child and his mother, flee to Egypt, and stay there until I tell you. Herod is going to search for the child to destroy him.'"* (Matthew 2:13) It is ironic that Egypt which was a land of slavery for their ancestors has now become a safe haven for the Holy Family. The Holy Family stayed in Egypt until the death of Herod who had ordered the slaughter of the innocent children two years and under. Matthew tells us that Jesus' return to Israel was in fulfillment of a prophecy made by Hosea 11:1: *"When Israel was a child I loved him, out of Egypt I called my son."* For Hosea, Israel began its existence with the Exodus event when God entered into a covenant relationship with His people. Matthew is telling us that in Jesus we are experiencing a new Exodus event which will establish us in a new and everlasting covenant with God. Jesus is inaugurating the new Israel!

KENOSIS IN THE BAPTISM OF JESUS:

In Matthew's account of the Baptism of Jesus, there is an interesting dialogue that takes place between John the Baptist whom Jesus approaches for the baptism of repentance: *"Then Jesus came from Galilee to John at the Jordan to be baptized by him. John tried to prevent him, saying, "I need to be baptized by you, and yet you are coming to me?" Jesus said to him in reply, "Allow it now, for thus it is fitting for us to fulfill all righteousness." Then he allowed him."* (Matthew 3:13-15) John was acutely aware of who he was vis-à-vis Jesus. In Luke 3, John sees himself as unworthy to loosen Jesus' sandal straps. John was much revered by the people as a great prophet and holy man. The Jewish leadership was even willing to consider him as the Messiah sent from God. *"Are you Elijah, or the prophet or the Messiah?"* In John's gospel we are told that they sent him a delegation to find out who he truly was. Yet, in the presence of Jesus, John sees himself as unfit to loosen Jesus' sandal straps. Only non-Jewish slaves were assigned the task of loosening the sandal straps of dinner guests before washing their feet. John sees himself as even lower than a non-Jewish slave in Jesus' presence. And yet Jesus humbles Himself even lower than John by asking to be baptized by him in the baptism of repentance. The Sinless One publicly identifies Himself as sinner in our stead, as the baptism of repentance was received only by sinners. Jesus, being our kinsperson-redeemer, takes upon Himself our burden of sin, and offers repentance and redemption through His own passion and death. His baptism is a sign of his eventual sacrifice on the cross, and in His identification with us as sinners, a true emptying of Himself.

Both the Father and the Holy Spirit have an enthusiastic response to this divine kenosis. Jesus is fulfilling God's demands for justice or the right order of things which is that we become God's true image and likeness, renounce sin, relate to God as Father in the way Jesus does, and share in God's divine nature. They are fully in accord with the kenotic Jesus, as fulfilling God's plan of salvation in this way is truly a Trinitarian decision. The Holy Spirit descended in visible form like a dove upon Jesus, and will stay with Jesus through every step of fulfilling God's magnanimous plan of salvation. And the Father's voice from heaven was heard to say: *"This is my beloved Son, with whom I am well pleased."* (Matthew 3:17)

KENOSIS IN JESUS' PUBLIC MINISTRY:

During Jesus' public ministry, His listeners were often struck with amazement at the wisdom that emanated from Him. Luke 4:22 expresses this sentiment very well: *"And all spoke highly of him and were amazed at the gracious words that came from his mouth."* At other times they were seized with fear and awe at the power that came forth from Jesus in the way He healed the sick! Luke 5:26 describes well the reaction people had when Jesus cured a paralyzed man: *"Then astonishment seized them all and they glorified God, and, struck with awe, they said, "We have seen incredible things today."* Even demons that were repeatedly cast out of individuals acknowledged Jesus' power over them and held Him in awe and fear. Luke 4:36, and 41, capture the reaction of the people and the demons themselves to Jesus' power over them: *"What is there about his word? For with authority and power he commands the unclean spirits, and they come out." ... And demons also came out from many, shouting, "You are the Son of God."* When Jesus raised the widow's son to life, the people reacted with fear and praise: *"Fear seized them all, and they glorified God exclaiming, "A great prophet has arisen in our midst," and "God has visited his people."* (Luke 7:16)

As an essential part of His kenotic experience, there was a very challenging and disruptive side to Jesus' ministry. He was not accepted among His own people and relatives in Nazareth. At the beginning of His sermon in the synagogue, His fellow villagers were impressed. However, when Jesus began showing them how closed they were to Him, and that no prophet was honored in his own country, they took exception and reacted violently: *"When the people in the synagogue heard this, they were all filled with fury. They rose up, drove him out of the town, and led him to the brow of the hill on which their town had been built, to hurl him down headlong. But he passed through the midst of them and went away."* (Luke 4:28-30)

Jesus was constantly heckled and challenged by the religious leadership, especially. Their minds and hearts were closed to the good news because Jesus threatened their religious authority and influence over the people. Their reaction to Jesus was always hostile and shocking, considering that they who were familiar with the works of God should have known better. Matthew 12:22-24 is a shocking indictment of their blasphemous ways: *"Then they brought to him a demoniac who was blind and mute. He cured the mute person so that he could speak and see. All the crowd was astounded, and said, "Could this perhaps be the Son of David?" But when the Pharisees heard this, they said, "This man drives out demons only by the power of Beelzebul, the prince of demons."* The leadership set traps for Him; they tried repeatedly to lure Him into heresy. They looked for any and every ruse they could conjure up to make a case for putting Him to death. Even after they arrest Jesus, they don't have a convincing case against Him. Matthew 26:59-60 expresses well this sentiment: *"The chief priests and the entire Sanhedrin kept trying to obtain false testimony against Jesus in order to put him to death, but they found none, though many false witnesses came forward."*

From Jesus' perspective, it was harrowing at times. At the same time, Jesus took this opposition to Him in stride, knowing fully well that it was necessary for Him to suffer and die and be raised from the dead on our behalf. In order to overcome sin, He had to confront it in every aspect. He predicted His passion, death, and resurrection, thereby setting at rest any cause to think that His death was the result of human design. Two men in dazzling garments stood before the women at the tomb and reiterated what Jesus had always said, that He was dying willingly and wholeheartedly and would be raised from the dead. He was doing this so that we could share in His very own life: *"They were terrified and bowed their faces to the ground. They said to them, 'Why do you seek the living one among the dead? He is not here, but he has been raised. Remember what he said to you while he was still in Galilee, that the Son of Man must be handed over to sinners and be crucified, and rise on the third day.'"* (Luke 24:5-7) All along, from all eternity, God had decided that Jesus would die on behalf of our sins! Through Him, God's justice would be fully requited! This was God's plan of salvation, and Jesus as the Suffering Messiah was no accident.

KENOSIS IN THE PASSION AND DEATH OF JESUS:

On three different occasions Jesus predicted His passion and death in the Synoptic gospels. Matthew 16 records the first prediction. Matthew offers a curious juxtaposition of two events that are at eerie odds with each other. Jesus has come to the neighborhood of Caesarea Philippi and poses this question to His disciples: *"Who do people say that the Son of Man is?"* Their reply was that some said He was John the Baptizer, others Elijah, still others, Jeremiah or one of the prophets. Then Jesus zeroed in on them and asked them a very personal question: *"But who do you say that I am?"* Simon Peter said in reply, *"You are the messiah, the Son of the living God."* (Matthew 16:15-16) Such a profound response could only have been inspired by the Holy Spirit. In reply Jesus says: *"Blessed are you, Simon son of Jonah. For flesh and blood has not revealed this to you, but my heavenly Father. And so I say to you, you are Peter, and upon this rock I will build my church, and the gates of the netherworld shall not prevail against it. I will give you the keys to the kingdom of heaven. Whatever you bind on earth shall be bound in heaven; and whatever you loose on earth shall be loosed in heaven."* (Matthew 16:15-20)

It is after Peter's powerful profession of faith in Jesus, that Matthew records Jesus' first prediction of His passion and death: *"From that time on, Jesus began to show his disciples that he must go to Jerusalem and suffer greatly from the elders, the chief priests, and the scribes, and be killed and on the third day be raised."* (Matthew 16:21) At this point, the same Peter who had been so impressive in his earlier response now offers a reply that is prompted by myopic self-interest: *"Then Peter took him aside and began to rebuke him, 'God forbid, Lord! No such thing shall ever happen to you.' He turned and said to Peter, 'Get behind me, Satan! You are an obstacle to me. You are thinking not as God does, but as human beings do.'"* (Matthew 16:22-23) Indeed, Jesus' reaction to His disciple is sharp and unequivocal!

The second prediction came after the Transfiguration when Jesus had cured the boy who had been possessed by an evil spirit. The disciples were all amazed, and their thinking was probably reinforced that He indeed would be Israel's political Messiah. That is when Jesus said to them: *"Pay attention to what I am telling you. The Son of Man is to be handed over to men." But they did not understand this saying; its meaning was hidden from them so that they should not understand it, and they were afraid to ask him about this saying."* (Luke 9:44-45)

The third time is when Jesus and His disciples are headed toward Jerusalem where He will be crucified: *"Then he took the Twelve aside and said to them, 'Behold, we are going up to Jerusalem and everything written by the prophets about the Son of Man will be fulfilled. He will be handed over to the Gentiles and he will be mocked and insulted and spat upon; and after they have scourged him they will kill him, but on the third day he will rise.'"* (Luke 18:31-33) Once again the disciples understood nothing of this. In fact, John and James who had witnessed the Transfiguration and should have known better, make the audacious request to be seated on either side of Jesus in heaven (Mark 10:35-45)! Their veiled and darkened faith remains firmly in place even after Jesus' resurrection. It is only after the Risen Lord appears to them on several occasions that their eyes are opened and they realize that Jesus has been raised from the dead and is indeed the Savior and Lord of the world!

Jesus who was always God became man. He emptied Himself of His glory and became one of us, becoming obedient to death, even to death on a cross. Only hardened criminals were subjected to death on a cross as their capital punishment. Even though He was God and totally innocent, Jesus was willing to humble himself out of love for us to the point of dying on the cross. Understandably there were varied reactions to His shameful death on the cross. Apart from John, the beloved disciple, none of the other disciples were present. They had all fled, either in fear or in shame. The leaders of the people kept jeering at Him, saying, *"He saved others, let him save himself if he is the chosen one, the Messiah of God."* (Luke 23:35) The soldiers too mocked Him, offering Him sour wine and taunting Him to save Himself if indeed He was the king of the Jews! One of the criminals blasphemed Him, as well as suggesting that if Jesus were the Messiah, He should save Himself and them as well.

There are some heartening strands, however, in this otherwise deplorable and seamy skein. One of the criminals experienced conversion in the presence of Jesus. He rebuked his fellow criminal and said, *"Have you no fear of God, for you are subject to the same condemnation? And indeed, we have been condemned justly, for the sentence we received corresponds to our crimes, but this man has done nothing criminal."* (Luke 23:40-42) Then he asked Jesus to remember him when He entered upon His reign. Jesus assured him that that very day he would be in paradise with Him! After His death, the centurion gave glory to God upon seeing what had happened, and offered the opinion that Jesus was the Son of God (Mark 15:39). And two prominent members of the Sanhedrin, Joseph of Arimathea and Nicodemus, made public their heretofore hidden discipleship, by approaching Pilate to request Jesus' body for burial: *"After this, Joseph of Arimathea, secretly a disciple of Jesus for fear of the Jews, asked Pilate if he could remove the body of Jesus. And Pilate permitted it. So he came and took his body. Nicodemus, the one who had first come to him at night, also came bringing a mixture of myrrh and aloes weighing about one hundred pounds. They took the body of Jesus and bound it with burial cloths along with the spices, according to Jewish burial custom. Now in the place where he had been crucified there was a garden, and in the garden a new tomb, in which no one had yet been buried. So they laid Jesus there because of the Jewish preparation day; for the tomb was close by."* (John 19:38-42) They defied the ban of according burial rites and a tomb to Jesus condemned as a criminal by Pilate and the Sanhedrin. They chose to give Jesus a tomb and complete the burial rites because they had come to believe that Jesus indeed was the Son of God who died on the cross for the forgiveness of sin and the salvation of the world.

PRAYER AND REFLECTION ON THE DIVINE KENOSIS

WEEK FIVE: *"When your kindred, having been so reduced to poverty, sell themselves to a resident alien who has become wealthy or to descendants of a resident alien's family, even after having sold themselves, they still may be redeemed by one of their kindred, by an uncle or cousin, or by some other relative from their family." (Leviticus 25:47-49)*

SPIRITUAL READING FOR THE WEEK:

- **Anoint Us in Your Covenant, Abba-Emmanuel:** Session Three
- **Old Testament:** Two or Three Chapters daily
- **New Testament:** Two or Three Chapters daily
- **Imitation of Christ:** One chapter daily

DAY ONE: MORNING SESSION

MORNING PRAYER: Acts of Faith, Hope, Charity; Daily Offering

Morning Face to Face with God:

Begin with Prayer to the Holy Spirit

REFLECTIONS ON KENOSIS IN THE INCARNATION:

(After pondering each bullet point, express your sentiments in a short prayer)

- We can reflect on several features of Jesus' incarnation and come to appreciate God's immeasurable love for us. In the genealogy of Jesus given to us in Matthew 1:1-17, three female ancestors are mentioned who clearly suggest that indeed, Jesus had very tainted blood lines.

- The story of Tamar is found in Genesis 38. She was the daughter-in-law of Judah, Jacob's fourth born son from Leah. She carried twins, Perez and Zerah, whose father was Judah, her father-in-law! Jesus descended from Perez and therefore had incest in his gene-pool.

- The story of Rahab, the prostitute, is found in the Book of Joshua, Chapters 2 and 6. Rahab's life was spared by Joshua because she hid the two Hebrew spies sent by him (Joshua 6:25). Rahab was married to Salmon and they had Boaz who was Jesus' ancestor. Boaz married Ruth, a Gentile woman, and together they had Obed, Jesus' ancestor (Book of Ruth, chapter 4).

- The birth of Jesus is rife with kenotic experiences as well. He was born to Mary, a virgin who conceived Jesus through the power of the Holy Spirit. While we don't have any specifics about how Mary and her family weathered this storm of her pregnancy outside of marriage, and why she was not stoned to death along with her son, we do have clear indications that Mary's pregnancy raised several suspicious questions.

- For one, Joseph was deeply disturbed when he first heard the news that his betrothed was with child, and knew for a fact that the child was not his. In the eyes of Jewish Law, Joseph had the power to expose Mary and have her stoned. Instead, *"Joseph her husband, since he was a righteous man, yet unwilling to expose her to shame, decided to divorce her quietly."* (Matthew 1:19)

- Once again as in Mary's conception, it is the Holy Spirit who made the impossible happen and delivered her from the jaws of death. Joseph changed his mind after he was visited by an angel in a dream: *"Joseph, son of David, do not be afraid to take Mary your wife into your home. For it is through the holy Spirit that this child has been conceived in her. She will bear a son and you are to name him Jesus, because he will save his people from their sins."* (Matthew 1:20-21)

- Another kenotic experience for the family is the unusual circumstances of Jesus' birth. In His kenotic birth, Jesus was seeking fellowship with the despised and sinful of humankind, symbolized by the shepherds whom He always appreciated. Jesus identified Himself with them in calling Himself the good shepherd. They were the lost sheep and He was there to find them.

- The Presentation in the Temple and Flight into Egypt veil the divinity and sovereignty of the Son of God now become flesh as a human baby. Mary and Joseph were there to fulfill their covenant obligation to God by offering Him their first-begotten son.

- Simeon had been told by the Holy Spirit that he would not experience death until he had seen the Anointed of the Lord. Accordingly he was led to Mary and Joseph and took the child in his arms and blessed God for displaying *"a light for revelation to the Gentiles, and glory for your people Israel."* (Luke 2:32)

- Then he changed the tone of his message: *"Behold, this child is destined for the fall and rise of many in Israel, and to be a sign that will be contradicted (and you yourself a sword will pierce) so that the thoughts of many hearts may be revealed."* (Luke 2:34-35) Once again, on behalf of their child, Mary and Joseph are invited into the kenotic experience of their son.

- Matthew tells us that Jesus' return to Israel was in fulfillment of a prophecy made by Hosea 11:1: *"When Israel was a child I loved him, out of Egypt I call my son."* For Hosea, Israel began its existence with the Exodus event when God entered into a covenant relationship with His people. Matthew is telling us that we are experiencing a new Exodus event in Jesus who will establish us in a new and everlasting covenant with God. Jesus is inaugurating the new Israel!

What is God saying to you?

End with Prayer to the Holy Trinity

NIGHT SESSION: Examination of Conscience

For what are you grateful? For what are you contrite?

Please review briefly your Morning Prayer topic. Make it your last thought of the day

DAY TWO: MORNING SESSION

MORNING PRAYER: Act of Faith; Act of Hope; Act of Charity; Daily Offering

Morning Face to Face with God:

Begin with Prayer to the Holy Spirit
Prayer on Leviticus 25:47-49: The Redemption of a Kinsperson by a Kinsperson
"When your kindred, having been so reduced to poverty, sell themselves to a resident alien who has become wealthy or to descendants of a resident alien's family, even after having sold themselves,

they still may be redeemed by one of their kindred, by an uncle or cousin, or by some other relative from their family."

Ponder the Reflection: ask the Holy Spirit for a deep appreciation of Jesus' love as manifested in His emptying of Himself on the cross!

Leviticus 25 gives us a detailed explanation of the implications of being a redeemer in the community. Moses is talking about the redemption of slaves. The word 'redeemer' or 'redemption,' stems from the Latin word 'redemptor,' which means 'to buy back.' In Hebrew, the term 'Goel' is used to translate 'redeemer,' and it means 'kinsperson.' Only a kinsperson could redeem a member of his family by paying his price for freedom. The kinsperson became the price by taking upon himself the slavery of his family member so that in exchange, his kinsperson would have his freedom. This passage is an amazing hint about what Jesus would do for us. In becoming incarnate, Jesus became our kinsperson or Goel, and has therefore earned the right/obligation of granting us a share in His freedom and life, by taking our enslavement to sin upon Himself. This obligation was freely undertaken in voluntary obedience to His Father's will. God so loved us that He sent His Son to offer eternal life to those who believed in Him through His sacrifice on the cross.

What is God saying to you?

End with Prayer to the Holy Trinity

NIGHT SESSION: Examination of Conscience

For what are you grateful? For what are you contrite?

Please review briefly your Morning Prayer topic. Make it your last thought of the day

DAY THREE: MORNING SESSION

MORNING PRAYER: Act of Faith; Act of Hope; Act of Charity; Daily Offering

Morning Face to Face with God:

Begin with Prayer to the Holy Spirit
Prayer on Isaiah 50:5-7: Third Suffering Servant Oracle
   "The Lord GOD opened my ear; I did not refuse, did not turn away. I gave my back to those who beat me, my cheeks to those who tore out my beard; my face I did not hide from insults and spitting. The Lord GOD is my help, therefore I am not disgraced; therefore I have set my face like flint,

knowing that I shall not be put to shame.” [Please read Isaiah 50:1-11 for a better appreciation of the passage].

Ponder the Reflection: ask the Holy Spirit for a deep appreciation of Jesus' love as manifested in His emptying of Himself on the cross!

In the Third Oracle, the redeemer is portrayed as one who has the right to issue a bill of divorce to His adulterous wife but has not. God can still wreak havoc on their enemies through plagues, as He did in Egypt. But most of all, the Suffering Servant speaks words of consolation and inspiration to the weary. He does not refuse the divine vocation and as a result submits willingly to insults and beatings: *"I gave my back to those who struck me, and my cheeks to those who pulled out the beard; I did not hide my face from insult and spitting."* (Verse 6) In the agony in the garden, after much struggle and travail, Jesus accepted willingly to go to His crucifixion and death. He set His face like flint on His road to Calvary.

What is God saying to you?

End with Prayer to the Holy Trinity

NIGHT SESSION: Examination of Conscience

For what are you grateful? For what are you contrite?

Please review briefly your Morning Prayer topic. Make it your last thought of the day

DAY FOUR: MORNING SESSION

MORNING PRAYER: Act of Faith; Act of Hope; Act of Charity; Daily Offering

Morning Face to Face with God:

Begin with Prayer to the Holy Spirit
Prayer on Isaiah 53:3; 5; 6; 10: Fourth Suffering Servant Oracle
"He was spurned and avoided by men, a man of suffering, knowing pain, like one from whom you turn your face, spurned, and we held him in no esteem…But he was pierced for our sins, crushed for our iniquity. He bore the punishment that makes us whole, by his wounds we were healed… But the LORD laid upon him the guilt of us all…But it was the LORD's will to crush him with pain." [Please read Isaiah 52:13 – 53:12 for a better appreciation of the passage].

Ponder the Reflection: ask the Holy Spirit for a deep appreciation of Jesus' love as manifested in His emptying of Himself on the cross!

In the Fourth and last Oracle, Isaiah gives us an extraordinary description of the Sinless Servant. By his voluntary suffering, he atones for the sins of his people, and saves them from just punishment at the hands of God: *"But the LORD laid upon him the guilt of us all."* (Verse 6) As redeemer, Jesus plunged His own life and goodness into the midst of Israel and the entire world. He bore the full brunt of our sin and suffering, and overcame evil by His own divine goodness: *"He bore the punishment that makes us whole, by his wounds we were healed."* (Verse 5) This act of redemption was a Trinitarian act. The Father and the Holy Spirit were in full accord. Out of love for us, God chose to have His Son harshly treated and mutilated, rather than send us to everlasting punishment and separation from Him: *"My servant, the just one, shall justify the many, their iniquity he shall bear... because he surrendered himself to death, was counted among the transgressors, bore the sins of many, and interceded for the transgressors."* (Verses 11; 12) The Father could not have loved us any more than *"by making his (Jesus') life a reparation offering."* (Verse 10)

What is God saying to you?

End with Prayer to the Holy Trinity

NIGHT SESSION: Examination of Conscience

For what are you grateful? For what are you contrite?

Please review briefly your Morning Prayer topic. Make it your last thought of the day

DAY FIVE: MORNING SESSION

MORNING PRAYER: Act of Faith; Act of Hope; Act of Charity; Daily Offering

Morning Face to Face with God:

Begin with Prayer to the Holy Spirit
Prayer on Matthew 3:14-17: The Baptism of Jesus:
> *"John tried to prevent him, saying, "I need to be baptized by you, and yet you are coming to me?" Jesus said to him in reply, "Allow it now, for thus it is fitting for us to fulfill all righteousness." Then he allowed him. After Jesus was baptized, he came up from the water and behold, the heavens were opened [for him], and he saw the Spirit of God descending like a dove [and] coming upon him. And a voice came from the heavens, saying, "This is my beloved Son, with whom I am well pleased."*

Ponder the Reflection: ask the Holy Spirit for a deep appreciation of Jesus' love as manifested in His emptying of Himself on the cross!

Jesus approaches John for the baptism of repentance. John tries to refuse Jesus' request by reminding Him that it is he who is in need of repentance. John was much revered by the people as a great prophet and holy man. The Jewish leadership was even willing to consider him as the Messiah sent from God. Yet, in the presence of Jesus, John sees himself as unfit to loosen His sandal straps (Luke 3:16). Only non-Jewish slaves were assigned the task of loosening the sandal straps of dinner guests before washing their feet. John sees himself as even lower than a non-Jewish slave in Jesus' presence. And yet Jesus humbles Himself even lower than John by asking to receive the baptism of repentance. The Sinless One publicly identifies Himself as a sinner in our stead, as the baptism of repentance was received only by sinners. Jesus, being our kinsperson-redeemer, takes upon Himself our burden of sin, and offers repentance and redemption through His own passion and death. His baptism is a sign of His eventual sacrifice on the cross, and a true emptying of Himself in His identification with us as sinners. Hence, as Paul says, we are baptized into the death of Jesus Christ.

What is God saying to you?

End with Prayer to the Holy Trinity

NIGHT SESSION: Examination of Conscience

For what are you grateful? For what are you contrite?

Please review briefly your Morning Prayer topic. Make it your last thought of the day

DAY SIX: MORNING SESSION

MORNING PRAYER: Act of Faith; Act of Hope; Act of Charity; Daily Offering

Morning Face to Face with God:

Begin with Prayer to the Holy Spirit

REPETITION OF DAYS TWO THROUGH FIVE:

Ask the Holy Spirit for a deep appreciation of Jesus' love as manifested in His emptying of Himself on the cross!

Today, you are doing a repetition of Days Two through Five of this week. In a repetition St. Ignatius says that *"we should pay attention to and dwell upon those points in which we have experienced greater consolation or desolation or greater spiritual appreciation."* (# 62) If you wish, you can do a triple colloquy: refer to #63 of the Spiritual Exercises.

What is God saying to you?

End with Prayer to the Holy Trinity

NIGHT SESSION: Examination of Conscience

For what are you grateful? For what are you contrite?

Please review briefly your Morning Prayer topic. Make it your last thought of the day

DAY SEVEN: MORNING SESSION

MORNING PRAYER: Act of Faith; Act of Hope; Act of Charity; Daily Offering

Morning Face to Face with God:

Begin with Prayer to the Holy Spirit

THE SPIRITUALITY OF ST. FRANCIS OF ASSISI:

(After pondering each bullet point, express your sentiments in a short prayer)

- St. Francis of Assisi is probably the most well-known and beloved Catholic saint. He was born in Assisi, Umbria, in 1181 or 1182. When about twenty, the town of Assisi was engaged in a skirmish against Perugia, a neighboring city. Francis was taken captive and held a prisoner for more than a year.
- A low fever during his imprisonment turned his thoughts towards God and eternity. Soon a yearning for the life of the spirit possessed him, and he gave himself to prayer.
- Thus began his spiritual awakening. While making a trip on horseback, he drew near a leper. He was disgusted by this repulsive sight and wanted to flee the scene. But an urge came upon him. He dismounted from his horse, embraced the unfortunate man, and gave him all his money. Francis now was acting on the grace of his spiritual awakening.
- Soon after, Francis made a pilgrimage to St. Peter's in Rome. He was disappointed at the meager offerings being made at the tomb of St. Peter's. He emptied his wallet, and then exchanged his expensive clothing with a tattered mendicant.
- A while later, Francis was praying before an ancient crucifix in the ruined chapel of San Damiano in Assisi. He heard the crucified Christ speak to him and say, "Go, Francis,

and repair my house which you see is falling to ruin." He took the summons literally. Consequently, he took some expensive drapery from his father's silk shop, and sold it to procure money to build the chapel.

- His father reacted violently to Francis' gesture. Francis hid from his father for a month. The pastor would not accept the gold that Francis offered him for the repair of San Damiano. When Francis finally met his father, there was a severe altercation. In front of the Bishop of Assisi, Francis was disowned by his father, and treated as a madman by his fellow townspeople. That is when he wedded himself to Lady Poverty.

- In doing so, he experienced the freedom that came from the total surrender of all worldly goods, honor, and privileges. In offering himself to God, Francis became totally free for God. He finally re-built the chapel of San Damiano and two other chapels. He engaged himself in works of mercy, especially tending to the lepers. In time he realized that Jesus was asking him to re-build the spiritual structure of the Church.

- In February 1208, the gospel at Mass struck him personally, where Jesus asked His disciples to possess neither gold, nor silver, nor scrip for their journey, nor two coats, nor shoes, nor a staff, and that they were to exhort sinners to repentance and announce the kingdom of God. He gave up everything and began wearing the coarse woolen tunic of the poorest peasants, tied around him with a knotted rope.

- His example of poverty, simplicity, and selfless service drew others to him. As a small band of disciples, they began to ask God what He wanted of them. On three occasions they opened the Scriptures at random in the church of St. Nicholas. Each time the Scripture passage exhorted them to leave everything behind and follow Christ.

- They forthwith went to the public square and gave away everything they owned, and made poverty their rule of life. Before long many were attracted to their way of life and began joining them. They came to be known as the Friars Minor.

- Pope Innocent III at first was not favorable to Francis. However, he was persuaded through a dream about the poor man of Assisi, to give Francis permission to start his community of Friars Minor, and to preach repentance wherever they went. Before they left their audience with the Pope, they all received the tonsure. Francis himself was ordained a deacon some time later.

What is God saying to you?

End with Prayer to the Holy Trinity

a part of a monk's or priest's head left bare on top by shaving off the hair.

NIGHT SESSION: *Examination of Conscience*

For what are you grateful? For what are you contrite?

What prayer would you compose to express what God has said to you this week?

Please review briefly your Morning Prayer topic. Make it your last thought of the day

PRAYER AND REFLECTION ON THE DIVINE KENOSIS – CONTINUED

WEEK SIX: *"EVERY PRIEST STANDS DAILY AT HIS MINISTRY, OFFERING FREQUENTLY THOSE SAME SACRIFICES THAT CAN NEVER TAKE AWAY SINS. BUT THIS ONE OFFERED ONE SACRIFICE FOR SINS, AND TOOK HIS SEAT FOREVER AT THE RIGHT HAND OF GOD; … FOR BY ONE OFFERING HE HAS MADE PERFECT FOREVER THOSE WHO ARE BEING CONSECRATED." (HEBREWS 10:11, 12, 14)*

SPIRITUAL READING FOR THE WEEK:

- **Anoint Us in Your Covenant, Abba-Emmanuel:** Session Three
- **Old Testament:** Two or Three Chapters daily
- **New Testament:** Two or Three Chapters daily
- **Imitation of Christ:** One chapter daily

DAY ONE: MORNING SESSION

MORNING PRAYER: Acts of Faith, Hope, Charity; Daily Offering

Morning Face to Face with God:

Begin with Prayer to the Holy Spirit

REFLECTIONS ON JESUS' KENOSIS IN HIS PASSION AND DEATH:

(After pondering each bullet point, express your sentiments in a short prayer)

- Jesus who was always God became man. He emptied Himself of His glory and became one of us, becoming obedient to death, even to death on a cross. Only criminals were subjected to death on a cross as their capital punishment.
- Even though He was God and totally innocent, Jesus was willing to humble Himself out of love for us to the point of dying on the cross.
- Apart from John, the beloved disciple, none of the other disciples were present. They had all fled, either in fear or in shame. The leaders of the people kept jeering at Him, saying He saved others, and if He were the Messiah of God, the chosen one, He should save Himself!
- The soldiers too mocked Him, offering Him sour wine and taunting Him to save Himself if indeed He was the king of the Jews! One of the criminals blasphemed Him,

as well as suggesting that if Jesus were the Messiah, He should save them and Himself as well.

- There are some heartening strands, however, in this otherwise deplorable and seamy skein. One of the criminals experienced conversion in the presence of Jesus. He rebuked his fellow criminal and said, *"Have you no fear of God, for you are subject to the same condemnation? And indeed, we have been condemned justly, for the sentence we received corresponds to our crimes, but this man has done nothing criminal."* (Luke 23:40-42)

- After His death, the centurion gave glory to God upon seeing what had happened, and offered the opinion that Jesus was the Son of God (Mark 15:39).

- Two prominent members of the Sanhedrin, Joseph of Arimathea and Nicodemus, made public their heretofore hidden discipleship, by approaching Pilate to request Jesus' body for burial (John 19:38-42).

- They defied the ban of according burial rites and a tomb to Jesus condemned as a criminal by Pilate and the Sanhedrin. They chose to give Jesus a tomb and complete the burial rites because they had come to believe that Jesus indeed was the Son of God who died on the cross for the forgiveness of sin and the salvation of the world.

What is God saying to you?

End with Prayer to the Holy Trinity

NIGHT SESSION: Examination of Conscience

For what are you grateful? For what are you contrite?

Please review briefly your Morning Prayer topic. Make it your last thought of the day

DAY TWO: MORNING SESSION

MORNING PRAYER: Act of Faith; Act of Hope; Act of Charity; Daily Offering

Morning Face to Face with God:

Begin with Prayer to the Holy Spirit
Prayer on Hebrews 10:11-14: One Sacrifice instead of many
> *"Every priest stands daily at his ministry, offering frequently those same sacrifices that can never take away sins. But this one offered one sacrifice for sins, and took his seat forever at the right hand of God; now he waits until his enemies are made his footstool. For by one offering he has made perfect forever those who are being consecrated." [Please read Hebrews 10:1-18 for a better appreciation of the passage]*

Ponder the Reflection: ask the Holy Spirit for a deep appreciation of Jesus' love as manifested in His emptying of Himself on the cross!

In different ways the Letter to the Hebrews offers a sharp contrast between the sacrifices of the Old Testament and the sacrifice of Jesus. The Old Testament sacrifices did not bring about the forgiveness of sin and all the spiritual benefits that go with it, but only prefigured them (Verse 1). Hebrews 10:2 then argues that if the sacrifices had actually brought about the forgiveness of sin, there would have been no reason for their constant repetition. The sacrifices were rather a continual reminder of the people's sins (Verse 3), which could not be erased or forgiven through the blood of animal sacrifices (Verse 4). Jesus came to end the tradition of imperfect animal sacrifices by obediently accepting His Father's will to die on the cross. Thus, *"we have been consecrated through the offering of the body of Jesus Christ once for all."* (Hebrews 10:10) Hebrews 10:11-14 reiterates the perfect recompense of one sacrifice instead of many. Jesus is now seated at the right hand of the Father, interceding for us. And through His offering on the cross *"he has made perfect forever those who are being consecrated."*

What is God saying to you?

End with Prayer to the Holy Trinity

NIGHT SESSION: Examination of Conscience

For what are you grateful? For what are you contrite?

Please review briefly your Morning Prayer topic. Make it your last thought of the day

DAY THREE: MORNING SESSION

MORNING PRAYER: Act of Faith; Act of Hope; Act of Charity; Daily Offering

Morning Face to Face with God:

Begin with Prayer to the Holy Spirit
Prayer on Luke 4:28-30: The Rejection at Nazareth
 "When the people in the synagogue heard this, they were all filled with fury. They rose up, drove him out of the town, and led him to the brow of the hill on which their town had been built, to hurl him down headlong. But he passed through the midst of them and went away." [Please read Luke 4:16-30 for a better appreciation of the passage]

Ponder the Reflection: ask the Holy Spirit for a deep appreciation of Jesus' love as manifested in His emptying of Himself on the cross!

Jesus has gone to Nazareth where He was raised. The news of His miracles in Capernaum has reached His hometown. Jesus went into the synagogue on the Sabbath day. He was given the scroll of the Prophet Isaiah which is found in Luke 4:16-18 and is a reference to Isaiah 61:1-3: *"The Spirit of the Lord is upon me, because he has anointed me to bring glad tidings to the poor, etc.…"* In His reflection, Jesus clearly points to Himself as the fulfillment of this prophecy. At first His audience is amazed at the gracious words that come forth from His mouth. But their hearts are hardened and they are unwilling to consider that Jesus is more than the son of Joseph, the carpenter. They are not willing to accept Jesus' message that He is the long-awaited Messiah. When Jesus confronts their stubborn disbelief by saying that Elijah and Elisha could only work miracles among the Gentiles because there was no faith in Israel, they become enraged and attempt to kill Him. Luke places this account at the beginning of Jesus' ministry even though Mark, who is his source, has it at the end of the Galilean ministry (Mark 6). In doing so, Luke is suggesting that the rejection of Jesus will persist throughout His ministry, leading eventually to His rejection by Israel. Later on, Acts 13:46 will echo this rejection of Jesus: *"Both Paul and Barnabas spoke out boldly and said, "It was necessary that the word of God be spoken to you first, but since you reject it and condemn yourselves as unworthy of eternal life, we now turn to the Gentiles."*

What is God saying to you?

End with Prayer to the Holy Trinity

NIGHT SESSION: Examination of Conscience

For what are you grateful? For what are you contrite?

Please review briefly your Morning Prayer topic. Make it your last thought of the day

DAY FOUR: MORNING SESSION

MORNING PRAYER: Act of Faith; Act of Hope; Act of Charity; Daily Offering

Morning Face to Face with God:

Begin with Prayer to the Holy Spirit
Prayer on Philippians 2:6-11: The Emptying of Christ

"Though he was in the form of God, [he] did not regard equality with God something to be grasped. Rather, he emptied himself, taking the form of a slave, coming in human likeness; and found human in appearance, he humbled himself, becoming obedient to death, even death on a cross. Because of this, God greatly exalted him and bestowed on him the name that is above every name, that at the name of Jesus every knee should bend, of those in heaven and on earth and under the earth, and every tongue confess that Jesus Christ is Lord, to the glory of God the Father."

Ponder the Reflection: ask the Holy Spirit for a deep appreciation of Jesus' love as manifested in His emptying of Himself on the cross!

Paul talks about Jesus emptying Himself of His divinity and taking the form of a slave. The Greek word for 'Emptying' is Kenosis. Out of unrestrained and compelling love for us, the Word of God emptied Himself of His glory, so that He could become flesh and make His dwelling among us. And the reason for emptying Himself of His divinity, as John 1:14 tells us, is that *"the Word became flesh and made his dwelling among us, and we saw his glory, the glory as of the Father's only Son, full of grace and truth."* Jesus emptied Himself, and being born in the likeness of men, he took the form of a slave. Satan tries to grasp at equality with God and attract worshipers who will proclaim him as God. Adam and Eve succumbed to Satan's temptation and tried to snatch at equality with God as well. Jesus was God by nature and therefore did not need to grasp at equality with God. Rather, Jesus did the very opposite, and out of love for us, emptied himself of His divinity so that we could be sharers in His divine nature! We share in the same illusion and desire to 'grasp at equality with God.' Only in and through Jesus can we become sharers in God's divine life! Jesus came to ransom us from our slavery to sin and pride.

What is God saying to you?

End with Prayer to the Holy Trinity

NIGHT SESSION: Examination of Conscience

For what are you grateful? For what are you contrite?

Please review briefly your Morning Prayer topic. Make it your last thought of the day

DAY FIVE: MORNING SESSION

MORNING PRAYER: Act of Faith; Act of Hope; Act of Charity; Daily Offering

Morning Face to Face with God:

Begin with Prayer to the Holy Spirit

Prayer on Hebrews 2:14-15: Exaltation through Abasement

"Now since the children share in blood and flesh, he likewise shared in them, that through death he might destroy the one who has the power of death, that is, the devil, and free those who through fear of death had been subject to slavery all their life… he had to become like his brothers in every way, that he might be a merciful and faithful high priest before God to expiate the sins of the people." [Please read Hebrews 2:5-18 for a better appreciation of the passage].

Ponder the Reflection: ask the Holy Spirit for a deep appreciation of Jesus' love as manifested in His emptying of Himself on the cross!

Jesus lived a truly human existence. He was lower than the angels (Verse 7) during His earthly life, especially in His suffering and death. Through His resurrection, Jesus was *crowned with glory and honor.* (Verse 7) He is now raised above all creation. All things are subject to Jesus because of His exaltation, (Verses 8-9) though we do not see this yet. Jesus is now our Leader, leading the people of God on their journey toward the Sabbath rest, (Hebrews 4:9) and into the heavenly sanctuary as our forerunner. (Hebrews 6:20) God made Jesus, our kinsperson, *"perfect through suffering,"* (Verse 10) consecrated (set apart for us by God) by obedient suffering. Because Jesus has been perfected as high priest, He is then able to *"be a merciful and faithful high priest before God to expiate the sins of the people,"* (Verse 15) consecrate us (set us apart) for God. Access to God is made possible through these two consecrations. We have been set apart for God by Jesus' consecration on our behalf. If Jesus is able to help us, it is because He has become one of us. Thus we are His brothers and sisters.

What is God saying to you?

End with Prayer to the Holy Trinity

NIGHT SESSION: Examination of Conscience

For what are you grateful? For what are you contrite?

Please review briefly your Morning Prayer topic. Make it your last thought of the day

DAY SIX: MORNING SESSION

MORNING PRAYER: Act of Faith; Act of Hope; Act of Charity; Daily Offering

Morning Face to Face with God:

Begin with Prayer to the Holy Spirit

REPETITION OF DAYS TWO THROUGH FIVE:

Ask the Holy Spirit for a deep appreciation of Jesus' love as manifested in His emptying of Himself on the cross!

Today, you are doing a repetition of Days Two through Five of this week. In a repetition St. Ignatius says that *"we should pay attention to and dwell upon those points in which we have experienced greater consolation or desolation or greater spiritual appreciation."* (# 62) If you wish, you can do a triple colloquy: refer to #63 of the Spiritual Exercises.

What is God saying to you?

End with Prayer to the Holy Trinity

NIGHT SESSION: Examination of Conscience

For what are you grateful? For what are you contrite?

Please review briefly your Morning Prayer topic. Make it your last thought of the day

DAY SEVEN: MORNING SESSION

MORNING PRAYER: Act of Faith; Act of Hope; Act of Charity; Daily Offering

Morning Face to Face with God:

Begin with Prayer to the Holy Spirit

THE SPIRITUALITY OF ST. FRANCIS OF ASSISI:

(After pondering each bullet point, express your sentiments in a short prayer)

- St. Francis was known to be downright sincere and had the simplicity of a child. When the guardian of the community insisted with Francis to have a fox skin sewn under his worn out tunic to provide some warmth, the saint consented only if another skin of the same size was sewn outside for all to see. His motto was never to hide anything from men that was known to God.
- His quote was, "What a man is in the sight of God, so much he is and no more." This was a saying that passed into the Imitation of Christ which was produced in the fifteenth century.
- St. Francis was unswerving in following an ideal. He always sought the truth. His biographer, Celano, who was a friar himself, says that Francis' "dearest desire so long as

he lived, was ever to seek among wise and simple, perfect and imperfect, the means to walk in the way of truth."

- For St. Francis, love was the greatest of all truths. Hence, he always displayed a deep sense of responsibility towards his fellow humans.

- The love of Christ and Him crucified permeated the whole of Francis' spirituality. He tried to imitate Jesus as literally as he could in his daily life. The distinctive mark of his spirituality was his heroic imitation of Christ's poverty.

- After money, St. Francis detested discord and divisions. He was well known as a peacemaker. In his opinion, the duty of a servant of God was to lift up the hearts of men and move them to spiritual gladness.

- St. Francis had great compassion for those who sinned as evidenced in his advice given to the Minister of one of his houses who wanted to retire to a hermitage because he had difficult community members: "I speak to you, as I can, concerning the state of your soul. You should accept as a grace all those things which deter you from loving the Lord God and whoever has become an impediment to you, whether they are brothers or others, even if they lay hands on you."

- St. Francis also wrote a letter to Saint Anthony of Padua. After joining the Order he was asked to teach the brothers. St. Anthony first wanted permission of St. Francis. Among other things, this is what St. Francis wrote: "I, Brother Francis send wishes of health to Brother Anthony, my bishop. It pleases me that you teach sacred theology to the brothers, as long as in the words of the Rule you 'do not extinguish the Spirit of prayer and devotion' with study of this kind."

- St. Francis died in 1226 at the age of 44, and was canonized in 1228. Before he died he founded three Orders. His imprint on history is the men and women who identify with his vision in the Franciscan way of life.

What is God saying to you?

End with Prayer to the Holy Trinity

NIGHT SESSION: Examination of Conscience

For what are you grateful? For what are you contrite?

What prayer would you compose to express what God has said to you this week?

Please review briefly your Morning Prayer topic. Make it your last thought of the day

SESSION FOUR: THE FRUITS OF DIVINE KENOSIS

"Because of this, God greatly exalted him and bestowed on him the name that is above every name, that at the name of Jesus every knee should bend, of those in heaven and on earth and under the earth, and every tongue confess that Jesus Christ is Lord, to the glory of God the Father."

– Philippians 2:9-11

THE RESURRECTION, PRIMARY FRUIT OF KENOSIS:

The Resurrection of Jesus is the primary fruit of His divine kenosis. All the other fruits described in this session follow from and reveal the deeper layers of the Resurrection. In the Risen Lord, God's glory or total otherness is made manifest to us. In His High Priestly prayer, Jesus prays, *"Father, the hour has come. Give glory to your son, so that your son may glorify you."* (John 17:1) The Resurrection of Jesus is both His hour of glory and the hour of glory for His Father! The Resurrection makes clear that Jesus is LORD and GOD! Jesus' Resurrection puts to rest any question or doubt that the disciples might have had about His divinity! They were hoping that He would be the political Messiah of Israel. But that He would be God? Even though several times one or the other of the disciples received the faith to see that indeed Jesus was God, after His death this incipient faith well-nigh perished. From the Resurrection accounts we know that after His death, Jesus' disciples were discombobulated and terrified out of their wits. They shut themselves behind closed doors for fear of the Jews. It might appear amazing to us that even after three years of being shaped and formed by Jesus, and being counseled repeatedly that their Master would suffer, be crucified and raised from the dead on the third day, that they still lost all hope in Him. They could not comprehend what it meant that Jesus would be raised from the dead. Jesus had emphasized the fact that as their Good Shepherd, He would lay down His life for His sheep. At His death, however, they locked themselves in the Upper Room, cringing and desperately forlorn.

Even after the Resurrection they found it hard to believe the eyewitness accounts that Jesus was raised from the dead! Luke 24:5-11 reports this eyewitness account of the women at the tomb: *"They were terrified and bowed their faces to the ground. They said to them, "Why do you seek the living one among the dead? He is not here, but he has been raised. Remember what he said to you while he was still in Galilee, that the Son of Man must be handed over to sinners and be crucified, and rise on the third day." And they remembered his words. Then they returned from the tomb and announced all these things to the eleven and to all the others. The women were Mary Magdalene, Joanna, and Mary the mother of James; the others who accompanied them also told this to the apostles, but their story seemed like nonsense and they did not believe them."*

Luke narrates another incident of doubt and hopelessness in the story of the disciples on their way to Emmaus. In their conversation with Jesus they revealed the source of their disbelief in the eyewitness account of some in their group: *"But we were hoping that he would be the one to redeem Israel; and besides all this, it is now the third day since this took place. Some women from our group, however, have astounded us: they were at the tomb early in the morning and did not find his body; they came back and reported that they had indeed seen a vision of angels who announced that he was alive. Then some of those with us went to the tomb and found things just as the women had described, but him they did not see."* (Luke 24:21-24) They found it hard to believe the eyewitness account because indeed they were hoping for a political messiah who would set Israel free!

Probably the most significant story of disillusionment and hopelessness is that of Doubting Thomas. The account is found in John 20:24-29. Thomas was not willing to believe the eyewitness accounts of his colleagues with whom he had spent three years of intense formation in discipleship with Jesus. He did not see the Risen Lord as the others did because he chose to absent himself from their company when Jesus appeared to them. His response to his colleagues was both stubborn and disbelieving: *"Unless I see the mark of the nails in his hands and put my finger into the nailmarks and put my hand into his side, I will not believe."* (John 20:25) A week later Jesus appeared to the group and this time Thomas was with them. Jesus invited Thomas to do what he said he needed to do in order to believe, namely, to probe the nail marks with his hand. Instead Thomas exclaimed in astonished belief: *"My Lord and my God!"*

After His Ascension, under the guidance and direction of the Holy Spirit, the disciples' eyes and ears and hearts were finally opened and they came to understand that Jesus indeed was their Lord and God! The progression in the disciples' understanding of the full implications of Jesus' Resurrection can be summed up in John's words from his first letter: *"What was from the beginning, what we have heard, what we have seen with our eyes, what we looked upon and touched with our hands concerns the Word of life – for the life was made visible; we have seen it and testify to it and proclaim to you the eternal life that was with the Father and was made visible to us – what we have seen and heard we proclaim now to you so that you too may have fellowship with us; for our fellowship is with the Father and with his Son, Jesus Christ."* (John 1:1-3)

THE ASCENSION:

There are three accounts of the Ascension. Mark 16:19 puts it very succinctly: *"So then the Lord Jesus, after he spoke to them, was taken up into heaven and took his seat at the right hand of God."* Two accounts are found in Luke's writings, his Gospel account and the Acts of the Apostles. The Ascension of Christ is presented as the climax to his Gospel and also as the most striking element in the introduction to his 'The Acts of the Apostles.' The disciples' experience of Jesus after His death on the cross involves four inseparable events, all emphasizing His glorification: his Resurrection, Exaltation, Ascension, and being seated at the right hand of

God, His Father. After His Resurrection, the River of Trinitarian Life did a split, so to speak. One branch, the Risen Lord, ascended to Heaven and is seated at the right hand of the Father, interceding for His flock on earth and gathering around Him the martyrs, witnesses, and disciples washed white in His blood. The other branch of the River of Trinitarian Life continues to flow among us, forming and expanding the Church, God's covenant family, under the tutelage and direction of the Holy Spirit.

In pondering the Ascension accounts, the reader receives some powerful insights into God's plan of salvation for us. The first fruit of the Risen Christ's Ascension is that the disciples will receive the gift of the Holy Spirit: *"On one occasion when he met with them, he told them not to leave Jerusalem: 'While meeting with them, he enjoined them not to depart from Jerusalem, but to wait for "the promise of the Father about which you have heard me speak; for John baptized with water, but in a few days you will be baptized with the holy Spirit."'"* (Acts 1:4-5) In the great discourse on the eve of His passion and death, Jesus had asked His Father to give us the Holy Spirit, to remain with us and within us (John 14:16-17), and to reveal everything to us that Jesus taught (John 14:26).

Secondly, while Jesus will return to His Father, He will continue to be Emmanuel, God among us, in the Eucharist and through His Holy Spirit, and with Him we will witness to the world about the saving deeds of God: *"But you will receive power when the holy Spirit comes upon you, and you will be my witnesses in Jerusalem, throughout Judea and Samaria, and to the ends of the earth."* (Acts 1:8)

Thirdly, an astonishing change takes place in the disciples at Jesus' Ascension. They are no longer afraid or feel orphaned. They have stopped living hidden lives, and are out in the marketplace, worshiping publicly in the Temple, engaging in constant prayer and praise of God, and letting the world know that indeed the Resurrection of Jesus has impacted their lives beyond measure: *"Then he led them [out] as far as Bethany, raised his hands, and blessed them. As he blessed them he parted from them and was taken up to heaven. They did him homage and then returned to Jerusalem with great joy, and they were continually in the temple praising God."* (Luke 24:50-53)

Perhaps the most telling dimension of Jesus' Ascension into Heaven is the fact that He continues to intercede for us before the throne of His Father: *"Therefore he is always able to save those who approach God through him, since he lives forever to make intercession for them."* (Hebrews 7:25) Romans 8:34 echoes the same sentiment: *"Who will condemn? It is Christ [Jesus] who died, rather, was raised, who also is at the right hand of God, who indeed intercedes for us."* These verses and others like them, tell us that although Christ's work to secure our salvation and bring us into the bosom of God's Trinitarian Life was completed on the cross, His care for His redeemed children will never be over. After all He will always be our Good Shepherd! If when humbled, despised, dying a crucified death, Jesus had the power to accomplish so great a work as reconciling us to God, how much more may we expect that He will be able to secure us within His flock, now that He is a living, exalted, and triumphant Redeemer, raised to life and interceding on our behalf before the throne of God: *"Indeed, if, while we were enemies, we were reconciled to God through the death of his Son, how much more, once reconciled, will we be saved by his life. Not only that, but we also boast of God through our Lord Jesus Christ, through whom we have now received reconciliation."* (Romans 5:10-11) We have the privilege of participating in this saving mystery every time we celebrate Eucharist.

After Jesus ascended to heaven and was seated at the right hand of God the Father, He returned to the glory He had had before His incarnation: *"Now glorify me, Father, with you, with the glory that I had with you before the world began."* (John 17:5) While the world continues to be 'won' for Christ by the Holy Spirit, Jesus is the Advocate for Christians. He is our Great Defender. This is the intercessory role He currently fulfills for those who are His: *"My children, I am writing this to you so that you may not commit sin. But if anyone does sin, we have an Advocate with the Father, Jesus Christ the righteous one. He is expiation for our sins, and not for our sins only but for those of the whole world."* (1 John 2:1-2) Jesus is always pleading our case before the Father, like a defense lawyer on our behalf. He is our Advocate; the Greek word is Advocatos whose meaning is best captured as defense attorney. God always sees in His children the perfect righteousness of Jesus. When Jesus died on the cross, His righteousness (perfect holiness) was given to us to share, while our sin was imputed to Him at His death. This is the great exchange Paul talks about in 2 Corinthians 5:21: *"For our sake he (God) made him to be sin who did not know sin, so that we might become the righteousness of God in him."* This incredible exchange took away forever our sinful state before God. Now God accepts us as blameless before Him through His Son.

SOVEREIGN ROLE OF CHRIST:

The Letter to the Hebrews highlights the sovereign and exalted role of Christ as our heavenly high priest. Hebrews 8:1-2 tells us that *"we have such a high priest, who has taken his seat at the right hand of the throne of the Majesty in heaven, a minister of the sanctuary and of the true tabernacle that the Lord, not man, set up."* And Hebrews 8:6 continues that *"he (Jesus) has obtained so much more excellent a ministry as he is mediator of a better covenant, enacted on better promises."* And in Hebrews 9:24-28, we are told very clearly what the sovereign role of Christ is: *"For Christ did not enter into a sanctuary made by hands, a copy of the true one, but heaven itself, that he might now appear before God on our behalf. Not that he might offer himself repeatedly, as the high priest enters each year into the sanctuary with blood that is not his own; if that were so, he would have had to suffer repeatedly from the foundation of the world. But now once for all he has appeared at the end of the ages to take away sin by his sacrifice. Just as it is appointed that human beings die once, and after this the judgment, so also Christ, offered once to take away the sins of many, will*

MF comment — when everything seems overwhelming, remember that God is the sovereign. Even if evil persists for awhile we trust in God. He will be our strength.

appear a second time, not to take away sin but to bring salvation to those who eagerly await him." We are now children of the sanctuary, gazed upon by the Father through the delight and love He experiences in His Son, Jesus, our Lord and Redeemer!

In the Book of Revelation, John reiterates the sovereign and exalted role of Christ as the Lamb who was slain. In his vision of heavenly worship, John saw the Lamb that was slain as the One who took the scroll in His hands and was able to break open its seals. All the four living creatures and the twenty-four elders fell down before the Lamb in worship and sang this hymn: *"Worthy are you to receive the scroll and to break open its seals, for you were slain and with your blood you purchased for God those from every tribe and tongue, people and nation. You made them a kingdom and priests for our God, and they will reign on earth."* (Revelation 5:9-10) There was another chorus of many angels along with the living creatures and elders who were countless in number, thousands upon tens of thousands and they all cried out: *"Worthy is the Lamb that was slain to receive power and riches, wisdom and strength, honor and glory and blessing."* (Revelation 5:12) Then there was an even larger assembly of voices of every creature in heaven and on earth and under the earth and in the sea; everything in the universe cried aloud: *"To the One who sits on the throne and to the Lamb be blessing and honor, glory and might, forever and ever."* (Revelation 5:13)

And in Colossians 2:15-20, Paul offers a paean exalting the sovereign role of Christ in our lives: *"He is the image of the invisible God, the first-born of all creation. For in him were created all things in heaven and on earth, the visible and the invisible, whether thrones or dominions or principalities or powers; all things were created through him and for him. He is before all things, and in him all things hold together. He is the head of the body, the church. He is the beginning, the firstborn from the dead, that in all things he himself might be preeminent. For in him all the fullness was pleased to dwell, and through him to reconcile all things for him, making peace by the blood of his cross [through him], whether those on earth or those in heaven."*

THE DESCENT OF THE HOLY SPIRIT:

As indicated earlier in the session, the River of Life took on a two-pronged direction in God's Plan of Salvation. With the Ascension, Jesus now gathers around Him thousands upon thousands of martyrs, witnesses, and disciples washed white in the blood of the Lamb. Seated at the right hand of the Father, Jesus is presenting us as sons and daughters of the living God. Meanwhile the River of Life flows through our world and the Church is being formed and strengthened through the action and power of the Holy Spirit. In Acts 1, Jesus tells His disciples not to leave Jerusalem before they had received the Father's promise of being baptized with the Holy Spirit. The Descent of the Holy Spirit upon the apostles was the event signaling the birth of the Church. It was momentous in the way it transformed this very ordinary and scared group of men and women into ardent and enthusiastic disciples and witnesses of Jesus.

After the Outpouring of the Holy Spirit, the disciples were no longer the same individuals. Acts 2:4 tells us that *"they were all filled with the holy Spirit and began to speak in different tongues, as the Spirit enabled them to proclaim."* Later in the chapter, through the action of the Holy Spirit, Peter and the disciples come to full faith in Jesus as Lord and Messiah: *"God raised this Jesus; of this we are all witnesses. Exalted at the right hand of God, he received the promise of the holy Spirit from the Father and poured it forth, as you (both) see and hear."* (Acts 2:32-33)

The Book of Acts is a glorious description of the power of the Holy Spirit at work in the formation and multiplication of Jesus' disciples, leading them to become powerful witnesses of their Lord and Savior. It is truly amazing to see how a small band of disciples, with no political and worldly power, were able to spread so fast, far, and wide, so that by the end of the first century there were communities of Christian disciples scattered all over the Roman Empire. Indeed the promise that Jesus made to His disciples about gifting them with His Holy Spirit was fulfilled beyond their wildest imagination: *"But when he comes, the Spirit of truth, he will guide you to all truth. He will not speak on his own, but he will speak what he hears, and will declare to you the things that are coming. He will glorify me, because he will take from what is mine and declare it to you."* (John 16:13-14)

PARTICIPATION IN GOD'S TRINITARIAN LIFE:

In Jesus we meet God as God really is: *"Whoever has seen me has seen the Father."* (John 14:9) Further John 1:18 says that *"No one has ever seen God. The only Son, God, who is at the Father's side, has revealed him."* In Jesus' words and actions the Father is revealed to us. Jesus tells us that the Father loves us unconditionally. He sent Jesus out of His immeasurable love so that in His blood we might be washed clean of our sins and share in God's divine life: *"And just as Moses lifted up the serpent in the desert, so must the Son of Man be lifted up, so that everyone who believes in him may have eternal life."* (John 3:14-16)

Jesus is the unique Word of God to humanity and the unique Word of humanity to God. Jesus Christ, the only Son of God, has become one with our flesh in order to be our saving kinsman-redeemer, and to represent us, His brothers and sisters, in the very presence of the Father: *"And the Word became flesh and made his dwelling among us, and we saw his glory, the glory as of the Father's only Son, full of grace and truth."* (John 1:14) Or as Paul would put it in Ephesians 1:22-23: *"And he put all things beneath his feet and gave him as head over all things to the church, which is his body, the fullness of the one who fills all things in every way."* Because of Christ, we have a relationship with God! Because of Christ and the Father, the Holy Spirit dwells among us and within us. We are now the abode of the Holy Trinity. We belong to the

Father, are in Christ, the beloved of the Father, and the Holy Spirit is in us as the Keeper of our souls.

Participation in God's Trinitarian Life means entering into and deepening four very personal relationships:

- *The internal relationships shared by Father, Son, and Holy Spirit from all eternity:* Their relationships can be characterized as perichoretic. The Greek Fathers of the Church describe the life of the Trinity as PERICHORESIS (peri = around; choresis = dancing). In the Great Discourse, Jesus gives us a deeper insight into why the Greek Fathers characterized God's life as a divine dance. In John 16:14-15, Jesus says: *"He will glorify me, because he will take from what is mine and declare it to you. Everything that the Father has is mine; for this reason I told you that he will take from what is mine and declare it to you."* Again in His high priestly prayer, Jesus says to His Father: *"and everything of mine is yours and everything of yours is mine, and I have been glorified in them."* (John 17:10) So in the divine dance there is a constant receiving and giving of one another among the Divine Persons. The Father goes out to the Son and gives all His life, love, wisdom, and power. And the Son in turn gives back to the Father all His life, love, wisdom and power, in total obedience to His will. This mutual self-giving is enacted in the Holy Spirit, the bond of love between Father and Son. Everything between Father and Son is done in the Holy Spirit, the giving and the receiving. These movements or 'missions' or processions are the intimate life of God and we have been invited to participate in their relationships in wonder and adoration.

- *The relationship of the eternal Son with humanity, in the Incarnation:* The Word became flesh and dwelt among us. Jesus is fully God and fully human and this will never change. His incarnation did not end with His death or with His resurrection and ascension. He was resurrected and ascended bodily. He will return bodily, the same as He departed. So when we talk of Jesus Christ, we are talking of the Second Person of the Trinity who through His incarnation has brought us into communion with God's Trinitarian Life!

- *The relationship of humanity with the Father through the Son and by the Holy Spirit:* In and through the life, death, resurrection, and ascension of Jesus, all humans are included in the life and love of God: Jesus is the one mediator for all people – past, present, and future: *"For there is one God. There is also one mediator between God and the human race, Christ Jesus, himself human, who gave himself as ransom for all."* (1Timothy 2:5) Jesus died for all humanity: *"Now is the time of judgment on this world; now the ruler of this world will be driven out. And when I am lifted up from the earth, I will draw everyone to myself."* (John 12:31-32)

- *The relationship of humans with one another as children of the Father redeemed by Jesus Christ:* "But God, who is rich in mercy, because of the great love he had for us, even when *we were dead in our transgressions, brought us to life with Christ (by grace you have been saved), raised us up with him, and seated us with him in the heavens in Christ Jesus, that in the ages to come he might show the immeasurable riches of his grace in his kindness to us in Christ Jesus."* (Ephesians 2:4-7) When Jesus died, all humanity died with Him. When Jesus rose, all humanity rose to new life with Him. When Jesus ascended, all humanity ascended and became seated with Him at the Father's side.

THE EUCHARIST:

The Eucharist contains and expresses all the fruits of Jesus' Kenosis. Lumen Gentium 11 proclaims the Eucharist as "the source and summit of the Christian life." From the very beginning Christians have celebrated the Eucharist in a form that has not changed despite the great diversity of times and liturgies. This is because we have been bound by the command Jesus gave us before he died: *"And after he (Jesus) had given thanks, broke it and said, "This is my body that is for you. Do this in remembrance of me." In the same way also the cup, after supper, saying, "This cup is the new covenant in my blood. Do this, as often as you drink in, in remembrance of me."* (1 Corinthians 11:24-25) We will spend four sessions on the Eucharist, because, indeed, it is the source and summit of Christian life.

PRAYER AND REFLECTION ON THE FRUITS OF KENOSIS

WEEK SEVEN: "THEN THE ANGEL SAID TO THE WOMAN IN REPLY, 'DO NOT BE AFRAID! I KNOW THAT YOU ARE SEEKING JESUS THE CRUCIFIED. HE IS NOT HERE, FOR HE HAS BEEN RAISED JUST AS HE SAID. COME AND SEE THE PLACE WHERE HE LAY.'" [MATTHEW 28:5-6]

SPIRITUAL READING FOR THE WEEK:

- **Anoint Us in Your Covenant, Abba-Emmanuel:** Session Four
- **Old Testament:** Two or Three Chapters daily
- **New Testament:** Two or Three Chapters daily
- **Imitation of Christ:** One chapter daily

DAY ONE: MORNING SESSION

MORNING PRAYER: Acts of Faith, Hope, Charity; Daily Offering

Morning Face to Face with God:

Begin with Prayer to the Holy Spirit
THE FRUITS OF KENOSIS:

(After pondering each bullet point, express your sentiments in a short prayer)

- The Resurrection of Jesus is the primary fruit of His divine Kenosis. In the Risen Lord, God's glory or total otherness is made manifest to us. The Resurrection of Jesus is both His hour of glory and the hour of glory for His Father!
- The Resurrection makes clear that Jesus is LORD and GOD! Jesus' Resurrection puts to rest any question or doubt that the disciples might have had about His divinity!
- After His Ascension, under the guidance and direction of the Holy Spirit the disciples' eyes and ears and hearts were finally opened and they came to understand that Jesus indeed was their Lord and God!
- After His Resurrection, the River of Trinitarian Life did a split, so to speak. One branch, the Risen Lord, ascended to Heaven and is seated at the right hand of the Father, interceding for His flock on earth and gathering around Him the martyrs, witnesses, and disciples washed white in His blood.
- The other branch of the River of Trinitarian Life continues to flow among us, forming and expanding the Church, God's covenant family, under the tutelage and direction of the Holy Spirit.
- The first fruit of the Risen Christ's Ascension is that the disciples will receive the gift of the Holy Spirit: *"On one occasion when he met with them, he told them not to leave Jerusalem: 'While meeting with them, he enjoined them not to depart from Jerusalem, but to wait for "the promise of the Father about which you have heard me speak; for John baptized with water, but in a few days you will be baptized with the holy Spirit.'"* (Acts 1:4-5)
- Secondly, while Jesus will return to His Father, He will continue to be Emmanuel, God among us, in the Eucharist and through His Holy Spirit, and with Him we will witness to the world about the saving deeds of God: *"But you will receive power when the holy Spirit comes upon you, and you will be my witnesses in Jerusalem, throughout Judea and Samaria, and to the ends of the earth."* (Acts 1:8)
- Perhaps the most telling dimension of Jesus' Ascension into Heaven is the fact that He continues to intercede for us before the throne of His Father: *"Therefore he is always able to save those who approach God through him, since he lives forever to make intercession for them."* (Hebrews 7:25)

- When Jesus died on the cross, His righteousness (perfect holiness) was given to us to share, while our sin was imputed to Him at His death. This is the great exchange Paul talks about in 2 Corinthians 5:21: *"For our sake he (God) made him to be sin who did not know sin, so that we might become the righteousness of God in him."*
- This incredible exchange took away forever our sinful state before God. Now God accepts us as blameless before Him through His Son.

What is God saying to you?

End with Prayer to the Holy Trinity

NIGHT SESSION: Examination of Conscience

For what are you grateful? For what are you contrite?

Please review briefly your Morning Prayer topic. Make it your last thought of the day

DAY TWO: MORNING SESSION

MORNING PRAYER: Act of Faith; Act of Hope; Act of Charity; Daily Offering

Morning Face to Face with God:

Begin with Prayer to the Holy Spirit
Prayer on Matthew 28:1-6: The Resurrection of Jesus

> *"After the Sabbath, as the first day of the week was dawning, Mary Magdalene and the other Mary came to see the tomb. And behold, there was a great earthquake; for an angel of the Lord descended from heaven, approached, rolled back the stone, and sat upon it. His appearance was like lightning and his clothing was white as snow. The guards were shaken with fear of him and became like dead men. Then the angel said to the women in reply, "Do not be afraid! I know that you are seeking Jesus the crucified. He is not here, for he has been raised just as he said. Come and see the place where he lay." [Please read Matthew 28:1-15 for a better appreciation of the passage].*

Read the Reflection; ask for the grace to be glad and rejoice intensely because of the great joy and the glory of Christ our Lord

Mary Magdalene and the other Mary came to the tomb of Jesus to complete His burial rites. They were not anticipating Jesus' resurrection. They were in the throes of intense sorrow and grief over the passing of their beloved Rabbi. In an instant their desperate frame of mind is replaced by earth-shattering Good News! Matthew begins his account in apocalyptic terms by stating that there was an earthquake. Heaven has descended upon earth in the form of an angel of the Lord, whose appearance is described in a similar way as the transfigured Jesus on Mount Tabor. The Resurrection of Jesus signals the turning of the ages! A paradigmatic change in the world has occurred. No longer will it be the same. Immediately, the Resurrection of Jesus puts its stamp on everything around, bringing it into subjection. The guards are shaken with fear and become like dead men. And the women are freed from their fear, and are filled with exceeding joy at knowing that Jesus has been raised from the dead. And then the angel gives them incontrovertible proof by showing them that the tomb is empty: *"He is not here, for he has been raised, just as he said. Come and see the place where he lay."* In subsequent appearances, the disciples will experience first-hand how the world has been transformed by the resurrection of Jesus!

What is God saying to you?

End with Prayer to the Holy Trinity

NIGHT SESSION: Examination of Conscience

For what are you grateful? For what are you contrite?

Please review briefly your Morning Prayer topic. Make it your last thought of the day

DAY THREE: MORNING SESSION

MORNING PRAYER: Act of Faith; Act of Hope; Act of Charity; Daily Offering

Morning Face to Face with God:

Begin with Prayer to the Holy Spirit
Prayer on Mark 16:9-11: The Appearance to Mary Magdalene:
   "When he had risen, early on the first day of the week, he appeared first to Mary Magdalene, out of whom he had driven seven demons. She went and told his companions who were mourning and weeping. When they heard that he was alive and had been seen by her, they did not believe."

Read the Reflection; ask for the grace to be glad and rejoice intensely because of the great joy and the glory of Christ our Lord

An amazing transformation took place in Mary Magdalene as a result of Jesus' ministrations. Mark 16:9 notes that *"Jesus rose from the dead early on the first day of the week. He first appeared to Mary Magdalene, out of whom he had cast seven demons."* We know from various references in the New Testament, that demons were fallen angels ruled by Satan. They knew who Jesus was.

They were in fear of him and there was no reconciliation possible between them and Jesus. If Mary had seven demons possessing her, the poor woman was wretched and overpowered by evil influences at their most destructive and powerful extent! In the eyes of society she would have been seen and despised as a sinner and lost sheep of Israel, thus causing unimaginable shame and anguish to herself and her family. Through Jesus, Mary was transformed. She has become His devoted disciple. Only Jesus could recognize God's own image and likeness in Mary, snatch her out of the hands of Satan, and claim her as His own. Mary is very special to Jesus, and the Risen Lord gives her the exquisite privilege of appearing to her. The apparition to Mary is the first one recorded in the Gospels, indicating the appreciation and importance the early Christian community accorded her.

What is God saying to you?

End with Prayer to the Holy Trinity

NIGHT SESSION: Examination of Conscience

For what are you grateful? For what are you contrite?

Please review briefly your Morning Prayer topic. Make it your last thought of the day

DAY FOUR: MORNING SESSION

MORNING PRAYER: ACT OF FAITH; ACT OF HOPE; ACT OF CHARITY; DAILY OFFERING

Morning Face to Face with God:

Begin with Prayer to the Holy Spirit
Prayer on John 20:19-23: Appearance to the Disciples:
> *"Jesus came and stood in their midst and said to them, "Peace be with you." When he had said this, he showed them his hands and his side. The disciples rejoiced when they saw the Lord. [Jesus] said to them again, "Peace be with you. As the Father has sent me, so I send you." And when he had said this, he breathed on them and said to them, "Receive the holy Spirit. Whose sins you forgive are forgiven them, and whose sins you retain are retained."*

Read the Reflection; ask for the grace to be glad and rejoice intensely because of the great joy and the glory of Christ our Lord

In John, the Resurrection, Ascension, and Imparting of the Holy Spirit are seen as different aspects of the same divine mystery. The disciples are transformed by the gift of the Holy Spirit being given to them by the Risen Jesus. This gift will be unleashed in them at the Outpouring of the Holy Spirit and after the Ascension. Two points are worthy of note in this resurrection event. Jesus, the Risen Lord, breathes the Holy Spirit into His apostles. He breathes into them His own divine life through His Holy Spirit. Secondly, through the Holy Spirit, Jesus gives His apostles the power to forgive and retain sin. God took an amazing risk to allow humans to exercise this power in His name. Twenty centuries of chosen humans, our bishops and priests, exercising this power in Jesus' name, has turned out to be an immense grace. God always knows best. As with Jesus, so with us, we will live and serve in the power and overshadowing of the Holy Spirit. The breathing of the Holy Spirit upon us by Jesus is our re-creation. We are begotten of the Spirit who will guide us to all truth and in doing so will give glory to Jesus!

What is God saying to you?

End with Prayer to the Holy Trinity

NIGHT SESSION: EXAMINATION OF CONSCIENCE

For what are you grateful? For what are you contrite?

Please review briefly your Morning Prayer topic. Make it your last thought of the day

DAY FIVE: MORNING SESSION

MORNING PRAYER: Act of Faith; Act of Hope; Act of Charity; Daily Offering

Morning Face to Face with God:

Begin with Prayer to the Holy Spirit
Prayer on John 20:27-29: The Doubting Thomas
> *"Then he said to Thomas, "Put your finger here and see my hands, and bring your hand and put it into my side, and do not be unbelieving, but believe." Thomas answered and said to him, "My Lord and my God!" Jesus said to him, "Have you come to believe because you have seen me? Blessed are those who have not seen and have believed." [Please read John 20:24-29 for a better appreciation of the passage].*

Read the Reflection; ask for the grace to be glad and rejoice intensely because of the great joy and the glory of Christ our Lord

Probably the most significant story of disillusionment and hopelessness is that of Doubting Thomas. Thomas was not willing to believe the eyewitness accounts of his colleagues with whom he had spent three years of intense discipleship with Jesus. He did not witness the Risen

Lord as the others did because he chose to absent himself from their company when Jesus appeared to them. His response to his colleagues was both stubborn and disbelieving: *"Unless I see the mark of the nails in his hands and put my finger into the nailmarks and put my hand into his side, I will not believe."* (Verse 25) A week later, Jesus appeared to the group. This time Thomas was with them. Jesus invited Thomas to do what he said he needed to do in order to believe, namely, to probe the nail marks with his hand. Instead Thomas exclaimed in astonished belief: *"My Lord and my God!"* Jesus then gave Thomas some salutary advice which we need to take to heart: *"Blessed are those who have not seen and have believed."* In the ultimate analysis, true discipleship can only be anchored in childlike trust and faith in Jesus.

What is God saying to you?

End with Prayer to the Holy Trinity

NIGHT SESSION: Examination of Conscience

For what are you grateful? For what are you contrite?

Please review briefly your Morning Prayer topic. Make it your last thought of the day

DAY SIX: MORNING SESSION

MORNING PRAYER: Act of Faith; Act of Hope; Act of Charity; Daily Offering

Morning Face to Face with God:

Begin with Prayer to the Holy Spirit
REPETITION OF DAYS TWO THROUGH FIVE:

Read the Reflection; ask for the grace to be glad and rejoice intensely because of the great joy and the glory of Christ our Lord

Today, you are doing a repetition of Days Two through Five of this week. In a repetition St. Ignatius says that *"we should pay attention to and dwell upon those points in which we have experienced greater consolation or desolation or greater spiritual appreciation."* (# 62) If you wish, you can do a triple colloquy: refer to #63 of the Spiritual Exercises.

What is God saying to you?

End with Prayer to the Holy Trinity

NIGHT SESSION: Examination of Conscience

For what are you grateful? For what are you contrite?

Please review briefly your Morning Prayer topic. Make it your last thought of the day

DAY SEVEN: MORNING SESSION

MORNING PRAYER: Act of Faith; Act of Hope; Act of Charity; Daily Offering

Morning Face to Face with God:

Begin with Prayer to the Holy Spirit
THE FIRST DWELLING PLACES OF THE INTERIOR CASTLE:

(After pondering each bullet point, express your sentiments in a short prayer)

- St. Teresa has a very definite starting point when one is talking about entering into a serious life of prayer. There has to be an honest and deliberate effort to root out sins, imperfections and disordered attachments which lead to dissipation and desolation. These are movements that draw us away from God and leave us lukewarm.
- The reason for this is that true prayer is the honest expression of a total commitment to Jesus in a covenant relationship with Him. Any meaningful relationship with Jesus can only be on His terms, as we are entering into covenant relationship with our holy, loving, and amazing God.
- Any form of self-centeredness where the emphasis is on self-aggrandizement rather than on humble discipleship, will destroy the relationship, or at best leave it tepid.
- This starting point was based on St. Teresa's own experience and journey. She had joined the Carmelite Order at the age of nineteen. It took her twenty long years before she arrived at her starting point of living her relationship with God with a forthright commitment to avoiding all deliberate sin.
- In her first Three Dwelling Places, the saint describes in sufficient detail how the beginner, even though in the state of grace, can and must emerge from a whole web of petty faults if their relationship with God is to become meaningful and move into any great depth.
- She offers us the image of the soul as being God's dwelling place with many rooms or mansions. God dwells in the heart of a person's being as we are indeed the image and likeness of God. The journey takes us from the outermost rooms to the room where God dwells.

- Most of us choose to live outside of ourselves, immersed completely in the world and its values that are contradictory to the spirit and teachings of Jesus. As a result we are strangers to ourselves and to God.

What is God saying to you?

End with Prayer to the Holy Trinity

NIGHT SESSION: Examination of Conscience

For what are you grateful? For what are you contrite?

What prayer would you compose to express what God has said to you this week?

Please review briefly your Morning Prayer topic. Make it your last thought of the day

PRAYER AND REFLECTION ON THE FRUITS OF KENOSIS - CONTINUED

WEEK EIGHT: *"The fruit of the spirit is love, joy, peace, patience, kindness, generosity, faithfulness, gentleness, self-control. Against such there is no law. Now those who belong to Christ [Jesus] have crucified their flesh with its passions and desires. If we live in the spirit, let us follow the spirit." [Galatians 5:22-25]*

SPIRITUAL READING FOR THE WEEK:

- **Anoint Us in Your Covenant, Abba-Emmanuel:** Session Four
- **Old Testament:** Two or Three Chapters daily
- **New Testament:** Two or Three Chapters daily
- **Imitation of Christ:** One chapter daily

DAY ONE: MORNING SESSION

MORNING PRAYER: Acts of Faith, Hope, Charity; Daily Offering

Morning Face to Face with God:

Begin with Prayer to the Holy Spirit

ON THE FRUITS OF KENOSIS:

(After pondering each bullet point, express your sentiments in a short prayer)

- The letter to the Hebrews highlights the sovereign role of Christ as our heavenly high priest. Hebrews 8:1-2 tells us that *"we have such a high priest, who has taken his seat at the right hand of the throne of the Majesty in heaven, a minister of the sanctuary and of the true tabernacle that the Lord, not man, set up."*

- In the Book of Revelation, John reiterates the sovereign role of Christ as the Lamb who was slain. All the four living creatures and the twenty-four elders fell down before the Lamb in worship and sang this hymn: *"Worthy are you to receive the scroll and to break open its seals, for you were slain and with your blood you purchased for God those from every tribe and tongue, people and nation. You made them a kingdom and priests for our God, and they will reign on earth."* (Revelation 5:9-10)

- There was another chorus of many angels along with the living creatures and elders who were countless in number, thousands upon tens of thousands and they all cried out: *"Worthy is the Lamb that was slain to receive power and riches, wisdom and strength, honor and glory and blessing."* (Revelation 5:12)

- Then there was an even larger assembly of voices of every creature in heaven and on earth and under the earth and in the sea; everything in the universe cried aloud: *"To the One who sits on the throne and to the Lamb be blessing and honor, glory and might, forever and ever."* (Revelation 5:13)

- And in Colossians 2:15-20, Paul offers a paean exalting the sovereign role of Christ in our lives: *"He is the image of the invisible God, the first-born of all creation. For in him were created all things in heaven and on earth, the visible and the invisible, whether thrones or dominions or principalities or powers; all things were created through him and for him. He is before all things, and in him all things hold together. He is the head of the body, the church. He is the beginning, the firstborn from the dead, that in all things he himself might be preeminent. For in him all the fullness was pleased to dwell, and through him to reconcile all things for him, making peace by the blood of his cross [through him], whether those on earth or those in heaven."*

- It is truly amazing to see how a small band of disciples, with no political and worldly power, were able to spread so fast, far and wide, so that by the end of the first century there were communities of Christian disciples scattered all over the Roman Empire.

- Indeed the promise that Jesus made to His disciples about gifting them with His Holy Spirit was fulfilled beyond their wildest imagination: *"But when he comes, the Spirit of truth, he will guide you to all truth. He will not speak on his own, but he will speak what he hears, and will declare to you the things that are coming. He will glorify me, because he will take from what is mine and declare it to you."* (John 16:13-14)

- In Jesus we meet God as God really is: *"Whoever has seen me has seen the Father."* (John 14:9) Further John 1:18 says, that *"No one has ever seen God. The only Son, God, who is at the Father's side, has revealed him."* In Jesus' words and actions the Father is revealed to us.

- Jesus tells us that the Father loves us unconditionally. He sent Jesus out of His immeasurable love so that in His blood we might be washed clean of our sins and share in God's divine life: *"And just as Moses lifted up the serpent in the desert, so must the Son of Man be lifted up, so that everyone who believes in him may have eternal life."* (John 3:14-16)

- Jesus is the unique Word of God to humanity and the unique Word of humanity to God. Jesus Christ, the only Son of God, has become one with our flesh in order to be our saving kinsman-redeemer, and to represent us, His brothers and sisters, in the very presence of the Father.

What is God saying to you?

End with Prayer to the Holy Trinity

NIGHT SESSION: Examination of Conscience

For what are you grateful? For what are you contrite?

Please review briefly your Morning Prayer topic. Make it your last thought of the day

DAY TWO: MORNING SESSION

MORNING PRAYER: Act of Faith; Act of Hope; Act of Charity; Daily Offering

Morning Face to Face with God:

Begin with Prayer to the Holy Spirit
Prayer on Acts 1:8-9: Jesus' Ascension:
   "But you will receive power when the holy Spirit comes upon you, and you will be my witnesses in Jerusalem, throughout Judea and Samaria, and to the ends of the earth." When he had said this, as they were looking on, he was lifted up, and a cloud took him from their sight." [Please read Acts 1:6–12 for a better appreciation of the passage].

Read the Reflection; ask for the grace to be glad and rejoice intensely because of the great joy and the glory of Christ our Lord

Along with Mark who has a brief account of the Ascension of Jesus in the longer ending, there are two accounts of the Ascension in Luke's writings, his Gospel account and the Acts of the Apostles which has the more detailed account. In pondering the Ascension accounts, the reader receives some powerful insights into God's plan of salvation for us. The first fruit of the Risen Christ's Ascension is the gift of the Holy Spirit: *"But you will receive power when the holy Spirit comes upon you, and you will be my witnesses in Jerusalem, throughout Judea and Samaria, and to the ends of the earth."* (Acts 1:8) And Mary, mother of Jesus, was present with the disciples as they prepared in prayer to receive the Holy Spirit. (Acts 1:14) Secondly, while Jesus will return to His Father, He will continue to be Emmanuel, God among us in the Eucharist and through His Holy Spirit. With Jesus dwelling in His covenant family, and in our hearts, we will witness to the world about the saving deeds of God. Thirdly, an astonishing change takes place in the disciples at Jesus' Ascension. They are no longer afraid or feel orphaned. They are out in the marketplace and worship publicly in the temple, engaging in constant prayer and praise of God: *"They did him homage and then returned to Jerusalem with great joy, and they were continually in the temple praising God."* (Luke 24:52-53)

What is God saying to you?

End with Prayer to the Holy Trinity

NIGHT SESSION: Examination of Conscience

For what are you grateful? For what are you contrite?

Please review briefly your Morning Prayer topic. Make it your last thought of the day

DAY THREE: MORNING SESSION

MORNING PRAYER: Act of Faith; Act of Hope; Act of Charity; Daily Offering

Morning Face to Face with God:

Begin with Prayer to the Holy Spirit
Prayer on Revelation 5:8-10 Worship of the Lamb that was slain
   "When he took it (the scroll), the four living creatures and the twenty-four elders fell down before the Lamb. Each of the elders held a harp and gold bowls filled with incense, which are the prayers of the holy ones. They sang a hymn: "Worthy are you to receive the scroll and to break open its seals, for you were slain and with your blood you purchased for God those from every tribe and tongue, people and nation. You made them a kingdom and priests for our God, and they will reign on earth." [Please read all of Chapter 5 for a better appreciation of the Lamb's role in heaven]

Read the Reflection; ask for the grace to be glad and rejoice intensely because of the great joy and the glory of Christ our Lord

The Risen Lord ascends to His Father and ours. His ascension signals the completion of His Father's mission to Him. The scroll symbolized God's plan of salvation which was to liberate us from our enslavement to Satan, sin, and permanent death. Through His death, the Lamb (Jesus is addressed as Lamb twenty eight times in Revelation) has broken open the seals of the scroll. Jesus has nailed once and for all our bondage to sin (Colossians 2:14). With His ascension, Jesus returns in triumph and glory to His Father. In heaven, the ascended Christ is worshiped and glorified by the twenty-four elders who represent the twelve tribes of Israel and the twelve apostles, and the four living creatures who represent all of creation. God's covenant family, made possible through the new and everlasting covenant established once and for all by the Lamb that was slain, now engages in worship of the Trinity through the Risen Jesus. And now the Risen Lord's role is to be the Intercessor for His covenant family. And the prayers of His covenant family rise to the Father as incense along with the intercession of His Son, our Lord and Savior.

What is God saying to you?

End with Prayer to the Holy Trinity

NIGHT SESSION: Examination of Conscience

For what are you grateful? For what are you contrite?

Please review briefly your Morning Prayer topic. Make it your last thought of the day

DAY FOUR: MORNING SESSION

MORNING PRAYER: Act of Faith; Act of Hope; Act of Charity; Daily Offering

Morning Face to Face with God:

Begin with Prayer to the Holy Spirit
Prayer on Acts 2:1-4: The Descent of the Holy Spirit:
   "When the time for Pentecost was fulfilled, they were all in one place together. And suddenly there came from the sky a noise like a strong driving wind, and it filled the entire house in which they were. Then there appeared to them tongues as of fire, which parted and came to rest on each one of them. And they were all filled with the holy Spirit and began to speak in different tongues, as

the Spirit enabled them to proclaim." [Please read Acts 2:1-13 for a better appreciation of the passage].

Read the Reflection; ask for the grace to be glad and rejoice intensely because of the great joy and the glory of Christ our Lord

The Descent of the Holy Spirit upon the apostles reverberated with the power and majesty of God, and brought about amazing transformation in the apostles and bystanders. The Outpouring of the Holy Spirit occasioned the birth of the Church. The Holy Spirit is described as *"a strong driving wind,"* and *"tongues of fire."* Fire symbolized the presence of God to initiate the covenant on Sinai. Here the Holy Spirit acts upon the apostles, preparing them to proclaim the new covenant with its unique gift of the Divine Spirit. The apostles were filled with the Holy Spirit and began to express themselves in foreign tongues and make bold proclamations. The bystanders were utterly amazed and dumbfounded because they could understand the apostles speaking to them in their own tongues. Being able to understand the apostles in their own languages was already signaling the catholicity of God's covenant family. What an amazing manifestation of God's power in and through the Holy Spirit!

What is God saying to you?

End with Prayer to the Holy Trinity

NIGHT SESSION: Examination of Conscience

For what are you grateful? For what are you contrite?

Please review briefly your Morning Prayer topic. Make it your last thought of the day

DAY FIVE: MORNING SESSION

MORNING PRAYER: Act of Faith; Act of Hope; Act of Charity; Daily Offering

Morning Face to Face with God:

Begin with Prayer to the Holy Spirit
Prayer on Galatians 5:22-25: The Fruit of the Spirit:
   "The fruit of the Spirit is love, joy, peace, patience, kindness, generosity, faithfulness, gentleness, self-control. Against such there is no law. Now those who belong to Christ [Jesus] have crucified their flesh with its passions and desires. If we live in the Spirit, let us also follow the Spirit."

Read the Reflection; ask for the grace to be glad and rejoice intensely because of the great joy and the glory of Christ our Lord

Through these gifts we receive an appreciation of God's life, of the Trinitarian relationships, and of the meaning of being in a new and everlasting covenant with the Triune God who is Covenant itself. We are heirs with Christ of God's eternal Life because of God's love for us. Joy and Peace are innate to the Risen Lord, and are offered to us as lasting signs of our insertion into God's divine life. Peace and Joy are our unassailable security in Jesus who has overcome Satan, sin, and death. Only Jesus can share His Peace and Joy with us because the Trinity is the Source, and Jesus is both the Source and the Way to receive the Trinitarian gifts of peace and joy through the Holy Spirit. As we enter more deeply into Trinitarian Life and put on the mind and heart of Jesus Christ, we learn to become as the Trinity is in relationship to us through the Holy Spirit. We learn to be patient and faithful as God, who throughout the history of human beings has been patient in endurance, both in His fidelity to the covenants, and to us in our sin and rebellion! Like God, under the tutelage of the Holy Spirit, we too learn to be kind and generous. Our gentleness and self-control are a sharing in God's own transparency of spirit.

What is God saying to you?

End with Prayer to the Holy Trinity

NIGHT SESSION: Examination of Conscience

For what are you grateful? For what are you contrite?

Please review briefly your Morning Prayer topic. Make it your last thought of the day

DAY SIX: MORNING SESSION

MORNING PRAYER: Act of Faith; Act of Hope; Act of Charity; Daily Offering

Morning Face to Face with God:

Begin with Prayer to the Holy Spirit

REPETITION OF DAYS TWO THROUGH FIVE:

Read the Reflection; ask for the grace to be glad and rejoice intensely because of the great joy and the glory of Christ our Lord

Today, you are doing a repetition of Days Two through Five of this week. In a repetition

St. Ignatius says that *"we should pay attention to and dwell upon those points in which we have experienced greater consolation or desolation or greater spiritual appreciation."* (# 62) If you wish, you can do a triple colloquy: refer to #63 of the Spiritual Exercises.

What is God saying to you?

End with Prayer to the Holy Trinity

NIGHT SESSION: Examination of Conscience

For what are you grateful? For what are you contrite?

Please review briefly your Morning Prayer topic. Make it your last thought of the day

DAY SEVEN: MORNING SESSION

MORNING PRAYER: Act of Faith; Act of Hope; Act of Charity; Daily Offering

Morning Face to Face with God:

Begin with Prayer to the Holy Spirit

THE FIRST DWELLING PLACES OF THE INTERIOR CASTLE - Continued:

(After pondering each bullet point, express your sentiments in a short prayer)

- In the First Dwelling Places, the relationship of the beginner with God is tenuous at best. The beginner is living on the periphery of his authentic self. While they have entered into God's dwelling place in their souls, they are still immersed in the things of the world. In fact they have contaminated themselves by bringing in the contrary values of the world.

- While they are conscientious and hard-working, their world revolves around their dreams and goals which occupy all their energies and passion. Too many things entice and distract them, and thus prevent them from taking the time to search for the true light. As a result, the divine light scarcely illuminates their lives and consciousness. They live in a permanent spiritual fog.

- God is kept at the periphery of their lives. They are so involved in worldly things, and so absorbed with its possessions, honor, or business affairs, that they are unable to satisfy their good and holy desires.

- If the beginner is to become a serious follower they must leave behind the spirit of the world which emphasizes their glorification at all costs, or else they will not proceed into the Second Dwelling Places.
- What kind of prayer does a beginner at this stage do? Because the beginner is still immersed in the affairs of the world which promote their own aggrandizement, their prayer will tend to be superficial and ritualistic.
- They will pray on occasion. They will go through their religious observances dutifully, albeit perfunctorily. To help such beginners enter into the deeper recesses of their soul where the Trinity dwells, St. Teresa emphasizes the necessity of practicing prayer and reflection that focuses on love and an honest relationship with God.
- She valued thoughtful reflection that moved the heart and connected with God: *"A prayer in which a person is not aware of whom he is speaking to, what he is asking, who it is who is asking and of whom, I do not call prayer however much the lips move."* (TIC- I:1:7)
- The Gospels are a fruitful source of meditative prayer as they offer the most profound revelation into the different mysteries of Trinitarian Life and God's Plan of Salvation.
- So for prayer there are no complicated steps. It is love, not reasoning that is primary. *"In order to profit by this path and ascend to the dwelling places we desire, the important thing is not to think much, but to love much; and to do that which is best stirs you to love."* (TIC - IV-1:7)
- To summarize then, a beginner in the First Dwelling Places would have to work on developing a habit of praying regularly, learning to pray from the heart with as much honesty and reverence towards God, to avoid sin and its occasions and move towards repentance, to consciously be present to God and reject values opposed to Jesus and His teachings.

What is God saying to you?

End with Prayer to the Holy Trinity

NIGHT SESSION: Examination of Conscience

For what are you grateful? For what are you contrite?

What prayer would you compose to express what God has said to you this week?

Please review briefly your Morning Prayer topic. Make it your last thought of the day

SESSION FIVE:
GATHERED AND ENLIVENED BY THE HOLY SPIRIT

"But you will receive power when the holy Spirit comes upon you, and you will be my witnesses in Jerusalem, throughout Judea and Samaria, and to the ends of the earth. When he had said this, as they were looking on, he was lifted up, and a cloud took him from their sight."

– Acts 1:8-9

HANDING OVER ADVOCACY TO THE HOLY SPIRIT:

Jesus has accomplished His mission on earth. As the Lamb that was slain and our High Priest, He has entered God's Sanctuary once and for all, and established on our behalf the new and everlasting covenant with our Triune God. He has fulfilled His Father's will and made us adopted sons and daughters of God. Seated at His Father's Right Hand, Jesus is now our Intercessor, gathering to Himself the fruits of His harvest, the holy men and women, martyrs and witnesses among them, who have been washed white in His blood, and participate in God's own life. They surround Jesus as His heavenly assembly, and through Him, along with the Cherubim and Seraphim, offer continual adoration, praise, and thanksgiving to the Trinity: *"Then I heard every creature in heaven and on earth and under the earth and in the sea, everything in the universe, cry out: "To the one who sits on the throne and to the Lamb be blessing and honor, glory and might, forever and ever. The four living creatures answered, "Amen," and the elders fell down and worshiped."* (Revelation 5:13-14)

Meanwhile, there are other sheep which need to be brought into the fold, as Jesus tells us in John 10:16: *"I have other sheep that do not belong to this fold. These also I must lead, and they will hear my voice, and there will be one flock, one shepherd."* Hanging on the cross, and just before He gave up His spirit, Jesus did one final survey of His mission on earth. John 20:28-30 tells us that *"after this, aware that everything was now finished, in order that the scripture might be fulfilled, Jesus said, 'I thirst.'"* There was a vessel filled with common wine. So they put a sponge soaked in wine on a sprig of hyssop and put it up to his mouth. When Jesus had taken the wine, he said, *"It is finished." And bowing his head, he handed over the spirit."* At that moment He had entered into His kingdom and accomplished covenant union with God on our behalf. It is significant that at His death, the separation in the Temple between God's abode in the Holy of Holies and the people's holy place was ripped apart: *"Then the veil of the temple was torn down the middle. Jesus cried out in a loud voice, 'Father, into your hands I commend my spirit'; and when he had said this he breathed his last."* (Luke 23:45b-46)

As Risen Lord, given the accomplishment of His mission on earth, the time to return to His Father has come. While He will be gathering in the harvest of His Exodus/Passover around

Him in heaven, His Holy Spirit will continue to assemble and strengthen God's covenant family on earth, sanctifying and blessing it with His gifts, and keeping the bride faithful to the teachings of the bridegroom: *"But when he comes, the Spirit of truth, he will guide you to all truth. He will not speak on his own, but he will speak what he hears, and will declare to you the things that are coming. He will glorify me, because he will take from what is mine and declare it to you. Everything that the Father has is mine; for this reason I told you that he will take from what is mine and declare it to you."* (John 16:12-15) The Holy Spirit will bring to completion, therefore, the work of salvation and restoration accomplished in Jesus by the Father.

THE BIRTH OF THE CHURCH OR GOD'S COVENANT FAMILY:

The Church, or God's universal covenant family, was born with a bang and sweep that was extraordinary and transformative. The Descent of the Holy Spirit brought about a paradigmatic change in the world. Since then the world has never been the same. After Jesus ascended to His Father, all the apostles, except for Judas Iscariot, along with some women, and Mary the mother of Jesus, and His brothers, went to the Upper Room where they were staying. They devoted themselves with one accord to prayer, in preparation and anticipation of the anointing of the Holy Spirit: *"All these devoted themselves with one accord to prayer, together with some women, and Mary the mother of Jesus, and his brothers."* (Acts 1:14)

Acts 2 describes the Descent of the Holy Spirit upon the apostles and those assembled with them. They were all in one place together during the feast of Pentecost. *"And suddenly there came from the sky a noise like a strong driving wind, and it filled the entire house in which they were. Then there appeared to them tongues as of fire, which parted and came to rest on each one of them. And they were all filled with the holy Spirit and began to speak in different tongues, as the Spirit enabled them to proclaim."* (Acts 2:2-4) The disciples heard a sudden noise like a strong driving wind which filled the entire house in which they were. John 3:8 tells us that *"the wind blows where it wills, and you can hear the sound it makes, but you do not know where it comes from or where it goes; so it is with everyone who is born of the Spirit."* While the disciples were preparing for this anointing from the Holy Spirit at Jesus' behest, they were incapable of knowing how exactly the Holy Spirit would behave, and what changes would take place in their lives as God fulfilled His Plan of Salvation in Jesus. The Holy Spirit indeed turned out to be a mighty wind of change!

After the Holy Spirit's first manifestation in the form of a strong wind, there came a second sign of the Spirit's Presence in the room: *"Then there appeared to them tongues as of fire, which parted and came to rest on each one of them."* In Exodus 19:18, God's presence is denoted by fire: *"Now Mount Sinai was completely enveloped in smoke, because the LORD had come down upon it in fire."* The same is true at the Burning Bush with Moses. In Matthew 3:11, John the Baptist confesses, *"I am baptizing you with water, for repentance, but the one who is coming after me is mightier than I. I am not worthy to carry his sandals. He will baptize you with the holy Spirit and fire."* The water baptism of John will be followed by a subsequent "immersion" of the repentant sinner in the cleansing power of the Spirit of God, and of the unrepentant in the destroying power of God's judgment. Some commentators see the *Holy Spirit* and *fire* as synonymous, and the effect of this "baptism," as either purification or destruction. And in John 1:32-34, John the Baptist testified further saying, *"I saw the Spirit come down like a dove from the sky and remain upon him. I did not know him, but the one who sent me to baptize with water told me, 'On whomever you see the Spirit come down and remain, he is the one who will baptize with the holy Spirit.' Now I have seen and testified that he is the Son of God."* Jesus is the one upon whom the Holy Spirit descended at His baptism. Jesus is also the one who is bringing about this same baptism of the Holy Spirit upon His disciples. In John 20:19-23, Jesus came and stood in the midst of His disciples while they were gathered together behind closed doors. He greeted them with His peace and then spoke to them in the following manner: *"As the Father has sent me, so I send you."* *And when he had said this, he breathed on them and said to them, "Receive the holy Spirit. Whose sins you forgive are forgiven them, and whose sins you retain are retained."* (John 20:21-23)

The Holy Trinity, Father, Son, and Holy Spirit, is present in the gathered covenant community at Pentecost. The Father, through His Son Jesus, is baptizing the disciples with His Holy Spirit. The disciples are being immersed in the power of the Holy Spirit as Jesus was upon his baptism: *"And they were all filled with the holy Spirit and began to speak in different tongues, as the Spirit enabled them to proclaim."* (Acts 2:4) As a result of the Holy Spirit's anointing upon them, the disciples began to proclaim the praises of God in ecstatic prayer, interpreted as speaking in foreign languages, symbolizing the catholic or worldwide mission of the church. This glorious and supernatural intervention of the Holy Spirit into the lives of the disciples created a mighty buzz in the people around them: *"Now there were devout Jews from every nation under heaven staying in Jerusalem. At this sound, they gathered in a large crowd, but they were confused because each one heard them speaking in his own language. They were astounded, and in amazement they asked, "Are not all these people who are speaking Galileans? Then how does each of us hear them in his own native language? ...yet we hear them speaking in our own tongues of the mighty acts of God."* (Acts 2:5-8; 11)

The Outpouring of the Holy Spirit upon the disciples inaugurates the genesis and expansion of God's covenant family, beginning in Jerusalem and moving to the ends of the earth. Just before Jesus ascended to His Father, He had this to say to His disciples: *"Thus it is written that the Messiah would suffer and rise and from the dead on the third day and that repentance, for the forgiveness of sins, would be preached in his name to all the nations, beginning from Jerusalem. You are witnesses of these things. And [behold] I am sending the promise of my Father upon you, but stay in the city until you are clothed with power from on high."* (Luke 24:46-49)

Peter begins his kerygma or proclamation of the Good News in the power of the Holy Spirit. The upshot of his preaching was to let all of Israel know for certain that *"God has made him*

(Jesus) both Lord and Messiah, this Jesus whom you crucified." (Acts 2:36) Peter's proclamation elicited a powerful response from his listeners. They were cut to the quick and asked Peter and the other apostles what they should do. In response, Peter said, *"Repent and be baptized, every one of you, in the name of Jesus Christ for the forgiveness of your sins; and you will receive the gift of the holy Spirit. For the promise is made to you and to your children and to all those far off, whomever the Lord our God will call."* (Acts 2:38-39). About three thousand persons accepted Peter's proclamation and were baptized.

Several changes are being orchestrated with the power of the Holy Spirit descending upon the apostles. Before the Resurrection, Peter denied Jesus. After the Resurrection and before the Outpouring of the Holy Spirit, Peter was hesitant to state categorically that he would love his Master and Lord to the death. In John 21, instead of offering Jesus agapé love, his response was mediocre. He said that he was prepared to love Jesus as a friend. Jesus did, however, predict that one day Peter would indeed love Him with agapé love, referring to his death by crucifixion. With the baptism of the Holy Spirit, Peter is emboldened, enthusiastic, and convincing. Later on, in Acts 4, Peter and John are brought before the Sanhedrin and one would have expected them to be intimidated by this powerful religious assembly. The exact opposite is the case. They are fearless in their witness of Jesus as their Risen Lord. Even after they have been threatened, they do not compromise: *"So they (the Sanhedrin) called them back and ordered them not to speak or teach at all in the name of Jesus. Peter and John, however, said to them in reply, "Whether it is right in the sight of God for us to obey you rather than God, you be the judges. It is impossible for us not to speak about what we have seen and heard. After threatening them further, they released them, finding no way to punish them, on account of the people who were all praising God for what had happened."* (Acts 4:18-21)

The power of the Holy Spirit kept being manifested in the lives of the apostles so that the community of believers, now called the New Way, began to grow rapidly. In Acts 3, Peter healed a crippled beggar and everyone was filled with amazement and astonishment at what had happened to him. The two apostles are hauled before the Sanhedrin and they remain fearless and steadfast in their witness of Jesus as their Risen Lord. Later they are released and when they return to their community, they resort to prayer: *"And now, Lord, take note of their threats, and enable your servants to speak your word with all boldness, as you stretch forth [your] hand to heal, and signs and wonders are done through the name of your holy servant Jesus. As they prayed, the place where they were gathered shook, and they were all filled with the holy Spirit and continued to speak the word of God with boldness."* (Acts 3:29-31)

A visible effect of the Outpouring of the Holy Spirit was the transformed life of the Christian community: *"The community of believers was of one heart and mind, and no one claimed that any of his possessions was his own, but they had everything in common. With great power the apostles bore witness to the resurrection of the Lord Jesus, and great favor was accorded them all. There was no needy person among them, for those who owned property or houses would sell them, bring the proceeds of the sale, and put them at the feet of the apostles, and they were distributed to each according to need."* (Acts 4:32-35)

THE SPREAD OF GOD'S COVENANT FAMILY:

Within the first century, the New Way, now called Christians in Antioch of Syria for the first time, spread throughout Asia Minor and Europe. This expansion happened through the apostles and others that the Holy Spirit garnered for the making of disciples among all nations and peoples. The chief among them, besides the apostles, was Paul of Tarsus who claimed to be an apostle because he had seen Jesus Christ, His Risen Lord, in a vision on his way to Damascus to persecute Jesus' followers. His vision of the Risen Lord led to his conversion and baptism: *"So Ananias went and entered the house; laying his hands on him, he said, "Saul, my brother, the Lord has sent me, Jesus who appeared to you on the way by which you came, that you may regain your sight and be filled with the holy Spirit."* (Acts 9:17) Paul made three missionary journeys covering Asia Minor and several countries in Europe. And in the course of his life as a missionary and apostle of the Lord Jesus, he was taught by the Holy Spirit Himself. When one reads his letters, there is amazement upon amazement about the way the Holy Spirit guided and guarded God's covenant family in his charge, making it expand, revealing to it the fuller implications of the Person, Presence, and teachings of the Lord Jesus, and continuing to nourish us, some twenty plus centuries later, with God's own divine life given to us through Jesus Christ, so that our participation in the Divine Life can be fuller and deeper. The insights that the Holy Spirit gave the apostles and Paul about God's Trinitarian Life and God's covenant family, that we call Church, are truly amazing and heart-warming.

COVENANT LIFE IN AND THROUGH THE HOLY SPIRIT:

Under the guidance of the Holy Spirit, Paul gives us a deep understanding of God's designs for us and what it really means to share God's life and love in covenant with Him. His letters are replete with profound insight and understanding into how the Holy Spirit fashions us into the image and likeness of Jesus and brings to fuller revelation all the things that Jesus taught us. This formation under the direction of the Holy Spirit is revealed, for instance, in his salutations at the beginning of several of his letters. Here is how Paul begins his Letter to the Romans: *"Paul, a slave of Christ Jesus, called to be an apostle and set apart for the gospel of God, which he promised previously through his prophets in the holy scriptures, the gospel about his Son, descended from David according to the flesh, but established as Son of God in power according to the spirit of holiness through resurrection from the dead, Jesus Christ our Lord. Through him we have received the grace of apostleship, to bring about the obedience of faith, for the sake of his name, among all the Gentiles, among whom are you also, who are called to belong to Jesus Christ; to all the beloved of God in Rome, called to be holy. Grace to you and peace from God our Father and the Lord Jesus Christ."* (Romans 1:1-7). St. Paul applies the term slave to himself in order to express his undivided allegiance to the Lord of the Church, the Master of all, including slaves and masters. He wants to imitate his Master who became a slave on our behalf. It is this aspect of the slave-master relationship rather than its degrading implications that St. Paul emphasizes when he discusses Christian commitment. When he talks about the obedience of faith, he is talking about faith in God's justifying action in Jesus Christ which relates one to God's gift of the new life that is made possible through the death and resurrection of Jesus Christ and the activity of the Holy Spirit. God's justifying action in Jesus Christ is the grace that Paul wishes his listeners to have from God our Father and the Lord Jesus Christ. And anyone who receives this justification in Jesus Christ, shares in the peace and joy of His resurrection.

In Romans 8:1-11, Paul tells us that holiness was impossible so long as the flesh, that is, self-interested hostility toward God (Verse 7), frustrated the divine objectives expressed in the law. What is worse, sin used the law to break forth into all manner of lawlessness (Verse 8). All this is now changed. On the cross, God broke the power of sin and pronounced sentence on it: *"For the law of the spirit of life in Christ Jesus has freed you from the law of sin and death."* (Romans 8:3). Christians still retain the flesh, but it is alien to their new being, which is life in the Spirit, namely the new self, governed by the Holy Spirit. Under the direction of the Holy Spirit, Christians are able to fulfill the divine will that formerly found expression in the law (Verse 4). The same Holy Spirit enlivens Christians for sharing in God's holiness, and will also resurrect their bodies at the last day: *"If the Spirit of the one who raised Jesus from the dead dwells in you, the one who raised Christ from the dead will give life to your mortal bodies also, through his Spirit that dwells in you."* (Romans 8:11). Christian life is therefore the experience of a constant challenge to put to death the evil deeds of the body through the life of the Spirit: *"For if you live according to the flesh, you will die, but if by the spirit you put to death the deeds of the body, you will live."* (Romans 8:13)

In 2 Corinthians 13:13, the last verse of Paul's letter, he offers us one of the clearest Trinitarian passages in the New Testament: *"The grace of the Lord Jesus Christ and the love of God and the fellowship of the holy Spirit be with all of you."* Everything in this verse points to a threefold companionship with God, who is Emmanuel, God-with-us. All three Persons of the Trinity, Father, Son, and Holy Spirit, are active in providing this companionship with us. Jesus brings grace and the Father brings love. Both grace and love are so powerful that they can only originate from God: *"For by grace you have been saved through faith, and this is not from you; it is the gift of God."* (Ephesians 2:8) And, *"God so loved the world that he gave his only Son, so that everyone who believes in him might not perish but might have eternal life."* (John 3:16) God's grace allows us entry into companionship with God. God's love keeps this companionship alive and vibrant. And this covenant life with our Triune God is made possible through communion with the Holy Spirit.

THE GIFTS OF THE HOLY SPIRIT:

In Galatians 5, Paul contrasts the fruits of the flesh against the fruits of the Holy Spirit: *"For the flesh has desires against the Spirit, and the Spirit against the flesh; these are opposed to each other, so that you may not do what you want. But if you are guided by the Spirit, you are not under the law."* (Galatians 5:17-18) Then Paul goes on to tell us what the fruits of the flesh are: *"Now the works of the flesh are obvious: immorality, impurity, licentiousness, idolatry, sorcery, hatreds, rivalry, jealousy, outbursts of fury, acts of selfishness, dissensions, factions, occasions of envy, drinking bouts, orgies, and the like. I warn you, as I warned you before, that those who do such things will not inherit the kingdom of God."* (Galatians 5:19-21). Such behaviors, as Paul delineates in this passage, clearly indicate servitude to evil and the prince of darkness. It is the world of desolation and darkness that we enter into when we have decided to grasp equality with God, and to stand up against Him, our Original, rather than with Him in humility, trust, and surrender. In Galatians 5:22, Paul then describes for us the fruit of the Holy Spirit: *"In contrast, the fruit of the Spirit is love, joy, peace, patience, kindness, generosity, faithfulness, gentleness, self-control. Against such there is no law."* When we experience these gifts we receive an appreciation of God's life, of the Trinitarian relationships and of the meaning of being in a new and everlasting covenant with the Triune God who is Covenant itself. Love being the first gift, 1 John 4:8-9 tells us that God is love: *"The man without love has known nothing of God, for God is love. God's love was revealed in our midst in this way: he sent his only Son to the world that we might have life through him."* We are heirs with Christ of God's eternal Life because of God's love for us. Joy and Peace are innate to the Risen Lord and are offered to us as lasting signs of our insertion into God's divine life: *"Even though the disciples had locked the doors of the place where they were for fear of the Jews, Jesus came and stood before them. "Peace be with you," he said. When he had said this, he showed them his hands and his side. At the sight of the Lord the disciples rejoiced. "Peace be with you," he said again."* (John 20:19) This peace and joy the world does not know. Only Jesus can share His Peace and Joy with us because the Trinity is the Source, and Jesus is both the Source and the Way to receive the Trinitarian gifts of peace and joy through the Holy Spirit.

Through the other fruits of the Holy Spirit, the Persons of the Trinity share with us their relational attributes that come so naturally to God. As we enter more deeply into Trinitarian Life and put on the mind and heart of Jesus Christ, we learn to become as the Trinity is in relationship to us through the Holy Spirit. We learn to be *patient and faithful* as God, throughout the history of human beings, has been patient in endurance, both in His fidelity to the covenants, and to us in our sin and rebellion! Like God, under the tutelage of the Holy Spirit, we too learn to be *kind and generous*. Our *gentleness and self-control* are a sharing in God's own transparency of spirit.

THE HOLY SPIRIT'S WORK IN OUR LIVES:

A central task entrusted to the Holy Spirit by Jesus is to instruct us in everything and remind us of all that Jesus told His disciples and us: *"The Advocate, the holy Spirit that the Father will send in my name – he will teach you everything and remind you of all that I told you."* (John 14:26) The Holy Spirit is our Mentor and Guide, the One who causes Jesus to be our Risen Lord, to take Him seriously and to live in constant covenant relationship with Him as our Lord. It is within this covenant with Jesus that we share in the Trinitarian Life of Father, Son, and Holy Spirit. In John 16, Jesus makes an interesting remark about the necessity of leaving us and ascending to the Father, or else the Comforter will never come to us. It is the Holy Spirit who fashions us into the image and likeness of Jesus, makes Jesus constantly present to us so that we will never be orphans, and unites heaven and earth as God's community of martyrs, witnesses, and saints.

The Holy Spirit has a very challenging task ahead of Him. He will prove the world wrong *about sin*, namely that Jesus is the only Savior of the world. Only through Jesus does forgiveness of sins come to us; *about justice,* because the ultimate justice or right order of things is that Jesus as our Risen Lord has restored us to the Father whose children we are now and sits at the right hand of His Father in glory and victory; *about condemnation,* because through his death, Jesus has vanquished Satan, prince of this world (John 16:8-11). The Holy Spirit, therefore, is the Spirit of Truth who will guide us to all truth. In doing so, the Holy Spirit will bring glory to Jesus through the visible manifestation of Jesus' holiness in our lives.

It is fitting that we end this session on The Holy Spirit's Gathering and Enlivening of God's Covenant Family, with the prayer to the Holy Spirit that has been recommended at the beginning of every prayer session that we do: *Come, Holy Spirit, and overshadow me with your gentle wisdom and power as I endeavor to sit at the feet of Jesus during this period of prayer. Purify my mind and heart as I seek to make the teachings of Jesus my priority in life, thinking, speaking and doing as He desires. You are the Keeper of my soul, leading me into God's heart. May I be docile and submissive to your wisdom and guidance, and may my life be a pleasing offering in your sight. AMEN.*

PRAYER AND REFLECTION ON GATHERED AND ENLIVENED BY THE HOLY SPIRIT

WEEK NINE: *"AND SUDDENLY THERE CAME FROM THE SKY A NOISE LIKE A STRONG DRIVING WIND, AND IT FILLED THE ENTIRE HOUSE IN WHICH THEY WERE. THEN THERE APPEARED TO THEM TONGUES AS OF FIRE, WHICH PARTED AND CAME TO REST ON EACH ONE OF THEM. AND THEY WERE ALL FILLED WITH THE HOLY SPIRIT AND BEGAN TO SPEAK IN DIFFERENT TONGUES, AS THE SPIRIT ENABLED THEM TO PROCLAIM." (ACTS 2:2-4)*

SPIRITUAL READING FOR THE WEEK:

- **Anoint Us in Your Covenant, Abba-Emmanuel:** Session Five
- **Old Testament:** Two or Three Chapters daily
- **New Testament:** Two or Three Chapters daily
- **Imitation of Christ:** One chapter daily

DAY ONE: MORNING SESSION

MORNING PRAYER: Acts of Faith, Hope, Charity; Daily Offering

Morning Face to Face with God:

Begin with Prayer to the Holy Spirit

THE BIRTH OF THE CHURCH OR GOD'S COVENANT FAMILY:

(After pondering each bullet point, express your sentiments in a short prayer)

- The Church, or God's universal covenant family, was born with a bang and sweep that was extraordinary and transformative. The Descent of the Holy Spirit brought about a paradigmatic change in the world. Since then the world has never been the same.
- While the disciples were preparing for this anointing from the Holy Spirit at Jesus' behest, they were incapable of knowing how exactly the Holy Spirit would behave, and what changes would take place in their lives as God fulfilled His Plan of Salvation in Jesus. The Holy Spirit indeed turned out to be a mighty wind of change!
- The Holy Trinity, Father, Son, and Holy Spirit, is present in the gathered covenant community at Pentecost. The Father, through His Son Jesus, is baptizing the disciples with His Holy Spirit. The disciples are being immersed in the power of the Holy Spirit

as Jesus was upon his baptism: *"And they were all filled with the holy Spirit and began to speak in different tongues, as the Spirit enabled them to proclaim."* (Acts 2:4)

- As a result of the Holy Spirit's influence upon them, the disciples began to proclaim the praises of God in ecstatic prayer, interpreted as speaking in foreign languages, symbolizing the catholic or worldwide mission of the church. This glorious and supernatural intervention of the Holy Spirit into the lives of the disciples created a mighty stir in the people around them.

- The power of the Holy Spirit kept being manifested in the lives of the apostles so that the community of believers, now called the New Way, began to grow rapidly. A visible effect of the outpouring of the Holy Spirit was the transformed life of the Christian community.

- Within the first century, the New Way, now called Christians in Antioch of Syria for the first time, spread throughout Asia Minor and Europe. This expansion happened through the apostles and others that the Holy Spirit garnered for the making of disciples among all nations and peoples.

- The chief among them, besides the apostles, was Paul of Tarsus who claimed to be an apostle because he had seen Jesus Christ, His Risen Lord, in a vision on his way to Damascus to persecute Jesus' followers. His vision of the Risen Lord led to his conversion and baptism.

- Paul made three missionary journeys covering Asia Minor and several countries in Europe. And in the course of his life as a missionary and apostle of the Lord Jesus, he was taught by the Holy Spirit Himself. The insights that the Holy Spirit gave the apostles and Paul about God's Trinitarian Life and God's covenant family, that we call Church, are truly amazing and heart-warming.

What is God saying to you?

End with Prayer to the Holy Trinity

NIGHT SESSION: Examination of Conscience

For what are you grateful? For what are you contrite?

Please review briefly your Morning Prayer topic. Make it your last thought of the day

DAY TWO: MORNING SESSION

MORNING PRAYER: Act of Faith; Act of Hope; Act of Charity; Daily Offering

Morning Face to Face with God:

Begin with Prayer to the Holy Spirit
Prayer on John 14:16-17: Promise of the Advocate:
"And I will ask the Father, and he will give you another Advocate to be with you always, the Spirit of truth, which the world cannot accept, because it neither sees nor knows it."

Read the Reflection; Thank the Holy Spirit for being the Keeper of your soul, and ask for the grace to be a dedicated temple of the Holy Trinity

Jesus is with His disciples in the Upper Room on the eve of His crucifixion and death. It is a moment of great intimacy and urgency. Jesus is sharing explicit details of His Father's plan for us that were alluded to in the past. The institution of the Eucharist, the declaration of our status as friends, and petitioning His Father to give us the Holy Spirit, are some of the special revelations that He offers us. Like Jesus, the Holy Spirit will be our Advocate. He will be the Keeper of our souls, guarding us jealously as Jesus did His disciples. The Holy Spirit will be with us always, re-creating us in the image and likeness of Jesus and making Jesus always present in us. Hence we will never be orphans. He is the Spirit of truth who will protect us from the evil ways of the world.

What is God saying to you?
End with Prayer to the Holy Trinity

NIGHT SESSION: Examination of Conscience

For what are you grateful? For what are you contrite?

Please review briefly your Morning Prayer topic. Make it your last thought of the day

DAY THREE: MORNING SESSION

MORNING PRAYER: Act of Faith; Act of Hope; Act of Charity; Daily Offering

Morning Face to Face with God:

Begin with Prayer to the Holy Spirit
Prayer on John 16:8-11: The Advocate's Role:

Proposal 3 enshrines a woman's right to abortion in the Michigan constitution

> *"And when he comes he will convict the world in regard to sin and righteousness and condemnation: sin, because they do not believe in me; righteousness, because I am going to the Father and you will no longer see me; condemnation, because the ruler of this world has been condemned."*

Read the Reflection; Thank the Holy Spirit for being the Keeper of your soul, and ask for the grace to be a dedicated temple of the Holy Trinity

The Holy Spirit will prove the world wrong about sin, namely, that Jesus is the only Savior of the world. Salvation comes through repentance and acceptance of Jesus as Savior and Lord; *about righteousness*, because the ultimate righteousness or right order of things is that Jesus, as our Risen Lord, has restored us to the Father whose children we now are, and He sits at the right hand of His Father in glory and victory; *about condemnation*, because through His death, Jesus has vanquished Satan, prince of this world, and ensured our victory over Satan and sin.

What is God saying to you?

Bill B – the Devil does not win.

End with Prayer to the Holy Trinity

NIGHT SESSION: Examination of Conscience

For what are you grateful? For what are you contrite?

Please review briefly your Morning Prayer topic. Make it your last thought of the day

DAY FOUR: MORNING SESSION

MORNING PRAYER: Act of Faith; Act of Hope; Act of Charity; Daily Offering

Morning Face to Face with God:

Begin with Prayer to the Holy Spirit
Prayer on John 16:13-15: The Advocate's Role:

> *"He will not speak on his own, but he will speak what he hears, and will declare to you the things that are coming. He will glorify me, because he will take from what is mine and declare it to you. Everything that the Father has is mine; for this reason I told you that he will take from what is mine and declare it to you."*

Read the Reflection; Thank the Holy Spirit for being the Keeper of your soul, and ask for the grace to be a dedicated temple of the Holy Trinity

Jesus is giving us an insider's view into the Trinitarian relationships. The Three Persons of the Holy Trinity do everything as One God because they share the same divine essence. Hence Jesus tells us that the Holy Spirit will work in harmony with Jesus: *"He will not speak on his own, but he will speak what he hears, and will declare to you the things that are coming."* The Holy Spirit's advocacy consists in re-creating us in the image and likeness of Jesus *(he will take from what is mine and declare it to you)*, our Master. In transforming us, the Holy Spirit will bring glory to Jesus who will be made visible through the disciples' witness. Then Jesus brings the Father into this wonderful Trinitarian dynamic of salvation: *"Everything that the Father has is mine; for this reason I told you that he will take from what is mine and declare it to you."* The source that the Holy Spirit will be tapping into to re-create us, is the same source that belongs to Jesus: divine life! The Holy Spirit's only intent and purpose as our Advocate is to offer us what belongs quintessentially to the Three Divine Persons: a share in the fullness of Divine Life!

What is God saying to you?

End with Prayer to the Holy Trinity

NIGHT SESSION: Examination of Conscience

For what are you grateful? For what are you contrite?

Please review briefly your Morning Prayer topic. Make it your last thought of the day

DAY FIVE: MORNING SESSION

MORNING PRAYER: Act of Faith; Act of Hope; Act of Charity; Daily Offering

Morning Face to Face with God:

Begin with Prayer to the Holy Spirit
Prayer on Acts 1:6-9: Imminent Coming of the Holy Spirit:
   "But you will receive power when the holy Spirit comes upon you, and you will be witnesses in Jerusalem, throughout Judea and Samaria, and to the ends of the earth." [Please read Acts 1:1-14 for a better appreciation of the passage].

Read the Reflection; Thank the Holy Spirit for being the Keeper of your soul, and ask for the grace to be a dedicated temple of the Holy Trinity

   "Lord, are you at this time going to restore the kingdom to Israel?" (Acts 1:6), is a question the disciples asked Jesus just before His Ascension. The question implies that in believing Jesus to

be the Christ, they had expected Him to be a political leader who would restore self-rule to Israel during His historical ministry. When this had not taken place, they ask if it is to take place at this time, the period of the church. Jesus makes it very clear that His kingdom is not of this world. And He goes on to describe its nature. Just as Jerusalem was the city of destiny in the Gospel of Luke, the place where salvation was accomplished, so here at the beginning of Acts, Jerusalem occupies a central position. It is the starting point for the mission of the disciples of Jesus, to begin in Jerusalem and go to the ends of the earth, which for Luke meant Rome. And for us who live in the Twenty First century, it means the whole world. This establishment and expansion of the true kingdom of Christ was to happen in the power of the Holy Spirit. Through His power, the disciples would become able and enthusiastic witnesses. And they prepare for the coming of the Holy Spirit through prayer in the Upper Room and Mary, the mother of Jesus was with them (Acts 1:13-14).

What is God saying to you?

End with Prayer to the Holy Trinity

NIGHT SESSION: Examination of Conscience

For what are you grateful? For what are you contrite?

Please review briefly your Morning Prayer topic. Make it your last thought of the day

DAY SIX: MORNING SESSION

MORNING PRAYER: Act of Faith; Act of Hope; Act of Charity; Daily Offering

Morning Face to Face with God:
Begin with Prayer to the Holy Spirit
REPETITION OF DAYS TWO THROUGH FIVE:

Read the Reflection; Thank the Holy Spirit for being the Keeper of your soul, and ask for the grace to be a dedicated temple of the Holy Trinity

Today, you are doing a repetition of Days Two through Five of this week. In a repetition St. Ignatius says that *"we should pay attention to and dwell upon those points in which we have experienced greater consolation or desolation or greater spiritual appreciation."* (# 62) If you wish, you can do a triple colloquy: refer to #63 of the Spiritual Exercises.

What is God saying to you?
End with Prayer to the Holy Trinity

NIGHT SESSION: Examination of Conscience

For what are you grateful? For what are you contrite?

Please review briefly your Morning Prayer topic. Make it your last thought of the day

DAY SEVEN: MORNING SESSION

MORNING PRAYER: Act of Faith; Act of Hope; Act of Charity; Daily Offering

Morning Face to Face with God:

Begin with Prayer to the Holy Spirit

THE SECOND DWELLING PLACES OF THE INTERIOR CASTLE:

(After pondering each bullet point, express your sentiments in a short prayer)

- The Second Dwelling Places are set apart for those who have taken some first steps in the practice of prayer. They have become more receptive to the promptings and invitations being offered to them by the Holy Spirit.
- Often at this stage, such promptings are given to them mainly through external resources, such as books, sermons, retreats, spiritual friendships, and trials that life brings everyone.
- Beginners in the Second Dwelling Places are making progress. They are pointed in God's direction but are still far from the destination. They are still engaged in worldly pursuits, both giving them up and still clinging to them. They see imperfectly through fogged spiritual lenses. Nevertheless they are making progress.
- They would characterize their relationship with God as becoming more personal. They know that God is calling them ceaselessly. God appeals to them in various ways, through conversations with good and holy persons, sermons, retreats, inspirational spiritual reading, sickness and trials, and insight and consolation from the Holy Spirit during prayer. They are able to hear God now whereas in the First Mansions they were quite deaf.
- However, they feel a certain restlessness and unease towards God because they are still kicking against the goad. The Second Dwelling Place is a battleground for the soul of the beginner. *The conflict is between the forces and values of the world, on the one hand, and the call to discipleship and union with God, on the other.*
- The world continues to exert an enormous pull. Earthly pleasures remain attractive and take on an air of permanence. There is an inordinate clinging to family and friends, and to their present lifestyle; being esteemed in the eyes of the world is still very important to them.

- Entering into a significant relationship with God conjures up unreasonable fears of having to give up or be stripped of everything that they know and love. As a result, there is almost a sense of doom that they imagine will come upon them.

- So they vacillate and beef up the argument that it is much wiser to return to the First Dwelling Places rather than embark on this uphill climb for God. After all, in the past they did not seem to be dissatisfied and restless as they now experience themselves.

- The battle has been joined as well by God. The Holy Spirit's tug is likewise felt in many ways. Their reason tells them clearly how mistaken the world's values are, as they are based on deceit and camouflage. They have witnessed the spiritual growth that has taken place in them. And they now have the conviction that their surety lies only in God! Thus their wills are inclined toward loving God and pressing on to leave behind the world and all its falsehoods, and embrace the person and values of Jesus.

- What then is the advice Saint Teresa offers a beginner in the Second Dwelling Places? Given that a beginner's foundations in the spiritual life are still weak, they should avoid any close association with mediocre people, and especially with those who are opposed to the values of Christ.

- Rather, they should take every opportunity and make every endeavor to associate with good people, especially with those who have advanced into the dwelling places nearer the center of their souls where the divine King dwells.

- They need to understand that any serious discipleship requires the embrace of the cross along with the suffering Christ. Life brings with it a fair share of trials and tribulations. It is not enough to be resigned to one's fate or hand that has been dealt to them.

- There must be a generous and purposeful acceptance of hardships and dryness in prayer and circumstances of daily life, as they are truly blessings to purify the beginner of self-centeredness and pride.

- The beginner needs to insist on being faithful on a daily basis to doing God's will as it manifests itself in everyday living. Union with God comes from doing God's will unstintingly, like Mary who was God's perfect handmaid.

- At this stage of the journey it is easy to get discouraged and start backsliding. St. Teresa encourages the beginner not to lose heart when they fall, but rather to continue making serious efforts toward making progress.

- Learning to ask and receive forgiveness, and to act upon one's repentance, is an important spiritual practice in the Second Dwelling Places.

- There is the need to exercise fidelity to prayer. We cannot enter heaven without first entering our own souls. It is only prayer that will bring us into God's Embrace.

What is God saying to you?

End with Prayer to the Holy Trinity

NIGHT SESSION: Examination of Conscience

For what are you grateful? For what are you contrite?

What prayer would you compose to express what God has said to you this week?

Please review briefly your Morning Prayer topic. Make it your last thought of the day

PRAYER AND REFLECTION ON GATHERED AND ENLIVENED BY THE HOLY SPIRIT – CONTINUED

WEEK TEN: *"God raised this Jesus; of this we are all witnesses. Exalted at the right hand of God, he received the promise of the Holy Spirit from the Father and poured it forth, as you (both) see and hear." (Acts 2:32-33)*

SPIRITUAL READING FOR THE WEEK:

- **Anoint Us in Your Covenant, Abba-Emmanuel:** Session Five
- **Old Testament:** Two or Three Chapters daily
- **New Testament:** Two or Three Chapters daily
- **Imitation of Christ:** One chapter daily

DAY ONE: MORNING SESSION

MORNING PRAYER: Acts of Faith, Hope, Charity; Daily Offering

Morning Face to Face with God:

Begin with Prayer to the Holy Spirit

THE VARIOUS FUNCTIONS OF THE HOLY SPIRIT:

(After pondering each bullet point, express your sentiments in a short prayer)

- The Holy Spirit "transports" our prayers from our hearts to the heart of the Father through Jesus: *"for we do not know how to pray as we ought, but the Spirit itself intercedes with inexpressible groanings. And the one who searches hearts knows what is the intention of the Spirit, because it intercedes for the holy ones according to God's will."* (Romans 8:26b-27)

- Another mode of transportation that the Holy Spirit uses is the gift of tongues. This amazing gift is available to all who are baptized in the Holy Spirit. This gift provides us with a safe and secure way to communicate with the Lord. By eliminating any fleshly or evil interference, we can pray effectively by utilizing the heavenly language the Lord gave us.

- In Galatians 5, Paul tells us that the fruits of the Holy Spirit are *"love, joy, peace, patience, kindness, generosity, faithfulness, gentleness, self-control. Against such there is no law."* When we experience these gifts we receive an appreciation of God's life, of the Trinitarian relationships and of the meaning of being in a new and everlasting covenant with the Triune God who is Covenant itself.

- *Love* being the first gift, 1 John 4:8-9 tells us that God is love: *"The man without love has known nothing of God, for God is love. God's love was revealed in our midst in this way: he sent his only Son to the world that we might have life through him."* We are heirs with Christ of God's eternal Life because of God's love for us.

- *Joy and Peace* are innate to the Risen Lord and are offered to us as lasting signs of our insertion into God's divine life. Only Jesus can share his Peace and Joy with us because the Trinity is the Source, and Jesus is both the Source and the Way to receive the Trinitarian gifts of peace and joy through the Holy Spirit.

- As we enter more deeply into Trinitarian Life and put on the mind and heart of Jesus Christ, we learn to become as the Trinity is in relationship to us through the Holy Spirit. We learn to be *patient and faithful* as God, throughout the history of human beings, has been patient in endurance, both in His fidelity to the covenants, and to us in our sin and rebellion!

- Like God, under the tutelage of the Holy Spirit, we too learn to be *kind and generous.*

- Our *gentleness and self-control* are a sharing in God's own transparency of spirit.

- A central task entrusted to the Holy Spirit by Jesus is to instruct us in everything and remind us of all that Jesus told His disciples and us. The Holy Spirit is our Mentor and Guide, the One who causes Jesus to be our Risen Lord, to take Him seriously and to live in constant covenant relationship with Him as our Lord.

- It is the Holy Spirit who fashions us into the image and likeness of Jesus, makes Jesus constantly present to us so that we will never be orphans, and unites heaven and earth as God's community of martyrs, witnesses, and saints.

- It is fitting that we end this session with the prayer to the Holy Spirit that has been recommended at the beginning of every prayer session that we do: *Come, Holy Spirit, and overshadow me with your gentle wisdom and power as I endeavor to sit at the feet of Jesus during this period of prayer. Purify my mind and heart as I seek to make the teachings of Jesus my priority in life, thinking, speaking and doing as He desires. You are the Keeper of my soul, leading me into God's heart. May I be docile and submissive to your wisdom and guidance, and may my life be a pleasing offering in your sight. AMEN.*

What is God saying to you?

End with Prayer to the Holy Trinity

NIGHT SESSION: Examination of Conscience

For what are you grateful? For what are you contrite?

Please review briefly your Morning Prayer topic. Make it your last thought of the day

DAY TWO: MORNING SESSION

MORNING PRAYER: Act of Faith; Act of Hope; Act of Charity; Daily Offering

Morning Face to Face with God:

Begin with Prayer to the Holy Spirit
Prayer on Acts 2:2-4: Empowered by the Holy Spirit:
> *"And suddenly there came from the sky a noise like a strong driving wind, and it filled the entire house in which they were. Then there appeared to them tongues as of fire, which parted and came to rest on each one of them. And they were all filled with the holy Spirit and began to speak in different tongues, as the Spirit enabled them to proclaim."*

Read the Reflection; Thank the Holy Spirit for being the Keeper of your soul, and ask for the grace to be a dedicated temple of the Holy Trinity

Of all the events connected with the Holy Spirit, this is probably the one with which we are most familiar. In our liturgy we celebrate the Feast of Pentecost every year after the Feast of the Ascension. In this Pentecost scene, the Presence and Power of the Holy Spirit is vivid, overwhelming, and transforming. God appears to humans with fire in both the Old and New Testaments. A profound cleansing takes place in us through the Holy Spirit, symbolized by tongues of fire. Through such a cleansing and transformation, the disciple comes to know that Jesus is alive and truly Savior and Lord of the universe! In faith, place yourself in the scene and experience the Presence and Power of the Holy Spirit along with Mary and the disciples.

What is God saying to you?

End with Prayer to the Holy Trinity

NIGHT SESSION: Examination of Conscience

For what are you grateful? For what are you contrite?

Please review briefly your Morning Prayer topic. Make it your last thought of the day

DAY THREE: MORNING SESSION

MORNING PRAYER: Act of Faith; Act of Hope; Act of Charity; Daily Offering

Morning Face to Face with God:

Begin with Prayer to the Holy Spirit
Prayer on Luke 11:13: The Answer to Prayer:

> *"If you then, who are wicked, know how to give good gifts to your children, how much more will the Father in heaven give the holy Spirit to those who ask him?"*

Read the Reflection; Thank the Holy Spirit for being the Keeper of your soul, and ask for the grace to be a dedicated temple of the Holy Trinity

No one knows the Holy Spirit more intimately and lovingly than the Father and Jesus. They desire that we live in covenant relationship with the Trinity. Hence, they are sharing everything with us without any reservation. The Father has given Himself to us through His Son. Jesus has given Himself to us by becoming one of us and rescuing us from the snatches of sin and Satan by dying on the cross. And now, they are giving us their Holy Spirit to be ours! Through the Holy Spirit we can surrender our lives and be in covenant union with the Holy Trinity.

What is God saying to you?

End with Prayer to the Holy Trinity

NIGHT SESSION: Examination of Conscience

For what are you grateful? For what are you contrite?

Please review briefly your Morning Prayer topic. Make it your last thought of the day

DAY FOUR: MORNING SESSION

MORNING PRAYER: Act of Faith; Act of Hope; Act of Charity; Daily Offering

Morning Face to Face with God:

Begin with Prayer to the Holy Spirit
Prayer on Romans 5:2-5: The Holy Spirit has been poured out:

"Through Him we have gained access [by faith] to this grace in which we stand, and we boast in hope of the glory of God. Not only that, but we even boast of our afflictions, knowing that affliction produces endurance, and endurance, proven character, and proven character, hope, and hope does not disappoint, because the love of God has been poured out into our hearts through the holy Spirit that has been given to us."

Read the Reflection; Thank the Holy Spirit for being the Keeper of your soul, and ask for the grace to be a dedicated temple of the Holy Trinity

The love of God has been poured out into our hearts through the holy Spirit that has been given to us: Through the outpouring of God's love for us through the Holy Spirit, Paul's life has been transformed. He has been able to identify with the crucified Christ in his ministry to God's covenant family. He accepts afflictions that come his way and even sees great blessings come to him through them: endurance, proven character, and hope. Such a transformation is wrought at the hands of the Holy Spirit. Like Paul we are disciples of Jesus. In having His Holy Spirit we are opposed to the values and spirit of the world. So like Paul we too will experience afflictions and suffering. But through the Holy Spirit we will be strengthened, purified, and transformed.

What is God saying to you?

End with Prayer to the Holy Trinity

NIGHT SESSION: Examination of Conscience

For what are you grateful? For what are you contrite?

Please review briefly your Morning Prayer topic. Make it your last thought of the day

DAY FIVE: MORNING SESSION

MORNING PRAYER: Act of Faith; Act of Hope; Act of Charity; Daily Offering

Morning Face to Face with God:

Begin with Prayer to the Holy Spirit
Prayer on 1 Corinthians 2:10b-13: The True Wisdom:

"For the Spirit scrutinizes everything, even the depths of God... No one knows what pertains to God except the Spirit of God. We have not received the spirit of the world but the Spirit that is from God, so that we may understand the things freely given us by God. And we speak about them not with words taught by human wisdom, but with words taught by the Spirit, describing spiritual realities in spiritual terms."

Read the Reflection; Thank the Holy Spirit for being the Keeper of your soul, and ask for the grace to be a dedicated temple of the Holy Trinity

1. *For the Spirit scrutinizes everything, even the depths of God...so that we may understand the things freely given us by God:* Here is an example of God sharing everything with us that belongs to Him. The Divine Spirit is familiar with the depths of God, because He shares the same divine essence with the Father and the Son. This same Holy Spirit dwells in the depths of our being and shares with us the depths of God! Amazing, but true, that God shares intimately with us everything that is His, all the time!

2. *And we speak about them not with words taught by human wisdom, but with words taught by the Spirit, describing spiritual realities in spiritual terms:* As we grow in discipleship and live under the authority of the Holy Spirit, we will begin to see that the Holy Spirit is revealing to us spiritual realities that we could never access through human wisdom. The Holy Spirit does indeed become our Mentor and Guide!

What is God saying to you?

End with Prayer to the Holy Trinity

NIGHT SESSION: Examination of Conscience

For what are you grateful? For what are you contrite?

Please review briefly your Morning Prayer topic. Make it your last thought of the day

DAY SIX: MORNING SESSION

MORNING PRAYER: Act of Faith; Act of Hope; Act of Charity; Daily Offering

Morning Face to Face with God:

Begin with Prayer to the Holy Spirit

REPETITION OF DAYS TWO THROUGH FIVE:

Read the Reflection; Thank the Holy Spirit for being the Keeper of your soul, and ask for the grace to be a dedicated temple of the Holy Trinity

Today, you are doing a repetition of Days Two through Five of this week. In a repetition St. Ignatius says that *"we should pay attention to and dwell upon those points in which we have experienced greater consolation or desolation or greater spiritual appreciation."* (# 62) If you wish, you can do a triple colloquy: refer to #63 of the Spiritual Exercises.

What is God saying to you?

End with Prayer to the Holy Trinity

NIGHT SESSION: Examination of Conscience

For what are you grateful? For what are you contrite?

Please review briefly your Morning Prayer topic. Make it your last thought of the day

DAY SEVEN: MORNING SESSION

MORNING PRAYER: Act of Faith; Act of Hope; Act of Charity; Daily Offering

Morning Face to Face with God:

Begin with Prayer to the Holy Spirit

THE THIRD DWELLING PLACES OF THE INTERIOR CASTLE:

(After pondering each bullet point, express your sentiments in a short prayer)

- There are many Christians in the world who reach the Third Dwelling Places. There are several positive characteristics that would describe a person in the Third Dwelling Places. These beginners are advancing in the spiritual life. An awakening has taken place in them! God has an important place in their lives.
- They are taking Jesus and His teachings seriously. As a result, they love to pray, and prayer is neither a burden nor an obligation. They converse with God throughout the day and this is something they love to do and enjoy.
- In many instances they have the awareness that God dwells within them. They guard against venial sin, and long not to offend God. They understand that to persevere in prayer, with the struggle it involves, is to make progress. They work on developing spiritual practices in their lives, like guarding their senses, using their time well,

practicing charity towards others, maintaining balance in the use of speech and dress, and in the management of their household.

- They are good, practicing Christians, and in the thinking of St. Teresa, the Lord will not deny them entrance into the final dwelling place if they so desire.

- However, *in the Third Dwelling Places, human nature is still an oppressive burden on the spirit.* Like the rich young man in the gospel, they could turn away from the requirements for becoming perfect. They love God very much, but they still want to do so conveniently, on their terms.

- Their spiritual self-image is very important to them. However, any threat to their wealth or honor or status quo will quickly uncover their attachments to these false gods. They tend to be judgmental and are easily shocked by the faults of others.

- In prayer they expect to have consolations as part of their normal experience, as their spiritual image is important. So they tend to get discouraged and distraught by dryness in prayer.

- The advancing beginner in the Third Dwelling Places finds more consolation in the spiritual life and things of God than they do in material comforts and all the attendant distractions. However, they are still straddling the fence. They are not yet willing to burn their bridges once and for all.

- In prayer, therefore, they seldom receive the deeper, more delectable peace and quiet of contemplation. However, occasionally they will receive a more profound experience of God which is an invitation to prepare better for what lies ahead.

- St. John of the Cross was of the opinion that the transition from here to contemplative prayer was short. St. Teresa of Avila, on the other hand, thought that the transition takes long.

- It is important for someone in the Third Dwelling Places to be able to talk and listen to someone who is free of the world's illusions. In other words, they would do well to associate with someone who is a contemplative.

- How does one pray in the Third Dwelling Places? The advancing beginner's prayer will still be discursive, with an emphasis on reverence and honesty. The tendency will be to speak less and listen more to God.

- *An active focusing on the indwelling presence is the best way to prepare for the Prayer of Quiet.* The advice given by Saints Teresa and John of the Cross to practice the active night of Senses is especially true for someone who is in the Third Dwelling Places and being invited into contemplative prayer.

What is God saying to you?

End with Prayer to the Holy Trinity

NIGHT SESSION: *Examination of Conscience*

For what are you grateful? For what are you contrite?

What prayer would you compose to express what God has said to you this week?

Please review briefly your Morning Prayer topic. Make it your last thought of the day

SESSION SIX: LIVING AS GOD'S COVENANT FAMILY

"Then he took the bread, said the blessing, broke it, and gave it to them saying, "This is my body, which will be given for you; do this in memory of me." And likewise the cup after they had eaten, saying, "This cup is the new covenant in my blood, which will be shed for you."
– Luke 22:19-20

PURPOSE OF OUR CREATION AS GOD'S IMAGE AND LIKENESS:

Both the Creation accounts in Genesis, Chapters One and Two, single out God's creation of us as being vastly different from the creation of the other creatures. The narratives go to great pains to single out this essential difference. When you read about the first five days of the Creation story, you are left with a sense of amazement and awe in the way God goes about the business of creating the universe. There is undivided focus, conscientious forethought, and stupendous activity on God's part. And all this intense divine energy and determination is directed towards setting the stage for the creation of humans to whom God will bequeath His glorious creation. At the end of each of the first five days of Creation, God expresses satisfaction at the work of His hands by exclaiming, "It is good." At the end of the sixth day, after God has created humans, He expresses His immense delight and satisfaction by exclaiming, "It is very good!" And the whole purpose of creating all the other creatures was so that humans would have dominion over them, in God's name and as God would: *"Let them have dominion over the fish of the sea, the birds of the air, the tame animals, all the wild animals, and all the creatures on the earth."* (Genesis 1:26)

But most importantly, God created humans in His image and likeness: *"God created mankind in his image; in the image of God he created them; male and female he created them."* (Genesis 1:27) As God provided the plants with seeds (Genesis 1:11, 12), and commanded the animals to be fertile and multiply (Genesis 1:22), so God gives sexuality to human beings as their means to continue in existence. The sole purpose for our creation in the image and likeness of God was to give us the capacity to participate in God's divine nature, as 2 Peter 1:4 tells us. God wanted humans to enter into covenant with Him, participating in the covenant love and life that exists in the Trinity of Father, Son, and Holy Spirit. In creating humans in His image and likeness, God gave us the gift of immortality, not only of our souls, but of our bodies as well, in fact, of our whole being. Through His resurrection, Jesus made sure that this decision on God's part would remain inviolate. We will, therefore, experience the resurrection of our bodies one day, at the end of time.

Two major aspects of covenant life are highlighted in the first two chapters of Genesis, giving us a deeper appreciation of God's designs in our creation. The first aspect is the fact of *a total sharing between the parties entering into covenant.* God alone has dominion over the work of His hands. God alone has sovereignty over all creation. However, God desires to enter into covenant with humans. Consequently, God shares with us what is His by right, His own divine life and love and to have dominion over all creatures. In the New Testament, it would have made good human sense if Jesus had kept to Himself sovereign jurisdiction over His Church. But Jesus shares with humans His sovereign power in the establishment and governance of the Church throughout history, till the end of time: *"And I say to you, you are Peter, and upon this rock I will build my church, and the gates of the netherworld shall not prevail against it. I will give you the keys to the kingdom of heaven. Whatever you bind on earth shall be bound in heaven; and whatever you loose on earth shall be loosed in heaven."* (Matthew 16:18-19)

The second aspect of covenant life is that in covenant living *focus on the other is foremost, and preoccupation with self is minimal to non-existent.* Genesis 2:25, tells us that *"The man and his wife were both naked, yet they felt no shame."* Adam and Eve were like little children. They were not tainted as yet by sin. They lived transparent lives with God and with each other. They were blissfully aware of the other in whom they had security, peace, and happiness. There was no preoccupation with self. Shame is supreme preoccupation with self, and suggests a battered self-image. We are also told that love and intimacy in each other's presence is the reason *"why a man leaves his father and mother and clings to his wife, and the two of them become one body."* (Genesis 2:24) Preoccupation with self leads one into isolation and alienation. Covenant living leads one into community and union with each other so that everything is shared, and they act as one entity. This was the case with Adam and Eve before the advent of sin. They were at ease with God and they enjoyed one another's company, as symbolized by the afternoon walks that they would take in the garden *"at the breezy time of the day."* (Genesis 3:8)

This image of God's covenant relationship with humans is in stark contrast to the sullied image after the advent of sin. Before sin, Adam and Eve are very comfortable with God. The image and likeness is at ease with the Original. God is truly Emmanuel, God-with-us. After sin, there was always a certain dread and fearful reverence toward God in the Old Testament, so that the Hebrews would never use God's name, and would address God using pseudonyms. This reticence and reserve toward God is well expressed in Exodus 21:18b-21: *"So they took up a position farther away and said to Moses, "You speak to us, and we will listen; but do not let God speak to us, or we shall die." Moses answered the people, "Do not be afraid, for God has come only to test you and put the fear of him upon you so you do not sin." So the people remained at a distance, while Moses approached the dark cloud where God was."*

There were instances in the Old Testament, however, that intimated the closeness and intimacy that God always desired with us, so that truly God would be Emmanuel, dwelling among us. Exodus 34:13-17 describes Moses' intimacy with God: *"Now, if I have found favor with you, please let me know your ways so that, in knowing you, I may continue to find favor with you. See, this nation is indeed your own people. The Lord answered: I myself will go along, to give you rest. Moses replied, "If you are not going yourself, do not make us go up from here. For how can it be known that I and your people have found favor with you, except by your going with us? Then we, your people and I, will be singled out from every other people on the surface of the earth." The LORD said to Moses: This request, too, which you have made, I will carry out, because you have found favor with me and you are my intimate friend."* After this most intimate exchange, Moses expresses a desire to see the LORD's glory, at which point God tells Him, *"You cannot see my face, for no one can see me and live."* (Exodus 34:20)

The fullness of time has not yet arrived when God's glory will be manifest in Jesus, and we will be brought into face to face intimacy with God through Jesus. As the Letter to the Hebrews puts it, *"In times past, God spoke in partial and various ways to our ancestors through the prophets; in these last days, he spoke to us through a son, whom he made heir of all things and through whom he created the universe, who is the refulgence of his glory, the very imprint of his being."* (Hebrews 1:1-3) Through Jesus we are brought back into the loving presence of God, calling Him, Abba, Father. In asking us to address God as Father, Jesus was sharing with us His relationship to His Father, thereby making us sons and daughters of His Father, and claiming us as His brothers and sisters. In receiving Jesus in Holy Communion, we abide in God and God in us, a profound experience and expression of covenant living with God. This Jesus was the Word who *"became flesh and made his dwelling among us, and we saw his glory, the glory as of the Father's only Son, full of grace and truth."* (John 1:14)

SIN IS A MASQUERADE OF COVENANT LIVING:

With the entrance of sin into human life, a masquerade of covenant living was offered to us. This depiction of a false set of covenant parameters is offered to us in the story of Adam and Eve and the serpent in Genesis 3. Adam and Eve are still living in covenant relationship with God when the serpent enters upon the scene. In response to the serpent's question, *"Did God really say, 'You shall not eat from any of the trees in the garden?,'"* Eve is still in covenant relationship with God and states the fact: *"We may eat of the fruit of the trees in the garden; it is only about the fruit of the tree in the middle of garden that God said, 'You shall not eat it or even touch it, or else you will die.'"* God is very solicitous about the well-being of His human friends with whom He is in covenant. Through this warning, God is covering their back and doing everything necessary to preserve and strengthen their covenant relationship by warning them of the dangers out there. It is at this point that Satan offers his own mockery of covenant living which is the antithesis of God's covenant life. The snake said to the woman: *"You certainly will not die! God knows well that when you eat of it your eyes will be opened and you will be like gods, who know good and evil."*

In covenant with God, Adam and Eve were standing up with God! In Satan's masquerade of covenant living, they are encouraged to stand up against God. In covenant living with God, the emphasis in relationship is on the other; in Satan's masquerade of covenant living, the emphasis in relationship is on self. Self is placed ahead of everybody and everything. Eve gives in to this deception of covenant living and in doing so experiences the destruction of covenant life with God, as well as covenant life with Adam: *"The woman saw that the tree was good for food and pleasing to the eyes, and the tree was desirable for gaining wisdom. So she took some of its fruit and ate it; and she also gave some to her husband, who was with her, and he ate it. Then the eyes of both of them were opened, and they knew that they were naked; so they sewed fig leaves together and made loincloths for themselves."* (Genesis 3:6-7)

In our own experience of married life and significant relationships, we share in the peace and joy of Jesus when we set aside preoccupation with self, and focus instead on the well-being of the other. By the same token, whenever we place self before everything and everyone else, we subscribe to Satan's masquerade of covenant living and experience desolation and alienation.

RESTORATION OF COVENANT LIVING IN JESUS:

Jesus came to return us to God's original plan of establishing covenant union with us as exemplified in the Garden of Eden, and in this way to put an end to our exile. We banished ourselves by choosing the masquerade rather than the truth of covenant life. We chose to stand up against God rather than with Him and in Him. The Holy Trinity, in their infinite compassion and mercy toward us, made the decision to restore us to covenant union in and with the Trinity, restoring the privilege to address God as 'Our Father,' and in this way to share intimately in the filial relationship between Father and Jesus, Son of God. This decision about our return to the Father through His Son and in the power of the Holy Spirit was not an afterthought, a course-correction. This decision was an integral part of God's original plan of salvation and entrance into God's very own life and love through Jesus Christ, who though He was Son of God, became son of man.

In order to liberate us from our sin and pride, Jesus emptied Himself and took the form of a slave, being born in the likeness of men. He became one of us so that in our stead He might die to our sin first, and as our Savior and Lord help us to die to sin in and through Him and live for God. Jesus took upon Himself our burden and slavery to sin so that we might enjoy His freedom as children of God. In the Word becoming flesh, Jesus became our *kinsman-redeemer*. In Romans 5:8-10, Paul describes this grace-filled swap that Jesus embraced for our salvation: *"It is precisely in this that God proves his love for us: that while we were still sinners, Christ died for us. Now that we have been justified by his blood, it is all the more certain that we shall be saved by him from God's wrath. For if, when we were God's enemies, we were reconciled to him by the death of his Son, it is all the more certain that we who have been reconciled will be saved by his life."*

Jesus came on this earth so that we might have abundant life. Having abundant life is sharing in God's own divine life. As John 14:19 tells us, *"In a little while the world will no longer see me, but you will see me, because I live and you will live."* We will come to know Jesus as the One who has life, and as His disciples we will have a share in this life. Jesus is referring to the divine life He shares with His Father and the Holy Spirit. The Triune God is Covenant itself and when we share in their divine life, we are in covenant with the Three Divine Persons. Jesus also tells us that when we participate in the divine life, we will know that Jesus is in the Father and we are in Him, and He in us!

Jesus emphasized this point of sharing God's covenant life with us so that we would live and act as one entity with the Trinity. Matthew 11:28-30 quotes Jesus as saying, *"Come to me, all you who are weary and find life burdensome, and I will refresh you. Take my yoke upon your shoulders and learn from me, for I am gentle and humble of heart. Your souls will find rest, for my yoke is easy and my burden light."* Jesus is alluding to the burdens of excessive moral and legal prescriptions of rabbinic Judaism that His listeners were shouldering. He was also talking about the necessity of accepting Him as their Savior against the ravages of sin. He was pointing to Himself as the only One who could grant them relief and freedom from these man-made regulations (the result of pride), and from sin of their making. He asks them to learn from Him for He is gentle and humble of heart. He is gentle and humble of heart because in His covenant love for us, he has made our lives His own. The burden that He places on our shoulders is our own life that He is now living with us. Our lives which were a suffocating and unbearable burden when we were carrying them on our own, have now become light and sweet because we have been made one with Jesus in covenant. When Jesus refers to a two oxen yoke, He is clearly suggesting that He will share all our burdens, and our very lives, as He is yoked with us. Consequently, we will experience the burdens of life as light and the yoke as sweet because Jesus is joined with us all the way.

THE TEACHINGS OF JESUS EMBODY HIS PERSON AND PRESENCE:

This idea of Jesus being yoked to us is further enhanced in His teachings. In John 15 Jesus talks of Himself as the Vine and us as His branches. In doing so He reveals several very interesting and profound truths. Jesus tells us that His Father is the Vine-Grower: *"He prunes away every barren branch, but the fruitful one he trims clean to increase their yield."* (John 15:2) The other Persons of the Trinity, along with Jesus, are equally committed to the business of ensuring our covenant life with God. Both the plan for our salvation and its execution are a Trinitarian endeavor. Here the Father is working closely with His Son and Holy Spirit in this work of sanctification. He is described as meticulous and totally dedicated to His vineyard. The Father prunes away every dead branch and He trims clean the fruitful ones in order to increase their yield. It is both heartening and overwhelming to realize how intimately involved each Person of the Trinity is in securing our covenant life with them!

Next, Jesus offers us the very profound truth that He and we are inextricably linked to one another. We cannot live without Him, do anything apart from Him, for we would then be like a withered, rejected branch, pruned by the Father to be thrown into the fire and burnt. While Jesus is our Life-Source, what is astounding is that He has bound himself to us inextricably, out of agapé love. Hence He will gladly die for us so that we might share in His life! And Jesus makes the promise, that if we lived in Him and His words became our life-style, we would have great power with God as Jesus does: *"If you live in me, and my words stay part of you, you may ask what you will – it will be done for you."* (John 15:7) Jesus' words are a personal and existential expression of Himself. Therefore, when He talks about His words being a part of us, He is talking about an inseparable relationship and union with Him that then brings us into the depths of God's Trinitarian Life and power!

Finally, Jesus says that we are His friends and not slaves. Slaves had no rights and therefore never did belong to or participate in the life and family of their Master. While such alienation from God was justified because of sin, Jesus would have none of it. In the Old Testament, and as an expression of the Mosaic Covenant, several individuals were addressed as 'servant of God.' Moses was hailed repeatedly as the servant of God, as for instance in Exodus 14:31; Joshua was called the servant of God in Joshua 24:29; David is referred to as the servant of God in Psalm 89. While this title is an expression of intimacy between God and specific humans, it also highlights a covenant union that is not quite complete. So, in calling us His friends, Jesus is revealing to us His true design which is participation in the divine life: *"There is no greater love than this: to lay down one's life for one's friends. You are my friends if you do what I command you. I no longer speak of you as slaves, for a slave does not know what his master is about. Instead, I call you friends, since I have made known to you all that I heard from my Father."* (John 15:13-15) As friends of Jesus we receive the unique privilege that only He has, namely to address His Father as 'Our Father.' As friends of Jesus, His teachings will be revealed to us in all their truth and power by His Holy Spirit: *"When he comes, however, being the Spirit of truth he will guide you to all truth. He will not speak on his own, but will speak only what he hears, and will announce to you the things to come."* (John 16:13) As friends of Jesus, we will learn to love one another as Jesus loves us, and recognize Jesus in one another as well. After all, He is the Head and we are the Body of Christ! Finally, Jesus assures us that He will bring to completion this covenant living with the Trinity because it is not we who have chosen Him. Rather it is He who has chosen us to go forth and bear fruit.

The Eucharist captures best our insertion into God's family. In His discourse on the Bread of Life in John 6, Jesus tells us that He is the Bread of Life. Jesus makes several assertions where He describes Himself as the Bread of Life resulting in the necessity of eating or feeding on His flesh and drinking His blood in order to have God's Life! We will not be able to access the divine Life unless we partake of divine food which is Jesus Himself! It is clear, therefore, that in His discourse Jesus is inviting us to a sacrificial covenant meal. In receiving His Body and drinking His blood we participate in His death and resurrection, thus becoming one with Him and sharing in His life. John 6:53-56 states categorically why Jesus came into the world and how He will save it: *"Let me solemnly assure you, if you do not eat the flesh of the Son of Man and drink his blood, you have no life in you. He who feeds on my flesh and drinks my blood has life eternal and I will raise him up on the last day. For my flesh is real food and my blood real drink. The man who feeds on my flesh and drinks my blood remains in me, and I in him."*

Through His death on the cross, the Risen Lord offered to His Father the perfect sacrifice that has brought about reconciliation and union with our Triune God. In receiving the Body and Blood of Jesus we become who we receive. In His Prayer for all believers, Jesus tells us what actually takes place when we receive His body and blood in Holy Communion at Eucharist: *"I have given them the glory you gave me that they may be one, as we are one – I living in them, you living in me – that their unity may be complete. So shall the world know that you sent me, and that you loved them as you loved me. Father, all those you gave me I would have in my company where I am, to see this glory of mine which is your gift to me, because of the love you bore me before the world began. Just Father, the world has not known you, but I have known you; and these men have known that you sent me. To them I have revealed your name, and I will continue to reveal it so that your love for me may live in them, and I may live in them."* (John 17:22-26) As Paul says in Colossians 1:27: *"God has willed to make known to them the glory beyond price which this mystery brings to the Gentiles – the mystery of Christ in you, your hope of glory."*

LIVING AS GOD'S COVENANT FAMILY:

Humility, the Basis of Living as God's Covenant Family:

Jesus emptied Himself of His divinity so that He could take upon Himself our sin, wash us clean in His blood, and bring us into His Father's embrace. In 2 Corinthians 5:21 Paul tells us that *"For our sakes God made him who did not know sin, to be sin, so that in him we might become the very holiness of God."* Jesus' kenosis served two purposes. On the one hand, in and through His kenosis He was being our *Goel*, kinsperson-Savior. On the other hand, Jesus was demonstrating to us that the only way we can participate in His divine life is by embracing His kenosis in our own lives as a way of eschewing sin. Eschewing sin would mean living one's life contrary to the standards of the world and in accordance with the teachings of Jesus.

There are therefore, two major strands in Jesus' teachings regarding kenosis: One, whenever Jesus asks us to empty ourselves, He is bidding us do what He did in the first place. In identifying ourselves with the kenotic Christ, paradoxically, we will experience the blessedness of His divine life. Here are some sayings of Jesus that invite us into His kenosis:

- *"Blest are you when they insult you and persecute you and utter every kind of slander against you because of me. Be glad and rejoice, for your reward is great in heaven; they persecuted the prophets before you in the same way."* (Matthew 5:11-12) Jesus experienced constant union with His Father and extraordinary love for us who were humiliating and rejecting Him as He went through His passion and death. Similarly, according to this beatitude, in sharing in His kenosis, we will experience union with the Risen Lord!

- *"My command to you is: love your enemies, pray for your persecutors. This will prove that you are sons of your heavenly Father, for his sun rises on the bad and the good, he rains on the just and the unjust…In a word, you must be made perfect as your heavenly Father is perfect."* (Matthew 5:44-48) Only God loves selflessly! Only God can share this selfless and generous love for sinners and enemies with us. Once again Jesus is offering us a share in God's perfection through the action of His Holy Spirit!

- *"You address me as 'Teacher' and 'Lord,' and fittingly enough, for that is what I am. But if I washed your feet – I who am Teacher and Lord – then you must wash each other's feet. What I just did was to give you an example: as I have done, so you must do."* (John 13:13-15) Jesus unleashed a revolution when as Teacher and Lord He identified Himself with a non-Jewish slave, thus holding nothing back in laying down His life for our salvation and sanctification. He is telling us that we will experience a revolution in our own lives if we insist on loving others no matter the challenges, rather than on being loved!

- *"Whoever wishes to be my follower must deny his very self, take up his cross each day, and follow in my steps. Whoever would save his life, will lose it, and whoever loses his life for my sake will save it."* (Luke 9:23-24) Jesus died in our stead and revealed two amazing truths: One is that He is God because only God could have died in our stead. And two, that in laying aside our wants and preferences and insisting on serving others as a generous and faithful servant would do, we would experience the power and joy of the Risen Lord!

The second major strand in Jesus' teachings regarding kenosis is that emptying ourselves of everything that is not of Jesus is necessary, or else covenant living with the Triune God is jeopardized. Hence, the Father, who is the Vine-Grower, prunes away all the dead branches and trims clean even the fruitful ones to increase their yield. Jesus places very high standards before us when it comes to avoiding sin in any form. For instance, it is not enough for Jesus that we refrain from murder. Even getting angry and holding on to our anger is forbidden (Matthew 5:21-22). And in the matter of forgiveness, Jesus is relentless in demanding that we be exactly as He is: *"If you forgive the faults of others, your heavenly Father will forgive you yours. If you do not forgive others, neither will your Father forgive you."* (Matthew 6:14-15)

Oddly enough, Jesus is immensely attractive in His lifestyle of humility. He has no hesitation to mingle with "sinners and tax-collectors," men and women who were loathed by established society and the religious leadership. He came for sinners and not for the just. Outcasts of society were thrilled at being accepted and loved by Jesus. It made sense to them to give up their former ways and return to God. Jesus brings them the good news of God's reign, inviting them to repent and receive God's forgiveness, and filling their hearts with peace and joy.

In His ministry Jesus is free of any attachment to His honor and reputation among the influential and powerful segments of society. He chose ordinary and unsophisticated men to be His inner circle of disciples. Even after three years of formation at the hands of the best Teacher in the world, they did not show much promise. Paradoxically, it seemed that the Holy Spirit could really "fill them up" with the transformative power and peace of the Risen Lord *only after* they had encountered the abyss of their own lack of faith and abject impotence.

While Jesus had all, He chose to live with very little wealth, convenience, and honor among circles that truly mattered in the eyes of the world. He steadfastly refused to kowtow to the ways of the world, rejecting riches, honor, and pride, and replacing them instead with a lifestyle of poverty, and humiliations leading to humility. His hour of greatest humiliation, and by the same token, greatest love, was His passion, crucifixion, and death. *"I am the good shepherd; the good shepherd lays down his life for the sheep."* (John 10:11) Jesus overcame Satan, sin, and death by always responding in love and truth, even to the point of offering His life for us. And He calls upon us to do the same, to not add to the evil in the world by responding with wrong doing, and even more, to minimize evil by responding with love and compassion.

Living in Covenant with Jesus and His Brothers and Sisters:

There are two divine realities that radiate through the lifestyle of Jesus and His call to covenant living. While Jesus worked miracles, He was not interested in showing the world what an extraordinary miracle-worker He was! Nor was His purpose to show what an extraordinary prophet or messenger from God He was. His one intent was to show the world that He came from His Father and that He was God. Disciples who steep themselves in the message and lifestyle of Jesus by entering into a covenant relationship with Him, slowly realize the power and peace that lie in forgiving and loving one's enemies, in loving without counting the cost, in trusting God over material security and comforts, in desiring to be the last rather than the first, in thanking God for and in every circumstance. Slowly they realize that Jesus walks with them in the messiness of their lives; that in the suffering and burdens of life the peace and joy of the Risen Lord are present. Gradually their faith in Jesus is strengthened to the point where His divinity is manifest in every circumstance of their lives. They begin to see that the Holy Spirit has strengthened their discipleship so that they are able to move mountains.

In other words the two divine realities are: 1) Jesus is God and the Second Person of the Trinity. 2) We will experience Him as Lord and Savior when we eschew every other pseudo-god or idol, and belong to Him alone, making His teachings our life style with the help of His Holy Spirit. Obviously this is a covenant relationship which will take patience and time to blossom and mature, but blossom and mature it will as the Holy Spirit is the architect and builder of our union with God.

Transformation of the World through God's Covenant Family:

Whatever analysis is made of the Church, or God's covenant family that has been in existence for twenty centuries, one would have to include the manifold blessings of covenant life that have been offered to our world. We have been edified and encouraged by the lives of thousands upon thousands of martyrs, witnesses, and saints who have witnessed to the power and covenant presence of God in their lives. Their transformation came through God's immense generosity and their total surrender to Him. We are reminded that even though we might have feet of clay, God will bring about our transformation because there is nothing more that God wants than to be Emmanuel, dwelling with and in us. Secondly, no earthly organization has done as much good for the benefit of humanity over twenty centuries than the Catholic Church. Throughout the world, the poor and disadvantaged have been helped through education, care of the sick, and thousands of charitable works provided by Catholic schools, colleges and universities, nursing homes and hospitals, medical colleges, orphanages and other Catholic Services. Unstinting service to the poor and downtrodden over twenty centuries has been provided by thousands upon thousands of Jesus' disciples who joined religious orders and communities for the sole purpose of glorifying God through a life of humble service. And thousands upon thousands of monasteries have been built all over the world to let the world know that God is central to their lives as God's covenant family, and their only purpose in life is to witness to the presence of Jesus as Savior and Lord of the Universe, and our Way to covenant union with the Blessed Trinity. The Church has been vilified and persecuted throughout the ages. The Church has suffered from inner rot, great and small, through the centuries, grieving immensely both the heart of God and His people. Through it all, the gates of hell have not prevailed against her, and the Holy Spirit continues to keep watch and bring about her transformation. And when scandals have been rife at different times in her history, God has always raised reformers and saints to do battle, and with God's help to bring His covenant family back to her roots of being founded in covenant with God.

PRAYER AND REFLECTION ON: LIVING AS GOD'S COVENANT FAMILY

WEEK ELEVEN: *"Then he took the bread, said the blessing, broke it, and gave it to them saying, 'This is my body, which will be given for you; do this in memory of me.' And likewise the cup after they had eaten, saying, 'This cup is the new covenant in my blood, which will be shed for you.'"* (Luke 22:19-20)

SPIRITUAL READING FOR THE WEEK:

- **Anoint Us in Your Covenant, Abba-Emmanuel:** Session Six
- **Old Testament:** Two or Three Chapters daily
- **New Testament:** Two or Three Chapters daily
- **Imitation of Christ:** One chapter daily

DAY ONE: MORNING SESSION

MORNING PRAYER: Acts of Faith, Hope, Charity; Daily Offering

Morning Face to Face with God:

Begin with Prayer to the Holy Spirit
LIVING AS GOD'S COVENANT FAMILY:
(After pondering each bullet point, express your sentiments in a short prayer)

Living a Transformed Life:
- John the beloved disciple was transformed after the resurrection of His Lord and Master, through the power of the Holy Spirit. He was able to shed many of his own self-centered attitudes that he had during his three year sojourn with Jesus. He came to a radical commitment to Him both in relationship and ministry, and he expressed this total surrender of his being to his Lord and Master in his writings.
- There is intimacy and oneness between Jesus and the disciple(s) that is palpable, tender, and very personal: *"What was from the beginning, what we have heard, what we have seen with our eyes, what we have looked upon and our hands have touched – we speak of the word of life."* (1 John 1:1)
- John goes on to make two very significant points: The first point is that *in his ministry John is witnessing to what he has seen and heard and touched.* John has witnessed the glory of God as made manifest in the Person of Jesus Christ: *"The Word became flesh and made*

his dwelling among us, and we have seen his glory: The glory of an only Son coming from the Father, filled with enduring love." (John 1:14)

- The second point is that he now has fellowship with the Father and the Son: *"What we have seen and heard we proclaim in turn to you so that you may share life with us. This fellowship of ours is with the Father and with his Son, Jesus Christ. Indeed, our purpose in writing you this is that our joy may be complete."* (1 John 1:3-4) John writes and preaches what the Holy Spirit has revealed to him in the depths of his heart.

- Like Mary, John had spent years pondering the mystery and majesty of the Father's love poured out upon us through His Son Jesus Christ: *"See what love the Father has bestowed on us in letting us be called children of God! Yet that is what we are... Dearly beloved, we are God's children now; what we shall later be has not yet come to light. We know that when it comes to light we shall be like him, for we shall see him as he is. Everyone who has this hope based on him keeps himself pure, as he is pure."* (1 John 3:1, 2-3)

- Paul's hatred for Christ's followers, and his zeal to have them exterminated, was both frightening and all consuming. How could anyone deal with such a maniacal zealot? In Paul's opinion, it was the grace and mercy of God shown to him in Jesus Christ that dealt with his obdurate heart.

- The Risen Lord opens the mind and heart of this rabid destroyer of Christ's followers and changes him into one of his most ardent, zealous, and generous apostles: *"I (Jesus) have appeared to you to designate you as my servant and as a witness to what you have seen of me and what you will see of me. I have delivered you from this people and from the nations, to open the eyes of those to whom I am sending you, to turn them from darkness to light and from the dominion of Satan to God; that through their faith in me they may obtain the forgiveness of their sins and a portion among God's people."* (Acts 26:16-18)

Witnessing to the Transformation in Ministry:
- When examining the ministry of the apostles in the New Testament, it becomes clear that for them ministry is witnessing to Jesus as He has been revealed to them in the depths of their hearts by the Holy Spirit.

- The same Jesus who came among us, suffered and died for us, and was raised by the Father in the power of the Holy Spirit, now dwells in their hearts and is in covenant relationship with them. Their message to the world is that Jesus Christ is the Resurrection and the Life. He is the Light of the World. He is the Way and the Truth and the Life.

- His disciples know all these truths in their covenant relationship with Jesus Christ who has become Emmanuel, God-with-us-and-in-us, to them. Their ministry is inviting everyone to believe that Jesus came into the world, not to condemn the world but to save it and to offer to them God's eternal life in Him that they have experienced and known.

- The disciples of Jesus were our first forebears in the faith. They have transmitted to us their own experience of Jesus and His gift of eternal life through His death and resurrection.
- Their life in Jesus consumed them. Nothing else mattered. We are temples of the Holy Trinity, and our lives need to become a constant hymn of gratitude, praise, and unstinted service of Jesus in His Body, the Church.

What is God saying to you?

End with Prayer to the Holy Trinity

NIGHT SESSION: Examination of Conscience

For what are you grateful? For what are you contrite?

Please review briefly your Morning Prayer topic. Make it your last thought of the day

DAY TWO: MORNING SESSION

MORNING PRAYER: Act of Faith; Act of Hope; Act of Charity; Daily Offering

Morning Face to Face with God:

Begin with Prayer to the Holy Spirit
Prayer on Matthew 5:3-10: The Beatitudes:
> *"Blessed are the poor in spirit, for theirs is the kingdom of heaven…Blessed are they who hunger and thirst for righteousness, for they will be satisfied…Blessed are the merciful, for they will be shown mercy…Blessed are they who are persecuted for the sake of righteousness, for theirs is the kingdom of heaven." [Please read Matthew 5:1-12 for a better appreciation of the passage].*

Read the Reflection; Ask for the grace that like your Teacher and Lord, you will be generous and wholehearted in your service of God's covenant family

The Beatitudes sum up all of Jesus' teachings. Jesus is asking us to be like Him, offering our lives to God and His people in sacrificial devotion and service. One experiences the joy and peace of the Kingdom of God when such an offering is made to the other, without reserve. The Beatitudes reach into the depths of our being and challenge every settled assumption we hold. In covenant fashion, they encourage living for the other: giving up comfort and security for the other *(poor in spirit)*; longing and working for the right order of things *(hunger and thirst for righteousness)*; showing mercy as God does, without counting the cost *(blessed are the merciful)*; being persecuted in working towards establishing righteousness *(persecuted for the sake of righteousness)*. The world does not think the way Jesus does. Through the Beatitudes, Jesus is offering us a different kind of existence. This new life of true happiness and union with God is considered to be foolishness by worldly standards. Disciples, who are guided by the norms set within the Beatitudes, harbor no enmity in their hearts. They seek peace and union of hearts. They are often misunderstood because they seek truth, and challenge others to do likewise. They experience joy even in the midst of suffering. Throughout the Beatitudes, Jesus extols the disciple who is willing to go to any lengths to seek and receive union with God. As you pray on the Beatitudes, ask the Holy Spirit to reveal to you their inner meaning and beauty.

What is God saying to you?

End with Prayer to the Holy Trinity

NIGHT SESSION: Examination of Conscience

For what are you grateful? For what are you contrite?

Please review briefly your Morning Prayer topic. Make it your last thought of the day

DAY THREE: MORNING SESSION

MORNING PRAYER: Act of Faith; Act of Hope; Act of Charity; Daily Offering

Morning Face to Face with God:

Begin with Prayer to the Holy Spirit
Prayer on Matthew 5:23-24: Teaching about Anger:
   "Therefore, if you bring your gift to the altar, and there recall that your brother has anything against you, leave your gift there at the altar, go first and be reconciled with your brother, and then come and offer your gift." [Please read Matthew 5:21-26 for a better appreciation of the passage].

Read the Reflection; Ask for the grace that like your Teacher and Lord, you will be generous and wholehearted in your service of God's covenant family

In Matthew 5:21-48, Jesus offers us six examples of conduct. Such conduct is asked of any true follower of Jesus. One of these is against anger which is the subject matter for our prayer. There is a thesis and an antithesis in the presentation of these six examples of conduct. Each one is introduced by a commandment of the law: *You have heard that it was said to your ancestors* or an equivalent formula. This is the thesis. It is then countered by Jesus' teaching in respect to that commandment, the antithesis: *But I say to you.* Three antitheses accept the Mosaic Law, as in the case with anger, but expand and give it deeper significance. In three instances the standard of conduct as presented in the Law is rejected: divorce, oaths, and retaliation. In the case with anger, reconciliation with an offended brother is urged. When examining the text, it becomes clear that Jesus wants us to eschew every trace of anger and resentment, as anger is the motive behind murder. The parable is severe in its message to us. The fate of the unrepentant sinner will be serious: *"Amen, I say to you, you will not be released until you have paid the last penny".* (Verse 26)

What is God saying to you?

End with Prayer to the Holy Trinity

NIGHT SESSION: Examination of Conscience

For what are you grateful? For what are you contrite?

Please review briefly your Morning Prayer topic. Make it your last thought of the day

DAY FOUR: MORNING SESSION

MORNING PRAYER: Act of Faith; Act of Hope; Act of Charity; Daily Offering

Morning Face to Face with God:

Begin with Prayer to the Holy Spirit
Prayer on Luke 6:27-30: Love of Enemies
> *"But to you who hear I say, love your enemies, do good to those who hate you, bless those who curse you, pray for those who mistreat you. To the person who strikes you on one cheek, offer the other one as well, and from the person who takes your cloak, do not withhold even your tunic. Give to everyone who asks of you, and from the one who takes what is yours do not demand it back."*
> *[Please read Luke 6:27-36 for a better appreciation of the passage].*

Read the Reflection; Ask for the grace that like your Teacher and Lord, you will be generous and wholehearted in your service of God's covenant family

Jesus tells us on several occasions that He came not for the just but to answer the needs of sinners. He expresses a special fondness for sinners and seeks their company. While He knows our human condition better than we do, especially our penchant for sabotaging the good within us, He believes with all His heart that sinners such as ourselves have been called to profound transformation. The purpose of His mission is to bring us salvation and union with God, to think, act, and be like Him. Like Jesus we are called to be forgiving, compassionate, and generous in our service of others: *"Bless those who curse you, pray for those who mistreat you (Verse 28)… Do to others as you would have them do to you (Verse 31)… Be merciful as [also] your Father is merciful."* (Verse 36)

What is God saying to you?

End with Prayer to the Holy Trinity

NIGHT SESSION: Examination of Conscience

For what are you grateful? For what are you contrite?

Please review briefly your Morning Prayer topic. Make it your last thought of the day

DAY FIVE: MORNING SESSION

MORNING PRAYER: Act of Faith; Act of Hope; Act of Charity; Daily Offering

Morning Face to Face with God:

Begin with Prayer to the Holy Spirit

Prayer on John 13:3-5; 12-16: The Washing of the Disciples' Feet:
"So, during supper, fully aware that the Father had put everything into his power and that he had come from God and was returning to God, he rose from supper and took off his outer garments. He took a towel and tied it around his waist. Then he poured water into a basin and began to wash the disciples' feet and dry them with the towel around his waist… "Do you realize what I have done for you? You call me 'teacher' and 'master,' and rightly so, for indeed I am. If I, therefore, the master and teacher, have washed your feet, you ought to wash one another's feet…No slave is greater than his master nor any messenger greater than the one who sent him." [Please read John 13:1-20 for a better appreciation of the passage].

Read the Reflection; Ask for the grace that like your Teacher and Lord, you will be generous and wholehearted in your service of God's covenant family

Jesus is in the Upper Room with His disciples. They are there to celebrate the Passover Meal of the Mosaic Covenant. And within the context of the Passover Meal, Jesus will institute the new and everlasting covenant through His forthcoming death on the cross, leading to His resurrection. Jesus institutes the new covenant (the New Testament) by giving His disciples His body to eat and His blood to drink, in anticipation of His death and resurrection. Jesus wants to make sure that this event of our salvation will always remain in our midst as a sacred memorial. He wants them to know that He went willingly to His passion and death. He was willing to be our slave in our stead, and pay the price for our freedom. He emphasizes this amazing swap He undertook on our behalf through a very concrete gesture: He washes the feet of His disciples in preparation for the new Passover Meal that is about to take place. He identifies Himself as a non-Jewish slave as He was willing to do anything for us. His love for us is indeed both unconditional and limitless, soon to be expressed through His sacrifice on the cross. And He asks us to do the same as is befitting anyone who takes living in covenant seriously.

What is God saying to you?

End with Prayer to the Holy Trinity

NIGHT SESSION: Examination of Conscience

For what are you grateful? For what are you contrite?

Please review briefly your Morning Prayer topic. Make it your last thought of the day

DAY SIX: MORNING SESSION

MORNING PRAYER: Act of Faith; Act of Hope; Act of Charity; Daily Offering

Morning Face to Face with God:

Begin with Prayer to the Holy Spirit
REPETITION OF DAYS TWO THROUGH FIVE:

Ask for the grace that like your Teacher and Lord, you will be generous and wholehearted in your service of God's covenant family

Today, you are doing a repetition of Days Two through Five of this week. In a repetition St. Ignatius says that *"we should pay attention to and dwell upon those points in which we have experienced greater consolation or desolation or greater spiritual appreciation."* (# 62) If you wish, you can do a triple colloquy: refer to #63 of the Spiritual Exercises.

What is God saying to you?

End with Prayer to the Holy Trinity

NIGHT SESSION: Examination of Conscience

For what are you grateful? For what are you contrite?

Please review briefly your Morning Prayer topic. Make it your last thought of the day

DAY SEVEN: MORNING SESSION

MORNING PRAYER: Act of Faith; Act of Hope; Act of Charity; Daily Offering

Morning Face to Face with God:

Begin with Prayer to the Holy Spirit

THE FOURTH DWELLING PLACES OF THE INTERIOR CASTLE:

(After pondering each bullet point, express your sentiments in a short prayer)

- The first Three Dwelling Places take up about 30 percent of the *Interior Castle*. The last Four Dwelling Places take up about 70 percent of the text, and are almost entirely about prayer in its infused stages.
- St. Teresa writes expansively about the Fourth Dwelling Places because she believes that very many beginners enter into the initial stage of infused or contemplative prayer.
- Another reason for writing in some detail is that there is a definite movement from discursive prayer which is the human way of doing things, to infused prayer which clearly is supernatural, given to us by the Holy Spirit directly.
- The transition can be bewildering, as the beginner will not be able to make sense of what is going on. The earlier criteria by which they judged prayer don't seem to be working. While they seem to be backsliding, paradoxically, their longing for God has intensified.
- At this stage, if the beginner is not helped properly, great harm can be done. Commonly, people do not know how to effect the transition from the one to the other. At this stage, wise spiritual direction is crucial.
- How then to explain the difference between discursive prayer and infused contemplation? St. Teresa made a distinction between consolations (*contentos*) and spiritual delight (*gustos*) in order to explain infused prayer or contemplation.
- The former (consolations) have their beginning in our human nature; they arise in the exercise of our human faculties like the mind, memory, imagination and will, and end in God.
- The latter (spiritual delight), on the other hand, have their beginning in God and overflow into our human nature. The Holy Spirit infuses this divine knowledge directly into our souls, bypassing so to speak, our human faculties.
- The consolations (*contentos*), then, result from our own efforts accompanied by God's grace; the spiritual delight (*gustos*) is received not through human efforts but passively or receptively from the Holy Spirit.
- Infused contemplation, therefore, is a divinely given, general, non-conceptual, loving awareness of God. Sometimes this awareness of God takes the form of a loving

attention, sometimes of a dry desire, sometimes of a strong thirsting. None of these experiences is the result of reading or reasoning – they are given, and therefore received.

- In *The Interior Castle*, (TIC VI:7:11) St. Teresa shows how a contemplative, having great difficulty doing discursive reflection, must still contemplate in and with the humanity of Christ: "*This prayer (discursive meditation) is the kind that those whom God has brought to supernatural things and to perfect contemplation are right in saying they cannot practice… But I say that a person will not be right if he says he does not dwell on these mysteries or often have them in mind, especially when the Catholic Church celebrates them…*"

- The infusion is serene, purifying. Always it is transformative of the person, usually imperceptibly and gradually, but on occasion obviously and suddenly.

- As the person grows into this new, infused prayer, God progressively takes over the will, and then the intellect and imagination. He occupies and absorbs them by what He gives.

- St. Teresa calls this *the suspension of the faculties; that is, they are relieved of the ordinary human necessity of working at thoughts, ideas, and affections.*

What is God saying to you?

End with Prayer to the Holy Trinity

NIGHT SESSION: Examination of Conscience

For what are you grateful? For what are you contrite?

What prayer would you compose to express what God has said to you this week?

Please review briefly your Morning Prayer topic. Make it your last thought of the day

PRAYER AND REFLECTION ON: LIVING AS GOD'S COVENANT FAMILY -CONTINUED

WEEK TWELVE: "*Go, therefore, and make disciples of all nations, baptizing them in the name of the Father, and of the Son, and of the Holy Spirit, teaching them to observe all that I have commanded you. And behold, I am with you always, until the end of the age.*" (MATTHEW 28:19-20)

SPIRITUAL READING FOR THE WEEK:

- **Anoint Us in Your Covenant, Abba-Emmanuel:** Session Six
- **Old Testament:** Two or Three Chapters daily

- **New Testament:** Two or Three Chapters daily
- **Imitation of Christ:** One chapter daily

DAY ONE: MORNING SESSION

MORNING PRAYER: Acts of Faith, Hope, Charity; Daily Offering

Morning Face to Face with God:

Begin with Prayer to the Holy Spirit

LIVING AS GOD'S COVENANT FAMILY:

(After pondering each bullet point, express your sentiments in a short prayer)

- Jesus' kenosis served two purposes. On the one hand, in and through His kenosis He was being our *Goel*, kinsperson-Savior. On the other hand, Jesus was demonstrating to us that the only way we can participate in His divine life is by embracing His kenosis in our own lives as a way of eschewing sin.
- Emptying ourselves of everything that is not of Jesus is necessary, or else covenant living with the Triune God is jeopardized. Hence, the Father, who is the Vine-Grower, prunes away all the dead branches and trims clean even the fruitful ones to increase their yield.
- Jesus places very high standards before us when it comes to avoiding sin in any form. And in the matter of forgiveness, Jesus is relentless in demanding that we be exactly as He is: *"If you forgive the faults of others, your heavenly Father will forgive you yours. If you do not forgive others, neither will your Father forgive you."* (Matthew 6:14-15)
- Paradoxically, it seemed that the Holy Spirit could really "fill them up" with the transformative power and peace of the Risen Lord *only after* they had encountered the abyss of their own lack of faith and abject impotence.
- While Jesus worked miracles, He was not interested in showing the world what an extraordinary miracle-worker He was! Nor was His purpose to show what an extraordinary prophet or messenger from God He was. His one intent was to show the world that He came from His Father and that He was God.
- Disciples who steep themselves in the message and lifestyle of Jesus by entering into a covenant relationship with Him, slowly realize the power and peace that lie in forgiving and loving one's enemies, in loving without counting the cost, in trusting God over material security and comforts, in desiring to be the last rather than the first, in thanking God for and in every circumstance.
- Slowly they realize that Jesus walks with them in the messiness of their lives; that in the suffering and burdens of life the peace and joy of the Risen Lord are present. Gradually

their faith in Jesus is strengthened to the point where His divinity is manifest in every circumstance of their lives.

- They begin to see that the Holy Spirit has strengthened their discipleship so that they are able to move mountains.

- Their discipleship hinges on two divine realities: 1) Jesus is God and the Second Person of the Trinity. 2) We will experience Him as Lord and Savior when we eschew every other pseudo-god or idol, and belong to Him alone, making His teachings our life style with the help of His Holy Spirit.

- Obviously this is a covenant relationship which will take patience and time to blossom and mature, but blossom and mature it will, as the Holy Spirit is the architect and builder of our union with God.

What is God saying to you?

End with Prayer to the Holy Trinity

NIGHT SESSION: Examination of Conscience

For what are you grateful? For what are you contrite?

Please review briefly your Morning Prayer topic. Make it your last thought of the day

DAY TWO: MORNING SESSION

MORNING PRAYER: Act of Faith; Act of Hope; Act of Charity; Daily Offering

Morning Face to Face with God:

Begin with Prayer to the Holy Spirit

Prayer on Matthew 6:19-21: True Riches
> *"Do not store up for yourselves treasures on earth, where moth and decay destroy, and thieves break in and steal. But store up treasures in heaven, where neither moth nor decay destroys, nor thieves break in and steal. For where your treasure is, there also will your heart be."*

Read the Reflection; Ask for the grace that like your Teacher and Lord, you will be generous and wholehearted in your service of God's covenant family

St. Ignatius of Loyola identified the path to alienation from God as being the insatiable desire for riches, which leads to a hunger for honor and power, which leads to pride or setting oneself up as the yardstick, instead of Jesus' teachings. The antidote to the way of the world is Jesus' way, which emphasizes poverty or freedom from attachment to material possessions and status: *"But store up treasures in heaven, where neither moth nor decay destroys, nor thieves break in and steal. For where your treasure is, there also will your heart be."* (Verses 20-21) Liberation from the bondage of materialism leads to the eye being sound and the body being filled with light (Verse 22). True freedom of spirit lies in the recognition and firm acceptance that no one can serve two masters. We cannot serve God and mammon. It can only be one or the other (Verses 24).

What is God saying to you?

End with Prayer to the Holy Trinity

NIGHT SESSION: Examination of Conscience

For what are you grateful? For what are you contrite?

Please review briefly your Morning Prayer topic. Make it your last thought of the day

DAY THREE: MORNING SESSION

MORNING PRAYER: Act of Faith; Act of Hope; Act of Charity; Daily Offering

Morning Face to Face with God:

Begin with Prayer to the Holy Spirit
Prayer on John 12:23-26: The Coming of Jesus' Hour
    "Jesus answered them, "The hour has come for the Son of Man to be glorified. Amen, amen, I say to you, unless a grain of wheat falls to the ground and dies, it remains just a grain of wheat; but if it dies, it produces much fruit. Whoever loves his life loses it, and whoever hates his life in this world will preserve it for eternal life. Whoever serves me must follow me, and where I am, there also will my servant be. The Father will honor whoever serves me."

Read the Reflection; Ask for the grace that like your Teacher and Lord, you will be generous and wholehearted in your service of God's covenant family

Lazarus has been raised from the dead. The crowds began to follow Jesus and to testify that He had done this great sign. Such enthusiasm led to Jesus' entry into Jerusalem. The Pharisees were disturbed and their reaction was, *"You see that you are gaining nothing. Look, the whole world has gone after him."* (Verse 19) John's surface meaning is that everyone is following Jesus. But his expression 'the whole world,' alludes to the universality of salvation both in this passage and in earlier references like 3:17 and 4:42. To highlight this universal invitation to salvation in Jesus, some Greeks approached the disciples and asked to see Jesus. It is then that in our passage for prayer, Jesus talks about his glorification by death: *"The hour has come for the Son of Man to be glorified."* (Verse 23) Only after the crucifixion could the gospel encompass both Jew and Gentile, as through His death, Jesus will be accessible to all. Only after His resurrection, did Jesus' disciples understand His crucifixion to be His hour of glory!

What is God saying to you?

End with Prayer to the Holy Trinity

NIGHT SESSION: Examination of Conscience

For what are you grateful? For what are you contrite?

Please review briefly your Morning Prayer topic. Make it your last thought of the day

DAY FOUR: MORNING SESSION

MORNING PRAYER: Act of Faith; Act of Hope; Act of Charity; Daily Offering

Morning Face to Face with God:

Begin with Prayer to the Holy Spirit
Prayer on 1 Peter 4:13-14: Blessings of Persecution
> *"But rejoice to the extent that you share in the sufferings of Christ, so that when his glory is revealed you may also rejoice exultantly. If you are insulted for the name of Christ, blessed are you, for the Spirit of glory and of God rests upon you."*

Read the Reflection; Ask for the grace that like your Teacher and Lord, you will be generous and wholehearted in your service of God's covenant family

Peter is talking about Christ being the cornerstone that is the foundation of the spiritual edifice of the Christian community. To unbelievers, Christ is an obstacle and a stumbling block on which they are destined to fail. Hence for the disciple, suffering is inevitable as there will always be a clash of world views: that of Satan and the world militating against the spirit of Jesus. In our passage for prayer, the suffering to which the author has already frequently referred is presented in more severe terms: *"Beloved, do not be surprised that a trial by fire is occurring among you, as if something strange were happening to you."* (Verse 12) The author seems to make reference to an actual persecution that is taking place among them. The epistle is reassuring its readers that in suffering persecution they are sharing in the sufferings of Jesus. In their union with the crucified Christ they will also experience the glory of the Risen Lord: *"Blessed are you, for the Spirit of glory and of God rests upon you."* (Verse 14)

What is God saying to you?

End with Prayer to the Holy Trinity

NIGHT SESSION: Examination of Conscience

For what are you grateful? For what are you contrite?

Please review briefly your Morning Prayer topic. Make it your last thought of the day

DAY FIVE: MORNING SESSION

MORNING PRAYER: Act of Faith; Act of Hope; Act of Charity; Daily Offering

Morning Face to Face with God:

Begin with Prayer to the Holy Spirit

Prayer on John 19:25-27: Jesus hands His Mother and John to each other

> *"Standing by the cross of Jesus were his mother and his mother's sister, Mary the wife of Clopas, and Mary of Magdala. When Jesus saw his mother and the disciple there whom he loved, he said to his mother, "Woman, behold your son." Then he said to the disciple, "Behold, your mother." And from that hour the disciple took her into his home."*

Read the Reflection; Ask for the grace that like your Teacher and Lord, you will be generous and wholehearted in your service of God's covenant family

Only John tells us that Our Lady was present at her son's crucifixion and death. As a mother, Mary must have wondered about the rest of the disciples who abandoned Jesus. As a devout Jewess, she must have wondered how it was possible for the Jewish leadership to be so prejudiced against her son. Yet from her own experience of the human condition, as she experienced and observed it in her son's kenosis and her own, she must have had His disposition: *"Father, forgive them; they do not know what they are doing."* (Luke 23:34) In this final act of love, before He surrendered His life to His Father, Jesus engages in an amazing act of covenant love and union. He bequeaths to His mother a special mission, in fact, the continuation of the same mission that was given to her at the Annunciation: to be His mother by becoming the mother of His covenant family, with whom He has become one, and symbolized by John, the beloved disciple. And in handing His mother to the safe-keeping of His beloved disciple, Jesus was asking His covenant family to always accord her a special place of honor and reverence in our hearts, similar to the honor and reverence Jesus always had for her. This has been the Church's understanding of the special connection between Mary, Mother of God, and God's Church, also known as God's covenant family.

What is God saying to you?

End with Prayer to the Holy Trinity

NIGHT SESSION: Examination of Conscience

For what are you grateful? For what are you contrite?

Please review briefly your Morning Prayer topic. Make it your last thought of the day

DAY SIX: MORNING SESSION

MORNING PRAYER: Act of Faith; Act of Hope; Act of Charity; Daily Offering

Morning Face to Face with God:

Begin with Prayer to the Holy Spirit

REPETITION OF DAYS TWO THROUGH FIVE:

Read the Reflection; Ask for the grace that like your Teacher and Lord, you will be generous and wholehearted in your service of God's covenant family

Today, you are doing a repetition of Days Two through Five of this week. In a repetition St. Ignatius says that *"we should pay attention to and dwell upon those points in which we have experienced greater consolation or desolation or greater spiritual appreciation."* (# 62) If you wish, you can do a triple colloquy: refer to #63 of the Spiritual Exercises.

What is God saying to you?

End with Prayer to the Holy Trinity

NIGHT SESSION: Examination of Conscience

For what are you grateful? For what are you contrite?

Please review briefly your Morning Prayer topic. Make it your last thought of the day

DAY SEVEN: MORNING SESSION

MORNING PRAYER: Act of Faith; Act of Hope; Act of Charity; Daily Offering

Morning Face to Face with God:

Begin with Prayer to the Holy Spirit

THE FOURTH DWELLING PLACES OF THE INTERIOR CASTLE - *Continued*:

(After pondering each bullet point, express your sentiments in a short prayer)

- It is not we who decide when this change shall take place. It is God who gives this new communion, and thus it is He who takes the initiative. As you can see, even someone who is beginning to experience infused contemplation will be confused and even distraught, because they will simply not be able to make sense of the transition, let alone deem it as being good and originating in God.

- What about someone who has not experienced even the beginnings of infused contemplation? Should they read anything on mystical prayer? St. Teresa believes that it could still benefit them as the Holy Spirit could whet their appetite and make them aware of what God has in store for them.

- In the Fourth Dwelling Places, St. Teresa distinguishes two kinds of infused prayer, the initial *"recollection,"* and the *"Prayer of Quiet."* Before the latter is given, almost always one will experience recollection, an infused and gentle awareness given by God and not produced by human effort.

- One is, as it were, gathered together in God and desires solitude to be with Him. The senses and external things slowly lose their hold upon the person. The beginnings of infused prayer occur in the Fourth Dwelling Places before the Prayer of Quiet. There is no absorption in God; rather, the inner person is serenely drawn to be occupied with Him.

- In *The Way of Perfection* St. Teresa defines the prayer of quiet as a state of prayer *"which is a quiet, deep and peaceful happiness in the will,"* and yet one does not understand what it is (Chapter 31). At the moment this prayer is given, the soul is captive and is not free to love anything but God.

- In her *Book of Life*, chapter 15, Teresa says, *"The soul is so satisfied with God that as long as the recollection lasts, the quiet and calm are not lost since the will is united with God even though the two faculties (intellect and memory) are distracted; in fact, little by little the will brings the intellect and the memory back to recollection. Even though the will may not be totally absorbed, it is so well occupied, without knowing how, that no matter what efforts the other two faculties make, they cannot take away its contentment and joy."*

- During the *Prayer of Quiet* some distractions are entirely possible, for while the memory and intellect may be somewhat stilled, they are not "completely lost," that is, absorbed in God. The person senses that they are close to the Lord and know Him better, but with no clear ideas. The quiet is felt in differing degrees at different times. It may last for a long while, even for a day or two. It follows then that one can enjoy this interior awareness even though engaged in exterior activities that require the attention of the mind.

- St. Teresa never divorces prayer from life. She lists numerous benefits of contemplative prayer in her various writings. The virtues grow better and deeper; the person loses their craving for worldly things; one's love for God has much less self-interest; there is a great desire for solitude, and so on.

What is God saying to you?

End with Prayer to the Holy Trinity

NIGHT SESSION: Examination of Conscience

For what are you grateful? For what are you contrite?

What prayer would you compose to express what God has said to you this week?

Please review briefly your Morning Prayer topic. Make it your last thought of the day

SESSION SEVEN:
KNOWING OUR FATHER IN THE TRINITY

"For God so loved the world that he gave his only Son, so that everyone who believes in him might not perish but might have eternal life. For God did not send his Son into the world to condemn the world, but that the world might be saved through him."

– John 3:16-17

TRINITARIAN RELATIONSHIPS FORESHADOWED IN THE OLD TESTAMENT:

Jesus tells us that He came not to abolish but to fulfill the Law and the Prophets. Regarding Himself, He fulfilled the Law's prophetic utterances: *"He said to them, "These are my words that I spoke to you while I was still with you, that everything written about me in the law of Moses and in the prophets and psalms must be fulfilled." Then he opened their minds to understand the scriptures."* (Luke 24:44-45) In myriad ways, the Old Testament was repeatedly foreshadowing the coming of Jesus Christ who once and for all would establish a new and everlasting covenant with God on our behalf. These signs, pointing to the coming of Jesus, reveal to us much of God's Trinitarian Life.

The Letter to the Hebrews encapsulates the full revelation of God's creative plan of salvation as originally presented in the Creation story and now fulfilled in Jesus Christ: *"In times past, God spoke in partial and various ways to our ancestors through the prophets; in these last days, he spoke to us through a son, whom he made heir of all things and through whom he created the universe, who is the refulgence of his glory, the very imprint of his being, and who sustains all things by his mighty word. When he had accomplished purification from sins, he took his seat at the right hand of the Majesty on high, as far superior to the angels as the name he inherited is more excellent than theirs."* (Hebrews 1:1-4) Through Jesus Christ we have come to know that God the Father is Creator of the Universe who brought about His creation with and through His Son. Jesus is the radiance or fullest brightness of His Father's glory, and shares the same divine essence as the Father. And because Jesus is God, He has accomplished our purification from sin, and is seated at the right hand of His Father. In the Prologue of his gospel, John reiterates the same point, thereby establishing the divinity of Jesus who shares the same divine essence as God, whom Jesus later reveals to us as His Father: *"In the beginning was the Word, and the Word was with God, and the Word was God. He was in the beginning with God. All things came to be through him, and without him nothing came to be."* (John 1:1-3)

The creation of the Universe is essentially a Trinitarian act, and the Holy Spirit is intimately involved as well. Genesis 1:2 tells us, *"In the beginning, when God created the heavens and the earth – and the earth was without form or shape, with darkness over the abyss and a mighty wind sweeping over the waters."* A *mighty wind* could literally be translated as *"spirit or breath [ruah] of God."* Many translations use the expression the "Spirit of God" hovering over the waters. Through the Holy Spirit, the Father, with the Son, brings about the creation of the Universe, with humans at the epicenter. In the Nicene Creed we pray, 'I believe in the Holy Spirit, the Lord, *the Giver of life,* who proceeds from the Father and the Son, who with the Father and the Son is adored and glorified, who has spoken through the prophets." Indeed, the Holy Spirit is the Giver of life.

Genesis 2:7 tells us that *"the LORD God formed the man out of the dust of the ground and blew into his nostrils the breath of life, and the man became a living being."* And in John 20:21-22, Jesus said, *"As the Father has sent me, so I send you."* Then He breathed on them and said: *"Receive the Holy Spirit."* St. Cyril of Alexandria, circa A.D. 435, commented on these two passages in the following way: "Seeing that he (Adam) ought to be not merely rational with an aptitude for doing good and right but also a participator in the Holy Spirit, he (God) breathed into him, so that he might have brighter marks of the divine nature within him, the breath of life. … Christ's act was a renewal of that primal gift and of the inbreathing bestowed on us, bringing us back to the form of the initial holiness and carrying man's nature up, as a kind of first fruits among the holy apostles, into the holiness bestowed on us initially at the first creation." God, indeed, offers His divine Life in and through His Holy Spirit!

JESUS, THE WAY TO GOD'S TRINITARIAN LIFE:

In Genesis 3:15 God says to the serpent and Adam and Eve: *"I will put enmity between you and the woman, and between your offspring and hers; they will strike at your head, while you strike at their heel."* From the New Testament we know that Eve's offspring is Jesus, born of Mary, who will fulfill the prophecy made in the Old Testament to their ancestor, Eve. This prophecy is reiterated by Jacob, now known as Israel, when he blesses his sons before his death and offers them his final testimony. He singles out Judah over his brothers, even though he is not the first-born: *"You, Judah, shall your brothers praise – your hand on the neck of your enemies; the sons of your father shall bow down to you… The scepter shall never depart from Judah, or the mace from between his feet, until tribute comes to him, and he receives the people's obedience.'"* (Genesis 49:8, 10) King David is a descendant of the tribe of Judah, and the promise made to Judah is now bequeathed to him. David's prophet, Nathan, communicates to him the word of the Lord: *"Moreover, the LORD also declares to you that the LORD will make a house for you: when your days have been completed and you rest with your ancestors, I will raise up your offspring after you, sprung from your loins, and I will establish his kingdom… Your house and your kingdom are firm forever before me; your throne shall be firmly established forever."* (2 Samuel 7:12, 16)

In the final age, the angel Gabriel will announce to Mary that this promise made by God to Adam and Eve, and reiterated throughout the history of God's people through Jacob, Judah, and David, is now being fulfilled in Jesus. As announced by the angel Gabriel to Mary, *"He (Jesus) will be great and will be called Son of the Most High, and the Lord God will give him the throne of David his father, and he will rule over the house of Jacob forever, and of his kingdom there will be no end."* (Luke 1:32-33) Jesus will fulfill the will and desire of His Father to crush the head of Satan and bring us back to His Father's embrace. Jesus will rule over the house of Jacob forever, and of His kingdom there will be no end. With Jesus the kingdom of God is now at hand. Jesus is the Son of God who has now become the son of man, so that God's divine life might be our inheritance, and we might be inhabitants of His kingdom which will have no end.

And the Holy Spirit, along with the Father, will be intimately involved in the salvific mission of Jesus as son of man and Son of God: *"The holy Spirit will come upon you, and the power of the Most High will overshadow you. Therefore the child to be born will be called holy, the Son of God."* (Luke 1:35) Luke uses the same word *episkiasei* as is used to describe the power of the Most High overshadowing the tent of meeting which held the Ark of the Covenant in the desert: *"Then the cloud covered the tent of meeting, and the glory of the LORD filled the tabernacle."* (Exodus 40:34) The same word is used as well when Solomon dedicated the Temple and God made His abode in it: *"When the priests left the holy place, the cloud filled the house of the LORD so that the priests could no longer minister because of the cloud, since the glory of the LORD had filled the house of the LORD."* (1 Kings 8:10-11) At the conception of Jesus in Mary's womb, the Father and Holy Spirit are intimately involved in the Trinity's most solemn decision to bring us back into Trinitarian covenant, through Jesus. The power of the Most High descends upon Mary who is now seen as the Ark of the Covenant.

In John's Gospel, Jesus reiterates the fulfillment of God's promise to restore us to His original plan to bring us into covenant life with Him. In His conversation with Nicodemus, Jesus said, *"Yes, God so loved the world that He gave his only Son, that whoever believes in him may not die but may have eternal life. God did not send the Son into the world to condemn the world, but that the world might be saved through him."* (John 3:16-17) The God whom Jesus revealed is a God who is full of love and compassion. As the Presence of His Father, Jesus amply demonstrated the Father's love and compassion through His life and ministry. As the Presence of the Father, on several occasions Jesus claimed oneness with His Father, and described Himself as 'I AM!' The last verses of John 3 capture well the purpose of Jesus' life on earth: *"For the one whom God sent speaks the words of God. He does not ration his gift of the Spirit. The Father loves the Son and has given everything over to him. Whoever believes in the Son has eternal life, but whoever disobeys the Son will not see life, but the wrath of God remains upon him."* (John 3:34-36)

IN PRAYER, JESUS LEADS US INTO THE FATHER'S TRINITARIAN HEART:

Jesus was asked by His disciples to teach them how to pray, as they had heard that John the Baptist had taught his disciples to pray. In teaching His disciples to pray Jesus revealed the whole purpose of His life and mission through the prayer He taught them. In asking His disciples to address God as Abba, Father, Jesus was offering as unmerited gift, the filial and tender relationship that He has as Son, with His Father. He held nothing back from us. In addressing God as Abba through Jesus, we enter into and participate in the love and total offering of self to each other between Father and Son. Understandably then, Jesus described Himself as the Way, the Truth, and the Life. He came so that we might have life, God's Life! We cannot come to the Father except through the Son who is the Way, the Truth, and the Life. The Father views us as His sons and daughters, and is exceedingly pleased with us in His Son. Through the Lord's Prayer that Jesus taught us, we will be able to explore in depth our relationship to our Trinitarian God and the Father's relationship to us, His sons and daughters. Let us look at the various components of the prayer:

OUR FATHER, WHO ART IN HEAVEN:

God's Trinitarian abode is inaccessible to us without Jesus. Through Jesus we are able to enter into God's abode where Father, Son, and Holy Spirit dwell. This access or gateway into the heart of God is granted by Jesus, making it possible for us through His death and resurrection to participate in the intimate divine relationship that exists between Father and Son in the Holy Spirit. This is the reason why the Father sent His Son into the world so that He could bring us back to Him and claim us as His sons and daughters, washed clean in His Son's blood, and now become His human covenant family, along the lines of His Trinitarian divine family. So it was appropriate for Jesus, in His High Priestly Prayer, to reveal to us the profound depths of our relationship to God as Abba, Father: *"And I have given them the glory you gave me, so that they may be one, as we are one, I in them and you in me, and that you loved them even as you loved me. Father, they are your gift to me. I wish that where I am they also may be with me, that they may see my glory that you gave me, because you loved me before the foundation of the world."* (John 17:22-24) Jesus is the Father's glory, His visible manifestation, and the Father has been revealed to us through Jesus. By God becoming our Father through Jesus, we have entered into the Holy Oneness that is uniquely the Trinity's: Jesus in us and the Father in Jesus. In knowing Jesus, we have come to realize that the Father loves us in the same way He loves Jesus. It is the Father who has gifted us to Jesus, and Jesus, as the Lamb that was slain, has guarded us jealously as a good shepherd would guard his flock, and returned us to the Father as the sweet smelling fruits of His bountiful harvest. And finally, Jesus prays that we might share His dwelling place or heaven that He has with the Father and the Holy Spirit. Whenever we pray the Lord's Prayer we enter into the profound depths of God's Father-Son relationship through the Holy Spirit, thereby sharing in all the blessings and graces of this Godly relationship.

HALLOWED BE THY NAME:

The name is the person. We pray that God's Person may be hallowed, that we may have the reverence and obedience that is due to the holiness of God in our relationship with Him. We acknowledge that God's divine being is totally other than ours. God is all light; there is no darkness in God. God is all Truth; there is no falsehood in God. God is all Beauty; there is no imperfection in God. God does not need to hallow His own name as He is without sin, and holiness is of God's essence. Because there is sin in us, we pray that in our relationship with God we might be free of sin, and thus participate in God's own holiness, as His true image and likeness. The Father's love for us is so intense and total, that His one desire is that we share in covenant union His own holiness which He has with His Son and the Holy Spirit. So when we pray that God's name be hallowed, we are asking to share in God's own holiness, through a life free of sin!

THY KINGDOM COME:

Through Jesus, God's reign has been firmly established in our midst through a new and everlasting covenant. Jesus is our Lord and King. At the request of His Father, Jesus became our suffering Messiah so that we might become children of God, members of God's covenant family, and disciples who have surrendered their lives to His authority and kingship. In our prayer we are asking that in God's covenant family we might fully subscribe to the Father's reign over our hearts, minds, and spirits, and that His reign be accepted by His children all over the world.

THY WILL BE DONE ON EARTH AS IT IS IN HEAVEN:

In the divine relationships there is no sin, or the slightest deviation from Truth, Goodness, and Beauty. The angels, saints, martyrs, and witnesses who have won the crown of victory over Satan, sin, and death, through the death and resurrection of the Lamb that was slain, are in perfect agreement with the Father's will. They now experience God's will in the love and total trust of the Trinitarian relationships in which they are participating. They join with the Lamb that was slain to intercede for us to express God's love and total oneness of will in our actions. Everyone is of one mind, heart, and spirit in heaven, as they all share in the holiness and life of the Trinity.

Here on earth the Father desires the same perfection in us as it exists in heaven. We are indeed God's covenant family in which the self-offering to the other is total and unreservedly selfless. Jesus therefore tells us to *"be perfect, just as your heavenly Father is perfect,"* (Matthew 5:48) and *"merciful, just as [also] your Father is merciful."* (Luke 6:36) The Father's desire, expressed to us through Jesus, is that we have the same high standards of being and doing as are the standards of God. We pray for such a transformation of our wills, so that they are in agreement with the Father's will. The strength of our prayer lies in our belief that the Holy Spirit will bring about such a transformation.

GIVE US THIS DAY OUR DAILY BREAD:

Bread was an essential commodity in the Palestine of Jesus' time, and was considered to be the staff of life. In this petition we are acknowledging our total dependence on God to provide for all our needs. Such dependence is the fruit of covenant union, and suggests that there is a deeper meaning to asking God for our daily bread. Daily bread is translated as *epi ousios* in the Greek, *substance from above*. The bread we are asking from the Father is compared and contrasted with the Manna that was 'substance from above' in the desert. Jesus says, *"Amen, amen, I say to you, it was not Moses who gave the bread from heaven; my Father gives you the true bread from heaven. For the bread of God is that which comes down from heaven and gives life to the world."* (John 6:32-33) We are asking the Father to give us Jesus who is the bread of life. Whoever comes to Him will never hunger, and whoever believes in Him will never thirst. It is necessary for us to receive Jesus from the Father, because *"unless you eat the flesh of the Son of Man and drink his blood, you do not have life within you."* (John 6:53)

FORGIVE US OUR TRESPASSES AS WE FORGIVE THOSE WHO TRESPASS AGAINST US:

It becomes clear as we pray the Lord's Prayer that the purpose is to enter into covenant union with the Trinity. In covenant there is a total offering of self to the other, and the focus in one's life is to be in accordance with the mind and heart of the other. God's Loving Kindness and mercy is what distinguishes God in relationship to us. We are children of God because we have been made adopted sons and daughters of the Living God through the sacrifice of Jesus on the Cross. As God desires nothing less for us than covenant union with Him, in this petition we ask to be as forgiving of those who trespass against us, as God is toward us. We are called to display covenant traits toward all, treating them as members of God's covenant family. Once again it is a very tall order that can only be fulfilled by the power and help of the Holy Spirit.

LEAD US NOT INTO TEMPTATION:

We pray that we might never become smug or complacent, and assume that we have the power within ourselves to resist temptation. Basically we are asking the Father to give us the humility to always depend upon Him, and never create a situation where we would perish because we did not rely on His mercy and love. We beg the Father to keep us humble and truly dependent upon Him, so that we might not be led into temptation.

BUT DELIVER US FROM THE EVIL ONE:

Deliver us from all evil or from Satan, the Evil One. In the battle with Satan we will not be capable of resisting his seductions and wiles if we rely on our own strength. We would be in danger of losing our souls. In covenant union with Christ, we are able to overcome all sin and evil. In this last petition we beseech the Father to preserve us from the snares of the Devil.

OUR PRAYER TO OUR FATHER:

Father, I am in your presence, awed by your tender compassion and love for me. In adoration, I acknowledge my total dependence upon you for my life, and all that I have and possess. In praise, I acknowledge you as the Giver of all good gifts to me and the whole world. In thanksgiving, I express my gratitude for your generosity and largesse. You are my God and my All, even when I choose to be willful and rebellious.

I am speechless at your generous decision to create me in your image and likeness, thereby giving me a limitless capacity to participate in your divine nature, and enter into covenant union with you. And when we were alienated because of our evil deeds, you reconciled us to yourself through your Son, Jesus, who is our Way back to you. Oh Father, you so loved us that You were willing to crush your Son Jesus, by making His life as a reparation offering on our behalf.

Now Father, you gaze upon me with the same tender love and intimacy that you have for your Son, Jesus. He has given us the privilege to share in His Son-ship, so that we can now address you as Abba, Father. You are immensely pleased with your Son's offering of us to you, to be your sons and daughters, to receive the gift of your total Self to us, and to make it possible for us to offer ourselves to you in total surrender and obedience, thus conforming ourselves to your own Son's image and likeness. Thank you for your wondrous plan of salvation and transformation.

Your Son, Jesus, has become my food and drink. I now have life in Him, your Life that He shares with you, Father, and the Holy Spirit. He abides in me, and I in Him. And you, Father, who dwell in Him, now make your abode in me. And with you and your Son, your Holy Spirit too dwells in my heart, revealing to me the depths of your Being. I praise you, glorify you, and adore you, Father, my God and my All. I offer myself to you, through your Son, Jesus Christ, the Lamb that was slain, thus becoming a pleasing offering in your sight. Living in your Embrace is your desire for me. I desire that you strengthen my resolve to live in total obedience to your Holy Will. I make this prayer through Christ our Lord. Amen. Triune God, be my all! Triune God, be my all! Triune God, be my all!

PRAYER AND REFLECTION ON KNOWING OUR FATHER IN THE TRINITY

WEEK THIRTEEN: *"FOR GOD SO LOVED THE WORLD THAT HE GAVE HIS ONLY SON, SO THAT EVERYONE WHO BELIEVES IN HIM MIGHT NOT PERISH BUT MIGHT HAVE ETERNAL LIFE. FOR GOD DID NOT SEND HIS SON INTO THE WORLD TO CONDEMN THE WORLD, BUT THAT THE WORLD MIGHT BE SAVED THROUGH HIM." (JOHN 3:16-18)*

SPIRITUAL READING FOR THE WEEK:

- **Anoint Us in Your Covenant, Abba-Emmanuel:** Session Seven
- **Old Testament:** Two or Three Chapters daily
- **New Testament:** Two or Three Chapters daily
- **Imitation of Christ:** One chapter daily

DAY ONE: MORNING SESSION

MORNING PRAYER: Acts of Faith, Hope, Charity; Daily Offering

Morning Face to Face with God:

Begin with Prayer to the Holy Spirit

IN PRAYER, JESUS LEADS US INTO THE FATHER'S TRINITARIAN HEART:

(After pondering each bullet point, express your sentiments in a short prayer)

- Prayer is that place where we come face to face with God and ourselves. In prayer we recognize ourselves in God, and our understanding and relationship with God goes beyond the mundane and superficial layers of our lives.

- In God's presence and love, all falsehood melts away, and we become transparent and desirous of offering ourselves to God in covenant. Prayer is also the place where God reveals His Trinitarian relationships to us and we come to understand that we belong to God's inner circle.

- In teaching His disciples to pray Jesus revealed the whole purpose of His life and mission through the prayer He taught them. In asking His disciples to address God as Abba, Father, Jesus was offering as unmerited gift, the filial and tender relationship that He has as Son, with His Father. He held nothing back from us.

- In addressing God as Abba through Jesus, we enter into and participate in the love and total offering of self to each other between Father and Son. Understandably then, Jesus described Himself as the Way, the Truth, and the Life. He came so that we might have life, God's Life!

- We cannot come to the Father except through the Son who is the Way, the Truth, and the Life. The Father views us as His sons and daughters, and is exceedingly pleased with us in His Son.

- Through the Lord's Prayer that Jesus taught us, we will be able to explore in depth our relationship to our Trinitarian God and the Father's relationship to us, His sons and daughters.

- God's Trinitarian abode is inaccessible to us without Jesus. Through Jesus we are able to enter into God's abode where Father, Son, and Holy Spirit dwell. This access or gateway into the heart of God is granted by Jesus, making it possible for us through His death and resurrection to participate in the intimate divine relationship that exists between Father and Son in the Holy Spirit.

- This is the reason why the Father sent His Son into the world so that He could bring us back to Him and claim us as His sons and daughters, washed clean in His Son's blood, and now become His human covenant family, along the lines of His Trinitarian divine family.

- By God becoming our Father through Jesus, we have entered into the Holy Oneness that is uniquely the Trinity's: Jesus in us and the Father in Jesus. In knowing Jesus, we come to realize that the Father loves us in the same way He loves Jesus.

- It is the Father who has gifted us to Jesus, and Jesus, as the Lamb that was slain, has guarded us jealously as a good shepherd would guard his flock, and returned us to the Father as the sweet smelling fruits of His bountiful harvest.

- Whenever we pray the Lord's Prayer we enter into the profound depths of God's Father-Son relationship through the Holy Spirit, thereby sharing in all the blessings and graces of this Godly Relationship.

What is God saying to you?

End with Prayer to the Holy Trinity

NIGHT SESSION: Examination of Conscience

For what are you grateful? For what are you contrite?

Please review briefly your Morning Prayer topic. Make it your last thought of the day

DAY TWO: MORNING SESSION

MORNING PRAYER: Act of Faith; Act of Hope; Act of Charity; Daily Offering

Morning Face to Face with God:

Begin with Prayer to the Holy Spirit

Prayer on Matthew 6:9-13: The Lord's Prayer:
"Our Father in heaven, hallowed be your name, your kingdom come, your will be done, on earth as in heaven. Give us today our daily bread; and forgive us our debts, as we forgive our debtors; and do not subject us to the final test, but deliver us from the evil one."

Read the Reflection; Thank God, Our Father, for the gift of covenant union with Him through Jesus in the Holy Spirit, and ask that you be a pleasing offering in His sight.

The Ten Commandments could be viewed as the Betrothal statement of the Mosaic Covenant. The spirit of the Ten Commandments was God's by nature. God wanted His people to incarnate that same spirit in their relationship with Him and one another through the observance of the Decalogue. In Jesus' New and Eternal covenant, the *Our Father* captures the essence of the covenant union between God and His covenant family. Through His death and resurrection, Jesus has offered us all the joys and privileges of His filial relationship with His Father. God is now our Father as well. We have become God's righteousness (2 Corinthians 5:21), we share in the divine nature (2 Peter 1:4) of the Blessed Trinity. It behooves us, therefore, to act like Jesus does, in total obedience to His Father. So we hallow God's name in the way Jesus did (John 17:11-12); we work tirelessly for the establishment of God's reign in our hearts and in the world, in union with and continuation of Jesus' redemption of the world. Jesus did His Father's will on earth as He always did in heaven, as the Perfect Son of the Perfect Father. Being made one with Jesus, it makes sense that we behave as He does towards His Father. In the second half of the Lord's Prayer, Jesus is reminding us that we are lost outside of Him. And so we ask for the unmerited gift of always being in union with Him through receiving our daily bread (the name given to the heavenly manna in the desert) which is His Body and Blood; we ask for the forgiveness of our sins in the same measure in which we forgive the sins of others; and we ask as well that we might always be faithful to our covenant bond with the Blessed Trinity, especially in the hour of death. Finally we ask to share in the victory of Jesus over Satan, the prince of darkness, and Evil incarnate. And we do all this through Jesus Christ. *(Pray the Lord's Prayer slowly and attentively several times).*

What is God saying to you?

End with Prayer to the Holy Trinity

NIGHT SESSION: Examination of Conscience

For what are you grateful? For what are you contrite?

Please review briefly your Morning Prayer topic. Make it your last thought of the day

DAY THREE: MORNING SESSION

MORNING PRAYER: Act of Faith; Act of Hope; Act of Charity; Daily Offering

Morning Face to Face with God:

Begin with Prayer to the Holy Spirit
Prayer on John 3:16-18: The Father's Love for us
> *"For God so loved the world that he gave his only Son, so that everyone who believes in him might not perish but might have eternal life. For God did not send his Son into the world to condemn the world, but that the world might be saved through him."*

Read the Reflection; Thank God, Our Father, for the gift of covenant union with Him through Jesus in the Holy Spirit, and ask that you be a pleasing offering in His sight.

In utterly astounding fashion, the Father demonstrates His total love for us by giving us His very own Son. Can there be any greater self-emptying and selfless giving than this act of God surrendering to us His Son Jesus as an infinite gift? And the reason why the Father so benevolently and magnanimously gave us His Son was so that we might not perish or be separated permanently from Him, but rather participate in God's very own eternal life. God's passionate desire was to redeem us by His Son becoming our slave (Philippians 2:5-11), taking upon Himself our burden of sin, and thus saving us from condemnation, and granting us the freedom of the children of God. The God whom Jesus revealed is a God who is full of love and compassion as Jesus amply demonstrated through His life. When the disciple has gotten in touch with the God of Jesus Christ, he/she is filled with love and an intense desire to reciprocate. Such a desire generally results in the disciple making a serious commitment to live a life of dedicated service to God and God's reign in the world. As intimacy with God deepens, so does reverence for God's holiness and goodness. And such love manifests itself in faithful service to God's people.

What is God saying to you?

End with Prayer to the Holy Trinity

NIGHT SESSION: Examination of Conscience

For what are you grateful? For what are you contrite?

Please review briefly your Morning Prayer topic. Make it your last thought of the day

DAY FOUR: MORNING SESSION

MORNING PRAYER: Act of Faith; Act of Hope; Act of Charity; Daily Offering

Morning Face to Face with God:

Begin with Prayer to the Holy Spirit
Prayer on Matthew 6:32-34: Dependence on God
> *"Your heavenly Father knows that you need them all. But seek first the kingdom (of God) and his righteousness, and all these things will be given you besides. Do not worry about tomorrow; tomorrow will take care of itself. Sufficient for a day is its own evil."*

Read the Reflection; Thank God, Our Father, for the gift of covenant union with Him through Jesus in the Holy Spirit, and ask that you be a pleasing offering in His sight.

In this passage taken from the Sermon on the Mount, Jesus is giving us keen understanding of our covenant relationship with our heavenly Father. Jesus is asking us to relate to His heavenly Father in the same way He does. The heavenly Father was engaged with His Son in every aspect of our salvation: *"The one (Father) who sent me is with me. He has not left me alone, because I always do what is pleasing to him."* (John 8:29). Hence Jesus trusted His Father completely and was totally obedient to Him. He asks us to do the same: to trust the Father completely that He will take care of our earthly affairs. Our priority needs always to be the priority of Jesus: working for the establishment of God's reign and righteousness. Everything else is secondary, of no importance if it does not serve the divine will. And Jesus assures us that if we live as if there were no tomorrow, wholeheartedly for today, our lives will be filled with the peace and joy of the Risen Lord!

What is God saying to you?

End with Prayer to the Holy Trinity

NIGHT SESSION: Examination of Conscience

For what are you grateful? For what are you contrite?

Please review briefly your Morning Prayer topic. Make it your last thought of the day

DAY FIVE: MORNING SESSION

MORNING PRAYER: Act of Faith; Act of Hope; Act of Charity; Daily Offering

Morning Face to Face with God:

Begin with Prayer to the Holy Spirit
Prayer on Matthew 11:25-27: The Praise of the Father:
> *"At that time Jesus said in reply, "I give praise to you, Father, Lord of heaven and earth, for although you have hidden these things from the wise and the learned you have revealed them to the childlike. Yes, Father, such has been your gracious will. All things have been handed over to me by my Father. No one knows the Son except the Father, and no one knows the Father except the Son and anyone to whom the Son wishes to reveal him."*

Read the Reflection; Thank God, Our Father, for the gift of covenant union with Him through Jesus in the Holy Spirit, and ask that you be a pleasing offering in His sight.

In several gospel passages, we are told how intimately involved the Father is in His Son's mission to bring eternal life to all who believed in Him. In fact it would be true to say that our salvation through Jesus is a Trinitarian act. This passage is one such that tells us clearly that all Three Divine Persons are involved. While eternal life is offered to all, only they will gain entrance into the kingdom of God who acknowledge their sins and ask for salvation in Jesus. They have a true spirit of repentance and humility. The wise and learned depend much too much on human wisdom earned by their learning and study. The childlike, on the other hand, have learned to trust God and depend completely on Him in true covenant fashion. An essential part of the Father's revelation to the childlike and trusting is the divine Father-Son relationship. The Father desires that we participate in this Father-Son relationship. Jesus is the one who will reveal to us His relationship with the Father, offering us gratis, all the blessings and privileges that He shares with His Father!

What is God saying to you?

End with Prayer to the Holy Trinity

NIGHT SESSION: Examination of Conscience

For what are you grateful? For what are you contrite?

Please review briefly your Morning Prayer topic. Make it your last thought of the day

DAY SIX: MORNING SESSION

MORNING PRAYER: Act of Faith; Act of Hope; Act of Charity; Daily Offering

Morning Face to Face with God:

Begin with Prayer to the Holy Spirit

OUR PRAYER TO THE FATHER:

> *Thank God, Our Father, for the gift of covenant union with Him through Jesus in the Holy Spirit, and ask that you be a pleasing offering in His sight.*

Today, you will pray with "Our Prayer to the Father" from the Session. You can go over this prayer once or twice, tasting and relishing the Father's great love for you as expressed in the gift of His Son, Jesus, as your Savior and Lord, and His Holy Spirit as your Advocate and Consoler. "Our Prayer to the Father" can act as a repetition of Days Two through Five of this week. In a repetition St. Ignatius says that *"we should pay attention to and dwell upon those points in which we have experienced greater consolation or desolation or greater spiritual appreciation."* (# 62)

What is God saying to you?

End with Prayer to the Holy Trinity

NIGHT SESSION: Examination of Conscience

For what are you grateful? For what are you contrite?

Please review briefly your Morning Prayer topic. Make it your last thought of the day

DAY SEVEN: MORNING SESSION

MORNING PRAYER: Act of Faith; Act of Hope; Act of Charity; Daily Offering

Morning Face to Face with God:

Begin with Prayer to the Holy Spirit

THE FIFTH DWELLING PLACES:

- St. Teresa thinks that many are invited into the varying degrees of union with God, described in the Fifth Dwelling Places. There are very few who never enter this mansion, presuming that they are in the Fourth Mansions. Some enter more, others less. However, only a few will experience some of the things that she talks about in the Fifth Dwelling Places.
- While this grace of union in prayer is wholly the work of the Holy Spirit, we can do our part to dispose ourselves to receive this grace. In order to purchase this pearl of great price, we need to ask for the grace to keep nothing back from God, little or great.
- Our reward in the spiritual life will be great or small in proportion to what we know we have given. When we have truly given God our all, and the Holy Spirit will let us know this, there is no more certain sign, whether or not we have reached the Prayer of Union.
- The best way to describe the contemplative process of greater and deeper union with God is in the Saint's own words: *"There is no need here to use any technique to suspend the mind since all the faculties are asleep in this state – and truly asleep – to the things of the world and to ourselves. As a matter of fact, during the time that the union lasts the soul is left as though without its senses, for it has no power to think even if it wants to… In sum, it is like one who in every respect has died to the world so as to live more completely in God. Thus the death is a delightful one, an uprooting from the soul of all the operations it can have while being in the body."* (TIC – V:1:4)

CONTRAST BETWEEN THE PRAYER OF QUIET AND PRAYER OF UNION:

- In the Prayer of Union, *"the intellect would want to be occupied in understanding something of what is felt. And since the soul does not have the energy to attain to this, it is so stunned that, even if consciousness is not completely lost, neither a hand nor a foot stirs, as we say here below when a person is in such a swoon that we think he is dead.*" (TIC – V:1:4)

- By contrast, in the Prayer of Quiet, "*the soul remains doubtful that it was union. It doubts whether it imagined the experience; whether it was asleep; whether the experience was given by God; or whether the devil transformed himself into an angel of light. It is left with a thousand suspicions. That it has them is good for, as I have said, even our own nature can sometimes deceive us in that dwelling place.*" (TIC – V:1:5)

- Although there is little chance of poisonous reptiles (temptation to grave sin) entering a soul in the Fourth Dwelling Places, some tiny lizards (imperfections and attachments) will enter, though they can do no harm, especially if they remain unnoticed. These are trivial fancies of the imagination, which are often very troublesome.

- In the Fifth Dwelling Places, "*these little lizards cannot enter this fifth dwelling place; there is neither imagination, nor memory, nor intellect that can impede this good. And I would dare say that if the prayer is truly that of union with God the devil cannot even enter or do any damage… Thus the soul is left with such wonderful blessings because God works within it without anyone disturbing Him, not even ourselves.*" (TIC – V:1:5)

- In the Prayer of Quiet, one seems only to touch the surface of the body, while in the Prayer of Union the other penetrates to the very marrow.

SIGN AND PROOF OF THE PRAYER OF UNION:

- St. Teresa offers us an unmistakable proof of the Prayer of Union: "*During the time of this union it neither sees, nor hears, nor understands, because the union is always short and seems to the soul even much shorter than it probably is. God so places Himself in the interior of that soul that when it returns to itself it can in no way doubt that it was in God and God was in it. This truth remains with it so firmly that even though years go by without God's granting that favor again, the soul can neither forget nor doubt that it was in God and God was in it. This certitude is what matters now.*" (TIC – V:1:11)

- St. Teresa is very emphatic about having this certitude: "*Whoever does not receive this certitude does not experience union of the whole soul with God, but union of some faculty, or that he experiences one of the many other kinds of favors God grants souls… Since we have no part at all to play in bringing it about no matter how much effort we put forth, but it is God who does so, let us not desire the capacity to understand this union.*" (TIC – V:1:11)

- She emphasizes the fact that this work of union is purely God's doing: "*And that He may show His marvels more clearly He doesn't want our will to have any part to play, for it has been entirely surrendered to Him. Neither does He want the door of the faculties and of the senses to be opened, for they are all asleep. But He wants to enter the center of the soul without going through any door, as He entered the place where His disciples were when He said, pax vobis; or as He left the tomb without lifting away the stone.*" (TIC – V:1:12)

What is God saying to you?

End with Prayer to the Holy Trinity

NIGHT SESSION: Examination of Conscience

For what are you grateful? For what are you contrite?

What prayer would you compose to express what God has said to you this week?

Please review briefly your Morning Prayer topic. Make it your last thought of the day

PRAYER AND REFLECTION ON KNOWING THE FATHER IN THE TRINITY – CONTINUED

WEEK FOURTEEN: *"AMEN, AMEN, I SAY TO YOU, IT WAS NOT MOSES WHO GAVE THE BREAD FROM HEAVEN; MY FATHER GIVES YOU THE TRUE BREAD FROM HEAVEN. FOR THE BREAD OF GOD IS THAT WHICH COMES DOWN FROM HEAVEN AND GIVES LIFE TO THE WORLD." (JOHN 6:32-33)*

SPIRITUAL READING FOR THE WEEK:

- **Anoint Us in Your Covenant, Abba-Emmanuel:** Session Seven
- **Old Testament:** Two or Three Chapters daily
- **New Testament:** Two or Three Chapters daily
- **Imitation of Christ:** One chapter daily

DAY ONE: MORNING SESSION

MORNING PRAYER: Acts of Faith, Hope, Charity; Daily Offering

Morning Face to Face with God:

Begin with Prayer to the Holy Spirit

KNOWING OUR FATHER IN THE TRINITY:

(After pondering each bullet point, express your sentiments in a short prayer)

- In the *Our Father*, We pray that we may have the reverence and obedience that is due to the holiness of God in our relationship with Him. We acknowledge that God's divine being is totally other than ours.
- God is all light; there is no darkness in God. God is all Truth; there is no falsehood in God. God is all Beauty; there is no imperfection in God. God does not need to hallow His own name as He is without sin, and holiness is of God's essence. Because there is sin in us, we pray that in our relationship with God we might be free of sin, and thus participate in God's own holiness, as His true image and likeness.
- The Father's love for us is so intense and total, that His one desire is that we share in His own holiness which He has with His Son and the Holy Spirit in covenant union. So when we pray that God's name be hallowed, we are asking to share in God's own holiness, through a life free of sin!
- Through Jesus, God's reign has been firmly established in our midst through a new and everlasting covenant. Jesus is our Lord and King. At the request of His Father, Jesus

became our suffering Messiah so that we might become children of God, members of God's covenant family, and disciples who have surrendered their lives to His authority and kingship.

- In our petition, *Thy kingdom come*, we are asking that in God's covenant family we might fully subscribe to the Father's reign over our hearts, minds, and spirits, and that His reign be accepted by His children all over the world.

- In the divine relationships there is no sin, or the slightest deviation from Truth, Goodness, and Beauty. The angels, saints, martyrs, and witnesses who have won the crown of victory over Satan, sin, and death, through the death and resurrection of the Lamb that was slain, are in perfect agreement with the Father's will.

- They now experience God's will in the love and total trust of the Trinitarian relationships in which they are participating, and join with the Lamb that was slain to intercede for us to express God's love and total oneness of will in our actions. Everyone is of one mind, heart, and spirit in heaven, as they all share in the holiness and life of the Trinity.

- Here on earth the Father desires the same perfection in us as it exists in heaven. We are indeed God's covenant family in which the self-offering to the other is total and unreservedly selfless. Jesus therefore tells us to *"be perfect, just as your heavenly Father is perfect,"* (Matthew 5:48) and *"merciful, just as [also] your Father is merciful."* (Luke 6:36)

- The Father's desire, expressed to us through Jesus, is that we have the same high standards of being and doing as are the standards of God. We pray for such a transformation of our wills, so that they are in agreement with the Father's will. The strength of our prayer lies in our belief that the Holy Spirit will bring about such a transformation.

- Our daily bread is translated as *epi ousios* in the Greek, substance from above. The bread we are asking from the Father is compared and contrasted with the Manna that was 'substance from above' in the desert (John 6:32-33). We are asking the Father to give us Jesus who is the bread of life. It is necessary for us to receive Jesus from the Father, because *"unless you eat the flesh of the Son of Man and drink his blood, you do not have life within you."* (John 6:53)

- It becomes clear as we pray the Lord's Prayer that the purpose is to enter into covenant union with the Trinity. God's Loving Kindness and mercy is what distinguishes God in relationship to us. We are children of God because we have been made adopted sons and daughters of the Living God through the sacrifice of Jesus on the Cross.

- As God desires nothing less for us than covenant union with Him, in this petition we ask to be as forgiving of those who trespass against us, as God is toward us. We are called to display covenant traits toward all, treating them as members of God's covenant family. Once again it is a very tall order that can only be fulfilled by the power and help of the Holy Spirit.

- We pray that we might never become smug or complacent, and assume that we have the power within ourselves to resist temptation. Basically we are asking the Father to give us the humility to always depend upon Him as Our Father, and never create a situation where we would perish because we did not rely on His mercy and love.

- Deliver us from all evil or from Satan, the Evil One. In the battle with Satan we will not be capable of resisting his seductions and wiles if we rely on our own strength. We would be in danger of losing our souls. In covenant union with Christ, we are able to overcome all sin and evil. In this last petition we beseech the Father to preserve us from the snares of the Devil.

What is God saying to you?

End with Prayer to the Holy Trinity

NIGHT SESSION: Examination of Conscience

For what are you grateful? For what are you contrite?

Please review briefly your Morning Prayer topic. Make it your last thought of the day

DAY TWO: MORNING SESSION

MORNING PRAYER: Act of Faith; Act of Hope; Act of Charity; Daily Offering

Morning Face to Face with God:

Begin with Prayer to the Holy Spirit

Prayer on John 5:20-23: The Work of the Son:
> *"Jesus answered and said to them, "… For the Father loves his Son and shows him everything that he himself does, and he will show him greater works than these, so that you may be amazed. For just as the Father raises the dead and gives life, so also does the Son give life to whomever he wishes. Nor does the Father judge anyone, but he has given all judgment to his Son, so that all may honor the Son just as they honor the Father."*

Read the Reflection; Thank God, Our Father, for the gift of covenant union with Him through Jesus in the Holy Spirit, and ask that you be a pleasing offering in His sight.

The opposition to Jesus is beginning to break out into the open. He has healed the sick and crippled man on the Sabbath and has claimed God as His own Father! On different occasions, in the midst of controversy, Jesus has spoken passionately and tenderly about His relationship with His Father. This passage is one such. Their Father-Son relationship is a covenant relationship. They share the same divine essence. They co-own and do everything together. Jesus' power to heal is a power He shares with His Father. Jesus' miracles are signs pointing to the greatest miracle that will cause amazement in us: His resurrection from the dead. Jesus shares in the same power of His Father to raise us from the dead. The judgment of this world will be done by Jesus. Jesus is making it very clear that He is divine and shares divinity with the Father and the Holy Spirit.

What is God saying to you?

End with Prayer to the Holy Trinity

NIGHT SESSION: Examination of Conscience

For what are you grateful? For what are you contrite?

Please review briefly your Morning Prayer topic. Make it your last thought of the day

DAY THREE: MORNING SESSION

MORNING PRAYER: Act of Faith; Act of Hope; Act of Charity; Daily Offering

Morning Face to Face with God:

Begin with Prayer to the Holy Spirit

Prayer on John 6:39-40: The Will of the Father:

> *"And this is the will of the one who sent me, that I should not lose anything of what he gave me, but that I should raise it [on] the last day. For this is the will of my Father, that everyone who sees the Son and believes in him may have eternal life, and I shall raise him [on] the last day."*

Read the Reflection; Thank God, Our Father, for the gift of covenant union with Him through Jesus in the Holy Spirit, and ask that you be a pleasing offering in His sight.

This passage is part of Jesus' Discourse on the Bread of Life. John 6 offers us two miracles, the multiplication of the Loaves and Jesus walking on the water. These two miracles have overtones of the crossing of the Red Sea and the feeding of Manna in the desert. Jesus is introducing a new Exodus. In the Discourse on the Bread of Life, Jesus will be talking about the new and eternal covenant that He will be establishing through His death on the cross and resurrection. We will receive the full inheritance of covenant life with God through Jesus, by eating His Body and drinking His blood. Most importantly, Jesus reveals the Father's deepest desire that we will all share in God's eternal life through His Son. One fruit of this participation in God's divine life is that we will have a share in Jesus' resurrection. As a result, our bodies too will be raised from the dead on the last day.

What is God saying to you?

End with Prayer to the Holy Trinity

NIGHT SESSION: Examination of Conscience

For what are you grateful? For what are you contrite?

Please review briefly your Morning Prayer topic. Make it your last thought of the day

DAY FOUR: MORNING SESSION

MORNING PRAYER: Act of Faith; Act of Hope; Act of Charity; Daily Offering

Morning Face to Face with God:

Begin with Prayer to the Holy Spirit

Prayer on John 8:25; 27-30: Jesus, the Father's Ambassador:
> *"So they said to him, "Who are you?" … They did not realize that he was speaking to them of the Father. So Jesus said (to them), "When you lift up the Son of Man, then you will realize that I AM, and that I do nothing on my own, but I say only what the Father taught me. The one who sent me is with me. He has not left me alone, because I always do what is pleasing to him." Because he spoke this way, many came to believe in him."*

Read the Reflection; Thank God, Our Father, for the gift of covenant union with Him through Jesus in the Holy Spirit, and ask that you be a pleasing offering in His sight.

Jesus has arrived at a critical point in His ministry. There are those who refuse to believe that He is the Son of God, no matter how many miracles He works or how authoritatively He speaks of God in fulfillment of the Law and the Prophets. There are others, however, who came to believe in Him. In these verses Jesus emphasizes the fact that He and the Father act as one because they are one. When the Son of Man (a Messianic title) is lifted up on the cross, meaning when the Son of Man is glorified through His resurrection from the dead after His death on the cross, those who accept Him will come to see that He is I AM or God! Jesus also reiterates the fact that His Father is closely involved in His work of salvation. He is always with His Son, and Jesus only does what is pleasing to His Father.

What is God saying to you?

End with Prayer to the Holy Trinity

NIGHT SESSION: Examination of Conscience

For what are you grateful? For what are you contrite?

Please review briefly your Morning Prayer topic. Make it your last thought of the day

DAY FIVE: MORNING SESSION

MORNING PRAYER: Act of Faith; Act of Hope; Act of Charity; Daily Offering

Morning Face to Face with God:

Begin with Prayer to the Holy Spirit

Prayer on John 10:17-18: Covenant Union of Father and Son:
> *"This is why the Father loves me, because I lay down my life in order to take it up again. No one takes it from me, but I lay it down on my own. I have power to lay it down, and power to take it up again. This command I have received from my Father."*

Read the Reflection; Thank God, Our Father, for the gift of covenant union with Him through Jesus in the Holy Spirit, and ask that you be a pleasing offering in His sight.

In John 10, Jesus speaks of Himself as the Good Shepherd. In the two verses that we will be praying with, Jesus expresses some very significant truths to us. He describes His covenant relationship with His Father as laying down His life on our behalf as this is the Father's will. In obeying His Father, Jesus experiences His Father's love for Him. Jesus is laying down His life on our behalf freely and under no compulsion. In obedience to His Father, Jesus lays down His life and will rise from the dead, thus making it clear that His death has brought about the conquest of Satan, sin, and permanent death.

What is God saying to you?

End with Prayer to the Holy Trinity

NIGHT SESSION: Examination of Conscience

For what are you grateful? For what are you contrite?

Please review briefly your Morning Prayer topic. Make it your last thought of the day

DAY SIX: MORNING SESSION

MORNING PRAYER: Act of Faith; Act of Hope; Act of Charity; Daily Offering

Morning Face to Face with God:

Begin with Prayer to the Holy Spirit

OUR PRAYER TO THE FATHER:

Thank God, Our Father, for the gift of covenant union with Him through Jesus in the Holy Spirit, and ask that you be a pleasing offering in His sight.

Today, you will pray with *"Our Prayer to the Father"* from the Session. You can go over this prayer once or twice, tasting and relishing the Father's great love for you as expressed in the gift of His Son, Jesus, as your Savior and Lord, and His Holy Spirit as your Advocate and Consoler. *"Our Prayer to the Father"* can act as a repetition of Days Two through Five of this week. In a repetition St. Ignatius says that *"we should pay attention to and dwell upon those points in which we have experienced greater consolation or desolation or greater spiritual appreciation."* (# 62)

What is God saying to you?

End with Prayer to the Holy Trinity

NIGHT SESSION: Examination of Conscience

For what are you grateful? For what are you contrite?

Please review briefly your Morning Prayer topic. Make it your last thought of the day

DAY SEVEN: MORNING SESSION

MORNING PRAYER: Act of Faith; Act of Hope; Act of Charity; Daily Offering

Morning Face to Face with God:

Begin with Prayer to the Holy Spirit

THE GRACES OF THE PRAYER OF UNION:

- Through the Prayer of Union, the transformation in the soul is the difference between the silkworm and the butterfly. The soul doesn't recognize itself. It receives graces and blessings that are God's pure gift to it: *"It sees within itself a desire to praise the Lord; it would want to dissolve and die a thousand deaths for Him. It soon begins to experience a desire to suffer great trials without its being able to do otherwise. There are the strongest desires for penance, for solitude, and that all might know God; and great pain comes to it when it sees that He is offended... if after God brings a soul here it makes the effort to advance, it will see great things."* (TIC – V:2:7).
- The soul does not have esteem for the works it did in the earlier dwelling places. It's attachment to honor and achievement dissipates.
- However much it might want to do for God, the soul realizes that it is all so very little in its own eyes. The reason for this is because it sees its transformation being brought about solely by God.
- The attachment to family, friends, and wealth wears thin, and while it carries out its obligations to family and friends, in some ways they become burdensome.
- Everything wearies it because it can no longer rest in creatures. Paradoxically, the soul experiences restlessness because it feels estranged from earthly things. It might even appear that they don't have peace. But St. Teresa re-assures us when she says, *"For the trials themselves are so valuable and have such good roots that although very severe they give rise to peace and happiness."* (TIC – V:2:10)
- There are some painful benefits as well that the soul receives in this state of union. The unhappiness caused by worldly things generates a great desire to leave this world. Any relief that the soul experiences, comes from the fact that it is here at God's desire.
- Also, another sorrow that the soul experiences is the fact that God is offended and little esteemed in this world and that many souls are lost. It feels this way both towards non-Christians and Christians as well. This sorrow is somewhat tempered by the fact that the soul wants to do everything in its power to praise, glorify, and serve God.
- Another sorrow is the fact that it is not yet fully surrendered to God even though it is doing its best to conform to God's will. The sorrow is based on the fact that only God can bring about deeper transformation and this grace has not yet been given to it.

- The disciple who has experienced the state of union becomes a powerful witness. *"For since the soul is left with these desires and virtues that were mentioned, it always brings profit to other souls during the time that it continues to live virtuously; and they catch fire from its fire. And even when the soul has itself lost this fire, the inclination to benefit others will remain, and the soul delights in explaining the favors God grants to whoever loves and serves Him."* (TIC– V:3:1).

- It is a sobering reality that even a soul who has experienced the grace of union with God in the Fifth Dwelling Places, can go astray. In the saint's words, *"Even in this state the soul is not so strong that it can place itself in the occasions as it will be after the betrothal is made… I have known persons who had ascended high and had reached this union, who were turned back and won over by the devil with his deep cunning and deceit. All hell must join for such a purpose because, as I have often said, in losing one soul of this kind, not only one is lost but a multitude."* (TIC – V:4:5 & 6)

- Hence, there is always great need to ask God in prayer to sustain us and to think that without His help we would soon end in the abyss.

- It is important to never get discouraged because God is not giving us the supernatural gifts described in the Prayer of Union. With the help of divine grace true union can always be attained by forcing ourselves to renounce our own will and be following the will of God in all things. If this be the case, then we have already obtained this grace from God.

- Hence we need not wish for that other delightful union described in the Fifth Dwelling Places, for its chief value lies in the resignation of our will to that of God without which it could not be reached. The happy soul which has attained it will live in this world and in the next without care of any sort.

What is God saying to you?

End with Prayer to the Holy Trinity

NIGHT SESSION: Examination of Conscience

For what are you grateful? For what are you contrite?

What prayer would you compose to express what God has said to you this week?

Please review briefly your Morning Prayer topic. Make it your last thought of the day

SESSION EIGHT
KNOWING JESUS IN THE TRINITY

"On the evening of that first day of the week, when the doors were locked, where the disciples were, for fear of the Jews, Jesus came and stood in their midst and said to them, "Peace be with you." When he had said this, he showed them his hands and his side. The disciples rejoiced when they saw the Lord. [Jesus] said to them again, "Peace be with you. As the Father has sent me, so I send you." And when he had said this, he breathed on them and said to them, "Receive the holy Spirit. Whose sins you forgive are forgiven them, and whose sins you retain are retained."

– John 20:19-23

JESUS, THE RESURRECTION AND THE LIFE:

The above quoted Scripture passage suggests a diametric contrast in the reaction the disciples had to Jesus before and after His resurrection. After Jesus' death and before His resurrection, the disciples were devastated, confused, and disillusioned. So they locked the doors of the place where they were for fear of the Jews. Jesus had both warned them and predicted His passion and death three times during His three years of ministry. However, He also kept reassuring them that He would be raised from the dead by His Father in the power of His Holy Spirit.

Jesus offered His disciples plenty of evidence that the promise of His resurrection would indeed be fulfilled. He healed the sick and the blind; He raised the dead to life as evidenced in the case of Lazarus in John 11, and the widow's son in Luke 7. He even forgave sins before working a miracle, thereby claiming to be God, as only God can forgive sins. The disciples grew in their faith and there were times when they displayed extraordinary depths of insight into Jesus, obviously given to them by the Holy Spirit. The reaction to Jesus' discourse on being the Bread of Life is especially revealing in John 6:66-69: *"As a result of this, many [of] his disciples returned to their former way of life and no longer accompanied him. Jesus then said to the Twelve, 'Do you also want to leave?' Simon Peter answered him, 'Master, to whom shall we go? You have the words of eternal life. We have come to believe and are convinced that you are the Holy One of God.'"*

There were other times, however, when the disciples revealed their feet of clay. They especially revealed their unredeemed characters during Jesus' passion and death. Judas betrayed Jesus for thirty pieces of silver. Peter denied and disowned his Master three times before the cock's crow, after he had made this grandiose boast: *"Even though I should have to die with you, I will not deny you."* (Matthew 26:35) And the other disciples all said the same. Except for John, who accompanied Jesus to His crucifixion along with Jesus' mother and some other women, including Mary Magdalene, all the other disciples scattered and fled in fear of the Jewish leadership! Their collective reaction to Jesus' death is captured in the verse: *"On the evening of that first day of the week, when the doors were locked, where the disciples were, for fear of the Jews..."* (John 20:19)

While the disciples are trapped in their anxiety and fear because of what has happened to their Master, in appearing to them, Jesus slowly begins their transformation. He shows them that it was necessary for Him to die for sinful humanity and raise them to new life in God. His resurrected appearance establishes the unassailable evidence that He could save us from our sins, and establish us as God's adopted sons and daughters! He is our Savior because He is our Lord and God! He appears in their midst and gives them His peace. Immediately the disciples experience a transformation. Their fear and anxiety dissipate and they begin rejoicing. There is a Power and Presence in their midst that has overcome Satan, sin, and death. No power on earth or in the heavens can withstand the victory of the Risen Lord. As Paul would say it later in his letter to the Colossians 2:15: *"Despoiling the principalities and the powers, he made a public spectacle of them, leading them away in triumph by it."* In some unmistakable way the disciples have finally grasped this truth in the Presence of their Risen Master and Lord! They rejoice because they are being transformed significantly by the Risen Lord's peace!

Eirene is the Greek word used to translate 'peace.' There are approximately 90 occurrences of *eirene* in the New Testament. Peace is defined by what God has done for human beings through Jesus Christ. So when Jesus appears to His disciples, they experience the transformation that He has brought about in the world through His death and resurrection. In the words of Paul in Colossians 1:19-20: *"For in him all the fullness was pleased to dwell, and through him to reconcile all things for him, making peace by the blood of his cross [through him], whether those on earth or those in heaven."* Jesus is Lord, and through Him, His disciples will be strong and steadfast in every circumstance of their lives. Through thick and thin, through trials and tribulations, they will remain steadfast in the peace and joy of the Risen Lord. They have now become hyphenated or grafted identities. They live in Christ and Christ lives in them. He is the vine, they are His branches. Outside of Him they can do nothing. In Him they can do all things. In persecution they will rejoice because they have borne hardship and insult for their Lord Jesus Christ. They are in covenant relationship with the Trinity through Jesus Christ and in the power of the Holy Spirit. They have been incorporated into God's Trinitarian Life through the Risen Lord, and this incorporation is being brought about by the Holy Spirit.

JESUS, THE WAY, THE TRUTH, AND THE LIFE:

Jesus is the Way, the Truth, and the Life because He is the Resurrection and the Life. In answer to Thomas, Jesus said, *"I am the way and the truth and the life. No one comes to the Father except through me. If you know me, then you will also know my Father. From now on you do know him and have seen him."* (John 14:6-7) In Jesus, God comes to meet us, holding nothing back, offering everything of who He is and what He has. Through Jesus, we have access to God to such an extent that we can now call Him Abba, Father. Jesus is the Truth, not just some truth, but the entire truth. He is God's definitive and perfect Word, expressing who God is, what He is like, who we are, and what we need to do to be saved through Him from our enslavement to Satan and sin. And Jesus is the Life. He gives us not only commandments and noble ideals, but also the power to live them out, the power to become God's covenant people, the grace to experience oneness in Him. That Power is the Lord and Giver of Life Himself, the Holy Spirit, whom Jesus pours out on those who accept Him. So there is only one Way, one Truth, one Life, and one High Priest in Jesus who offers the perfect sacrifice for sins.

Once we have been baptized in Christ, there is no longer a separation between Jesus and us. We have been baptized into His death and have risen with Him in His resurrection. We are baptized into Him, have become members of His body. So He begins to live His life and exercise His priesthood in and through us. If we let Him, He will use our lips to spread His truth, our lives to show the way, and our love to give others life. And the works He will accomplish through us will far surpass what He did in His three short years of public ministry: *"Amen, amen, I say to you, whoever believes in me will do the works that I do, and will do greater ones than these, because I am going to the Father."* (John 14:12) More hungry will be fed, more sick healed, more books written. The Good News will be preached not just in Galilee, but all over the world, not just in person, but touching millions at a time, through various mass media.

But the greatest work that He will accomplish through us is to teach us to be priests, to offer the spiritual sacrifice of our own lives to the Father through Him, with Him, and in Him: *"I urge you therefore, brothers, by the mercies of God, to offer your bodies as a living sacrifice, holy and pleasing to God, your spiritual worship."* (Romans 12:1) For the meaning of human life is to love, and the greatest gift we have received from Jesus is the power to give ourselves away in selfless love like Him.

At the center of Christian discipleship then, is the disciple's experience of Jesus. Without Jesus, the disciple's life and ministry are meaningless. Many followers enter into ministry with enthusiasm and fervor because their lives have been touched in dramatic and poignant ways, but, all too often, they quickly slip away from a solid reliance on their true source and sustenance, Jesus, their Way, Truth, and Life! They are the grains of wheat that fell by the wayside, or on rocky ground, or among thorns.

The ardent follower develops the practice of depending on Jesus in every aspect of life. Imagine Jesus to be your heart, beating constantly all the days of your life, without any respite, so that you might have life consistently and restfully. Jesus restores and renews divine lifeblood in us continuously, so that we might live God's life to the fullest! The Gospels speak of the disciple as the branch that receives its sap and nourishment from Jesus, the Vine. Apart from this Vine, the branch is fit only to be cast into the fire. The disciple flourishes in his or her dependence on Christ. Abiding union with Jesus brings about a profound change in the disciple's lifestyle. Knowing how central this union with Jesus is, the disciple has spent countless hours sitting at the feet of the Master. Within this hunger to be mentored by Jesus are sown the seeds of conviction that Jesus indeed is the source of the disciple's life and ministry.

Jesus, then, is our Way, Truth, and Life! It is through Him that we are incorporated into the Life of the Trinity. Our discipleship is the witness to this explicit flowering of divine life in us who are indwelt by the Father, Son, and Holy Spirit. We are now the branches, inextricably linked to the vine and living abundantly the divine life which courses through Jesus who indwells us. Jesus has been raised from the dead and is seated at the right hand of the Father, as Son and Second Person of the Trinity, as well as our Savior-Intercessor because He is the 'Lamb that was slain.'

JESUS REVEALS THE FATHER TO US:

Jesus is the Father's ambassador. His purpose on earth was to show us the way back to His Father. He was sent by His Father and always did what was pleasing to Him. He did not do anything on His own. His Father sent Jesus to be lifted up on the cross, so that everyone who believes in Him may have eternal life. In doing so the world will realize that Jesus is God and is the Way to the Father's Trinitarian Life: *"So they said to him, 'Who are you?' Jesus said to them, 'What I told you from the beginning. I have much to say about you in condemnation. But the one who sent me is true, and what I heard from him I tell the world.' They did not realize that he was speaking to them of the Father. So Jesus said (to them), 'When you lift up the Son of Man, then you will realize that I AM, and that I do nothing on my own, but I say only what the Father taught me. The one who sent me is with me. He has not left me alone, because I always do what is pleasing to him.' Because he spoke this way, many came to believe in him."* (John 8:25-30)

In the course of His ministry, Jesus revealed His Father to us. For one, Jesus told us that His Father so loved the world that He gave us His only begotten Son, Jesus, so that we might not perish eternally but might receive eternal life, God's own life. Jesus also shared with us that He and the Father are one. If we know Him, we will know the Father. It is not possible to know Jesus and not know the Father at the same time. Jesus was talking about having oneness of being and essence with His Father. And this oneness is gradually revealed to us in and by the Holy Spirit who makes clear to us all the things that Jesus taught us: *"Philip said to him, 'Master, show us the Father, and that will be enough for us.' Jesus said to him, 'Have I been with you for so long a time and you still do not know me, Philip? Whoever has seen me has seen the Father. How can you say, "Show us the Father?" Do you not believe that I am in the Father and the Father is in me? The words that I speak to you I do not speak on my own. The Father who dwells in me is doing his works. Believe me that I am in the Father and the Father is in me, or else, believe because of the works themselves.'"* (John 14:8-11)

In revealing the Father to us, Jesus also makes it clear that He and the Father share in one essence, and they are consequently always engaged in the same works. Hence, the words that Jesus speaks are not only His own words. They are His Father's words as well. Similarly, His works are His Father's works as well. The Father witnesses the special works of Jesus during His ministry and expresses His delight and satisfaction as He did at the Baptism of Jesus and His Transfiguration. Jesus also tells us that His Father is engaged in all the works that Jesus engages in, on our behalf: *"I am the true vine, and my Father is the vine grower. He takes away every branch in me that does not bear fruit, and every one that does he prunes so that it bears more fruit. You are already pruned because of the word that I spoke to you."* (John 15:1-3)

However, the special revelation that Jesus offers us is that through His death and resurrection on our behalf, He has washed us clean in His blood. We are now children of the sanctuary and with our High Priest we sit with Him at the Father's right hand: *"But God, who is rich in mercy, because of the great love he had for us, even when we were dead in our transgressions, brought us to life with Christ (by grace you have been saved), raised us up with him, and seated us with him in the heavens in Christ Jesus."* (Ephesians 2:4-6) Paul addresses God as *"the God and Father of our Lord Jesus Christ"* because through Jesus we have been made adopted sons and daughters of His Father: *"In love he destined us for adoption to himself through Jesus Christ, in accord with the favor of his will, for the praise of the glory of his grace that he granted us in the beloved."* (Ephesians 1:5-6)

Another special revelation that Jesus has offered us is that through Him we have become the Body of Christ or God's human covenant family sharing the Trinity's divine life and love, and living within God's Embrace. We now surround the Lamb that was slain and together with Him, offer continual praise and adoration to the Father. This covenant family has been won for the Father through the blood of the Lamb, and engages in Trinitarian life through the power and umbrage of the Holy Spirit: *"Then I heard every creature in heaven and on earth and under the earth and in the sea, everything in the universe, cry out: 'To the one who sits on the throne and to the Lamb be blessing and honor, glory and might, forever and ever.'"* (Revelation 5:13) And the Lamb is the Bridegroom and we are the bride called to the wedding supper of the Lamb: *"For the wedding day of the Lamb has come, his bride has made herself ready. She was allowed to wear a bright, clean linen garment." (The linen represents the righteous deeds of the holy ones)* (Revelation 19:7-8)

JESUS REVEALS THE HOLY SPIRIT TO US:

Just as Jesus revealed the Father to us, so that we know that they share one divine essence, in the same way, Jesus reveals to us the Holy Spirit. Just as the Father was intimately involved in every facet of Jesus' life and ministry because they shared the same vision and plan of salvation for us, in the same way, the Holy Spirit, along with the Father, was intimately involved in every facet of Jesus' life and ministry. God's Trinitarian Life was manifested in every aspect of the 'Works of God' or the Economy of Salvation. Just as the Father mediates everything through His Son, in the same way Jesus goes about fulfilling every step of His Father's plan of salvation in the power of the Holy Spirit. The angel Gabriel tells Mary in Luke 1:35: *"The holy Spirit will come upon you and the power of the Most High will overshadow you. Therefore the child to be born will be called holy, the Son of God."* At His Baptism, the Holy Spirit descended on Jesus in visible form like a dove. Luke 4:1-2 tells us that *"Filled with the holy Spirit, Jesus returned from the Jordan and was led by the Spirit into the desert for forty days, to be tempted by the devil."* After His forty days in the desert, Jesus entered His public life and ministry in the power of the Holy Spirit. Again and again in the gospels, we are told that Jesus was moved by the Spirit when He worked His miracles and did His teachings. Hebrews 9:14 observes that Christ *"through the eternal spirit offered himself up unblemished to God."* His resurrection was the climax of His ministry and our entrance into God's life, and it was orchestrated by the Holy Spirit: *"If the Spirit of the one who raised Jesus from the dead dwells in you, the one who raised Christ from the dead will give life to your mortal bodies also, through his Spirit that dwells in you."* (Romans 8:11)

Just as Jesus acted in His Trinitarian relationships by carrying out His Father's wishes in every detail of the divine plan of salvation and did everything in the power of His Holy Spirit, in the same way He made sure that we would live our lives in the power of the Holy Spirit who would re-create us in the image and likeness of Jesus, so that like Him we too would be faithful to 'Our' common Father's will in every detail. Jesus made sure that we would receive the Holy Spirit from His Father: *"I will ask the Father and he will give you another Advocate to be with you always…But you know it, because it remains with you, and will be in you."* (John 14:16-17) And the Holy Spirit acts in Trinitarian communion and harmony with the Father and Jesus: *"But when he comes, the Spirit of truth, he will guide you to all truth. He will not speak on his own, but he will speak what he hears, and will declare to you the things that are coming. He will glorify me, because he will take from what is mine and declare it to you. Everything that the Father has is mine; for this reason I told you that he will take from what is mine and declare it to you."* (John 16:13-15)

PRAYING TO JESUS IN THE TRINITY:

It is only through Jesus that we have access into the covenant life of our Triune God, Father, Son, and Holy Spirit. It is in and through Jesus that the Father and the Holy Spirit make their abode in us. Our entrance and participation in the life of God happens through Jesus who is the Bread of Life and our spiritual drink. In prayer we come into the Trinity's inner circle and are privileged to share in their divine relationships and union. In prayer and solitude the disciple imbibes God's yearnings for humankind and makes them their own. Prayer is the place where the Holy Spirit mentors the disciple, bringing about understanding of God's designs for self and the salvation of the world. Gradually, the disciple experiences a transformation in mind and heart and begins to put on the mind and heart of Jesus.

As the disciple is led deeper into the mystery of God's Trinitarian love, there is a profound sense of the limitation of the human mind and its incapacity to comprehend God's holiness and goodness. So disciples ask rhetorical questions for which they seek no answers. The questions attempt to delineate dimly the deep impact the Holy Spirit has made on them as He recreates them into Jesus' image and likeness. Why did God never give up on us and why did He choose to allow Jesus to become incarnate and become our sacrifice for sin and reparation? Why would Jesus go to such extreme lengths to demonstrate God's love for us? Why would Jesus, out of pure love, share His filial relationship with us and give us the gift of sharing in His Father-Son relationship? Why did the Father and Jesus offer us their Holy Spirit to be the Keeper of our souls and reveal to us the depths of Jesus' teachings and thus bring us into God's heart?

As much as the mind is befuddled by this indescribable profundity, the heart is moved toward transformation. And faith ventures forth into deeper waters. The disciple is in the presence of the Trinity's inexpressible mystery. Silent awe and adoration seem to be the natural response, unless God chooses to give words and expression to the experience. An overwhelming sense of gratitude and humility permeates this reverence. The disciple is confronted with the remarkable reality that through Jesus, God would expect us to be *"holy and without blemish before him."* (Ephesians 1:4) In prayer, the disciple receives the answer that what is impossible for humans is possible for God. In prayer, the awareness grows that indeed God has begun a good work and is bringing it to completion.

The disciple has made it a practice to live conjointly with Jesus. Everything in the disciple's life is open to scrutiny and supervision by Jesus. Nothing is private or out of bounds in the relationship. The disciple does everything along with Jesus, for the disciple is no longer alone. And along with Jesus, the disciple expresses and lives from the presence and love of the Father and the Holy Spirit who are present in union with Jesus. Within this Triune union of grace, the disciple's true integrity and authenticity rests.

Finally, just as every prayer is begun and ended in and through Jesus who is the Way to the Father, similarly all of life is begun and continues in and through Jesus, making us witnesses of the Father's love for us and the Holy Spirit's overshadowing of us.

OUR PRAYER TO JESUS:

Jesus, I begin my prayer with adoration and praise of you as my Savior. I have always known you as Jesus, and your name was revealed to us by your Father. Your name tells us who you are on our behalf: *God is salvation* or *God saves!* You have the perfect credentials to be my Savior, because you are the Son of God, I AM, who shares the same divine essence and nature with the Father and the Holy Spirit. As Savior, you plumbed the depths of sacrificial love on our behalf, in our stead. Through your ignominious death on the cross you became sin so that we might become your righteousness! You became our slave so that we might claim your freedom and have your Father as Our Father! As our High Priest you are now seated at the right hand of Our Father, interceding for us and gathering us around you as your Covenant Family.

Jesus, I address you as my Lord and God! With Mary, your Mother, and all the apostles and saints, I believe that you are my Lord and my God. With Thomas the Apostle, I fall on my knees and acclaim you as My Lord and my God! Your resurrection from the dead is the triumphant Amen and fulfillment of all the promises God made from the beginning of time. In your resurrection, I know that you are Lord and God! In your resurrection, I know that your death on the cross was not the wasted death of a criminal, but rather the death of the Lamb of sacrifice, offered as a perfect oblation on behalf of our sins. In baptism I was buried with you in your death, and rose with you in your resurrection. As my Risen Lord, I know that my repentant heart will always receive your forgiveness of my sins. As my Risen Lord, I know that you have gained access for me into God's divine life and love. With the Father and the Holy Spirit, I believe that you are One God in Three Persons and Three Persons in one God!

Jesus, you were raised from the dead because in the first place you deemed it necessary to become incarnate, to take on our human flesh, to become Emmanuel, God-with-us-and-in-us! After your resurrection, you left your disciples with no doubt that you had flesh and bones just as they did. You asked if they had something that you could eat (Luke 24:42-43). In becoming man, you became the covenant knot between the Trinity and us. It was always the Trinity's intention to bind us in covenant love and union with God. Hence, the Father created us in the divine image and likeness through you. Through your death and resurrection, you sealed this bond once and for all. Your sacrifice on the Cross was the perfect offering on our behalf. It has restored the right order between God and us. As our High Priest, you have entered into God's Sanctuary once and for all, and we have entered with you. In amazement and awe, I whelm myself with the fact that through you we have entered into God's Trinitarian embrace. In you, the Father loves us with the same love He has for you. Through you, we have the Holy Spirit as our Advocate and Comforter. He is re-creating us in your divine image and likeness, the first-born of all creation, the first-born from the dead.

Finally, I accept you as the Way, the Truth, and the Life, and surrender myself to you. I acknowledge you as the Resurrection and the Life, as the Alpha and the Omega, as the Source and Summit of my life. You will come to judge the living and the dead, and with you, we too will be raised from the dead. I pledge my life to you, and ask that you join my offering with yours to the Father so that I might become a pleasing offering in His sight. Amen. Triune God, be my all! Triune God, be my all! Triune God, be my all!

PRAYER AND REFLECTION ON KNOWING JESUS IN THE TRINITY

WEEK FIFTEEN: *"AND THE WORD BECAME FLESH AND MADE HIS DWELLING AMONG US, AND WE SAW HIS GLORY, THE GLORY AS OF THE FATHER'S ONLY SON, FULL OF GRACE AND TRUTH." (JOHN 1:14)*

SPIRITUAL READING FOR THE WEEK:

- **Anoint Us in Your Covenant, Abba-Emmanuel:** Session Eight
- **Old Testament:** Two or Three Chapters daily
- **New Testament:** Two or Three Chapters daily
- **Imitation of Christ:** One chapter daily

DAY ONE: MORNING SESSION

MORNING PRAYER: Acts of Faith, Hope, Charity; Daily Offering

Morning Face to Face with God:

Begin with Prayer to the Holy Spirit

KNOWING JESUS IN THE TRINITY:

(After pondering each bullet point, express your sentiments in a short prayer)

- The Risen Lord appears to the apostles and gives them His peace. Immediately the disciples experience a transformation. Their fear and anxiety dissipate and they begin rejoicing. There is a Power and Presence in their midst that has overcome Satan, sin, and death. No power on earth or in the heavens can withstand the victory of the Risen Lord.
- In some unmistakable way the disciples have finally grasped this truth in the Presence of their Risen Master and Lord! They rejoice because they are being transformed significantly by the Risen Lord's peace!
- *Eirene* is the Greek word used to translate 'peace.' There are approximately 90 occurrences of *eirene* in the New Testament. Peace is defined by what God has done for human beings through Jesus Christ. So when Jesus appears to His disciples, they experience the transformation that He has brought about in the world through His death and resurrection.

- Jesus is Lord, and through Him, His disciples will be strong and steadfast in every circumstance of their lives. Through thick and thin, through trials and tribulations, they will remain steadfast in the peace and joy of the Risen Lord. They have now become hyphenated or grafted identities. They live in Christ and Christ lives in them.

- He is the vine, they are His branches. In Him they can do all things. In persecution they will rejoice because they have borne hardship and insult for their Lord Jesus Christ. They are in covenant relationship with the Trinity through Jesus Christ and in the power of the Holy Spirit. They have been incorporated into God's Trinitarian Life through the Risen Lord.

- Jesus is the Way, the Truth, and the Life because He is the Resurrection and the Life. In Jesus, God comes to meet us, holding nothing back, offering everything of who He is and what He has. Through Jesus, we have access to God to such an extent that we can now call him Abba, Father.

- Jesus is the Truth, not just some truth, but the entire truth. He is God's definitive and perfect Word, expressing who God is, what He is like, who we are, and what we need to do to be saved through Him from our enslavement to Satan and sin.

- And Jesus is the Life. He gives us not only commandments and noble ideals, but also the power to live them out, the power to become God's covenant people. That Power is the Lord and Giver of Life Himself, the Holy Spirit, whom Jesus pours out on those who accept Him. So there is only one Way, one Truth, one Life, and one High Priest in Jesus who offers the perfect sacrifice for sins.

- Once we have been baptized in Christ, there is no longer a separation between Jesus and us. We have been baptized into His death and have risen with Him in His resurrection.

- We are baptized into Him, become members of His body. So He begins to live His life and exercise His priesthood in and through us. If we let Him, He will use our lips to spread His truth, our lives to show the way, and our love to give others life. And the works He will accomplish through us will far surpass what He did in His three short years of public ministry (John 14:12).

- But the greatest work that He will accomplish through us is to teach us to be priests, to offer the spiritual sacrifice of our own lives to the Father through Him, with Him, and in Him (Romans 12:1) For the meaning of human life is to love, and the greatest gift we have received from Jesus is the power to give ourselves away in selfless love like Him.

What is God saying to you?

End with Prayer to the Holy Trinity

NIGHT SESSION: Examination of Conscience

For what are you grateful? For what are you contrite?

Please review briefly your Morning Prayer topic. Make it your last thought of the day

DAY TWO: MORNING SESSION

MORNING PRAYER: Act of Faith; Act of Hope; Act of Charity; Daily Offering

Morning Face to Face with God:

Begin with Prayer to the Holy Spirit

Prayer on John 1:14: The Word became Flesh
"And the Word became flesh and made his dwelling among us, and we saw his glory, the glory as of the Father's only Son, full of grace and truth."

Read the Reflection; Thank Jesus for being your Risen Lord who has brought you into covenant union with our Triune God, and ask to be His devoted disciple

   In the first few verses of the Prologue, John goes to great pains to establish the believers' faith in Jesus as God. John addresses Jesus as the Word of God who already existed at the beginning and therefore preceded time and creation. The ultimate manifestation of God's Word is to now become flesh. What an amazing paradox! 'Flesh' is all that is ephemeral, subject to death, imperfect, and at first glance, incompatible with God. In the incarnation, the Eternal Word took on our exact human nature, becoming one with us in everything except sin. The Father rejoices in His Son's identification with us in our sinfulness and brokenness, knowing fully well that in this identification lay our redemption and participation in the divine life! Through taking on our flesh, Jesus has made His dwelling (The Hebrew word *shekinah* is used to denote God's dwelling place in the temple which was the Ark of the Covenant) among us. He is our Temple in our flesh. His disciples saw His glory, the glory of God's only Son, full of grace and truth. In His flesh, we have seen that Jesus is God!

What is God saying to you?

End with Prayer to the Holy Trinity

NIGHT SESSION: Examination of Conscience

For what are you grateful? For what are you contrite?

Please review briefly your Morning Prayer topic. Make it your last thought of the day

DAY THREE: MORNING SESSION

MORNING PRAYER: Act of Faith; Act of Hope; Act of Charity; Daily Offering

Morning Face to Face with God:

Begin with Prayer to the Holy Spirit

Prayer on John 2:19-22: Cleansing of the Temple
> *"Jesus answered and said to them, "Destroy this temple and in three days I will raise it up." The Jews said, "This temple has been under construction for forty-six years, and you will raise it up in three days?" But he was speaking about the temple of his body. Therefore, when he was raised from the dead, his disciples remembered that he had said this, and they came to believe the scripture and the word Jesus had spoken."*

Read the Reflection; Thank Jesus for being your Risen Lord who has brought you into covenant union with our Triune God, and ask to be His devoted disciple

Among the several themes that John develops in his gospel, two stand out: the Word of God became flesh and Jesus is the temple. Through the course of his gospel, John marshals several witnesses who give evidence of the fact that Jesus, the Word made flesh, is God. Along with the apostles, John the Baptist is a very important witness. Similarly, in chapter after chapter, John alludes to the fact that Jesus pointed to Himself as the temple, the place where God resides as Emmanuel. Jesus had come to establish the new and eternal covenant and replace the old Mosaic covenant whose symbol was the Temple built in stone. Jesus Himself would become the temple of the new and everlasting covenant. The cleansing of the Temple suggests that God's dwelling place had been desecrated. It was no longer a sacred place where God was given first priority. Hence Jesus saw it fitting to cleanse it and highlight the real purpose of its existence. More importantly, Jesus made the point that this earthly temple would be replaced by Him: *"Destroy this temple and in three days I will raise it up."* Obviously Jesus was referring to His resurrection, and many of His disciples came to believe in Him when they remembered what He had said. The temple built by human hands was destroyed by the Romans in A.D. 70, and has never been re-built since.

What is God saying to you?

End with Prayer to the Holy Trinity

NIGHT SESSION: Examination of Conscience

For what are you grateful? For what are you contrite?

Please review briefly your Morning Prayer topic. Make it your last thought of the day

DAY FOUR: MORNING SESSION

MORNING PRAYER: Act of Faith; Act of Hope; Act of Charity; Daily Offering

Morning Face to Face with God:

Begin with Prayer to the Holy Spirit

Prayer on John 6:54-58: Jesus, the Bread of Life

"Whoever eats my flesh and drinks my blood remains in me and I in him. Just as the living Father sent me and I have life because of the Father, so also the one who feeds on me will have life because of me. This is the bread that came down from heaven. Unlike your ancestors who ate and still died, whoever eats this bread will live forever."

Read the Reflection; Thank Jesus for being your Risen Lord who has brought you into covenant union with our Triune God, and ask to be His devoted disciple

In five verses, Jesus emphasizes the necessity of eating His body and drinking His blood five times! In one instance, Jesus is very graphic in His description, to allay any doubt about what He means when He says that *"the one who feeds on me [the way a carnivore gnaws at its carcass] will have life because of me."* In these verses, Jesus also gives us the true intent as to why it is necessary for us to eat His body and drink His blood: *"Whoever eats my flesh and drinks my blood remains in me and I in him."* Through Eucharistic communion, we become one with Jesus in covenant union. We abide in Him, and He in us. Through Jesus, we are given a share in the perfect indwelling of the Three Divine Persons in each other. Through eating His body and drinking His blood, we are given a share in the fullness of God's divine Life: *"Just as the living Father sent me and I have life because of the Father, so also the one who feeds on me will have life because of me."*

What is God saying to you?

End with Prayer to the Holy Trinity

NIGHT SESSION: Examination of Conscience

For what are you grateful? For what are you contrite?

Please review briefly your Morning Prayer topic. Make it your last thought of the day

DAY FIVE: MORNING SESSION

MORNING PRAYER: Act of Faith; Act of Hope; Act of Charity; Daily Offering

Morning Face to Face with God:

Begin with Prayer to the Holy Spirit

Prayer on John 8:12: Jesus, the Light of the World
> *"Jesus spoke to them again, saying, "I am the light of the world. Whoever follows me will not walk in darkness, but will have the light of life."*

Read the Reflection; Thank Jesus for being your Risen Lord who has brought you into covenant union with our Triune God, and ask to be His devoted disciple

Light is a very powerful image that symbolizes freedom from sin symbolized by darkness. Light also symbolizes transparency, openness, joy, holiness, and truth. Jesus uses the imagery of light to illumine our minds and hearts about the fact that He is divine. *'I am the light of the world,'* is the second of seven "I AM" statements made by Jesus and found in John's gospel. As God, Jesus is our Savior who has overcome Satan, sin, and permanent death. Whoever accepts Jesus as Lord and Savior will not walk in darkness because in Jesus there is no darkness. Jesus is the Light of the World, and through Him we share in the fullness of *'the light of life.'* Jesus was referring to our sharing of His divine life, He who is *'the light of life,'* when in Matthew 5:14-16, He says, *"You are the light of the world. A city set on a mountain cannot be hidden. Nor do they light a lamp and then put it under a bushel basket; it is set on a lampstand, where it gives light to all in the house. Just so, your light must shine before others, that they may see your good deeds and glorify your heavenly Father."*

What is God saying to you?

End with Prayer to the Holy Trinity

NIGHT SESSION: Examination of Conscience

For what are you grateful? For what are you contrite?

Please review briefly your Morning Prayer topic. Make it your last thought of the day

DAY SIX: MORNING SESSION

MORNING PRAYER: Act of Faith; Act of Hope; Act of Charity; Daily Offering

Morning Face to Face with God:

Begin with Prayer to the Holy Spirit

OUR PRAYER TO JESUS: *p. 196*

> *Thank Jesus for being your Risen Lord who has brought you into covenant union with our Triune God, and ask to be His devoted disciple*

Today, you will pray with *"Our Prayer to Jesus"* from the Session. You can go over this prayer once or twice, tasting and relishing the boundless and inexhaustible love Jesus has for you as your Savior and Lord, as well His passionate love and devotion to His Father into whose embrace He has brought you. You can spend time tasting and relishing the gift of His Holy Spirit to you as the Keeper of your soul. *"Our Prayer to Jesus"* can act as a repetition of Days Two through Five of this week. In a repetition St. Ignatius says that *"we should pay attention to and dwell upon those points in which we have experienced greater consolation or desolation or greater spiritual appreciation."* (# 62)

What is God saying to you?

End with Prayer to the Holy Trinity

NIGHT SESSION: Examination of Conscience

For what are you grateful? For what are you contrite?

Please review briefly your Morning Prayer topic. Make it your last thought of the day

DAY SEVEN: MORNING SESSION

MORNING PRAYER: Act of Faith; Act of Hope; Act of Charity; Daily Offering

Morning Face to Face with God:

Begin with Prayer to the Holy Spirit

THE SIXTH DWELLING PLACES:

- St. Teresa sees the Sixth Dwelling Places as the place where the betrothal takes place. In her day for the arrangement of a marriage, the following stages were followed: 1) meetings between the young man and woman; 2) exchanging of gifts; 3) falling in love; 4) the joining of hands; 5) betrothal; 6) marriage.

- The union experienced in the Fifth Dwelling Places continues to deepen. Now the soul is determined to take no other spouse. But Jesus wants to intensify the desire and determination of the soul for this betrothal. And this strengthening takes place through interior and exterior trials that the soul suffers.

- At this stage of union, the disciple's lifestyle and behavior become a lightning rod in a sense. Some are threatened by their example and resort to gossip; others feel convicted and avoid their company; still others are appreciative but do not want to change. The upshot of it all is that the disciple feels isolated and rejected.

- When the disciple is praised, it becomes a suffering indeed. People are as quick to say good things as bad; secondly, since Our Lord is the source of all good, praise of them rings hollow. Since their concern for the honor and glory of God, is greater than for their own glory, they will not be led astray by praise that is directed to them. They are very pleased if God is glorified even if it means that they have to suffer.

- When God liberates a soul so that it pays scant attention to praise being directed towards it, it pays much less attention to disapproval; on the contrary it rejoices and finds it to be sweet music. *"This is an amazing truth. Blame does not intimidate the soul but strengthens it. Experience has already taught it the wonderful gain that comes through this path... And since it clearly experiences the benefits of persecution, it acquires a special and very tender love for its persecutors. It seems to it that they are greater friends and more advantageous than those who speak well of it."* (TIC – VI:1:5)

- Severe illness can be an exterior trial that a disciple can face in this dwelling place. *"For in some way, if these pains are severe, the trial is, it seems to me, the greatest on earth – I mean the greatest exterior trial, however many the other pains."* (TIC – VI:1:6)

- An interior trial can be the result of a confessor or spiritual director being out of their depth when listening to a disciple in the betrothal stage of union. You can have a confessor *"who is so discreet and has so little experience that there is nothing he is sure of; he fears everything and finds in everything something to doubt because he sees these unusual experiences. He becomes especially doubtful if he notices some imperfection in a soul that has them, for it seems to such confessors that the ones to whom God grants these favors must be angels – but that is impossible as long as they are in this body."* TIC – VI:1:8)

- This situation gets aggravated when the disciple has a fearful temperament: *"Even though they feel secure and cannot believe that the favor when granted by His Majesty, is from any other spirit than from God, the torment returns immediately since the favor is something that passes quickly, and the remembrance of sins is always present, and the soul sees faults in itself, which are never lacking."* (TIC – VI:1:8)

- Along with this sense of doubt, there is the inability to explain what is going on to the confessor or spiritual director. *"The soul's understanding is so darkened that it becomes incapable of seeing the truth and believes whatever the imagination represents to it (for the imagination is then its master) or whatever foolish things the devil wants to represent...*

Many are the things that war against it with an interior oppression so keen and unbearable that I don't know what to compare this experience to if not to the oppression of those that suffer in hell, for no consolation is allowed in the midst of this tempest." (TIC – VI:1:9)

- The disciple has no choice except to wait for God's mercy to intervene. And just like that, the Lord can calm the storm and fill the soul with consolation, leading to thanksgiving and praise of God.

- This experience of feeling totally incapacitated leads to a profound sense of sin, to a sense that one does not have any love of God, to a sense that everything is gift. When it prays, it feels its efforts are useless as there is a total absence of consolation. It cannot pray discursively, as the faculties are incapable of meditation. In such a dark night, St. Teresa proposes that we *"engage in external works of charity and hope in the mercy of God who never fails those who hope in Him."* (TIC – VI:1:13)

What is God saying to you?

NIGHT SESSION: Examination of Conscience

For what are you grateful? For what are you contrite?

What prayer would you compose to express what God has said to you this week?

Please review briefly your Morning Prayer topic. Make it your last thought of the day

PRAYER AND REFLECTION ON KNOWING JESUS IN THE TRINITY – CONTINUED

WEEK SIXTEEN: *"WHOEVER EATS MY FLESH AND DRINKS MY BLOOD REMAINS IN ME AND I IN HIM. JUST AS THE LIVING FATHER SENT ME AND I HAVE LIFE BECAUSE OF THE FATHER, SO ALSO THE ONE WHO FEEDS ON ME WILL HAVE LIFE BECAUSE OF ME." (JOHN 6:56-57)*

WHAT IS AT THE HEART OF SESSION EIGHT, WEEK SIXTEEN?

SPIRITUAL READING FOR THE WEEK:

- **Anoint Us in Your Covenant, Abba-Emmanuel:** Session Eight
- **Old Testament:** Two or Three Chapters daily
- **New Testament:** Two or Three Chapters daily
- **Imitation of Christ:** One chapter daily

DAY ONE: MORNING SESSION

MORNING PRAYER: Acts of Faith, Hope, Charity; Daily Offering

Morning Face to Face with God:

Begin with Prayer to the Holy Spirit

ON KNOWING JESUS IN THE TRINITY:

(After pondering each bullet point, express your sentiments in a short prayer)

- At the center of Christian discipleship is the disciple's experience of Jesus. Without Jesus, the disciple's life and ministry are meaningless. Many followers slip away from a solid reliance on their true sustenance, Jesus, their Way, Truth, and Life! They are the grains of wheat that fall by the wayside, or on rocky ground, or among thorns.
- The ardent follower develops the practice of depending on Jesus in every aspect of life. The disciple flourishes in his or her dependence on Christ. Abiding union with Jesus brings about a profound change in the disciple's lifestyle.
- Knowing how central this union with Jesus is, the disciple has spent countless hours sitting at the feet of the Master. Within this hunger to be mentored by Jesus are sown the seeds of conviction that Jesus indeed is the source of the disciple's life and ministry.
- Our discipleship is the witness to this explicit flowering of divine life in us who are indwelt by the Father, Son, and Holy Spirit. We are now the branches, inextricably

linked to the vine and living abundantly the divine life which courses through Jesus who indwells us.

- In the course of His ministry, Jesus revealed His Father to us. For one, Jesus told us that His Father so loved the world that He gave us His only begotten Son, Jesus, so that we might not perish eternally but might receive eternal life, God's own life.

- Jesus also shared with us that He and the Father are one. If we know Him, we will know the Father. It is not possible to know Jesus and not know the Father at the same time. Jesus was talking about having oneness of being and essence with His Father. And this oneness is gradually revealed to us in and by the Holy Spirit who makes clear to us all the things that Jesus taught us.

- However, the special revelation that Jesus offers us is that through His death and resurrection on our behalf, He has washed us clean in His blood. We are now children of the sanctuary and with our High Priest we sit with Him at the Father's right hand.

- Another special revelation that Jesus has offered us is that through Him we have become the Body of Christ or God's human covenant family sharing the Trinity's divine life and love, and living within God's Embrace. We now surround the Lamb that was slain and together with Him, offer continual praise and adoration to the Father.

- Just as the Father was intimately involved in every facet of Jesus' life and ministry because they shared the same vision and plan of salvation for us, in the same way, the Holy Spirit, along with the Father, was intimately involved in every facet of Jesus' life and ministry. God's Trinitarian Life was manifested in every aspect of the 'Works of God' or the Economy of Salvation.

- Just as the Father mediates everything through His Son, in the same way Jesus goes about fulfilling every step of His Father's plan of salvation in the power of the Holy Spirit. Jesus acted in His Trinitarian relationships by carrying out His Father's wishes in every detail of the divine plan of salvation and did everything in the power of his Holy Spirit.

- In the same way Jesus made sure that we would live our lives in the power of the Holy Spirit who would re-create us in the image and likeness of Jesus, so that like Him we too would be faithful to 'Our' common Father's will in every detail.

What is God saying to you?

End with Prayer to the Holy Trinity

NIGHT SESSION: Examination of Conscience

For what are you grateful? For what are you contrite?

Please review briefly your Morning Prayer topic. Make it your last thought of the day

DAY TWO: MORNING SESSION

MORNING PRAYER: Act of Faith; Act of Hope; Act of Charity; Daily Offering

Morning Face to Face with God:

Begin with Prayer to the Holy Spirit

Prayer on John 10:7-11: Jesus, the Good Shepherd

"So Jesus said again, "Amen, amen, I say to you, I am the gate for the sheep. All who came [before me] are thieves and robbers, but the sheep did not listen to them. I am the gate. Whoever enters through me will be saved, and will come in and go out and find pasture… I came so that they might have life and have it more abundantly. I am the good shepherd. A good shepherd lays down his life for the sheep."

Read the Reflection; Thank Jesus for being your Risen Lord who has brought you into covenant union with our Triune God, and ask to be His devoted disciple

In the Old Testament, God was described as the Good Shepherd. The prophets preached incessantly that the leaders of God's flock had to be good shepherds. Jesus is excoriating the present religious leadership that has turned out to be hirelings, concerned only about their own welfare. Consequently, the sheep do not listen to them. By contrast, Jesus is the Good Shepherd. He is the Way to God. He is the gate through which we come to God. Along with being the Way, Jesus is the Truth and the Life. Through Him we will be saved: "We will go out and find pasture." Through Jesus we will have life. And the reason why we will have this life more abundantly is because it is God's own life which is limitless and unfathomable. For His sheep, Jesus is willing to give His life. His mission as shepherd is to create a covenant relationship between the Blessed Trinity and us, His sheep.

What is God saying to you?

End with Prayer to the Holy Trinity

NIGHT SESSION: Examination of Conscience

For what are you grateful? For what are you contrite?

Please review briefly your Morning Prayer topic. Make it your last thought of the day

DAY THREE: MORNING SESSION

MORNING PRAYER: Act of Faith; Act of Hope; Act of Charity; Daily Offering

Morning Face to Face with God:

Begin with Prayer to the Holy Spirit

Prayer on John 11:25-27: Jesus is the Resurrection and the Life
"Jesus told her, "I am the resurrection and the life; whoever believes in me, even if he dies, will live, and everyone who lives and believes in me will never die. Do you believe this?" She said to him, "Yes, Lord. I have come to believe that you are the Messiah, the Son of God, the one who is coming into the world."

Read the Reflection; Thank Jesus for being your Risen Lord who has brought you into covenant union with our Triune God, and ask to be His devoted disciple

John offers us seven signs or miracles in his gospel, and the raising of Lazarus is the last sign that he offers. The synoptic gospels do not mention this miracle. There are several ironies that John makes note of in the circumstances of this miracle. In His ministry Jesus has been projecting Himself as the source of light and life. The raising of Lazarus is an emphatic exclamation mark to His assertion. Oddly enough, it is after such a declaration that the Sanhedrin makes the decision to put Jesus to death. Because of their blindness to Jesus, the light of the world, they could not envisage that if they put Him to death, He would indeed rise from the dead. The resurrection of Lazarus was a harbinger of the resurrection of Jesus Himself. The raising of Lazarus is a sign of the divine life that Jesus, raised from the dead, will offer to anyone who accepts Him as their Savior and Lord. In spite of the crisis that Martha was undergoing, she came to believe that Jesus was the Messiah, the Son of God. Jesus is indeed the Resurrection and the Life! Her faith was deeply enhanced after Lazarus was raised to life, and especially after Jesus was raised from the dead! We can ask to have the same deep faith and trust in Jesus that Martha had, especially in our own times of crisis.

What is God saying to you?

End with Prayer to the Holy Trinity

NIGHT SESSION: Examination of Conscience

For what are you grateful? For what are you contrite?

Please review briefly your Morning Prayer topic. Make it your last thought of the day

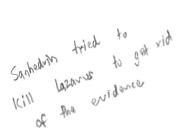
Sanhedrin tried to kill Lazarus to get rid of the evidence

DAY FOUR: MORNING SESSION

MORNING PRAYER: Act of Faith; Act of Hope; Act of Charity; Daily Offering

Morning Face to Face with God:

Begin with Prayer to the Holy Spirit

Prayer on John 14:6-7: Jesus, the Way and the Truth and the Life
> *"Jesus said to him, "I am the way and the truth and the life. No one comes to the Father except through me. If you know me, then you will also know my Father. From now on you do know him and have seen him."*

Read the Reflection; Thank Jesus for being your Risen Lord who has brought you into covenant union with our Triune God, and ask to be His devoted disciple

1. *I am the way and the truth and the life:* This too is one of the seven "I AM" statements of Jesus. This statement is taken from the Great Discourse made in the Upper Room on the eve of Jesus' death. It is a very solemn moment, and Jesus is revealing the depths of His Being and Life in the midst of the uncertainty and anxiety of His disciples. Jesus is the only way, the only truth, and the only life, because He is God. It is only in, with, and through Him that we can share in God's Life!

2. *No one comes to the Father except through me:* This statement makes it clear that Jesus alone is the Savior and Lord of this world. There is no other savior besides Jesus. One can come to the Father only through Jesus who is the Way, the Truth, and the Life!

3. *If you know me, then you will also know my Father. From now on you do know him and have seen him:* Jesus is speaking of His life in the Blessed Trinity. God is One in Three, Three in One. In knowing Jesus, we share the knowledge and life that Jesus has with the Father and the Holy Spirit. Through Jesus we come to know that the Father, the Son of God, and the Holy Spirit are one. When we know Jesus, therefore, we also know the Father and the Holy Spirit.

What is God saying to you?

End with Prayer to the Holy Trinity

NIGHT SESSION: Examination of Conscience

For what are you grateful? For what are you contrite?

Please review briefly your Morning Prayer topic. Make it your last thought of the day

DAY FIVE: MORNING SESSION

MORNING PRAYER: Act of Faith; Act of Hope; Act of Charity; Daily Offering

Morning Face to Face with God:

Begin with Prayer to the Holy Spirit

Prayer on John 20:19b-23: Jesus is the Risen Lord

> *"Jesus came and stood in their midst and said to them, "Peace be with you." When he had said this, he showed them his hands and his side. The disciples rejoiced when they saw the Lord. [Jesus] said to them again, "Peace be with you. As the Father has sent me, so I send you." And when he had said this, he breathed on them and said to them, "Receive the holy Spirit. Whose sins you forgive are forgiven them, and whose sins you retain are retained."*

Read the Reflection; Thank Jesus for being your Risen Lord who has brought you into covenant union with our Triune God, and ask to be His devoted disciple

In John, the Resurrection, Ascension, and Imparting of the Holy Spirit are seen as different aspects of the same divine mystery. The disciples are transformed by the gift of the Holy Spirit being given to them by the Risen Jesus. Two points are worthy of note in this resurrection event. Jesus, the Risen Lord, breathes the Holy Spirit into His apostles. He breathes into them His own divine life through His Holy Spirit. Secondly, through the Holy Spirit, Jesus gives His apostles the power to forgive and retain sin. God took an amazing risk, to allow humans to exercise this power in His name. Twenty centuries of chosen humans, our bishops and priests, exercising this power in Jesus' name, has turned out to be an immense grace. God always knows best. As with Jesus, so with us, we will live and serve in the power and overshadowing of the Holy Spirit. In baptism, the breathing of the Holy Spirit upon us by Jesus is our re-creation. We are begotten of the Spirit who will guide us to all truth and in doing so we will give glory to Jesus!

What is God saying to you?

End with Prayer to the Holy Trinity

NIGHT SESSION: Examination of Conscience

For what are you grateful? For what are you contrite?

Please review briefly your Morning Prayer topic. Make it your last thought of the day

DAY SIX: MORNING SESSION

MORNING PRAYER: Act of Faith; Act of Hope; Act of Charity; Daily Offering

Morning Face to Face with God:

Begin with Prayer to the Holy Spirit

OUR PRAYER TO JESUS:

p. 196

Thank Jesus for being your Risen Lord who has brought you into covenant union with our Triune God, and ask to be His devoted disciple

Today, you will pray with "Our Prayer to Jesus" from the Session. You can go over this prayer once or twice, tasting and relishing the boundless and inexhaustible love Jesus has for you as your Savior and Lord, as well His passionate love and devotion to His Father into whose embrace He has brought you. You can spend time tasting and relishing the gift of His Holy Spirit to you as the Keeper of your soul. "Our Prayer to Jesus" can act as a repetition of Days Two through Five of this week. In a repetition St. Ignatius says that "we should pay attention to and dwell upon those points in which we have experienced greater consolation or desolation or greater spiritual appreciation (# 62).

What is God saying to you?

End with Prayer to the Holy Trinity

NIGHT SESSION: Examination of Conscience

For what are you grateful? For what are you contrite?

Please review briefly your Morning Prayer topic. Make it your last thought of the day

DAY SEVEN: MORNING SESSION

MORNING PRAYER: Act of Faith; Act of Hope; Act of Charity; Daily Offering

Morning Face to Face with God:

Begin with Prayer to the Holy Spirit

THE SIXTH DWELLING PLACES: AWAKENING IMPULSES:

- In the Sixth Dwelling Place the soul receives delicate and refined impulses that proceed from deep within the interior part of the soul. And they are far different than the impulses offered in the Fifth Dwelling Place.

- One such impulse is that often when a person is distracted, suddenly *"His Majesty will awaken it. His action is quick as a falling comet. And as clearly as it hears a thunderclap, even though no sound is heard, the soul understands that it was called by God..."*
- *It feels that it is wounded in the most exquisite way, but it doesn't learn how or by whom it was wounded... And the pain is great, although delightful and sweet. And even if the soul does not want this wound, the wound cannot be avoided. But the soul, in fact, would never want to be deprived of this pain. The wound satisfies it much more than the delightful and painless absorption of the prayer of quiet."* (TIC – VI:2:2)
- St. Teresa tells us that this favor cannot be explained. This delightful pain is not continuous, and it is not really pain. It is described as pain because it is overwhelming and indescribable.
- It is never permanent and therefore does not set the soul on fire. *"But just as the fire is about to start, the spark goes out and the soul is left with the desire to suffer again that loving pain the spark causes."* (TIC – VI:2:4)
- St. Teresa offers some important reasons as to why such an impulse of exquisite pain can only come from God and not the devil: *(The devil) doesn't have the power to join pain – and so much of it – to the spiritual quiet and delight of the soul... the pain he causes are never delightful or peaceful, but disturbing and contentious... the favor brings wonderful benefits to the soul, the more customary of which are the determination to withdraw from earthly satisfactions and conversations and other similar things."* (TIC – VI:2:6)
- There are other awakenings that the soul might receive that do not have this element of intense and exquisite pain: *"When it is praying vocally and not thinking of anything interior, it seems a delightful enkindling will come upon it... The soul is moved with a delightful desire to enjoy Him, and thereby it is prepared to make intense acts of love and praise of our Lord."* (TIC – VI:2:8)

AWAKENING THROUGH LOCUTIONS:

- St. Teresa speaks at great length about the various kinds of locutions. Our reflection will be informative and not exhaustive. St. Teresa believes that locutions can come from God or from the devil or from one's own imagination. Some are so exterior that they come through the sense of hearing. They are audible through a spoken word.
- There is great need for proper discernment in the matter of locutions. To help us in this, she gives us clear signs of a true and authentic locution as coming from God: *"the first and truest is the power and authority they bear, for locutions from God effect what they say... A soul finds itself in the midst of ... tribulation and disturbance... in darkness of the intellect and in dryness; with one word alone of these locutions ("don't be distressed") from the Lord, it is left calm and free from all distress...*

- *The second sign is the great quiet left in the soul, the devout and peaceful recollection, the readiness to engage in the praises of God…*
- *The third sign is that these words remain in the memory for a very long time, and some are never forgotten."* (TIC – VI:3:5-7)
- There are occasions when the devil can play his part. The words given in a locution, while they are held on to steadfastly, can still be doubted, because their certainty is being questioned, thus causing doubt and anxiety. And sometimes one can be imprudent in the way they set about carrying out God's will as they think has been revealed to them through the locution. In such matters help from a confessor or spiritual director might be necessary.

What is God saying to you?

End with Prayer to the Holy Trinity

NIGHT SESSION: Examination of Conscience

For what are you grateful? For what are you contrite?

What prayer would you compose to express what God has said to you this week?

Please review briefly your Morning Prayer topic. Make it your last thought of the day

SESSION NINE
KNOWING THE HOLY SPIRIT IN THE TRINITY

"But as it is written: "What eye has not seen, and ear has not heard, and what has not entered the human heart, what God has prepared for those who love him," this God has revealed to us through the Spirit. For the Spirit scrutinizes everything, even the depths of God. Among human beings, who knows what pertains to a person except the spirit of the person that is within? Similarly, no one knows what pertains to God except the Spirit of God. We have not received the spirit of the world but the Spirit that is from God, so that we may understand the things freely given us by God. And we speak about them not with words taught by human wisdom, but with words taught by the Spirit, describing spiritual realities in spiritual terms."

– 1 Corinthians 2:9-13

THE HOLY SPIRIT IN TRINITARIAN LIFE:

Paul gives us a profound insight into the inner life of God and how the Holy Spirit is the bond of knowledge and union between Father and Son. In the text cited above, Paul asks an intriguing question: *"Who, for example, knows a man's innermost self but the man's own spirit within him?"* Outside of God, no one really knows us the way we know ourselves. We have only to go over the chapters of our lives, lingering upon the details of our experiences. Invariably we realize that there are so many intricate and delicate layers in our experiences, and when we talk about them, much of what we say, while true, only reveals in part our inner depths. In verbalizing our experiences we offer wisps of tenderness or intricate layers of sorrow and pain, or complex movements of joy and jubilation, but most of it remains indescribable. So we try to describe our experiences to others, noting at the same time that we are simply not able to communicate the depths of our being.

It therefore comes as a momentous revelation when Paul tells us that the Holy Spirit scrutinizes all matters, even the deep things of God. God's Spirit has the power to probe God's innermost depths that He indwells. The Holy Spirit picks up every nuance in God's depths and gives voice to it through Jesus, the Word of God. We can assume with confidence therefore that the Holy Spirit will reveal to us even the tiniest wisps of divine tenderness and love within the Trinity and toward us, what eye has not seen, what ear has not heard! The Father and the Son know themselves and each other in their Holy Spirit. It is therefore only in the Holy Spirit that we can know the Father and the Son: *"Therefore, I tell you that nobody speaking by the spirit of God says, "Jesus be accursed." And no one can say, "Jesus is Lord," except by the holy Spirit."* (1 Corinthians 12:3) It makes eminent sense therefore, that Jesus asked and received the promise of the Holy Spirit from His Father to continue the work of revealing the Father and the Son to His disciples. It was also necessary that Jesus return to His Father, or else the Holy Spirit would not come: *"But I tell you the truth, it is better for you that I go. For if I do not go, the Advocate will not come to you. But if I go, I will send him to you."* (John 16:7) Without the baptism of the Holy Spirit, the Kingdom of God, firmly established by Jesus, could not be inaugurated. The inauguration could only happen in and through the Outpouring of the Holy Spirit.

FATHER AND SON ACT IN AND THROUGH THEIR HOLY SPIRIT:

It is through the words and actions of the Father and the Son that the Holy Spirit is manifested to us. The Father creates in the power of His Holy Spirit. God created the heavens and the earth with *"a mighty wind sweeping over the waters."* (Genesis 1:2) Thus began the establishment of order and harmony over chaos and darkness. In the second story of Creation, *"the LORD God formed the man out of the dust of the ground and blew into his nostrils the breath of life, and the man became a living being."* (Genesis 2:7) In commenting on John 20:21-22 where Jesus breathed on His disciples and gave them the Holy Spirit, St. Cyril of Alexandria commented that "Christ's act was a renewal of that primal gift and of the inbreathing bestowed on us, bringing us back to the form of the initial holiness and carrying man's nature up, as a kind of first fruits among the holy apostles, into the holiness bestowed on us initially at the first creation."

God always intended that we would be filled with "the breath of life," namely the Holy Spirit, or else we could not be the image and likeness of God or ever be capable of entering into covenant with God! God would not allow 'the breath of life' to be destroyed in us by sin. Our restoration to the fullness of the Holy Spirit, our Breath of life, has been made possible through the death and resurrection of Jesus who is LORD! *"He (Jesus) breathed on them and said to them: "Receive the Holy Spirit."* (John 20:22) And in Acts 2:3-4, we are told that *"there appeared to them tongues as of fire, which parted and came to rest on each one of them. And they were filled with the holy Spirit and began to speak in different tongues, as the Spirit enabled them to proclaim."*

Jesus accomplished His mission on earth in the power of the Holy Spirit, thus revealing to us the depths of His Father's heart and His own as well. Mary, His mother, conceived Jesus through the power of the Holy Spirit: *"The holy Spirit will come upon you, and the power of the Most High will overshadow you. Therefore the child to be born will be called holy, the Son of God."* (Luke 1:35) In His Baptism, Jesus is viewed differently by different audiences. There is the human audience that assumed He was a sinner because He was receiving John's baptism of repentance for the forgiveness of sins. In a public manner Jesus identifies Himself as a sinner. He knows He is our *Goel*, kinsman-redeemer, taking upon Himself our sins so that we might be fully restored and be able to claim His Father as Our Father! John the Baptist recognizes 'the Lamb of God' and insists on being baptized by Jesus. Jesus, on the other hand, asks John to give in for now and to go ahead and offer him the baptism of repentance. The Father and the Holy Spirit, on the other hand, respond to Jesus with enthusiasm and support, and offer a resounding 'Amen' so to speak, in the way they affirm Jesus. *"After Jesus was baptized, he came up from the water and behold, the heavens were opened [for him], and he saw the Spirit of God descending like a dove [and] coming upon him. And a voice came from the heavens, saying, "This is my beloved Son, with whom I am well pleased."* (Matthew 3:16-17)

In Matthew 4:1 we are told that Jesus was led into the desert by the Spirit of God to be tempted by the devil. Jesus continues to take upon Himself the burdens and consequences of sin, temptation being one of them, so that He can vanquish Satan, sin, and death, and in the process offer us the privilege of sharing in the fullness of His life (Colossians 2:9). This is a momentous confrontation with principalities and powers and the Holy Spirit's mission is to hover over Jesus! Jesus continues the establishment of God's reign in our midst through His public ministry, and for this *"Jesus returned to Galilee in the power of the Spirit, and news of him spread throughout the whole region. He taught in their synagogues and was praised by all."* (Luke 4:14-15) Jesus continued to be full of the power of the Spirit unto His death and resurrection. Peter sums it up well in his discourse: *"You who are Israelites, hear these words. Jesus the Nazorean was a man commended to you by God with mighty deeds, wonders, and signs, which God worked through him in your midst, as you yourselves know. This man, delivered up by the set plan and foreknowledge of God, you killed, using lawless men to crucify him. But God raised him up, releasing him from the throes of death, because it was impossible for him to be held by it… God raised this Jesus; of this we are all witnesses. Exalted at the right hand of God, he received the promise of the holy Spirit from the Father and poured it forth, as you (both) see and hear."* (Acts 2:22-23, 24, 32-33)

OUTPOURING OF THE HOLY SPIRIT UPON US:

On several occasions during Jesus' ministry, mention is made of the Holy Spirit and how there will be an outpouring upon us as Jesus Himself was filled by His Holy Spirit. During Jesus' public ministry, John the Baptist contrasts His baptism of repentance with the baptism that Jesus would be offering: *"I am baptizing you with water, but one mightier than I is coming. I am not worthy to loosen the thongs of his sandals. He will baptize you with the holy Spirit and with fire."* (Luke 3:16) During the Great Discourse, Jesus tells us that He will ask the Father and He will give us another Advocate to be with us always. He is the Spirit of Truth who will remain with us and in us (John 14:16-17). Jesus describes the Holy Spirit as 'another Advocate.' Jesus Himself is our first Advocate, and He assures us that the Holy Spirit will offer us the same kind of assurance, strength, and peace that the world cannot give. And in the workings of the Holy Spirit in our lives we will recognize the Presence and Life of Jesus. Furthermore, like

Jesus and the Father, the Holy Spirit will be our Emmanuel, God who dwells among us and within us. In the quotation offered in the very beginning of this session, we were told that the Holy Spirit scrutinizes all matters, even the deep things of God. The Holy Spirit's abode will be in our hearts as it is in God's innermost being. On the eve of His Ascension Jesus reiterates the necessity of being baptized by the Holy Spirit: *"While meeting with them, he enjoined them not to depart from Jerusalem, but to wait for "the promise of the Father about which you have heard me speak; for John baptized with water, but in a few days you will be baptized with the holy Spirit."* (Acts 1:4-5)

DESCENT OF THE HOLY SPIRIT:

The Descent of the Holy Spirit upon the apostles reverberated with the power and majesty of God and brought about amazing transformation in the apostles and the bystanders. We are told that *"… suddenly there came from the sky a noise like a strong driving wind, and it filled the entire house in which they were. Then there appeared to them tongues as of fire, which parted and came to rest on each one of them. And they were all filled with the holy Spirit and began to speak in different tongues, as the Spirit enabled them to proclaim."* (Acts2:2-4) The reaction of the bystanders, all of whom understood the apostles speaking to them in their own tongues, was astounding: *"(We are) both Jews and converts to Judaism, Cretans and Arabs, yet we hear them speaking in our own tongues of the mighty acts of God"* They were all astounded and bewildered, and said to one another, *"What does this mean?"* (Acts 2:11-12) The reaction of Peter to the whole experience, in particular, is amazing. Before the resurrection of Jesus and his baptism in the Holy Spirit, Peter was unreliable and testy. His protestations of loyalty and courage rang hollow so that Jesus predicted that Peter would deny him three times. And that is exactly what happened. Peter denied his Master three times and fled the scene of Jesus' Passion and death. However, now that he has been imbued with the power and grace of the Holy Spirit, a momentous transformation has been wrought in him. He is no longer afraid and is willing to go forth unshaken in his Master's footsteps, and witness boldly to Jesus: *"Therefore let the whole house of Israel know for certain that God has made him both Lord and Messiah, this Jesus whom you crucified." Now when they heard this, they were cut to the heart, and they asked Peter and the other apostles: "What are we to do, my brothers? Peter said to them, "Repent and be baptized, every one of you, in the name of Jesus Christ for the forgiveness of your sins; and you will receive the gift of the holy Spirit."* (Acts 2:36-38)

THE HOLY SPIRIT'S WORK IN OUR LIVES:

A central task entrusted to the Holy Spirit by Jesus is to instruct us in everything and remind us of all that Jesus told His disciples and us (John 14:26). The Holy Spirit is our mentor and guide, the One who causes Jesus to be our Risen Lord, to take Him seriously and to live in constant covenant relationship with Him as our Lord. It is within this covenant with Jesus that we share in the Trinitarian Life of Father, Son, and Holy Spirit. In John 16, Jesus makes an interesting remark about the necessity of leaving us and ascending to the Father, or else the Comforter will never come to us. It is the Holy Spirit who fashions us into the image and likeness of Jesus, makes Jesus constantly present to us so that we will never be orphans, and unites heaven and earth as God's community of martyrs, witnesses, and saints.

The Holy Spirit has a very challenging task ahead of Him. He will prove the world wrong *about sin*, namely that Jesus is the only Savior of the world. Only through Him does forgiveness of sins come to us; *about justice*, because the ultimate justice or right order of things is that Jesus as our Risen Lord has restored us to the Father whose children we now are and sits at the right hand of His Father in glory and victory; *about condemnation*, because through His death, Jesus has vanquished Satan, prince of this world (John 16:8-11). The Holy Spirit, therefore, is the Spirit of Truth who will guide us to all truth. In doing so, the Holy Spirit will bring glory to Jesus through the visible manifestation of Jesus' holiness in our lives.

In his Letter to the Galatians, Paul spells out very clearly the fruits of the Holy Spirit. Anyone who is under the umbrage of the Holy Spirit will produce these fruits. According to Paul, *"the fruit of the Spirit is love, joy, peace, patience, kindness, generosity, faithfulness, gentleness, self-control. Against such there is no law. Now those who belong to Christ [Jesus] have crucified their flesh with its passions and desires. If we live in the Spirit, let us also follow the Spirit."* (Galatians 5:22-25) The Holy Spirit is the bond between Father and Son, their Spirit in and through whom the Trinity reveals itself to us in loving kindness, always drawing us to share in the fullness of their divine life. The Holy Spirit reveals to us the innermost depths of God, transforming us into Christ, replacing our own minds and hearts with the mind and heart of our Savior and Lord, Jesus Christ. Through the Holy Spirit we cry 'Abba,' Father! Through the Holy Spirit we belong to God and no longer to ourselves.

FALLING IN LOVE WITH THE HOLY SPIRIT:

Throughout the history of Christian discipleship, holy men and women have excelled in the formation imparted to them through the Holy Spirit. The Holy Spirit became a real and loving presence in their lives, guiding them in their everyday decisions and activities and leading them into the heart of God's mystery. People like Saint Antony of the Desert, Saint Benedict, Saint Francis of Assisi, Saint Catherine of Siena, Saint Ignatius of Loyola, Saint Teresa of Avila, Saint John of the Cross, have given us marvelous insights as to how the Holy Spirit works in our lives. Here are some of their conclusions:

- The gift of discernment flows from the disciple's passionate commitment to live according to Jesus' teachings.
- Commitment is about serving God through service of God's people. True love expresses itself in deeds: *"Children, let us love not in word or speech but in deed and truth."* (1 John 3:18)
- When the opposing spirit is moving within us creating desolation, it is important to counter it with boldness. Any form of secrecy needs to be exposed. A good spiritual director or companion is always a great help.
- It is not enough to be generous in the spiritual life. One needs to develop wisdom that only the Holy Spirit can give. The disciple is constantly alert, even when all seems to be going well. Those who seek God's will in everyday life soon learn that they can never let their spiritual guard down. Vigilance, in both consolation and desolation, is the price of true discipleship: *"Be sober and vigilant. Your opponent the devil is prowling around like a roaring lion looking for [someone] to devour. Resist him, steadfast in faith, knowing that your fellow believers throughout the world undergo the same sufferings."* (1 Peter 5:8-9)
- Discernment is a gift and a task. It is a gift that the Holy Spirit will grant us if we ask assiduously for it. It is a task because the Holy Spirit desires our cooperation in making every effort to do God's will in our lives.
- Constant companionship with the Holy Spirit, during formal prayer and the day's events, will create a discerning lifestyle in the disciple.

PRAYER TO THE HOLY SPIRIT:

O Holy Spirit, I praise and adore you as God, as the Third Person of the Blessed Trinity. You are the Giver of God's Life. You are the divine Breath of my life, the Keeper of my soul. You scrutinize all matters, even the depths of God. In days of old, you spoke through the prophets, preparing God's covenant family for the coming of Jesus. In these last days, you speak to us through Jesus, the Word of God, revealing to us the profound truths of His teaching, and re-creating us in His image and likeness. You are the gift of the Father's love, given to us at the request of Jesus, our Savior and Lord.

Jesus described you as another Advocate who would dwell among us and in us. You are Emmanuel, dwelling among us and in us. Jesus also told us that you would reveal the inner truths of His teachings. I thank you for revealing Jesus to me, for probing the depths of my being with His compassion and love, and strengthening my resolve to be His faithful disciple. I thank you for revealing the Father to me through Jesus, for experiencing the Father's love for me in the fullness and tenderness of His love for Jesus. I thank you for deepening my relationship with you, for mentoring me in covenant union and life with God.

Jesus said that you would have a forensic role, convicting the world regarding sin and righteousness, and condemning Satan. I thank you for deepening my faith in Jesus as my Savior and Lord. I acknowledge Jesus as my Lord and Savior who sits at the right hand of the Father in glory, interceding on our behalf. I thank you for convicting the values of the world in me, showing me how deceptive and illusory they are. I thank you for showing me that Satan has been vanquished and condemned through the Risen Lord's victory on the cross. I thank you for giving me dominion over Satan in the name of Jesus.

I have been baptized in the death and resurrection of Jesus. In Jesus' death I have been empowered to conquer sin in my life, to carry my cross on a daily basis with trust and patience. In the resurrection of Jesus, I share in the victory of the Lamb that was slain, and His peace and joy reign in my heart. I was baptized in the name of the Father, Son, and Holy Spirit. As Emmanuel, you now dwell in the depths of my being, as the Keeper of my soul, as my Advocate who is leading me to the Father through Jesus, my Savior and Lord. As the Dweller of my soul, along with the Father and the Son, I am now privileged to be God's abode and your Sanctuary.

I thank you for journeying with me on a daily basis, comforting and strengthening me in my daily trials and tribulations. I thank you for convicting me when I pay scant heed to your voice, or even ignore it. You then leave me in sadness and dissatisfaction, inviting me back to repentance and obedience to your authority over me. And while you convict me in my sin, I never feel condemned, because you are the Holy Spirit, incarnating divine love and compassion through Jesus, and with the Father and the Son, deeply committed to my covenant union with the Blessed Trinity.

Come, Holy Spirit, and continue to overshadow me with your gentle wisdom and power. Purify my mind and heart as I seek to make the teachings of Jesus my priority in life, thinking, speaking, and doing as He desires. You are the Keeper of my soul, leading me into God's heart. May I be docile and submissive to your wisdom and guidance, and may my life be a pleasing offering in your sight, through Christ our Lord. Amen. Triune God, be my all! Triune God, be my all! Triune God, be my all!

PRAYER AND REFLECTION ON KNOWING THE HOLY SPIRIT IN THE TRINITY

WEEK SEVENTEEN: *"I HAVE BAPTIZED YOU WITH WATER; HE WILL BAPTIZE YOU WITH THE HOLY SPIRIT." (MARK 1:8)*

SPIRITUAL READING FOR THE WEEK:

- **Anoint Us in Your Covenant, Abba-Emmanuel:** Session Nine
- **Old Testament:** Two or Three Chapters daily
- **New Testament:** Two or Three Chapters daily
- **Imitation of Christ:** One chapter daily

DAY ONE: MORNING SESSION

MORNING PRAYER: Acts of Faith, Hope, Charity; Daily Offering

Morning Face to Face with God:

Begin with Prayer to the Holy Spirit

REFLECTIONS ON KNOWING THE HOLY SPIRIT IN THE TRINITY:

(After pondering each bullet point, express your sentiments in a short prayer)

- The Holy Spirit scrutinizes all matters, even the deep things of God. God's Spirit has the power to probe God's innermost depths that He indwells. The Holy Spirit picks up every nuance in God's depths and gives voice to it through Jesus, the Word of God.
- We can assume with confidence therefore that the Holy Spirit will reveal to us even the tiniest wisps of divine tenderness and love within the Trinity and toward us, what eye has not seen, what ear has not heard!
- The Father and the Son know themselves and each other in their Holy Spirit. It is therefore only in the Holy Spirit that we can know the Father and the Son: *"Therefore, I tell you that nobody speaking by the spirit of God says, "Jesus be accursed." And no one can say, "Jesus is Lord," except by the holy Spirit."* (1 Corinthians 12:3)
- It makes eminent sense therefore, that Jesus asked and received the promise of the Holy Spirit from His Father to continue the work of revealing the Father and the Son to His disciples.
- It was also necessary that Jesus return to His Father, or else the Holy Spirit would not come. Without the baptism of the Holy Spirit, the Kingdom of God, firmly established

by Jesus, could not be inaugurated. The inauguration could only happen in and through the Outpouring of the Holy Spirit.

- God always intended that we would be filled with "the breath of life," namely the Holy Spirit, or else we could not be the image and likeness of God, or ever be capable of entering into covenant with God! God would not allow 'the breath of life' to be destroyed in us by sin. Our restoration to the fullness of The Holy Spirit, our Breath of life, has been made possible through the death and resurrection of Jesus who is LORD!
- Jesus describes the Holy Spirit as 'another Advocate.' Jesus Himself is our first Advocate, and He assures us that the Holy Spirit will offer us the same kind of assurance, strength, and peace that the world cannot give. And in the workings of the Holy Spirit in our lives we will recognize the Presence and Life of Jesus.
- Furthermore, like Jesus and the Father, the Holy Spirit will be our Emmanuel, God who dwells among us and within us. The Holy Spirit's abode will be in our hearts as it is in God's innermost being.
- On the eve of His Ascension Jesus reiterates the necessity of being baptized by the Holy Spirit: *"While meeting with them, he enjoined them not to depart from Jerusalem, but to wait for 'the promise of the Father about which you have heard me speak; for John baptized with water, but in a few days you will be baptized with the holy Spirit.'"* (Acts 1:4-5)

What is God saying to you?

End with Prayer to the Holy Trinity

NIGHT SESSION: Examination of Conscience

For what are you grateful? For what are you contrite?

Please review briefly your Morning Prayer topic. Make it your last thought of the day

DAY TWO: MORNING SESSION

MORNING PRAYER: Act of Faith; Act of Hope; Act of Charity; Daily Offering

Morning Face to Face with God:

Begin with Prayer to the Holy Spirit
Prayer on John 7:37-39: Rivers of Living Water
> *"On the last and greatest day of the feast, Jesus stood up and exclaimed, "Let anyone who thirsts come to me and drink. Whoever believes in me, as scripture says: 'Rivers of living water will flow*

from within him.'" He said this in reference to the Spirit that those who came to believe in him were to receive. There was, of course, no Spirit yet, because Jesus had not yet been glorified."

Read the Reflection; Thank the Holy Spirit for being the Keeper of your soul, and ask for the grace to be a dedicated temple of the Holy Trinity

This is the second time that Jesus has gone up to Jerusalem in the gospel of John. He is there for the celebration of Sukkot, or the feast of Booths, a fall harvest festival. It also commemorated the 40 years of Jewish wandering in the desert after the enactment of the Sinai Covenant. In His teaching, Jesus is doing several things. He is clearly laying claim to the fact that He is the Source of Life: *"Let anyone who thirsts come to me and drink."* Jesus is the Way, the Truth, and the Life for anyone, not just for a select few. We gain entrance to the Source of eternal life, symbolized by living water, through faith in Jesus: *"Rivers of living water will flow from within him."* Jesus is also proclaiming the advent of the new and everlasting covenant which He would bring about through His death on the cross and resurrection. And through the Holy Spirit this covenant bond with our Triune God would be sealed: *"He said this in reference to the Spirit that those who came to believe in him were to receive."*

What is God saying to you?

End with Prayer to the Holy Trinity

NIGHT SESSION: Examination of Conscience

For what are you grateful? For what are you contrite?

Please review briefly your Morning Prayer topic. Make it your last thought of the day

DAY THREE: MORNING SESSION

MORNING PRAYER: Act of Faith; Act of Hope; Act of Charity; Daily Offering

Morning Face to Face with God:

Begin with Prayer to the Holy Spirit
Prayer on Luke 11:13: The Answer to Prayer

"If you then, who are wicked, know how to give good gifts to your children, how much more will the Father in heaven give the holy Spirit to those who ask him?"

Read the Reflection; Thank the Holy Spirit for being the Keeper of your soul, and ask for the grace to be a dedicated temple of the Holy Trinity

No one knows the Holy Spirit more intimately and lovingly than the Father and Jesus. They desire that we live in covenant relationship with the Trinity. Hence, they are sharing everything with us without any reservation. The Father has given Himself to us through His Son. In the power of the Holy Spirit, Jesus has given Himself to us by becoming one of us and rescuing us from the snatches of sin and Satan by dying on the cross. And now, the Father and Son are giving us their Holy Spirit to be ours, so that we might be obedient to the Father's will in the power of the Holy Spirit! Through the Holy Spirit we can surrender our lives and be in covenant union with the Holy Trinity. If we ask earnestly, we will receive the Holy Spirit in abundance.

What is God saying to you?

End with Prayer to the Holy Trinity

NIGHT SESSION: Examination of Conscience

For what are you grateful? For what are you contrite?

Please review briefly your Morning Prayer topic. Make it your last thought of the day

DAY FOUR: MORNING SESSION

MORNING PRAYER: Act of Faith; Act of Hope; Act of Charity; Daily Offering

Morning Face to Face with God:

Begin with Prayer to the Holy Spirit
Prayer on Acts 1:6-9: "Imminent Coming of the Holy Spirit":
"But you will receive power when the holy Spirit comes upon you, and you will be witnesses in Jerusalem, throughout Judea and Samaria, and to the ends of the earth." [Please read Acts 1:1-14 for a better appreciation of the passage].

Read the Reflection; Thank the Holy Spirit for being the Keeper of your soul, and ask for the grace to be a dedicated temple of the Holy Trinity

"Lord, are you at this time going to restore the kingdom to Israel?" (Acts 1:6), is a question the disciples asked Jesus just before His Ascension. The question implies that in believing Jesus to

be the Christ, they had expected Him to be a political leader who would restore self-rule to Israel during His historical ministry. When this had not taken place, they ask if it is to take place at this time, the period of the church. Just as Jerusalem was the city of destiny in the Gospel of Luke, the place where salvation was accomplished, so here at the beginning of Acts, Jerusalem occupies a central position. It is the starting point for the mission of the disciples of Jesus, to begin in Jerusalem and go to the ends of the earth, which for Luke meant Rome. This establishment and expansion of the true kingdom of Christ was to happen in the power of the Holy Spirit. Through His power, the disciples would become able and enthusiastic witnesses. And they prepare for the coming of the Holy Spirit through prayer in the Upper Room, and Mary, the mother of Jesus, was with them (Acts 1:13-14).

What is God saying to you?

End with Prayer to the Holy Trinity

NIGHT SESSION: Examination of Conscience

For what are you grateful? For what are you contrite?

Please review briefly your Morning Prayer topic. Make it your last thought of the day

DAY FIVE: MORNING SESSION

MORNING PRAYER: Act of Faith; Act of Hope; Act of Charity; Daily Offering

Morning Face to Face with God:

Begin with Prayer to the Holy Spirit
Prayer on Matthew 28:18-20: The Commissioning of the Disciples
   "Then Jesus approached and said to them, "All power in heaven and on earth has been given to me. Go, therefore, and make disciples of all nations, baptizing them in the name of the Father, and of the Son, and of the holy Spirit, teaching them to observe all that I have commanded you.""

Read the Reflection; Thank the Holy Spirit for being the Keeper of your soul, and ask for the grace to be a dedicated temple of the Holy Trinity

Jesus is now the Risen Lord, the great I AM! He is the one to whom *"all power in heaven and on earth has been given."* Just before His ascension to become our Intercessor in heaven, Jesus sends His disciples on a very important mission. He commissions them to make disciples of all nations, *"baptizing them in the name of the Father, and of the Son, and of the Holy Spirit, teaching them to observe all that I have commanded you."* The Risen Lord has accomplished His Father's mission to bring eternal life to all who believe in Him as Lord and Savior, to make them sharers in the divine nature (2 Peter 1:4). Just as Jesus was sent by the Father, in the same vein and with the same divine power, He sends His disciples to make disciples of everyone who believes in Jesus through baptism. The Greek word 'Baptizo' means to dip repeatedly, and is used 63 times in the New Testament. Our baptism with water goes hand in hand with faith in Jesus: *"Whoever believes and is baptized will be saved."* (Mark 16:16) Mere intellectual assent is not enough. A real change needs to take place. In baptism, this change happens in the name of the Father, Son, and Holy Spirit. We now belong to our Triune God in a covenant relationship. We now share in the fullness of divine life, in the secure knowledge that we are sons and daughters of the Living God whom we now address with Jesus as Abba, Father. This verse from Matthew is a clear statement of the divinity of the Holy Spirit and the oneness of God in Three Persons.

What is God saying to you?

End with Prayer to the Holy Trinity

NIGHT SESSION: Examination of Conscience

For what are you grateful? For what are you contrite?

Please review briefly your Morning Prayer topic. Make it your last thought of the day

DAY SIX: MORNING SESSION

MORNING PRAYER: Act of Faith; Act of Hope; Act of Charity; Daily Offering

Morning Face to Face with God:

Begin with Prayer to the Holy Spirit

OUR PRAYER TO THE HOLY SPIRIT: p.221

> *Thank Jesus for being your Risen Lord who has brought you into covenant union with our Triune God, and ask to be His devoted disciple*

Today, you will pray with *"Our Prayer to the Holy Spirit"* from the Session. You can go over this prayer once or twice, tasting and relishing the Holy Spirit's compassionate care of your soul, re-creating you constantly in the image and likeness of Jesus, and leading you to the Father in and through His Son. *"Our Prayer to the Holy Spirit"* can act as a repetition of Days Two through Five of this week. In a repetition St. Ignatius says that *"we should pay attention to and dwell upon those points in which we have experienced greater consolation or desolation or greater spiritual appreciation."* (# 62)

What is God saying to you?

End with Prayer to the Holy Trinity

NIGHT SESSION: Examination of Conscience

For what are you grateful? For what are you contrite?

Please review briefly your Morning Prayer topic. Make it your last thought of the day

DAY SEVEN: MORNING SESSION

MORNING PRAYER: Act of Faith; Act of Hope; Act of Charity; Daily Offering

Morning Face to Face with God:

Begin with Prayer to the Holy Spirit

THE SIXTH DWELLING PLACES: LOCUTIONS FROM THE IMAGINATION:

- St. Teresa maintains that when locutions come from the imagination they do not have the signs of a true and authentic locution. There is neither certitude, nor peace, nor interior delight.
- These imagined locutions could be experienced during the time of prayer, and the person might feel strongly that these locutions are spoken to them and even that they see things. However, they clearly lack the true signs of an authentic locution.

INTELLECTUAL LOCUTIONS:

- St. Teresa is very positive that intellectual locutions are definitely from God: *"The locution takes place in such intimate depths and a person with the ears of the soul seems to hear those words from the Lord Himself so clearly and so in secret that this very way in which they are heard, together with the acts that the vision itself produces, assures that person and gives him certitude that the devil can have no part to play in the locution."* (TIC – VI:3:12)
- There are several signs given to the soul to say that such a locution is authentic and from God. The locution is so clear that the soul remembers every syllable and whether

it is said in one style or another, even if it is a whole sentence. In a locution from the imagination, the words will not be so clear or distinct but like something dreamed up.

- Secondly, these locutions come to one most unexpectedly, about matters in the future that never entered the mind.
- Thirdly, *"the one locution comes as in the case of a person who hears* (intellectual locution), *and that of the imagination* (locution from the imagination) *as in the case of a person who gradually composes what he himself wants to be told…"*
- Fourthly, *"the words are very different, and with one of them much is comprehended. Our intellect could not compose them so quickly…"*
- Fifth, *"together with the words … there is often given much more to understand than is ever dreamed possible without words."* (TIC – VI:3:14-16)

RAPTURE, ECSTASY, TRANSPORT:

- The whole purpose of being subjected to trials and suffering is in order to prepare the soul for many graces of deeper union. One such grace is rapture or ecstasy, or transport, all of which are the same in St. Teresa's opinion.
- She describes them in Chapter 4 of The Sixth Dwelling Places. *"One kind of rapture is that in which the soul even though not in prayer is touched by some word it remembers or hears about God. It seems that His Majesty from the interior of the soul… is moved with compassion in seeing the soul suffer so long a time from its desire. All burnt up, the soul is renewed like the phoenix, and one can devoutly believe that its faults are pardoned. Now that it is so pure, the Lord joins it with Himself, without anyone understanding what is happening except these two."* (TIC – VI:4:3)
- One result of such rapture is that the soul experiences a deep enlightenment and knowledge of God. In a state of rapture, the soul can have imaginative and intellectual visions. They are so memorable that they are never forgotten.
- St. Teresa talks about ecstasy and describes it in the following manner: *"He takes away the breath so that, even though the other senses sometimes last a little longer, a person cannot speak at all; although at other times everything is taken away at once, and the hands and the body grow cold so that the person doesn't seem to have any life; nor sometimes is it known whether he is breathing. This situation lasts but a short while. I mean in its intensity; for when this extreme suspension lets up a little, it seems that the body returns to itself somewhat and is nourished so as to die again and give more life to the soul. Nevertheless so extreme an ecstasy doesn't last long."* (TIC – VI:4:13)
- The result of such an experience is that *"the will becomes so absorbed and the will so withdrawn, for a day or even days, that the latter seems incapable of understanding anything*

that doesn't lead to awakening the will to love; and the will is wide awake to this love and asleep to becoming attached to any creature." (TIC – VI:4:14)

- St. Teresa describes another kind of rapture that she describes as a flight of the spirit. It is experienced differently interiorly. *"Suddenly a movement of the soul is felt so swift that it seems the spirit is carried off, and at a fearful speed especially in the beginning… At the beginning of this swift movement there is not so much certitude that the rapture is from God."* (TIC – VI:5:1)

- According to St. Teresa, great courage is required on the part of the soul as this favor (flight of the spirit) is something frightening. If God did not give the soul this courage it would be deeply distressed.

- In this quick rapture of the spirit, the spirit seems to go forth from the body into an entirely different region where the light is so different from earth's light. When he comes to his senses, the soul would be unable to imagine that light and all the other things that it experienced in that realm.

- And the soul while in rapture would not be able to tell whether the soul is in the body or that the body is without a soul.

What is God saying to you?

End with Prayer to the Holy Trinity

NIGHT SESSION: Examination of Conscience

For what are you grateful? For what are you contrite?

What prayer would you compose to express what God has said to you this week?

Please review briefly your Morning Prayer topic. Make it your last thought of the day

PRAYER AND REFLECTION ON KNOWING THE HOLY SPIRIT IN THE TRINITY – CONTINUED

WEEK EIGHTEEN: *"AND HOPE DOES NOT DISAPPOINT, BECAUSE THE LOVE OF GOD HAS BEEN POURED OUT INTO OUR HEARTS THROUGH THE HOLY SPIRIT THAT HAS BEEN GIVEN TO US."* *(ROMANS 5:5)*

SPIRITUAL READING FOR THE WEEK:

- **Anoint Us in Your Covenant, Abba-Emmanuel:** Session Nine
- **Old Testament:** Two or Three Chapters daily
- **New Testament:** Two or Three Chapters daily
- **Imitation of Christ:** One chapter daily

DAY ONE: MORNING SESSION

MORNING PRAYER: Acts of Faith, Hope, Charity; Daily Offering

Morning Face to Face with God:

Begin with Prayer to the Holy Spirit

ON KNOWING THE HOLY SPIRIT IN THE TRINITY:

(After pondering each bullet point, express your sentiments in a short prayer)

- Before the resurrection of Jesus and his baptism in the Holy Spirit, Peter was unreliable and testy. His protestations of loyalty and courage rang hollow so that Jesus predicted that Peter would deny him three times. And that is exactly what happened. Peter denied his Master three times and fled the scene of Jesus' Passion and death.
- However, now that he has been imbued with the power and grace of the Holy Spirit, a momentous transformation has been wrought in him. He is no longer afraid and is willing to go forth unshaken in his Master's footsteps and witness boldly to Jesus.
- A central task entrusted to the Holy Spirit by Jesus is to instruct us in everything and remind us of all that Jesus told His disciples and us (John 14:26). The Holy Spirit is our mentor and guide, the One who causes Jesus to be our Risen Lord, to take Him seriously and to live in constant covenant relationship with Him as our Lord.
- Throughout the history of Christian discipleship, holy men and women have excelled in the formation imparted to them through the Holy Spirit. The Holy Spirit became

a real and loving presence in their lives, guiding them in their everyday decisions and activities and leading them into the heart of God's mystery.

- The gift of discernment flows from the disciple's passionate commitment to live according to Jesus' teachings. Discernment is a gift and a task. It is a gift that the Holy Spirit will grant us if we ask assiduously for it. It is a task because the Holy Spirit desires our cooperation in making every effort to do God's will in our lives.

- It is not enough to be generous in the spiritual life. One needs to develop wisdom that only the Holy Spirit can give. The disciple is constantly alert, even when all seems to be going well. Those who seek God's will in everyday life soon learn that they can never let their spiritual guard down. Vigilance, in both consolation and desolation, is the price of true discipleship.

- Constant companionship with the Holy Spirit, during formal prayer and during the day's events, will create a discerning lifestyle in the disciple.

- To bring about this covenant union of God with His human covenant family, the fellowship or communion of the Holy Spirit has been offered to us. Through the Holy Spirit, the Trinity invites us into God's life and relationships. For us it is communion because we are being brought to participate in God's union.

- From being aliens and outsiders, we are brought into union with God, given entrance into God's Sanctuary, offered the privilege of praising, adoring, and thanking the Trinity ceaselessly, as the Father's sons and daughters.

What is God saying to you?

End with Prayer to the Holy Trinity

NIGHT SESSION: Examination of Conscience

For what are you grateful? For what are you contrite?

Please review briefly your Morning Prayer topic. Make it your last thought of the day

DAY TWO: MORNING SESSION

MORNING PRAYER: Act of Faith; Act of Hope; Act of Charity; Daily Offering

Morning Face to Face with God:

Begin with Prayer to the Holy Spirit
Prayer on Romans 5:2-5: The Holy Spirit has been poured out:

"Through Him we have gained access [by faith] to this grace in which we stand, and we boast in hope of the glory of God. Not only that, but we even boast of our afflictions, knowing that affliction produces endurance, and endurance, proven character, and proven character, hope, and hope does not disappoint, because the love of God has been poured out into our hearts through the holy Spirit that has been given to us."

Read the Reflection; Thank the Holy Spirit for being the Keeper of your soul, and ask for the grace to be a dedicated temple of the Holy Trinity

The love of God has been poured out into our hearts through the holy Spirit that has been given to us: Through the outpouring of God's love for us through the Holy Spirit, Paul's life has been transformed. He has been able to identify with the crucified Christ in his ministry to God's covenant family. He accepts afflictions that come his way and even sees great blessings come to him through them: endurance, proven character, and hope. Such a transformation is wrought at the hands of the Holy Spirit

What is God saying to you?

End with Prayer to the Holy Trinity

NIGHT SESSION: Examination of Conscience

For what are you grateful? For what are you contrite?

Please review briefly your Morning Prayer topic. Make it your last thought of the day

DAY THREE: MORNING SESSION

MORNING PRAYER: Act of Faith; Act of Hope; Act of Charity; Daily Offering

Morning Face to Face with God:

Begin with Prayer to the Holy Spirit
Prayer on 1 Corinthians 2:10b-13: The True Wisdom:

"For the Spirit scrutinizes everything, even the depths of God… No one knows what pertains to God except the Spirit of God. We have not received the spirit of the world but the Spirit that is from God, so that we may understand the things freely given us by God. And we speak about them not with words taught by human wisdom, but with words taught by the Spirit, describing spiritual realities in spiritual terms."

Read the Reflection; Thank the Holy Spirit for being the Keeper of your soul, and ask for the grace to be a dedicated temple of the Holy Trinity

1. *For the Spirit scrutinizes everything, even the depths of God...so that we may understand the things freely given us by God:* Here is another example of God sharing everything with us that belongs to Him. The Divine Spirit is familiar with the depths of God, because He shares the same divine essence with the Father and the Son. This same Holy Spirit dwells in the depths of our being and shares with us the depths of God! Amazing, but true, that God shares intimately with us everything that is His, all the time!

2. *And we speak about them not with words taught by human wisdom, but with words taught by the Spirit, describing spiritual realities in spiritual terms:* As we grow in discipleship and live under the authority of the Holy Spirit, we begin to see that the Holy Spirit is revealing to us spiritual realities that we could never access through human wisdom. The Holy Spirit does indeed become our Mentor and Guide!

What is God saying to you?

End with Prayer to the Holy Trinity

NIGHT SESSION: Examination of Conscience

For what are you grateful? For what are you contrite?

Please review briefly your Morning Prayer topic. Make it your last thought of the day

DAY FOUR: MORNING SESSION

MORNING PRAYER: Act of Faith; Act of Hope; Act of Charity; Daily Offering

Morning Face to Face with God:

Begin with Prayer to the Holy Spirit
Prayer on 1 John 5:6-9: The Holy Spirit's Testimony
   "This is the one who came through water and blood, Jesus Christ, not by water alone, but by water and blood. The Spirit is the one that testifies, and the Spirit is truth. So there are three that testify, the Spirit, the water, and the blood, and the three are of one accord. If we accept human testimony, the testimony of God is surely greater."

Read the Reflection; Thank the Holy Spirit for being the Keeper of your soul, and ask for the grace to be a dedicated temple of the Holy Trinity

1John is reflecting on the important landmarks in the accomplishment of God's plan of salvation through Jesus. Jesus is *"the one who came through water."* Through His baptism at the hands of John the Baptist, the Sinless One identified with us sinners. He became sin on our behalf. He accepted John's baptism of repentance on our behalf. He continued with this identification on our behalf throughout His public ministry, leading Him to come *"through water and blood ... not by water alone, but by water and blood." Through blood* is a clear reference to Jesus' death on the cross. The Holy Spirit testified at both times. The Holy Spirit came upon Jesus after His baptism and Jesus did His public ministry in the power of the Holy Spirit, leading Him to shed His blood on the cross as a reparation offering. John says that the testimony of God is greater than the testimony of humans. God offers three witnesses: the Holy Spirit at Jesus' baptism and in His ministry, including His death and resurrection; water, referring to His baptism by John; and blood, referring to His death on the cross. In Deuteronomy 17:6 only two witnesses were required for ratification.

What is God saying to you?

End with Prayer to the Holy Trinity

NIGHT SESSION: Examination of Conscience

For what are you grateful? For what are you contrite?

Please review briefly your Morning Prayer topic. Make it your last thought of the day

DAY FIVE: MORNING SESSION

MORNING PRAYER: Act of Faith; Act of Hope; Act of Charity; Daily Offering

Morning Face to Face with God:

Begin with Prayer to the Holy Spirit
Prayer on Ephesians 1:13-14: Inheritance through the Spirit:
> *"In him (Jesus) you also, who have heard the word of truth, the gospel of your salvation, and have believed in him, were sealed with the promised holy Spirit, which is the first installment of our inheritance toward redemption as God's possession, to the praise of his glory."*

Read the Reflection; Thank the Holy Spirit for being the Keeper of your soul, and ask for the grace to be a dedicated temple of the Holy Trinity

The Holy Spirit is the first and perfect installment of our inheritance toward redemption as God's possession. Jesus is the purchaser. He has purchased our inheritance for us, which is participation in God's life as His children. The Holy Spirit is our down payment, so to speak. The Holy Trinity, out of their amazing love for us, has made sure, that our salvation and inheritance would be ensured every step of the way! This promise of salvation is assured, because through Jesus' death and resurrection it is founded in the Power and Presence of the Holy Spirit who dwells among us and within us!

What is God saying to you?

End with Prayer to the Holy Trinity

NIGHT SESSION: Examination of Conscience

For what are you grateful? For what are you contrite?

Please review briefly your Morning Prayer topic. Make it your last thought of the day

DAY SIX: MORNING SESSION

MORNING PRAYER: Act of Faith; Act of Hope; Act of Charity; Daily Offering

Morning Face to Face with God:

Begin with Prayer to the Holy Spirit

OUR PRAYER TO THE HOLY SPIRIT: p. 221

Thank Jesus for being your Risen Lord who has brought you into covenant union with our Triune God, and ask to be His devoted disciple

Today, you will pray with *"Our Prayer to the Holy Spirit"* from the Session. You can go over this prayer once or twice, tasting and relishing the Holy Spirit's compassionate care of your soul, re-creating you constantly in the image and likeness of Jesus, and leading you to the Father in and through His Son. *"Our Prayer to the Holy Spirit"* can act as a repetition of Days Two through Five of this week. In a repetition St. Ignatius says that *"we should pay attention to and dwell upon those points in which we have experienced greater consolation or desolation or greater spiritual appreciation."* (# 62)

What is God saying to you?

End with Prayer to the Holy Trinity

NIGHT SESSION: Examination of Conscience

For what are you grateful? For what are you contrite?

Please review briefly your Morning Prayer topic. Make it your last thought of the day

DAY SEVEN: MORNING SESSION

MORNING PRAYER: Act of Faith; Act of Hope; Act of Charity; Daily Offering

Morning Face to Face with God:

Begin with Prayer to the Holy Spirit

THE SIXTH DWELLING PLACES: INTELLECTUAL VISIONS:

- St. Teresa describes an intellectual vision as follows: *"It will happen while the soul is heedless of any thought about such a favor being granted to it, and though it never had a thought that it deserved this vision, that it will feel Jesus Christ, our Lord, beside it. Yet, it does not see Him, either with the eyes of the body or with those of the soul. This is called an intellectual vision."* (TIC – VI:8:2)

- The soul has certainty about the presence of Jesus and the effects that the soul experiences leaves it in no doubt: *"The vision was a great help toward walking with a habitual remembrance of God and a deep concern about avoiding anything displeasing to Him, for it seemed to her that He was always looking at her. And each time she wanted to speak with His Majesty in prayer, and even outside of it, she felt He was so near that He couldn't fail to hear her. But she didn't hear words spoken whenever she wanted; only unexpectedly when they were necessary… Afterward she understood clearly that the vision was not caused by the devil, which became more and more clear as time went on."* (TIC – VI:8:3)

- Such a grace is a great favor given to the soul without any merits on its part. The soul would not exchange this blessing for any earthly treasure or delight. And when the Lord chooses to take the vision away, the soul feels very much alone. An intellectual vision can also be of a saint or Mary, Mother of God.

IMAGINATIVE VISIONS:

- In the imaginative vision, St. Teresa says that *"He shows it (the soul) His most sacred humanity in the way He desires; either as He was when He went about in the world or as He is after His resurrection. And even though the vision happens so quickly that we could compare it to a streak of lightning, this most glorious image remains so engraved on the imagination that I think it would be impossible to erase it until it is seen by the soul in that place where it will be enjoyed without end."* (TIC – VI:9:3)
- St. Teresa says that this Presence bears such extraordinary majesty that is causes the soul extreme fright. In the interior world of the soul, a great stirring takes place; the soul is so well instructed about so many great truths that it has no need of any other master.
- *"True Wisdom has taken away the mind's dullness and leaves a certitude, which lasts for some time, that this favor is from God. However much the soul is told the contrary, others cannot then cause it fear that there could be any deception… The devil can present a vision, but not with this truth and majesty and these results."* (TIC – VI:9:10)
- St. Teresa cautions us against desiring imaginative visions. Desiring such a favor shows a lack of humility; we are asking for something that we do not deserve.
- Secondly, such a person, who desires imaginative visions, will be prone to be led astray by the devil.
- Thirdly, when the imagination is backed by strong desire, it tends to see and hear what it desires.
- Fourthly, it would be foolishness to choose a path while being ignorant about what is best for us. Such matters are best left to the Lord.
- Fifthly, such imaginative visions are given to souls who have been purified by severe trials.
- Lastly, such an inordinate desire will spell the soul's ruin.

What is God saying to you?

End with Prayer to the Holy Trinity

NIGHT SESSION: Examination of Conscience

For what are you grateful? For what are you contrite?

What prayer would you compose to express what God has said to you this week?

Please review briefly your Morning Prayer topic. Make it your last thought of the day

SESSION TEN
EUCHARIST: GATHERED WITH THE LAMB
IN THE HOLY SPIRIT

"Everyone who commits sin commits lawlessness, for sin is lawlessness. You know that he was revealed to take away sins, and in him there is no sin. No one who remains in him sins; no one who sins has seen him or known him."

– James 3:4-5

THE GATHERING OF GOD'S COVENANT FAMILY:

Every Sunday we begin our Eucharistic celebration with the Gathering of God's covenant family through a hymn, appropriately called the Gathering Song or Processional Hymn. This is a very momentous assembly. It consists of the Lamb that was slain, with His covenant family congregated around Him in heaven, inviting us, His body, who are the Holy Spirit's Gathering of God's covenant family here on earth, to join in the heavenly Eucharistic celebration. Holy Mother Church, or God's covenant family, is acutely aware of this extra-terrestrial or supernatural dimension, as is evidenced in her prayer throughout the Eucharistic celebration. The Church also remembers, through her intercessory prayer, another very significant segment of God's covenant family that is present in this august assembly: God's holy people being purified of their sins in Purgatory. In the Eucharistic Prayer, the holy souls in Purgatory are given a prominent place in the assembly's intercessory prayer.

We, the pilgrim Church, join with our heavenly family and celebrate covenant union with the Trinity, centered in the Eucharistic banquet of the Lamb that was slain. This glorious celebration of both the Triumphant and Pilgrim church is taking place continually, as envisaged in Revelation 5:13: *"Then I heard every creature in heaven and on earth and under the earth and in the sea, everything in the universe, cry out: "To the one who sits on the throne and to the Lamb be blessing and honor, and glory and might, forever and ever."* It is a celebration that goes on all day, every day.

BEING SIGNED WITH THE CROSS:

The Presider, acting in the name of Jesus, begins the Eucharistic celebration with the Sign of the Cross. The cross is our symbol of salvation, as Jesus died on the cross for our sins. The cross was the ultimate sign of degradation, as it was the symbol of capital punishment. Jesus accepted the abysmal humiliation of the cross on our behalf, to free us from our bondage to

Satan and sin. In this way, the cross was made the ultimate sign of triumph over Satan and sin, of grace and entrance into God's love and life!

In Catholic homes and institutions the crucifix is given a place of prominence. In her wisdom, Mother Church has asked us to begin and end our day, and all we do and say, with the Sign of the Cross. In baptism we were baptized into the death of Jesus on the Cross, and rose with Him in His resurrection. As Paul tells us in his Letter to the Colossians, *"You were buried with him in baptism, in which you were also raised with him through faith in the power of God, who raised him from the dead."* (Colossians 2:12) In this way we were brought into the life and love of the Father, Son, and Holy Spirit through Jesus' death on the cross.

In signing ourselves with the name of our Triune God, we are stating boldly and uncompromisingly that we belong to God in covenant union. In return for His total offering of Himself to us through His Son, Jesus Christ, we have surrendered ownership of our lives to God. We trust completely in the power and protection of our Triune God. In the early centuries of Christianity, this ritual of signing ourselves with the cross was always understood to be a source of divine power and protection. God is our Good Shepherd and even though we walk *"through the valley of the shadow of death"* (Psalm 23), no harm will come to us because we walk with Him in the saving event of His death and resurrection.

Therefore, as we begin our celebration with the Sign of the Cross, we express our profound gratitude to the Trinity for sharing with us the divine life made possible through the crucifixion and death of Jesus on the cross. In the Sign of the Cross, we pray that our lives will be lived in ever greater harmony with God, and that we will do everything only in God's name. It is important, then, that we put our whole heart and soul into the making of the Sign of the Cross upon ourselves. It makes sense to make a deliberate, unhurried Sign of the Cross, from forehead to breast, and shoulder to shoulder, offering our thoughts, actions, every part of our being, in loving surrender to our loving God. Through this gesture, we are stating very deliberately that we belong to God's covenant family. Through the Sign of the Cross, we consecrate ourselves in the strength and salvation of Christ, in the Name of the Father, Son, and Holy Spirit.

THE GREETING SAYS IT ALL:

In the name of Jesus, the Presider then welcomes us and chooses one of several greetings. The following is the greeting we usually hear on Sunday: *"The grace of the Lord Jesus Christ, the love of God, and the communion of the Holy Spirit be with you all."* This greeting is taken from 2 Corinthians 13:13. It is the last verse of the last chapter of Paul's Second Letter to the Corinthians. It is probably one of the best recapitulations of God's Plan of Salvation on our behalf. *'The grace of the Lord Jesus Christ'* is the unmerited gift to us of sharing in God's divine life, made possible through the death and resurrection of Jesus Christ. Jesus is our Savior because He is Lord. As one of us, He has bridged the chasm between God and us, caused by our sin. As Son of God, Jesus could do what we could not. And now we share in His relationship with the Father and the Holy Spirit. With Him, in Him, and through Him, we now address His Father as Our Father!

'The love of God' has made possible this indescribable gift of participation in the divine nature through Jesus. John 3:16 highlights this passionate commitment of the Father to us, and His generous decision to give us His only Son: *"For God so loved the world that he gave his only Son, so that everyone who believes in him might not perish but might have eternal life."*

To bring about this covenant union of God with His human covenant family, *the communion or fellowship of the Holy Spirit* has been offered to us. Through the Holy Spirit, the Trinity invites us into God's life and relationships. From being aliens and outsiders, we are brought into union with God, given entrance into God's Sanctuary, offered the privilege of praising, adoring, and thanking the Trinity ceaselessly, as the Father's sons and daughters. Communion is God's gift to us to share in what belongs quintessentially only to God: the Divine Life. In His magnanimous love for us, God has fostered an inextricable bond between Him and us through communion or fellowship with Him.

Another greeting that the Presider might use is, *"The Lord be with you."* We have been gathered by the Holy Spirit in the name of Jesus. We are a community of believers assembled in His name. Jesus said in Matthew 18:20: *"Where two or three are gathered together in my name, there I am in the midst of them."* This greeting makes it clear that Jesus is present in our midst. The response, *"And with your spirit,"* expresses the profound reality that we are temples of the Blessed Trinity by virtue of our baptism. Through this greeting, therefore, the priest is asking God to increase the growth of divine life that we received in baptism.

The Lord be with you, reminds us of similar words of assurance that God spoke to a wide variety of biblical stalwarts whenever He sent them on a perilous mission. The mission could only be done in the power of God, and total trust on the part of the one being missioned was required. God told Moses that He would go with him to liberate His people from bondage in Egypt: *"God answered: I will be with you; and this will be your sign that I have sent you. When you have brought the people out of Egypt, you will serve God at this mountain."* (Exodus 3:12) After Moses died, God called Joshua to the daunting task of leading the people into the Promised Land, where there were many large armies resisting their entry. There were many battles to be fought. Yet God asked Joshua to be stout of heart and confident that he would succeed: *"No man shall be able to stand before you all the days of your life; as I was with Moses, so I will be with you; I will not fail you or forsake you. Be strong and of good courage; for you shall cause this people to inherit the land which I swore to their fathers to give them... for the Lord your God is with you wherever you go."* (Joshua 1:5-6, 9)

From a biblical perspective, like Moses, Gideon, David, Mary, the apostles, God sends us too on a mission, with the same words that reassured our ancestors in the faith: *"The Lord be with you."* This reassurance from God through the priest, reminds us that God is with us. We are not alone. In fact, Jesus is living our lives with us. We can be faithful in trials and tribulations because God is with us as Emmanuel.

At the start of the Mass, then, we are reminded that we are about to embark on the most important mission of the day and of our lives. We are about to enter into the Sacred Mysteries, to participate in Christ's death and resurrection, and receive Christ's body, blood, soul and divinity in communion. We are also being asked to live out Christ's death and resurrection in our own lives. We could never be worthy of such a great honor and challenge. But we are being invited by the Lord to this Eucharistic Banquet. The Lord's Loving Kindness and tender Mercy will compensate for all our failings and imperfections.

THE NEED FOR REPENTANCE:

In this gathering that has assembled to celebrate the death and resurrection of the Lamb, there can be no tolerance and acceptance of sin. Only a contrite and repentant heart can make the Pilgrim Church ready for this celebration, as no one who remains in Jesus sins. As John tells us in his First Letter, *"Whoever sins belongs to the devil, because the devil has sinned from the beginning. Indeed, the Son of God was revealed to destroy the works of the devil. No one who is begotten by God commits sins, because God's seed remains in him; he cannot sin because He is begotten by God."* (1 John 3:8-9) Hence, as pilgrims, on our way to the everlasting heavenly Eucharistic Celebration, we acknowledge the need for forgiveness and mercy and we ask God to cleanse us in the Penitential Rite.

The first three chapters of the Book of Revelation highlight the importance of the spirit of repentance. Jesus sent His angel to John to give the seven churches of Asia a special message, inviting them back to their first love and warning them of the consequences that would befall them in their laxity. Interestingly enough, John receives this revelation from Jesus Christ, the Alpha and the Omega, on the Lord's Day, when the Eucharist is celebrated: *"I was caught up in spirit on the Lord's day and heard behind me a voice as loud as a trumpet, which said, "Write on a scroll what you see and send it to the seven churches."* (Revelation 1:10-11) Chapter Three ends with words from Jesus that capture the essence of the Penitential Rite: *"Behold, I stand at the door and knock. If anyone hears my voice and opens the door [then] I will enter his house and dine with him, and he with me. I will give the victor the right to sit with me on my throne, as I myself first won the victory and sit with my Father on his throne."* (Revelation 3:20-21) The invitation to covenant life with God has been offered to us. Jesus has demonstrated the importance of this invitation by dying on our behalf to make possible this union between God and us. And the Father and Jesus together have given us their Holy Spirit to re-create us in the image and likeness of Jesus, and thus make us a new creation. The only way we can enter into covenant life with God is by offering ourselves to God wholeheartedly and selflessly, holding nothing back. We will then be seated on Jesus' throne, sharing in His victory over Satan, sin, and permanent death. As we see in the assessment made of the seven churches, some held back nothing and gave their all to God; others received a mixed review. And Laodicea was tepid and lukewarm fit to be spit out of God's mouth. Jesus re-iterates the invitation and makes it clear that it is an invitation that only we can accept. The Penitential Rite highlights the necessity of the spirit of repentance.

THE CONFITEOR AND KYRIE ELEISON:

The Penitential Rite is focused around the "Confiteor" and "Kyrie Eleison." The "I confess" prayer stands in a long biblical tradition of confessing one's sins. The Old Testament Law required people to confess certain sins: *"Tell the Israelites: If a man or a woman commits any offense against another person, thus breaking faith with the LORD, and thereby becomes guilty, that person shall confess the wrong that has been done, make restitution in full, and in addition give one fifth of its value to the other that has been wronged."* (Numbers 5:6-7) In the New Testament, the practice of confessing one's sins takes on a sense of urgency. John the Baptist preached a baptism of repentance, with people confessing their sins and being baptized by John. People from the whole Judean countryside and even from Jerusalem went out to him to be baptized. The Baptist was also ruthless in his indictment of those who came to be baptized and did not have true repentance in their hearts. *"He said to the crowds who came out to be baptized by him, "You brood of vipers! Who warned you to flee from the coming wrath? Produce good fruits as evidence of your repentance; and do not begin to say to yourselves, 'We have Abraham as our father,' for I tell you, God can raise up children to Abraham from these stones."* (Luke 3:7-8)

In His preaching, Jesus always emphasized repentance. In the parable of the Lost Sheep, Jesus ends by saying, *"Rejoice with me because I have found my lost sheep.' I tell you, in just the same way there will be more joy in heaven over one sinner who repents than over ninety-nine righteous people who have no need of repentance."* (Luke 15:6b-7) In his First Letter, John asks us to confess our sins with confidence and we will be forgiven them: *"If we say, "We are without sin," we deceive ourselves, and the truth is not in us. If we acknowledge our sins, he is faithful and just and will forgive our sins and cleanse us from every wrongdoing. If we say, "We have not sinned," we make him a liar, and his word is not in us."* (1 John 1:8-10)

This tradition of confessing sin was taken up by the early Christians and became an essential preparation for the celebration of the Eucharist. By the eleventh century the "Confiteor" or "I confess" prayer became a part of the preparation for the Eucharistic celebration. The "I confess" is done to God and to our brothers and sisters gathered by the Holy Spirit for the celebration. It challenges us to consider seriously four areas in which we may have fallen into sin: *"in my thoughts and in my words, in what I have done and in what I have failed to do."*

These four areas serve as an excellent examination of conscience: *In my thoughts:* Jesus tells us that it is not important what goes into the stomach. More important is what comes out of our hearts into our relationships. Jesus warns us about several ways in which we can fail in our thoughts. Without ever physically harming someone, we can sin through our anger toward others. Judging others, being anxious about the future, or falling into deep discouragement are other ways our thoughts can lead us into sin.

In my words: The letter of James warns us that the tongue is a fire. The spoken word can be used to bless and to curse, and when it is used for evil it causes great turmoil: *"How great a forest is set ablaze by a small fire."* (James 3:5) The Bible mentions many ways our speech can be used for harm, through gossip, slander, insult, lying, and boasting.

In what I have done: This area encompasses what most people commonly think about sin – actions that directly hurt other people or our relationship with God. Along these lines, the Ten Commandments are often used as the basis for an examination of conscience.

In what I have failed to do: This is the most challenging part. Not only are we responsible for our sinful actions, but we also will be held accountable for the good that we failed to do! As the Letter of James teaches, *"Whoever knows what is right to do and fails to do it, for him it is sin."* (James 4:17) This part of the *Confiteor* reminds us that the Christian path is about putting on the mind and heart of Christ, becoming like Him in all things and every circumstance. Jesus does not want us merely to avoid sin; He wants us to grow in His self-giving love.

After the *Confiteor*, we pray the *Kyrie Eleison*. Jesus is our Savior and Lord. He is our Savior because He is Lord, the title given to Him after His resurrection that acknowledges His divinity. In the **Kyrie Eleison, Christe Eleison** prayer, we acknowledge Jesus as Savior and Lord: **Kyrie Eleison** is Greek for Lord, have mercy. **Christe Eleison** is Greek for Christ, have mercy. Christ, from the Greek Christos, is the Anointed One or Messiah, or Savior.

THE GLORIA IN EXCELSIS:

We have emerged from the Penitential Rite with gratitude in our hearts and praise on our lips because we have experienced God's mercy and forgiveness and are left with the conviction that God will never abandon us. Very aptly, therefore, we express our sentiments of joy and praise through the *Gloria in Excelsis Deo*. This glorious Prayer of Praise, in honor of the Trinity, was introduced into the Western Liturgy sometime in the Fifth Century and most likely by St. Hilary of Poitiers (d 368). This hymn was first composed in the Second Century in Greek. St. Hilary became acquainted with this marvelous hymn that was used in the Eastern rites of the Liturgy. When he returned from the East to Poitiers in France, he introduced it to the

Western Church. The Latin translation of this hymn is attributed to St. Hilary.

The opening lines are taken from Luke's gospel when the choir of angels appears to the shepherds: *"Glory to God in the highest and on earth peace to those on whom his favor rests."* (Luke 2:14) St. Hilary was an uncompromising foe of Arianism which denied the divinity of Christ, and by implication, the Trinity. Through this hymn of praise and adoration, we affirm our faith in the Trinity, and especially in the divinity of Christ. Most of the song of praise focuses on Jesus. The hymn singles out each Person of the Trinity, beginning with God the Father: *"We praise you, we bless you, we adore you, we glorify you, we give you thanks for your great glory, Lord God, heavenly King, O God, almighty Father."* There is a majesty and sweep to the praise of the Father as it gushes out of our hearts, upon our lips, and out to the Father. Our prayer is worthy of God, and right and just for us to do, as the image and likeness of God.

And then the hymn proceeds to lay great emphasis upon the Lordship and divinity of Jesus, as our salvation hinges on the fact that Jesus is both man and God: *"Lord Jesus Christ, Only Begotten Son, Lord God, Lamb of God, Son of the Father, you take away the sins of the world, have mercy on us; you take away the sins of the world, receive our prayer; you are seated at the right hand of the Father, have mercy on us. For you alone are the Holy One, you alone are the Lord, you alone are the Most High, Jesus Christ, with the holy Spirit, in the glory of God the Father. Amen."* His divinity is acknowledged in various ways: three times Jesus is addressed as Lord, a title that was given to Him after His resurrection to acknowledge His divinity; He is addressed as 'Son of the Father,' to emphasize His place in the Blessed Trinity, and 'Lamb of God' who takes away the sins of the world by His death on the cross. Only God can take away sin. Jesus alone is the 'Holy One,' a title given only to God. Finally, Jesus is acknowledged in Trinitarian fellowship with the Father and the Holy Spirit. The Holy Spirit is acknowledged as the Third Person of the Trinity, and therefore as God, in fellowship with the Father and Jesus.

THE OPENING PRAYER OR COLLECT:

The Introductory Rites are brought to a close with the Opening Prayer or Collect. The Presider gathers or collects the prayers of the whole Church and offers them to God. While the whole Liturgy is interspersed with prayers of praise, adoration, and intercession, in particular places the Church intercedes on behalf of her covenant family with the Father through Jesus who is her Head. The Opening Prayer is the first of such places. Such intercession is done with great sincerity and trust in the saving power of the Lamb who was slain on the cross for the forgiveness of sin. On week days when we are celebrating the feast day of a saint, the Presider will gather the prayers of the whole Church and offer them to the Father through the intercession of the saint of the day. With this concluding prayer we are ready to enter into the Liturgy of the Word.

PRAYER AND REFLECTION ON EUCHARIST: GATHERED WITH THE LAMB IN THE HOLY SPIRIT

WEEK NINETEEN: *"The grace of the Lord Jesus Christ and the love of God and the fellowship of the Holy Spirit be with all of you." (2 Corinthians 13:13)*

SPIRITUAL READING FOR THE WEEK:

- **Anoint Us in Your Covenant, Abba-Emmanuel:** Session Ten
- **Old Testament:** Two or Three Chapters daily
- **New Testament:** Two or Three Chapters daily
- **Imitation of Christ:** One chapter daily

DAY ONE: MORNING SESSION

MORNING PRAYER: Acts of Faith, Hope, Charity; Daily Offering

Morning Face to Face with God:

Begin with Prayer to the Holy Spirit

GATHERING OF THE ASSEMBLY:

Prayer on Revelation 19:5-8: The Victory Song

"Then I heard something like the sound of a great multitude or the sound of rushing water or mighty peals of thunder, as they said: "Alleluia! The Lord has established his reign, [our] God, the almighty. Let us rejoice and be glad and give him glory. For the wedding day of the Lamb has come, his bride has made herself ready. She was allowed to wear a bright, clean linen garment." *(The linen represents the righteous deeds of the holy ones.)*

Read the Reflection; Ask the Holy Spirit to give you a deep appreciation for the Eucharist, and that your participation might always be wholehearted and generous.

Every Sunday we assemble for the wedding day of the Lamb. We are there as His bride and we prepare to make ourselves ready for the wedding feast. God's covenant family, assembled around the Lamb, begins the Eucharistic celebration with a gathering song. This momentous assembly consists of God's covenant family in heaven gathered around the Lamb that was slain. The heavenly assembly is celebrating the establishment of God's reign through the Lamb that was slain. It is the wedding day of the Lamb and His bride. And in heaven, God's covenant family has made itself ready. Here on earth the Holy Spirit has gathered God's covenant family to join in the heavenly wedding feast. Holy Mother Church, or God's covenant family, is acutely aware of this extra-terrestrial and supernatural dimension. In this celebration, the Church also remembers another very significant segment of God's covenant family that is present at this assembly: God's holy people being purified of their sins in Purgatory. In the Eucharistic Prayer, the holy souls in Purgatory are given a prominent place in the assembly's prayer of intercession. We, the pilgrim Church, join with this heavenly assembly and celebrate covenant union with the Trinity, centered in the Eucharistic banquet of the Lamb, the bridegroom. This glorious celebration of both the Triumphant and Pilgrim church is already taking place as envisaged in Revelation 5:13: *"Then I heard every creature in heaven and on earth and under the earth and in the sea, everything in the universe, cry out: "To the one who sits on the throne and to the Lamb be blessing and honor, and glory and might, forever and ever."*

What is God saying to you?

End with Prayer to the Holy Trinity

NIGHT SESSION: Examination of Conscience

For what are you grateful? For what are you contrite?

Please review briefly your Morning Prayer topic. Make it your last thought of the day

DAY TWO: MORNING SESSION

MORNING PRAYER: Act of Faith; Act of Hope; Act of Charity; Daily Offering

Morning Face to Face with God:

Begin with Prayer to the Holy Spirit

PRAYER ON THE SIGN OF THE CROSS:

> *In the name of the Father, and of the Son, and of the Holy Spirit, Amen.*

Read the Reflection; Ask the Holy Spirit to give you a deep appreciation for the Eucharist, and that your participation might always be wholehearted and generous.

Acting in the name of Jesus our High Priest, our Presider begins the Eucharistic celebration with the Sign of the Cross. The Cross was the ultimate sign of degradation, the symbol of capital punishment in Roman times. Jesus accepted the humiliation of the Cross on our behalf, and offered it as an atonement offering, to free us from our bondage to Satan and sin. In this way, the cross became the ultimate sign of triumph over Satan and sin, of grace and entrance into God's love and life! In baptism we were baptized into the death of Jesus on the Cross, and rose with Him in His resurrection (Colossians 2:12). In this way we were brought into the life and love of the Father, Son, and Holy Spirit through the cross. In signing ourselves with the name of our Triune God, we are declaring boldly and uncompromisingly that we belong to God in covenant union. In return for the Father's total offering of Himself to us through His Son, Jesus Christ, we have surrendered ownership of our lives to the Blessed Trinity. Therefore, as we begin our celebration with the sign of the cross, we express our profound gratitude to the Trinity for sharing with us the divine life made possible through the crucifixion and death of Jesus on the cross. In the Sign of the Cross, we pray that our whole lives will be lived in ever greater harmony with God, and that we will do everything only in God's name.

What is God saying to you?

End with Prayer to the Holy Trinity

NIGHT SESSION: Examination of Conscience

For what are you grateful? For what are you contrite?

Please review briefly your Morning Prayer topic. Make it your last thought of the day

DAY THREE: MORNING SESSION

MORNING PRAYER: Act of Faith; Act of Hope; Act of Charity; Daily Offering

Morning Face to Face with God:

Begin with Prayer to the Holy Spirit

PRAYER ON THE GREETING:

> *"The grace of our Lord Jesus Christ, and the love of God, and the communion of the Holy Spirit be with you all." (2 Corinthians 13:13)*

Read the Reflection; Ask the Holy Spirit to give you a deep appreciation for the Eucharist, and that your participation might always be wholehearted and generous.

The priest welcomes the gathering of God's covenant family by using St. Paul's greeting.

  1. *'The grace of the Lord Jesus Christ'* is the unmerited gift to us of sharing in God's divine life, made possible through the death and resurrection of Jesus Christ. Jesus has

bridged the chasm between God and us, caused by our sin. And now we share in His relationship with the Father and Holy Spirit. With Him, in Him, and through Him, we now can address His Father as Our Father!

2. *'The love of God'* the Father has made possible this indescribable gift of participation in the divine nature through Jesus: *"For God so loved the world that he gave his only Son, so that everyone who believes in him might not perish but might have eternal life."* (John 3:16)

3. *'The fellowship (communion) of the Holy Spirit':* To bring about this covenant union of God with His human covenant family, **the fellowship or communion of the Holy Spirit** has been offered to us. Through the Holy Spirit, the Trinity invites us into God's life and relationships, to share in their Trinitarian fellowship.

What is God saying to you?

End with Prayer to the Holy Trinity

NIGHT SESSION: Examination of Conscience

For what are you grateful? For what are you contrite?

Please review briefly your Morning Prayer topic. Make it your last thought of the day

DAY FOUR: MORNING SESSION

MORNING PRAYER: Act of Faith; Act of Hope; Act of Charity; Daily Offering

Morning Face to Face with God:

Begin with Prayer to the Holy Spirit

PRAYER ON 'I CONFESS':

"I confess to almighty God and to you, my brothers and sisters, that I have greatly sinned, in my thoughts and in my words, in what I have done and in what I have failed to do, through my fault, through my fault, through my most grievous fault."

Read the Reflection; Ask the Holy Spirit to give you a deep appreciation for the Eucharist, and that your participation might always be wholehearted and generous.

By the eleventh century the "I confess" prayer became a part of the preparation for the Eucharistic celebration. The confession of our sins is done before the members of God's covenant family, to God and to our brothers and sisters gathered by the Holy Spirit for the celebration. In acknowledging our sins we admit our need of Jesus as our Savior, as we cannot save ourselves through our own merit. We look at four areas of our sinfulness: *In my thoughts:* An unsanctified mind is the devil's workshop. Without ever physically harming someone, we can sin through our anger toward others. Judging others, being anxious about the future, or falling into deep discouragement are other ways our thoughts can lead us into sin. *In my words:* The spoken word can be used to bless and to curse, and when used for evil it causes great turmoil: *"How great a forest is set ablaze by a small fire."* (James 3:5) *In what I have done:* This is the area we commonly relate to sin – our actions that directly hurt our relationship with God or other people. The Ten Commandments are often used as the basis for an examination of conscience. *In what I have failed to do:* Not only are we responsible for our sinful actions we have committed, but we will also be held accountable for the good that we failed to do! As the Letter of James teaches, *"Whoever knows what is right to do and fails to do it, for him it is sin."* (James 4:17) The *'I confess'* prayer reminds us that the Christian path is about putting on the mind and heart of Christ, becoming like Him in all things and every circumstance. Jesus does not want us merely to avoid sin; He wants us to grow in His self-giving love.

What is God saying to you?

End with Prayer to the Holy Trinity

NIGHT SESSION: Examination of Conscience

For what are you grateful? For what are you contrite?

Please review briefly your Morning Prayer topic. Make it your last thought of the day

DAY FIVE: MORNING SESSION

MORNING PRAYER: Act of Faith; Act of Hope; Act of Charity; Daily Offering

Morning Face to Face with God:

Begin with Prayer to the Holy Spirit

PRAYER ON THE 'I CONFESS' – CONTINUED:

"Therefore I ask blessed Mary ever-Virgin, all the Angels and Saints, and you, my brothers and sisters, to pray for me to the Lord our God."

Read the Reflection; Ask the Holy Spirit to give you a deep appreciation for the Eucharist, and that your participation might always be wholehearted and generous.

As followers of Jesus, we live out our discipleship within God's covenant family, with our

Triune God at the center, being Emmanuel, God-with-us. While our prayer is personal, it always has a community dimension. We are the Body of Christ, united to the Bridegroom as His bride. Our prayer, therefore, is always made within the context of our covenant bond with God and His family. Prayer is a ceaseless activity in God's covenant family because it is the best expression and experience of our union with God and one another. Our heavenly brothers and sisters are interceding for us, and their prayers rise like incense to the Father, through and along with the intercession of Jesus, our Lamb that was slain on our behalf (Revelation 5:8). We also seek the intercession of our brothers and sisters who are members of God's covenant family here on earth. We express these powerful bonds in the 'I confess' prayer at the beginning of our celebration, in preparation for our participation in the wedding feast of the Lamb (Revelation 19:7-9)

What is God saying to you?

End with Prayer to the Holy Trinity

NIGHT SESSION: Examination of Conscience

For what are you grateful? For what are you contrite?

Please review briefly your Morning Prayer topic. Make it your last thought of the day

DAY SIX: MORNING SESSION

MORNING PRAYER: Act of Faith; Act of Hope; Act of Charity; Daily Offering

Morning Face to Face with God:

Begin with Prayer to the Holy Spirit

Prayer on the Kyrie Eleison:

"KYRIE ELEISON, CHRISTE ELEISON, KYRIE ELEISON."

Ask the Holy Spirit to give you a deep appreciation for the Eucharist, and that your participation might always be wholehearted and generous.

Jesus always emphasized repentance. In the parable of the Lost Sheep, Jesus ends by saying, *"Rejoice with me because I have found my lost sheep.' I tell you, in just the same way there will be more joy in heaven over one sinner who repents than over ninety-nine righteous people who have no need of repentance."* (Luke 15:6b-7) In their letters, the apostles of Jesus emphasize repentance through confession of our sins: *"If we say, 'We are without sin,' we deceive ourselves, and the truth is not in us. If we acknowledge our sins, he is faithful and just and will forgive our sins and cleanse us from every wrongdoing."* (1 John 1:8-9) This tradition of confessing sin became an essential preparation for the celebration of the Eucharist. The Didache, an early second century text, talks about the practice of confessing sin: "Assemble on the Lord's Day, and break bread and offer the Eucharist; but first make confession of faults, so that your sacrifice may be a pure one." (Didache 14) In the *Kyrie Eleison, Christe Eleison* prayer, we acknowledge Jesus as Savior and Lord. *Kyrie Eleison* is Greek for Lord, have mercy. Jesus can forgive sin because He is Lord. *Christe Eleison* is Greek for Christ, have mercy. Christ, from the Greek Christos, is the Anointed One or Messiah, or Savior. Because Jesus is Lord, a title for God in the Old Testament which was given to Him after the resurrection, He can be our Savior who forgives our sins.

What is God saying to you?

End with Prayer to the Holy Trinity

NIGHT SESSION: Examination of Conscience

For what are you grateful? For what are you contrite?

Please review briefly your Morning Prayer topic. Make it your last thought of the day

DAY SEVEN: MORNING SESSION

MORNING PRAYER: Act of Faith; Act of Hope; Act of Charity; Daily Offering

Morning Face to Face with God:

Begin with Prayer to the Holy Spirit

THE SIXTH DWELLING PLACES: KEEPING THE HUMANITY OF CHRIST EVER PRESENT:
- St. Teresa is adamant about keeping the humanity of Jesus present in our minds, no matter how spiritually advanced one might be. She is advocating very strongly against the mistaken notion that when a disciple arrives at contemplative prayer, they should disregard anything that is corporeal and tied to the imagination.
- Now that they have passed the beginning stages of prayer and union with God, they think it is better for them to deal with the divinity of Christ exclusively, and avoid the humanity of Christ and corporeal things.

- It is best for us to listen to St. Teresa herself on this matter and to receive proper guidance for our spiritual lives: *"To be always withdrawn from corporeal things and enkindled in love is the trait of angelic spirits not of those who live in mortal bodies."*

- *"It's necessary that we speak to, think about, and become the companions of those who having had a mortal body accomplished such great feats for God. How much more is it necessary not to withdraw through one's own efforts from all our good and help which is the most sacred humanity of our Lord Jesus Christ."*

- *"I cannot believe that these souls do so, but they just don't understand; and they will do harm to themselves and to others. At least I assure them that they will not enter these last two dwelling places. For if they lose the guide, who is the good Jesus, they will not hit upon the right road. It will be quite an accomplishment if they remain safely in the other dwelling places."* (TIC – VI:7:6)

- Later in the same chapter, St. Teresa shows how a contemplative, having great difficulty doing discursive reflection, must still contemplate in and with the humanity of Christ: *"This prayer (discursive meditation) is the kind that those whom God has brought to supernatural things and to perfect contemplation are right in saying they cannot practice... But I say that a person will not be right if he says he does not dwell on these mysteries or often have them in mind, especially when the Catholic Church celebrates them..."*

- *"The intellect (in contemplative prayer) represents them in such a way, and they are so stamped on the memory, that the mere sight of the Lord fallen to the ground in the garden with that frightful sweat is enough to last the intellect not only an hour but many days, while it looks with a simple gaze at who He is and how ungrateful we have been for so much suffering."*

- *"Soon the will responds even though it may not do so with tender feelings, with the desire to serve somehow for such a great favor and to suffer something for One who suffered so much, and with other similar desires relating to what the memory and intellect are dwelling upon."* (TIC – VI:7:11)

What is God saying to you?

End with Prayer to the Holy Trinity

NIGHT SESSION: Examination of Conscience

For what are you grateful? For what are you contrite?

What prayer would you compose to express what God has said to you this week?

Please review briefly your Morning Prayer topic. Make it your last thought of the day

PRAYER AND REFLECTION ON EUCHARIST: GATHERED WITH THE LAMB IN THE HOLY SPIRIT – CONTINUED

WEEK TWENTY: *"GLORY TO GOD IN THE HIGHEST AND ON EARTH PEACE TO THOSE ON WHOM HIS FAVOR RESTS." (LUKE 2:14)*

SPIRITUAL READING FOR THE WEEK:

- **Anoint Us in Your Covenant, Abba-Emmanuel:** Session Ten
- **Old Testament:** Two or Three Chapters daily
- **New Testament:** Two or Three Chapters daily
- **Imitation of Christ:** One chapter daily

DAY ONE: MORNING SESSION

MORNING PRAYER: Acts of Faith, Hope, Charity; Daily Offering

Morning Face to Face with God:

Begin with Prayer to the Holy Spirit

THE GLORIA PRAYER:

Read the Reflection; Ask the Holy Spirit to give you a deep appreciation for the Eucharist, and that your participation might always be wholehearted and generous.

This hymn was first composed in Greek in the Second Century. St. Hilary of Poitiers, France, became acquainted with this marvelous hymn that was used in the Eastern rites of the Liturgy. When he returned from the East to France, he introduced it to the Western Church. The Latin translation of this hymn is attributed to St. Hilary. The opening lines are taken from Luke's gospel when the choir of angels appears to the shepherds: *"Glory to God in the highest and on earth peace to those on whom his favor rests."* (Luke 2:14) St. Hilary was an uncompromising foe of Arianism which denied the divinity of Christ and therefore, the Trinity or one God in three divine Persons. Arius was a priest of Alexandria, Egypt, and lived in the fourth century. The heresy is named after him. Through this hymn of praise and adoration, we affirm our faith in the Trinity, and especially in the divinity of Christ. *(Recite the Gloria slowly and reverently several times during your prayer.)*

What is God saying to you?

End with Prayer to the Holy Trinity

NIGHT SESSION: Examination of Conscience

For what are you grateful? For what are you contrite?

Please review briefly your Morning Prayer topic. Make it your last thought of the day

DAY TWO: MORNING SESSION

MORNING PRAYER: Act of Faith; Act of Hope; Act of Charity; Daily Offering

Morning Face to Face with God:

Begin with Prayer to the Holy Spirit

PRAYER ON THE GLORIA: PRAISE OF THE FATHER

"Glory to God in the highest, and on earth peace to people of good will. We praise you, we bless you, we adore you, we glorify you, we give you thanks for your great glory, Lord God, heavenly King, O God, almighty Father."

Read the Reflection; Ask the Holy Spirit to give you a deep appreciation for the Eucharist, and that your participation might always be wholehearted and generous.

The opening line, taken from Luke 2:14, announces the glorious tidings of the birth of Jesus, our Savior. The angel is heralding the time of fulfillment of God's plan of salvation. God's desire to bring us into covenant union with Him is being accomplished through His Son. Any one of good will, persons who have repentance in their hearts and faith in Jesus as their Savior, will have the peace of Christ. Then the hymn goes into praise and adoration of the Father. We address God as *Lord God*, a name and title that is used extensively to address God in the Old Testament. In addressing God as *heavenly King*, we are stating that the kingdom of God is in our midst through Jesus. God is also addressed as *almighty Father*. We have become sons and daughters of the living God and can address Him as Father because Jesus has made this possible through His death on the cross. We now participate in His Son-ship. Our Father is almighty because only God could accomplish our salvation through Jesus' death and resurrection. There is a majesty and sweep to the praise and adoration of the Father as it gushes out of our hearts, upon our lips, and out to the Father. Since we relate to the Father and the Holy Spirit through Jesus, our praise and thanksgiving of the Father is our participation in the praise, thanksgiving, and obedience of Jesus towards His Father. *(Recite the Gloria slowly and reverently several times during your prayer.)*

What is God saying to you?

End with Prayer to the Holy Trinity

NIGHT SESSION: Examination of Conscience

For what are you grateful? For what are you contrite?

Please review briefly your Morning Prayer topic. Make it your last thought of the day

DAY THREE: MORNING SESSION

MORNING PRAYER: Act of Faith; Act of Hope; Act of Charity; Daily Offering

Morning Face to Face with God:

Begin with Prayer to the Holy Spirit

PRAYER ON THE GLORIA: PRAISE AND ADORATION OF THE SON:

"Lord Jesus Christ, Only Begotten Son, Lord God, Lamb of God, Son of the Father, you take away the sins of the world, have mercy on us; you take away the sins of the world, receive our prayer; you are seated at the right hand of the Father, have mercy on us. For you alone are the Holy One, you alone are the Lord, you alone are the Most High, Jesus Christ."

Read the Reflection; Ask the Holy Spirit to give you a deep appreciation for the Eucharist, and that your participation might always be wholehearted and generous.

And then the hymn lays great emphasis upon the Lordship and divinity of Jesus, as our salvation hinges on the fact that Jesus is both man and God. Jesus is the fullness of the deity in bodily form: *"For in him dwells the whole fullness of the deity bodily, and you share in this fullness in him."* (Colossians 2:9) Jesus' divinity is acknowledged in various ways: three times Jesus is addressed as Lord, a title that was given to him after His resurrection to acknowledge His divinity; He is addressed as 'Son of the Father.' Jesus shares in the same divine essence as the Father and is the Second Person of the Trinity. Jesus is the 'Lamb of God' who takes away the sins of the world. Only God can take away sin. Jesus alone is the 'Holy One,' a title given only to God. Finally, Jesus is acknowledged in Trinitarian fellowship with the Father and the Holy Spirit: *"With the holy Spirit, in the glory of God the Father. Amen."* (Recite the Gloria slowly and reverently several times during your prayer.)

What is God saying to you?

End with Prayer to the Holy Trinity

NIGHT SESSION: Examination of Conscience

For what are you grateful? For what are you contrite?

Please review briefly your Morning Prayer topic. Make it your last thought of the day

DAY FOUR: MORNING SESSION

MORNING PRAYER: Act of Faith; Act of Hope; Act of Charity; Daily Offering

Morning Face to Face with God:

Begin with Prayer to the Holy Spirit

PRAYER ON THE GLORIA: ADORATION OF THE HOLY SPIRIT:

"With the Holy Spirit, in the glory of God the Father. Amen.

Read the Reflection; Ask the Holy Spirit to give you a deep appreciation for the Eucharist, and that your participation might always be wholehearted and generous.

Thus far we have acknowledged the Godhead of the Father and the Son. At the end of our prayer we acknowledge the Holy Spirit as the Third Person of the Trinity, and therefore as God, in fellowship with the Father and Jesus. In His high priestly prayer, Jesus prayed that through His life and ministry He had brought glory to His Father, namely, made Him visibly present to the world through the presence of Jesus. Jesus then asked the Father to bring glory to Him (Jesus) through His death on the cross leading to His being raised from the dead. In this way the world would know that Jesus is God, thus bringing glory to His Father and to Himself. The phrase 'in the glory of God the Father' makes clear that the Holy Spirit shares in the glory of our Trinitarian God. Through Jesus, the Holy Spirit, like the Father, has been made known to the world through Jesus who is our Lord and Savior. *(Recite the Gloria slowly and reverently several times during your prayer.)*

What is God saying to you?

End with Prayer to the Holy Trinity

NIGHT SESSION: Examination of Conscience

For what are you grateful? For what are you contrite?

Please review briefly your Morning Prayer topic. Make it your last thought of the day

DAY FIVE: MORNING SESSION

MORNING PRAYER: Act of Faith; Act of Hope; Act of Charity; Daily Offering

Morning Face to Face with God:

Begin with Prayer to the Holy Spirit

PRAYER ON THE OPENING PRAYER OR COLLECT:

"O God, who through your Word reconcile the human race to yourself in a wonderful way, grant, we pray, that with prompt devotion and eager faith the Christian people may hasten toward the solemn celebrations to come. Through our Lord Jesus Christ, your Son, who lives and reigns with you in the unity of the Holy Spirit, one God, for ever and ever. Amen. (4th Sunday of Lent, March 15, 2015)

Read the Reflection; Ask the Holy Spirit to give you a deep appreciation for the Eucharist, and that your participation might always be wholehearted and generous.

The Introductory Rites conclude with the Opening Prayer, also called the Collect. The presider begins with the invitation to the congregation to pray, and after a brief pause, proclaims the prayer of the day. The prayer is called the 'Collect' because the presider is collecting the prayers of God's covenant family scattered throughout the world, and as family, offering the prayer to the Father through the Son. Throughout the world, therefore, on any given Sunday or weekday, the same Opening Prayer or Collect is prayed. Once again, it becomes clear to us that our prayer will always have a universal dimension because we will always be praying within the context of God's covenant family. And we will always do this through, with, and in Jesus Christ, the Lamb of God who sealed us in a new and everlasting covenant with the Father, in the power of the Holy Spirit, through His death on the cross. *(With gratitude reflect on the indescribable gift of sharing and celebrating God's life and love within the communion of saints.)*

What is God saying to you?

End with Prayer to the Holy Trinity

NIGHT SESSION: Examination of Conscience

For what are you grateful? For what are you contrite?

Please review briefly your Morning Prayer topic. Make it your last thought of the day

DAY SIX: MORNING SESSION

MORNING PRAYER: Act of Faith; Act of Hope; Act of Charity; Daily Offering

Morning Face to Face with God:

Begin with Prayer to the Holy Spirit

REPETITION OF DAYS ONE THROUGH FIVE:

Ask the Holy Spirit to give you a deep appreciation for the Eucharist, and that your participation might always be wholehearted and generous.

Today, you are doing a repetition of Days One through Five of this week. In a repetition St. Ignatius says that *"we should pay attention to and dwell upon those points in which we have experienced greater consolation or desolation or greater spiritual appreciation."* (# 62) If you wish, you can do a triple colloquy: refer to #63 of the Spiritual Exercises.

What is God saying to you?

End with Prayer to the Holy Trinity

NIGHT SESSION: Examination of Conscience

For what are you grateful? For what are you contrite?

Please review briefly your Morning Prayer topic. Make it your last thought of the day

DAY SEVEN: MORNING SESSION

MORNING PRAYER: Act of Faith; Act of Hope; Act of Charity; Daily Offering

Morning Face to Face with God:

Begin with Prayer to the Holy Spirit

THE SEVENTH DWELLING PLACES:

- The Seventh Dwelling Places is where the spiritual marriage or perfect union between God and the soul takes place. Since the illuminations in both the Sixth and Seventh Dwelling Places are extraordinary, there are no closed doors between these last two mansions.

- St. Teresa's reason for dividing them is because God gives some revelations that are not given in the Sixth Dwelling Places. God has prepared the soul through its sufferings, caused especially by its insatiable hunger and desire for God. *"He brings it, before the spiritual marriage is consummated, into His dwelling place which is this seventh."* (TIC – VII:1:3)

- In the previous two dwelling places, the Lord joined the soul to Himself. The soul couldn't understand what was going on for all the faculties were lost.

- In the Seventh Dwelling Places, however, God grants the soul a fair measure of understanding of the favors He grants it. Through an intellectual vision, the Most Blessed Trinity, all three Persons, are revealed to the soul.

- *"First there comes an enkindling in the spirit in the manner of a cloud of magnificent splendor; and these Persons are distinct, and through an admirable knowledge the soul understands as a most profound truth that all three Persons are one substance and one power and one knowledge and one God alone."*

- *"It knows in such a way that what we hold by faith, it understands, we can say, through sight – although the sight is not with the bodily eyes nor with the eyes of the soul, because we are not dealing with an imaginative vision. Here all three Persons communicate themselves to it, speak to it, and explain those words of the Lord in the Gospel: that He and the Father and the Holy Spirit will come to dwell with the soul that loves Him and keeps His commandments."* (TIC – VII:1:6)

- Instead of being absorbed and incapable of engaging in other activities, the paradox is that the soul is even more occupied in the service of God. Once it has carried out its duties it remains with the enjoyable company of the Blessed Trinity.

- St. Teresa maintains that this Presence of the Blessed Trinity is not felt fully, as it will in heaven, or else the soul would be incapable of doing anything else or even live among people. However, it is vibrant and constant, and the soul finds itself in this holy company every time it takes notice.

- In this Presence of the Blessed Trinity in her soul, St. Teresa noticed a division in her soul, so to speak. One part of her soul was suffering great trials in her ministry, while the other part was enjoying blessed quietude and rest.

- St. Teresa also mentions the presence of the Risen Jesus in the soul: *"The Lord appears in this center of the soul, not in an imaginative vision but in an intellectual one, although more delicate than those mentioned (in the Sixth Dwelling Places), as He appeared to the apostles without entering through the door when He said to them pax vobis."*

- *"What God communicates here to the soul in an instant is a secret so great and a favor so sublime – and the delight the soul experiences so extreme – that I don't know what to compare it to. I can say only that the Lord wishes to reveal for that moment, in a more sublime manner than through any spiritual vision or taste, the glory of heaven."* (TIC – VII:2:3)

- The difference in the Presence of the Lord in the Sixth and Seventh Dwelling Places is that in the latter, the Lord has desired to be so joined with the creature that He doesn't want to be separated from the soul. In the Sixth Dwelling Places, spiritual betrothal is the joining of two things into one. However, the two can be separated and each can remain by itself.

What is God saying to you?

End with Prayer to the Holy Trinity

NIGHT SESSION: Examination of Conscience

For what are you grateful? For what are you contrite?

What prayer would you compose to express what God has said to you this week?

Please review briefly your Morning Prayer topic. Make it your last thought of the day

SESSION ELEVEN
EUCHARIST: CELEBRATING THE LITURGY OF THE WORD

"Blessed is the one who reads aloud and blessed are those who listen to this prophetic message and heed what is written in it, for the appointed time is near."

– Revelation 1:3

THE TABLE OF HOLY SCRIPTURE:

The Penitential rite has prepared us to encounter the Living God through His divine word in Holy Scripture. God's living word reveals to us the plan and purpose of our lives. God created us in His image and likeness so that He could offer us covenant living with Him, giving us the awesome privilege to share in His divine life and love, as His sons and daughters. In order to bring His divine plan of salvation to completion, God revealed to us that His Word is the living Person of His Son, Jesus Christ. Hence, the Church has offered us the image of the "two tables" from which we share the life of God: from the table of His divine word during the Liturgy of the Word which leads us to the table of the Eucharist where we eat and drink the Word of God incarnated in Jesus who died on the cross, rose from the dead, and made us sons and daughters of His Father whom we now claim as our Father. The table of Holy Scripture prepares us for a deeper encounter with the living God in the reception of Jesus in Holy Communion. These two very significant aspects of our celebration have an inner unity, highlighting for us both our history with God, and our journey into covenant union with our Trinitarian God through the death and resurrection of Jesus Christ. Thus the word of God, read and proclaimed by the Church in the Liturgy of the Word, leads inexorably to the new Passover sacrificial meal of Jesus, consummated in Holy Communion as to its natural end.

GOD'S WORD SPOKEN TO YOU:

The Liturgy of the Word of God is essentially a proclamation or *kerygma*, making it clear that the reign of God is at hand. There is urgent need for repentance and turning towards God. We cannot be straddling the fence as we listen to God's word. God's word creates a crisis which compels us to make a decision. The encounter is very personal and demands a response, either leading to surrender and commitment, or to resistance and even rejection of God's invitation to covenant living.

The lector proclaims the word of God in God's name. The lector is lending his human voice so that God's revelation can be spoken to us in the hope that we will heed God's voice: *"Blessed is the one who reads aloud and blessed are those who listen to this prophetic message and heed what is written in it, for the appointed time is near."* (Revelation 1:3)

The Bible is primarily an account in which God talks about Himself in relationship to us. It is God's own voice, spoken to us personally, and through the authorship of human beings. Each book of the Bible is marked by the personality of the sacred author, and by the cultural background, theological perspectives and pastoral concerns of the community which the sacred author was addressing. Such communities extended over several countries and continents. In brief, the Scriptures were inspired by the Holy Spirit. God spoke to us through the instrumentality of human authors: *"Know this first of all, that there is no prophecy of scripture that is a matter of personal interpretation, for no prophecy ever came through human will; but rather human beings moved by the holy Spirit spoke under the influence of God."* (2 Peter 1:20-21)

The nature of the authorship of the Sacred Scriptures speaks to the covenant nature of God's relationship with us. God communicates His life, love, and relationship with us through the full involvement of human effort and authorship. The Scriptures are like Jesus Himself – fully divine and fully human. In the Dogmatic Constitution on Divine Revelation (Dei Verbum), Chapter III, Vatican II says: "Holy Mother Church, relying on the belief of the apostles, holds that the books of both the Old and New Testament in their entirety, with all their parts, are sacred and canonical because, having been written under the inspiration of the Holy Spirit (John 20:31; 2 Timothy 3:16; 2 Peter 1:19-21; 3:15-16) they have God as their author and have been handed on as such to the Church herself. In composing the sacred books, God chose men and while employed by Him they made use of their powers and abilities, so that with Him acting in them and through them, they, as true authors, consigned to writing everything and only those things which He wanted" (Dei Verbum 11). Hearing and taking to heart the word of God is therefore a serious matter.

THE FIRST READING:

The first reading is taken from the Old Testament. During the Easter season it is taken from the Acts of the Apostles. The Old Testament has been accepted by the Church as authentic divine teaching in which the mystery of salvation is present in a hidden manner. Our understanding of Jesus and the New Testament will remain incomplete and diminished if we don't have a true appreciation of the Old Testament. As the Letter to the Hebrews says very eloquently, *"In times past, God spoke in partial and various ways to our ancestors through the prophets; in these last days, he spoke to us through a son."* (Hebrews 1:1-2) Jesus and His new kingdom established through His new and eternal covenant, is the climax of God's revelation begun in the Old Testament. One cannot, therefore, understand Jesus and the New Testament without having a true appreciation of the story of Israel in the Old Testament. The Old Testament reading at Mass helps us enter into the story of Israel and thus see the unity of the Bible more clearly. Thus Vatican II echoes St. Augustine very well, in singling out the dovetail connection between the Old and New Testaments: "God, the inspirer and author of both testaments, wisely arranged that the New Testament be hidden in the Old and the Old be made manifest in the New. For, though Christ established the New Covenant in His blood, still the books of the Old Testament with all their parts, caught up into the proclamation of the gospel acquire and show forth their full meaning in the New Testament and in turn shed light on it and explain it" (Dei Verbum 16).

The First Reading is related thematically to the Gospel Reading, highlighting continuity, and sometimes, contrast between the two Testaments. At other times, the First Reading prefigures Christ and the Church. Thus images of the Passover are linked with the Eucharist, and the Exodus story with the new Exodus in Jerusalem brought about by Jesus' death on the cross. The Crossing of the Red Sea is a pre-figuration of our Baptism.

THANKS BE TO GOD:

At the end of the first reading, the lector ends with *"The Word of the Lord,"* and our response is "Thanks be to God." Our response is a fitting one for we have just heard God speak directly to us through the lector! Our exclamation of gratitude is the most appropriate response to the amazing fact that God would speak to us through the Scriptures. Gratitude is the most fitting response we can have to God's love and saving action in our lives. Gratitude was constantly expressed by God's people in the psalms. This particular expression of thanksgiving was used by Paul because God had delivered him from sin and death: *"The sting of death is sin, and the power of sin is the law. But thanks be to God who gives us the victory through our Lord Jesus Christ."* (1 Corinthians 15:56-57) After we have expressed our enthusiastic and awe-filled response to God's direct revelation to us, we then spend some time in silence to taste and relish the full import of God's word. Like Mary who *"kept all these things, pondering them in her heart,"* (Luke 2:18) we spend some time in awe and adoration of the God who just spoke to us.

THE RESPONSORIAL PSALM:

We respond to God's word spoken to us in the First Reading, by using God's inspired words in the Book of Psalms, instructing us as to how we are to praise and thank Him. We do this through the Responsorial Psalm. The singing of the Psalm helps us to enter more deeply into the meaning of the First Reading. St. Paul encouraged the use of the psalms in our prayer: *"Let the word of God dwell in you richly, as in all wisdom you teach and admonish one another, singing psalms, hymns, and spiritual songs with gratitude in your hearts to God."* (Colossians 3:16) The Psalms were used extensively in the Temple liturgy, and would often be sung by two alternating choirs, with the antiphon being sung at the beginning and end of the psalm. The Church has adopted this back-and-forth movement in our recitation and singing of the Responsorial Psalm. This movement is also found during other parts of the Mass, as for instance, at the start of the Preface: *"The Lord be with you; And with your spirit,* etc. Moses used this antiphonal movement during the covenant ceremony at Sinai. He proclaimed the words of the LORD to the people and they answered in unison, proclaiming, *"All that the Lord has spoken we will do."* (Exodus 19:8) We see this same liturgical movement in the Book of Revelation, when John beholds thousands of angels praising the Lord: *"Worthy is the Lamb who was slain, to receive power and wealth and wisdom and might and honor and glory and blessing!"* Then all the creatures reply, *"To him who sits upon the throne and to the Lamb be blessing and honor and glory and might forever and ever!"* And the angelic four living creatures answer back, *"Amen."* (Revelation 5:11-14)

In the heavenly liturgy, the angels and saints are in ecstasy in the beatific vision of the Blessed Trinity. Their proclamations of praise, adoration, and worship express their awe-filled joy. They are in covenant union with the Blessed Trinity. There is total and joyful agreement and oneness in the heavenly assembly. Their joy is contagious, causing each heavenly choir to reciprocate the other's praise and adoration. Standing in the presence of God and experiencing His love and goodness, the angels and saints cannot help but praise and thank Him. In our Eucharistic celebration we have joined with them in praising and adoring the Blessed Trinity through the Lamb that was slain. In our liturgy we are being introduced into this blissful antiphonal chorus. When we respond to the Psalm (therefore called Responsorial Psalm) we are taking our first steps into the eternal *Perichoresis*, or the Divine Dance.

THE SECOND READING:

The second reading is taken from the New Testament. On many Sundays the Second Reading will be picked out from one of Paul's letters. We will also hear selections from the Acts of the Apostles, the Catholic Letters, or the Book of Revelation. The Second Reading reflects on the saving mystery of Jesus' death and resurrection, and the meaning it has for us in our lives. The Second Reading also encourages us in our discipleship, stressing the need to repent and put on Christ. In many instances, the Second Reading will not reflect the theme that is being offered and explored in the First Reading and the Gospel.

THE GOSPEL:

The Liturgy of the Word approaches its climax with the proclamation of the Gospel. Vatican II taught that the gospels rightly have "a special place… because they are our principal source for the life and teaching of the Incarnate Word, our Savior." (Dei Verbum 18) The celebration shows a special reverence for the reading of the Gospel, and accordingly has developed an elaborate ritual to express it. The congregation stands during the proclamation of the Gospel. Standing is a posture of reverence, and a serious expression of our intent to listen and accept the Word of God in Jesus Christ. Jesus will speak to us directly and we are ready to receive Him into our hearts as Emmanuel. We are following in a revered tradition that existed in the time of Ezra and Nehemiah. The assembled Jews stood and listened to Ezra as he read from the book of the Law (Nehemiah 8:5).

Alleluia: The people say or sing "Alleluia," which is a Hebrew expression of joy, meaning "Praise Yahweh!" or "Praise the Lord," in response to the Gospel acclamation. It was used by the angels in heaven to praise God for His work of salvation and to announce the coming of Christ to His people in the wedding supper of the Lamb: *"After this I heard what sounded like the loud voice of a great multitude in heaven, saying: "Alleluia! Salvation, glory, and might belong to our God, for true and just are his judgments. He has condemned the great harlot who corrupted the earth with her harlotry. He has avenged on her the blood of his servants."* (Revelation 19:1-2) In this way we welcome Jesus into our midst, with joy and anticipation for what He will reveal to us in the Gospel.

Procession: As the Alleluia is being sung, the priest (or deacon) quietly processes to the altar to prepare for the proclamation of the gospel. He prays, "Cleanse my heart and my lips, almighty God, that I may worthily proclaim your holy Gospel." His prayer echoes the sentiments of the prophet Isaiah whose lips were cleansed before he became God's messenger and prophet: *"Then I heard the voice of the Lord saying, 'Whom shall I send? Who will go for us?' Here I am,' I said, 'send me!'"* (Isaiah 6:8) If a deacon reads the Gospel, the priest recites a similar prayer for him at the beginning of the procession.

The Sign of the Cross: The presider begins the proclamation of the gospel with the greeting dialogue that is used several times during the celebration: *"The Lord be with you… And with you spirit,"* praying that we will be filled with peace and boldness as we receive Jesus through the gospel proclamation. The priest then announces the gospel reading by making three signs of the cross: on his forehead, lips, and heart, and one on the book. The congregation follows suit by signing themselves on the forehead, lips, and heart. The ritual symbolizes our decision to consecrate our thoughts, words, and actions to the Lord through the reception of the Incarnate Word in the gospel proclamation.

ENCOUNTERING JESUS:

The gospels are God's living word. The Church teaches that *"when the Sacred Scriptures are read in the Church, God himself speaks to his people, and Christ present in his own word, proclaims the Gospel."* (General Instructions for the Roman Missal 29) So when Jesus speaks through the gospel account, He is addressing each one of us personally and as His covenant family. We are not listening about Jesus in the past; we are listening to Him in the here and now. He is our Savior and Lord. He is here to bring us forgiveness of sin and transformation. So for instance, when we listen to the account of the woman caught in the act of adultery, or the woman healed of her hemorrhage, or the demoniac who was healed in the synagogue, Jesus is offering us the same invitation to be forgiven, and healed, and saved that He offered them. As our Savior and Lord, Jesus is asking that we encounter Him so that our lives will be transformed and no longer be the same. The proclamation of the Gospel, therefore, makes Jesus' life present to us in a real and profound way.

THE HOMILY:

The word *homily* means 'explanation.' Offering an explanation of the Scriptures was a long standing tradition in the OT. After the Babylonian exile, the synagogues continued this tradition. Jesus Himself practiced this tradition as did the Apostles. In Mark 1:21-22, we are told that *"then they came to Capernaum, and on the Sabbath he entered the synagogue and taught. The people were astonished at his teaching, for he taught them as one having authority and not as the scribes."* In Acts 13:15, Paul and his companions are invited by the synagogue officials to offer a homily: *"After the reading of the law and the prophets, the synagogue officials sent word to them, "My brothers, if one of you has a word of exhortation for the people, please speak."* The early Church continued with this tradition and it is with us to this day. In the early Church, the bishop was typically the presider at Eucharist, and it was he who gave the homily. This old practice produced the great homilies of several Fathers of the Church like St. Augustine, St. Ambrose, and St. John Chrysostom. The homily has always been held as an important teaching tool in the tradition of the Church. It is seen as being crucial for the instruction of the faithful so that they can understand and apply the readings to their lives. Vatican II states emphatically that the homily should hold "pride of place" among the various forms of Christian instruction (Dei Verbum 24).

The homily is to be given only by an ordained minister of the Church, a deacon, priest, or bishop. The same is true for the reading of the Gospel at Mass. Jesus gave His disciples and their successors the authority and the responsibility to teach His disciples to observe all that He had commanded them: *"All power in heaven and on earth has been given to me. Go, therefore, and make disciples of all nations, baptizing them in the name of the Father, and of the Son, and of the holy Spirit, teaching them to observe all that I have commanded you. And behold, I am with you always, until the end of the age."* (Matthew 28:18-20) Ultimately, the homily is meant to be an unequivocal statement that the preaching is passing on the Church's apostolic faith and not merely the private thoughts and experiences of an individual. It is the particular responsibility of the bishop as a successor of the apostles to teach the apostolic faith. And his union with the pope and the other bishops throughout the world gives further visible, concrete witness to the apostolic faith. Priests and deacons, by virtue of their ordination, share in this particular responsibility as well. So they also may proclaim the Gospel and deliver the homily at Mass.

THE CREED:

The Nicene Creed was formulated at the Council of Nicaea in 325, and was formally ratified at the Council of Constantinople in 381. Specifically, it refuted the heresy promulgated by Arius, a Libyan presbyter in Alexandria. Arius held that although 'the Son' was divine, he was a created being. There was a time when he was not. Therefore he was not co-essential or consubstantial with the Father. This made Jesus less than the Father and posed serious questions about Jesus being the Savior of the world. The Nicene Creed explicitly affirms the divinity of Jesus and His consubstantiality with the Father or sharing the same divine essence with the Father.

The Creed is a summary statement of our faith. It was used in the early Church as the standard for Christian belief. After the Council of Nicaea, it became a means for ensuring right doctrine and curbing heresy. Our profession of faith emphasizes the role of the Three Divine Persons who are the principal actors in the enactment of God's plan of salvation on our behalf. The role of each divine Person is emphasized and clarified so that our faith is affirmed and substantiated. Moving from creation to Christ's incarnation, death and resurrection, to the sending of the Holy Spirit, to the era of the Church and finally to the Second Coming, the Creed carries us through the entire story of salvation history.

I believe in one God, the Father almighty, maker of heaven and earth, of all things visible and invisible: We begin the Creed by focusing on the place of God the Father in the divine plan of salvation.   The Creed proclaims that the universe was brought into existence by the one true God, "the maker of heaven and earth," and is moving in a certain direction according to God's plan.

I believe in one Lord Jesus Christ, the only Begotten Son of God, born of the Father before all ages. God from God, Light from Light, true God from true God, begotten, not made, consubstantial with the Father … and his kingdom will have no end: The Nicene Creed asserts the fact that God's divine plan was fully revealed in God's Son, the *"one Lord Jesus Christ."* Jesus is called Lord, because we affirm our faith in Him as divine. He is "true God from true God," as Jesus shares the same divine essence with the Father. We proclaim that Jesus is *"eternally begotten of the*

Father;" He is *"begotten, not made, consubstantial (one in Being or homoousios in Greek) with the Father."* Already in the third Century, in a council at Antioch, the Church had to affirm against Paul of Samosata that Jesus Christ is Son of God by nature and not by adoption. The first ecumenical Council of Nicaea in 325 affirmed in its creed that the Son of God is *"begotten, not made, of the same substance as the Father,"* and condemned Arius who had affirmed that the Son of God was "from another substance" than that of the Father. The distinction between 'beget' and 'make' was made to avoid any confusion about who Jesus is. You beget someone of the same kind as yourself. But you make something of a different kind from yourself. What God begets is God; what God creates is not God. The Creed also notes that Jesus became man *"for our salvation."* Jesus is a divine Person with two natures, divine and human. Jesus suffered and died on the cross and rose from the dead to bring us the forgiveness of sins. Jesus is our Savior. He saves us as Son of God who became son of man. At the end of our lives, Jesus *"will come again in glory to judge the living and the dead." "His kingdom will have no end"* is a categorical statement, highlighting the overthrow of the kingdom of Satan and the complete victory of the kingdom of God.

I believe in the Holy Spirit, the Lord, the giver of life, who proceeds from the Father and the Son, who with the Father and the Son is adored and glorified, who has spoken through the prophets: The last section of the Nicene Creed emphasizes our faith in the Holy Spirit and His place in the Triune Godhead. The Spirit is called 'holy' because He proceeds from the Father and the Son: The Holy Spirit shares the same divine essence as the Father and the Son. The Source of Holiness, or total Otherness, is found in the Father, the Son, and the Holy Spirit. The Spirit is also holy because He is the source of sanctification in God's covenant family. The Holy Spirit is also referred to as 'Lord,' just as Jesus was, because He is truly divine, and co-equal with the Father and the Son. Hence it fitting that the Holy Spirit is adored along with the Father and the Son. The Holy Spirit is the *'giver of life'* as well. Breath (the literal meaning of spirit) is the sign of life in us. In Genesis 1:2, the creation of the world is described as *"a mighty wind (the Spirit of God) sweeping over the waters,"* or breathing over the waters. The Holy Spirit is also the source of eternal life, as a person has to be born of *water and the spirit* (John 3:5). According to Paul, *"the Spirit gives life."* (2 Corinthians 3:6) Finally, *"through the Spirit, by faith, we await the hope of righteousness."* (Galatians 5:5) The Holy Spirit came to be understood as the Source of life. So indeed, the Holy Spirit is the Giver of life. The Holy Spirit has been acting in the world since Old Testament times, even though there was no awareness that the Holy Spirit was a divine Person and was distinct from the Father. The Holy Spirit spoke through the prophets in the Old Testament. In the New Testament Jesus tells us that the Holy Spirit will be our Advocate, abiding in us, and revealing who Jesus is and all that He taught.

I believe in one, holy, catholic and apostolic Church. I confess one Baptism for the forgiveness of sins, the resurrection of the dead and the life of the world to come: There are four characteristics that distinguish the true nature of the Church. Jesus reveals these qualities of His Church through the Holy Spirit. The Church is one because Jesus Christ, the Founder of the Church, brought us back to the Father and made us one family of God. The Church is one in the Holy Spirit who dwells in our hearts and is constantly re-creating us into becoming the Body of Christ. The Church is holy because she is united with her head, Jesus Christ, the Source of holiness. The Church also leads others to holiness through the Holy Spirit. While we are sinners, the holiness of the Church is seen in her Head who shares it with His body who lives in union with Him, and one another, offering sacrificial love and service for the benefit of the world. The Church is catholic or universal because the Church has been commissioned by Jesus to proclaim the good news that salvation is for all peoples and nations, and to baptize in the name of the Father, Son, and Holy Spirit. Finally, the Church is apostolic as there is an unbroken link with the teaching of the apostles. The pope and bishops are the successors of the apostles, and in the Catholic Church, the succession from Peter, the first Pope, to the present pope has remained unbroken. Acknowledging our belief in one Baptism for the forgiveness of sins, the resurrection of the dead, and the life of the world to come are further creedal statements that we profess in the Nicene Creed.

THE PRAYER OF THE FAITHFUL:

The Liturgy of the Word ends with "The Prayer of the Faithful." This is one of the most ancient parts of the Mass, already attested to by St. Justin Martyr in A.D. 155: "Then we all rise together and offer prayers for ourselves… and for all others, wherever they may be, so that we may be found righteous by our life and actions, and faithful to the commandments, so as to obtain eternal salvation." (CCC 1345) The *Prayer of the Faithful* highlights the Catholic dimension of the Church. The congregation therefore prays in response to the Word of God which they have heard with their ears and received into their hearts. In union with Jesus, their High Priest, they exercise their baptismal priesthood, and offer prayers to God for the salvation of the world. This is the second time in the Liturgy (the Opening Prayer was the first) where the Church offers intentions for the needs of the universal Church, for national and world leaders, the salvation of the world, for those with specific needs, and for the local Church. Almost always, the lector will ask the congregation to add their own intentions in silence to the litany of intercessory prayers that are wafting to the throne of the Father through Jesus, Our Lamb who is seated at the right hand of the Father. It helps as part of our preparation to consider the intentions that we wish to bring to the altar of Christ's sacrifice.

PRAYER AND REFLECTION ON EUCHARIST: CELEBRATING THE LITURGY OF THE WORD

WEEK TWENTY ONE: *"Then all the people began to eat and drink, to distribute portions, and to celebrate with great joy, for they understood the words that had been explained to them." (Nehemiah 8:12)*

SPIRITUAL READING FOR THE WEEK:

- **Anoint Us in Your Covenant, Abba-Emmanuel:** Session Eleven
- **Old Testament:** Two or Three Chapters daily
- **New Testament:** Two or Three Chapters daily
- **Imitation of Christ:** One chapter daily

DAY ONE: MORNING SESSION

MORNING PRAYER: Acts of Faith, Hope, Charity; Daily Offering

Morning Face to Face with God:

Begin with Prayer to the Holy Spirit
(After pondering each bullet point, express your sentiments in a short prayer)

Prayer on Revelation 1:1-3: Listening to the Word of God
"The revelation of Jesus Christ, which God gave to him, to show his servants what must happen soon. He made it known by sending his angel to his servant John, who gives witness to the word of God and to the testimony of Jesus Christ by reporting what he saw. Blessed is the one who reads aloud and blessed are those who listen to this prophetic message and heed what is written in it, for the appointed time is near."

Read the Reflection; Ask the Holy Spirit to give you a deep appreciation for the Liturgy of the Word, and that your participation might always be wholehearted and generous.

The Penitential Rite has prepared us to encounter the Living God through His divine word in Holy Scripture. The Liturgy of the Word of God is essentially a proclamation or *kerygma*, making it clear that the reign of God is at hand and there is urgent need for repentance. We cannot be straddling the fence as we listen to God's word. God's word creates a crisis which compels us to make a decision, for or against God's word to us. The encounter is very personal and demands a response, either leading to surrender and commitment or to resistance to accepting God's invitation to covenant living. The lector, therefore, has the responsibility of proclaiming the word of God in God's name. The lector, in the spirit of Revelation 1:3, is lending his/her human voice so that God's revelation can be spoken to us during the liturgy of the word, and that we will heed God's voice: *"Blessed is the one who reads aloud and blessed are those who listen to this prophetic message and heed what is written in it, for the appointed time is near."* In order to bring His divine plan of salvation to completion, God revealed to us that His Word is the living Person of His Son, Jesus Christ. The faithful are fed at the table of Holy Scripture or God's word, which nourishment has its culmination in us being fed at the table of the Eucharist. Thus the word of God, read and proclaimed by the Church in the liturgy of the Word, leads inexorably to the consummation of the body, blood, soul and divinity of Jesus in communion, as to its natural end.

What is God saying to you?

End with Prayer to the Holy Trinity

NIGHT SESSION: Examination of Conscience

For what are you grateful? For what are you contrite?

Please review briefly your Morning Prayer topic. Make it your last thought of the day

DAY TWO: MORNING SESSION

MORNING PRAYER: Acts of Faith, Hope, Charity; Daily Offering

Morning Face to Face with God:

Begin with Prayer to the Holy Spirit

THE FIRST READING FROM THE OLD TESTAMENT:

Prayer on Hebrews 1:1-3a: Transition from the OT:

"In times past, God spoke in partial and various ways to our ancestors through the prophets; in these last days, he spoke to us through a son, whom he made heir of all things and through whom he created the universe, who is the refulgence of his glory, the very imprint of his being, and who sustains all things by his mighty word."

Read the Reflection; Ask the Holy Spirit to give you a deep appreciation for the Liturgy of the Word, and that your participation might always be wholehearted and generous.

The Bible is God's own voice, spoken to us personally, and through the authorship of human beings. The communities being addressed by God through these human authors extended over several countries and continents. Peter attests to the Scriptures being God's word spoken through human authorship: *"Know this first of all, that there is no prophecy of scripture that is a matter of personal interpretation, for no prophecy ever came through human will; but rather human beings moved by the holy Spirit spoke under the influence of God."* (2 Peter 1:20-21) The first reading is mostly taken from the Old Testament and is related thematically to the reading from the Gospel, highlighting continuity or contrast between the two Testaments. Jesus and His new kingdom is the climax of God's revelation, begun in the Old Testament. Vatican II echoes St. Augustine very well in singling out the dovetail connection between the Old and New Testaments: "God, the inspirer and author of both testaments, wisely arranged that the New Testament be hidden in the Old and the Old be made manifest in the New. For, though Christ established the New Covenant in His blood, still the books of the Old Testament with all their parts, caught up into the proclamation of the gospel acquire and show forth their full meaning in the New Testament and in turn shed light on it and explain it." (Dei Verbum 16)

What is God saying to you?

End with Prayer to the Holy Trinity

NIGHT SESSION: Examination of Conscience

For what are you grateful? For what are you contrite?

Please review briefly your Morning Prayer topic. Make it your last thought of the day

DAY THREE: MORNING SESSION

MORNING PRAYER: Acts of Faith, Hope, Charity; Daily Offering

Morning Face to Face with God:

Begin with Prayer to the Holy Spirit

PRAYER ON 'THANKS BE TO GOD':

"The sting of death is sin, and the power of sin is the law. But thanks be to God who gives us the victory through our Lord Jesus Christ. Therefore, my beloved brothers, be firm, steadfast, always

fully devoted to the work of the Lord, knowing that in the Lord your labor is not in vain." (1 Corinthians 15:56-58)

Read the Reflection; Ask the Holy Spirit to give you a deep appreciation for the Liturgy of the Word, and that your participation might always be wholehearted and generous.

At the end of the First Reading, the lector ends with "The Word of the Lord," and our response is "Thanks be to God." Our response is very fitting as we have just heard God speak directly to us through the lector! We exclaim our gratitude in response to the amazing fact that God would speak to us through the Scriptures. Essentially we can never really express enough gratitude for the indescribable act of love and saving action in our lives on God's part. In the psalms and numerous canticles, God's people expressed their gratitude in the Old Testament. The expression 'Thanks be to God' was used by Paul because God had delivered him from sin and death: *"The sting of death is sin, and the power of sin is the law. But thanks be to God who gives us the victory through our Lord Jesus Christ."* (1 Corinthians 15:56-57) After we have expressed our heartfelt thanksgiving to God for His direct revelation to us, we then spend some time in silence to taste and relish the full significance of God's word. Like Mary who *"kept all these things, pondering them in her heart,"* (Luke 2:18) we spend some time in awe and adoration of the God who just spoke to us.

What is God saying to you?

End with Prayer to the Holy Trinity

NIGHT SESSION: Examination of Conscience

For what are you grateful? For what are you contrite?

Please review briefly your Morning Prayer topic. Make it your last thought of the day

DAY FOUR: MORNING SESSION

MORNING PRAYER: Acts of Faith, Hope, Charity; Daily Offering

Morning Face to Face with God:

Begin with Prayer to the Holy Spirit

PRAYER ON THE RESPONSORIAL PSALM:

Read the Reflection; Ask the Holy Spirit to give you a deep appreciation for the Liturgy of the Word, and that your participation might always be wholehearted and generous.

The Responsorial Psalm is chosen to respond to the First Reading. The Psalms are the inspired word of God. They give us God's insight into how we should manage our human condition with its highs and lows. There are psalms of praise and adoration and thanksgiving. And there are psalms of repentance, trust, and urgent prayer in very difficult circumstances. After hearing God's word proclaimed in the first reading, we respond with God's own inspired words of praise, thanksgiving, repentance, and petition. Responding with our own words would seem inadequate and inappropriate. The singing of the responsorial psalm helps to create an atmosphere of prayer conducive for meditation on the reading. Using the psalms in their worship of God was quite natural in the Old Testament. Jesus prayed the psalms and Paul exhorted his followers to sing psalms: *"Let the word of God dwell in you richly, as in all wisdom you teach and admonish one another, singing psalms, hymns, and spiritual songs with gratitude in your hearts to God."* (Colossians 3:16)

What is God saying to you?

End with Prayer to the Holy Trinity

NIGHT SESSION: Examination of Conscience

For what are you grateful? For what are you contrite?

Please review briefly your Morning Prayer topic. Make it your last thought of the day

DAY FIVE: MORNING SESSION

MORNING PRAYER: Acts of Faith, Hope, Charity; Daily Offering

Morning Face to Face with God:

Begin with Prayer to the Holy Spirit

PRAYER ON THE SECOND READING FROM THE NEW TESTAMENT:

Read the Reflection; Ask the Holy Spirit to give you a deep appreciation for the Liturgy of the Word, and that your participation might always be wholehearted and generous.

The second reading comes from the New Testament: it is taken from one of the letters, the Acts of the Apostles, or the book of Revelation. Though often selected independently of the first reading and the Gospel, these New Testament writings reflect on the saving mystery of Jesus Christ, and advise us on the meaning it has for our lives. They also draw out the practical applications of our life in Christ and exhort us ever more to "put on Christ" and turn away from sin.

What is God saying to you?

End with Prayer to the Holy Trinity

NIGHT SESSION: Examination of Conscience

For what are you grateful? For what are you contrite?

Please review briefly your Morning Prayer topic. Make it your last thought of the day

DAY SIX: MORNING SESSION

MORNING PRAYER: Acts of Faith, Hope, Charity; Daily Offering

Morning Face to Face with God:

Begin with Prayer to the Holy Spirit

PRAYER ON THE THIRD READING OR GOSPEL:

Ask the Holy Spirit to give you a deep appreciation for the Liturgy of the Word, and that your participation might always be wholehearted and generous.

An elaborate liturgical ritual precedes the proclamation of the gospel, implying that it is the most important reading in the Liturgy of the Word. We all stand and recite together the gospel acclamation. The deacon or priest then proceeds to the ambo along with the altar servers who are carrying lighted candles. On occasion there is the use of incense, and the threefold sign of the cross is made on the forehead, lips, and breast prior to the proclamation. This elaborate ceremony indicates clearly that we have arrived at a most sacred moment when the gospel is read. These gospel accounts written by human authors, under the guidance and inspiration of the Holy Spirit, are therefore God's own words about Christ's life. The proclamation of the Gospel makes Jesus' life present to us in a profound way. Christ speaks personally to each one of us through the divinely inspired words in the Gospel. We do not merely hear about Jesus calling people to repent and follow Him; we hear Jesus Himself say to us: *"Repent for the kingdom of heaven is at hand.*" (Matthew 4:17) We do not simply hear about Jesus forgiving a woman who was caught in adultery. It is as if we hear Jesus say to us in our sorrow over our sins, *"Neither do I condemn you; go, and do not sin again."* (John 8:11) Every gospel account that is proclaimed challenges us to answer Jesus' question to us: *"Who do you say that I am?"*

What is God saying to you?

End with Prayer to the Holy Trinity

NIGHT SESSION: Examination of Conscience

For what are you grateful? For what are you contrite?

Please review briefly your Morning Prayer topic. Make it your last thought of the day

DAY SEVEN: MORNING SESSION

MORNING PRAYER: Acts of Faith, Hope, Charity; Daily Offering

Morning Face to Face with God:

Begin with Prayer to the Holy Spirit

THE SEVENTH DWELLING PLACES – CONTINUED:

(After pondering each bullet point, express your sentiments in a short prayer)

- St. Teresa answers the question whether a soul can be sure of its salvation when it has arrived in the Seventh Dwelling Places. In her opinion the soul is secure as long as *"the divine Majesty keeps it in His hand and it does not offend Him…"*
- *"The soul doesn't consider itself safe even though it sees itself in this state and the state has lasted for some years. But it goes about with much greater fear than before, guarding itself from any small offense against God and with the strongest desires to serve Him, … and with habitual pain and confusion at seeing the little it can do and the great deal to which it is obliged. This pain is no small cross but a very great penance."* (TIC – VII:2:9)
- St. Teresa talks about several graces that a soul receives in the Seventh Dwelling Places. The first grace is a forgetfulness of self: *"The soul doesn't worry about all that can happen. It experiences strange forgetfulness, for, as I say, seemingly the soul no longer is or would want to be anything in anything, except when it understands that there can come from itself something by which the glory and honor of God may increase even one degree. For this purpose the soul would very willingly lay down its life."* (TIC – VII:3:2)

- The second grace is that the soul has a great desire to suffer: *"The desire left in these souls that the will of God be done in them reaches such an extreme that they think everything His Majesty does is good. If He desires the soul to suffer, well and good; it not, it doesn't kill itself as it used to."* (TIC – VII:3:4)

- The amazing transformation is that these souls have a deep interior joy when they are persecuted, with much peace and no hostile feelings toward their persecutors. On the contrary, they have a special love for their persecutors. The soul has no fear of death.

- They no longer desire consolations or spiritual delights, since God Himself dwells in them. *"There is a great detachment from everything and a desire to be always either alone or occupied in something that will benefit some soul. There are no interior trials or feelings of dryness, but the soul lives with a remembrance and tender love of our Lord. It would never want to go without praising Him. When it becomes distracted, the Lord Himself awakens it…"* (TIC – VII:3:8)

- The Lord and the soul rejoice together in the deepest silence. The faculties are not lost or confused; they do not work because they are in constant amazement.

- In Chapter Four, St. Teresa offers very salutary advice by way of conclusion: *"It is necessary that your foundation consist of more than prayer and contemplation. If you do not strive for the virtues and practice them, you will always be dwarfs…"*

- *"Let us desire and be occupied in prayer not for the sake of our enjoyment but so as to have this strength to serve… Believe me, Martha and Mary must join together in order to show hospitality to the Lord and have Him always present and not host Him badly by failing to give Him something to eat."*

- *"How would Mary, always seated at His feet, provide Him with food if her sister did not help her? His food is that in every way possible we draw souls that they may be saved and praise Him always…"*

- *"In sum, my Sisters, what I conclude with is that we shouldn't build castles in the air. The Lord doesn't look so much at the greatness of our works as at the love with which they are done. And if we do what we can, His Majesty will enable us each day to do more and more, provided that we do not quickly tire…"*

- *"His Majesty will join it with that which He offered on the cross to the Father for us. Thus even though works are small they will have the value our love for Him would have merited had they been great."* (TIC – VII:4:12 & 15)

What is God saying to you?

End with Prayer to the Holy Trinity

NIGHT SESSION: Examination of Conscience

For what are you grateful? For what are you contrite?

What prayer would you compose to express what God has said to you this week?

Please review briefly your Morning Prayer topic. Make it your last thought of the day

PRAYER AND REFLECTION ON EUCHARIST: CELEBRATING THE LITURGY OF THE WORD – CONTINUED

WEEK TWENTY TWO: *"BLESSED IS THE ONE WHO READS ALOUD AND BLESSED ARE THOSE WHO LISTEN TO THIS PROPHETIC MESSAGE AND HEED WHAT IS WRITTEN IN IT, FOR THE APPOINTED TIME IS NEAR." (REVELATION 1:3)*

SPIRITUAL READING FOR THE WEEK:

- **Anoint Us in Your Covenant, Abba-Emmanuel:** Session Eleven
- **Old Testament:** Two or Three Chapters daily
- **New Testament:** Two or Three Chapters daily
- **Imitation of Christ:** One chapter daily

DAY ONE: MORNING SESSION

MORNING PRAYER: Acts of Faith, Hope, Charity; Daily Offering

Morning Face to Face with God:

Begin with Prayer to the Holy Spirit
(After pondering each bullet point, express your sentiments in a short prayer)

PRAYER ON THE HOMILY

"Ezra read clearly from the book of the law of God, interpreting it so that all could understand what was read. Then Nehemiah, that is, the governor, and Ezra the priest-scribe, and the Levites who were instructing the people said to all the people: "Today is holy to the LORD your God. Do

not lament, do not weep!"... Then all the people began to eat and drink, to distribute portions, and to celebrate with great joy, for they understood the words that had been explained to them." (Nehemiah 8:8-12)

Read the Reflection; Ask the Holy Spirit to give you a deep appreciation for the Liturgy of the Word, and that your participation might always be wholehearted and generous.

From the earliest days of Christian liturgy, the Word of God was read and then accompanied by a homily which explained the meaning of the Scriptural readings and drew out the application for people's lives. The word homily means "explanation" in Greek. In the early Church, the bishop typically was the one who celebrated Sunday Mass and gave the homily. From this early practice came the homilies of St. Augustine, St. Ambrose, St. John Chrysostom, and many other celebrated texts from the Church Fathers. The liturgical practice of explaining the Scripture readings is rooted in ancient Jewish custom. In the book of Ezra, for example, the book of the law was not merely read to the people. The Levites *"helped the people to understand the law."* (Nehemiah 8:7) They read from God's law *"and they gave the sense, so that the people understood the reading."* (Nehemiah 8:8) The Jewish synagogues followed a similar practice. Readings from Scripture were accompanied by explanations. Jesus Himself practiced this custom. He expounded on a reading from Scripture in His hometown synagogue in Nazareth (Luke 4:18-30), and He also regularly taught in the synagogues throughout Galilee (Mark 1:21; Luke 4:15). The homily is crucial for the instruction of the faithful, so that they can understand the readings and apply it to their lives. Vatican II saw the homily as holding "pride of place" among the various forms of Christian instruction (Dei Verbum 24). It is our common experience that a nourishing and heart-warming homily greatly strengthens and renews us.

What is God saying to you?

End with Prayer to the Holy Trinity

NIGHT SESSION: Examination of Conscience

For what are you grateful? For what are you contrite?

Please review briefly your Morning Prayer topic. Make it your last thought of the day

DAY TWO: MORNING SESSION

MORNING PRAYER: Acts of Faith, Hope, Charity; Daily Offering

Morning Face to Face with God:

Begin with Prayer to the Holy Spirit

PRAYER ON THE NICENE CREED

"I believe in one God, the Father almighty, maker of heaven and earth, of all things visible and invisible.

Read the Reflection; Ask the Holy Spirit to give you a deep appreciation for the Liturgy of the Word, and that your participation might always be wholehearted and generous.

The Nicene Creed was formulated at the Council of Nicaea in 325, and was formally ratified at the Council of Constantinople in 381. Specifically, it refuted the heresy promulgated by Arius, a Libyan presbyter in Alexandria. Arius held that although 'the Son' was divine, he was a created being. There was a time when he was not. Therefore he was not co-essential or consubstantial with the Father. This made Jesus less than the Father and posed serious questions about Jesus being the Savior of the world. The Nicene Creed explicitly affirms the divinity of Jesus and His consubstantiality with the Father or sharing the same divine essence with the Father.

The Creed is a summary statement of our faith. It was used in the early Church as the standard for Christian belief. After the Council of Nicaea, it became a means for ensuring right doctrine and curbing heresy. Our profession of faith emphasizes the role of the Three Divine Persons who are the principal actors in the enactment of God's plan of salvation on our behalf. The role of each divine Person is emphasized and clarified so that our faith is affirmed and substantiated. Moving from creation to Christ's incarnation, death and resurrection, to the sending of the Holy Spirit, to the era of the Church and finally to the Second Coming, the Creed carries us through the entire story of salvation history. Our prayer for today focuses on the place of God the Father in the divine plan of salvation.   The Creed proclaims that the universe was brought into existence by the one true God, *"the maker of heaven and earth,"* and is moving in a certain direction according to God's plan. *(For your prayer, recite the Nicene Creed, with reverent attention and pauses for reflection, to the words and the Presence of the Blessed Trinity.)*

What is God saying to you?

End with Prayer to the Holy Trinity

NIGHT SESSION: Examination of Conscience

For what are you grateful? For what are you contrite?

Please review briefly your Morning Prayer topic. Make it your last thought of the day

DAY THREE: MORNING SESSION

MORNING PRAYER: Acts of Faith, Hope, Charity; Daily Offering

Morning Face to Face with God

Begin with Prayer to the Holy Spirit

PRAYER ON THE NICENE CREED – CONTINUED

"I believe in one Lord Jesus Christ, the Only Begotten Son of God, born of the Father before all ages, God from God, Light from Light, true God from true God, begotten, not made, consubstantial with the Father; through him all things were made. For us men and for our salvation he came down from heaven, and by the Holy Spirit was incarnate of the Virgin Mary, and became man. For our sake he was crucified under Pontius Pilate, he suffered death and was buried, and rose again on the third day in accordance with the Scriptures. He ascended into heaven and is seated at the right hand of the Father. He will come again in glory to judge the living and the dead and his kingdom will have no end."

Read the Reflection; Ask the Holy Spirit to give you a deep appreciation for the Liturgy of the Word, and that your participation might always be wholehearted and generous.

The Nicene Creed asserts the fact that God's divine plan was fully revealed in God's Son, the *"one Lord Jesus Christ."* Jesus is called Lord, because we affirm our faith in Him as divine. He is *"true God from true God,"* as Jesus shares the same divine essence with the Father. We proclaim that Jesus is *"eternally begotten of the Father;"* He is *"begotten, not made, consubstantial (one in Being or homoousios in Greek) with the Father."* Already in the third Century, in a council at Antioch, the Church had to affirm against Paul of Samosata that Jesus Christ is Son of God by nature and not by adoption. The first ecumenical Council of Nicaea in 325 affirmed in its creed that the Son of God is *"begotten, not made, of the same substance as the Father,"* and condemned Arius who had affirmed that the Son of God was "from another substance" than that of the Father. The distinction between 'beget' and 'make' was made to avoid any confusion about who Jesus is. You beget someone of the same kind as yourself. But you make something of a different kind from yourself. What God begets is God; what God creates is not God. The

Creed also notes that Jesus became man *"for our salvation."* Jesus is a divine Person with two natures, divine and human. Jesus suffered and died on the cross and rose from the dead to bring us the forgiveness of sins. Jesus is our Savior. He saves us as Son of God who became son of man. At the end of our lives Jesus *"will come again in glory to judge the living and the dead." "His kingdom will have no end"* is a categorical statement, highlighting the overthrow of the kingdom of Satan and the complete victory of the kingdom of God.

What is God saying to you?

End with Prayer to the Holy Trinity

NIGHT SESSION: Examination of Conscience

For what are you grateful? For what are you contrite?

Please review briefly your Morning Prayer topic. Make it your last thought of the day

DAY FOUR: MORNING SESSION

MORNING PRAYER: Acts of Faith, Hope, Charity; Daily Offering

Morning Face to Face with God:

Begin with Prayer to the Holy Spirit

PRAYER ON THE NICENE CREED – CONTINUED

> *"I believe in the Holy Spirit, the Lord, the giver of life, who proceeds from the Father and the Son, who with the Father and the Son is adored and glorified, who has spoken through the prophets."*

Read the Reflection; Ask the Holy Spirit to give you a deep appreciation for the Liturgy of the Word, and that your participation might always be wholehearted and generous.

   This last section of the Nicene Creed emphasizes our faith in the Holy Spirit and His place in the Triune Godhead. The Spirit is called 'holy' because He proceeds from the Father and the Son: The Holy Spirit shares the same divine essence as the Father and the Son. The Source of Holiness, or total Otherness, is found in the Father, the Son, and the Holy Spirit. The Spirit is also holy because He is the source of sanctification in God's covenant family. The Holy Spirit is also referred to as 'Lord', just as Jesus was, because He is truly divine, and co-equal with the Father and the Son. Hence it fitting that the Holy Spirit is adored along with the Father and the Son. The Holy Spirit is the 'giver of life' as well. Breath (the literal meaning of spirit) is the sign of life in us. In Genesis 1:2, the creation of the world is described as *"a mighty wind (the Spirit of God) sweeping over the waters,"* or breathing over the waters. The Holy Spirit is also the source of eternal life, as a person has to be born of *water and the spirit* (John 3:5). According to St. Paul, "the Spirit gives life." (2 Corinthians 3:6) Finally, *"through the Spirit, by faith, we await the hope of righteousness."* (Galatians 5:5) The Holy Spirit came to be understood as the Source of life. So indeed, the Holy Spirit is the Giver of life. The Holy Spirit has been acting in the world since Old Testament times, even though there was no awareness that the Holy Spirit was a divine Person and was distinct from the Father. The Holy Spirit spoke through the prophets in the Old Testament. In the New Testament Jesus tells us that the Holy Spirit will be our Advocate, abiding in us, and revealing who Jesus is and all that He taught.

What is God saying to you?

End with Prayer to the Holy Trinity

NIGHT SESSION: Examination of Conscience

For what are you grateful? For what are you contrite?

Please review briefly your Morning Prayer topic. Make it your last thought of the day

DAY FIVE: MORNING SESSION

MORNING PRAYER: Acts of Faith, Hope, Charity; Daily Offering

Morning Face to Face with God:

Begin with Prayer to the Holy Spirit

PRAYER ON THE NICENE CREED - CONTINUED:

> *"I believe in one, holy, catholic and apostolic Church. I confess one Baptism for the forgiveness of sins and I look forward to the resurrection of the dead and the life of the world to come. Amen."*

Read the Reflection; Ask the Holy Spirit to give you a deep appreciation for the Liturgy of the Word, and that your participation might always be wholehearted and generous.

There are four characteristics that distinguish the true nature of the Church. Jesus reveals these qualities of His Church through the Holy Spirit. The Church is one because Jesus Christ, the Founder of the Church, brought us back to the Father and made us one family of God. The Church is one in the Holy Spirit who dwells in our hearts and is constantly re-creating us into becoming the Body of Christ. The Church is holy because she is united with her head, Jesus Christ, the Source of holiness. The Church also leads others to holiness through the Holy Spirit. While we are sinners, the holiness of the Church is seen in her Head who shares it with His body who lives in union with Him, and one another, offering sacrificial love and service for the benefit of the world. The Church is catholic or universal because the Church has been commissioned by Jesus to proclaim the good news to all nations and baptize in the name of the Father, Son, and Holy Spirit. Finally, the Church is apostolic as there is an unbroken link with the teaching of the apostles. The pope and bishops are the successors of the apostles, and in the Catholic Church the succession from Peter, the first Pope, to the present pope has remained unbroken. Acknowledging our belief in one Baptism for the forgiveness of sins, the resurrection of the dead, and the life of the world to come are further creedal statements that we profess in the Nicene Creed.

What is God saying to you?

End with Prayer to the Holy Trinity

NIGHT SESSION: Examination of Conscience

For what are you grateful? For what are you contrite?

Please review briefly your Morning Prayer topic. Make it your last thought of the day

DAY SIX: MORNING SESSION

MORNING PRAYER: Acts of Faith, Hope, Charity; Daily Offering

Morning Face to Face with God:

Begin with Prayer to the Holy Spirit

PRAYER ON THE PRAYER OF THE FAITHFUL:

Read the Reflection; Ask the Holy Spirit to give you a deep appreciation for the Liturgy of the Word, and that your participation might always be wholehearted and generous.

The *Prayer of the Faithful* highlights the Catholic dimension of the Church. The congregation therefore prays in response to the Word of God which they have heard with their ears and received into their hearts. In union with Jesus, their High Priest, they exercise their baptismal priesthood, and offer prayers to God for the salvation of the world. This is the second time in the Liturgy (the Opening Prayer was the first) where the Church offers intentions for the needs of the universal Church, for national and world leaders, the salvation of the world, for those with specific needs, and for the local Church. Almost always, the Lector will ask the congregation to add their own petitions in silence to the litany of intercessory prayers that are wafting to the throne of the Father through Jesus, Our Lamb who is seated at the right hand of the Father. It helps as part of our preparation to consider the intentions that we wish to bring to the altar of Christ's sacrifice.

What is God saying to you?

End with Prayer to the Holy Trinity

NIGHT SESSION: Examination of Conscience

For what are you grateful? For what are you contrite?

Please review briefly your Morning Prayer topic. Make it your last thought of the day

DAY SEVEN: MORNING SESSION

MORNING PRAYER: Acts of Faith, Hope, Charity; Daily Offering

Morning Face to Face with God:

Begin with Prayer to the Holy Spirit

THE DARK NIGHT OF THE SENSES BY ST. JOHN OF THE CROSS

(After pondering each bullet point, express your sentiments in a short prayer)

- St. John of the Cross makes a distinction between the Dark Night of the Senses and the Dark Night of the Spirit. He devotes his entire treatise *The Dark Night*, on these two nights of purification/transformation.
- In Book One he deals with the Night of the Senses, and Book Two focuses on the Night of the Spirit. In the sensory night, the senses are purged and made docile and submissive to the spirit. The night of the senses is common and happens to many a soul.

- From the way of the Beginner they are being invited to the way of the Proficient. The Dark Night of the Senses was the next step that the Holy Spirit took in leading the disciple to become a 'proficient.'
- They were going about their prayer and spiritual practices with eagerness and fidelity and were experiencing satisfaction and consolation. In their opinion, God was pleased with them.
- Just when they think all is well, *"God now leaves them in such darkness that they do not know which way to turn in their discursive imaginings. They cannot advance a step in meditation, as they used to, now that the interior sense faculties are engulfed in this night. He leaves them in such dryness that they not only fail to receive satisfaction and pleasure from their spiritual exercises and works, as they formerly did, but also find these exercises distasteful and bitter."* (TDN – Book One: Chapter 8:3) With this change everything seems to be going in reverse causing them confusion and doubt.
- Discursive prayer was becoming progressively more difficult to do. Discursive forms of prayer, like meditation and Ignatian Contemplation (imaging prayer) did not have the same appeal as before. Consequently, in prayer the disciple began noticing a reluctance to exercise the intellect, imagination, and memory.
- Earlier, there was a great need to satisfy one's religious curiosity which at times seemed insatiable. That desire has waned to a great extent because the longing to know God and be in covenant with Him has exceeded the eagerness to know about God and be satisfied intellectually.
- *"And he (God) desires to liberate them from the lowly exercise of the senses and of discursive meditation, by which they go in search of him so inadequately and with so many difficulties, and lead them into the exercise of the spirit, in which they become capable of a communion with God that is more abundant and more free of imperfections."* (TDN – Book One: Chapter 8:3)
- God does this only after beginners have exercised themselves in prayer on a consistent basis and have practiced virtue seriously. Through serious prayer they become detached from worldly things and gain spiritual strength in God.
- This shift in prayer is now experienced as distraction, boredom, inability to stay focused, and dryness. God appears vague, removed, and beyond their reach. Needless to say, this state is confusing and discouraging. They feel that a dark night has descended upon them.

What is God saying to you?

End with Prayer to the Holy Trinity

NIGHT SESSION: Examination of Conscience

For what are you grateful? For what are you contrite?

What prayer would you compose to express what God has said to you this week?

Please review briefly your Morning Prayer topic. Make it your last thought of the day

SESSION TWELVE
EUCHARIST: CELEBRATING THE LITURGY OF THE EUCHARIST

WORDS OF INSTITUTION:

"Take this, all of you, and eat of it, for this is my body, which will be given up for you… Take this, all of you, and drink from it, for this is the chalice of my Blood, the Blood of the New and Eternal Covenant, which will be poured out for you and for many for the forgiveness of sins. Do this in memory of me." (Eucharistic Prayer II)

In the second half of the Mass, called the Liturgy of the Eucharist, Jesus' sacrifice on the cross is made present by the priest, who carries out what Jesus did at the Last Supper and what He commanded the apostles to do in His memory. Bread and wine are offered as gifts by the people and then consecrated and changed into the Body and Blood of Christ, whom we receive in Holy Communion. There are three principal parts to the Liturgy of the Eucharist: 1. The Preparation of the Gifts; 2. The Eucharistic Prayer; 3. The Communion Rite. In this Session we will consider parts 1 and 2.

THE PREPARATION OF THE GIFTS:

In offering the bread and wine, we are offering ourselves to God, as these gifts represent our sustenance, and therefore, our very lives. Clearly then, the presentation of the gifts has sacrificial tones. The early Christians were familiar with the Presentation of the Gifts in their liturgy. Already in A.D. 155, St. Justin Martyr mentioned the custom of someone bringing bread and wine to the priest after the prayers of intercession. St. Hippolytus (A.D. 225) notes the practice as well. In putting together the Liturgy, the Church was taking her cue from Israel's sacrificial rites in the Old Testament. Every sacrifice was a covenant ritual, as the victim represented the one making the offering. Our offering to God through bread and wine has special significance as God will accept our offering and transform it into the Body, Blood, Soul, and Divinity of Jesus. This ability to offer ourselves with the assurance that we will be transformed into Jesus was made possible for us through Jesus' incarnation. In His incarnation, Jesus, Son of God, ratified such an offering. He offered to become one of us, and Mary, as the new Eve and our representative, accepted the Father's invitation to become the mother of His Son through the power of the Holy Spirit. So Jesus first became one of us, so that as Paul would put it, He could become sin and we His righteousness. Now, through our offering of bread and wine, we can and will be transformed into Jesus, thus participating in God's righteousness.

MIXING OF WATER AND WINE:

This transformation into Jesus is indicated in the mingling of the water with the wine. Before the wine is offered, the priest pours a drop of water into the wine. Wine symbolizes Christ's divinity, and water symbolizes our humanity. In assuming our humanity, Jesus was able to become our Lamb of sacrifice, thus enabling us to share in His divinity: *"By the mystery of this water and wine may we come to share in the divinity of Christ who humbled himself to share in our humanity."* The prayer brings out the kenosis or emptying of Christ in accepting our humanity. As Philippians 2:7 tells us, *"Rather, he emptied himself, taking the form of a slave, coming in human likeness."* During our Sunday Eucharist, the priest will pray this prayer softly and you will not hear him, as the congregation is singing. However, his prayer is ours as well.

ENTERING THE HOLY OF HOLIES:

The priest then prepares himself to enter into the Sacred Mysteries. Soon we will be in the august presence of the whole heavenly assembly, with the Father at the center, with Jesus, our Lamb that was slain, surrounded by His disciples whom He has washed clean in His blood. The priest and the congregation are acutely aware of their unworthiness and ask God to make them worthy: *"With humble spirit and contrite heart may we be accepted by you, O Lord, and may our sacrifice in your sight this day be pleasing to you, Lord God."* The priest then washes his hands, knowing that only God can make him acceptable in His sight: *"Wash me, O Lord, from my iniquity and cleanse me from my sin."*

We have arrived at a climactic moment in the Mass. The bread and wine will soon be transformed into the Body and Blood of Jesus, and Our Lord will come to us in Holy Communion and become one with us. Our divine High Priest will make this happen through the priest who is acting in His place. The priest then asks for prayer as he is about to begin the Eucharistic Prayer: *"Pray, brethren, that my sacrifice and yours may be acceptable to God, the almighty Father."* The priest is acting in the Person of Christ; in a real sense then the sacrifice is his. And it is our sacrifice as well, as the entire Church is offering herself in union with Christ's sacrifice. So the congregation responds: *"May the Lord accept the sacrifice at your hands for the praise and glory of his name, for our good and the good of all his holy Church."*

THE EUCHARISTIC PRAYER:

There are thirteen Eucharistic Prayers that are approved by Rome for use in the United States. There are nine Eucharistic Prayers in the Sacramentary (altar missal). They include four universal Eucharistic Prayers, the Roman Canon and three others. On Sundays, generally, the priest can choose from the first three. The fourth Eucharistic Prayer has its own Preface and is used when a proper Preface is not specified. There are three Eucharistic Prayers for Masses with children, and two for Masses of Reconciliation which are used during the Season of Lent.

The various Eucharistic Prayers have been modeled after Jewish table prayers and follow the same format. The format consisted of the Prayer of Praise of God for His creation; Praise and Thanksgiving for God's Redemptive work in the past, similar to the proclamation of God's saving act in the Exodus made during the Passover Meal; and Intercession for the future, praying that God would continue His saving work among them and that God would send the Messiah to restore the Davidic kingdom. When you listen closely to the Eucharistic Prayer you will notice a threefold structure as well. There is a blessing over the bread and wine; the proclamation of the central event of Jesus' death and resurrection, and our restoration as God's covenant family; praise to God for creation, thanksgiving for His saving deeds, and intercession.

The Old Testament sacrifices pre-figured Christ's sacrifice on the cross. Perhaps, more than any other sacrifice in the Old Testament, the events surrounding Abraham's sacrifice prefigure Christ's sacrifice on Calvary. Genesis 22 tells how Abraham took his only beloved son Isaac to Mount Moriah on a donkey. Isaac carried the wood for the sacrifice up the mountain and was bound on the wood to be offered as a sacrifice for sin. In response to this heroic act of total surrender God swore that He would bless the whole human family through Abraham's descendants. Many centuries later, God the Father offers up His *only beloved son*, Jesus, in Jerusalem – a city associated with *Moriah*, the very place where Abraham offered up Isaac, and King Solomon built the first Temple (2 Chronicles 3:1). Like Isaac, Jesus travels to this place on a *donkey*, and like Isaac, He *carries the wood* of the cross to Calvary. There, like Isaac again, Jesus is bound to the wood and offered as a *sacrifice* for sin – a sacrifice that brings about the *worldwide blessing* that God swore to Abraham in Genesis 22. On Good Friday, God the Father and God the Son, therefore, bring to fulfillment what was prefigured by Abraham and Isaac long ago, and God's oath to Abraham that He would bless the human family is realized through His Son.

As the Eucharistic Prayers near their conclusion, the priest makes various intercessions. First, he prays for all who will soon be nourished by the body and blood of Christ. He prays that "they may become one body, one spirit in Christ (EP III) – an echo of St. Paul's words in 1 Corinthians 10:17: *"Because there is one bread, we who are many are one body, for we all partake of the one bread."* The priest also prays that our participation in Christ's sacrifice might make us "an eternal offering to you (EP III)", or "a living sacrifice (EP IV)," echoing St. Paul's exhortation to the Romans: *"Present your bodies as a living sacrifice, holy and acceptable to God, which is your spiritual worship."* (Romans 12:1) Secondly, the priest prays for the Church universal, naming the pope and the local bishop and then interceding for all bishops, clergy, and the entire people of God, both the living and the dead. Some intercessions have a universal scope, interceding for "all who seek you with a sincere heart (EP IV)," and praying that the sacrifice of the Mass "advance the peace and salvation of all the world (EP III)."

THE PREFACE:

The Preface to the Eucharistic Prayer disposes us to enter deeply into the Sacred Mysteries of Jesus, the Lamb of God, being made present in our midst through His sacrifice on the cross. The Preface also is a summary of what is about to take place. Because the Preface introduces us to the thirteen Eucharistic Prayers, and there is so much richness and variety in the Eucharistic Celebrations of the three-year Liturgical Cycle, the Church offers us 50 different Prefaces in the Order of the Mass. These Prefaces are tailored for each liturgical season. For instance, there are two Prefaces for the season of Advent, two for Christmas, four for Lent and two for the Passion of the Lord, five for the Easter Season, eight for Sundays in Ordinary Time, five for the Dead, and the list goes on.

Every Preface opens with the three part dialogue. We are familiar with the first exchange as we have used it in other places of our celebration. We ask the Lord to be with us as we prepare ourselves to participate in the death and resurrection of our Risen Lord. This is the most radical and comprehensive mission of our lives: to be present to the Lamb that was slain, and through Him to the Father in the power of the Holy Spirit, in true covenant so that our lives belong to Him as a pleasing offering. Then we are asked to lift up our hearts and in unison we respond that we have lifted them up on high. Our hearts symbolize the depths of our being. We express the seriousness of our intent to enter fully into the new and everlasting covenant when we say that we have lifted up our hearts to the Lord. And then we pray the third exchange: we are asked to give thanks to the Lord. We gave thanks during the Gloria Prayer, and during the Liturgy of the Word. And we will continue in the same vein throughout our celebration. The Mass is a thanksgiving celebration, Eucharist meaning thanksgiving. We have been redeemed by the blood of the Lamb. Everything we have and are is God's gift to us, especially the gift of sharing in the fullness of divine life, made possible through Jesus, the Lamb of God. Very appropriately therefore we respond to the invitation to give thanks by proclaiming that 'It is right and just' to do so.

The priest then goes into the Prayer of the Preface which is essentially a prayer of thanksgiving and praise. The Prayer is always addressed to the Father and the opening lines are always the same. They bear some resemblance to the prayer of adoration and praise addressed to the Father in the Gloria Prayer. In the Preface, one dimension or the other of our history of salvation is highlighted for which we are giving thanks and praise. In Preface IV for Sundays in Ordinary Time, for example, we are offered a brief history of our salvation: *"For by his birth he brought renewal to humanity's fallen state, and by his suffering, canceled out our sins; by his rising from the dead, he has opened the way to eternal life, and by ascending to you, O Father, he has unlocked the gates of heaven. And so, with the company of Angels and Saints, we sing the hymn of your praise, as without end we acclaim."* In Preface III for Sundays in Ordinary Time, we highlight the salvation of man by a man: *"It is truly right and just, our duty and our salvation, always and everywhere to give you thanks, Lord, Holy Father, almighty and eternal God. For we know it belongs to your boundless glory, that you came to the aid of mortal beings with your divinity and even fashioned for us a remedy out of mortality itself, that the cause of our downfall might become the means of our salvation through Christ our Lord. Through him the host of angels adores your majesty and rejoices in your presence forever. May our voices, we pray, join with theirs in one chorus of exultant praise, as we acclaim:"* You would do well to pray on your own with the various Prefaces and come to appreciate the wealth and spiritual wisdom of our Eucharistic prayers that have been fashioned by the Church over centuries.

THE SANCTUS:

In response to the Preface we express our thanksgiving and praise by praying the Sanctus Prayer: *"Holy, Holy, Holy Lord God of hosts. Heaven and earth are full of your glory. Hosanna in the highest. Blessed is he who comes in the name of the Lord. Hosanna in the highest."* As with the Responsorial Psalm, the most adequate way of responding to God's Loving Kindness, is through the revealed word of God. In Isaiah 6:3, one Seraph cried out to the other in the Presence of God: *"Holy, holy, holy is the LORD of hosts! All the earth is filled with his glory!"* In beholding this vision, Isaiah felt doomed, a man of unclean lips whom the Seraph cleansed. Similarly, on the Day of the Lord when the Eucharist was celebrated, John had a similar experience of unworthiness before the presence of God: *"When I caught sight of him, I fell down at his feet as though dead. He touched me with his right hand and said, 'Do not be afraid. I am the first and the last, the one who lives. Once I was dead, but now I am alive forever and ever. I hold the keys to death and the netherworld.'"* (Revelation 1:17-18) In proclaiming God's holiness, we are uniting with the Seraphim and saints, with the full confidence that we will be cleansed of our sins by the blood of the Lamb. Understandably, we direct our praise and thanksgiving toward the Messiah: *"Blessed is he who comes in the name of the Lord."* We join with the crowds who welcomed Jesus as the Messiah into Jerusalem on the eve of His death by crucifixion: *"Hosanna! Blessed is he who comes in the name of the Lord, [even] the king of Israel."* (John 12:13) *Hosanna* is a Hebrew word, meaning *"Save us."* In liturgical worship it became an expression of praise. We welcome Jesus into our midst. Soon and very soon, He will be present on our altar as the Lamb of God, our Risen Lord.

THE EPICLELSIS:

Epiclesis from the Greek means *"an invocation upon."* Already the early Christians asked for an invocation of the Holy Spirit upon the gifts of bread and wine so that they would be transformed into the body and blood of Jesus. Jesus authorized his apostles and their successors to change bread and wine into the body and blood of Christ as a memorial of what He did when He instituted the Eucharist in the Upper Room. Jesus also breathed the Holy Spirit upon His apostles and through them upon their successors. The manifestation of the Holy Spirit's presence and power was seen at the Outpouring of the Holy Spirit after Jesus' Ascension. Jesus did everything in the power of the Holy Spirit, from conception to resurrection. Jesus wants His followers to do the same. The Church is very aware of this Trinitarian truth. The priest exercises his priesthood given to him by Jesus in the power of the Holy Spirit. *"Make holy, therefore, these gifts, we pray, by sending down your Spirit upon them like the dewfall, so that they may become for us the Body and Blood of our Lord, Jesus Christ."* (Eucharistic Prayer II); or *"Therefore, O Lord, we humbly implore you: by the same Spirit graciously make holy these gifts we have brought to you for consecration, that they may become the Body and Blood of your Son our Lord Jesus Christ."* (Eucharistic Prayer III)

THE WORDS OF INSTITUTION AND CONSECRATION:

"Take this, all of you, and eat of it, for this is my body, which will be given up for you… Take this, all of you, and drink from it, for this is the chalice of my Blood, the Blood of the New and Eternal Covenant, which will be poured out for you and for many for the forgiveness of sins. Do this in memory of me."

Jesus is instituting the Eucharist within the Passover Feast which was a sacrifice: *"It is the Passover sacrifice for the LORD, who passed over the houses of the Israelites in Egypt; when he struck down the Egyptians, he delivered our houses."* (Exodus 12:27) In speaking of His Body and Blood, Jesus is referring to Himself as the Lamb of sacrifice of the new covenant. Jesus uses the phrase, *'which will be given up for you,'* (didomai in Greek), which in the gospels is associated with sacrifice: *"and the bread that I will give is my flesh for the life of the world"* (John 6:51); *"For the Son of Man did not come to be served but to serve and to give his life as a ransom for many."* (Mark 10:45) Similarly, when Jesus talks about His *"blood being poured out for you and for many,"* He is alluding to His sacrificial death on the cross. In the sacrifices of atonement in the Temple, the blood of the animals was poured out upon the altar: *"He shall also put some of the blood on the horns of the altar which is before the LORD in the tent of meeting. The rest of the blood he shall pour out at the base of the altar for burnt offerings which is at the entrance of the tent of meeting."* (Leviticus 4:18) Jesus also speaks of the blood of the new and eternal covenant. This is the only place in the Gospels where Jesus speaks of the new and eternal covenant that He is establishing through His death and resurrection. Jesus' words echo Moses' words when the Mosaic covenant was established: *"Then he took the blood and splashed it on the people, saying, 'This is the blood of the covenant which the LORD has made with you according to all these words.'"* (Exodus 24:8) Through His blood the new and everlasting covenant is being established. Jesus' words also indicate a replacement of the Mosaic covenant by His new and eternal covenant established in His blood: *"When he (the prophet Jeremiah) speaks of a "new" covenant, he declares the first one obsolete. And what has become obsolete and has grown old is close to disappearing."* (Hebrews 8:13) In anticipation of His impending sacrifice on the cross by crucifixion, Jesus offers us His body to eat and His blood to drink in the Passover meal.

Lastly, *"for you and for many for the forgiveness of sins:"* Jesus is speaking as the Suffering Servant, prophesied in Isaiah: *"My servant, the just one, shall justify the many, their iniquity he shall bear."* (Isaiah 53:11) In the phrase 'one for many,' the sacrifice of the Suffering Servant (Jesus) on behalf of His kinsfolk (covenant family) is being emphasized. 'Many' therefore, does include everybody. Elsewhere in Isaiah, salvation is a universal gift (grace), as for instance in Isaiah 49:6: *"It is too little, he says, for you to be my servant, to raise up the tribes of Jacob, and restore the survivors of Israel; I will make you a light to the nations, that my salvation may reach to the ends of the earth."* 1Timothy 2:5-6 tells us that Jesus died for all: *"There is also one mediator between God and the human race, Christ Jesus, himself human, who gave himself as ransom for all."* The sober reality is that while Jesus died for all, not everyone will choose to accept the salvation offered by Jesus. To do so, one would have to accept Him as Savior and Lord.

There is an intimate connection between the Epiclesis and Pronouncement of the Words of Consecration. The Catechism of the Catholic Church makes this point very clear. 1106 says, "Together with the anamnesis, the epiclesis is at the heart of each sacramental celebration, most especially of the Eucharist: You ask how the bread becomes the Body of Christ, and the wine… the Blood of Christ. I shall tell you: the Holy Spirit comes upon them and accomplishes what surpasses every word and thought… Let it be enough for you to understand that it is by the Holy Spirit, just as it was of the Holy Virgin and by the Holy Spirit that the Lord, through and in himself, took flesh." (St. John Damascene, De Fide orth. 4, 13)

THE MYSTERY OF FAITH:

Through the power of the Holy Spirit, the words of consecration pronounced by the priest have changed the bread and wine into the Body and Blood of Jesus. The priest genuflects in silent adoration, and we adore with him, Christ's Body in the host, and His Blood in the chalice. We are before the heavenly throne of God, with the Lamb that was slain in our midst, with the heavenly covenant family of angels, Mary, Mother of God and the saints, martyrs and witnesses, gathered around Him. The sacredness of the entire liturgy rises to an awe-inspiring crescendo, leading to silent adoration. The priest echoes the solemn moment and reality by saying very solemnly: *"The mystery of faith."* The congregation in reply expresses its own amazement and wonder by choosing one of several acclamations: *"We proclaim your Death, O Lord, and profess your Resurrection until you come again,"* or *"When we eat this Bread and drink this Cup, we proclaim your Death, O Lord, until you come again."*

THE ANAMNESIS OR DO THIS IN MEMORY OF ME:

Jesus ends the words of consecration or the institution narrative with the command: *"Do this in memory of me."* Immediately after the Consecration, we tell Jesus that we are fulfilling His command through the following prayer: *"Therefore, O Lord, as we celebrate the memorial of the saving Passion of your Son, his wondrous Resurrection and Ascension into heaven, and as we look forward to his second coming, we offer you in thanksgiving this holy and living sacrifice (EP III)."* This prayer is called the Anamnesis (Greek for Remembrance). In Hebrew it is Zikaron. The *Catechism of the Catholic Church* tells us what Anamnesis is: "In the sense of Sacred Scripture the *memorial* is not merely the recollection of past events but the proclamation of the mighty works wrought by God for men. In the liturgical celebration of these events, they become in a certain way present and real (1363)... In the New Testament, the memorial takes on new meaning. When the Church celebrates the Eucharist, she commemorates Christ's Passover, and it is made present: the sacrifice Christ offered once for all on the cross remains ever present (1364)." Jesus, our Risen Lord is present in our midst and the saving event of His death and resurrection is present in His Person. While this event took place in time, it is eternally present in the Person of the Risen Lord. As a memorial of the Lord's Supper, the Eucharist makes the events of the Upper Room and Calvary sacramentally present to us today.

INTERCESSIONS:

At this stage of the Eucharistic Prayer, the priest then proceeds to make a series of intercessions. The first intercession is a second *epiclesis*, invoking the Holy Spirit to form us into God's covenant family through our partaking of the Body and Blood of Christ: *"Humbly we pray that, partaking of the Body and Blood of Christ, we may be gathered into one by the Holy Spirit (EP II)."* Similarly, in Eucharistic Prayer III, the *epiclesis* is expressed thus: *"Look, we pray, upon the oblation of your Church, and, recognizing the sacrificial Victim by whose death you willed to reconcile us to yourself, grant that we, who are nourished by the Body and Blood of your Son and filled with his Holy Spirit, may become one body, one spirit in Christ."*

The next intercessory prayer is for the Church at large, as well as for our Church leaders, our Pope, bishops, and clergy. Eucharistic Prayer III is more elaborate than Eucharistic Prayer II, for instance: *"May he make of us an eternal offering to you, so that we may obtain an inheritance with your elect, especially with the most blessed Virgin Mary, Mother of God, with your blessed Apostles and glorious Martyrs (with Saint N.: the Saint of the day or Patron Saint) and with all the*

Saints, on whose constant intercession in your presence we rely for unfailing help. May this Sacrifice of our reconciliation, we pray, O Lord, advance the peace and salvation of all the world. Be pleased to confirm in faith and charity your pilgrim Church on earth, with your servant N. our Pope and N. our Bishop, the Order of Bishops, all the clergy, and the entire people you have gained for your own. Listen graciously to the prayers of this family, whom you have summoned before you: in your compassion, O merciful Father, gather to yourself all your children scattered throughout the world."

The third intercessory prayer is for the repose of the holy souls in Purgatory. They are remembered at every Eucharist during the Intercessory Prayers after the consecration: *"Remember also our brothers and sisters who have fallen asleep in the hope of the resurrection and all who have died in your mercy: welcome them into the light of your face (EP II)."*

The last prayer of intercession is made for the congregation: *"Have mercy on us all, we pray, that with the blessed Virgin Mary, Mother of God, with the blessed Apostles, and all the Saints who have pleased you throughout the ages, we may merit to be co-heirs to eternal life, and may praise and glorify you through your Son, Jesus Christ (EP II)."* At the conclusion of the Intercessory Prayers, the Eucharistic Prayer draws to an end in the Doxology and Great Amen. As you can see, the Church followed the format that was modeled in the Jewish Table Presentation of the Gifts; the proclamation of the central event of Jesus' death and resurrection, and our restoration as God's covenant family; praise to God for creation, thanksgiving for His saving deeds, and intercession for the Church.

THE DOXOLOGY:

"Through him, and with him, and in him, O God, almighty Father, in the unity of the Holy Spirit, all glory and honor is yours, for ever and ever. Amen."

This is a very significant prayer that re-caps all that has been taking place so far and leads us into the preparation for Holy Communion. The saving mystery in Jesus is clearly a Trinitarian action, accomplished by the Father, through His Son, in the power of the Holy Spirit. This prayer of adoration and praise to God (*doxa* in Greek means glory) is joined to the continual adoration and praise that is being offered by the Lamb seated at the right hand of the Father, and joined with His heavenly assembly. This prayer has its echoes in St. Paul's Letter to the Romans 11:6: *"For from him and through him and for him are all things. To him be glory forever. Amen."* Here, the liturgy expresses the Trinitarian nature of our worship in the Mass. Quintessentially it is the covenant offering of ourselves to God in return for God's gift of Himself to us through Jesus. So, we praise the almighty Father best by offering our lives through, with, and in the Son who surrendered Himself completely on Calvary. And we make our offering to the Father in the unity and power of His Holy Spirit who abides in us.

GREAT AMEN:

'Amen' is a Hebrew word that is used extensively both in the Old Testament and New. It affirms the validity of what has been said and expresses a wholehearted commitment to it. It was often used in liturgical settings. 1Chronicles 16:36 is a good example. King David had appointed Asaph and his brothers to sing for the first time the praises of the LORD before the Ark of the Covenant. Verse 36 is the conclusion: *"Blessed be the LORD, the God of Israel, from everlasting to everlasting! Let all the people say, Amen! Hallelujah."* In his letters, St. Paul used 'Amen' to express validity and commitment: *"To him be glory in the church and in Christ Jesus to all generations, forever and ever. Amen."* (Ephesians 3:21) It is in the Book of Revelation that we receive a true appreciation of 'Amen,' as it is expressed in the heavenly liturgy. Here is one example: *"All the angels stood around the throne and around the elders and the four living creatures. They prostrated themselves before the throne, worshiped God, and exclaimed: Amen. Blessing and glory, wisdom and thanksgiving, honor, power, and might be to our God forever and ever. Amen."* (Revelation 7:11-12) St. Jerome compared the angelic acclamation to a heavenly thunderclap. In our response, we join with the communion of saints in expressing our joyful and wholehearted commitment to the saving mystery of participation in the life of the Blessed Trinity through Jesus Christ in the power of the Holy Spirit.

PRAYER AND REFLECTION ON CELEBRATING THE LITURGY OF THE EUCHARIST

WEEK TWENTY THREE: *"BY THE MYSTERY OF THIS WATER AND WINE MAY WE COME TO SHARE IN THE DIVINITY OF CHRIST WHO HUMBLED HIMSELF TO SHARE IN OUR HUMANITY." (PRAYER OVER THE WINE IN THE PREPARATION OF THE GIFTS)*

SPIRITUAL READING FOR THE WEEK:

- **Anoint Us in Your Covenant, Abba-Emmanuel:** Session Twelve
- **Old Testament:** Two or Three Chapters daily
- **New Testament:** Two or Three Chapters daily
- **Imitation of Christ:** One chapter daily

DAY ONE: MORNING SESSION

MORNING PRAYER: Acts of Faith, Hope, Charity; Daily Offering

Morning Face to Face with God:

Begin with Prayer to the Holy Spirit

What is God saying to you?

PRAYER ON THE PREPARATION OF THE GIFTS:

"Blessed are you, Lord God of all creation, for through your goodness we have received the bread we offer you: fruit of the earth and work of human hands, it will become for us the bread of life."

Ask the Holy Spirit to give you a deep appreciation for the Liturgy of the Eucharist, and that your participation might always be wholehearted and generous

In offering the bread and wine, we are offering ourselves to God, as these gifts represent our sustenance, and therefore, our very lives. Clearly then, the presentation of the gifts has sacrificial tones. Every sacrifice in the Old Testament was a covenant ritual, as the victim represented the one making the offering. Our offering to God through bread and wine has special significance as God will accept our offering and transform it into the Body, Blood, Soul, and Divinity of Jesus. This ability to offer ourselves with the assurance that we will be transformed into Jesus was made possible for us through Jesus' incarnation. In His incarnation, Jesus, Son of God, ratified such an offering. He offered to become one of us, and Mary as the new Eve and our representative, accepted the Father's invitation to become the mother of His Son through the power of the Holy Spirit. So Jesus first became one of us, as Paul would put it, so that He could become sin and we His righteousness. So now, through our offering of bread and wine, we can and will be transformed into Jesus, thus participating in God's righteousness.

What is God saying to you?

End with Prayer to the Holy Trinity

NIGHT SESSION: Examination of Conscience

For what are you grateful? For what are you contrite?

Please review briefly your Morning Prayer topic. Make it your last thought of the day

DAY TWO: MORNING SESSION

MORNING PRAYER: Acts of Faith, Hope, Charity; Daily Offering

Morning Face to Face with God:

Begin with Prayer to the Holy Spirit

PRAYER ON THE MIXING OF WATER AND WINE:

"By the mystery of this water and win may we come to share in the divinity of Christ who humbled himself to share in our humanity."

[handwritten: mingling above "mystery of"; wine above "win"]

"Blessed are you, Lord God of all creation, for through your goodness we have received the wine we offer you: fruit of the vine and work of human hands, it will become our spiritual drink."

Ask the Holy Spirit to give you a deep appreciation for the Liturgy of the Eucharist, and that your participation might always be wholehearted and generous

This transformation into Jesus is indicated in the mixing of the water with the wine. Before the wine is offered, the priest pours a drop of water into the wine. Wine symbolizes Christ's divinity, and water symbolizes our humanity. In assuming our humanity, Jesus was able to become our Lamb of sacrifice, thus enabling us to share in His divinity: *"By the mystery of this water and wine may we come to share in the divinity of Christ who humbled himself to share in our humanity."* The prayer brings out the kenosis or emptying of Christ in accepting our humanity. As Philippians 2:7 tells us, *"Rather, he emptied himself, taking the form of a slave, coming in human likeness."*

What is God saying to you?

End with Prayer to the Holy Trinity

NIGHT SESSION: Examination of Conscience

For what are you grateful? For what are you contrite?

Please review briefly your Morning Prayer topic. Make it your last thought of the day

DAY THREE: MORNING SESSION

MORNING PRAYER: Acts of Faith, Hope, Charity; Daily Offering

Morning Face to Face with God:

Begin with Prayer to the Holy Spirit

PRAYER ON ENTERING THE HOLY OF HOLIES:

Ask the Holy Spirit to give you a deep appreciation for the Liturgy of the Eucharist, and that your participation might always be wholehearted and generous

The priest then prepares himself to enter into the Sacred Mysteries. Soon we will be in the august presence of the whole heavenly assembly, with the Father at the center, with Jesus, our Lamb that was slain, surrounded by His disciples whom He has washed clean in His blood. The priest and the congregation are acutely aware of their unworthiness and ask God to make them worthy: *"With humble spirit and contrite heart may we be accepted by you, O Lord, and may our sacrifice in your sight this day be pleasing to you, Lord God."* The priest then washes his hands, knowing that only God can make him acceptable in His sight: *"Wash me, O Lord, from my iniquity and cleanse me from my sin."*

We have arrived at a climactic moment in the Mass. The bread and wine will soon be transformed into the Body and Blood of Jesus, and Our Lord will come to us in Holy Communion and become one with us. Our divine High Priest will make this happen through the priest who is acting in His place. The priest then asks for prayer as he is about to begin the Eucharistic prayer: *"Pray, brethren, that my sacrifice and yours may be acceptable to God, the almighty Father."* The priest is acting in the Person of Christ; in a real sense then, the sacrifice is his. And it is our sacrifice as well, as the entire Church is offering herself in union with Christ's sacrifice. So the congregation responds: *"May the Lord accept the sacrifice at your hands for the praise and glory of his name, for our good and the good of all his holy Church."*

What is God saying to you?

End with Prayer to the Holy Trinity

NIGHT SESSION: Examination of Conscience

For what are you grateful? For what are you contrite?

Please review briefly your Morning Prayer topic. Make it your last thought of the day

DAY FOUR: MORNING SESSION

MORNING PRAYER: Acts of Faith, Hope, Charity; Daily Offering

Morning Face to Face with God:

Begin with Prayer to the Holy Spirit

PRAYER ON THE PREFACE:

Ask the Holy Spirit to give you a deep appreciation for the Liturgy of the Eucharist, and that your participation might always be wholehearted and generous

Every Preface opens with the three part dialogue. We are familiar with the first exchange as we have used it in other places of our celebration. We ask the Lord to be with us as we prepare ourselves to participate in the death and resurrection of our Risen Lord. This is the most radical and comprehensive mission of our lives: to be present to the Lamb that was slain and through Him to the Father in the power of the Holy Spirit in true covenant so that our lives belong to Him as a pleasing offering. Then we are asked to lift up our hearts and in unison we respond that we have lifted them up on high. Our hearts symbolize the depths of our being. We express the seriousness of our intent to enter fully into the new and everlasting covenant when we say that we have lifted up our hearts to the Lord. And then we pray the third exchange: we are asked to give thanks to the Lord. We gave thanks during the Gloria Prayer and during the Liturgy of the Word. And we will continue in the same vein throughout our celebration. The Mass is a thanksgiving celebration, Eucharist meaning thanksgiving. We have been redeemed by the blood of the Lamb. Everything we have and are is God's gift to us, especially the gift of sharing in the fullness of divine life, made possible through Jesus, the Lamb of God. Very appropriately therefore we respond to the invitation to give thanks by proclaiming that 'It is right and just' to do so.

The priest then goes into the Prayer of the Preface which is essentially a prayer of thanksgiving and praise. The Prayer is always addressed to the Father and the opening lines are always the same. In the Preface, one dimension or the other of our history of salvation is highlighted for which we are giving thanks and praise. In Preface IV for Sundays in Ordinary Time, for example, we are offered a brief history of our salvation. In Preface III for Sundays in Ordinary Time we highlight the salvation of man by a man. You would do well to pray with the various Prefaces on your own, and come to appreciate the wealth and spiritual wisdom of our Eucharistic prayers that have been fashioned by the Church over centuries.

What is God saying to you?

End with Prayer to the Holy Trinity

NIGHT SESSION: Examination of Conscience

For what are you grateful? For what are you contrite?

Please review briefly your Morning Prayer topic. Make it your last thought of the day

DAY FIVE: MORNING SESSION

MORNING PRAYER: Acts of Faith, Hope, Charity; Daily Offering

Morning Face to Face with God:

Begin with Prayer to the Holy Spirit

PRAYER ON THE SANCTUS:

Ask the Holy Spirit to give you a deep appreciation for the Liturgy of the Eucharist, and that your participation might always be wholehearted and generous

In response to the Preface we express our thanksgiving and praise by praying the Sanctus Prayer: *"Holy, Holy, Holy Lord God of hosts. Heaven and earth are full of your glory. Hosanna in the highest. Blessed is he who comes in the name of the Lord. Hosanna in the highest."* In Isaiah 6:3, one Seraph cried out to the other in the Presence of God: *"Holy, holy, holy is the LORD of hosts! All the earth is filled with his glory!"* In beholding this vision, Isaiah felt doomed, a man of unclean lips whom the Seraph cleansed. In proclaiming God's holiness we are uniting with the Seraphim and saints, with the full confidence that we will be cleansed of our sins by the blood of the Lamb. Understandably, we direct our praise and thanksgiving toward the Messiah: *"Blessed is he who comes in the name of the Lord."* We join with the crowds who welcomed Jesus as the Messiah into Jerusalem on the eve of His death by crucifixion: *"Hosanna! Blessed is he who comes in the name of the Lord, [even] the king of Israel."* (John 12:13) *Hosanna* is a Hebrew word, meaning *"Save us."* In liturgical worship it became an expression of praise. We welcome Jesus into our midst. Soon and very soon, He will be present on our altar as the Lamb of God, our Risen Lord.

What is God saying to you?

End with Prayer to the Holy Trinity

NIGHT SESSION: Examination of Conscience

For what are you grateful? For what are you contrite?

Please review briefly your Morning Prayer topic. Make it your last thought of the day

DAY SIX: MORNING SESSION

MORNING PRAYER: Acts of Faith, Hope, Charity; Daily Offering

Morning Face to Face with God:

Begin with Prayer to the Holy Spirit

PRAYER ON THE EPICLESIS:

Ask the Holy Spirit to give you a deep appreciation for the Liturgy of the Eucharist, and that your participation might always be wholehearted and generous

Epiclesis from the Greek means *"an invocation upon."* Already the early Church asked for an invocation of the Holy Spirit upon the gifts of bread and wine so that they would be transformed into the Body and Blood of Jesus. Jesus authorized His apostles and their successors to change bread and wine into the Body and Blood of Christ as a memorial of what He did when He instituted the Eucharist in the Upper Room. Jesus also breathed the Holy Spirit upon His apostles and through them upon His successors. The manifestation of the Holy Spirit's presence and power was seen at the Outpouring of the Holy Spirit after Jesus' Ascension. Jesus did everything in the power of the Holy Spirit, from conception to resurrection. Jesus wants His followers to do the same. The Church is very aware of this Trinitarian truth. The priest exercises his priesthood given to him by Jesus in the power of the Holy Spirit. *"Make holy, therefore, these gifts, we pray, by sending down your Spirit upon them like the dewfall, so that they may become for us the Body and Blood of our Lord, Jesus Christ;"* (Eucharistic Prayer II) or *"Therefore, O Lord, we humbly implore you: by the same Spirit graciously make holy these gifts we have brought to you for consecration, that they may become the Body and Blood of your Son our Lord Jesus Christ".* (Eucharistic Prayer III).

What is God saying to you?

End with Prayer to the Holy Trinity

NIGHT SESSION: Examination of Conscience

For what are you grateful? For what are you contrite?

Please review briefly your Morning Prayer topic. Make it your last thought of the day

DAY SEVEN: MORNING SESSION

MORNING PRAYER: Acts of Faith, Hope, Charity; Daily Offering

Morning Face to Face with God:

Begin with Prayer to the Holy Spirit

SIGNS OF THE TRANSITION TO CONTEMPLATION:

(After pondering each bullet point, express your sentiments in a short prayer)

- *The Dark Night*, Book One, Chapter 9 deals with the signs of transition to contemplative prayer. *"The first sign is that since these souls do not get satisfaction or consolation from the things of God, they do not get any from creatures either. Since God puts a soul in this dark night in order to dry up and purge its sensory appetite, he does not allow it to find sweetness or delight in anything."* (TDN – Book One: Chapter 9:2)

- At this stage of discipleship, one is serious about loving and serving God. There is a definite solicitude about the things of God. So it is quite disconcerting to the disciple when the second sign begins to emerge: *"The memory ordinarily turns to God solicitously and with painful care, and the soul thinks it is not serving God but turning back, because it is aware of this distaste for the things of God."* (TDN – Book One: Chapter 9:3)

- This second sign is not an indication of a lukewarm attitude. The lukewarm tend to be lax and negligent about serving God. Those suffering from this sensory night are ordinarily serious about their commitment to God. Consequently they are pained that they are not serving God better, given their sense of helplessness.

- The Third sign is *"the powerlessness, in spite of one's efforts, to meditate and make use of the imagination, the interior sense, as was one's previous custom. At this time God does not communicate himself through the senses as he did before, by means of the discursive analysis and synthesis of ideas, but begins to communicate himself through pure spirit by an act of simple contemplation in which there is no discursive succession of thought."* (TDN – Book One: Chapter 9:8)

- God is bringing about a transition from the discursive to the contemplative through this sensory night of affliction and purgation. The soul feels powerless as it cannot meditate on the things of God with its intellect, imagination, and memory.

- They feel very afflicted and abandoned by God. While the dryness and distraction in prayer is difficult to handle and calls for patience and trust, what is more difficult to handle is their fear that they are going astray and will not receive any spiritual blessings again.

- In trying to resolve these difficult straits, they make an effort to go back to discursive forms of prayer. *"They fatigue and overwork themselves, thinking God is conducting them along another road, which is contemplation and is very different from the first, for the one road belongs to discursive meditation and the other is beyond the range of the imagination and discursive reflection.*" (TDN – Book One: Chapter 10:2)

- The advice to them is to "*persevere patiently and not be afflicted. Let them trust in God who does not fail those who seek him with a simple and righteous heart; nor will he fail to impart what is needful for the way until getting them to the clear and pure light of love. God will give them this light by means of that other night, the night of spirit, if they merit that he place them in it.*" (TDN – Book One: Chapter 10:3)

- Furthermore, one should not pay attention to discursive meditation but learn "*to remain in rest and quietude even though it may seem obvious to them that they are doing nothing and wasting time, and even though they think this disinclination to think about anything is due to their laxity. Through patience and perseverance in prayer, they will be doing a great deal without activity on their part.*" (TDN – Book One: Chapter 10:4)

- In the early stages of the sensory night, the disciple is preoccupied with the dryness and inability to utilize the faculties well in prayer. Gradually, however, the disciple will begin to feel a certain longing for God which could intensify to become urgent longings of love for God. In time the disciple begins to reap many benefits from this purification in which one feels helpless and hopeless.

What is God saying to you?

End with Prayer to the Holy Trinity

NIGHT SESSION: Examination of Conscience

For what are you grateful? For what are you contrite?

What prayer would you compose to express what God has said to you this week?

Please review briefly your Morning Prayer topic. Make it your last thought of the day

Be Hot or Cold
If you are lukewarm,
I'll spit you out of
my mouth.

PRAYER AND REFLECTION ON CELEBRATING THE LITURGY OF THE EUCHARIST- CONTINUED

WEEK TWENTY FOUR: *"TAKE THIS, ALL OF YOU, AND EAT OF IT, FOR THIS IS MY BODY, WHICH WILL BE GIVEN UP FOR YOU… TAKE THIS ALL OF YOU, AND DRINK FROM IT, FOR THIS IS THE CHALICE OF MY BLOOD, THE BLOOD OF THE NEW AND ETERNAL COVENANT, WHICH WILL BE POURED OUT FOR YOU AND FOR MANY FOR THE FORGIVENESS OF SINS. DO THIS IN MEMORY OF ME." (WORDS OF CONSECRATION)*

SPIRITUAL READING FOR THE WEEK:

- **Anoint Us in Your Covenant, Abba-Emmanuel:** Session Twelve
- **Old Testament:** Two or Three Chapters daily
- **New Testament:** Two or Three Chapters daily
- **Imitation of Christ:** One chapter daily

DAY ONE: MORNING SESSION

MORNING PRAYER: Acts of Faith, Hope, Charity; Daily Offering

Morning Face to Face with God:

Begin with Prayer to the Holy Spirit

PRAYER ON THE WORDS OF INSTITUTION AND CONSECRATION:

Take this, all of you, and eat of it, for this is my body, which will be given up for you… Take this, all of you, and drink from it, for this is the chalice of my Blood, the Blood of the New and Eternal Covenant, which will be poured out for you and for many for the forgiveness of sins. Do this in memory of me.

Ask the Holy Spirit to give you a deep appreciation for the Liturgy of the Eucharist, and that your participation might always be wholehearted and generous

In speaking of His body and blood, Jesus is referring to Himself as the Lamb of sacrifice of the new covenant. Jesus uses the phrase, *'which will be given up for you,' (didomai* in Greek), which in the gospels is associated with sacrifice. He is alluding to His sacrificial death on the cross. Jesus also speaks of the *blood of the new and eternal covenant.* This is the only place in the Gospels where Jesus speaks of the new and eternal covenant that He is establishing through His death and resurrection. Jesus' words also indicate a replacement of the Mosaic covenant by His new and eternal covenant established in His blood: *"When he (the prophet Jeremiah) speaks of a "new" covenant, he declares the first one obsolete. And what has become obsolete and has grown old is close to disappearing."* (Hebrews 8:13) At the Last Supper Jesus offers His own body and blood in sacrifice on the cross for the forgiveness of sins. In anticipation of His impending sacrifice on the cross by crucifixion, Jesus offers us His body to eat and His blood to drink in the Passover meal. Lastly, *"for you and for many for the forgiveness of sins"*: Jesus is speaking as the Suffering Servant, prophesied in Isaiah: *"My servant, the just one, shall justify the many, their iniquity he shall bear."* (Isaiah 53:11) In the phrase 'one for many,' the sacrifice of the Suffering Servant (Jesus) on behalf of His kinsfolk (covenant family) is being emphasized. 'Many' therefore, does include everybody. The sober reality is that while Jesus died for all, not everyone will choose to accept the salvation offered by Jesus. One would have to accept Him as Savior and Lord.

What is God saying to you?

End with Prayer to the Holy Trinity

NIGHT SESSION: Examination of Conscience

For what are you grateful? For what are you contrite?

Please review briefly your Morning Prayer topic. Make it your last thought of the day

DAY TWO: MORNING SESSION

MORNING PRAYER: Acts of Faith, Hope, Charity; Daily Offering

Morning Face to Face with God:

Begin with Prayer to the Holy Spirit

PRAYER ON THE MYSTERY OF FAITH:

Ask the Holy Spirit to give you a deep appreciation for the Liturgy of the Eucharist, and that your participation might always be wholehearted and generous

Through the power of the Holy Spirit, the words of consecration pronounced by the priest have changed the bread and wine into the Body and Blood of Jesus. The priest genuflects in silent adoration, and we adore with him, the Risen Christ present in His Body in the host, and His Blood in the chalice. We are before the heavenly throne of God, with the Lamb that was slain in our midst, with the heavenly covenant family of angels and saints, Mary, Mother of God, martyrs and witnesses, gathered around Him. The sacredness of the entire liturgy rises to an awe-inspiring crescendo, leading to silent adoration. The priest echoes the solemn moment and reality by saying very solemnly: *The mystery of faith.* The congregation in reply expresses its own amazement and wonder by choosing one of several acclamations: *"We proclaim your Death, O Lord, and profess your Resurrection until you come again,"* or *"When we eat this Bread and drink this Cup, we proclaim your Death, O Lord, until you come again."*

What is God saying to you?

End with Prayer to the Holy Trinity

NIGHT SESSION: Examination of Conscience

For what are you grateful? For what are you contrite?

Please review briefly your Morning Prayer topic. Make it your last thought of the day

DAY THREE: MORNING SESSION

MORNING PRAYER: Acts of Faith, Hope, Charity; Daily Offering

Morning Face to Face with God:

Begin with Prayer to the Holy Spirit

PRAYER ON THE ANAMNESIS OR DO THIS IN MEMORY OF ME:

Ask the Holy Spirit to give you a deep appreciation for the Liturgy of the Eucharist, and that your participation might always be wholehearted and generous

Jesus ends the words of consecration or the institution narrative with the command: *"Do this in memory of me."* Immediately after the Consecration, we tell Jesus that we are fulfilling His command through the following prayer: *"Therefore, O Lord, as we celebrate the memorial of the saving Passion of your Son, his wondrous Resurrection and Ascension into heaven, and as we look forward to his second coming, we offer you in thanksgiving this holy and living sacrifice."* (EP III) This prayer is called the Anamnesis (Greek for Remembrance). In Hebrew it is Zikaron. The Catechism of the Catholic Church tells us what Anamnesis is: "In the sense of Sacred

Scripture the *memorial* is not merely the recollection of past events but the proclamation of the mighty works wrought by God for men. In the liturgical celebration of these events, they become in a certain way present and real (1363)... In the New Testament, the memorial takes on new meaning. When the Church celebrates the Eucharist, she commemorates Christ's Passover, and it is made present: the sacrifice Christ offered once for all on the cross remains ever present (1364)." Jesus, our Risen Lord is present in our midst and the saving event of His death and resurrection is present in His Person. While this event took place in time, it is eternally present in the Person of the Risen Lord. As a memorial of the Lord's Supper, the Eucharist makes the events of the Upper Room and Calvary sacramentally present to us today.

What is God saying to you?

End with Prayer to the Holy Trinity

NIGHT SESSION: Examination of Conscience

For what are you grateful? For what are you contrite?

Please review briefly your Morning Prayer topic. Make it your last thought of the day

DAY FOUR: MORNING SESSION

MORNING PRAYER: Acts of Faith, Hope, Charity; Daily Offering

Morning Face to Face with God:

Begin with Prayer to the Holy Spirit

PRAYER ON THE INTERCESSIONS:

Ask the Holy Spirit to give you a deep appreciation for the Liturgy of the Eucharist, and that your participation might always be wholehearted and generous

At this stage of the Eucharistic Prayer, the priest makes a series of intercessions. The first intercession is a second *epiclesis*, invoking the Holy Spirit to form us into God's covenant family through our partaking of the Body and Blood of Christ: *"Humbly we pray that, partaking of the Body and Blood of Christ, we may be gathered into one by the Holy Spirit."* (EP II) The next intercessory prayer is for the Church at large, as well as for our Church leaders, our Pope, bishops, and clergy. *"Remember, Lord, your Church, spread throughout the world, and bring her to the fullness of charity, together with N. our Pope and N, our Bishop and all the clergy ."* (EP II) The third intercessory prayer is for the repose of the holy souls in Purgatory. They are remembered at every Eucharist during the Intercessory Prayers after the consecration: *"Remember also our brothers and sisters who have fallen asleep in the hope of the resurrection and all who have died in your mercy: welcome them into the light of your face."* (EP II) The last prayer of intercession is made for the congregation: *"Have mercy on us all, we pray, that with the blessed Virgin Mary, Mother of God, with the blessed Apostles, and all the Saints who have pleased you throughout the ages, we may merit to be co-heirs to eternal life, and may praise and glorify you through your Son, Jesus Christ."* (EP II) At the conclusion of the Intercessory Prayers, the Eucharistic Prayer draws to an end in the Doxology and Great Amen.

What is God saying to you?

End with Prayer to the Holy Trinity

NIGHT SESSION: Examination of Conscience

For what are you grateful? For what are you contrite?

Please review briefly your Morning Prayer topic. Make it your last thought of the day

DAY FIVE: MORNING SESSION

MORNING PRAYER: Acts of Faith, Hope, Charity; Daily Offering

Morning Face to Face with God:

Begin with Prayer to the Holy Spirit

PRAYER ON THE DOXOLOGY:

> *"Through him, and with him, and in him, O God, almighty Father, in the unity of the Holy Spirit, all glory and honor is yours, for ever and ever. Amen."*

Ask the Holy Spirit to give you a deep appreciation for the Liturgy of the Eucharist, and that your participation might always be wholehearted and generous

This is a very significant prayer that re-caps all that has been taking place so far and leads us into the preparation for Holy Communion. The saving mystery in Jesus is clearly a Trinitarian action, accomplished by the Father, through His Son, in the power of the Holy Spirit. This prayer of adoration and praise to God (*doxa* in Greek means glory) is joined to the continual adoration and praise that is being offered by the Lamb seated at the right hand of the Father, and joined with His heavenly assembly. This prayer has its echoes in St. Paul's

Letter to the Romans 11:36: *"For from him and through him and for him are all things. To him be glory forever. Amen."* Here, the liturgy expresses the Trinitarian nature of our worship in the Mass. Quintessentially it is the covenant offering of ourselves to God in return for God's gift of Himself to us through Jesus. So we praise the almighty Father best by offering our lives through, with, and in the Son who surrendered Himself completely on Calvary. And we make our offering to the Father in the unity of His Holy Spirit who abides in us.

What is God saying to you?

End with Prayer to the Holy Trinity

NIGHT SESSION: Examination of Conscience

For what are you grateful? For what are you contrite?

Please review briefly your Morning Prayer topic. Make it your last thought of the day

DAY SIX: MORNING SESSION

MORNING PRAYER: Acts of Faith, Hope, Charity; Daily Offering

Morning Face to Face with God:

Begin with Prayer to the Holy Spirit

PRAYER ON THE GREAT AMEN:

Ask the Holy Spirit to give you a deep appreciation for the Liturgy of the Eucharist, and that your participation might always be wholehearted and generous

'Amen' is a Hebrew word that is used extensively both in the Old Testament and New. It affirms the validity of what has been said and expresses a wholehearted commitment to it. It was often used in liturgical settings. 1Chronicles 16:36 is a good example. King David had appointed Asaph and his brothers to sing for the first time the praises of the LORD before the Ark of the Covenant. Verse 36 is the conclusion: *"Blessed be the LORD, the God of Israel, from everlasting to everlasting! Let all the people say, Amen! Hallelujah."* In his letters, St. Paul used 'Amen' to express validity and commitment: *"To him be glory in the church and in Christ Jesus to all generations, forever and ever. Amen."* (Ephesians 3:21) It is in the Book of Revelation that we receive a true appreciation of 'Amen' as it is expressed in the heavenly liturgy. Here is one example: *"All the angels stood around the throne and around the elders and the four living creatures. They prostrated themselves before the throne, worshiped God, and exclaimed: Amen. Blessing and glory, wisdom and thanksgiving, honor, power, and might be to our God forever and ever. Amen."* (Revelation 7:11-12) St. Jerome compared the angelic acclamation to a heavenly thunderclap. In our response, we join with the communion of saints in expressing our joyful and wholehearted commitment to the saving mystery of participation in the life of the Blessed Trinity through Jesus Christ in the power of the Holy Spirit.

What is God saying to you?

End with Prayer to the Holy Trinity

NIGHT SESSION: Examination of Conscience

For what are you grateful? For what are you contrite?

Please review briefly your Morning Prayer topic. Make it your last thought of the day

DAY SEVEN: MORNING SESSION

MORNING PRAYER: Acts of Faith, Hope, Charity; Daily Offering

Morning Face to Face with God:

Begin with Prayer to the Holy Spirit

BENEFITS OF THE SENSORY NIGHT:

(After pondering each bullet point, express your sentiments in a short prayer)

- The soul gains intimate knowledge of self and one's own misery. This purification makes the soul realize its own lowliness and misery which seemed hidden and even non-existent before the sensory night began.
- This acute sense of self leads to relating with God more respectfully and reverently as befitting God's holiness.
- Accompanying this sense of its own misery and unworthiness before God, the soul also by contrast becomes aware of God's grandeur and majesty.
- Through the sensory night, the soul receives the gift of humility which can only be built on a true understanding of self. Such an attitude goes against spiritual pride, one of the capital sins.
- Such humility creates love of neighbor and a reluctance to judge anyone as they did when they enjoyed God's favors and consolations.
- They become pliant and malleable in the hands of God and willingly seek direction and correction. Gradually, the roots of pride are destroyed.

- *"The soul undergoes a thorough reform in its imperfections of avarice, in which it craved various spiritual objects and was never content with many of its spiritual exercises because of the covetousness of its appetite and the gratification it found in spiritual things."* (TDN – Book One: Chapter 13:1)
- Regarding spiritual lust, its craving for spiritual gifts and its performance in prayer and spiritual disciplines lessens and undergoes a thorough reform.
- *"God so curbs concupiscence and bridles the appetite through this arid and dark night that the soul cannot feast on any sensory delight from earthly or heavenly things."* (TDN – Book One: Chapter 13:3) When God does this, the soul dwells in peace and tranquility. There is no disturbance as there used to be.
- The soul is aware of God throughout the day and has a great fear that it will backslide spiritually.
- It practices all the virtues. Individuals become meek toward God, themselves, and others. They are more accepting of self and others, less argumentative and impatient.
- Their struggle with envy lessens. They are more charitable toward others and are able to rejoice in their well-being. Their love for spiritual matters begins to return.
- In the midst of dryness and a sense of abandonment, *"God frequently communicates to the soul, when it least expects, spiritual sweetness, a very pure love, and a spiritual knowledge that is sometimes most delicate."* (TDN – Book One: Chapter 13:10)
- Lastly, in all they do, they are motivated more by the desire to please God rather than by their own delight and satisfaction acting as the criterion or motivation.

What is God saying to you?

End with Prayer to the Holy Trinity

NIGHT SESSION: Examination of Conscience

For what are you grateful? For what are you contrite?

What prayer would you compose to express what God has said to you this week?

Please review briefly your Morning Prayer topic. Make it your last thought of the day

SESSION THIRTEEN
EUCHARIST: THE COMMUNION RITE

"Let us rejoice and be glad and give him glory. For the wedding day of the Lamb has come, his bride has made herself ready. She was allowed to wear a bright, clean linen garment." (The linen represents the righteous deeds of the holy ones.)

– Revelation 19:7-8

THE LORD'S PRAYER:

"At the Savior's command and formed by divine teaching, we dare to say: Our Father, who art in heaven, hallowed by thy name; thy kingdom come, thy will be done on earth as it is in heaven. Give us this day our daily bread, and forgive us our trespasses, as we forgive those who trespass against us; and lead us not into temptation, but deliver us from evil."

Very appropriately we begin our preparation for Holy Communion with the recitation of the Lord's Prayer. You received an elaborate reflection on the 'Our Father' in *Session 7: Knowing Our Father in the Trinity*. Please re-read it along with the reflections here presented. I will limit myself to highlighting some key truths revealed to us in this prayer. The prayer itself is an excellent preparation for Holy Communion. We begin by addressing God as Father. Through the institution of God's new and eternal covenant with us through the death and resurrection of Jesus, we have been brought into covenant union with the Blessed Trinity. The Father-Son relationship in God has been offered to us. We can address and relate to God as Jesus does. We are now the Father's sons and daughters; we are sons and daughters in the Son; God is now our Father! Our participation in God's life through Jesus is at the heart of our Eucharistic celebration. In Holy Communion, we will have entered profoundly into the reality of this indescribable mystery of us becoming partakers of God's divine nature (2 Peter 1:4).

In the Lord's Prayer we are asking for our daily bread: *epi ousios* in the Greek, or *substance from above*. This was the description of manna, food from above that was given to the Israelites in the desert. In John 6, Jesus tells us that He is manna, food from heaven that will never perish. By eating His Body and drinking His Blood, we will have entered into covenant union with the Father, Son, and Holy Spirit. We will have become God's temple or abode, God dwelling in us, and we in God. So in our prayer we ask that we have the true sentiments of covenant union: forgiveness of our sins which implies repentance; forgiveness of others which implies agapé love; protection against our own sinful tendencies and the wiles of the Evil One. In this way we prepare ourselves to receive Our Lord in Holy Communion.

PRAYER FOR PEACE AND ITS OFFERING:

Deliver us, Lord, we pray, from every evil, graciously grant peace in our days, that, by the help of your mercy, we may be always free from sin and safe from all distress, as we await the blessed hope and the coming of our Savior, Jesus Christ. For the kingdom, the power and the glory are yours now and for ever.

Lord Jesus Christ, who said to your Apostles: Peace I leave you, my peace I give you; look not on our sins, but on the faith of your Church, and graciously grant her peace and unity in accordance with your will. Who live and reign for ever and ever. Amen.

The peace of the Lord be with you always. And with your spirit.

Let us offer each other the sign of peace.

After the Lord's Prayer, the priest first implores the Father to deliver us from every evil. The best way for this to happen is by receiving peace so that we will be free from sin and safe from every distress as we await the blessed hope and coming of our Savior, Jesus Christ. Then we make the same petition of Jesus, asking Him to graciously grant His peace to His Church. Through His death and resurrection which we are participating in and celebrating, we have received Jesus' peace. Peace is the victory over Satan, sin, and permanent death that Jesus has won. It is decisive, conclusive, and unassailable. In believing and accepting Jesus as our Savior and Lord, we are now permeated with this peace! Only sin and our rebellion can take away this peace which is the Presence of the Risen Lord. In Holy Communion we will receive the peace of Christ in abundance!

Before we receive Jesus in the Eucharist, we ask for the gift of peace, which is abiding, because it is the peace of the Risen Lord. And because we are God's covenant family, we can only have God's peace if we share it with one another. The priest therefore invites us to offer each other the Sign of peace. Before we offer the peace of Christ to one another, we have removed every trace of un-forgiveness from our hearts. When we offer peace to one another, we are joined together by the bond of the peace of Christ!

THE FRACTION OR BREAKING OF THE BREAD:

After the sign of peace is given, the priest breaks the host in a symbolic action known as the Fraction or the Breaking of the bread. In the Old Testament, the father of the family would recite a blessing and then break bread and distribute it to his family. There are several instances of the breaking of the bread in the New Testament, either prefiguring the Eucharist as in the multiplication of the loaves: *"Then, taking the five loaves and the two fish and looking up to heaven, he said the blessing, broke the loaves, and gave them to [his] disciples..."* (Mark 6:41), or actually signifying the Eucharist: *"And it happened that, while he was with them at table, he took bread, said the blessing, broke it, and gave it to them."* (Luke 24:30) In Acts the Eucharist was described as the breaking of bread: *"Every day they devoted themselves to meeting together in the temple area and to breaking bread in their homes."* (Acts 2:46) Soon the meal will begin and we will partake of the Body and Blood of Jesus Christ. The breaking of the bread is a clear indication that the meal will soon begin.

COMMINGLING:

May this mingling of the Body and Blood of our Lord Jesus Christ bring eternal life to us who receive it.

Then the priest does the commingling. In the early Church, the mingling denoted the unity of the Church, between the Pope and His priests: a small particle from the host (called *fermentum*) he had consecrated would be sent to the priests in the city to place in their chalices. In 8th century Syria, the understanding emerged that the separate consecrations of the bread and wine symbolized the separation of Christ's Body and Blood in His death. The commingling rite expresses the reunion of Jesus' Body and Blood in His resurrection. In the first commingling of the Eucharist that took place at the Preparation of the Gifts, we prayed that the mingling of the drop of water representing us, with the wine representing Jesus, would make us share in Christ's divinity who shared in our humanity. Soon that prayer will be answered in Holy Communion.

LAMB OF GOD:

Lamb of God, you take away the sins of the world, have mercy on us. Lamb of God, you take away the sins of the world, have mercy on us. Lamb of God, you take away the sins of the world, grant us peace.

Jesus, as our Lamb of God, is mentioned in several places in the New Testament. In the Book of Revelation, Jesus is given different titles. But most of all He is addressed as the Lamb who was slain, 28 times. The heavenly liturgy is focused around the Lamb that was slain, offering praise and worship to the Father with His host of angels, martyrs and witnesses. The heavenly Eucharist is described in great detail in Revelation, Chapters 4 through 7 and reaches its climax in Chapter 19: *"When he (the Lamb) took it, the four living creatures and the twenty-four elders fell down before the Lamb. Each of the elders held a harp and gold bowls filled with incense, which are the prayers of the holy ones. They sang a hymn: "Worthy are you to receive the scroll and to break open its seals, for you were slain and with your blood you purchased for God those from every tribe and tongue, people and nation. You made them a kingdom and priests for our God and they will reign on earth."* (Revelation 4:8-10) In Revelation 5:13 we are told that John saw all the creatures worshiping the Lamb: *"Then I heard every creature in heaven and on earth and under the earth and in the sea, and everything in the universe, cry out: "To the one who sits on the throne and to the Lamb be blessing and honor, glory and might, forever and ever."* (Revelation 5:13) It becomes clear that Jesus is our Intercessor in heaven as the 'Lamb that was slain.' Life in heaven is about God's covenant family engaged in a continual Eucharistic liturgy of adoration, praise, thanksgiving, and intercession through Jesus, the Lamb that was slain. This reality of heaven being a continual Eucharistic celebration is emphasized even more emphatically in Revelation 7:9-12: *"After this I had a vision of a great multitude, which no one could count, from every nation, race, people, and tongue. They stood before the throne and before the Lamb, wearing white robes and holding palm branches in their hands. They cried out in a loud voice: "Salvation comes from our God, who is seated on the throne, and from the Lamb."… They prostrated themselves before the throne, worshiped God, and exclaimed: "Amen. Blessing and glory, wisdom and thanksgiving, honor, power, and might be to our God forever and ever. Amen."* We are in unison with God's covenant family that is joined in worship of God and Jesus, through the infinite merits of the Lamb that shed His blood on the Cross. The Lamb is Jesus, Son of God, and we ask Him to forgive us our sins and to prepare us for the wedding feast described in Revelation 19.

John's gospel identifies Jesus as the Lamb that was slain. In John 19:14 we are told that *"It was preparation day for Passover, and it was about noon."* The priests slaughtered the lambs between noon and 3:00 PM for the Passover Meal which took place after sunset, when it was dark. In being handed over to the Jewish leadership, Jesus was being led to the slaughter. Since it was preparation day and the crucified bodies could not remain on the crosses during the Sabbath, the Jews asked Pilate to hasten their death by having their legs broken and their bodies taken down. John 19:33-36 tells us *"when they came to Jesus and saw that he was already dead, they did not break his legs, but one soldier thrust his lance into his side, and immediately blood and water flowed out…For this happened so that the scripture passage might be fulfilled: "Not a bone of it will be broken."* The victim of sacrifice had to be a perfect specimen, with no broken bones or twisted limbs. Once again, John is identifying Jesus as the perfect victim of sacrifice on our behalf.

However, the most pertinent reference to Jesus as the Lamb of God is made by John the Baptist. He does this on two different occasions. In both cases he addresses Jesus as the Lamb of God. In the first instance found in John 1:29; 34: *"The next day he saw Jesus coming toward him and said, "Behold, the Lamb of God, who takes away the sin of the world… Now I have seen and testified that he is the Son of God."* In the Fourth Suffering Servant Oracle, the suffering servant is described as a lamb of sacrifice: *"Though harshly treated, he submitted and did not open his mouth; like a lamb led to slaughter or a sheep silent before shearers, he did not open his mouth."* (Verse 7) And in verse 10, we are told that *"it was the LORD's will to crush him with pain. By making his life as a reparation offering… the LORD's will shall be accomplished through him."* John is clearly describing Jesus as the suffering servant Messiah who as Son of God can and will take away the sins of the world, and our sins.

By this time in our celebration, we have confessed our sins and acknowledged our sinfulness several times. The Church is acutely aware of the fact that during our celebration we have entered deeper into the Holy Presence of God. The congregation expresses this privilege through praise, thanksgiving, and adoration. However, the holy Presence of God also reveals to us our sinfulness and constant need of salvation. And now the sacred moment has arrived for us to receive the Body, Blood, Soul and Divinity of Jesus in Holy Communion. We will be sealed in the new and everlasting covenant with the Blessed Trinity through Jesus, our Lamb that was slain. We realize our unworthiness and only the Lamb can make us worthy. So the 'Lamb of God' prayer is the prayer of a sinner being invited to become a saint through our Lamb that was slain. That was His intent in the first place when He allowed Himself to be led to the slaughter. In our third invocation, we ask the Lamb of God to grant us peace which is His presence in our midst and in our hearts. He is present with us as the Risen Lord who is victorious over sin and Satan. We share in His victory over Satan and eternal separation from God through Jesus who is our assurance of redemption and transformation.

PREPARATION FOR HOLY COMMUNION:

"Lord Jesus Christ, Son of the living God, who, by the will of the Father and the work of the Holy Spirit, through your Death gave life to the world, free me by this, your most holy Body and Blood, from all my sins and from every evil; keep me always faithful to your commandments, and never let me be parted from you." OR "May the receiving of your Body and Blood, Lord Jesus Christ, not bring me to judgment and condemnation, but through your loving mercy be for me protection in mind and body and a healing remedy."

The preparation for Communion hinges on two obvious realities that lie at the heart of our relationship with God, and are the context of every prayer we make, especially now, as we are about to receive the Body, Blood, Soul, and Divinity of Jesus in Holy Communion. The fundamental realities of our lives are first, that Jesus has given life to the world and to us by His death on the cross, and second, that we are sinners, always in need of salvation, who have great hope that our sins will be forgiven because we approach the throne of grace with contrite hearts. So we pray, not only that our sins will be forgiven, but that we might be faithful to the teachings of Jesus and always be united with Him. The Church, in her wisdom, deems this prayer as a worthy preparation for the reception of Jesus. Such a prayer is soon going to be eminently fulfilled when we receive Holy Communion.

RECEPTION OF HOLY COMMUNION:

Behold the Lamb of God, behold him who takes away the sins of the world. Blessed are those called to the supper of the Lamb.

As we get ready to receive Jesus in Holy Communion and in this way enter into covenant union with the Blessed Trinity, we are reminded that Jesus is the Lamb of God. We have been redeemed through His sacrifice on the cross; we have been washed clean in His blood shed on our behalf. Jesus, as our Lamb of sacrifice, is the Son of God. He does indeed take away the sins of the world, and our sins. And we are being invited to the supper of the Lamb.

We receive a proper understanding of the supper of the Lamb from Revelation 19. The heavenly liturgy reaches its climax in the wedding feast between the Lamb of God who is presented as the Bridegroom, and the bride, who is the Church: *"Alleluia! The Lord has established his reign, [our] God, the almighty. Let us rejoice and be glad and give him glory. For the wedding day of the Lamb has come, his bride has made herself ready. She was allowed to wear a bright, clean linen garment. (The linen represents the righteous deeds of the holy ones.)"* (Revelation 19:6-8) The context for this wedding feast celebration is the New Passover Meal. In all of the New Testament, we find only four Alleluias, and they are all found in Revelation 19:1-8. They are reminiscent of the Hallel Psalms 113-118, which were sung during the Mosaic Passover Meal. They were Psalms of praise, and hallelujah or the praises of God are echoed in these Psalms of praise (hallel). The first Alleluia is a song of praise and thanksgiving: *"Alleluia! Salvation, glory, and might belong to our God, for true and just are his judgments."* (Revelation 19:1-2) The second alleluia praises God for destroying Satan: *"He has condemned the great harlot…He has avenged on her the blood of his servants."* *They said a second time: "Alleluia! Smoke will rise from her forever and ever."* (Revelation 19:2-3). The third Alleluia is a reiteration: *"The twenty-four elders and the four living creatures fell down and worshiped God who sat on the throne, saying, "Amen. Alleluia."* (Revelation 19:4). The last alleluia trumpets the commencement of the wedding feast of the Lamb: *"Alleluia! The Lord has established his reign, [our] God, the almighty. Let us rejoice and be glad and give him glory. For the wedding day of the Lamb has come, his bride has made herself ready."* (Revelation 19:6-7)

Holy Communion then is seen as the wedding supper of the Lamb. We truly become one with Jesus who dwells in us and we in Him, and through Him, the Father who dwells in Him now dwells in us, and with them, the Holy Spirit who indwells us as our Advocate.

"Lord, I am not worthy that you should enter under my roof, but only say the word and my soul shall be healed."

In our response to the invitation to come to the wedding feast of the Lamb and be united with Him in Holy Communion, we respond with the sentiments of the Roman Centurion: *"Lord, I am not worthy to have you enter under my roof; only say the word and my servant will be healed… When Jesus heard this, he was amazed and said to those following him, 'Amen, I say to you, in no one in Israel have I found such faith.'"* (Matthew 8:8; 10) Part of his unworthiness might have stemmed from being a Gentile into whose home no Jewish person would enter. But he felt unworthy because he had the faith to realize he was in the Presence of God. He addressed Jesus as Lord. So his faith in Jesus prompted him to make a simple and heart-warming plea to Jesus: Please heal my servant, Lord. The centurion's faith was so compelling and extraordinary that Jesus was amazed. He was a Roman officer who had profound compassion for his slave. His deep love and concern for him made him come to Jesus with his request: *"Lord, my servant is lying at home paralyzed, suffering dreadfully."* When Jesus offered to come to his home, he expressed his unworthiness and total faith in Him. Jesus sends home the officer and his friends, with the knowledge that his request has been granted. We are invited as we approach the wedding feast of the Lamb as His bride, to have total faith and trust in Jesus as the Roman Centurion did.

THE CONCLUDING RITES: PRAYER, GREETING, BLESSING AND DISMISSAL:

"May your holy gifts purify us, O Lord, we pray, and by their working render us fully pleasing to you. Through Christ our Lord." "Amen."

"The Lord be with you." "And with your spirit."

"May almighty God bless you, the Father, and the Son, and the Holy Spirit." "Amen."

"Go forth, the Mass is ended." OR *"Go and announce the Gospel of the Lord."* OR *"Go in peace, glorifying the Lord by your life."* OR *"Go in peace."* "Thanks be to God."

The concluding rites begin with the Prayer after Communion. Generally, the Prayer echoes our gratitude to God and makes an earnest entreaty that the gifts we have received will be to the greater praise and service of God and the salvation of our soul.

We are then greeted with a very familiar greeting that has already been used several times during our celebration: *"The Lord be with you…* And we respond: *"And with your spirit."* Then we are blessed in the name of the Father, Son, and Holy Spirit.

The greeting and blessing signify a solemn moment as our celebration comes to a close. Once again, as at other important moments in our celebration, when there was special need for God's help so that we could accept His mission, at this point in our Eucharistic celebration, we are going to be dismissed or sent on a mission. We have experienced covenant union with the Blessed Trinity through the death and resurrection of Jesus, and the Risen Lord is present in us as Emmanuel. On behalf of the Blessed Trinity who dwells in our hearts, the priest, in the name of Jesus, is sending us forth: *"It was not you who chose me, but I who chose you and appointed you to go and bear fruit that will remain, so that whatever you ask the Father in my name he may give you. This I command you: love one another."* (John 15:16-17) Even with Jesus, this is a daunting mission. Without Jesus, this would be mission impossible. The priest is praying that the Lord will be with us as He was on numerous occasions when He sent His prophets and apostles on difficult and impossible missions. As with them, so with us and through us, He will accomplish His will. As disciples, we need to remain faithful and steadfast, to be branches that produce abundant fruit. The Lord will make that happen. And we pray in the same manner for our priest when we say, 'And with your spirit.' The mission is to be a Eucharistic people, to be victims of sacrifice like the Lamb that was slain, in our service and love of Jesus in His covenant family members. We pledge to become what we celebrated.

PRAYER AND REFLECTION ON EUCHARIST: THE COMMUNION RITE

WEEK TWENTY FIVE: *"Through him, and with him, and in him, O God, almighty Father, in the unity of the Holy Spirit, all glory and honor is yours, for ever and ever. Amen." (Doxology and the Great Amen)*

SPIRITUAL READING FOR THE WEEK:

- **Anoint Us in Your Covenant, Abba-Emmanuel:** Session Thirteen
- **Old Testament:** Two or Three Chapters daily
- **New Testament:** Two or Three Chapters daily
- **Imitation of Christ:** One chapter daily

DAY ONE: MORNING SESSION

MORNING PRAYER: Acts of Faith, Hope, Charity; Daily Offering

Morning Face to Face with God:

Begin with Prayer to the Holy Spirit

EUCHARIST: THE COMMUNION RITE

(After pondering each bullet point, express your sentiments in a short prayer)

- Our participation in God's life through Jesus is at the heart of our Eucharistic celebration. In Holy Communion we will have entered profoundly into the reality of this indescribable mystery of us becoming partakers of God's divine nature (2 Peter 1:4).

- By eating His Body and drinking His Blood, we will have entered into covenant union with the Father, Son, and Holy Spirit. We will have become God's temple or abode, God dwelling in us, and we in God.

- Through His death and resurrection which we are participating in and celebrating, we have received Jesus' peace. Peace is the victory over Satan, sin, and permanent death that Jesus has won. It is decisive, conclusive, and unassailable. In believing and accepting Jesus as our Savior and Lord, we are now permeated with this peace!

- Before we offer the peace of Christ to one another, we have removed every trace of un-forgiveness from our hearts. When we offer peace to one another, we are joined together by the bond of the peace of Christ!

- In 8th century Syria, the understanding emerged that the separate consecrations of the bread and wine symbolized the separation of Christ's Body and Blood in His death. The commingling rite expresses the reunion of Jesus' Body and Blood in His resurrection.

- Jesus is our Intercessor in heaven as the 'Lamb that was slain.' Life in heaven is about God's covenant family engaged in a continual Eucharistic liturgy of adoration, praise, thanksgiving, and intercession through Jesus, the Lamb that was slain.

- We will be sealed in the new and everlasting covenant with the Blessed Trinity through Jesus, our Lamb that was slain. We realize our unworthiness and only the Lamb can make us worthy. So the 'Lamb of God' prayer is the prayer of a sinner being invited to become a saint through our Lamb that was slain. That was Jesus' intent in the first place when He allowed Himself to be led to the slaughter.

- The preparation for Communion hinges on two obvious realities that lie at the heart of our relationship with God, especially now, as we are about to receive the Body, Blood, Soul, and Divinity of Jesus in Holy Communion. One, Jesus has given life to the world and to us by His death on the cross.

- And two, that we are sinners, always in need of salvation, who have great hope that our sins will be forgiven because we approach the throne of grace with contrite hearts. So we pray, not only that our sins will be forgiven, but that we might be faithful to the teachings of Jesus and always be united with Him.

- In our response to the invitation to come to the wedding feast of the Lamb and be united with Him in Holy Communion, we respond with the sentiments of the Roman

Centurion. His faith was so compelling and extraordinary that Jesus is amazed. We are invited as we approach the wedding feast of the Lamb as His bride, to have total faith and trust in Jesus as the Roman Centurion did.

- The Dismissal sends us on a mission. The mission is to be a Eucharistic people, to be victims of sacrifice like the Lamb that was slain, in our service and love of Jesus in His covenant family members. We pledge to become what we celebrated.

What is God saying to you?

End with Prayer to the Holy Trinity

NIGHT SESSION: Examination of Conscience

For what are you grateful? For what are you contrite?

Please review briefly your Morning Prayer topic. Make it your last thought of the day

DAY TWO: MORNING SESSION

MORNING PRAYER: Acts of Faith, Hope, Charity; Daily Offering

Morning Face to Face with God:

Begin with Prayer to the Holy Spirit

PRAYER ON THE LORD'S PRAYER

> *"At the Savior's command and formed by divine teaching, we dare to say: Our Father, who art in heaven, hallowed by thy name; thy kingdom come, thy will be done on earth as it is in heaven. Give us this day our daily bread, and forgive us our trespasses, as we forgive those who trespass against us; and lead us not into temptation, but deliver us from evil."*

Ask the Holy Spirit to give you a deep appreciation for the Liturgy of the Eucharist, and that your participation might always be wholehearted and generous

Very appropriately we begin our preparation for Holy Communion with the recitation of the Lord's Prayer. The prayer is an excellent preparation for Holy Communion. We begin by addressing God as Father. Through the institution of God's new and everlasting covenant with us through the death and resurrection of Jesus, we have been brought into covenant union with the Blessed Trinity. The Father-Son relationship in God has been offered to us. We can both address and relate to God as Jesus does. We are now the Father's sons and daughters; we are sons and daughters in the Son; God is now our Father! Our participation in God's life through

Jesus is at the heart of our Eucharistic celebration. In Holy Communion, we will have entered profoundly into the reality of this indescribable mystery of us becoming partakers of God's divine nature (2 Peter 1:4).

In the Lord's Prayer we are asking for our daily bread: *epi ousios* in the Greek, or *substance from above*. This was the description of manna, food from above that was given to the Israelites in the desert. In John 6, Jesus tells us that He is manna, food from heaven that will never perish. By eating His body and drinking His blood, we will have entered into covenant union with the Father, Son, and Holy Spirit. We will have become God's temple or abode, God dwelling in us, and we in God. So in our prayer we ask that we have the true sentiments of covenant union: forgiveness of our sins which implies repentance; forgiveness of others which implies agapé love; protection against our own sinful tendencies and the wiles of the Evil One. In this way we prepare ourselves to receive Our Lord in Holy Communion.

What is God saying to you?

End with Prayer to the Holy Trinity

NIGHT SESSION: Examination of Conscience

For what are you grateful? For what are you contrite?

Please review briefly your Morning Prayer topic. Make it your last thought of the day

DAY THREE: MORNING SESSION

MORNING PRAYER: Acts of Faith, Hope, Charity; Daily Offering

Morning Face to Face with God:

Begin with Prayer to the Holy Spirit

PRAYER FOR PEACE

> *Deliver us, Lord, we pray, from every evil, graciously grant peace in our days, that, by the help of your mercy, we may be always free from sin and safe from all distress, as we await the blessed hope and the coming of our Savior, Jesus Christ.*

For the kingdom, the power and the glory are yours now and for ever.

> *Lord Jesus Christ, who said to your Apostles: Peace I leave you, my peace I give you; look not on our sins, but on the faith of your Church, and graciously grant her peace and unity in accordance with your will. Who live and reign for ever and ever.* Amen.

Ask the Holy Spirit to give you a deep appreciation for the Liturgy of the Eucharist, and that your participation might always be wholehearted and generous

After the Lord's Prayer, the priest first implores the Father to deliver us from every evil. The best way for this to happen is by receiving peace in our days. We reiterate the same plea we have made in the Lord's Prayer and elsewhere that we be forgiven our sins by receiving God's mercy. In this way we will be free from sin and safe from every distress as we await the blessed hope and coming of our Savior, Jesus Christ. In the next prayer, we make the same petition of Jesus, asking Him to graciously grant peace to His Church. Through His death and resurrection which we are celebrating in this Eucharist, we have received Jesus' peace. Peace is the victory over Satan, sin, and permanent death that Jesus has won. It is decisive, conclusive, and unassailable. In believing and accepting Jesus as our Savior and Lord, we are now permeated with this peace! Only sin and our rebellion can take away this peace which is the presence of the Risen Lord, from our hearts. In Holy Communion we will receive the peace of Christ in abundance! Before we receive Jesus in the Eucharist, we ask for the gift of peace, which is abiding, because it is the peace of the Risen Lord.

What is God saying to you?

End with Prayer to the Holy Trinity

NIGHT SESSION: Examination of Conscience

For what are you grateful? For what are you contrite?

Please review briefly your Morning Prayer topic. Make it your last thought of the day

DAY FOUR: MORNING SESSION

MORNING PRAYER: Acts of Faith, Hope, Charity; Daily Offering

Morning Face to Face with God:

Begin with Prayer to the Holy Spirit

PRAYER ON THE SIGN OF PEACE

The peace of the Lord be with you always. And with your spirit.

Let us offer each other the sign of peace.

Ask the Holy Spirit to give you a deep appreciation for the Liturgy of the Eucharist, and that your participation might always be wholehearted and generous

And to demonstrate that we are God's covenant family, the priest first offers us the Lord's peace and we reciprocate by making the same prayer for him as well. We can only have God's peace if we share it with one another. This exchange of God's peace among us, highlights two significant truths. The first is that God has established an unbreakable bond between Himself and us, when He created us in the divine image and likeness. This bond was always intended to be a covenant relationship. Consequently, we cannot say we love God and not love His image and likeness. In the Ten Commandments, three commandments focus on our relationship with God and seven on our relationship with our neighbor and fellow humans. The second truth is that we have always to have forgiveness in our hearts. We are to forgive 490 (70X7) times a day if necessary. After giving us the Lord's Prayer, Jesus makes forgiveness of others a necessary condition to receive forgiveness for ourselves: *"If you forgive others their transgressions, your heavenly Father will forgive you. But if you do not forgive others, neither will your Father forgive your transgressions."* (Matthew 6:14-15) Our willingness to offer each other Christ's peace suggests the seriousness of our commitment to a covenant relationship with God and one another. We are willing to lay down our lives in generous and selfless service, to be foot-washers to one another, as Jesus has asked us. When we offer Christ's peace to one another, we need to remind ourselves that living for the other is possible because He abides in us and we have His peace, and therefore share in His victory over Satan and sin. We are joined together and with one another by the bond of the peace of Christ!

What is God saying to you?

End with Prayer to the Holy Trinity

NIGHT SESSION: Examination of Conscience

For what are you grateful? For what are you contrite?

Please review briefly your Morning Prayer topic. Make it your last thought of the day

DAY FIVE: MORNING SESSION

MORNING PRAYER: Acts of Faith, Hope, Charity; Daily Offering

Morning Face to Face with God:

Begin with Prayer to the Holy Spirit

PRAYER ON THE FRACTION AND COMMINGLING

May this mingling of the Body and Blood of our Lord Jesus Christ bring eternal life to us who receive it.

Ask the Holy Spirit to give you a deep appreciation for the Liturgy of the Eucharist, and that your participation might always be wholehearted and generous

After the sign of peace is given, the priest breaks the host in a symbolic action known as the fraction or the breaking of the bread. In the Old Testament, the father of the family would recite a blessing and then break bread and distribute it to his family. There are several instances of the breaking of the bread in the New Testament, either prefiguring the Eucharist as in the multiplication of the loaves: *"Then, taking the five loaves and the two fish and looking up to heaven, he said the blessing, broke the loaves, and gave them to [his] disciples…"* (Mark 6:41), or actually signifying the Eucharist: *"And it happened that, while he was with them at table, he took bread, said the blessing, broke it, and gave it to them."* (Luke 24:30) In Acts the Eucharist was described as the breaking of bread: *"Every day they devoted themselves to meeting together in the temple area and to breaking bread in their homes."* (Acts 2:46) Soon the meal will begin and we will partake of the body and blood of Jesus Christ. The breaking of the bread is a clear indication that the meal will soon begin.

Then the priest does the commingling. In the early Church, the mingling denoted the unity of the Church, between the Pope and His priests: a small particle from the host (called *fermentum*) he had consecrated would be sent to the priests in the city to place in their chalices. In 8th century Syria the understanding emerged that the separate consecrations of the bread and wine symbolized the separation of Christ's body and blood in His death. The commingling rite expresses the reunion of Jesus' body and blood in His resurrection. In the first commingling of the Eucharist that took place we prayed that the mingling of the drop of water representing us, with the wine representing Jesus, make us share in Christ's divinity who shared in our humanity. Soon that prayer will be answered in Holy Communion.

What is God saying to you?

End with Prayer to the Holy Trinity

NIGHT SESSION: Examination of Conscience

For what are you grateful? For what are you contrite?

Please review briefly your Morning Prayer topic. Make it your last thought of the day

DAY SIX: MORNING SESSION

MORNING PRAYER: Acts of Faith, Hope, Charity; Daily Offering

Morning Face to Face with God:

Begin with Prayer to the Holy Spirit

REPETITION OF DAYS ONE THROUGH FIVE:

Ask the Holy Spirit to give you a deep appreciation for the Liturgy of the Eucharist, and that your participation might always be wholehearted and generous

  Today, you are doing a repetition of Days One through Five of this week. In a repetition St. Ignatius says that *"we should pay attention to and dwell upon those points in which we have experienced greater consolation or desolation or greater spiritual appreciation."* (# 62) If you wish, you can do a triple colloquy: refer to #63 of the Spiritual Exercises.

What is God saying to you?

End with Prayer to the Holy Trinity

NIGHT SESSION: Examination of Conscience

For what are you grateful? For what are you contrite?

Please review briefly your Morning Prayer topic. Make it your last thought of the day

DAY SEVEN: MORNING SESSION

MORNING PRAYER: Acts of Faith, Hope, Charity; Daily Offering

Morning Face to Face with God:

Begin with Prayer to the Holy Spirit

THE DARK NIGHT OF THE SPIRIT:

(After pondering each bullet point, express your sentiments in a short prayer)

- In Book Two of *The Dark Night* St. John of the Cross deals with the Dark Night of the Spirit. When the process of the Dark Night of the Senses is completed or far advanced, the disciple sees clearly how the Holy Spirit has transformed them.

- They are brought into a different world. They understand the teachings of Jesus with a clarity and insight they did not have before. If God wishes to lead the soul into the dark night of the spirit, He does not do so immediately. In fact the disciple could spend many years as a proficient.

- In this state, the disciple *"as one liberated from a cramped cell, (it) goes about the things of God with much more freedom and satisfaction of spirit and with more abundant interior delight than it did in the beginning before entering the night of sense... The soul readily finds in its spirit, without the work of meditation, a very serene, loving contemplation and spiritual delight."* (TDN – Book Two: Chapter 1:1).

- St. John of the Cross gives us two important reasons as to why God first leads the soul through the sensory night prior to the passive dark night of the spirit. The first reason is because *"All good and evil habits reside in the spirit and until these habits are purged, the senses cannot be completely purified of their rebellions and vices."* (TDN – Book Two: Chapter 3:1)

- The second reason is because *"In this night that follows both parts are jointly purified. This was the purpose of the reformation of the first night and the calm that resulted from it: that the sensory part, united in a certain way with the spirit, might undergo purgation and suffering with greater fortitude. Such is the fortitude necessary for so strong and arduous a purgation that if the lower part in its weakness is not reformed first, and afterward strengthened in God through the experience of sweet and delightful communion with him, it has neither the fortitude nor the preparedness to endure it."* (TDN – Book Two: Chapter 3:2)

- The dark night of the spirit is a twofold experience, of intense purification and transformation. The soul describes its purification in the following manner: *"Poor, abandoned, and unsupported by any of the apprehensions of my soul (in the darkness of my intellect, the distress of my will, and the affliction and anguish of my memory), left to darkness in pure faith, which is a dark night for these natural faculties, and with my will touched only by sorrows, afflictions, and longings of love of God, I went out from myself."* (TDN – Book Two: Chapter 4:1)

- On the other hand, a re-creation is taking place which might not be noticeable at first: *"This was great happiness and a sheer grace for me, because through the annihilation and calming of my faculties, passions, appetites, and affections, by which my experience and satisfaction in God were base, I went out from my human operation and way of acting to God's operation and way of acting... My intellect departed from itself, changing from human and natural to divine...And my will departed from itself and became divine. United with the divine love, it no longer loves in a lowly manner, with its natural strength, but with the strength and purity of the Holy Spirit; and thus the will does not operate humanly in relation to God. The memory, too, was changed into eternal apprehensions of glory."* (TDN – Book Two: Chapter 4:2)

- Consequently, through this spiritual night of purification and illumination, God initiates the soul in the perfection of love without its doing anything or even knowing how it happens.

What is God saying to you?

NIGHT SESSION: Examination of Conscience

For what are you grateful? For what are you contrite?

What prayer would you compose to express what God has said to you this week?

Please review briefly your Morning Prayer topic. Make it your last thought of the day

PRAYER AND REFLECTION ON EUCHARIST: THE COMMUNION RITE

WEEK TWENTY SIX: *"Behold the lamb of God, behold him who takes away the sins of the world. Blessed are those called to the supper of the lamb."*

SPIRITUAL READING FOR THE WEEK:

- **Anoint Us in Your Covenant, Abba-Emmanuel:** Session Thirteen
- **Old Testament:** Two or Three Chapters daily
- **New Testament:** Two or Three Chapters daily
- **Imitation of Christ:** One chapter daily

DAY ONE: MORNING SESSION

MORNING PRAYER: Acts of Faith, Hope, Charity; Daily Offering

Morning Face to Face with God:

Begin with Prayer to the Holy Spirit

PRAYER ON LAMB OF GOD:

"Lamb of God, you take away the sins of the world, have mercy on us. Lamb of God, you take away the sins of the world, have mercy on us. Lamb of God, you take away the sins of the world, grant us peace."

Ask the Holy Spirit to give you a deep appreciation for the Liturgy of the Eucharist, and that your participation might always be wholehearted and generous

The Church is acutely aware of the fact that during our celebration we have entered deeper into the Holy Presence of God. The congregation expresses this privilege through praise, thanksgiving, and adoration. However, the holy Presence of God also reveals to us our sinfulness and constant need of salvation. And now the sacred moment has arrived for us to receive the Body, Blood, Soul and Divinity of Jesus in Holy Communion. We will be sealed in the new and everlasting covenant with the Blessed Trinity through Jesus, our Lamb that was slain. We realize our unworthiness and only the Lamb can make us worthy. So the 'Lamb of God' prayer is the prayer of a sinner being invited to become a saint through our Lamb that was slain. That was His intent in the first place when He allowed Himself to be led to the slaughter. In our third invocation, we ask the Lamb of God to grant us peace which is His presence in our midst and in our hearts. He is present with us as the Risen Lord who is victorious over sins and Satan. We share in His victory over Satan and eternal separation from God through Jesus who is our assurance of redemption and transformation.

What is God saying to you?

End with Prayer to the Holy Trinity

NIGHT SESSION: Examination of Conscience

For what are you grateful? For what are you contrite?

Please review briefly your Morning Prayer topic. Make it your last thought of the day

DAY TWO: MORNING SESSION

MORNING PRAYER: Acts of Faith, Hope, Charity; Daily Offering

Morning Face to Face with God:

Begin with Prayer to the Holy Spirit

PRAYER ON PREPARATION FOR HOLY COMMUNION:

"Lord Jesus Christ, Son of the living God, who, by the will of the Father and the work of the Holy Spirit, through your Death gave life to the world, free me by this, your most holy Body and Blood, from all my sins and from every evil; keep me always faithful to your commandments, and never let me be parted from you."

OR "May the receiving of your Body and Blood, Lord Jesus Christ, not bring me to judgment and condemnation, but through your loving mercy be for me protection in mind and body and a healing remedy."

Ask the Holy Spirit to give you a deep appreciation for the Liturgy of the Eucharist, and that your participation might always be wholehearted and generous

The preparation for Communion hinges on two obvious realities that lie at the heart of our relationship with God, and are the context of every prayer we make, especially now, as we are about to receive the body, blood, soul, and divinity of Jesus in Holy Communion. The fundamental realities of our lives is first, that Jesus has given life to the world and to us by his death on the cross, and second, that we are sinners, always in need of salvation, who have great hope that our sins will be forgiven because we approach the throne of grace with contrite hearts. So we pray, not only that our sins will be forgiven, but that we might be faithful to the teachings of Jesus and always be united with Him. The Church, in her wisdom, deems this prayer as a worthy preparation for the reception of Jesus. Such a prayer is soon going to be eminently fulfilled when we receive Holy Communion.

What is God saying to you?

End with Prayer to the Holy Trinity

NIGHT SESSION: Examination of Conscience

For what are you grateful? For what are you contrite?

Please review briefly your Morning Prayer topic. Make it your last thought of the day

DAY THREE: MORNING SESSION

MORNING PRAYER: Acts of Faith, Hope, Charity; Daily Offering

Morning Face to Face with God:

Begin with Prayer to the Holy Spirit

PRAYER ON RECEPTION OF HOLY COMMUNION:

Behold the Lamb of God, behold him who takes away the sins of the world. Blessed are those called to the supper of the Lamb.

Ask the Holy Spirit to give you a deep appreciation for the Liturgy of the Eucharist, and that your participation might always be wholehearted and generous

As we get ready to receive Jesus in Holy Communion and in this way enter into covenant union with the Blessed Trinity, we are reminded that Jesus is the Lamb of God. We have been redeemed through His sacrifice on the cross; we have been washed clean in His blood shed on our behalf. Jesus, as our Lamb of sacrifice, is the Son of God. He does indeed take away the sins of the world, and our sins. And we are being invited to the supper of the Lamb.

The heavenly liturgy reaches its climax in the wedding feast between the Lamb of God who is presented as the Bridegroom, and the bride, who is the Church: *"Alleluia! The Lord has established his reign, [our] God, the almighty. Let us rejoice and be glad and give him glory. For the wedding day of the Lamb has come, his bride has made herself ready. She was allowed to wear a bright, clean linen garment." (The linen represents the righteous deeds of the holy ones.)* (Revelation 19:6-8) Holy Communion then is seen as the wedding supper of the Lamb. We truly become one with Jesus who dwells in us and we in Him, and through Him, the Father who dwells in Him now dwells in us, and with them, the Holy Spirit who in indwells us as our Advocate.

What is God saying to you?

End with Prayer to the Holy Trinity

NIGHT SESSION: Examination of Conscience

For what are you grateful? For what are you contrite?

Please review briefly your Morning Prayer topic. Make it your last thought of the day

DAY FOUR: MORNING SESSION

MORNING PRAYER: Acts of Faith, Hope, Charity; Daily Offering

Morning Face to Face with God:

Begin with Prayer to the Holy Spirit

PRAYER ON RECEPTION OF HOLY COMMUNION:

"Lord, I am not worthy that you should enter under my roof, but only say the word and my soul shall be healed."

Ask the Holy Spirit to give you a deep appreciation for the Liturgy of the Eucharist, and that your participation might always be wholehearted and generous

In our response to the invitation to come to the wedding feast of the Lamb and be united with Him in Holy Communion, we respond with the sentiments of the Roman Centurion: *"Lord, I am not worthy to have you enter under my roof; only say the word and my servant will be healed… When Jesus heard this, he was amazed and said to those following him, "Amen, I say to you, in no one in Israel have I found such faith."* (Matthew 8:8; 10) Part of his unworthiness might have stemmed from being a Gentile into whose home no Jewish person would enter. But he felt unworthy because he had faith to realize he was in the Presence of God. He addressed Jesus as Lord. So his faith in Jesus prompted him to make a simple and heart-warming plea to Jesus: Please heal my servant, Lord. The centurion's faith was so compelling and extraordinary that Jesus was amazed. He was a Roman officer who had profound compassion for his slave. His deep love and concern for him made him come to Jesus with his request: *"Lord, my servant is lying at home paralyzed, suffering dreadfully."* When Jesus offered to come to his home, he expressed his unworthiness and total faith in Him. Jesus sends home the officer and his friends, with the knowledge that his request has been granted. We are invited as we approach the wedding feast of the Lamb as His bride, to have total faith and trust in Jesus as the Roman Centurion did.

What is God saying to you?

End with Prayer to the Holy Trinity

NIGHT SESSION: Examination of Conscience

For what are you grateful? For what are you contrite?

Please review briefly your Morning Prayer topic. Make it your last thought of the day

DAY FIVE: MORNING SESSION

MORNING PRAYER: Acts of Faith, Hope, Charity; Daily Offering

Morning Face to Face with God:

Begin with Prayer to the Holy Spirit

PRAYER ON THE CONCLUDING RITES: PRAYER, GREETING, BLESSING, AND DISMISSAL:

"May your holy gifts purify us, O Lord, we pray, and by their working render us fully pleasing to you. Through Christ our Lord." "Amen."

"The Lord be with you." "And with your spirit." *"May almighty God bless you, the Father, and the Son, and the Holy Spirit."* "Amen."

"Go forth, the Mass is ended." OR *"Go and announce the Gospel of the Lord."* OR *"Go in peace, glorifying the Lord by your life."* OR *"Go in peace."* "Thanks be to God."

Ask the Holy Spirit to give you a deep appreciation for the Liturgy of the Eucharist, and that your participation might always be wholehearted and generous

The concluding rites begin with the *Prayer after Communion*. Generally, the Prayer echoes our gratitude to God and makes an earnest entreaty that the gifts we have received will be to the greater praise and service of God and the salvation of our soul.

We are then greeted with a very familiar greeting that has already been used several times during our celebration: *"The Lord be with you… And with your spirit."* Then we are blessed in the name of the Father, Son, and Holy Spirit.

The *greeting and blessing* signify a solemn moment as our celebration comes to a close. Once again, as at other important moments in our celebration, when there was special need for God's help so that we could accept His mission, at this point in our Eucharistic celebration, we are going to be *dismissed or sent on a mission*. We have experienced covenant union with the Blessed Trinity through the death and resurrection of Jesus, and the Risen Lord is present in us as Emmanuel. On behalf of the Blessed Trinity who dwells in our hearts, the priest, in the name of Jesus, is sending us forth: *"It was not you who chose me, but I who chose you and appointed you to go and bear fruit that will remain, so that whatever you ask the Father in my name he may give you. This I command you: love one another."* (John 15:16-17) Even with Jesus, this is a daunting mission. Without Jesus, this would be mission impossible. The priest is praying that the Lord will be with us as He was on numerous occasions when He sent His prophets and apostles on difficult and impossible missions which He accomplished through them. As disciples, we need to remain faithful and steadfast, to be branches that produce abundant fruit. The Lord will make that happen. And we pray in the same manner for our priest when we say, 'And with your spirit.' The mission is to be a Eucharistic people, to be victims of sacrifice like the Lamb that was slain, in our service and love of Jesus in His covenant family members. We pledge to become what we celebrated.

What is God saying to you?

End with Prayer to the Holy Trinity

NIGHT SESSION: Examination of Conscience

For what are you grateful? For what are you contrite?

Please review briefly your Morning Prayer topic. Make it your last thought of the day

DAY SIX: MORNING SESSION

MORNING PRAYER: Acts of Faith, Hope, Charity; Daily Offering

Morning Face to Face with God:

Begin with Prayer to the Holy Spirit

REPETITION OF DAYS ONE THROUGH FIVE:

Ask the Holy Spirit to give you a deep appreciation for the Liturgy of the Eucharist, and that your participation might always be wholehearted and generous

Today, you are doing a repetition of Days One through Five of this week. In a repetition St. Ignatius says that *"we should pay attention to and dwell upon those points in which we have experienced greater consolation or desolation or greater spiritual appreciation."* (# 62) If you wish, you can do a triple colloquy: refer to #63 of the Spiritual Exercises.

What is God saying to you?

End with Prayer to the Holy Trinity

NIGHT SESSION: Examination of Conscience

For what are you grateful? For what are you contrite?

Please review briefly your Morning Prayer topic. Make it your last thought of the day

DAY SEVEN: MORNING SESSION

MORNING PRAYER: Acts of Faith, Hope, Charity; Daily Offering

Morning Face to Face with God:

Begin with Prayer to the Holy Spirit

AFFLICTIONS IN THE DARK NIGHT OF THE SPIRIT:

(After pondering each bullet point, express your sentiments in a short prayer)

- Some of these afflictions have to do with the blinding and paralyzing effect the divine light has on our human faculties when God is bringing about union with the soul. The soul is blinded by the divine light and experiences it as *"spiritual darkness, for it not only surpasses the act of natural understanding but it also deprives the soul of this act and darkens it."* (TDN – Book Two: Chapter 5:3)

- This divine light exposes all that is impure and sinful in the soul, resulting in the disciple experiencing unworthiness and sinfulness before God. They feel wretched and miserable and think that God is against them and has abandoned them. The disciple realizes how utterly devoid they are without God and everything is pure gift.

- At times death would be preferable to the intensity of this purification: *"They suffer so much in their weakness that they almost die, particularly at times when the light is more powerful. Both the sense and the spirit, as though under an immense and dark load, undergo such agony and pain that the soul would consider death a relief."* (TDN – Book Two: Chapter 5:6)

- The paradox is that God's aim is to grant the soul favors and not to chastise it. However, the soul is still so weak and vulnerable that it experiences new life from God as the rigors of death.

- They are convinced that God has rejected them and such abandonment is a very heavy burden to bear. They also feel forsaken and despised by people, particularly by their friends. They can feel useless and insignificant in themselves, and sidelined by family and friends.

- Another affliction is a sense of emptiness that they experience. Their talent and giftedness don't have the same appeal; material possessions don't satisfy in the same way; since they feel rejected and abandoned by God, their spiritual gifts don't mean much. They are miserable about their imperfections, none of their faculties can function, and the darkness in and around them is great indeed.

- The disciple is made very aware of the evils (past sins and present sinfulness) in which it is immersed through this purification, and is uncertain of any remedy to it.

- Furthermore, God will not allow the soul to have any respite or reassurance from other sources. The words of the spiritual director, or a spiritual master, or a teaching, don't appeal or provide any relief. *"They remain in this condition until their spirit is humbled, softened, and purified, until it becomes so delicate, simple, and refined that it can be one with the Spirit of God, according to the degree of union of love that God, in his mercy, desires to grant."* (TDN – Book Two: Chapter 7:3)

- Such purification will last for some years; however, every now and then God's light will shine upon the soul and illumine it greatly, giving it a foretaste of that for which it hopes. However, such relief is fleeting.

- Just when the soul assumes it is safe, the purgation returns and darkens the soul in a more severe affliction that could last longer than the previous one. In all of this suffering, they know that they love God and would do anything for Him.

- However, they find no relief from their affliction and are unable to believe that God loves them. In fact they are convinced that they should be abhorred by God and everybody else.

- The prayer of intercession becomes almost impossible as they feel the chasm between God and them, and they don't have it in them to bridge it. And even when they try, God does not hear them or pay any attention to them.

- The saint offers salutary advice in this situation: *"This is not the time to speak with God… but to suffer this purgation patiently… God it is who is working now in the soul, and for this reason the soul can do nothing."* (TDN – Book Two: Chapter 8:1)

What is God saying to you?

End with Prayer to the Holy Trinity

NIGHT SESSION: Examination of Conscience

For what are you grateful? For what are you contrite?

What prayer would you compose to express what God has said to you this week?

Please review briefly your Morning Prayer topic. Make it your last thought of the day

SESSION FOURTEEN
LIVING AS DISCIPLE IN GOD'S COVENANT FAMILY

"But blessed are your eyes, because they see, and your ears, because they hear. Amen, I say to you, many prophets and righteous people longed to see what you see but did not see it, and to hear what you hear but did not hear it."

– Matthew 13:16-17

APPRECIATING YOUR CALLING:

There is perhaps no better way to sum up Jesus' life and teachings than by mulling over the fulfillment of God's plan of salvation through Him as recorded by Paul in his letter to the Ephesians: *"Blessed by the God and Father of our Lord Jesus Christ, who has blessed us in Christ with every spiritual blessing in the heavens, as he chose us in him, before the foundation of the world, to be holy and without blemish before him. In love he destined us for adoption to himself through Jesus Christ, in accord with the favor of his will, for the praise of the glory of his grace that he granted us in the beloved."* (Ephesians 1:3-6) Through Jesus Christ, God adopted us and made us integral members of the divine family, perfectly bridging the gap between Him and us, created by rebellion and sin. Even more startling is the fact that God is a blatant optimist when it comes to creating dreams in our regard. Given the unfaithful history of God's people, it seems rather astonishing, that our God continually hopes and dreams that we will come to live in Christ's image. Yet such is the power of God's salvation through Jesus. This is the transformation that takes place in any individual who, like the Blind Man in John 9, accepts Jesus as Savior and Lord, and humbles his entire being in submission to Him as the Son of the Living God. God's dream for us is holiness, blamelessness, and genuine son-ship in Jesus.

God's plan of salvation in and through Jesus, challenges conscious thought and ignites the imagination. God chose to unite us with the Triune God through Jesus becoming human. Jesus identified with us in all things while defeating sin, and through Him we have been guaranteed access into God's life and heart. We have been made God's very own sons and daughters, and it is our privilege and birthright to share in God's dream to live holy and blameless lives, full of love, as God is full of love. God's plan for us, envisaged from all eternity, and given the breath of life in our creation at the beginning of time, has now been brought to fulfillment and completion in Jesus Christ.

Probably there is no more eloquent description than Paul's of how God calls us into covenant life with Him, and desires that we share in the fullness of His divine nature. For many years Paul lived as a devout Pharisee, a keen observer of the Law in its minutest detail, and was thus blameless in righteousness based on the Law. As he says in his letter to the Philippians 3:5-6: *"Circumcised on the eighth day, of the race of Israel, of the tribe of Benjamin, a Hebrew of Hebrew parentage, in observance of the law a Pharisee, in zeal I persecuted the church, in righteousness based on the law I was blameless."* But then he was encountered on the road to Damascus where he met Jesus face to face. A life-altering dialogue ensued between them, and Paul was never the same after that: *"But Ananias replied, "Lord, I have heard from many sources about this man, what evil things he has done to your holy ones in Jerusalem. And here he has authority from the chief priests to imprison all who call upon your name." But the Lord said to him, "Go, for this man is a chosen instrument of mine to carry my name before the Gentiles, kings, and Israelites, and I will show him what he will have to suffer for my name."* (Acts 9:13-16)

In his letter to the Galatians, Paul underscores his conversion and calling from the Lord: *"Now I want you to know, brothers, that the gospel preached by me is not of human origin. For I did not receive it from a human being, nor was I taught it, but it came through a revelation of Jesus Christ."* (Galatians 1:11-12) Paul's whole life and ministry is founded on this call from Jesus Christ. He followed it wholeheartedly, getting himself baptized by Ananias, receiving the fullness of the Holy Spirit, and witnessing to His Lord and Savior, Jesus Christ: *"So Ananias went and entered the house; laying his hands on him, he said, "Saul, my brother, the Lord has sent me, Jesus who appeared to you on the way by which you came, that you may regain your sight and be filled with the holy Spirit." Immediately things like scales fell from his eyes and he regained his sight. He got up and was baptized, and when he had eaten, he recovered his strength."* (Acts 9:17-19)

In his letter to the Philippians, Paul reflects on his past life in light of his covenant life with the Trinity through Jesus Christ, His Lord and Savior: *"[But] whatever gains I had, these I have come to consider a loss because of Christ. More than that, I even consider everything as a loss because of the supreme good of knowing Christ Jesus my Lord. For his sake I have accepted the loss of all things and I consider them so much rubbish, that I may gain Christ and be found in him, not having any righteousness of my own based on the law but that which comes through faith in Christ, the righteousness from God, depending on faith to know him and the power of his resurrection and [the] sharing of his sufferings by being conformed to his death, if somehow I may attain the resurrection from the dead."* (Philippians 3:7-11)

In the course of his life and ministry, Paul experienced the full benefits of his covenant life gifted to him by Jesus through the power of the Holy Spirit. He experienced this transformation through intimate participation in the Life and Love of our Triune God. And when we examine the lives and writings of the followers of Jesus in the New Testament we realize that they did their ministry because they were sent by their Lord and Savior, Jesus Christ. They were sent on mission after being transformed by the Holy Spirit. They did everything in the power of the Holy Spirit, and subsequent disciples were like Paul, baptized in water and the Holy Spirit, and thus brought into the Life and Love of Father, Son, and Holy Spirit.

It behooves us as disciples of Jesus, to ponder deeply our call to be incorporated into Trinitarian Life through the tender compassion and mercy of our heavenly Father who sent His Son, Jesus Christ into the world so that we might not perish but might have eternal life. Our Heavenly Father has made it clear that Jesus Christ came not to condemn the world but that the world might be saved through Him. As 1John 3:1-3 says: *"See what love the Father has bestowed on us that we may be called the children of God. Yet so we are. The reason the world does not know us is that it did not know him. Beloved, we are God's children now; what we shall be has not yet been revealed. We do know that when it is revealed we shall be like him, for we shall see him as he is. Everyone who has this hope based on him makes himself pure, as he is pure."*

HAVING THE RIGHT APPROACH TO DISCIPLESHIP:

God's love for us is so tender and wholehearted in that the Father, Son, and Holy Spirit have given their Life and Love to us in covenant. The Trinity has thereby made it clear through their involvement in our lives that God will hold back nothing of Himself from us. Given this amazing truth, any authentic approach to discipleship would have to be grounded in God's infinite love and mercy toward us. Paul was tireless in proclaiming this plan of God's salvation to the early Christians because he was convinced that the heritage of being God's sons and daughters was indeed the bedrock of our meaning and joy in life. To the Ephesians he proclaims that *"He chose us in him (Christ), before the foundation of the world, to be holy and without blemish before him. In love he destined us for adoption to himself through Jesus Christ, in accord with the favor of his will, for the praise of the glory of his grace that he granted us in the beloved."* (Ephesians 1:4-6) This message that we are precious to God, who wants a very special relationship with us as sons and daughters, is reiterated numerous times in Scripture.

While every disciple sincerely longs for this loving intimacy with God, many are hesitant to take this step. The committed disciple who calls on God as Abba with trust and conviction soon realizes that being God's child is at the core of their reality. And such a truth sets us free. In other words, God's way of understanding us is very different from the way we understand ourselves. True spiritual and psychological health and freedom begin only when we put on the mind and heart of God, when we learn to look at and understand ourselves through God's eyes and thoughts. In the parable of the Prodigal Son, the message seems to be that salvation and the process of becoming God-like can occur only when we have a genuine experience of being loved beyond measure, regardless of how wretched and perverse we might have been and/or perceive ourselves to be. God never gives up on us, no matter how many times we might have given up on ourselves. And so it is always worth our while to pick up the broken pieces of our lives and return to God, who is always watchful and solicitous for our arrival home.

Like the older son, many of us continue to be baffled by God's attitude and treatment of us as exemplified in the father of the parable. God's way of understanding reality just doesn't make sense. It takes simple, childlike faith to accept God's word, to believe that we are different from the way we perceive ourselves because God created us in His own divine image and likeness, and therefore views us differently. We are precious in God's eyes because from all eternity we have been made in God's image and likeness, and no one can change that essential reality of our beings. It is not possible to become a true disciple if one has not experienced deeply God's all-encompassing love, where God is unwavering and faithful in good times and bad, in good conduct and bad, in holiness and sinfulness, in gloomy darkness and bright sunshine.

The right start is to understand clearly that the most important facet of discipleship is being loved by God, rather than our love of God. The two will go together, hand in hand, because the disciple in being overwhelmed by God's love will have no option except to love wholeheartedly in return. Unfortunately, many a discipleship has foundered because the disciple worked tirelessly and fruitlessly on loving God without first having had a profound encounter with the Father's love and forgiveness through His Son, Jesus. The emphasis on loving rather than being loved by God, or to put it more bluntly, the assumption that one can be the architect of one's own salvation in which God plays a secondary role, was condemned as a heresy by the Church. The particular circumstances had to do with Pelagius (circa 354-420 AD), an English monk of the Fifth Century, who held that Jesus might be useful in our quest for salvation but was not necessary; that, in fact, we can save ourselves. Pelagius was condemned as a heretic because of his teaching that Jesus no longer had any relevance. In essence, a true disciple is someone who sits at the feet of the Master, constantly amazed and overwhelmed by the extraordinary love and acceptance of God for them. True holiness begins and ends in the heart of God. In God the disciple enters into covenant relationship. In this relationship the disciple's mind and heart are transformed, and a life focused on loving and serving God and others becomes a passionate lifestyle. True religion is a matter of the heart. Understandably, one of Christianity's central tenets is that we cannot save ourselves. Salvation is God's business; allowing ourselves to be saved and transformed by falling into God's arms is ours.

The distinguishing mark of Christian discipleship is that the seeker is called by Jesus Christ to be a disciple or follower. If discipleship is about being called by the Master, then its power and mystery originate in the caller and not the one being called. God often seems to call a person who in the eyes of the world is a misfit for the job. Paul's words, *"When I am weak, then I am strong"* (2 Corinthians 12:10), echo this paradox. The power of God comes forth in the weakness of the disciple because they depend more completely on God's power. There is a clear sense on the seeker's part that Jesus is invested in the disciple's life. The seeker is awed by this commitment and passion, and in turn, give themselves to the Master in humble and ardent following. If there was one lesson the disciples learned from the events of Jesus' passion and death, it was that they were powerless. Only a total trust and dependence on their Master and His mission could redeem their discipleship and make it authentic. They realized this truth through the Outpouring of the Holy Spirit in the resurrection and ascension of their Lord and Master, Jesus.

SITTING AT THE FEET OF THE MASTER:

Where there is love, joy and peace are present. This is a fact of our lived experience. In the presence of love we feel nourished and ennobled, and there arises in our hearts a desire to reciprocate the love we have received by doing something special for the giver. When a disciple has spent hours at the feet of the Lord tasting and relishing the loving kindness of the Master, gradually there arises in the heart a desire that grows ever stronger and deeper to respond in kind. When disciples are consumed by the gift of God's love to them, they feel called to give themselves entirely to God's service in whatever way God might call them.

Mary experienced this constant urge to ponder and relish the workings and presence of God in her life. She was filled with gratitude and praise, and when her horizons were darkened by uncertainty and doubt, she trusted completely in the tender and constant faithfulness of God: *"My soul proclaims the greatness of the Lord; my spirit rejoices in God my savior. For he has looked upon his handmaid's lowliness; behold, from now on will all ages call me blessed. The Mighty One has done great things for me, and holy is his name. His mercy is from age to age to those who fear him."* (Luke 1:46-50) Indeed, Mary was always "the handmaid of the Lord," and her sitting at the feet of her Lord enhanced and strengthened her total dedication to God.

Mary Magdalene was a person who related to the Lord with the same passion that a beloved has for her lover. After her conversion, Jesus was the light of her life. Wherever she went, she was consumed by the thought of Him. She followed Him wherever He went and was the first one to meet the Risen Lord. Early on in her discipleship she understood the importance and even necessity of sitting at the feet of the Master.

Another Mary, Martha's sister, had the same spirit and devotion towards Jesus that Mary Magdalene had. Jesus complimented her about sitting at His feet and taking in His words of life: *"As they continued their journey he entered a village where a woman whose name was Martha welcomed him. She had a sister named Mary [who] sat beside the Lord at his feet listening to him speak. Martha, burdened with much serving, came to him and said, "Lord, do you not care that my sister has left me by myself to do the serving? Tell her to help me." The Lord said to her in reply, "Martha, Martha, you are anxious and worried about many things. There is need of only one thing. Mary has chosen the better part and it will not be taken from her"* (Luke 10:38-42).

The secret to changing a sinner's heart is love. A sinner becomes capable of living and acting like a saint when his or her heart has been moved powerfully by God's love and compassion. The history of the Church is replete with examples of great sinners becoming great saints after God touched their hearts. Hence, sitting daily at the feet of the Master and receiving His words of Life is of paramount importance.

PRAYER IS CONTINUAL IMMERSION INTO THE LORD'S PRESENCE:

There is one prevailing truth that pilots the disciple's life: the conviction that Jesus is the source of salvation and meaningful transformation. He alone is the foundation on which the Christian disciple's personal commitment and faith are fashioned. Such confidence in the power of Jesus and the workings of the Holy Spirit in the disciple's life and consciousness can only develop through the assiduous practice of prayer. Through prayer, the mind and heart of Jesus are formed in the disciple. Without prayer the disciple is like parched land thirsting for water. Scripture suggests that without fervent prayer, disciples are like sheep without a shepherd, living in spiritual confusion and exhaustion. In prayer the follower comes face to face with the tender mercies, as well as the holiness of God. In such a presence the sincere seeker has no alternative except to become transparent and authentic. At home in the presence of God's love and compassion, the transformed disciple is refocused, and fears and anxieties are seen in their true perspective.

In the creative hands of the Holy Spirit, the disciple is brought to a renewed appreciation of prayer as an experience of recognizing God's presence. This holy presence becomes both nurturing and necessary for the seeker's existence. The disciple begins to appreciate God's intimate yearnings for the salvation of the world and begins to sense that he or she has a special place in God's heart. A reading of Ephesians 1:7-10 provides an inkling of God's dynamic love for us: *"In him we have redemption by his blood, the forgiveness of transgressions, in accord with the riches of his grace that he lavished upon us. In all wisdom and insight, he has made known to us the mystery of his will in accord with his favor that he set forth in him as a plan for the fullness of times, to sum all things in Christ, in heaven and on earth."*

It is incomprehensible to the human mind that God would desire holiness and blamelessness for each of us. Essentially these are qualities of the divine. Yet, through this grace given to us by the Holy Spirit, the disciple gradually learns to put on the mind and heart of Jesus. Slowly, realization of the transformation that is taking place gains momentum. There is progressive movement toward becoming holy, blameless, and full of love.

In prayer, as Jesus promised, the Holy Spirit reveals and puts meaning into the teachings that are recorded in Scripture. Blessed with such revelation, the disciple experiences a peace and integrity that is not of this world. As the transformation progresses, the disciple journeys further into God's mystery and is privileged with wisdom and special insight about God.

Standing face to face with God's mystery, falsehood and hypocrisy begin to be exposed. Close proximity to the divine Presence can sometimes create a deep sense of sinfulness and unworthiness, similar to what Moses and Isaiah experienced. This same experience of humility carries through in the writings of our Christian mystics such as St. Teresa of Avila and St. John of the Cross. In this context, prayer becomes a place where one gets to know oneself as God knows us.

God's power is clearly visible in the life and works of the disciple when they stay true to the teachings and spirit of Jesus. Their discipleship brings about the establishment of God's reign in human hearts when they are single-minded in their focus on God's mission for them, and conform their own desires to God's will for them. A disciple is a seeker who tries to be in constant touch with God during all of his or her waking hours. Only then does being created in God's image and likeness become a living reality and not just wishful thinking. Discipleship becomes walking in the footsteps of the Master. The disciple's feet will never quite fill out the imprints of the Master's steps, but in walking and being with the Master, a slow and profound transformation takes place. The Master's voice is heard and His presence felt in and through the disciple. Much of ministry becomes the communication of the good news that the disciple has received and personalized.

Discipleship, or the continual process of looking into the eyes of God, is God's gift to us. It becomes a gift difficult to receive when we have convinced ourselves that conversion of heart is our doing and we are not up to it. However, when we understand that it is God who brings about the change in us and our job is to ask for this gift with childlike faith, we will receive it. Doubt and confusion, great and small, are always present in faith. The believer knows there will be light at the end of the tunnel even though there is darkness and sagging hope all around. In times of crisis the questioning mind seems stronger than the trusting will. Thomas trusted until he was thrown into chaos and despair. His world shattered with his Master's crucifixion. It took his Master's resurrection to restore him to a renewed commitment of faith and trust in Jesus. Discipleship is God's gift to us. It can only be fully appreciated when we place our trust in God's continual help along the way. Our faith might bend; hopefully it will not break. When true discipleship becomes a reality, wanting to fulfill all of the beatitudes becomes a way of life.

CONTINUAL FORMATION IN DISCIPLESHIP WITH MUCH FRUIT:

True discipleship can only come with patience and perseverance, forgiveness of self and others, and efforts to abide in God's will, with God's help. As the disciple sits at the feet of the Master, prayer becomes a school of formation. Under the guidance of the Holy Spirit, the disciple's faith is cleansed of inner doubts and fears. The Holy Spirit begins to exhibit influence in the disciple's consciousness, and other spirits are not allowed to dominate and encumber the disciple's thoughts and actions.

Prayer becomes a haven and refuge from the burdens of the day and the yoke of life. Every now and then, when we experience the rough edges of our lives, desperation and hopelessness may invade our space and being. For many, the outcome of such travail is despair. Living then becomes painful and unworkable. Yet the disciple is taught an alternative in the words of Jesus, *"Come to me, all you who are weary and find life burdensome, and I will refresh you."* (Matthew 11:28)

The disciple learns to distinguish between the burdens that Jesus wants us to carry and the burdens that are creations of our own egoism and pride. In doing God's will we might well be expected to carry a burden on our shoulders, but Jesus promises us that He will help us carry that load. He tells us His burden gives rest to our souls because His yoke is easy and His burden light.

Prayer is the place where many of the faithful have moved mountains. We recall the stories of Hannah and her son Samuel, and of Abraham and Sarah and the birth of Isaac. In the New Testament, we have the remarkable account of Zechariah and Elizabeth, parents of John the Baptist. These biblical texts are stunning and moving examples of lives being changed and destinies transformed through the prayer of faithful followers. Elizabeth expresses the walk of faith profoundly, *"In these days the Lord is acting on my behalf; he has seen fit to remove my reproach among men."* (Luke 1:25) The disciple knows that God will indeed deliver as promised.

Through prayer, a hunger and yearning for God develops that a once-a-day visitation with the Master cannot satisfy. A need germinates to make Jesus a constant companion wherever the disciple goes. The Trinity is present with the disciple through life's daily tasks and hurdles. There is the distinct sense that the disciple is no longer alone in whatever transpires. At some point in this process, the disciple links up with some of the age-old traditions that have grown out of a similar process in the lives of countless holy men and women. The practice of the presence of God through the constant recitation of a prayer formula might become the disciple's way of keeping God in the heart and consciousness. Gradually there is a profound sense of the indwelling presence of God and the words of the formula are recited in the heart as an automatic response. Along with the formula, the disciple may well have the need to express sentiments of gratitude and intercession continually during the course of the day. And some will report that they are constantly conversing with God in their hearts, both talking and listening. Prayer has become an intimate reality in the disciple's life, as necessary to discipleship as breathing is to life. As transformation at the hands of the Holy Spirit progresses, with generous cooperation from the disciple, the disciple can truly say what they experience: *"I live now, not I, but Christ lives in me."*

PRAYER AND REFLECTION ON LIVING AS DISCIPLE IN GOD'S COVENANT FAMILY

WEEK TWENTY SEVEN: *"THE WAY WE CAME TO KNOW LOVE WAS THAT HE LAID DOWN HIS LIFE FOR US; SO WE OUGHT TO LAY DOWN OUR LIVES FOR OUR BROTHERS." (1 JOHN 3:16)*

SPIRITUAL READING FOR THE WEEK:

- **Anoint Us in Your Covenant, Abba-Emmanuel:** Session Fourteen
- **Old Testament:** Two or Three Chapters daily
- **New Testament:** Two or Three Chapters daily
- **Imitation of Christ:** One chapter daily

DAY ONE: MORNING SESSION

MORNING PRAYER: Acts of Faith, Hope, Charity; Daily Offering

Morning Face to Face with God:

Begin with Prayer to the Holy Spirit

REFLECTIONS ON LIVING AS DISCIPLE IN GOD'S COVENANT FAMILY:

(After pondering each bullet point, express your sentiments in a short prayer)

- Through Jesus Christ, God adopted us and made us integral members of the divine family, perfectly bridging the gap between Him and us, created by rebellion and sin. Even more startling is the fact that God is a blatant optimist when it comes to creating dreams in our regard.
- Given the unfaithful history of God's people, it seems rather astonishing, that our God continually hopes and dreams that we will come to live in Christ's image. Yet such is the power of God's salvation through Jesus.
- This is the transformation that takes place in any individual who accepts Jesus as Savior and Lord, and humbles his entire being in submission to Him as the Son of the Living God. God's dream for us is holiness, blamelessness, and genuine son-ship in Jesus.
- God's plan of salvation in and through Jesus, challenges conscious thought and ignites the imagination. God chose to unite us with the Triune God through Jesus becoming

human. Jesus identified with us in all things while defeating sin, and through Him we have been guaranteed access into God's life and heart.

- We have been made God's very own sons and daughters, and it is our privilege and birthright to share in God's dream to live holy and blameless lives, full of love, as God is full of love. God's plan for us, envisaged from all eternity, and given the breath of life in our creation at the beginning of time, has now been brought to fulfillment and completion in Jesus Christ.

- Probably there is no more eloquent description than Paul's of how God calls us into covenant life with Him, and desires that we share in the fullness of His divine nature. In his letter to the Galatians, Paul underscores his conversion and calling from the Lord: *"Now I want you to know, brothers, that the gospel preached by me is not of human origin. For I did not receive it from a human being, nor was I taught it, but it came through a revelation of Jesus Christ."* (Galatians 1:11-12)

- Paul experienced this transformation through intimate participation in the Life and Love of our Triune God. And when we examine the lives and writings of the followers of Jesus in the New Testament we realize that they did their ministry because they were sent by their Lord and Savior, Jesus Christ. They were sent on mission after being transformed by the Holy Spirit.

- They did everything in the power of the Holy Spirit, and subsequent disciples were like Paul, baptized in water and the Holy Spirit, and thus brought into the Life and Love of Father, Son, and Holy Spirit.

- It behooves us as disciples of Jesus, to ponder deeply our call to be incorporated into Trinitarian Life through the tender compassion and mercy of our heavenly Father who sent His Son, Jesus Christ into the world so that we might not perish but might have eternal life.

What is God saying to you?

End with Prayer to the Holy Trinity

NIGHT SESSION: Examination of Conscience

For what are you grateful? For what are you contrite?

Please review briefly your Morning Prayer topic. Make it your last thought of the day

DAY TWO: MORNING SESSION

MORNING PRAYER: Acts of Faith, Hope, Charity; Daily Offering

Morning Face to Face with God:

Begin with Prayer to the Holy Spirit

Prayer on John 7:45-52: Nicodemus speaks up for Jesus

"So the guards went to the chief priests and Pharisees, who asked them, "Why did you not bring him?" The guards answered, "Never before has anyone spoken like this one." So the Pharisees answered them, "Have you also been deceived? Have any of the authorities or the Pharisees believed in him? But this crowd, which does not know the law, is accursed." Nicodemus, one of their members who had come to him earlier, said to them, "Does our law condemn a person before it first hears him and finds out what he is doing?" They answered and said to him, "You are not from Galilee also, are you? Look and see that no prophet arises from Galilee." [Please read John 7:32-52 for a better appreciation of the passage].

Read the Reflection; Ask for the grace to be wholehearted in your discipleship, constantly giving yourself in loving and generous service to God's covenant family

This passage is a clear indication that the visit with Jesus has had a powerful impact on Nicodemus. Jesus had gone up to Jerusalem when the Feast of Booths was half over. He began to teach in the temple area. Before long Jesus has entered into controversy regarding His origins. While being impressed by Jesus, His bystanders are unwilling to take Him seriously. The controversy heats up and before long the Sanhedrin is involved. They send temple guards to arrest Jesus. An interesting turn of events occurs: *"So the guards went to the chief priests and Pharisees, who asked them, "Why did you not bring him?" The guards answered, "Never before has anyone spoken like this one."* The Sanhedrin went apoplectic in their condemnation of the guards, and of the people choosing Jesus over them, and describing them as 'lost anyway.' It is then that Nicodemus came to Jesus' defense. True to form, they denounce his opinion and are derogatory towards him: *'You are not from Galilee also are you?'"*

What is God saying to you?

"Lost to the world"

End with Prayer to the Holy Trinity

NIGHT SESSION: Examination of Conscience

For what are you grateful? For what are you contrite?

Please review briefly your Morning Prayer topic. Make it your last thought of the day

DAY THREE: MORNING SESSION

MORNING PRAYER: Acts of Faith, Hope, Charity; Daily Offering

Morning Face to Face with God:

Begin with Prayer to the Holy Spirit

Prayer on John 19:38-42: The Burial of Jesus

"After this, Joseph of Arimathea, secretly a disciple of Jesus for fear of the Jews, asked Pilate if he could remove the body of Jesus. And Pilate permitted it. So he came and took his body. Nicodemus, the one who had first come to him at night, also came bringing a mixture of myrrh and aloes weighing about one hundred pounds. They took the body of Jesus and bound it with burial cloths along with the spices, according to the Jewish burial custom. Now in the place where he had been crucified there was a garden, and in the garden a new tomb, in which no one had yet been buried. So they laid Jesus there because of the Jewish preparation day; for the tomb was close by."

Read the Reflection; Ask for the grace to be wholehearted in your discipleship, constantly giving yourself in loving and generous service to God's covenant family

After Jesus' death, Nicodemus and Joseph of Arimathea came out in public and declared their commitment and loyalty to Jesus. They were now willing to help in the burial rituals required for Jesus. They knew full well that in doing so they would incur the wrath of the Sanhedrin, as they were defying the ban to not offer burial rites to criminals. For them, Jesus was the lamb of sacrifice, not a criminal. They were no longer afraid, and as far as their discipleship was concerned, they no longer needed to be denizens of the dark or closet disciples. They were now disciples of Jesus in the light of day. At this time of peril, Nicodemus and Joseph came forward in fearless avowal of their faith in the crucified Savior. Were it not for their generosity, Jesus would have been buried as a criminal, with no burial rites. When Jesus had been lifted up on the cross, Nicodemus remembered the words that He had spoken to him in the night interview: *"Just as Moses lifted up the serpent in the desert, so much the Son of Man be lifted up, that all who believe may have eternal like in him."* (John 3:14-15) Nicodemus and Joseph of Arimathea came to believe!

What is God saying to you?

End with Prayer to the Holy Trinity

NIGHT SESSION: Examination of Conscience

For what are you grateful? For what are you contrite?

Please review briefly your Morning Prayer topic. Make it your last thought of the day

DAY FOUR: MORNING SESSION

MORNING PRAYER: Acts of Faith, Hope, Charity; Daily Offering

Morning Face to Face with God:

Begin with Prayer to the Holy Spirit

Prayer on John 9:35-38: The Cure of the Blind Man:

> *"When Jesus heard that they had thrown him out, he found him and said, "Do you believe in the Son of Man?" He answered and said, "Who is he, sir that I may believe in him?" Jesus said to him, "You have seen him and the one speaking with you is he." He said, "I do believe, Lord," and he worshiped him."*

Read the Reflection; Ask for the grace to be wholehearted in your discipleship, constantly giving yourself in loving and generous service to God's covenant family.

1. *"Do you believe in the Son of Man:?"* All of John 9 is taken up with the cure and testimony of the man born blind from birth. Because of his passionate testimony of Jesus before the Sanhedrin, he was excommunicated from the temple and synagogue. Jesus meets the healed man and asks whether he accepts Jesus as the Son of Man. Son of Man was a title in Daniel 7:13-14, that Jesus applied to Himself as the Messiah.

2. *"I do believe, Lord, and he worshiped him:* The title 'Lord' was applied to Jesus after His resurrection when the disciples knew beyond any doubt that Jesus was God. In the New Testament writings they address Jesus as Lord because in light of their resurrection experience they saw that Jesus was God all along during His earthly ministry. The man, healed of his blindness, came to recognize Jesus as Savior and Lord, and his spontaneous gesture is to worship Jesus.

What is God saying to you?

End with Prayer to the Holy Trinity

Do you have spiritual blindness.

NIGHT SESSION: Examination of Conscience

For what are you grateful? For what are you contrite?

Please review briefly your Morning Prayer topic. Make it your last thought of the day

DAY FIVE: MORNING SESSION

MORNING PRAYER: Acts of Faith, Hope, Charity; Daily Offering

Morning Face to Face with God:

Begin with Prayer to the Holy Spirit

Prayer on Luke 19:9-10: Zacchaeus, the Tax Collector:
> *"And Jesus said to him, "Today salvation has come to this house because this man too is a descendant of Abraham. For the Son of Man has come to seek and to save what was lost."*

Read the Reflection; Ask for the grace to be wholehearted in your discipleship, constantly giving yourself in loving and generous service to God's covenant family.

1. *Salvation has come to this house because this man too is a descendant of Abraham:* Zacchaeus was a chief tax collector. According to Rabbinic wisdom, he could never be saved, as his sins were beyond the pale of forgiveness. Consequently, as a Jew, he was condemned to be a lost sheep of Israel. Jesus brings salvation to Zacchaeus, and restores his spiritual lineage with Abraham. He is able to receive salvation from Jesus because he believes and wants to be his disciple. In response, Zacchaeus is willing to tithe 50% of his possessions, and return fourfold to anyone whom he might have cheated inadvertently.

2. *The Son of Man has come to seek out and to save what was lost:* God's compassion for us, revealed in Jesus, is boundless and non-discriminatory. Jesus is there, especially for those who feel lost and abandoned, as He is the Incarnate Presence of God's mercy and love for us.

What is God saying to you?

End with Prayer to the Holy Trinity

NIGHT SESSION: Examination of Conscience

For what are you grateful? For what are you contrite?

Please review briefly your Morning Prayer topic. Make it your last thought of the day

Office in Jerico
Crossing of many highways
excellent locations

Sycamore Tree

DAY SIX: MORNING SESSION

MORNING PRAYER: Acts of Faith, Hope, Charity; Daily Offering

Morning Face to Face with God:

Begin with Prayer to the Holy Spirit

REPETITION OF DAYS TWO THROUGH FIVE:

Read the Reflection; Ask for the grace to be wholehearted in your discipleship, constantly giving yourself in loving and generous service to God's covenant family.

Today, you are doing a repetition of Days Two through Five of this week. In a repetition St. Ignatius says that *"we should pay attention to and dwell upon those points in which we have experienced greater consolation or desolation or greater spiritual appreciation."* (# 62) If you wish, you can do a triple colloquy: refer to #63 of the Spiritual Exercises.

What is God saying to you?

End with Prayer to the Holy Trinity

NIGHT SESSION: Examination of Conscience

For what are you grateful? For what are you contrite?

Please review briefly your Morning Prayer topic. Make it your last thought of the day

DAY SEVEN: MORNING SESSION

MORNING PRAYER: Acts of Faith, Hope, Charity; Daily Offering

Morning Face to Face with God:

Begin with Prayer to the Holy Spirit

ILLUMINATION THROUGH THE DARK NIGHT:
(After pondering each bullet point, express your sentiments in a short prayer)

- St. John of the Cross tells us what the real purpose of the spiritual night is: *"Even though this happy night darkens the spirit, it does so only to impart light concerning all things; and even though it humbles individuals and reveals their miseries, it does so only to exalt them; and even though it impoverishes and empties them of all possessions and natural affection, it does so only that they may reach out divinely to the enjoyment of all earthly and heavenly things, with a general freedom of spirit in them all."* (TDN – Book Two: Chapter 9:1)

- St. John of the Cross uses the image of a 'ladder' to describe the graces that God grants a soul, through the dark night of the spirit. With a ladder there is a descent and an ascent; the soul is both humbled and exalted. He describes ten different steps or graces by which the soul ascends to God.

- The first step is that the soul can't find satisfaction or support, or any kind of consolation or resting place in anything. This utter dissatisfaction in earthly things points it heavenward toward God.

- The second step creates an incessant search for God that never stops. In everything it thinks, says, and does, it is seeking for its Beloved. In all things it centers its loving attention on God.

- In the third step of the ladder, the disciple is very eager to do as much as possible for God. Their fervor is such that they will not get dissipated. However, along with this ardor for God's glory, there is an accompanying sorrow and pain that so little is being done for God. As Saint John of the Cross would say, *"On this third step the soul is far removed from vainglory, presumption, and the practice of condemning others."* (TDN – Book Two: Chapter 19:3)

- In the fourth step, there is a habitual and constant suffering because of its intense desire for God. *"The soul in no way seeks consolation or satisfaction either in God or in anything else; neither does it desire or ask favors of God, for it is clearly aware that it has already received many from him. All its care is directed toward how it might give some pleasure to God and render him some service because of what he deserves and the favors he has bestowed, even though the cost might be high."* (TDN – Book Two: Chapter 19:4)

- In the fifth step there is an impatient desire and longing for God that can never be quenched. This delay is burdensome and frustrating.

- *"The sixth step makes the soul run swiftly toward God and experience touches in him. And it runs without fainting by reason of its hope. The love that has invigorated it makes it fly swiftly... The soul's charity is now highly increased and almost completely purified."* (TDN – Book Two: Chapter 20:1)

- *"The seventh step of the ladder gives it an ardent boldness. At this stage love neither profits by the judgment to wait nor makes use of the counsel to retreat, neither can it be curbed through shame. For the favor God now gives it imparts an ardent daring."* (TDN – Book Two: Chapter 20:2)

- *"The eighth step of love impels the soul to lay hold of the Beloved without letting him go. Although the soul satisfied its desire on this step of union, it does not do so continually. Some manage to get to it, but soon turn back and leave it. If one were to remain on this step, a certain glory would be possessed in this life, and so the soul rests on it for only short periods of time."* (TDN – Book Two: 20:3)

- *"The ninth step of love causes the soul to burn gently. It is the step of the perfect who burn gently in God. The Holy Spirit produces this gentle and delightful ardor by reason of the perfect soul's union with God."* (TDN – Book Two: Chapter 20:4)
- *"The tenth and last step of this secret ladder of love assimilates the soul to God completely because of the clear vision of God that a person possesses at once on reaching it. After arriving at the ninth step in this life, the soul departs from the body. Since these souls – few that there be – are already extremely purged through love, they do not enter purgatory."* (TDN – Book Two: Chapter 20:5)

What is God saying to you?

End with Prayer to the Holy Trinity

NIGHT SESSION: Examination of Conscience

For what are you grateful? For what are you contrite?

What prayer would you compose to express what God has said to you this week?

Please review briefly your Morning Prayer topic. Make it your last thought of the day

PRAYER AND REFLECTION ON LIVING AS DISCIPLE IN GOD'S COVENANT FAMILY – CONTINUED

WEEK TWENTY EIGHT: *"But the hour is coming, and is now here, when true worshipers will worship the Father in spirit and truth; and indeed the Father seeks such people to worship him. God is spirit, and those who worship him must worship in spirit and truth." – John 4:23-24*

SPIRITUAL READING FOR THE WEEK:

- **Anoint Us in Your Covenant, Abba-Emmanuel:** Session Fourteen
- **Old Testament:** Two or Three Chapters daily
- **New Testament:** Two or Three Chapters daily
- **Imitation of Christ:** One chapter daily

DAY ONE: MORNING SESSION

MORNING PRAYER: Acts of Faith, Hope, Charity; Daily Offering

Morning Face to Face with God:

Begin with Prayer to the Holy Spirit

REFLECTIONS ON LIVING AS DISCIPLE IN GOD'S COVENANT FAMILY:

(After pondering each bullet point, express your sentiments in a short prayer)

- God's love for us is so tender and wholehearted in that Father, Son, and Holy Spirit have given their Life and Love to us in covenant. The Trinity has thereby made it clear through their involvement in our lives that God will hold back nothing of Himself from us.
- Given this amazing truth, any authentic approach to discipleship would have to be grounded in God's infinite love and mercy toward us. Paul was tireless in proclaiming this plan of God's salvation to the early Christians because he was convinced that the heritage of being God's sons and daughters was indeed the bedrock of our meaning and joy in life.
- While every disciple sincerely longs for this loving intimacy with God, many are hesitant to take this step. The committed disciple who calls on God as Abba with trust and conviction soon realizes that being God's child is at the core of their reality. And such a truth sets us free.
- God never gives up on us, no matter how many times we might have given up on ourselves. And so it is always worth our while to pick up the broken pieces of our lives and return to God, who is always watchful and solicitous for our arrival home.
- It is not possible to become a true disciple if one has not experienced deeply God's all-encompassing love, where God is unwavering and faithful in good times and bad, in good conduct and bad, in holiness and sinfulness, in gloomy darkness and bright sunshine.
- The distinguishing mark of Christian discipleship is that the seeker is called by Jesus Christ to be a disciple or follower. If discipleship is about being called by the Master, then its power and mystery originate in the caller and not the one being called.
- There is one prevailing truth that pilots the disciple's life: the conviction that Jesus is the source of salvation and meaningful transformation. He alone is the foundation on which the Christian disciple's personal commitment and faith are fashioned. Such confidence in the power of Jesus and the workings of the Holy Spirit in the disciple's life and consciousness can only develop through the assiduous practice of prayer.

- Through prayer, the mind and heart of Jesus are formed in the disciple. Without prayer the disciple is like parched land thirsting for water. Scripture suggests that without fervent prayer, disciples are like sheep without a shepherd, living in spiritual confusion and exhaustion.

- In prayer the follower comes face to face with the tender mercies, as well as the holiness of God. In such a presence the sincere seeker has no alternative except to become transparent and authentic. At home in the presence of God's love and compassion, the transformed disciple is refocused, and fears and anxieties are seen in their true perspective.

- In the creative hands of the Holy Spirit, the disciple is brought to a renewed appreciation of prayer as an experience of recognizing God's presence. This holy presence becomes both nurturing and necessary for the seeker's existence. The disciple begins to appreciate God's intimate yearnings for the salvation of the world and begins to sense that he or she has a special place in God's heart.

- In prayer, as Jesus promised, the Holy Spirit reveals and puts meaning into the teachings that are recorded in Scripture. Blessed with such revelation, the disciple experiences a peace and integrity that is not of this world. As the transformation progresses, the disciple journeys further into God's mystery and is privileged with wisdom and special insight about God.

What is God saying to you?

End with Prayer to the Holy Trinity

NIGHT SESSION: Examination of Conscience

For what are you grateful? For what are you contrite?

Please review briefly your Morning Prayer topic. Make it your last thought of the day

DAY TWO: MORNING SESSION

MORNING PRAYER: Acts of Faith, Hope, Charity; Daily Offering

Morning Face to Face with God:

Begin with Prayer to the Holy Spirit

Prayer on John 4:17-19; 21-26: From Openness to Belief

"Jesus answered her, "You are right in saying, 'I do not have a husband.' For you have had five husbands, and the one you have now is not your husband. What you have said is true." The woman said to him, "Sir, I can see that you are a prophet…" "Jesus said to her, "…But the hour is coming,

and is now here, when true worshipers will worship the Father in Spirit and truth; and indeed the Father seeks such people to worship him. God is Spirit, and those who worship him must worship in Spirit and truth." The woman said to him, "I know that the Messiah is coming, the one called the Anointed; when he comes, he will tell us everything." Jesus said to her, "I am he, the one who is speaking with you."

Read the Reflection; Ask for the grace to be wholehearted in your discipleship, constantly giving yourself in loving and generous service to God's covenant family.

1. *For you have had five husbands, and the one you have now is not your husband:* In response to Jesus' request to bring her husband, the woman spoke truthfully that she did not have a husband. However, she did not reveal the whole truth that she had had five husbands. Jesus does that for her. He is not flattering in revealing this truth of her life. However, the woman's heart has been stirred, and says, "I can see that you are a prophet."

2. *I know that the Messiah is coming, the one called the Anointed, when he comes, he will tell us everything:* The Samaritans believed that they would recognize the Messiah because he would tell them everything. Jesus will reveal everything to her because he has told her shameful details of her life as a total stranger. She is ready to accept Jesus as her Savior.

3. *Jesus said to her, "I am he, the one who is speaking with you:"* Jesus then reveals to her that indeed He is the Lord and Messiah for whom she has been waiting.

What is God saying to you?

End with Prayer to the Holy Trinity

NIGHT SESSION: Examination of Conscience

For what are you grateful? For what are you contrite?

Please review briefly your Morning Prayer topic. Make it your last thought of the day

DAY THREE: MORNING SESSION

MORNING PRAYER: Acts of Faith, Hope, Charity; Daily Offering

Morning Face to Face with God:

Begin with Prayer to the Holy Spirit

Prayer on John 4:41-42: The Belief of the Samaritans

> *"Many more began to believe in him (Jesus) because of his word, and they said to the woman, 'We no longer believe because of your word; for we have heard for ourselves, and we know that this is truly the savior of the world.'"*

Read the Reflection; Ask for the grace to be wholehearted in your discipleship, constantly giving yourself in loving and generous service to God's covenant family.

This passage gives us insight into how the Holy Spirit operates. The Samaritan villagers first came to Jesus because they heard and accepted the witness of their fellow villager, the Samaritan woman. Under ordinary circumstances they should have rejected her testimony. After all she was a woman whose testimony could not be accepted, and a shameful and sinful person at that! However, the Holy Spirit was moving powerfully in her. Her countenance was radiating the joy and peace at having found the Messiah. What she had to tell them was irresistible. So they followed her to go and meet Jesus. Once they met Jesus, they came under His divine spell! They were mesmerized by His word. They came to believe. They no longer needed the woman's testimony. She had fulfilled her mission of bringing them to Jesus. And Jesus did the rest. As disciples, Jesus sends us out to witness to the world that indeed He is the risen Lord and Savior of the world. Through our testimony our listeners will come to Jesus who then will bring them into a covenant relationship with Him through the Holy Spirit.

What is God saying to you?

End with Prayer to the Holy Trinity

NIGHT SESSION: Examination of Conscience

For what are you grateful? For what are you contrite?

Please review briefly your Morning Prayer topic. Make it your last thought of the day

DAY FOUR: MORNING SESSION

MORNING PRAYER: Acts of Faith, Hope, Charity; Daily Offering

Morning Face to Face with God:

Begin with Prayer to the Holy Spirit

Prayer on Luke 17:15-16; 19: The Cleansing of the Samaritan Leper:

> *"And one of them, realizing he had been healed, returned, glorifying God in a loud voice; and he fell at the feet of Jesus and thanked him. He was a Samaritan… Then he said to him, "Stand up*

and go; your faith has saved you." [Please read Luke 17:11-19 for a better appreciation of the passage].

Read the Reflection; Ask for the grace to be wholehearted in your discipleship, constantly giving yourself in loving and generous service to God's covenant family.

1. *Realizing he had been healed, returned, glorifying God in a loud voice; and he fell at the feet of Jesus and thanked him. He was a Samaritan:* It must have taken the Samaritan leper great courage and trust to come to Jesus, along with the nine other Jewish lepers. As a Samaritan, he was considered an outcast. Jesus was a Jew. Would Jesus turn him down? Owing to his degrading sickness, his misery was great indeed! But even greater was his faith and trust in Jesus. His healing produced in him the authentic results of repentance or conversion: He returned to glorify God, and falling at the feet of Jesus, thanked him!

2. *Then he (Jesus) said to him, "Stand up and go; your faith has saved you:* Jesus came to save us from our sin and offer us a share in God's divine life through Him. Having faith in Jesus, as the Samaritan did, is surrendering to Jesus as Savior and Lord. Jesus exercises His power within the context of faith, as He has come to bring us salvation from Satan, sin, and permanent death. His dismissal of the Samaritan is very moving: *"Stand up and go; your faith has saved you."*

What is God saying to you?

End with Prayer to the Holy Trinity

NIGHT SESSION: Examination of Conscience

For what are you grateful? For what are you contrite?

Please review briefly your Morning Prayer topic. Make it your last thought of the day

DAY FIVE: MORNING SESSION

MORNING PRAYER: Acts of Faith, Hope, Charity; Daily Offering

Morning Face to Face with God:

Begin with Prayer to the Holy Spirit

Prayer on Ephesians 4:31: Renewal in Christ:
"All bitterness, fury, anger, shouting, and reviling must be removed from you, along with all malice."

Read the Reflection; Ask for the grace to be wholehearted in your discipleship, constantly giving yourself in loving and generous service to God's covenant family.

Paul is talking about unity in the Body of Christ. He is urging the Ephesians to live in a manner that is worthy of their covenant union with God through Jesus. The body can't be different from the head. This unity is to be expressed in every facet of our lives and is made possible through the Holy Spirit. Everything that is the opposite of covenant union with God has got to be rejected. Bitterness, fury, anger, shouting, and reviling one another, along with malice, are the hallmarks of the evil one and enslavement to sin.

What is God saying to you?

End with Prayer to the Holy Trinity

NIGHT SESSION: Examination of Conscience

For what are you grateful? For what are you contrite?

Please review briefly your Morning Prayer topic. Make it your last thought of the day

DAY SIX: MORNING SESSION

MORNING PRAYER: Acts of Faith, Hope, Charity; Daily Offering

Morning Face to Face with God:

Begin with Prayer to the Holy Spirit

REPETITION OF DAYS TWO THROUGH FIVE:

Read the Reflection; Ask for the grace to be wholehearted in your discipleship, constantly giving yourself in loving and generous service to God's covenant family.

Today, you are doing a repetition of Days Two through Five of this week. In a repetition St. Ignatius says that *"we should pay attention to and dwell upon those points in which we have experienced greater consolation or desolation or greater spiritual appreciation."* (# 62) If you wish, you can do a triple colloquy: refer to #63 of the Spiritual Exercises.

What is God saying to you?

End with Prayer to the Holy Trinity

NIGHT SESSION: Examination of Conscience

For what are you grateful? For what are you contrite?

Please review briefly your Morning Prayer topic. Make it your last thought of the day

DAY SEVEN: MORNING SESSION

MORNING PRAYER: Acts of Faith, Hope, Charity; Daily Offering

Morning Face to Face with God:

Begin with Prayer to the Holy Spirit

THE SPIRITUALITY OF BLESSED MOTHER TERESA OF CALCUTTA

(After pondering each bullet point, express your sentiments in a short prayer)

- Blessed Teresa's strength as a disciple came from her constant union with God. She was always at God's beck and call, asking and receiving guidance from Him. She received all her strength from Him. And when we consider how her Missionaries of Charity have spread all over the world, the decisions that she had to make were many and difficult. However, she went about her daily tasks with a serenity and peace that could only come from Jesus.
- In brief, all she ever wanted to do was God's will. After her death, it was revealed that Blessed Teresa had spent many years in the dark night of the soul. In analyzing her deeds and achievements Pope St. John Paul II answered the question as to where she found the strength and perseverance to place herself completely at the service of others.
- His answer was that Blessed Teresa found it in prayer and the silent contemplation of Jesus Christ, His holy face, His Sacred Heart. However, from her letters we have gathered that she experienced severe doubts and struggles over her beliefs which she felt over nearly 50 years.
- During that time she had very little respite. Her postulator, Reverend Brian Kolodiejchuk, said that Blessed Teresa "felt no presence of God whatsoever, neither in her heart or in the Eucharist."
- Blessed Teresa herself expressed grave doubts about God's existence and pain over her lack of faith: "Where is my faith? Even deep down … there is nothing but emptiness and darkness… If there be God – please forgive me. When I try to raise my thoughts to Heaven, there is such convicting emptiness that those very thoughts return like sharp knives and hurt my very soul… How painful is this unknown pain – I have no faith. Repulsed, empty, no faith, no love, no zeal… What do I labor for? If there be no God, there can be no soul. If there be no soul then, Jesus, You also are not true."

- The supreme paradox is that while she went through this intense dark night of the soul for so many years, her faith that God was working through her calling and mission remained undiminished. The Missionaries of Charity continued to flourish and vocations to her community increased greatly all over the world.

- While she was deprived of any semblance of closeness to God or assurance that He loved her, she did not question His existence and remained ever faithful to her Eucharistic Adoration and life of continual prayer and service.

- Many of our Catholic saints have had similar experiences and describe them in their writings. St. Therese of Lisieux termed it a "night of nothingness," which she experienced during the last eighteen months of her life on earth. Blessed Teresa was called by God to love unconditionally, to love in nothingness, even if there were never any response from God.

- In his first encyclical *Deus caritas est,* Pope Benedict XVI mentioned Blessed Teresa three times to clarify one of his main points of the encyclical: "In the example of Blessed Teresa of Calcutta we have a clear illustration of the fact that time devoted to God in prayer not only does not detract from effective and loving service to our neighbor but is in fact the inexhaustible source of that service."

- There are definite similarities between Blessed Teresa and St. Francis of Assisi. Like St. Francis of Assisi, Blessed Teresa served and met Christ in her service of the poor. Her profound love and respect for the poor suggests that Jesus had given her His very own love and devotion for the poor in whose image and likeness they had been created.

- Like Jesus and St. Francis, Blessed Teresa deemed it an honor and privilege to serve the poor as their servant. They both embraced radical poverty; they both loved and served the poorest of the poor, especially lepers. They both submitted themselves to religious vows of poverty, chastity, and obedience. St. Francis was wedded to Lady Poverty and Blessed Teresa took a fourth vow to serve free the poorest of the poor.

- They were both outstanding in their submission to Jesus, no matter how challenging the circumstances were. Blessed Teresa was a great admirer of St. Francis. She stipulated that every morning, during thanksgiving after Communion, the Sisters of Charity would recite the Peace Prayer of St. Francis.

- In one sentence, this might be a synthesis of the spirituality of Mother Teresa. All she ever wanted to do in life was the will of God. But she knew there was no other way to know what God wanted, every moment of the day, except by asking Him for the grace to know His divine will and then to do it with all her heart.

What is God saying to you?

End with Prayer to the Holy Trinity

NIGHT SESSION: Examination of Conscience

For what are you grateful? For what are you contrite?

What prayer would you compose to express what God has said to you this week?

Please review briefly your Morning Prayer topic. Make it your last thought of the day

SESSION FIFTEEN
THE REVIEW OF OUR JOURNEY

"You yourselves can testify that I said [that] I am not the Messiah, but that I was sent before him. The one who has the bride is the bridegroom; the best man, who stands and listens to him, rejoices greatly at the bridegroom's voice. So this joy of mine has been made complete. He must increase; I must decrease."

– John 3:28–30

REVIEWING OUR SPIRITUAL JOURNEY: THE FIRST PHASE OF FORMATION:

We began the First Phase with Lead me into the Deep, Lord. The manual was designed to help you accept generously and wholeheartedly God's invitation to enter into covenant union with Him. On God's part, making this offer to you was both urgent and enthusiastic as Jesus made this invitation a reality through His death and resurrection: *"Behold, I stand at the door and knock. If anyone hears my voice and opens the door, [then] I will enter his house and dine with him, and he with me. I will give the victor the right to sit with me on my throne, as I myself first won the victory and sit with my Father on his throne."* (Revelation 3:20-21) Over 12 weeks you prayed with the Scriptures and various aspects of the spiritual life. In doing so you came to a deep appreciation of Jesus and the urgent necessity of surrendering your life to Him in return for the gift of His own life to you. Furthermore, under the guidance of the Holy Spirit, you began to develop your own internal authority about your life of covenant union with God, of which you were having a first-hand experience in prayer.

In time, the third assumption that we had made, became a reality. Your relationship with God had become significant and consequently, you began following the dictates of the Holy Spirit rather than the dictates of your own anxious mind. The Holy Spirit began to re-order your priorities, and teach you how best to deepen your discipleship with God through a greater investment of your time, and even your life. You began to appreciate with profound gratitude that God has given Himself to you completely, through His Son, Jesus, and the Holy Spirit was making it possible for you to surrender your entire life to God in joyful trust. You then realized the true meaning of covenant: *the mutual and total offering of oneself to the other:* of God to me, and me to God through the Holy Spirit.

With this personal formation at the hands of the Holy Spirit, you embarked on the next leg of the First Phase by making *Instruct Me in Your Ways, Lord* your daily manual of prayer. You became familiar with the Old Testament, without which our understanding of Jesus and the New Testament is jeopardized. The major focus throughout the First Phase was to get a proper understanding of who God really is from His revelation of Himself. An accompanying focus was to understand who we truly are in God's eyes, so that we will live our lives in the appropriate context of a covenant relationship with God.

FRUITS OF THE FIRST PHASE OF FORMATION:

At the end of Phase One, you had a clear sense that you were no longer mere beginners. You now had a familiarity with the process and dynamics of prayer, and had entered into a personal, meaningful, and transformative relationship with our Triune God. As a result, you were experiencing significant changes in your lives. Let us look at some of the fruits that you experienced at the end of the First Phase of Formation:

1. In your estimation, the First Phase has been a *significant experience* for you, and you wanted to continue into the Second Phase of the Program.

2. Whether you considered yourselves to be beginners, or were already committed disciples when you joined the Program, now you realized more clearly that humility is the foundation of the spiritual life, that all progress is a pure blessing and gift from God. You realized that you would make progress in the spiritual life only when *you relied on God in everything.*

3. Your day or weekend retreat experiences have given you a *security and confidence* about the dynamics of prayer, and you are learning to appreciate the *great benefits* of belonging to a community of believers.

4. You are *becoming familiar with Scripture*, and developing a hunger to delve more deeply into the Word of God who is both *Person and Revelation.* You are slowly beginning to realize that you can't separate the teachings from the Person of Jesus.

5. You have *become consistent* in setting aside time *daily* for a person-to-person, heart-to-heart, honest dialogue with God that often times became an encounter. An encounter took place when there was definite divine intervention in your lives!

6. You have *become more consistent* in your habit of daily spiritual reading, concentrating on reading the *whole Bible in one year,* and the Imitation of Christ at least once a year.

7. You were coming to a deeper appreciation of your Catholic Faith, and the mediation of God's Presence and Life through the sacraments. The celebration of Eucharist and the sacrament of Reconciliation were becoming meaningful and very enriching.

8. Consolation became your normal state of soul. If you moved out of consolation, you learned how to more effectively counter your desolation through the sacrament of reconciliation, spiritual practices, and the Practice of the Presence of God.

9. Besides your daily time for prayer and spiritual reading, you conversed with God more often during the day. This awareness of God's presence grew deeper and became an integral part of your life style.

10. You have now come to know Jesus in a personal way, experiencing intimacy with Him during the day, and becoming more familiar with the other Persons of the Trinity. You have been bringing the Father and the Holy Spirit more easily into your prayer.

11. Your commitment to God was significant enough that you began moving towards not committing deliberate sin. No sin is small and insignificant.

12. As disciple you began developing a delicate conscience and were immediately contrite and repentant whenever you sinned.

13. Gratitude and joy became consistent features of your discipleship.

14. You became familiar with the Rules for Recognizing the Voice and Presence of the Holy Spirit, and made the Discernment of Spirits a regular feature of your spiritual lives.

15. You slowly came to understand that the Church is God's covenant family. Any meaningful relationship with God will necessitate committed service to God's Church.

16. You sensed that an awakening took place in your heart because God entered into your life. The Holy Spirit created within you an intense longing and desire to become one with God. Such an awakening began to re-order your priorities in life.

THE SECOND PHASE OF FORMATION:

We began the Second Phase doing *The Spiritual Exercises of St. Ignatius* translated by Louis J. Puhl, S.J., using *Mold Me as Your Disciple, Lord* as the accompanying manual. You saw that *The Spiritual Exercises of St. Ignatius* were undoubtedly an excellent tool of formation in discipleship. And you were well prepared through the First Phase of formation in God's Embrace to undergo such a momentous journey over six months. Perhaps the best summary of your retreat experience would be *perfect freedom to serve God and His people selflessly.* St. Ignatius characterized this attitude of always being disposed to choose whatever God willed or permitted in one's daily circumstances as Indifference.

Hallow Me as Your Disciple, Lord was a follow-up to *The Spiritual Exercises of St. Ignatius.* At the end of the 24-week long Nineteenth Annotation retreat, you came to realize that *The Spiritual Exercises of St. Ignatius* are undoubtedly an excellent tool of formation in discipleship. You saw that at the end of the Spiritual Exercises, St. Ignatius invited you to ponder all that you have received from God. The list of blessings was exhaustive and overwhelming. In response, you made a total offering of self to God. The true nature of love, manifested in deeds, especially God's offering of His Son to us as Savior and Lord, prompted you to give God everything, especially liberty, memory, understanding and your entire will, all that you have and possess. Such a prayer is perfect abandonment and was made freely and wholeheartedly, *after* you experienced God's largesse overwhelmingly. Such an offering is the quintessential expression of a covenant relationship.

After the retreat, you realized that no other vision or agenda could hold up against such a world-view of discipleship. Your mind and heart had been washed clean of any resistance. When resistance arose in the future you addressed it in the same way as during the retreat: through incessant petitioning and childlike trust in God's ability to bring about transformation. At an even deeper level than in the First Phase, you now made sense of Christ's values and embraced them wholeheartedly. *Hallow Me as Your Disciple, Lord* built upon your profound retreat experience. It tapped into your intense desire to live out this covenant offering of self on a daily basis, generously and wholeheartedly.

FRUITS OF THE SECOND PHASE OF FORMATION:

Whatever helps and methods of prayer you needed and used in the preliminary stages of the relationship have now served their purpose. They have brought you as a burgeoning disciple into the Presence and Heart of God. You still use discursive methods of prayer as needed, but communication with God has moved into the realm of communion, leading to greater and deeper union. Fewer words are now being used in prayer, as the emphasis in the relationship with God is on communion. There is a greater emphasis on being receptive to God's Presence and voice. Listening to God is more important than being listened to. Hence, the emphasis in the relationship has shifted from God serving your interests and well-being, to God becoming the focus and center of your life. As an advancing disciple you now want to belong to God and to be faithful to Him, to do His will generously and joyfully, to make God the center of discipleship. You are now at God's beck and call.

Gradually, you have been finding out that God's way of revealing Himself is through infused knowledge. Prayer has shifted from communication with God through words, thoughts, and images into communion through fewer words, greater affect, and quiet. This transition into communion through loving attention in silence, can and will be disconcerting and sometimes baffling. At times you have wondered whether anything was happening as the faculties of mind, imagination, and memory don't seem to work as facilely as before. In fact they appear unruly; distraction and even boredom seem like the norm. However, the heart was being drawn through a lively longing for God as the Cloud of Unknowing would describe it. Every now and then you have received assurance that indeed God is taking you into a deeper place. The Holy Spirit provided faint brushes of consolation which led to a firmer commitment and surrender to God. Gradually, you learned to be lovingly attentive to God in adoration and worship, without worrying or being concerned whether prayer is satisfying or not. Trust and surrender to God have become the bedrock of your relationship with God. Meanwhile, a deeper connection and commitment was being established between God and you as disciple, and you moved toward wholehearted commitment.

At this stage then, you were moving towards or into contemplative prayer. Contemplative prayer is the process which the Holy Spirit uses to bring about a genuine and total surrender of the disciple to Jesus. Contemplative prayer is an opening of one's whole being to the loving Presence of the Divine, trusting in the work of the Holy Spirit to reveal to them all the things that Jesus had taught his disciples: *"But when he comes, the Spirit of truth, he will guide you to all truth. He will not speak on his own, but he will speak what he hears, and will declare to you the things that are coming. He will glorify me, because he will take from what is mine and declare it to you."* (John 16:13-14) Let us look at some of the fruits that the participants have experienced at the end of their Second Phase of formation:

1. Discipleship is more about greater and greater surrender to God, making Him alone the center of your lifestyle and discipleship.

2. When disciples have become humble, nothing can be taken away from them, because their heart is with God and where their heart is, there their treasure lies. No matter what, they have it all.

3. They keep paring their needs to a minimum, concerned about doing what is right rather than from preference.

4. Their hearts are filled to overflowing with gratitude. They don't need any more of God's gifts, even when some are taken away, because they have received God's abundance.

5. There is a definite eschewing of deliberate sin and an intense desire to help in the establishment of God's reign. The disciple operates on the *Principle of Agere Contra:* to go against anything in one's desires and will that is contrary to God's will, and to seek constantly only what God desires.

6. The disciple is acutely aware that whatever transformation is taking place is at the behest of the Holy Spirit. Their heart is therefore filled with constant gratitude to God.

7. The disciple is praying the whole day, offering gratitude and praise as they go through their day with God. God is constantly present, and remembering God's deeds of love and mercy is a devotion of love and gratitude. There is an eager desire to reciprocate God's love for them by their own generous deeds of loving and selfless service.

8. They are content to bloom where they have been planted, to live in the now, to let bygones be bygones because God has forgiven them and is managing their daily affairs. The future is of relevance only when it shows up in the present moment.

9. Sunday worship has become very meaningful. The disciple becomes very aware of the community dimension of the Eucharistic celebration. Eucharist and communion can only be meaningful when the celebration leads the disciple to lay down their lives for the community.

10. Covenant living continues to shape the disciple's identity. They see themselves as hyphenated identities: self-Jesus.

11. Prayer is an essential part of the disciple's lifestyle. The disciple lives and breathes God. Their formal times for prayer are very important. So are their informal conversations with God.

12. The disciple moves towards a more contemplative way of communicating and knowing God. Both in prayer and daily life, their knowledge and understanding of God that they have received from study and prayer, is now being supplemented by knowledge and wisdom being given to them directly by the Holy Spirit. The saints would call this infused knowledge.

13. Prayer is more and more a waiting on God, receptive to whatever God desires. The disciple has moved into contemplative prayer. At times it is very taxing to wait on God who seems to be so elusive and distant. Dark faith is the name of the game. Hopefully as prayer advances, the disciple will develop night vision, knowing that the Presence silhouettes the darkness.

14. Prayer is about God rather than about self. They are more intent on the God of consolations than the consolations of God. The disciple is not concerned about how they are performing. They are more concerned about what it is that God desires of them.

15. Oftentimes prayer seems to be without results, as it can be dry and distracting. However, as the disciple learns, the results of prayer come to them at odd and unexpected times, through insights, consolations, affirmations and deeper convictions.

16. The senses and external things slowly lose their hold upon the person. The beginnings of infused prayer are taking place. The disciple is entering into the Prayer of Quiet. There is no absorption in God; rather, the inner person is serenely drawn to be occupied with Him.

THE THIRD PHASE OF FORMATION

With *'Anoint Us in Your Covenant, Abba-Emmanuel'* we began the Third Phase of our Formation Program in God's Embrace Renewal Centers. In the first two phases we attempted to lay a solid foundation so that the Holy Spirit could build our spiritual home on solid rock. The titles of the manuals emphasized the development of this very personal and intimate covenant relationship between Jesus and His disciple, leading into covenant union with our Triune God. The development in discipleship was both progressive and intensive: from *Lead* to *Instruct* to *Mold* to *Hallow*. And the focus was always the participant. During this intensive spiritual journey the awareness began to dawn upon the participant that Jesus has become one with His covenant family. He is the Bridegroom and the Church is His bride. He is the Head and we are His body. While we can distinguish Jesus from us, we cannot separate ourselves from Him. Hence, entering into covenant union with the Trinity through Jesus also means loving, serving, and laying down one's life for God's covenant family.

In the Third Phase of our Formation you explored this intimate and unbreakable bond between our Triune God and His covenant family. You celebrated God's Life and Presence within His covenant family: *"Do this in memory of me."* (Luke 22:19) You participated in God's divine life through the sacramental life of God's covenant family. During this Phase you took to heart God's immense love for us as manifested in the way He has established His covenant family. And we explored our identity as God's covenant family.

FRUITS OF THE THIRD PHASE OF FORMATION:

Saints Teresa of Avila and John of the Cross have enumerated many benefits and graces that are given to the advancing disciple. The aim of our Third Phase was to move towards becoming a proficient, in the words of St. John of the Cross, and appreciating the journey into the way of the perfect. I would like to highlight a few of the many benefits that a proficient experiences through the dark night of the senses. You can complete your review by reflecting on *The Interior Castle* and *The Dark Night*, found in Part II of the Manual. You will have to determine what benefits you have experienced in your discipleship.

1. The soul gains intimate knowledge of self and one's own misery. This purification makes the soul realize its own lowliness and misery which seemed hidden and even non-existent before the sensory night began.

2. This acute sense of self leads to relating with God more respectfully and reverently as befitting God's holiness.

3. Accompanying this sense of its own misery and unworthiness before God, the soul also by contrast becomes aware of God's grandeur and majesty.

4. Through the sensory night, the soul receives the gift of humility which can only be built on a true understanding of self. Such an attitude goes against spiritual pride, one of the capital sins.

5. Such humility creates love of neighbor and a reluctance to judge anyone as they did when they enjoyed God's favors and consolations.

6. They become pliant and malleable in the hands of God and willingly seek direction and correction. Gradually, the roots of pride are destroyed.

7. *"The soul undergoes a thorough reform in its imperfections of avarice, in which it craved various spiritual objects and was never content with many of its spiritual exercises because of the covetousness of its appetite and the gratification it found in spiritual things."*

8. Regarding spiritual lust, its craving for spiritual gifts and its performance in prayer *and spiritual disciplines lessens and undergoes a thorough reform.*

9. *"God so curbs concupiscence and bridles the appetite through this arid and dark night that the soul cannot feast on any sensory delight from earthly or heavenly things."* When God does this, the soul dwells in peace and tranquility. There is no disturbance as there used to be.

10. The soul is aware of God throughout the day and has a great fear that it will backslide spiritually.

11. It practices all the virtues. Individuals become meek toward God, themselves, and others. They are more accepting of self and others, less argumentative and impatient.

12. Their struggle with envy lessens. They are more charitable toward others and are able to rejoice in their well-being. Their love for spiritual matters begins to return.

13. In the midst of dryness and a sense of abandonment, *"God frequently communicates to the soul, when it least expect, spiritual sweetness, a very pure love, and a spiritual knowledge that is sometimes most delicate."*

14, Lastly, in all they do, they are motivated more by the desire to please God rather than by their own delight and satisfaction acting as the criterion or motivation.

PRAYER AND REFLECTION ON THE REVIEW OF OUR JOURNEY

WEEK TWENTY NINE: *"THREE TIMES I BEGGED THE LORD ABOUT THIS, THAT IT MIGHT LEAVE ME, BUT HE SAID TO ME, "MY GRACE IS SUFFICIENT FOR YOU, FOR POWER IS MADE PERFECT IN WEAKNESS." (2 CORINTHIANS 12:8)*

SPIRITUAL READING FOR THE WEEK:

- **Anoint Us in Your Covenant, Abba-Emmanuel:** Session Fifteen
- **Old Testament:** Two or Three Chapters daily
- **New Testament:** Two or Three Chapters daily
- **Imitation of Christ:** One chapter daily

DAY ONE: MORNING SESSION

MORNING PRAYER: Acts of Faith, Hope, Charity; Daily Offering

Morning Face to Face with God:

Begin with Prayer to the Holy Spirit

THE FIRST PHASE OF THE JOURNEY:

(After pondering each bullet point, express your sentiments in a short prayer)

- *Lead Me into the Deep, Lord* was designed to help you accept generously and wholeheartedly God's invitation to enter into covenant union with Him.
- On God's part, making this offer to you was both urgent and enthusiastic as Jesus made this invitation a reality through His death and resurrection: *"Behold, I stand at the door and knock. If anyone hears my voice and opens the door, [then] I will enter his house and dine with him, and he with me. I will give the victor the right to sit with me on my throne, as I myself first won the victory and sit with my Father on his throne."* (Revelation 3:20-21)
- Over 12 weeks you prayed with the Scriptures and various aspects of the spiritual life. In doing so you came to a deep appreciation of Jesus and the urgent necessity of surrendering your life to Him in return for the gift of His own life to you.

- Furthermore, under the guidance of the Holy Spirit, you began to develop your own internal authority about your life of covenant union with God, of which you were having a first-hand experience in prayer.
- In time, the third assumption became a reality. Your relationship with God had become significant and consequently, you began following the dictates of the Holy Spirit rather than the dictates of your own anxious mind.
- The Holy Spirit began to re-order your priorities, and teach you how best to deepen your discipleship with God through a greater investment of your time, and even your life.
- You began to appreciate with profound gratitude that God has given Himself to you completely, through His Son, Jesus, and the Holy Spirit is making it possible for you to surrender your entire life to God in joyful trust.
- You then realized the true meaning of covenant: *the mutual and total offering of oneself to the other:* of God to me, and me to God through the Holy Spirit.
- With this personal formation at the hands of the Holy Spirit, you embarked on the next leg of the First Phase by making *Instruct Me in Your ways, Lord* your daily manual of prayer. You became familiar with the Old Testament, without which our understanding of Jesus and the New Testament is jeopardized.
- The major focus throughout the first phase was to get a proper understanding of who God really is from His revelation of Himself. An accompanying focus was to understand who we truly are in God's eyes, so that we will live our lives in the appropriate context of a covenant relationship with God.

What is God saying to you?

End with Prayer to the Holy Trinity

NIGHT SESSION: Examination of Conscience

For what are you grateful? For what are you contrite?

Please review briefly your Morning Prayer topic. Make it your last thought of the day

DAY TWO: MORNING SESSION

MORNING PRAYER: Acts of Faith, Hope, Charity; Daily Offering

Morning Face to Face with God:

Begin with Prayer to the Holy Spirit

FRUITS OF THE FIRST PHASE OF FORMATION:

(After pondering each bullet point, express your sentiments in a short prayer)

- In your estimation, the First Phase has been *a significant experience* for you, and you wanted to continue into the Second Phase of the Program.
- Whether you considered yourselves to be beginners, or were already committed disciples when you joined the Program, now you realize more clearly that humility is the foundation of the spiritual life, that all progress is a pure blessing and gift from God. You realize that you will make progress in the spiritual life only when *you rely on God in everything*.
- Your day or weekend retreat experiences have given you a *security and confidence* about the dynamics of prayer, and you are learning to appreciate the great benefits of belonging to a community of believers.
- You are *becoming familiar with Scripture*, and developing a hunger to delve more deeply into the Word of God who is both *Person and Revelation*. You are slowly beginning to realize that you can't separate the teachings from the Person of Jesus.
- You have *become consistent* in setting aside time *daily* for a person-to-person, heart-to-heart, honest dialogue with God that often times became an encounter. An encounter took place when there was definite divine intervention in your lives!
- You have *become more consistent* in your habit of daily spiritual reading, concentrating on reading the *whole Bible in one year,* and the Imitation of Christ at least once a year.
- You were coming to a deeper appreciation of your Catholic Faith, and the mediation of God's Presence and Life through the sacraments. The celebration of Eucharist and the sacrament of Reconciliation were becoming meaningful and very enriching.
- Consolation became your normal state of soul. If you moved out of consolation, you learned how to more effectively counter your desolation through the sacrament of reconciliation, spiritual practices, and the Practice of the Presence of God.
- Besides your daily time for prayer and spiritual reading, you conversed with God more often during the day. This awareness of God's presence grew deeper and became an integral part of your life style.
- You have now come to know Jesus in a personal way, experiencing intimacy with Him during the day, and becoming more familiar with the other Persons of the Trinity. You have been bringing the Father and the Holy Spirit more easily into your prayer.
- Your commitment to God was significant enough that you began moving towards not committing deliberate sin. No sin is small and insignificant.
- As disciple you began developing a delicate conscience and were immediately contrite and repentant whenever you sinned.
- Gratitude and joy became consistent features of your discipleship.

- You became familiar with the Rules for Recognizing the Voice and Presence of the Holy Spirit, and made the Discernment of Spirits a regular feature of your spiritual lives.
- You slowly came to understand that the Church is God's covenant family. Any meaningful relationship with God will necessitate committed service to God's Church.
- You sensed that an awakening took place in your hearts because God entered into your lives. The Holy Spirit created within you an intense longing and desire to become one with God. Such an awakening began to re-ordering your priorities in life.

What is God saying to you?

End with Prayer to the Holy Trinity

NIGHT SESSION: Examination of Conscience

For what are you grateful? For what are you contrite?

Please review briefly your Morning Prayer topic. Make it your last thought of the day

DAY THREE: MORNING SESSION

MORNING PRAYER: Acts of Faith, Hope, Charity; Daily Offering

Morning Face to Face with God:

Begin with Prayer to the Holy Spirit

ABANDONMENT TO GOD BRINGS ABOUT PERFECT FREEDOM

(After pondering each bullet point, express your sentiments in a short prayer)

- The true nature of love prompts the disciple to give God everything, especially liberty, memory, understanding and his/her entire will, all that they have and possess.
- In giving God our liberty, we are saying that we will make the concerted effort to seek and find His will in our daily circumstances rather than prefer our own choices which can and do lead us astray.
- In giving God our memory, we are saying that we will not live in the past. We will let bygones be bygones. We will make every effort to forgive and to live in the present moment. Most of all, we will live in the present moment because our God is our Good Shepherd. Our God is our Rock on which we can build our union. Hence, we will trust!

- In giving God our understanding, we are saying that we will go by God's understanding provided to us by the Holy Spirit, and always bring our understanding to close scrutiny to make sure that we are aligned with God's understanding.
- In giving God our entire will, we are saying that God's will is perfect and our will is burdened by inordinate attachments. The only way to free our wills of sin is to replace them with God's will. This replacement occurs at the hands of the Holy Spirit!
- Such a prayer then, is perfect abandonment. Such abandonment is made freely and wholeheartedly *after* the disciple has experienced God's largesse overwhelmingly.
- No other vision or agenda can hold up against this world-view of discipleship. The disciple's mind and heart have been washed clean of any resistance. When resistance arises in the future it will be addressed in the same way as during the retreat: through incessant petitioning and childlike trust in God's ability to bring about transformation.
- The disciple now makes sense of Christ's values and embraces them wholeheartedly. In such a joyous and wholehearted commitment lies perfect freedom.

What is God saying to you?

End with Prayer to the Holy Trinity

NIGHT SESSION: General and Particular Examination of Conscience

For what are you grateful? For what are you contrite?

Please review briefly your Morning Prayer topic. Make it your last thought of the day

DAY FOUR: MORNING SESSION

MORNING PRAYER: Act of Faith; Act of Hope; Act of Charity; Daily Offering

Morning Face to Face with God:

Begin with Prayer to the Holy Spirit

THE SPIRITUAL UNDERPINNINGS OF ABANDONMENT TO GOD

(After pondering each bullet point, express your sentiments in a short prayer)

- *Becoming Holy, Blameless, and Loving through Christ:* At this juncture, God has become the center of the disciple's life and being, and they have become God's satellite. The gravitational pull toward God is constant and reliable so that there is less likelihood that the disciple will spin off into another orbit. The satellite derives its purpose and life from spinning around the Son.

- They are living in covenant union with the Blessed Trinity. Each Person takes on a special significance and there is greater appreciation of God's love and life.
- Their sole preoccupation is now to be in the service of God and others, living their lives as a holy offering of reverent adoration and loving service.
- It is now a joy and a way of life for the disciple to conform themselves in all things to Jesus. The cross has become a willing step that the disciple takes because it gives them an opportunity to engage in a humble washing of others' feet, even of enemies.
- Their lives are permeated with constant gratitude and increasing humility. In times of humiliation, they bless their critics and detractors and trust that God will bring good out of every circumstance.
- This transformation leaves no room in the disciple's heart for hostility and enmity even though others might consider them to be an enemy. The disciple understands how the apostles could rejoice in their sufferings as recorded in Acts 5:40-41, because they too are beginning to have similar experiences.

What is God saying to you?

End with Prayer to the Holy Trinity

NIGHT SESSION: Examination of Conscience

For what are you grateful? For what are you contrite?

Please review briefly your Morning Prayer topic. Make it your last thought of the day

DAY FIVE: MORNING SESSION

MORNING PRAYER: Acts of Faith, Hope, Charity; Daily Offering

Morning Face to Face with God:

Begin with Prayer to the Holy Spirit

THE SECOND PHASE OF FORMATION:

(After pondering each bullet point, express your sentiments in a short prayer)

- You saw that *The Spiritual Exercises of St. Ignatius* were undoubtedly an excellent tool of formation in discipleship. And you were well prepared through the First Phase of formation in God's Embrace to undergo such a momentous journey over six months.
- Perhaps the best summary of your retreat experience would be *perfect freedom to serve God and His people selflessly.*

- St. Ignatius characterized this attitude of always being disposed to choose whatever God willed or permitted in one's daily circumstances as Indifference.
- *Hallow Me as Your Disciple, Lord* was a follow-up to *The Spiritual Exercises of St. Ignatius*. At the end of the retreat, you came to realize that *The Spiritual Exercises of St. Ignatius* are undoubtedly an excellent tool of formation in discipleship.
- You saw that at the end of the Spiritual Exercises, St. Ignatius invited you to ponder all that you have received from God. The list of blessings was exhaustive and overwhelming. In response, you made a total offering of self to God.
- The true nature of love, manifested in deeds, especially God's offering of His Son to us as Savior and Lord, prompted you to give God everything, especially liberty, memory, understanding and your entire will, all that you have and possess.
- Such a prayer is perfect abandonment and was made freely and wholeheartedly *after* you experienced God's largesse overwhelmingly. Such an offering is the quintessential expression of a covenant relationship.
- After the retreat, your mind and heart had been washed clean of any resistance. When resistance arose in the future you addressed it in the same way as during the retreat: through incessant petitioning and childlike trust in God's ability to bring about transformation.
- At an even deeper level than in the First Phase, you now made sense of Christ's values and embraced them wholeheartedly. *Hallow Me as Your Disciple, Lord* built upon your profound retreat experience. It tapped into your intense desire to live out this covenant offering of self on a daily basis, generously and wholeheartedly.

What is God saying to you?

End with Prayer to the Holy Trinity

NIGHT SESSION: Examination of Conscience

For what are you grateful? For what are you contrite?

Please review briefly your Morning Prayer topic. Make it your last thought of the day

DAY SIX: MORNING SESSION

MORNING PRAYER: Acts of Faith, Hope, Charity; Daily Offering

Morning Face to Face with God:

Begin with Prayer to the Holy Spirit

TRANSITION INTO THE SECOND PHASE OF FORMATION:

(After pondering each bullet point, express your sentiments in a short prayer)

- Whatever helps and methods of prayer you needed and used in the preliminary stages of the relationship have now served their purpose. They have brought you as a burgeoning disciple into the Presence and Heart of God.

- You still use discursive methods of prayer as needed, but communication with God has moved into the realm of communion, leading to greater and deeper union. Fewer words are now being used in prayer, as the emphasis in the relationship with God is on communion.

- There is greater emphasis on being receptive to God's Presence and voice. Listening to God is more important than being listened to. Hence, the emphasis in the relationship has shifted from God serving your interests and well-being, to God becoming the focus and center of your life.

- As an advancing disciple you now want to belong to God and to be faithful to Him, to do His will generously and joyfully, to make God the center of discipleship. You are now at God's beck and call.

- Gradually, you have been finding out that God's way of revealing Himself is through infused knowledge. Prayer has shifted from communication with God through words, thoughts, and images into communion through fewer words, greater affect, and quiet.

- This transition into communion through loving attention in silence, can and will be disconcerting and sometimes baffling. At times you have wondered whether anything was happening as the faculties of mind, imagination, and memory don't seem to work as facilely as before.

- In fact they appear unruly; distraction and boredom seemS like the norm. However, the heart was being drawn through a lively longing for God as *The Cloud of Unknowing* would describe it.

- Every now and then you have received assurance that indeed God is taking you into a deeper place. The Holy Spirit provided faint brushes of consolation which led to a firmer commitment and surrender to God.

- Gradually, you learned to be lovingly attentive to God in adoration and worship, without worrying or being concerned whether prayer is satisfying or not. Trust and surrender to God have become the bedrock of your relationship with God.

- Meanwhile, a deeper connection and commitment was being established between God and you as disciple, and you moved toward wholehearted commitment. At this stage then, you were moving towards or into contemplative prayer.

- Contemplative prayer is the process which the Holy Spirit uses to bring about a genuine and total surrender of the disciple to Jesus. Contemplative prayer is an opening of one's whole being to the loving Presence of the Divine, trusting in the work of the Holy Spirit to reveal to them all the things that Jesus had taught his disciples.

What is God saying to you?

End with Prayer to the Holy Trinity

NIGHT SESSION: Examination of Conscience

For what are you grateful? For what are you contrite?

Please review briefly your Morning Prayer topic. Make it your last thought of the day

DAY SEVEN: MORNING SESSION

MORNING PRAYER: Acts of Faith, Hope, Charity; Daily Offering

Morning Face to Face with God:

Begin with Prayer to the Holy Spirit

FRUITS OF THE SECOND PHASE OF FORMATION:

(After pondering each bullet point, express your sentiments in a short prayer)

- Discipleship is more about greater and greater surrender to God, making Him alone the center of your lifestyle and discipleship.
- When disciples have become humble, nothing can be taken away from them, because their heart is with God and where their heart is, there their treasure lies. No matter what, they have it all.
- They keep paring their needs to a minimum, concerned about doing what is right rather than from preference. Their hearts are filled to overflowing with gratitude. They don't need any more of God's gifts, even when some are taken away, because they have received God's abundance.
- There is a definite eschewing of deliberate sin and an intense desire to help in the establishment of God's reign.
- The disciple operates on the *Principle of Agere Contra:* to go against anything in one's desires and will that is contrary to God's will, and to seek constantly only what God desires.
- The disciple is acutely aware that whatever transformation is taking place is at the behest of the Holy Spirit. Their heart is therefore filled with constant gratitude to God.

- The disciple is praying the whole day, offering gratitude and praise as they go through their day with God. God is constantly present, and remembering God's deeds of love and mercy is a devotion of love and gratitude.
- There is an eager desire to reciprocate God's love for them by their own generous deeds of loving and selfless service. They are content to bloom where they have been planted, to live in the now, to let bygones be bygones because God has forgiven them and is managing their daily affairs. The future is of relevance only when it shows up in the present moment.
- Sunday worship has become very meaningful. The disciple becomes very aware of the community dimension of the Eucharistic celebration. Eucharist and communion can only be meaningful when the celebration leads the disciple to lay down their lives for the community.
- Covenant living continues to shape the disciple's identity. They see themselves as hyphenated identities: self-Jesus. Prayer is an essential part of the disciple's lifestyle. The disciple lives and breathes God.
- Their formal times for prayer are very important. So are their informal conversations with God. The disciple moves towards a more contemplative way of communicating and knowing God.
- Both in prayer and daily life, their knowledge and understanding of God that they have received from study and prayer, is now being supplemented by knowledge and wisdom being given to them directly by the Holy Spirit. The saints would call this infused knowledge.
- Prayer is more and more a waiting on God, receptive to whatever God desires. The disciple has moved into contemplative prayer. At times it is very taxing to wait on God who seems to be so elusive and distant. Dark faith is the name of the game.
- Hopefully as prayer advances, the disciple will develop night vision, knowing that the Presence silhouettes the darkness. Prayer is about God rather than about self. They are more intent on the God of consolations than the consolations of God.
- The disciple is not concerned about how they are performing. They are more concerned about what it is that God desires of them.
- Oftentimes prayer seems to be without results, as it can be dry and distracting. However, as the disciple learns, the results of prayer come to them at odd and unexpected times, through insights, consolations, affirmations and deeper convictions.
- The senses and external things slowly lose their hold upon the person. The beginnings of infused prayer are taking place. The disciple is entering into the Prayer of Quiet. There is no absorption in God; rather, the inner person is serenely drawn to be occupied with Him.

What is God saying to you?

End with Prayer to the Holy Trinity

NIGHT SESSION: Examination of Conscience

For what are you grateful? For what are you contrite?

What prayer would you compose to express what God has said to you this week?

Please review briefly your Morning Prayer topic. Make it your last thought of the day

PRAYER AND REFLECTION ON THE REVIEW OF OUR JOURNEY – CONTINUED

WEEK THIRTY: *"I KNOW SOMEONE IN CHRIST WHO, FOURTEEN YEARS AGO (WHETHER IN THE BODY OR OUT OF THE BODY I DO NOT KNOW, GOD KNOWS), WAS CAUGHT UP TO THE THIRD HEAVEN. AND I KNOW THAT THIS PERSON (WHETHER IN THE BODY OR OUT OF THE BODY I DO NOT KNOW, GOD KNOWS) WAS CAUGHT UP INTO PARADISE AND HEART INEFFABLE THINGS, WHICH NO ONE MAY UTTER."* *(2 CORINTHIANS 12:2-4)*

SPIRITUAL READING FOR THE WEEK:

- **Anoint Us in Your Covenant, Abba-Emmanuel:** Session Fifteen
- **Old Testament:** Two or Three Chapters daily
- **New Testament:** Two or Three Chapters daily
- **Imitation of Christ:** One chapter daily

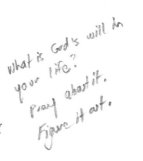

what is God's will in your life? Pray about it. Figure it out.

DAY ONE: MORNING SESSION

MORNING PRAYER: Acts of Faith, Hope, Charity; Daily Offering

Morning Face to Face with God:

Begin with Prayer to the Holy Spirit

THE THIRD PHASE OF FORMATION:

(After pondering each bullet point, express your sentiments in a short prayer)

- In the first two phases of the Program, we attempted to lay a solid foundation so that the Holy Spirit could build our spiritual home on solid rock. The titles of the manuals emphasized the development of this very personal and intimate covenant relationship between Jesus and His disciple, leading into covenant union with our Triune God.

- The development in discipleship was both progressive and intensive: from *Lead* to *Instruct* to *Mold* to *Hallow*. And the focus was always the participant.
- During this intensive spiritual journey the awareness began to dawn upon the participant that Jesus has become one with His covenant family. He is the Bridegroom and the Church is His bride. He is the Head and we are His body.
- While we can distinguish Jesus from us, we cannot separate ourselves from Him. Hence, entering into covenant union with the Trinity through Jesus also means loving, serving, and laying down one's life for God's covenant family.
- In the Third Phase of our Formation you explored this intimate and unbreakable bond between our Triune God and His covenant family. You celebrated God's Life and Presence within His covenant family: *"Do this in memory of me."* (Luke 22:19)
- You participated in God's divine life through the sacramental life of God's covenant family. During this phase you took to heart God's immense love for us as manifested in the way He has established His covenant family. And we explored our identity as God's covenant family.

What is God saying to you?

End with Prayer to the Holy Trinity

NIGHT SESSION: Examination of Conscience

For what are you grateful? For what are you contrite?

Please review briefly your Morning Prayer topic. Make it your last thought of the day

DAY TWO: MORNING SESSION

MORNING PRAYER: Acts of Faith, Hope, Charity; Daily Offering

Morning Face to Face with God:

Begin with Prayer to the Holy Spirit

PRACTICING THE PRESENCE OF GOD: THE JESUS PRAYER (or Your own Prayer Aspiration):

Are you familiar with the Jesus Prayer?

Have you practiced the Jesus Prayer?

Have you used the longer version of the Prayer?

Have you used the shorter version of the Prayer?

Have you experienced forgiveness through the Prayer?

Have you experienced peace through the Prayer?

Have you experienced hope and strength through the Prayer?

Have you experienced trust and security through the Prayer?

Do you pray with loving attention to the words of the prayer?

Do you pray with loving attention to the Presence of Jesus?

Have you created a rhythm to your recitation of the Prayer?

Has this Prayer increased your commitment to Jesus?

Do you try to pray this Prayer unceasingly?

Do you pray this Prayer only occasionally?

Do you pray this Prayer primarily with your lips?

Do you now pray this Prayer in your heart?

Through this practice, has prayer become a matter of the heart?

Through this practice, do you sense a sacred space within you?

Does this Prayer continue in you even when you are very busy?

Does this Prayer create a longing in you to be alone with God?

Is Jesus becoming a familiar Presence during the day?

Has Jesus become a Presence within you?

When upset/disturbed, do you pray the Jesus Prayer?

When anxious and worried, do you pray the Jesus Prayer?

When angry, do you resort to the Jesus Prayer?

When hurt, do you resort to the Jesus Prayer?

When envious or jealous, do you pray the Jesus Prayer?

When tempted to gossip, do you pray the Jesus Prayer?

When lustful, do you pray the Jesus Prayer?

When in doubt and confusion, do you pray the Jesus Prayer?

Do you pray the Jesus Prayer in all circumstances?

Has the Jesus Prayer become your way of life?

When you awaken at night, are you praying the Prayer?

Has the Prayer helped you to forgive others?

Does the Prayer help you remain in consolation?

[Handwritten marginal notes:]

Jesus, have mercy on me, a sinner.

Jesus Christ, son of the living God, have mercy on me, a sinner.

Lord Jesus Christ, son of God, have mercy on me, a sinner.

Christogram, medal

Has the practice increased your longing for God?

Has the practice deepened your awareness of God's love?

Is the practice healing you of your past hurts and resentments?

Is the practice healing you of your past guilt and shame?

Are you are now living with God more in the present moment?

Is your attitude toward the future one of peace and trust?

What is God saying to you?

End with Prayer to the Holy Trinity

NIGHT SESSION: Examination of Conscience

For what are you grateful? For what are you contrite?

Please review briefly your Morning Prayer topic. Make it your last thought of the day

DAY THREE: MORNING SESSION

MORNING PRAYER: Acts of Faith, Hope, Charity; Daily Offering

Morning Face to Face with God:

Begin with Prayer to the Holy Spirit

CONSTANT GRATITUDE:

> *Constant Gratitude as a way of life was recommended by Paul in his letters, for instance to the Philippians and Thessalonians. St. Ignatius of Loyola also recommended highly the practice of constant gratitude.*

Would you say that you are a grateful person? Y

Do you express your gratitude several times a day? Y

Do you express your gratitude to God in prayer?

Do you express your gratitude to God during the day?

Do you express your gratitude to God frequently?

Or mostly do you express your gratitude to yourself?

Do you express your gratitude to others frequently? ✔

Do you seldom express your gratitude to others?

Do you thank God for your blessings? ✔

Do you thank God for the gift of life?
Do you thank God for His Providence?
Do you thank God for the gift of Divine Life?
Are you consciously grateful for knowing the Father? ✓
Are you consciously grateful for knowing Jesus? ✓
Are you consciously grateful for knowing the Holy Spirit? ✓
Are you deeply grateful for the gift of Eucharist? ✓
Are you in grateful awe at receiving Jesus Himself in communion?
Are you deeply grateful for your Catholic Faith? ✓
Are you grateful to God for your talents? ✓
Do you expressly mention your talents in your gratitude?
Do you rejoice at the success of others? ✓
Can you be grateful when others are doing well and you are not?
Do you bless others when they do not bless you?
Do you want to bless others when they do not bless you?
Have you come to thank God for all that has been?
Are you grateful that your weaknesses make you humble? ✓
Are you grateful that God has healed your past hurts?
Are you grateful that your past does not haunt you?
Can you thank God for your failures becoming stepping-stones?
Can you thank God for all your past circumstances?
Can you thank God for all your present circumstances?
Can you thank God for all the circumstances of your life?
Have you gained perspective from hurts caused to you?
Have you recognized God's presence in trial and tribulation?
Are you becoming more non-judgmental as you grow in gratitude?
Are you becoming compassionate as you grow in gratitude?
Are you becoming humble as you grow in gratitude?
Do you place others before you as you grow in gratitude?
Are you becoming more loving toward others as a result?
Are you becoming more trusting of God's ways in your life?
Are you becoming patient and long-suffering?
What is God saying to you?
End with Prayer to the Holy Trinity

NIGHT SESSION: Examination of Conscience

For what are you grateful? For what are you contrite?

Please review briefly your Morning Prayer topic. Make it your last thought of the day

DAY FOUR: MORNING SESSION

MORNING PRAYER: Acts of Faith, Hope, Charity; Daily Offering

Morning Face to Face with God:

Begin with Prayer to the Holy Spirit

CONTANT CONVERSATION:

Constant

In his book on "The Practice of the Presence of God," Brother Lawrence recommends continual conversation with God throughout the day. It was his experience that such a way of life would bring about profound union with God. In fact, Brother Lawrence claims that it was God Himself who taught him this way of living.

Do you think about God during the day?
Do you think a lot about God during the day?
Do you talk to God during the day?
Do you talk to God several times a day?
Do you talk to God the whole day about everything in your life?
Upon awakening, do you want to converse with God?
Do you still converse with God when you are with others?
(How would you describe this experience?) — Help me to know what to say in this instance.
Does your conversation with God keep you focused during the day?
Is gratitude a big topic in your conversation with God?
Is petition a big portion of your conversation with God?
Do you sense God by your side when you speak to Him?
Do you sense God in you when you speak to Him?
Does God speak to you as well?
Are you slow in recognizing God's voice and movements?
Has your spirit become quite sensitive to God's stirrings?
Are you moved to tears when God speaks to you?
Are you moved to sorrow for sin when God speaks to you? ✓
Are you moved to gratitude when God speaks to you?

Does God speak to you through Scripture?
Does God speak to you in whispers and nudges? ✓
Are there times when you commune with God in silence?
Are you living your life within this conversation with God?
Has reverence for God become a special trait of this communion?
Is singleness of purpose a benefit of this communion?
Is humility a benefit of this communion? ✓
What is God saying to you?
End with Prayer to the Holy Trinity

NIGHT SESSION: Examination of Conscience

For what are you grateful? For what are you contrite?

Please review briefly your Morning Prayer topic. Make it your last thought of the day

DAY FIVE: MORNING SESSION

MORNING PRAYER: Acts of Faith, Hope, Charity; Daily Offering

Morning Face to Face with God:

Begin with Prayer to the Holy Spirit

RECOGNIZING GOD'S VOICE AND PRESENCE

Is your discipleship lived out under the influence of the Holy Spirit?
Do you have peace and trust in God most of the time?
Do you have peace and joy for the most part?
Is consolation your normal state of soul?
When in consolation, do you guard against movements of desolation?
When in consolation, do you experience devotion and fervor in prayer?
When in consolation, do you think you are better than others?
When in consolation, do you tend to judge others who seem to be lax?
Do you make decisions immediately, when in consolation?
Or, do you sift God's will from your own interpretation of it?
Is it easy for you to be in a state of consolation?
Do you make decisions only when you are in consolation?
Is being in a state of consolation a struggle for you?
Is desolation your normal state?

Does lust and sexual addictions cause desolation?

Does pornography cause desolation?

Does rejection cause you desolation?

Does gambling cause you desolation?

Do you tend to postpone and neglect prayer when in desolation?

Do you abandon your decisions made in time of consolation?

Do you feel convicted by the Holy Spirit in time of desolation?

In desolation do you feel convicted or condemned by the Holy Spirit?

Do you do extra prayer in time of desolation?

Do you do spiritual reading and penance in time of desolation?

Do you try not to make new decisions in time of desolation?

Do you try to stick to your decisions made in time of consolation?

When assailed by doubts, do you try to resolve them by yourself?

Or, when assailed by doubts and confusion, do you seek counsel?

When assailed by desolation, do you seek the sacrament of Penance?

When assailed by desolation, do you practice patience and trust?

When in desolation, do you blame God and others?

When in desolation, do you make excuses for your behavior?

When in desolation, do you regress into your past failures?

Do you benefit from the lessons learned in time of desolation?

Are you grateful when you return to a state of consolation?

Do you guard against your ego when you return to consolation?

Is consolation becoming a state of quiet sobriety and humble gratitude?

In time of consolation is God asking you to keep your eyes on Him alone?

Is consolation becoming the Sabbath when you restore your strength?

What is God saying to you?

End with Prayer to the Holy Trinity

NIGHT SESSION: Examination of Conscience

For what are you grateful? For what are you contrite?

Please review briefly your Morning Prayer topic. Make it your last thought of the day

DAY SIX: MORNING SESSION

MORNING PRAYER: Acts of Faith, Hope, Charity; Daily Offering

Morning Face to Face with God:

Begin with Prayer to the Holy Spirit

REPETITION: MY RULE OF LIFE IN GOD'S EMBRACE:

(Ponder each item prayerfully; ask the Holy Spirit to strengthen your resolve)

In the presence of the most Holy Trinity, and surrounded by the whole heavenly assembly of Mary, Mother of God and our Mother, the archangels and angels, the saints and holy witnesses of Jesus Christ, I, _____, do solemnly declare that it is my intent, with the Holy Spirit's gracious and bountiful help, to commit myself to spending an hour daily in strengthening and deepening my call to discipleship through the following means offered to me by the Holy Spirit in the 3-year Program of God's Embrace:

1. SPIRITUAL READING: 20 Minutes

The Bible: I will choose to read either three chapters of the Old Testament and three chapters of the New Testament on a daily basis, beginning with the book of Genesis and the Gospel of Matthew, or two chapters of the Old Testament and one chapter of the New Testament on a daily basis. Please specify your option:

The Catholic Catechism: I will read three pages a day or fifteen pages over the weekend.

The Imitation of Christ: I will read one chapter a day.

The Manual: I will read the Sessions that have been allotted for the month, and two or three pages from Part Two of the Manual.

2. DEVOTIONAL PRACTICES:

Please indicate which practices you will do on a daily/weekly/monthly basis:

Weekly Mass:

Rosary:

Chaplet of Divine Mercy:

Adoration before the Blessed Sacrament:

Sacrament of Reconciliation:

Daily Mass Readings:

Liturgy of the Hours:

3. DAILY FACE TO FACE SESSION WITH JESUS: 15-20 minutes
Daily Examination of Conscience: 10 minutes

4. SPIRITUAL PRACTICES DURING THE DAY: EXPERIMENTS WITH TRUTH
The Holy Spirit will reveal your spiritual practices to you through your daily discernment of spirits. The Holy Spirit will let you know God's will through your spiritual reading, devotional practices, daily Morning Face to Face with God, Examination of Conscience, and practice of the Presence of God. The Person of Jesus will be revealed to you as you practice forgiveness, humility, trust, surrender, loving without counting the cost, and patience in difficult situations.

What is God saying to you?

End with Prayer to the Holy Trinity

NIGHT SESSION: Examination of Conscience

For what are you grateful? For what are you contrite?

Please review briefly your Morning Prayer topic. Make it your last thought of the day

DAY SEVEN: MORNING SESSION

MORNING PRAYER: Acts of Faith, Hope, Charity; Daily Offering

Morning Face to Face with God:

Begin with Prayer to the Holy Spirit

FRUITS OF THE THIRD PHASE OF FORMATION:

(After pondering each bullet point, express your sentiments in a short prayer)

- Saints Teresa of Avila and John of the Cross have enumerated many benefits and graces that are given to the advancing disciple. The aim of our Third Phase was to move towards becoming a proficient, in the words of St. John of the Cross, and appreciating the journey into the way of the perfect.
- Here are some of the many benefits that a proficient experiences through the dark night of the senses. You can complete your review by reflecting on *The Interior Castle* and *The Dark Night*, found in Part II of the Manual. You will have to determine what benefits you have experienced in your discipleship.

- The soul gains intimate knowledge of self and one's own misery. This purification makes the soul realize its own lowliness and misery which seemed hidden and even non-existent before the sensory night began.
- This acute sense of self leads to relating with God more respectfully and reverently as befitting God's holiness.
- Accompanying this sense of its own misery and unworthiness before God, the soul also by contrast becomes aware of God's grandeur and majesty.
- Through the sensory night, the soul receives the gift of humility which can only be built on a true understanding of self. Such an attitude goes against spiritual pride, one of the capital sins.
- Such humility creates love of neighbor and a reluctance to judge anyone as they did when they enjoyed God's favors and consolations.
- They become pliant and malleable in the hands of God and willingly seek direction and correction. Gradually, the roots of pride are destroyed.
- *"The soul undergoes a thorough reform in its imperfections of avarice, in which it craved various spiritual objects and was never content with many of its spiritual exercises because of the covetousness of its appetite and the gratification it found in spiritual things."*
- Regarding spiritual lust, its craving for spiritual gifts and its performance in prayer and spiritual disciplines lessens and undergoes a thorough reform.
- *"God so curbs concupiscence and bridles the appetite through this arid and dark night that the soul cannot feast on any sensory delight from earthly or heavenly things."* When God does this, the soul dwells in peace and tranquility. There is no disturbance as there used to be.
- The soul is aware of God throughout the day and has a great fear that it will backslide spiritually.
- It practices all the virtues. Individuals become meek toward God, themselves, and others. They are more accepting of self and others, less argumentative and impatient.
- Their struggle with envy lessens. They are more charitable toward others and are able to rejoice in their well-being. Their love for spiritual matters begins to return.
- In the midst of dryness and a sense of abandonment, *"God frequently communicates to the soul, when it least expect, spiritual sweetness, a very pure love, and a spiritual knowledge that is sometimes most delicate."*
- Lastly, in all they do, they are motivated more by the desire to please God rather than by their own delight and satisfaction acting as the criterion or motivation.

What is God saying to you?

End with Prayer to the Holy Trinity

NIGHT SESSION: Examination of Conscience

For what are you grateful? For what are you contrite?

What prayer would you compose to express what God has said to you this week?

Please review briefly your Morning Prayer topic. Make it your last thought of the day

PART TWO:

PART TWO

SPIRITUALITY OF THE DESERT FATHERS AND MOTHERS

In the Third and Fourth Centuries, there was a mass movement into the deserts of the Middle East, especially Egypt, after the proclamation of the Edict of Milan in 313 A.D. by the Roman Emperors, Constantine and Licinius. After Christianity became the official religion of the Roman Empire through the Edict of Milan, it became acceptable and even respectable to be known as a Christian. One unfortunate consequence was a watering down of the practice of the faith. Consequently, a major transition began in the Church, leading to a blossoming of monasticism in the desert. The Spirituality of the Desert, especially in the Scetes desert of Egypt, emerged from an intense desire on the part of many Christians to live an authentic life of discipleship. In time they became known as the Desert Fathers and Mothers.

The most well-known of these monks was St. Antony the Great who moved to the desert in AD 270-271. He is universally acknowledged as the father and founder of desert monasticism. St. Antony died in 356 AD. By then there were thousands of monks and nuns living in the desert. St. Athanasius of Alexandria, St. Antony's biographer, wrote that the "desert had become a city." In 270 AD, St. Antony heard a Sunday sermon stating that perfection could be achieved by selling one's possessions, distributing the proceeds to the poor, and following Christ (Matthew 19:21). St. Antony did just that, and took the step of moving deep into the desert to seek complete solitude. He soon realized that separating himself physically from material possessions did not necessarily ensure freedom from attachment to them. In the solitude of the desert he came to see that his mind and heart needed to be purified of inordinate tendencies and attachments. Indeed, the mind was the chief battleground of the spiritual life. The spiritual life was very much about directing all one's thoughts and desires to the praise and service of God, under the guidance of the Holy Spirit. St. Antony viewed the solitude, austerity, and sacrifice of the desert as an alternative to martyrdom, considered as the highest form of perfection. This was especially true after the Edict of Milan, when dissipation and mediocrity had permeated the life of the Church.

Life in the desert was a clear invitation to a life of simplicity, a separation from material goods, and focusing one's attention on refining and purifying the spirit. The life and example of St. Antony and the other hermits attracted many followers. They either lived alone or in small clusters. They were ascetics, renouncing a life of comfort and sense-pleasure. Instead they spent their days in prayer, singing psalms, fasting, giving alms to the needy, preserving love and harmony with one another, while keeping their thoughts and desires on God alone. They exerted an immense moral and spiritual influence on the Church. Many either joined them in the desert or sought their advice. As more pilgrims began visiting the desert communities and leaders to benefit from their spiritual wisdom, the early sayings and reflections of the desert Abbas and Ammas began circulating in the wider community. Latin versions of the original

Greek stories and monastic rules guided the early monastic development in the Byzantine world and eventually in the western Christian world. By the time of St. Antony's death in 356 AD, there were tens of thousands of Christians living in the desert as monks and hermits. Benedictine monasteries in the West used *The Sayings of the Desert Fathers* as their staple spiritual reading.

The monasticism of the desert had a major influence on the development of Christian Spirituality and monasticism. And the informal gathering of hermits later on became the model for Christian monasticism. Three types of monasticism emerged in Egypt around the Desert Fathers: The Solitary Hermit: St. Antony and his followers practiced this model in Lower Egypt. Then there were the Cenobites: They were communities of monks and nuns in Upper Egypt, founded by St. Pachomius. The third model was Small Groups of Monks and Nuns which was a combination of the first two. They had a common spiritual elder, called an Abba or Amma. St. Amun was the founder of this model. Several such communities would come together in larger gatherings to worship on weekends. The Sayings of the Desert Fathers were compiled by these small communities of monks and nuns.

The first fully organized community of monks under St. Pachomius included men and women living in separate quarters. They supported themselves by weaving cloth and baskets, and doing other tasks. Each monk or nun had a three year probationary period, after which they gained full admittance into the community. All property was held in common, meals were eaten together and in silence. They fasted twice a week and wore simple peasant clothing with a hood. They spent time, together and alone, in prayer and spiritual reading, meditating on the scriptures, and working to support the community. St. Pachomius established the tradition of every community needing to have a spiritual elder – abba or amma – to keep the monks honest and accountable. Ideally, the abba or amma was one who had journeyed along the way of the desert and could speak with authority and compassion. On the basis of their own experience they could also provide the subjects with a road map of the spiritual journey. The spiritual elder was a central component in the establishment of community life.

From the wisdom of the Desert Fathers and Mothers we learn that our souls too can be viewed as a desert: lonely, desolate, broken, and in need of water. The Desert Fathers realized that their souls harbored the same distractions and turmoil that they had left behind in the towns and villages. They developed a different set of values in the desert: God is to be found in the silence of our hearts. Silence is arrived at through repentance, through the awareness that we are disordered and deceitful, and the realization that we can be saved only in surrender to Jesus. 'Desert' (*eremos* in the Greek) means 'abandonment.' 'Hermit' is derived from this Greek word.

The spiritual life is about abandonment, surrender to God. In the physical desert out there, and in the desert of your soul, you face up to yourself, to your temptations and passions. You confront your heart as honestly and forthrightly as possible, without any preoccupation about what others will think and say about you. You reject all scapegoats, facing your demons squarely and honestly. Your sole objective is to know and do what God wants of you. While the desert is a place of quiet and silence, it is also the place where transformation is born and carried out. It is a place of confrontation, not withdrawal. It is a place of encounter where you will no longer be the same. The desert is where you move into repentance and stay in it permanently. In the desert, one does not withdraw from people. To live in the desert means to live for God.

The hermit lived in a cell which symbolizes the soul. We can never escape from our soul, however much we might try to do so. We will find God first and foremost in our soul. Our spiritual progress will be reflective of the way we treat our soul. When we have become comfortable with God through repentance and forgiveness of sin, we will reflect God's goodness and joy. The desert teaches us that in the ultimate analysis, we have no control of much of life and our circumstances. What we do have is God's presence in our lives and His promise to be with us in all aspects of our lives. Through slow and arduous acceptance of self, we learn to be patient and loving, compassionate and forgiving, non-judgmental and humble.

THE SPIRITUALITY OF SAINT BENEDICTINE

INTRODUCTION:

St. Benedict was born in 480 AD in the Italian town of Norcia, and died between 543 and 547 AD. The Roman Empire was in crisis in the 5th century. The Visigoths, under King Alaric, attacked the city of Rome in 408 AD. The City fell in August of 410 AD. With the destruction of Rome and the Western Roman Empire, the dark ages descended upon Europe and lasted for seven centuries. The chaos and anxiety in secular society was having a major negative impact on the life of the Church. As in previous times of danger and crisis, the Holy Spirit began a movement of renewal in the Church through Saint Benedict. At first St. Benedict became a hermit to counter the malaise and rot that had set in. Before long, he was identified as a leader and reformer, and thus began a great movement of renewal in the Church. He founded twelve communities for monks at Subiaco, about 40 miles east of Rome. He then moved to Monte Cassino in the mountains of Southern Italy where he died. St. Benedict is acknowledged as the Founder of Western Monasticism. His main contribution to the monastic and spiritual life is his 'Rule of Saint Benedict.' There are seventy three short chapters, and it offers wisdom in two areas: how to live a Christ-centered life in this world, and monastic governance, or how to run the monastery efficiently.   St. Benedict established the tradition of living the monastic life in community. Thus began the great movement in the West of living an intentional spiritual life behind four walls in monasteries. His Rule of Life established the Benedictine Way of Life in the monastery. Let us look at some of his traditions that he established in monastic life that reveal the charism and understanding of discipleship that was given to him by the Holy Spirit:

PRAYER, STUDY, WORK, AND REST:

They are the daily components of monastic living, and of our own lives. For St. Benedict, prayer, study, work, and rest were all equally significant in God's eyes as we were doing all for the glory of God. They are all equally important for us, because balance and a rhythmic pattern of living are essential to a healthy spiritual life. Prayer is obviously of the utmost importance. However, it becomes an obstacle if it is done to the exclusion of other necessary tasks that are God's will for us. The same holds true for study where we immerse ourselves in the Word of God, and neglect our daily duties and need for rest and relaxation. The emphasis is always to maintain a proper balance between these four very important aspects of daily life. They are all equally holy because they are all God's will for us. When they are done in proper balance and rhythm, they provide excellent scaffolding for the building of a solid spiritual life.

PRAYER:

Prayer is squarely centered on the Divine Office in the Benedictine tradition. Chapters 8 through 20 of the Rule give us the structure of the Divine Office and how life in the Benedictine monastery revolves around a healthy and organic balance between prayer, work, study/reading and rest. In the Rule of Saint Benedict, there were eight prayer periods, interspersed throughout the day: Matins or Vigils, done around 1:00 AM, Lauds or Morning Prayer, Prime Prayer at the first hour of daylight, Terce or Midmorning Prayer, Sext or Midday Prayer, None or Midafternoon Prayer, Vespers or Evening Prayer, and Compline or Night Prayer. Within the week all 150 psalms were prayed in song, along with hymns, antiphons, and commentaries. The Liturgy of the Hours, as we know it in the Catholic Church, and prayed by priests and deacons, is actually an abbreviation of the fuller, complete monastic office. In the current abbreviated form of the Liturgy of the Hours, the Office of Readings would be Matins. Morning Prayer (Lauds), and Evening Prayer (Vespers) are the major hours, and Terce, Sext, None, and Compline, are the minor hours.

In the Rule, St. Benedict tells us to "hold nothing dearer than Christ," and to drop everything immediately when it is time for prayer. Every now and then we will be tempted to postpone or even neglect our daily prayer because we are in desolation, or tired and unbalanced in the way we feel. According to St. Benedict, being committed consistently to our daily prayer is of the utmost importance. If we are to hold nothing dearer than Christ, then it follows that prayer becomes our constant companion throughout the day.

Prayer is both individual and communal. Lectio Divina, also known as the Benedictine Method of Prayer, is the method of prayer attributed to St. Benedict and his followers. We have used this method extensively in our first two phases of formation in *God's Embrace Renewal Centers*. It is a method that can be used for prayer as well as for spiritual reading. According to the Rule, prayer is also 'Opus Dei,' the work of God. Prayer is inseparable from the rest of the day. Hence it is to be used frequently and throughout the day to express our praise, adoration, thanksgiving, petition, contrition in the midst of our daily activities and challenges. In times past, the church bells called us to pray the Angelus. We can create similar summons to prayer throughout the day: whenever our phone rings, to say a prayer for the person calling; every time the clock in our home chimes, to pray for our family members; after we have read an email, to pray for the sender; to say a prayer of adoration and praise every time we get into and come out of our vehicles, and so on.

WORK AND STUDY:

St. Benedict treats daily manual labor in Chapter 48 of his Rule. He was of the opinion that the spiritual life needed to have a proper rhythm and order to it, as an idle mind is the devil's workshop. *"When they live by the labor of their hands, as our fathers and the apostles did, then they are really monks. Yet, all things are to be done with moderation on account of the fainthearted."* Interspersed in the daily manual labor are periods of reading (study) and prayer, beginning with Prime around 6:00 AM. The hours for manual labor would amount to five, the hours for reading/study to two. And they would be done in between the hours of the Divine Office. *"From the first of October to the beginning of Lent, the brothers ought to devote themselves to reading until the end of the second hour. At this time Terce is said and they are to work at their assigned tasks until None. At the first signal for the hour of None, all are to put aside their work to be ready for the second signal. Then after their meal they will devote themselves to their reading or to the psalms. During the days of Lent, they should be free in the morning to read until the third hour, after which they will work at their assigned tasks until the end of the tenth hour... On Sunday all are to be engaged in reading except those who have been assigned various duties. If anyone is so remiss and indolent that he is unwilling or unable to study or to read, he is to be given some work in order that he may not be idle. Brothers who are sick or weak should be given a type of work or craft that will keep them busy without overwhelming them or driving them away. The abbot must take their infirmities into account."*

VOWS OF STABILITY, CONVERSION, AND OBEDIENCE:

The Benedictines take the vow of Stability. The monastery they enter becomes their abode and community for the rest of their lives. They would need special permission to transfer their membership to another monastery. Stability was of the utmost importance for St. Benedict and it countered effectively the sense of hopelessness and chaos that existed in secular society. Stability is the antidote to boredom which creates the illusion that there is a more exciting and interesting opportunity out there. Stability advocates against a deep-seated tendency in us to give up what we are doing because it is boring or requires too much effort. And given the fact that our lives are characterized by great mobility and a plethora of gadgets, the mundane becomes quite boring and interminable. Stability calls for obedience to God as manifested in our daily responsibilities. And often times, in these responsibilities we are called to be obedient to humans who are our superiors. St. Benedict tells us that we are obeying God in obeying them. In everyday life, our stability will manifest itself as consistent and dependable behavior in our relationships and responsibilities.

CONVERSION:

Conversion is the second vow that the Benedictines take. Through this attitude of conversion, we are always pointed in God's direction, always at God's beck and call, like Mary was. With her we say, "Behold the handmaid of the Lord." Conversion becomes eminently attractive, because God's total gift of Himself to us through Jesus undergirds our own desire to give ourselves totally to Him. When we are converted, we belong to God. Our focus is on God rather than on ourselves. Our surrender to God makes feasible our ability to be stable toward God in all our actions, and towards our fellow humans in all our relationships.

OBEDIENCE:

Jesus was obedient to His Father. Jesus always placed His Father before Himself. It was His immense pleasure to do so. Jesus also placed us before His very own life. It was His immense joy to lay down His life on our behalf. The only authentic way to express ourselves in our covenant relationship with God, who has given Himself to us in and through Jesus, is to be obedient to God in the minutest details of our lives, and to everyone else who is our religious superior, or supervisor at work, or spouse at home. Joyful and wholehearted obedience leads to true stability in our lives and is the finest expression of conversion.

SIMPLICITY:

The Benedictine way of life calls for doing the ordinary things of daily life with loving attention and reverence because they are God's desire for us. It behooves us to do them carefully and with thought. A deep awareness of God's loving presence in our lives is at the heart of an attitude of simplicity. We feel secure and deeply loved by Him. We are the abode of the Blessed Trinity. Consequently, we live and act in a spirit of calmness and joy. Such a spirit creates a transparency in us which leads to being uncomplicated and obtuse. Simplicity, therefore, is devoid of exaggeration, of a need to impress, of a desire to be better than others. Simplicity leads to making moderation a priority in our lives.

MODERATION:

St. Benedict was an astute assessor of the pitfalls in human behavior that affect the spiritual life. Excess in material possessions can lead to an obtuseness of spirit and lack of freedom to know and do God's will. On the other hand, struggling to have the necessities of life can also be an unhealthy preoccupation that has a negative impact on one's relationship with God. St.

Benedict desired that we live in a 'state of enough.' We need to keep this rule of conduct before us on a daily basis. Unfortunately, in our homes we can easily have much more than we need. We can mistakenly think that what we want is really what we need. When material excess has become part and parcel of our lives, our spirits get dimmed and become phlegmatic. The moderation that St. Benedict advocates, will lead to a better balance in one's life, a necessary platform to build a solid spiritual life.

BALANCE:

Moderation leads to balance in one's life. There is a well-known Latin phrase that expresses the essence of balance: 'In medio stat virtus.' Virtue, or the ability to do good freely, lies in moderation, or the ability to remain free of excesses, either too much or too little. Balance is an attitude that does not come naturally to us. Unfortunately, there is too much rushing from one task to another, multi-tasking because we allot insufficient time for our duties. Consequently, we are in a frenzy, or depressed, because we are feeling overwhelmed. Because of our inordinate attachments, we will tend towards doing too much or too little, towards having too much, towards placing ourselves before others. Balance is being in a state of consolation or pointed consistently in God's direction. When one is in balance, one has time for one's duties because one takes the time to do every duty well. Accordingly, there is purposefulness in one's actions throughout the day.

HOSPITALITY:

St. Benedict wanted his monks to treat everybody as 'the guest,' and that 'all guests should be welcomed as Christ." Even the stranger should be welcomed as Christ the guest. And according to the teachings of Jesus, even our enemy should be loved. At the heart of hospitality is our covenant relationship with Jesus. He has become one with us. We are His body, and He is the Head. We are the bride, and He is the bridegroom. We cannot, therefore, say that we love Jesus and hate His body/bride. Hence, every person, stranger and even enemy, should be welcomed as Christ.

SILENCE:

'Listen' is the first word of the Rule. To listen is to place the other ahead of us, treat the other as more important than ourselves, or else we will not be disposed toward the other in generous service. Such a disposition of being there for the other requires respect for the other as God's image and likeness. One will not be able to listen unless there is inner stillness in one's heart and mind. Lectio Divina or The Benedictine Method of Prayer helps very much in the development of listening to God and being receptive to His presence. Such prayer develops a lifestyle of humble service where the focus of one's attention and priority is on the other rather than on self, on God and the well-being of others. Silence calls for the understanding that one has got to march to a different drum beat if one is to have true peace and serenity. The values of the world which emphasize material possessions, honor, and power, lead to dissipation, unhappiness, and emptiness. Developing silence requires us to swim against the current; it calls for openness to the Holy Spirit to guide our lives and to make God our Center.

HUMILITY:

In Chapter 7 of his Rule, St. Benedict gives us 12 different steps in humility. These steps give us true insight into the holiness of St. Benedict and his understanding of discipleship. *The first step of humility is to keep the fear of God ever before one's eyes.* Such fear is reverence that the disciple experiences when being overwhelmed by God's love and forgiveness. The realization generates much gratitude and a sober appreciation of one's waywardness. Such awareness leads to developing this first and basic step in humility: keeping the fear of God ever before our eyes.

The second step of humility is that a man loves not his own will nor takes pleasure in the satisfaction of his desires; rather he does the will of Him who sent him. When there is covenant love and union, this second step in humility becomes a priority. The other rather than self becomes one's priority in life. Love of God and service of neighbor become more important and meaningful than pleasure and satisfaction of one's own desires.

The third step of humility is that a man submits to his superior in all obedience for the love of God: "He became obedient even to death." (Philippians 2:8) Total trust in God's providence undergirds this step of humility. Both in religious life and in the world, we will have others who are our superiors. Oftentimes we will be asked to do what is not to our liking, imputing ulterior motives to our superiors when we do not like to do what has been asked of us. Jesus and the saints tell us that we please God when we set aside our own wills and obey sincerely and generously the superior's directives.

The fourth step of humility is that "in this obedience under difficult, unfavorable, or even unjust conditions, his heart quietly embraces suffering and endures it without weakening or seeking escape." This step is the behavior of a disciple who is deeply united with his Master, Jesus. They have come to love everyone in Jesus, and therefore, as more significant to them than they are to themselves. Such love is sacrificial and covenant-like. Jesus loved us under, difficult, unfavorable, and unjust conditions. Paradoxically, the reign of God or righteousness (justice) will be well served and strengthened when a supposed injustice is being done to us.

The fifth step of humility is that "a man does not conceal from his abbot any sinful thoughts entering his heart, or any wrongs committed in secret, but rather confesses them humbly." St. Ignatius of Loyola has a similar expectation of his community known as the manifestation of conscience. All our saints emphasize the importance of accountability and transparency if one is to make progress in the spiritual life. Twelve step programs require such transparency towards the sponsor. Our sinfulness will convince us to live in the shadows. Accountability brings us into the light of God.

The sixth step of humility is that "a monk is content with the lowest and most menial treatment, and regards himself as a poor and worthless workman in whatever task he is given." Jesus loved us to the point of swapping places with us: He became sin so that we might become God's righteousness (2 Corinthians 5:21). We were more significant to Him that His very own life was to Him. St. Benedict wants us to be like our Master. So Jesus says in Luke 17:10: *"So should it be with you. When you have done all you have been commanded, say, 'We are unprofitable servants; we have done what we were obliged to do.'"*

The seventh step of humility is that "a man not only admits with his tongue but is also convinced in his heart that he is inferior to all and of less value." This step of humility is the result of a profound purification/transformation at the hands of the Holy Spirit, talked about by our saints like Saints Teresa of Avila and John of the Cross. The disciple has come to understand that everything in life, especially sharing in God's life and love is pure gift. An offshoot of this awareness is the realization that one has sinned grievously and been forgiven. The conviction grows that everyone else is better than he, and this is not the result of self-hatred but of humility.

The eighth step of humility is that "a monk does only what is endorsed by the common rule of the monastery and the example set by his superiors." This rule applies both to monks in the monastery and to family life. In both places there is a 'rule' that the right order of things establishes. We know what that rule is, because when we obey it, there is harmony and love and peace in the community/family. It is placing the common good above our own desires. When we choose to do our own thing, putting ourselves before the others, we create disharmony, turmoil, disturbance, and aid in the establishment of the wrong order of things. This step asks us to safeguard the common good of the community/family.

The ninth step of humility is that a monk controls his tongue and remains silent, not speaking unless asked a question." This step of humility is endorsing what James 3:6 says: *"The tongue is also a fire. It exists among our members as a world of malice, defiling the whole body and setting the entire course of our lives on fire, itself set on fire by Gehenna."* The Desert Fathers and Mothers insisted on guarding our thoughts and being vigilant against sinning through them because the spiritual life is won or lost depending on who rules your mind: your allegiance to evil or obedience to the Holy Spirit.

The tenth step of humility is that he is not given to ready laughter, for it is written: "Only a fool raises his voice in laughter." (Sirach 21:23) This step of humility is guarding against behavior that is boisterous and focused on making oneself the center of attention. It is not against laughter that expresses one's joy and gratitude.

The eleventh step of humility is that a monk speaks gently and without laughter, seriously and with becoming modesty, briefly and reasonable, but without raising his voice, as it is written: "A wise man is known by his few words." The eleventh step of humility continues the theme expressed in the tenth step. When a disciple is grounded in God, they are grounded in themselves. Their behavior does not draw attention to themselves.

The twelfth step of humility is that "a monk always manifests humility in his bearing no less than in his heart, so that it is evident… in all matters." This twelfth step is the embodiment of all the other steps in humility. A humble person truly reflects God's presence. The peace and joy of the Risen Lord is present in them.

THE SPIRITUALITY OF SAINT FRANCIS OF ASSISI

St. Francis of Assisi is probably the most well-known and beloved Catholic saint. He was born in Assisi, Umbria, in 1181 or 1182. He received some elementary education from the priests of St. George Church at Assisi. He was not diligent, and his literary accomplishments remained negligible. He helped his father, Pietro Bernardone, a wealthy cloth merchant, in the family business, but showed little inclination for a merchant's career. He was frivolous and fun loving and the center of the party. His parents indulged his whims and Francis lived a life of leisure and revelry. In spite of his penchant for loose living, Francis displayed an instinctive sympathy for the poor. When he was about twenty, the town of Assisi was in an armed skirmish against Perugia, a neighboring city. Francis was taken captive and held a prisoner for more than a year. A low fever during his imprisonment turned his thoughts towards God and eternity.

Upon his release, a yearning for the life of the spirit possessed him, and he gave himself to prayer. Thus began his spiritual awakening. On one occasion he was making a trip on horseback and drew near a leper. He was disgusted by this repulsive sight and wanted to flee the scene. But an urge came upon him. He dismounted from his horse, embraced the unfortunate man, and gave him all his money. Francis now was acting on the grace of his spiritual awakening. Soon after, he made a pilgrimage to St. Peter's Basilica in Rome. He was disappointed at the meager offerings that were being made at the tomb of St. Peter's. Prompted by the Holy Spirit, he emptied his wallet, and then exchanged his expensive clothing with a tattered mendicant.

Shortly thereafter, Francis was praying before an ancient crucifix, in the ruined chapel of San Damiano, in Assisi. He heard the Crucified Christ speak to him and say, "Go, Francis, and repair my house which you see is falling to ruin." He took the summons literally. In response, he took some expensive drapery from his father's silk store without his permission, and sold it to procure money to build the chapel. Pietro Bernardone reacted violently to his son's gesture. In fear of his father, Francis hid himself for a month near the chapel of San Damiano. To make matters worse, the pastor would not accept the gold that Francis offered him for the repair of San Damiano. When Francis finally met his father, there was a severe altercation. His father took him to the Bishop of Assisi to settle the matter. He wanted the gold returned to him, and to disinherit his son. Francis was disowned by his father, and treated as a madman by his fellow townspeople. That is when he wedded himself to Lady Poverty, and said that from then on he had God as his Father. In doing so, he experienced the freedom that came from the total surrender of all worldly goods, honor, and privileges. In offering himself to God, Francis became totally free for God. He finally re-built the chapel of San Damiano and two other chapels. He engaged in works of mercy, especially tending to the lepers. In time he realized that Jesus was asking him to re-build the spiritual structure of the Church, to pastor souls.

In February 1208, Francis received a special summons from Jesus through the gospel reading at Mass which struck him very personally. Jesus was commissioning the Twelve in Matthew 10:7-14: *"As you go, make this proclamation: 'The kingdom of heaven is at hand.' Cure the sick, raise the dead, cleanse lepers, drive out demons. Without cost you are to give. Do not take gold or silver or copper for your belts; no sack for the journey, or a second tunic, or sandals, or walking stick... Whoever will not receive you or listen to your words – go outside that house or town and shake the dust from your feet."* Francis took this summons literally. He saw himself as needing to give everything up, to announce the kingdom of God, and exhort sinners to repentance. He gave up everything and began wearing the coarse woolen tunic of the poorest peasants, tied around him with a knotted rope. His example of poverty, simplicity, and selfless service drew others to him. As a small band of disciples, they began to ask God what He wanted of them. On three occasions they opened the Scriptures at random in the church of St. Nicholas, one of the three that Francis had rebuilt. Each time the Scripture passage exhorted them to leave everything behind and follow Christ. They forthwith went to the public square in Assisi and gave away everything they owned, and made poverty their Rule of life. Before long many were attracted to their way of life and began joining them.

After Francis put together a rudimentary Rule of Life, he and his companions set out for Rome to seek the approval of the Holy See. The Bishop of Assisi was in Rome and he commended Francis and his companions to the Holy See. At first Pope Innocent III was not favorable towards Francis. However, through a dream where he saw the poor man of Assisi upholding the tottering Church of St. John Lateran, he was persuaded to give Francis permission to start his community of Friars Minor, and to preach repentance wherever they went. Before they left their audience with the Pope, they all received the tonsure. Francis himself was ordained a deacon some time later.

Upon their return to Assisi, Francis and his companions came to be known as Friars Minor. It is not clear why Francis wanted his community to be knows as Friars Minor. Some think it is because they were identifying themselves with the minor or lower classes. Others believe that the last judgement in Matthew had to do with it: *"Amen, I say to you, whatever you did for one of these least brothers of mine, you did for me."* (Matthew 25:40) The name was a perpetual reminder to them of the need to be humble. In about 1211 they found a permanent home near Assisi through the generosity of the Benedictines of Monte Subasio who gave them the chapel of St. Mary of the Angels or the Porziuncola, the same chapel where the gospel reading at Mass so stirred him. It was there that the first Franciscan convent was formed. It consisted of the erection of a few small huts made from wattle, straw, and mud and enclosed by a hedge. This first convent became the cradle of the Franciscan Order, the Caput et Mater Ordinis (the Head and Mother of the Order). From here the friars went in pairs to the surrounding countryside to preach repentance to Jesus Christ. They were filled with joy, and called themselves the Lord's minstrels. The world was their home: they slept in haylofts, grottoes, church porches, and labored with the peasants in their fields. When they were not hired, they begged for their livelihood. Soon their influence spread far and wide, and men of different grades of life began joining their ranks.

During the Lent of 1212, Francis was greeted with some unexpected news. Clare, a young heiress of Assisi asked to be allowed to embrace the new life that Francis had started. She was moved by his preaching at the church of St. George where Francis had received his initial education. Francis received her, her sister, St. Agnes, and a band of other pious women to the new life of poverty, penance, and seclusion, by cutting off their hair and clothing them with the religious habit. They were eventually established at San Damiano, in a dwelling near the chapel that Francis had rebuilt with his own hands. Once again, thanks to the generosity of the Benedictines, this chapel was given to Francis, and it became the first monastery of the Second Franciscan Order of Poor Ladies, now known as Poor Clares.

Francis had a great desire to convert the Saracens (Muslims). He made two unsuccessful attempts to do so. In the autumn of 1212 he sailed for Syria and was shipwrecked on the coast of present-day Slavonia. Instead, the following spring of 1213 he devoted himself to evangelizing Central Italy. In 1214, Francis made a second attempt to convert the Muslims and set out for Morocco via Spain. However, in Spain he came down with a severe illness which forced him to return to Italy.

Between 1214 and his death in 1226, Francis' Order of Friars Minor expanded rapidly all over Europe, spreading through Italy, into France, Spain, Germany, and even England. Francis wanted to evangelize France but was dissuaded by Cardinal Ugolino who had been made the Protector of the Order. Instead, Francis preached before the Pope and cardinals at the Lateran. During this visit to the Eternal City, between 1217 and 1218, Francis is reputed to have met St. Dominic, Founder of the Dominican Order. During 1218, Francis went on missionary tours of Italy. He was a very powerful evangelist. Wherever he went, people followed him, eager to listen to the Good News. Francis preached in marketplaces, from church steps, and outdoors. His exhortations were short, compelling, and from the heart. People brought their sick to Francis, wanting him to pray with them, lay hands on them, and heal them. While he was preaching at Camara, a small village near Assisi, the whole congregation was so moved by his words, that as a group they asked to be admitted into his Order. To accede to this request and similar ones in the future, Francis instituted his Third Order of the Brothers and Sisters of Penance. It was meant specifically for those in the world who could not leave their homes and their various avocations. Francis prescribed certain duties for these tertiaries: they were not to carry arms, take oaths, or engage in lawsuits, etc. 1221 is considered to be the accepted year when the Third Order was established.

At the second General Chapter in May 1219, Francis, still keen on realizing his dream of evangelizing the Muslims, assigned separate missions to each of his foremost disciples in this regard. He himself chose the disastrous Fifth Crusade that was being waged against al-Kamil, the Sultan of Egypt and a nephew of the great Muslim warrior Saladin. He crossed enemy lines to gain an audience with the Sultan who was camped on the banks of the River Nile. Francis hoped to bring about peace by converting al-Kamil, as he was opposed to warfare. The encounter was very peaceful. The Sultan regarded Francis highly. However, his efforts were unsuccessful to convert al-Kamil. Francis came away with the clear understanding that Christians should live in peace with Muslims.

Francis was gone from Italy for about a year, during which time he visited the Holy Land, and obtained for the friars the presence that they still retain as guardians of the holy sites. While he was away, several crises arose within the Order. Francis had appointed Matthew of Narni and Gregory of Naples as the two Vicars General of the Order in his absence. They summoned a chapter, and among other practices, sought to impose new fasts upon the friars, more severe than the rule required. And Cardinal Ugolino, the Protector of the Order, conferred on the Poor Clares a written rule that was the one followed by the Benedictine nuns. Brother Philip, whom Francis had put in charge of the interests of the Poor Clares, accepted this imposition. As if all of this wasn't enough, John of Capella, one of the saint's first companions, brought together a large number of lepers, men and women, with the idea of forming them into a new religious order. He had even set out for Rome to seek approval for the rule he had drawn up for these unfortunate people. The final nail in Francis' coffin of woes was the rumor that he had died while in the East.

When Francis arrived in Venice in July 1220 along with Brother Elias, a general feeling of unease and unrest prevailed among the friars. Compounding all these woes was the fact that the Order was in transition. The simple, childlike, and joyful ways that had marked the Franciscan movement at the start, were gradually disappearing. The heroic and radical poverty that had been practiced by Francis and his first companions became less easy and desirable as the friars increased in number rapidly. Cardinal Ugolino, who later on became Pope Gregory IX, was one of the chief architects in bringing about the lofty ideals of Francis within range and practice. Francis saw all these changes taking place upon his return.

The Order held another Chapter in 1220 or 1221 at the Porziuncola. About 5,000 friars showed up for it. At this Chapter, Francis was disheartened by the tendency of many friars to relax the rigors of the rule. He felt unsuited in his organizing abilities to govern with all these changes taking place. So he resigned as General of the Order in favor of Peter of Cattaneo. But Peter died in less than a year and was succeeded by Brother Elias who remained the vicar general of the Order until Francis' death in 1226.

In the last five years of his life on earth, Francis sought to teach his friars by personal example. When he passed through Bologna on his return from the East, he saw that the convent was called the 'House of the Friars' and a school was attached to it. He saw clearly that times were changing. As for his attitude toward study, he had desired that his monks have enough theological knowledge that was in keeping with the mission of the Order which was to preach by example. He therefore regarded the accumulation of books as contrary to the poverty his friars professed. He also resisted the desire for mere book knowledge which was a prevalent tendency in his time. In his mind, the spirit of prayer was based on simplicity of life on which his ideals were based.

The tradition of celebrating Christmas with a crib or crèche in church or in our homes goes back to 1223 when Francis conceived the idea of celebrating the Birth of Our Lord in a novel manner. He is the one who introduced the Crib in a church at Greccio. From then on the tradition and devotion of having the Crib in our churches and homes became popular.

In early August, 1224, Francis retired to La Verna along with three companions to keep a forty day fast. He always had a deep devotion to the Crucified Christ. During these days of retreat, the Passion of Christ became the overriding theme of his prayer. Around the feast of the Exaltation of the Cross (September 14), as he was praying on the mountain side, Francis beheld a vision of the seraph. This was followed by the stigmata: the five wounds of the crucified Christ were imprinted on his body. Brother Leo was with him and recorded the miracle in an account that is preserved at Assisi. After he received the stigmata, Francis suffered increasing pains throughout his frail body, already broken by continual mortification. In the last months of his life, he was worn out and exhausted. His eyesight failed him to the point where he was almost completely blind. In September 1225, Francis paid a last visit to St. Clare at San Damiano. They prepared a little hut of reeds in the garden for him. It was there that he composed his 'Canticle of the Sun.' Between 1225 and 1226, Francis received medical treatment for his eyes. His eyesight improved to some extent. In April 1226, Francis was moved to Cortona where he dictated his last testament, which he described as a 'reminder, a warning, and an exhortation.' He exhorted his friars to remain faithful to obedience to superiors holding the place of God, literal observance of the Rule without gloss and exaggeration, especially regarding poverty, enjoining the solemn duty of manual labor on all the friars. In July 1226, Francis' health took a turn for the worse. He was brought to Assisi and carried to his favorite Porziuncula where he first began his foundation. On his way there, he invoked a blessing upon Assisi. His prayer expressed gratitude for the change that had taken place in the city and among its inhabitants. Whereas formerly it was a dwelling place of wicked men given to evil ways, God in His infinite mercy and goodness had transformed it into a place where the people now acknowledged God in truth and gave glory to His holy Name. Assisi had become a place where Christians were edified by the holy life and earnest gospel teaching present there. Francis died in 1226 at the age of 44, and was canonized in 1228. Before he died he founded three Orders. His imprint on history is the men and women who identify with his vision in the Franciscan way of life.

THE SPIRITUALITY OF SAINT FRANCIS:

St. Francis had some unique spiritual traits that show us how greatly transformed he was at the hands of the Holy Spirit. He was known to be downright sincere, and had the simplicity of a child. When the guardian of the community insisted that he have a fox skin sewn under his worn out tunic to provide some warmth, the saint consented only if another skin of the same size was sewn outside for all to see. His motto was never to hide anything from men that was known to God. His quote was, "What a man is in the sight of God, so much he is and no more." This was a saying that passed into the Imitation of Christ which was produced in the Fifteenth century.

St. Francis was unswerving in following an ideal. He always sought the truth. His biographer Celano, who was a friar himself, says that Francis' "dearest desire so long as he lived, was ever to seek among wise and simple, perfect and imperfect, the means to walk in the way of truth." For St. Francis, love was the greatest of all truths. Hence, he always displayed a deep sense of responsibility towards his fellow humans.

The love of Christ and Him crucified permeated the whole of Francis' spirituality. He tried to imitate Jesus as literally as he could in his daily life. The distinctive mark of his spirituality was his heroic imitation of Christ's poverty. After money, St. Francis detested discord and divisions. He was well known as a peace-maker. In his opinion, the duty of a servant of God was to lift up the hearts of men and move them to spiritual gladness.

St. Francis had great compassion for those who sinned as evidenced in his advice given to the Minister of one of his houses who wanted to retire to a hermitage because he was dealing with difficult community members: "I speak to you, as I can, concerning the state of your soul. You should accept as a grace all those things which deter you from loving the Lord God and whoever has become an impediment to you, whether they are brothers or others, even if they lay hands on you."

St. Francis also wrote a letter to Saint Anthony of Padua. After joining the Order he was asked to teach the brothers. Anthony first wanted permission of St. Francis. Among other things, this is what Francis wrote: "I, Brother Francis send wishes of health to Brother Anthony, my bishop. It pleases me that you teach sacred theology to the brothers, as long as in the words of the Rule you 'do not extinguish the Spirit of prayer and devotion' with study of this kind."

St. Francis, pray for us!

THE INTERIOR CASTLE OF ST. TERESA OF AVILA

(All quotes are taken from "The Collected Works of St. Teresa of Avila, translated by Kieran Kavanaugh, O.C.D. and Otilio Rodriguez, O.C.D.)

INTRODUCTION:

St. Teresa of Avila was born in 1515 and died in 1582. Her feast day is celebrated on October 15. The Church proclaimed Saints Teresa of Avila and Catherine of Siena the first women *Doctors of the Church* in 1970. St. Teresa's writings on prayer are unparalleled, and one of her favorite prayers for many years was the *Our Father*. Through it she was raised to the heights of contemplation despite numerous distractions, much travel, and diversified duties in her efforts to reform the Order of Mount Carmel, called the Discalced Carmelites. Despite poor health and a host of spiritual challenges, she was mainly responsible for the reform and expansion of the Carmelites throughout Spain. She rebuilt the Order at a time when laxity and an easy lifestyle permeated the convents and monasteries.

St. Teresa was a wise and practical woman who was extraordinarily gifted in explaining simply the highest degrees of prayer and union with God. She assures us that those who practice prayer faithfully will receive all they ask beyond their greatest hopes and expectations. Shortly after writing *The Book of Her Life* for her confessor, St. Teresa wrote *The Way of Perfection* at the request of her nuns who were eager to learn about prayer and contemplation. Toward the end of her life, after she had experienced both the spiritual betrothal and spiritual marriage, St. Teresa wrote *The Interior Castle*, giving us her own panoramic view of her relationship with God, from the lower stages to the highest. St. Teresa's gift is her ability to write of that relationship and to attract us to explore the possibility of having that same involvement. This reflection makes an attempt to offer the wisdom offered in *The Interior Castle*.

THE FIRST DWELLING PLACES:

St. Teresa has a very definite starting point when one is talking about entering into a serious life of prayer. There has to be an honest and deliberate effort to root out sins, imperfections and disordered attachments which lead to dissipation and desolation. These are movements that draw us away from God and leave us lukewarm. The reason is that true prayer is the honest expression of a total commitment to Jesus in a covenant relationship with Him. Any meaningful relationship with Jesus can only be on His terms, as we are entering into covenant relationship with our holy, loving, and amazing God. Any form of self-centeredness, where the emphasis is on self-aggrandizement rather than on humble discipleship, will destroy the relationship, or at best leave it tepid. This starting point was based on St. Teresa's own experience and journey. She had joined the Carmelite Order at the age of nineteen. It took her twenty long years before she arrived at her starting point of living her relationship with God with a forthright commitment to avoiding all deliberate sin.

In her first Three Dwelling Places, the saint describes in sufficient detail how the beginner, even though in the state of grace, can and must emerge from a whole web of petty faults if their relationship with God is to become meaningful and move into any great depth. She offers us the image of the soul as being God's dwelling place with many rooms or mansions. God dwells in the heart of a person's being as we are indeed the image and likeness of God. The journey takes us from the outermost rooms to the room where God dwells. Most of us choose to live outside of ourselves, immersed completely in the world and its values that are contradictory to the spirit and teachings of Jesus. Consequently, we are strangers to ourselves and to God.

In the First Dwelling Places, the relationship of the beginner with God is tenuous at best. The beginner is living on the periphery of their authentic self. While they have entered into God's dwelling place in their souls, they are still immersed in the things of the world. In fact they have contaminated themselves by bringing in the contrary values of the world. While they are conscientious and hard-working, their world revolves around their dreams and goals which occupy all their energies and passion. Too many things entice and distract them, and thus prevent them from taking the time to search for the true light. Consequently, the divine light scarcely illuminates their lives and consciousness. They live in a permanent spiritual fog. God is kept at the periphery of their lives. They are so involved in worldly things, and so absorbed with its possessions, honor, or business affairs, that they are unable to satisfy their good and holy desires. If the beginner is to become a serious follower, they must leave behind the spirit of the world which emphasizes their glorification at all costs, or else they will not proceed into the Second Dwelling Places.

What kind of prayer does a beginner at this stage do? Because the beginner is still immersed in the affairs of the world which promote their own aggrandizement, their prayer will tend to be superficial and ritualistic. They will pray on occasion. They will go through their religious observances dutifully, albeit perfunctorily. To help such beginners enter into the deeper recesses of their soul where the Trinity dwells, St. Teresa emphasizes the necessity of practicing prayer and reflection that *focuses on love and an honest relationship with God.* She valued thoughtful reflection that moved the heart and connected with God: *"A prayer in which a person is not aware of whom he is speaking to, what he is asking, who it is who is asking and of whom, I do not call prayer however much the lips move."* (TIC – 1:1: 7) The Gospels are a fruitful source of meditative prayer as they offer the most profound revelation into the different mysteries of Trinitarian Life and God's Plan of Salvation.

So for prayer there are no complicated steps. It is love, not reasoning that is primary. *"If you would progress a long way on this road and ascend to the Mansions of your desire, the important thing is not to think much, but to love much."* (TIC – 4:1:7) She offers the same advice to Don Antonio in a letter where she advised him not to think a great deal, nor worry about meditation; rather to keep occupying himself all the time with the praise of the Lord. To summarize then, a beginner in the First Dwelling Places would have to work on developing a habit of praying regularly, learning to pray from the heart with as much honesty and reverence towards God, to avoid sin and its occasions and move towards repentance, to consciously be present to God and reject values opposed to Jesus and His teachings.

THE SECOND DWELLING PLACES:

The Second Dwelling Places are set apart for those who have taken some first steps in the practice of prayer. They have become more receptive to the promptings and invitations being offered to them by the Holy Spirit. Often at this stage, such promptings are given to them through external resources, such as books, sermons, retreats, spiritual friendships, and trials that life brings everyone. Beginners in the Second Dwelling Places are making progress. They are pointed in God's direction but are still far from the destination. They are still engaged in worldly pursuits, both trying to give them up and still clinging to them. They see imperfectly through fogged spiritual lenses. Nevertheless they are making progress. They would characterize their relationship with God as becoming more personal. They know that God is calling them ceaselessly. God appeals to them in various ways, through conversations with good and holy persons, sermons, retreats, inspirational spiritual reading, sickness and trials, and insight and consolation from the Holy Spirit during prayer. They are able to hear God now whereas in the First Dwelling Places they were both deaf and resistant.

However, they feel a certain restlessness and unease towards God because they are still kicking against the goad. The Second Dwelling places are a battleground for the soul of the beginner. *The conflict is between the forces and values of the world, on the one hand, and the call to discipleship and union with God, on the other.* The world continues to exert an enormous pull. Earthly pleasures remain attractive and still have an air of permanence. There is an inordinate clinging to family and friends, and to their present lifestyle. Being esteemed in the eyes of the world is still very important to them. Entering into a significant relationship with God conjures up unreasonable fears of having to give up or be stripped of everything that they know and love. Consequently, there is almost a sense of doom that they imagine will come upon them. So they vacillate and beef up the argument that it is much wiser to return to the First Dwelling Places rather than embark on this uphill climb for God. After all, in the past they did not seem to be dissatisfied and restless as they now experience themselves. The battle has been joined as well by God. The Holy Spirit's tug is likewise felt in many ways. Their reason tells them clearly how mistaken the world's values are as they are based on deceit and camouflage. They have witnessed the spiritual growth that has taken place in them. And they now have the conviction that their surety lies only in God! Thus their wills are inclined towards loving God and pressing on to leave behind the world and all its falsehoods, and embrace the person and values of Jesus.

What then is the advice Saint Teresa offers a beginner in the Second Dwelling Places? Given that a beginner's foundations in the spiritual life are still weak, they should avoid any close association with mediocre people, and especially with those who are opposed to the values of Christ. Rather, they should take every opportunity and make every endeavor to associate with good people, especially with those who have advanced into the Dwelling Places nearer the center of their souls where the divine Majesty dwells. Secondly, they need to understand that any serious discipleship requires the embrace of the cross along with the suffering Christ. Life brings with it a fair share of trials and tribulations. It is not enough to be resigned to one's fate or hand that has been dealt. There must be a generous and purposeful acceptance of hardships and dryness in prayer and circumstances of life, as they are truly blessings to purify the beginner of self-centeredness and pride. Thirdly, the beginner needs to insist on being faithful on a daily basis to doing God's will as it manifests itself in everyday living. Union with God comes from doing God's will unstintingly, like Mary who was God's perfect handmaid. Fourthly, at this stage of the journey it is easy to get discouraged and start backsliding. St. Teresa encourages the beginner not to lose heart when they fall, but rather to continue making serious efforts toward making progress. Learning to ask and receive forgiveness, and act upon one's repentance, is an important spiritual practice in the Second Dwelling Places. Fifthly, there is the need to exercise fidelity to prayer. We cannot enter heaven without first entering our own souls. It is only prayer that will bring us into God's Embrace.

THE THIRD DWELLING PLACES:

There are many Christians in the world who reach the Third Dwelling Places. There are several positive characteristics that would describe a person at this stage. These beginners are advancing in the spiritual life. God has an important place in their lives. They are taking Jesus and His teachings seriously. As a result, they love to pray, and prayer is neither a burden nor an obligation. They converse with God throughout the day and this is something they love to do and enjoy. In many instances, they have the awareness that God dwells within them. They guard against venial sin and long not to offend God. They understand that to persevere in prayer, with the struggle involved, is to make progress. They work on developing spiritual practices in their lives, like guarding their senses, using their time well, practicing charity toward others, maintaining balance in the use of speech and dress, and in the management of their household. They are good, practicing Christians, and in the thinking of St. Teresa, the Lord will not deny them entrance into the final dwelling places if they so desire.

However, in the *Third Dwelling Places, human nature is still an oppressive burden on the spirit.* Like the rich young man in the gospel, they could turn away from the requirements for becoming perfect. They love God very much, but they still want to do so conveniently, on their terms. Their spiritual self-image is very important to them. However, any threat to their wealth or honor or status quo will quickly uncover their attachments to these false gods. They tend to be judgmental and are easily shocked by the faults of others. In prayer they expect to have consolations as part of their normal experience, as their spiritual image is important to them. So they tend to get discouraged and distraught by dryness in prayer.

The advancing beginner in the Third Dwelling Places finds more consolation in the spiritual life and things of God than they do in material comforts and all the attendant distractions. However, they are still straddling the fence. They are not yet willing to burn their bridges. In prayer, therefore, they seldom receive the deeper, more satisfying peace and quiet of contemplation. However, occasionally they will receive a more profound experience of God which is an invitation to prepare better for what lies ahead. St. John of the Cross was of the opinion that the transition from here to contemplative prayer was short. St. Teresa of Avila, on the other hand, thought that the transition takes long. It is important for someone in the Third Dwelling Places to be able to talk and listen to someone who is free of the world's illusions. In other words, they would do well to associate with someone who is a contemplative.

How does one pray in the Third Dwelling Places? The advancing beginner's prayer will still be discursive, with an emphasis on reverence and honesty. The tendency will be to speak less and listen more to God. *An active focusing on the indwelling presence is the best way to prepare for the Prayer of Quiet.* The advice given by Saints Teresa and John of the Cross to practice the active night of Senses is especially true for someone who is in the Third Dwelling Places and is being invited into contemplative prayer.

THE FOURTH DWELLING PLACES:

The first Three Dwelling Places take up about 30 percent of *The Interior Castle.* The last Four take up about 70 percent of the text, and are almost entirely about prayer in its infused stages. St. Teresa devotes three chapters to the Fourth Dwelling Places because she believes that very many beginners enter into the initial stage of infused or contemplative prayer. Another reason for writing in some detail is that there is a definite movement from discursive prayer which is the human way of doing things, to infused prayer which clearly is supernatural, given to us by the Holy Spirit directly. The transition can be bewildering, as the beginner will not be able to make sense of what is going on. The earlier criteria by which they judged prayer don't seem to be working. While they seem to be backsliding, paradoxically, their longing for God has intensified. Commonly, people do not know how to effect the transition from the one to the other. At this stage, wise spiritual direction is crucial.

How then to explain the difference between discursive prayer and infused contemplation? St. Teresa made a distinction between consolations (*contentos*) and spiritual delight (*gustos*) in order to explain infused prayer or contemplation. Consolations (*contentos*) in prayer are the result of the exercise of our human faculties like the mind, memory, imagination, and will. While the emphasis is on human activity, the experience is orchestrated by the Holy Spirit and ends in God. Because these consolations have a human dimension to them, there is the danger that we might want to extend their duration. Also, because they are mixed with our own emotions, they could affect us bodily as well. Consolations can also come to us in the course of our daily lives. For instance, we experience much joy and happiness at the sight of a good friend whom we have not seen for many years. St. Teresa tells us that consolations are the experience in prayer of disciples who are in the first Three Dwelling Places. They have these devout feelings as they work with the intellect, memory, and imagination, engaging in discursive thought and meditation (TIC – IV:1:4-6). Spiritual delight (*gustos*), on the other hand, has its beginning in God and overflows into our human nature. The Holy Spirit infuses this divine knowledge directly into our souls, bypassing, so to speak, our human faculties. In other words, human activity cannot produce spiritual delight. Consolations (*contentos*), then, are the result of God's grace working in and through our human faculties and efforts. Spiritual delight (*gustos*), on the other hand, is received directly through the action of the Holy Spirit and not through human efforts. The action is that of the Holy Spirit. The disciple receives the infusion passively or receptively.

St. Teresa offers a contrasting image of water to tell the difference between consolation and spiritual delight. In the case of consolation, the water comes from far away through canals and aqueducts. There is much effort and ingenuity involved, implying the need for human effort in cooperation with God's grace. In the case of spiritual delight, on the other hand, the source of water is right there. "*The trough fills without any noise. If the spring is abundant, as is this one we are speaking about, the water overflows once the trough is filled, forming a large stream. There is no need of any skill, nor does the building of aqueducts have to continue; but water is always flowing from the spring.*" (TIC – IV:2:3)

Spiritual delight or infused contemplation, therefore, originates in God. The Holy Spirit produces spiritual delight "*with the greatest peace and quiet and sweetness in the very interior part of ourselves. I don't know from where or how, nor is that happiness and delight experienced, as are earthly consolations, in the heart. I mean there is no similarity at the beginning, for afterward the delight fills everything; this water overflows through all the dwelling places and faculties until reaching the body. That is why I said that it begins in God and ends in ourselves.*" (TIC – IV:2:4) Spiritual delight cannot be imagined by us, because our efforts cannot acquire it. As St. Teresa tells us, "*The very experience of it makes us realize that it is not of the same metal as we ourselves but fashioned from the purest gold of the divine wisdom. Here, in my opinion, the faculties are not united but absorbed and looking as though in wonder at what they are."* (TIC – IV:2:6)

While infused prayer is a gift that God wishes to give us, such a gift is best left to His wisdom and providence to dispense. St. Teresa tells us how we can obtain such a favor. Above all we need humility, and the saint offers us several signs to tell us whether we have this humility. The first sign is to realize that we do not *"deserve these favors and spiritual delights from the Lord or that you will receive them in your lifetime."* (TIC – IV:2:9) She asks us to always place God's will and wisdom ahead of our own aspirations and ambitions. In her opinion, the best way to receive these favors is by not seeking them or striving after them. Such an attitude brings about true humility that is the hallmark of authentic discipleship: we learn to love God without self-interest; we realize that there is a lack of humility in thinking that we deserve such great favors "for our miserable services;" thirdly, given that we are sinners, we should be more interested in imitating the crucified Lord rather than in having spiritual delights; fourthly, the Lord doesn't need to give us these signal favors for our salvation; the fifth reason is that such favors cannot be acquired. There is no use in exhausting ourselves because no amount of human effort will bring this about. This spiritual delight (water) is given to whomever God wills to give it. And often God gives it when the soul is least thinking of it.

It is not we who decide when this change shall take place. It is God who gives this new communion, and thus it is He who takes the initiative. As you can see, even someone who is beginning to experience infused contemplation will be confused and even distraught, because they will simply not be able to make sense of the transition, let alone deem it as being very good and originating in God. What about someone who has not experienced even the beginnings of infused contemplation? Should they read anything on mystical prayer? St. Teresa believes that it could still benefit them as the Holy Spirit could whet their appetite and make them aware of what God has in store for them.

In the Fourth Dwelling Places, St. Teresa distinguishes two kinds of infused prayer, the initial *"recollection,"* and the *"Prayer of Quiet."* Before the latter is given, almost always one will experience recollection, an infused and gentle awareness given by God and not produced by human effort. It doesn't come to us when we want it, but rather when God gives it to us. St. Teresa holds that *"when His Majesty grants it, He does so to persons who are already beginning to despise the things of the world… for He calls such persons especially so that they might be attentive to interior matters. So I believe that if we desire to make room for His Majesty, He will give not only this but more, and give it to those whom He begins to call to advance further."* (TIC – IV:3:3) Then she goes on to say that such recollection helps the soul to remain attentive and aware of what the Lord is working in it rather than striving to engage in discourse. The imagination will continue to remain active, and even distractive, because it will only be quiet when God begins to absorb the soul. St. Teresa is cautioning against the practice of stopping the imagination from engaging in any activity. Rather it is important to focus on awakening love in one's heart. She offers salutary advice: *"In this work of the spirit the one who thinks less and has less desire to act does more… The soul does become quite a fool when it tries to induce this prayer, and it is left much drier; and the imagination perhaps becomes more restless through the effort made not to think of anything."* (TIC – IV:3:5)

St. Teresa also tells us what our approach should be in Recollection and the Prayer of Quiet: *"And without any effort or noise the soul should strive to cut down the rambling of the intellect – but not suspend either it or the mind (imagination); it is good to be aware that one is in God's presence and of who God is. If what it feels within itself absorbs it, well and good… Let the soul enjoy it without any endeavors other than some loving words, for even though we may not try in this prayer to go without thinking of anything, I know that often the intellect will be suspended, even though for only a very brief moment."* (TIC – IV:3:7) The Prayer of Recollection is much less intense than the Prayer of Quiet. It is the transition to the Prayer of Quiet. Hence, in the Prayer of Recollection, meditation, or the work of the intellect, must not be set aside. One will notice however that the intellect works at a much slower pace with a reduction of reflection and images, and an increased desire to listen and be receptive to the Presence of God. It can be likened to a sense of life being meaningful only in God, with everything else becoming secondary. The senses and external things slowly lose their hold upon the person. The beginnings of infused prayer occur in the Fourth Dwelling Places during Recollection and before the Prayer of Quiet. There is no absorption in God; rather, the inner person is serenely drawn to be occupied with Him.

In the Prayer of Quiet, *"the mind (imagination) wanders from one extreme to the other, like a fool unable to rest in anything… The will has such deep rest in its God that the clamor of the intellect is a terrible bother to it. There is no need to pay any attention to this clamor, for doing so would make the will lose much of what it enjoys. But one should leave the intellect and go surrender oneself into the arms of love, for His Majesty will teach the soul what it must do at that point. Almost everything lies in finding oneself unworthy of so great a good and in being occupied with giving thanks."* (TIC – IV:3:8) At the moment this prayer is given, the soul is captive and is not free to love anything but God. In her *Book of Life, chapter 15,* St. Teresa says, *"The soul is so satisfied with God that as long as the recollection lasts, the quiet and calm are not lost since the will is united with God even though the two faculties (intellect and memory) are distracted; in fact, little by little the will brings the intellect and the memory back to recollection. Even though the will may not be totally absorbed, it is so well occupied, without knowing how, that no matter what efforts the other two faculties make, they cannot take away its contentment and joy."*

During the *Prayer of Quiet* some distractions are entirely possible, for while the memory and intellect may be somewhat stilled, they are not "completely lost," that is, absorbed in God. The person senses that they are close to the Lord and know Him better, but with no clear ideas. The quiet is felt in differing degrees at different times. It may last even for a day or two. It follows then that one can enjoy this interior awareness even though one is engaged in exterior activities that require the attention of the intellect.

In her writings St. Teresa tells us about numerous benefits that a disciple derives from contemplative prayer. Regarding the *Prayer of Quiet*, in *The Book of Her Life, Chapter 14*, she says, *"it makes the virtues grow incomparably better than in the previous degree of prayer, for the soul is now ascending above its misery and receiving a little knowledge of the delights of glory... it begins soon to lose its craving for earthly things – and little wonder!... He is so close it no longer needs to send Him messengers but can speak with Him itself and not be shouting since He is so near that when it merely moves its lips, He understands it... this delight (as contrasted with earthly delights) seems to fill the void that through our sins we have caused in the soul. This satisfaction takes place in its very intimate depths, and the soul doesn't know where the satisfaction comes from or how, nor frequently does it know what to do or what to desire or what to ask for."*

In TIC – IV:3:9, St. Teresa lists several other benefits as well: *"the soul is not as tied down as it was before in things pertaining to the service of God, but has much more freedom. Thus in not being constrained by the fear of hell (because although there is even greater fear of offending God it loses servile fear here), this soul is left with great confidence that it will enjoy Him... The fear it used to have of trials it now sees to be tempered. Its faith is more alive; it knows that if it suffers trials for God, His Majesty will give it the grace to suffer them with patience. Sometimes it even desires them because there also remains a strong will to do something for God. Since its knowledge of God's grandeur grows, it considers itself to be more miserable. Because it has already experienced spiritual delight from God, it sees that worldly delights are like filth. It finds itself withdrawing from them little by little, and it is more master of itself for so doing. In sum, there is an improvement in all the virtues. It will continue to grow if it doesn't turn back now to offending God; because if it does, then everything will be lost however high on the summit the soul may be. Nor should it be understood that if God grants this favor once or twice to a soul all these good effects will be caused. It must persevere in receiving them, for in this perseverance lies all our good."*

THE FIFTH DWELLING PLACES:

St. Teresa devotes four chapters to the Fifth Dwelling Places in *The Interior Castle*. In the first chapter she thinks that many are invited into the varying degrees of union with God, described in the Fifth Dwelling Places. In the Saint's opinion there are very few who never enter this mansion, presuming that they are in the Fourth Dwelling Places. Some enter more, others less. Most gain at least some admittance into these rooms.

However, only a few will experience some of the things that she talks about in the Fifth Dwelling Places. While this grace of union in prayer is wholly the work of the Holy Spirit, we can do our part to dispose ourselves to receive this grace. In order to purchase this pearl of great price, we need to ask for the grace to keep nothing back from God, little or great. When we have truly given God our all, and the Holy Spirit will let us know this, there is no more certain sign, whether or not we have reached the prayer of union.

The best way to describe the next stage or the Fifth Dwelling Places in the contemplative process of greater and deeper union with God is in the Saint's own words: *"Don't think this union is some kind of dreamy state like the one I mentioned before. I say "dreamy state" because it only seems that the soul is asleep; for neither does it really think it is asleep nor does it feel awake. There is no need here to use any technique to suspend the mind since all the faculties are asleep in this state – and truly asleep – to the things of the world and to ourselves. As a matter of fact, during the time that the union lasts the soul is left as though without its senses, for it has no power to think even if it wants to… In sum, it is like one who in every respect has died to the world so as to live more completely in God. Thus the death is a delightful one, an uprooting from the soul of all the operations it can have while being in the body."* (TIC – V:1:4)

CONTRAST BETWEEN THE PRAYER OF QUIET AND PRAYER OF UNION:

There is a definite contrast between the Prayer of Quiet and the Prayer of Union. In the Prayer of Union, *"the intellect would want to be occupied in understanding something of what is felt. And since the soul does not have the energy to attain to this, it is so stunned that, even if consciousness is not completely lost, neither a hand nor a foot stirs, as we say here below when a person is in such a swoon that we think he is dead."* (TIC – V:1:4) By contrast, in the Prayer of Quiet, *"the soul remains doubtful that it was union. It doubts whether it imagined the experience; whether it was asleep; whether the experience was given by God; or whether the devil transformed himself into an angel of light. It is left with a thousand suspicions. That it has them is good for, as I have said, even our own nature can sometimes deceive us in that dwelling place."* (TIC – V:1:5)

Although there is little chance of poisonous reptiles (temptation to grave sin) entering a soul in the Fourth Dwelling Places, some tiny lizards (imperfections and attachments) will enter, though they can do no harm, especially if they remain unnoticed. These are trivial fancies of the imagination, which are often very troublesome. In the Fifth Dwelling Places, *"these little lizards cannot enter this fifth dwelling place; there is neither imagination, nor memory, nor intellect that can impede this good. And I would dare say that if the prayer is truly that of union with God the devil cannot even enter or do any damage… Thus the soul is left with such wonderful blessings because God works within it without anyone disturbing Him, not even ourselves."* (TIC – V:1:5) In the Prayer of Quiet, one seems only to touch the surface of the body, while in the Prayer of Union the other penetrates to the very marrow.

PROOF OF THE PRAYER OF UNION:

In Chapter One of The Fifth Dwelling Places of *The Interior Castle*, St. Teresa offers us an unmistakable sign or proof of the Prayer of Union: *"During the time of this union it neither sees, nor hears, nor understands, because the union is always short and seems to the soul even much shorter than it probably is. God so places Himself in the interior of that soul that when it returns to itself it can in no way doubt that it was in God and God was in it. This truth remains with it so firmly that even though years go by without God's granting that favor again, the soul can neither forget nor doubt that it was in God and God was in it. This certitude is what matters now."* (TIC – V:1:9) St. Teresa is very emphatic about having this certitude regarding the experience of the Prayer of Union, without which one cannot say that they have received the experience from the Holy Spirit: *"Whoever does not receive this certitude does not experience union of the whole soul with God, but union of some faculty, or that he experiences one of the many other kinds of favors God grants souls… Since we have no part at all to play in bringing it about no matter how much effort we put forth, but it is God who does so, let us not desire the capacity to understand this union."* (TIC – V:1:11) She emphasizes the fact that this work of union is purely God's doing: *"And that He may show His marvels more clearly He doesn't want our will to have any part to play, for it has been entirely surrendered to Him. Neither does He want the door of the faculties and of the senses to be opened, for they are all asleep. But He wants to enter the center of the soul without going through any door, as He entered the place where His disciples were when He said, pax vobis; or as He left the tomb without lifting away the stone."* (TIC – V:1:12)

Through the Prayer of Union, the transformation in the soul is the difference between the silkworm and the butterfly, the image that St. Teresa uses in Chapter Two of The Fifth Dwelling Places. The soul doesn't recognize itself. It receives graces and blessings that are God's pure gift to it: *"It sees within itself a desire to praise the Lord; it would want to dissolve and die a thousand deaths for Him. It soon begins to experience a desire to suffer great trials without its being able to do otherwise. There are the strongest desires for penance, for solitude, and that all might know God; and great pain comes to it when it sees that He is offended… if after God brings a soul here it makes the effort to advance, it will see great things."* (TIC – V:2:7)

St. Teresa enumerates other benefits that come to a soul in this union. It does not have esteem for the works it did in the earlier dwelling places. It's attachment to honor and achievement dissipates. However much it might want to do for God, the soul realizes that it is all so very little in its own eyes. The reason for this is because it sees its transformation being brought about solely by God. The attachment to family, friends, and wealth wears thin, and while it carries out its obligations to family and friends, in some ways they become burdensome. Everything wearies it because it can no longer rest in creatures. Paradoxically, the soul experiences restlessness because it feels estranged from earthly things. It might even appear that they don't have peace. But St. Teresa re-assures us when she says, *"For the trials themselves are so valuable and have such good roots that although very severe they give rise to peace and happiness."* (TIC – V:2:10)

There are some painful benefits as well that the soul receives in this state of union. The unhappiness caused by worldly things generates a great desire to leave this world. Any relief that the soul experiences, comes from the fact that it is here at God's desire. Also, another sorrow that the soul experiences is the fact that God is offended and little esteemed in this world and that many souls are lost. It feels this way both towards non-Christians and Christians as well. This sorrow is somewhat tempered by the fact that the soul wants to do everything in its power to praise, glorify, and serve God. Another sorrow is the fact that it is not yet fully surrendered to God even though it is doing its best to conform to God's will. The sorrow is based on the fact that only God can bring about deeper transformation and this grace has not yet been given to it.

The disciple who has experienced the state of union becomes a powerful witness. *"For since the soul is left with these desires and virtues that were mentioned, it always brings profit to other souls during the time that it continues to live virtuously; and they catch fire from its fire. And even when the soul has itself lost this fire, the inclination to benefit others will remain, and the soul delights in explaining the favors God grants to whoever loves and serves Him."* (TIC– V:3:1). It is a sobering reality that even a soul who has experienced the grace of union with God in the Fifth Dwelling Places, can go astray. In the saint's words, *"I have known persons who had ascended high and had reached this union, who were turned back and won over by the devil with his deep cunning and deceit. All hell must join for such a purpose because, as I have often said, in losing one soul of this kind, not only one is lost but a multitude."* (TIC – V:4:6) Hence, there is always great need to ask God in prayer to sustain us and to think that without His help we would soon end in the abyss.

THE CONSOLATION OF LIVING IN TRUST:

It is important to never get discouraged because God is not giving us the supernatural gifts described in the Prayer of Union. With the help of divine grace true union can always be attained by forcing ourselves to renounce our own will and follow the will of God in all things. If this be the case, then we have already obtained this grace from God. Hence we need not wish for that other delightful union described in the Fifth Dwelling Places, for its chief value lies in the resignation of our will to that of God without which it could not be reached. The happy soul which has attained it will live in this world and in the next without care of any sort.

THE SIXTH DWELLING PLACES:

St. Teresa devotes eleven chapters to The Sixth Dwelling Places. She sees the Sixth Dwelling Places as the place where the betrothal takes place. In her day for the arrangement of a marriage, the following stages were followed: 1) meetings between the young man and woman;

2) exchanging of gifts; 3) falling in love; 4) the joining of hands; 5) betrothal; 6) marriage. The union experienced in the Fifth Dwelling Places continues to deepen. Now the soul is determined to take no other spouse. But Jesus wants to intensify the desire and determination of the soul for this betrothal. And this strengthening takes place through interior and exterior trials that the soul suffers.

INTERIOR AND EXTERIOR TRIALS:

At this stage of union, the disciple's lifestyle and behavior become a lightning rod in a sense. Some are threatened by their example and resort to gossip; others feel convicted and avoid their company; still others are appreciative of them but do not want to change. The upshot of it all is that the disciple feels isolated and rejected. When the disciple is praised, it becomes a suffering indeed. People are as quick to say good things as bad; secondly, since Our Lord is the source of all good, praise of them rings hollow. Since their concern for the honor and glory of God is greater than for their own glory, they will not be led astray by praise that is directed to them. They are very pleased if God is glorified even if it means that they have to suffer. When God liberates a soul so that it pays scant attention to praise being directed towards it, it pays much less attention to disapproval; on the contrary it rejoices: *"This is an amazing truth. Blame does not intimidate the soul but strengthens it. Experience has already taught it the wonderful gain that comes through this path... And since it clearly experiences the benefits of persecution, it acquires a special and very tender love for its persecutors. It seems to it that they are greater friends and more advantageous than those who speak well of it."* (TIC – VI:1:5)

Severe illness can be an exterior trial that a disciple can face in this dwelling place. *"For in some way, if these pains are severe, the trial is, it seems to me, the greatest on earth – I mean the greatest exterior trial, however many the other pains."* (TIC – VI:1:6)

An interior trial can be the result of a confessor or spiritual director being out of their depth when listening to a disciple in the betrothal stage of union. You can have a confessor *"who is so discreet and has so little experience that there is nothing he is sure of; he fears everything and finds in everything something to doubt because he sees these unusual experiences. He becomes especially doubtful if he notices some imperfection in a soul that has them, for it seems to such confessors that the ones to whom God grants these favors must be angels – but that is impossible as long as they are in this body."* (TIC – VI:1:8) This situation gets aggravated when the disciple has a fearful temperament: *"Even though they feel secure and cannot believe that the favor when granted by His Majesty, is from any other spirit than from God, the torment returns immediately since the favor is something that passes quickly, and the remembrance of sins is always present, and the soul sees faults in itself, which are never lacking."* (TIC – VI:1:8)

Along with this sense of doubt, there is the inability to explain what is going on to the confessor or spiritual director. *"The soul's understanding is so darkened that it becomes incapable of seeing the truth and believes whatever the imagination represents to it (for the imagination is then its master) or whatever foolish things the devil wants to represent… Many are the things that war against it with an interior oppression so keen and unbearable that I don't know what to compare this experience to if not to the oppression of those that suffer in hell, for no consolation is allowed in the midst of this tempest."* (TIC – VI:1:9) The disciple has no choice except to wait for God's mercy to intervene. And just like that, the Lord can calm the storm and fill the soul with consolation, leading to praise and thanksgiving to God. This experience of feeling totally incapacitated leads to a profound sense of sin, to a sense that one does not have any love of God, to a sense that everything is gift. When it prays, if feels its efforts are useless as there is a total absence of consolation. It cannot pray discursively, as the faculties are incapable of meditation. In such a dark night, St. Teresa proposes that we *"engage in external works of charity and hope in the mercy of God who never fails those who hope in Him."* (TIC – VI:1:13)

AWAKENING IMPULSES:

In the Sixth Dwelling Place the soul receives delicate and refined impulses that proceed from deep within the interior part of the soul. And they are far different than the impulses offered in the Fifth Dwelling Place. One such impulse is that often when a person is distracted, suddenly *"His Majesty will awaken it. His action is quick as a falling comet. And as clearly as it hears a thunderclap, even though no sound is heard, the soul understands that it was called by God… It feels that it is wounded in the most exquisite way, but it doesn't learn how or by whom it was wounded… And the pain is great, although delightful and sweet. And even if the soul does not want this wound, the wound cannot be avoided. But the soul, in fact, would never want to be deprived of this pain. The wound satisfies it much more than the delightful and painless absorption of the prayer of quiet."* (TIC – VI:2:2) St. Teresa tells us that this favor cannot be explained. This delightful pain is not continuous, and it is not really pain. It is described as pain because it is overwhelming and indescribable. It is never permanent and therefore does not set the soul on fire. *"But just as the fire is about to start, the spark goes out and the soul is left with the desire to suffer again that loving pain the spark causes."* (TIC – VI:2:4)

St. Teresa offers some important reasons as to why such an impulse of exquisite pain can only come from God and not the devil: *"(The devil) doesn't have the power to join pain – and so much of it – to the spiritual quiet and delight of the soul… the pain he causes are never delightful or peaceful, but disturbing and contentious… the favor brings wonderful benefits to the soul, the more customary of which are the determination to withdraw from earthly satisfactions and conversations and other similar things."* (TIC – VI:2:6) There are other awakenings that the soul might receive that do not have this element of intense and exquisite pain: *"When it is praying vocally and not thinking of anything interior, it seems a delightful enkindling will come upon it… The soul is moved with a delightful desire to enjoy Him, and thereby it is prepared to make intense acts of love and praise of our Lord."* (TIC – VI:2:8)

AWAKENING THROUGH LOCUTIONS:

St. Teresa speaks at great length about the various kinds of locutions. Our reflection will be informative and not exhaustive. St. Teresa believes that locutions can come from God or from the devil or from one's own imagination. Some are so exterior that they come through the sense of hearing. They are audible through a spoken word. There is great need for proper discernment in the matter of locutions. To help us in this, St. Teresa gives us clear signs of a true and authentic locution as coming from God: *"the first and truest (sign) is the power and authority they bear, for locutions from God effect what they say… A soul finds itself in the midst of … tribulation and disturbance… in darkness of the intellect and in dryness; with one word alone of these locutions ("don't be distressed") from the Lord, it is left calm and free from all distress… The second sign is the great quiet left in the soul, the devout and peaceful recollection, the readiness to engage in the praises of God… The third sign is that these words remain in the memory for a very long time, and some are never forgotten."* (TIC – VI:3:5-7) There are occasions when the devil can play his part. The words given in a locution, while they are held on to steadfastly, can still be doubted, because their certainty is being questioned, thus causing doubt and anxiety. And sometimes one can be imprudent in the way they set about carrying out God's will as they think has been revealed to them through the locution. In such matters help from a confessor or spiritual director might be necessary.

LOCUTIONS FROM THE IMAGINATION AND THE INTELLECT:

St. Teresa maintains that when locutions come from the imagination they do not have the signs of a true and authentic locution. There is neither certitude, nor peace, nor interior delight. These imagined locutions could be experienced during the time of prayer, and the person might feel strongly that these locutions are spoken to them and even that they see things. However, they clearly lack the true signs of an authentic locution, as stated above.

St. Teresa is very positive that intellectual locutions are definitely from God: *"The locution takes place in such intimate depths and a person with the ears of the soul seems to hear those words from the Lord Himself so clearly and so in secret that this very way in which they are heard, together with the acts that the vision itself produces, assures that person and gives him certitude that the devil can have no part to play in the locution."* (TIC – VI:3:12) There are several signs given to the soul to say that such a locution is authentic and from God. The locution is so clear that the soul remembers every syllable and whether it is said in one style or another, even if it is a whole sentence. In a locution from the imagination, the words will not be so clear or distinct but like something dreamed up. Secondly, these locutions come to one most unexpectedly, about matters in the future that never entered the mind. Thirdly, *"the one locution comes as in the case of a person who hears, and that of the imagination as in the case of a person who gradually composes what he himself wants to be told… Fourth, the words are very different, and with one of them much is comprehended. Our intellect could not compose them so quickly… Fifth, together with the words … there is often given much more to understand than is ever dreamed possible without words."* (TIC – VI:3:14-16)

RAPTURE, ECSTASY, TRANSPORT:

The whole purpose of being subjected to trials and suffering is in order to prepare the soul for many graces of deeper union. One such grace is rapture or ecstasy, or transport, all of which are the same in St. Teresa's opinion, and she describes them in Chapter 4 of The Sixth Dwelling Places. *"One kind of rapture is that in which the soul even though not in prayer is touched by some word it remembers or hears about God. It seems that His Majesty from the interior of the soul… is moved with compassion in seeing the soul suffer so long a time from its desire. All burnt up, the soul is renewed like the phoenix, and one can devoutly believe that its faults are pardoned. Now that it is so pure, the Lord joins it with Himself, without anyone understanding what is happening except these two."* (TIC – VI:4:3) One result of such rapture is that the soul experiences a deep enlightenment and knowledge of God. In a state of rapture, the soul can have imaginative and intellectual visions. They are so memorable that they are never forgotten.

St. Teresa talks about ecstasy and describes it in the following manner: *"He takes away the breath so that, even though the other senses sometimes last a little longer, a person cannot speak at all; although at other times everything is taken away at once, and the hands and the body grow cold so that the person doesn't seem to have any life; nor sometimes is it known whether he is breathing. This situation lasts but a short while. I mean in its intensity; for when this extreme suspension lets up a little, it seems that the body returns to itself somewhat and is nourished so as to die again and give more life to the soul. Nevertheless so extreme an ecstasy doesn't last long."* (TIC – VI:4:13) The result of such an experience is that *"the will becomes so absorbed, and the will so with-drawn for a day or even days, that the latter seems incapable of understanding anything that doesn't lead to awakening the will to love; and the will is wide awake to this love and asleep to becoming attached to any creature."* (TIC – VI:4: 4)

St. Teresa describes another kind of rapture that she describes as a flight of the spirit. It is experienced differently interiorly. *"Suddenly a movement of the soul is felt so swift that it seems the spirit is carried off, and at a fearful speed especially in the beginning… At the beginning of this swift movement there is not so much certitude that the rapture is from God."* (TIC – VI:5:1) According to her, great courage is required on the part of the soul as this favor is something frightening. If God did not give the soul this courage it would be deeply distressed. In this quick rapture of the spirit, the spirit seems to go forth from the body into an entirely different region where the light is so different from earth's light. When he comes to his senses, the soul would be unable to imagine that light and all the other things that it experienced in that realm. And the soul while in rapture would not be able to tell whether the soul is in the body or that the body is without a soul.

INTELLECTUAL VISIONS:

St. Teresa describes an intellectual vision as follows: *"It will happen while the soul is heedless of any thought about such a favor being granted to it, and though it never had a thought that it deserved this vision, that it will feel Jesus Christ, our Lord, beside it. Yet, it does not see Him, either with the eyes of the body or with those of the soul. This is called an intellectual vision."* (TIC – VI:8:2) The soul has certainty about the presence of Jesus, and the effects that the soul experiences leaves it in no doubt: *"The vision was a great help toward walking with a habitual remembrance of God and a deep concern about avoiding anything displeasing to Him, for it seemed to her that He was always looking at her. And each time she wanted to speak with His Majesty in prayer, and even outside of it, she felt He was so near that He couldn't fail to hear her. But she didn't hear words spoken whenever she wanted; only unexpectedly when they were necessary… Afterward she understood clearly that the vision was not caused by the devil, which became more and more clear as time went on."* (TIC – VI:8:3) Such a grace is a great favor given to the soul without any merits on its part. The soul would not exchange this blessing for any earthly treasure or delight. And when the Lord chooses to take the vision away, the soul feels very much alone. An intellectual vision can also be of a saint or Mary, Mother of God.

IMAGINATIVE VISIONS:

In the imaginative vision, St. Teresa says that *"He shows it (the soul) His most sacred humanity in the way He desires; either as He was when He went about in the world or as He is after His resurrection. And even though the vision happens so quickly that we could compare it to a streak of lightning, this most glorious image remains so engraved on the imagination that I think it would be impossible to erase it until it is seen by the soul in that place where it will be enjoyed without end."* (TIC – VI:9:3) St. Teresa says that this Presence bears such extraordinary majesty that is causes the soul extreme fright. In the interior world of the soul, a great stirring takes place; the soul is so well instructed about so many great truths that it has no need of any other master.

"True Wisdom has taken away the mind's dullness and leaves a certitude, which lasts for some time, that this favor is from God. However much the soul is told the contrary, others cannot then cause it fear that there could be any deception… The devil can present a vision, but not with this truth and majesty and these results." (TIC – VI:9:10)

St. Teresa cautions us against desiring imaginative visions. Desiring such a favor shows a lack of humility; we are asking for something that we do not deserve. Secondly, such a person will be prone to be led astray by the devil. Thirdly, when the imagination is backed by strong desire, it tends to see and hear what it desires. Fourthly, it would be foolishness to choose a path while being ignorant about what is best for us. Such matters are best left to the Lord. Fifthly, such imaginative visions are given to souls who have been purified by severe trials. Lastly, such an inordinate desire will spell the soul's ruin.

KEEPING THE HUMANITY OF CHRIST EVER PRESENT:

St. Teresa is adamant about keeping the humanity of Jesus present in our minds, no matter how spiritually advanced one might be. She is advocating very strongly against the mistaken notion that when a disciple arrives at contemplative prayer, they should disregard anything that is corporeal and tied to the imagination. Now that they have passed the beginning stages of prayer and union with God, it is better for them to deal with the divinity of Christ exclusively, and avoid the humanity of Christ and corporeal things. She devotes the larger part of Chapter Seven in the Sixth Dwelling Places to debunk the disciple of such a notion. It is best for us to listen to St. Teresa herself on this matter and to receive proper guidance for our spiritual lives: *"To be always withdrawn from corporeal things and enkindled in love is the trait of angelic spirits not of those who live in mortal bodies. It's necessary that we speak to, think about, and become the companions of those who having had a mortal body accomplished such great feats for God. How much more is it necessary not to withdraw through one's own efforts from all our good and help which is the most sacred humanity of our Lord Jesus Christ. I cannot believe that these souls do so, but they just don't understand; and they will do harm to themselves and to others. At least I assure them that they will not enter these last two dwelling places. For if they lose the guide, who is the good Jesus, they will not hit upon the right road. It will be quite an accomplishment if they remain safely in the other dwelling places."* (TIC – VI:7:6)

Later in the same chapter, St. Teresa shows how a contemplative, having great difficulty doing discursive reflection, must still contemplate in and with the humanity of Christ: *"This prayer (discursive meditation) is the kind that those whom God has brought to supernatural things and to perfect contemplation are right in saying they cannot practice… But I say that a person will not be right if he says he does not dwell on these mysteries or often have them in mind, especially when the Catholic Church celebrates them… The intellect (in contemplative prayer) represents them in such a way, and they are so stamped on the memory, that the mere sight of the Lord fallen to the ground in the garden with that frightful sweat is enough to last the intellect not only an hour but many days, while it looks with a simple gaze at who He is and how ungrateful we have been for so much suffering. Soon the will responds even though it may not do so with tender feelings, with the desire to serve somehow for such a great favor and to suffer something for One who suffered so much, and with other similar desires relating to what the memory and intellect are dwelling upon."* (TIC – VI:7:11)

THE SEVENTH DWELLING PLACES:

The Seventh Dwelling Places is where the spiritual marriage or perfect union between God and the soul takes place. Since the illuminations in both the Sixth and Seventh Dwelling Places are extraordinary, there are no closed doors between these last two Mansions. Her reason for dividing them is because God gives some revelations that are not given in the Sixth Dwelling Places. God has prepared the soul through its sufferings, caused especially by its insatiable hunger and desire for God. *"He brings it, before the spiritual marriage is consummated, into His dwelling place which is this seventh."* (TIC – VII:1:3) In the previous two Mansions, the Lord joined the soul to Himself. The soul couldn't understand what was going on for all the faculties were unable to function.

In the Seventh Dwelling Places, however, God grants the soul a fair measure of understanding of the favors He grants it. Through an intellectual vision, the Most Blessed Trinity, all three Persons, are revealed to the soul: *"First there comes an enkindling in the spirit in the manner of a cloud of magnificent splendor; and these Persons are distinct, and through an admirable knowledge the soul understands as a most profound truth that all three Persons are one substance and one power and one knowledge and one God alone. It knows in such a way that what we hold by faith, it understands, we can say, through sight – although the sight is not with the bodily eyes nor with the eyes of the soul, because we are not dealing with an imaginative vision. Here all three Persons communicate themselves to it, speak to it, and explain those words of the Lord in the Gospel: that He and the Father and the Holy Spirit will come to dwell with the soul that loves Him and keeps His commandments."* (TIC – VII:1:6)

Instead of being absorbed and incapable of engaging in other activities, the paradox is that the soul is even more occupied in the service of God. Once it has carried out its duties it remains with the enjoyable company of the Blessed Trinity. St. Teresa maintains that this Presence of the Blessed Trinity is not felt fully, as it will in heaven, or else the soul would be incapable of doing anything else or even live among people. However, it is vibrant and constant, and the soul finds itself in this holy company every time it takes notice. In this Presence of the Blessed Trinity in her soul, St. Teresa noticed a division in her soul, so to speak. One part of her soul was suffering great trials in her ministry, while the other part was enjoying blessed quietude at its own pleasure.

St. Teresa also mentions the presence of the Risen Jesus in the soul: *"The Lord appears in this center of the soul, not in an imaginative vision but in an intellectual one, although more delicate than those mentioned (in the Sixth Dwelling Places), as He appeared to the apostles without entering through the door when He said to them pax vobis. What God communicates here to the soul in an instant is a secret so great and a favor so sublime – and the delight the soul experiences so extreme – that I don't know what to compare it to. I can say only that the Lord wishes to reveal for that moment, in a more sublime manner than through any spiritual vision or taste, the glory of heaven."* (TIC – VII:2:3) The difference in the Presence of the Lord in the Sixth and Seventh Dwelling Places is that in the latter, the Lord has desired to be so joined with the disciple that He doesn't want to be separated from the soul. In the Sixth Dwelling Places, spiritual betrothal is the joining of two things into one. However, the two can be separated and each remain by itself.

St. Teresa answers the question whether a soul can be sure of its salvation when it has arrived in the Seventh Dwelling Places. In her opinion the soul is secure as long as *"the divine Majesty keeps it in His hand and it does not offend Him… The soul doesn't consider itself safe even though it sees itself in this state and the state has lasted for some years. But it goes about with much greater fear than before, guarding itself from any small offense against God and with the strongest desires to serve Him, … and with habitual pain and confusion at seeing the little it can do and the great deal to which it is obliged. This pain is no small cross but a very great penance."* (TIC – VII:2:9)

In Chapter Three, St. Teresa talks about several graces that a soul receives in the Seventh Dwelling Places. The first grace is a forgetfulness of self: *"The soul doesn't worry about all that can happen. It experiences strange forgetfulness, for, as I say, seemingly the soul no longer is or would want to be anything in anything, except when it understands that there can come from itself something by which the glory and honor of God may increase even one degree. For this purpose the soul would very willingly lay down its life."* (TIC – VII:3:2)

The second grace is that the soul has a great desire to suffer: *"The desire left in these souls that the will of God be done in them reaches such an extreme that they think everything His Majesty does is good. If He desires the soul to suffer, well and good; it not, it doesn't kill itself as it used to."* (TIC – VII:3:4) The amazing transformation is that these souls have a deep interior joy when they are persecuted, with much peace and no hostile feelings toward their persecutors. On the contrary, they have a special love for their persecutors. The soul has no fear of death.

They no longer desire consolations or spiritual delights, since God Himself dwells in them. *"There is a great detachment from everything and a desire to be always either alone or occupied in something that will benefit some soul. There are no interior trials or feelings of dryness, but the soul lives with a remembrance and tender love of our Lord. It would never want to go without praising Him. When it becomes distracted, the Lord Himself awakens it…"* (TIC – VII:3:8) The Lord and the soul rejoice together in the deepest silence. The faculties are not lost or confused; they do not work because they are in constant amazement.

In Chapter Four, St. Teresa offers very salutary advice by way of conclusion: *"It is necessary that your foundation consist of more than prayer and contemplation. If you do not strive for the virtues and practice them, you will always be dwarfs… let us desire and be occupied in prayer not for the sake of our enjoyment but so as to have this strength to serve… Believe me, Martha and Mary must join together in order to show hospitality to the Lord and have Him always present and not host Him badly by failing to give Him something to eat. How would Mary, always seated at His feet, provide Him with food if her sister did not help her? His food is that in every way possible we draw souls that they may be saved and praise Him always…*

In sum, my Sisters, what I conclude with is that we shouldn't build castles in the air. The Lord doesn't look so much at the greatness of our works as at the love with which they are done. And if we do what we can, His Majesty will enable us each day to do more and more, provided that we do not quickly tire… His Majesty will join it with that which He offered on the cross to the Father for us. Thus even though works are small they will have the value our love for Him would have merited had they been great." (TIC – VII:4:12 & 15)

St. Teresa of Avila, pray for us!

THE DARK NIGHT
ST. JOHN OF THE CROSS

INTRODUCTION:

St. John of the Cross makes a distinction between the Dark Night of the Senses and the Dark Night of the Spirit. He devotes his entire treatise *The Dark Night,* on these two nights of purification/transformation. In Book One he deals with the Night of the Senses, and Book Two focuses on the Night of the Spirit. In the sensory night, the senses are purged and made docile and submissive to the spirit. The night of the senses is common and happens to many a soul. From the way of the Beginner they are being invited to the way of the Proficient. The night of the spirit, on the other hand, is a far more intense purification at the hands of the Holy Spirit. The spiritual night is the lot of very few. It is for disciples who are being led from the way of the Proficient to that of the Perfect. The sensory night, then, prepares one for the more intense night of the spirit.

THE DARK NIGHT OF THE SENSES:

In *Hallow Me as Your Disciple, Lord*, Phase Two of our Formation Program, we looked at the Dark Night of the Senses. One has transitioned from the Way of the Beginner to the Way of the Proficient or the Illuminative Way. This transition or first purgation is bitter to the senses. In the Way of the Beginner, the seeker responded to the invitation offered to them through an awakening that took place in their hearts. They realized that they had to make Jesus their first priority in life, reordering all their other priorities to conform to the Person and teachings of Jesus. On their part, they embraced the Active Night of purification that St. John treats in *The Ascent of Mount Carmel.* With serious intent, both in their prayer and daily actions, they sought God's will rather than their own willful preferences, choosing to do what is right rather than what is pleasurable and convenient, thus placing God and others before themselves. They made the decision not to commit deliberate sin, big or small. Prayer became a daily practice and the presence of God became habitual. However, they also realized that even with the help of God's actual grace, they could go only so far when it came to eradicating the roots of sin in their lives. The Holy Spirit had to intervene directly.

The Dark Night of the Senses was the next step that the Holy Spirit took in leading the disciple to become a 'proficient.' Various signs began to appear in the disciple's prayer which indicated that the Holy Spirit was initiating the Dark Night of the Senses. They were going about their prayer and spiritual practices with eagerness and fidelity and were experiencing satisfaction and consolation. In their opinion, God was pleased with them. Just when they think all is well, *"God now leaves them in such darkness that they do not know which way to turn in their discursive imaginings. They cannot advance a step in meditation, as they used to, now that the interior sense faculties are engulfed in this night. He leaves them in such dryness that they not only fail to receive satisfaction and pleasure from their spiritual exercises and works, as they formerly did, but also find these exercises distasteful and bitter"*. (TDN – Book One: Chapter 8:3) With this change everything seems to be going in reverse causing them confusion and doubt.

Discursive prayer was becoming progressively more difficult to do. Discursive forms of prayer, like meditation and Ignatian Contemplation (imaging prayer) did not have the same appeal as before. Consequently, in prayer the disciple began noticing a reluctance to exercise the intellect, imagination, and memory. Earlier, there was a great need to satisfy one's religious curiosity which at times seemed insatiable. That desire has waned to a great extent because the longing to know God and be in covenant with Him has exceeded the eagerness to know about God and be satisfied intellectually. *"And he (God) desires to liberate them from the lowly exercise of the senses and of discursive meditation, by which they go in search of him so inadequately and with so many difficulties, and lead them into the exercise of the spirit, in which they become capable of a communion with God that is more abundant and more free of imperfections."* (TDN – Book One: Chapter 8:3) God does this only after beginners have exercised themselves in prayer on a consistent basis and have practiced virtue seriously. Through serious prayer they become detached from worldly things and gain spiritual strength in God. This shift in prayer is now experienced as distraction, boredom, inability to stay focused, and dryness. God appears vague, removed, and beyond their reach. Needless to say, this state is confusing and discouraging. They feel that a dark night has descended upon them.

SIGNS OF THE TRANSITION TO CONTEMPLATION:

Book One, Chapter 9 deals with the signs of transition to contemplative prayer. *"The first sign is that since these souls do not get satisfaction or consolation from the things of God, they do not get any from creatures either. Since God puts a soul in this dark night in order to dry up and purge its sensory appetite, he does not allow it to find sweetness or delight in anything."* (TDN – Book One: Chapter 9:2) At this stage of discipleship, one is serious about loving and serving God. There is a definite solicitude about the things of God. So it is quite disconcerting to the disciple when the second sign begins to emerge: *"The memory ordinarily turns to God solicitously and with painful care, and the soul thinks it is not serving God but turning back, because it is aware of this distaste for the things of God."* (TDN – Book One: Chapter 9:3) This sign is not a sign of a lukewarm attitude. The lukewarm tend to be lax and negligent about serving God. Those suffering from this sensory night are ordinarily serious about their commitment to God. Consequently they are pained that they are not serving God better. The Third sign is *"the powerlessness, in spite of one's efforts, to meditate and make use of the imagination, the interior sense, as was one's previous custom. At this time God does not communicate himself through the senses as he did before, by means of the discursive analysis and synthesis of ideas, but begins to communicate himself through pure spirit by an act of simple contemplation in which there is no discursive succession of thought."* (TDN – Book One: Chapter 9:8)

CONDUCT REQUIRED DURING THE SENSORY DARK NIGHT:

God is bringing about a transition from the discursive to the contemplative through this sensory night of affliction and purgation. The soul feels powerless as it cannot meditate on the things of God with its intellect, imagination, and memory. They feel very afflicted and abandoned by God. While the dryness and distraction in prayer is difficult to handle and calls for patience and trust, what is more difficult to handle is their fear that they are going astray and will not receive any spiritual blessings again. In trying to resolve these difficult straits, they make an effort to go back to discursive forms of prayer. *"They fatigue and overwork themselves, thinking God is conducting them along another road, which is contemplation and is very different from the first, for the one road belongs to discursive meditation and the other is beyond the range of the imagination and discursive reflection."* (TDN – Book One: Chapter 10:2) The advice to them from St. John of the Cross is to *"persevere patiently and not be afflicted. Let them trust in God who does not fail those who seek him with a simple and righteous heart; nor will he fail to impart what is needful for the way until getting them to the clear and pure light of love. God will give them this light by means of that other night, the night of spirit, if they merit that he place them in it."* (TDN – Book One: Chapter 10:3) Furthermore, one should not pay attention to discursive meditation but learn *"to remain in rest and quietude even though it may seem obvious to them that they are doing nothing and wasting time, and even though they think this disinclination to think about anything is due to their laxity. Through patience and perseverance in prayer, they will be doing a great deal without activity on their part."* (TDN – Book One: Chapter 10:4)

In the early stages of the sensory night, the disciple is preoccupied with the dryness and inability to utilize the faculties well in prayer. Gradually, however, the disciple will begin to feel a certain longing for God which could intensify to become urgent longings of love for God. In time the disciple begins to reap many benefits from this purification in which one feels helpless and hopeless.

BENEFITS OF THE SENSORY NIGHT:

St. John of the Cross enumerates numerous benefits in Book One, Chapters 12 and 13. He notes the following benefits in Chapter 12:

- The soul gains intimate knowledge of self and one's own misery. This purification makes the soul realize its own lowliness and misery which seemed hidden and even non-existent before the sensory night began.
- This acute sense of self leads to relating with God more respectfully and reverently as befitting God's holiness.
- Accompanying this sense of its own misery and unworthiness before God, the soul also by contrast becomes aware of God's grandeur and majesty.
- Through the sensory night, the soul receives the gift of humility which can only be built on a true understanding of self. Such an attitude goes against spiritual pride, one of the capital sins.
- Such humility creates love of neighbor and a reluctance to judge anyone as they did when they enjoyed God's favors and consolations.
- They become pliant and malleable in the hands of God and willingly seek direction and correction.
- Gradually, the roots of pride are destroyed.

In Chapter 13, St. John of the Cross notes the following benefits:

- *"The soul undergoes a thorough reform in its imperfections of avarice, in which it craved various spiritual objects and was never content with many of its spiritual exercises because of the covetousness of its appetite and the gratification it found in spiritual things."*
- Regarding spiritual lust, its craving for spiritual gifts and its performance in prayer and spiritual disciplines lessens and undergoes a thorough reform.
- *"God so curbs concupiscence and bridles the appetite through this arid and dark night that the soul cannot feast on any sensory delight from earthly or heavenly things."* When God does this, the soul dwells in peace and tranquility. There is no disturbance as there used to be.
- The soul is aware of God throughout the day and has a great fear that it will backslide spiritually.
- It practices all the virtues. Individuals become meek toward God, themselves, and others. They are more accepting of self and others, less argumentative and impatient.
- Their struggle with envy lessens. They are more charitable toward others and are able to rejoice in their well-being. Their love for spiritual matters begins to return.
- In the midst of dryness and a sense of abandonment, *"God frequently communicates to the soul, when it least expects, spiritual sweetness, a very pure love, and a spiritual knowledge that is sometimes most delicate."*
- Lastly, in all they do, they are motivated more by the desire to please God rather than by their own delight and satisfaction acting as the criterion or motivation.

CONCLUDING COMMENTS ON THE SENSORY NIGHT:

According to St. John of the Cross, God is actually shining upon the soul much more brightly than before. However, the disciple's capacity thus far is very limited to receive such a bright divine presence. The disciple is blinded by such a divine advent. It is like the human eye being blinded by looking directly at the sun. The sense faculties are overwhelmed and go haywire. Their experience is one of the 'absence' of God. God is choosing to communicate directly with them, giving them knowledge and love of God directly, and not through their minds and sense faculties which are quite limited in their scope. The saints call this direct communion with God infused prayer. God might permit external difficulties and crises which force the disciple to trust God and hold on to Him in their moments of doubt and darkness. In the Dark Night of the Senses, the disciple learns to live with childlike trust and faith. Gradually, the Holy Spirit increases the disciple's capacity to receive God and be in a deeper covenant relationship with Him. The Dark Night of the Senses purifies the soul and leads it upon the way of holiness and mystical prayer.

Finally, in Book One, Chapter 14, St. John of the Cross addresses the question of how long the Dark Night of the Senses will last: *"Yet we cannot say certainly how long the soul will be kept in this fast and penance of the senses. Not everyone undergoes this in the same way, neither are the temptations identical. In the measure of the degree of love to which God wishes to raise a soul, he humbles it with greater or less intensity, or for a longer or shorter period. Those who have more considerable capacity and strength for suffering, God purges more intensely and quickly. But those who are very weak he keeps in this night for a long time. Their purgation is less intense and their temptations abated, and he frequently refreshes their senses to keep them from backsliding."*

THE DARK NIGHT OF THE SPIRIT:

In Book Two of *The Dark Night* St. John of the Cross deals with the Dark Night of the Spirit. When the process of the Dark Night of the Senses is completed or far advanced, the disciple sees clearly how the Holy Spirit has transformed them. They are brought into a different world. They understand the teachings of Jesus with a clarity and insight they did not have before. If God wishes to lead the soul into the dark night of the spirit, He does not do so immediately. In fact the disciple could spend many years as a proficient. In this state, the disciple *"as one liberated from a cramped cell, it goes about the things of God with much more freedom and satisfaction of spirit and with more abundant interior delight than it did in the beginning before entering the night of sense... The soul readily finds in its spirit, without the work of meditation, a very serene, loving contemplation and spiritual delight."* (TDN – Book Two: Chapter 1:1). However, the purgation is not complete. The sensory purgation was the first step preparing for the purification of the spirit.

St. John of the Cross gives us two important reasons as to why God first leads the soul through the sensory night prior to the passive dark night of the spirit. The first reason is because *"All good and evil habits reside in the spirit and until these habits are purged, the senses cannot be completely purified of their rebellions and vices."* (TDN – Book Two: Chapter 3:1) The second reason is because *"In this night that follows both parts are jointly purified. This was the purpose of the reformation of the first night and the calm that resulted from it: that the sensory part, united in a certain way with the spirit, might undergo purgation and suffering with greater fortitude. Such is the fortitude necessary for so strong and arduous a purgation that if the lower part in its weakness is not reformed first, and afterward strengthened in God through the experience of sweet and delightful communion with him, it has neither the fortitude nor the preparedness to endure it."* (TDN – Book Two: Chapter 3:2)

St. John then describes the experience of the dark night of the spirit when he comments on the first stanza of his poem *The Dark Night.* It is a twofold experience, of intense purification and transformation. The soul describes its purification in the following manner: *"Poor, abandoned, and unsupported by any of the apprehensions of my soul (in the darkness of my intellect, the distress of my will, and the affliction and anguish of my memory), left to darkness in pure faith, which is a dark night for these natural faculties, and with my will touched only by sorrows, afflictions, and longings of love of God, I went out from myself."* (TDN – Book Two: Chapter 4:1) On the other hand, a re-creation is taking place which might not be noticeable at first: *"This was great happiness and a sheer grace for me, because through the annihilation and calming of my faculties, passions, appetites, and affections, by which my experience and satisfaction in God were base, I went out from my human operation and way of acting to God's operation and way of acting... My intellect departed from itself, changing from human and natural to divine...And my will departed from itself and became divine. United with the divine love, it no longer loves in a lowly manner, with its natural strength, but with the strength and purity of the Holy Spirit; and thus the will does not operate humanly in relation to God. The memory, too, was changed into eternal apprehensions of glory."* (TDN – Book Two: Chapter 4:2) Consequently, through this spiritual night of purification and illumination, God initiates the soul in the perfection of love without its doing anything or even knowing how it happens.

DARK NIGHT OF AFFLICTIONS:

St. John of the Cross goes on to enumerate the various types of afflictions that the soul endures in this night of the spirit. Some of these afflictions have to do with the blinding and paralyzing effect the divine light has on our human faculties when God is bringing about union with the soul. The soul is blinded by the divine light and experiences it as *"spiritual darkness, for it not only surpasses the act of natural understanding but it also deprives the soul of this act and darkens it."* (TDN – Book Two: Chapter 5:3) This divine light exposes all that is impure and sinful in the soul, resulting in the disciple experiencing unworthiness and sinfulness before God. They feel wretched and miserable and think that God is against them and has abandoned them. The disciple realizes how utterly devoid they are without God and everything is pure gift.

At times death would be preferable to the intensity of this purification: *"They suffer so much in their weakness that they almost die, particularly at times when the light is more powerful. Both the sense and the spirit, as though under an immense and dark load, undergo such agony and pain that the soul would consider death a relief."* (TDN – Book Two: Chapter 5:6) The paradox is that God's aim is to grant the soul favors and not to chastise it. However, the soul is still so weak and vulnerable that it experiences new life from God as the rigors of death.

In Book Two, Chapter 6, St. John of the Cross continues enumerating other afflictions that befall the disciple in the dark night of the spirit. They are convinced that God has rejected them and such abandonment is a very heavy burden to bear. They also feel forsaken and despised by people, particularly by their friends. They can feel useless and insignificant in themselves, and sidelined by family and friends. Another affliction is a sense of emptiness that they experience. Their talent and giftedness don't have the same appeal; material possessions don't satisfy in the same way; since they feel rejected and abandoned by God, their spiritual gifts don't mean much. They are miserable about their imperfections, none of their faculties can function, and the darkness in and around them is great indeed.

In Book Two, Chapter 7, St. John of the Cross describes the afflictions of the will. The disciple is made very aware of the evils (past sins and present sinfulness) in which it is immersed through this purification, and is uncertain of any remedy to it. Furthermore, God will not allow the soul to have any respite or reassurance from other sources. The words of the spiritual director, or a spiritual master, or a teaching, don't appeal or provide any relief. *"They remain in this condition until their spirit is humbled, softened, and purified, until it becomes so delicate, simple, and refined that it can be one with the Spirit of God, according to the degree of union of love that God, in his mercy, desires to grant."* (TDN – Book Two: Chapter 7:3)

He makes the reflection that such purification will last for some years; however, every now and then God's light will shine upon the soul and illumine it greatly, giving it a foretaste of that for which it hopes. However, such relief is fleeting. Just when the soul assumes it is safe, the purgation returns and darkens the soul in a more severe affliction that could last longer than the previous one. In all of this suffering, they know that they love God and would do anything for Him. However, they find no relief from their affliction and are unable to believe that God loves them. In fact they are convinced that they should be abhorred by God and everybody else.

In Book Two, Chapter 8, St. John of the Cross deals with other afflictions. The prayer of intercession becomes almost impossible as they feel the chasm between God and them, and they don't have it in them to bridge it. And even when they try, God does not hear them or pay any attention to them. The saint offers salutary advice in this situation: *"This is not the time to speak with God… but to suffer this purgation patiently… God it is who is working now in the soul, and for this reason the soul can do nothing."* (TDN – Book Two: Chapter 8:1)

ILLUMINATION THROUGH THE DARK NIGHT:

In Book Two, Chapter 9:1, St. John of the Cross tells us what the real purpose of the spiritual night is: *"Even though this happy night darkens the spirit, it does so only to impart light concerning all things; and even though it humbles individuals and reveals their miseries, it does so only to exalt them; and even though it impoverishes and empties them of all possessions and natural affection, it does so only that they may reach out divinely to the enjoyment of all earthly and heavenly things, with a general freedom of spirit in them all."*

St. John of the Cross describes the graces that God grants a soul, through the dark night of the spirit. He does so in Book Two, Chapters 19 and 20. He uses the image of a 'ladder', as simultaneously there is a descent and an ascent; the soul is both humbled and exalted. He describes ten different steps or graces by which the soul ascends to God.

The first step is that the soul can't find satisfaction or support, or any kind of consolation or resting place in anything. This utter dissatisfaction in earthly things points it heavenward toward God.

The second step creates an incessant search for God that never stops. In everything it thinks, says, and does, it is seeking for its Beloved. In all things it centers its loving attention on God.

In the third step of the ladder, the disciple is very eager to do as much as possible for God. Their fervor is such that they will not get dissipated. However, along with this ardor for God's glory, there is an accompanying sorrow and pain that so little is being done for God. As Saint John of the Cross would say, *"On this third step the soul is far removed from vainglory, presumption, and the practice of condemning others."* (TDN – Book Two: Chapter 19:3)

In the fourth step, there is a habitual and constant suffering because of its intense desire for God. *"The soul in no way seeks consolation or satisfaction either in God or in anything else; neither does it desire or ask favors of God, for it is clearly aware that it has already received many from him. All its care is directed toward how it might give some pleasure to God and render him some service because of what he deserves and the favors he has bestowed, even though the cost might be high."* (TDN – Book Two: Chapter 19:4)

In the fifth step there is an impatient desire and longing for God that can never be quenched. This delay is burdensome and frustrating.

Book Two, Chapter 20, St. John of the Cross enumerates the remaining steps of the ladder leading up to God. *"The sixth step makes the soul run swiftly toward God and experience touches in him. And it runs without fainting by reason of its hope. The love that has invigorated it makes it fly swiftly… The soul's charity is now highly increased and almost completely purified."* (TDN – Book Two: Chapter 20:1)

"The seventh step of the ladder gives it an ardent boldness. At this stage love neither profits by the judgment to wait nor makes use of the counsel to retreat, neither can it be curbed through shame. For the favor God now gives it imparts an ardent daring." (TDN – Book Two: Chapter 20:2)

"The eighth step of love impels the soul to lay hold of the Beloved without letting him go. Although the soul satisfied its desire on this step of union, it does not do so continually. Some manage to get to it, but soon turn back and leave it. If one were to remain on this step, a certain glory would be possessed in this life, and so the soul rests on it for only short periods of time." (TDN – Book Two: 20:3)

"The ninth step of love causes the soul to burn gently. It is the step of the perfect who burn gently in God. The HS produces this gentle and delightful ardor by reason of the perfect soul's union with God." (TDN – Book Two: Chapter 20:4)

"The tenth and last step of this secret ladder of love assimilates the soul to God completely because of the clear vision of God that a person possesses at once on reaching it. After arriving at the ninth step in this life, the soul departs from the body. Since these souls – few that there be – are already extremely purged through love, they do not enter purgatory." (TDN – Book Two: Chapter 20:5)

St. John of the Cross, pray for us!

BLESSED MOTHER TERESA OF CALCUTTA

We are familiar with the life and example of Blessed Mother Teresa of Calcutta as she died on September 5, 1997 and was beatified by then Pope John Paul II on October 19, 2003, now St. John Paul II. In this segment we will take a look at some traits of Blessed Teresa's spiritual life in order to be edified by her example and encouraged in our own following of Jesus.

Blessed Teresa was born circa August 26, 1910 in Skopje, the current capital of the Republic of Macedonia, of Albanian parents. She was baptized as Agnes Gonxha Bojaxhiu on August 27, 1910 which is often cited as her birthday. In 1928, as an 18 year old, Blessed Teresa decided to become a nun. She traveled to Ireland to join the Loreto Sisters of Dublin. She took the name of Sister Mary Teresa after St. Thérese of Lisieux. After a year in Ireland, Blessed Teresa was sent to Darjeeling, India for her novitiate. In May 1931 she made her First Profession of Vows. Her first mission was to teach at Saint Mary's High School for girls in Calcutta. It was a school run by the Loreto Sisters and was dedicated to teaching girls from the poorest Bengali families. She learned Bengali and Hindi and taught Geography and History. On May 24, 1937, Blessed Teresa pronounced her Final Profession of Vows to a life of poverty, chastity, and obedience. In the tradition of the Loreto nuns, she took the title of 'mother' upon making her final vows and from then on was known as Mother Teresa. In 1944 Mother Teresa became the School Principal.

On September 19, 1946, Mother Teresa experienced a second calling that would forever change her life. She received a powerful locution from Jesus which made it clear to her that He wanted her to found the Missionaries of Charity. She was riding a train from Calcutta to Darjeeling in the Himalayan foothills for a retreat. Christ spoke to her and told her that her mission as a teacher had come to an end and He wanted her to work among Calcutta's poorest and sickest people: "I want Indian nuns, Missionaries of Charity, who would be my fire of love amongst the poor, the sick, the dying and the little children. You are, I know, the most incapable person – weak and sinful but just because you are that, I want to use you for my glory. Wilt thou refuse?"

This locution raised several questions for Mother Teresa. She was under obedience and therefore could not leave the convent without official permission. In January 1948, she finally received approval from Archbishop Périer to pursue this new calling. In August 1948, wearing the blue and white sari that she would always wear in public and became the religious garb of her congregation, Mother Teresa left the Loreto Convent and went out into the city. She took the first step of receiving basic medical training for six months and then made the slums of Calcutta her home with the goal of helping "the unwanted, the unloved, the uncared for."

Mother Teresa quickly translated this vague and generalized stirring into concrete actions to help the urban poor. She began an open-air school and established a home for the dying destitute in a dilapidated building that the city owned. She convinced the city officials to donate it to her cause. In October 1950 Mother Teresa received canonical recognition to establish a new congregation, the Missionaries of Charity. She began with 12 members, most of them former teachers or pupils from St. Mary's School. Interestingly enough, during her 15 years or so as an educator at St. Mary's School, Mother Teresa's prayer for her teachers and students was: "Give me the strength to be ever the light of their lives, so that I may lead them at last to you." In ways she never could have imagined, this prayer turned out to be prophetic. Besides the vows of poverty, chastity, and obedience, her sisters take a fourth vow to give "wholehearted free service to the poorest of the poor."

Her congregation began to expand rapidly. Donations from around India and the world began pouring in to help her apostolate. She established leper colonies, orphanages, nursing homes, family clinics and mobile health clinics. In 1971, Mother Teresa opened her first American-based House of Charity. In 1985, she returned to New York and spoke at the 40th anniversary of the United Nations General Assembly. While there, she also opened 'Gift of Love,' a home to care for those infected with HIV/AIDS. Presently, the Missionaries of Charity number around 4500 and live and work in 133 countries.

Blessed Teresa had *a deep faith in the Real Presence of Jesus* in the Blessed Sacrament. This faith was the bedrock of her spirituality as well as the strength of her ministry and religious congregation. This is basically what she had to say about the way she translated this devotion and love in daily action: *"I make a holy hour every day in the presence of Jesus in the Blessed Sacrament. Our holy hour (done in community) is our daily family prayer where we get together and pray the Rosary the first half hour and the second half hour in silence. Our adoration has doubled the number of our vocations."* This daily practice of adoration before the Blessed Sacrament should inspire us to make Eucharistic Adoration an important spiritual discipline. It should also make us realize that this intimate face to face visit with Our Lord will work wonders in our relationship with God and the good we seek to do to help with the establishment of God's kingdom.

Blessed Teresa was greatly admired by the Indian people. The Central Government of India and the State Government of Bengal treated her with great respect and admiration. However, she would not accept any financial help from the Government. She wanted her sisters to be completely free in serving the poor. She believed that God would provide through the generosity of people. And in her conviction she has been proven correct. She knew in her heart that if people stopped supporting the ministry of the Missionaries of Charity they would cease to exist.

Blessed Teresa and her community had a strictly regulated daily life. They are up at 4:40 AM, on feast days at 5:10 AM, with set times for prayer, meals, and work. They do everything in community. There is little to no emphasis on personal time and privacy. There is a remarkable relationship between poverty and regularity. A very poor person has little to no time for leisure and idleness, as their lives are preoccupied with making ends meet. Their poverty chooses the lifestyle for them. They learn to live contentedly within the restrictions that life places upon them. The Missionaries of Charity live a life of great simplicity, prayer, work, and life in common. Amazingly enough, through this life style, the sisters exude joy and hope for all those around them.

Blessed Teresa's zeal for the true faith is well known. After serving the poorest of the poor for some thirty five years, Pope St. John Paul II inserted a change in their Constitution to include taking care of the spiritual needs of people in their ministry. At first the community felt very inadequate as they had not received any formal training in evangelization and catechesis. They are located in about 100 countries. Included in their mission is to teach the faith and evangelize. And they have made a huge impact. Their strength comes from being obedient to their calling and in daily Eucharistic Adoration.

Blessed Teresa's strength as a disciple came from her constant union with God. She was always at God's beck and call, asking and receiving guidance from him. She received all her strength from Him. And when we consider how her Missionaries of Charity have spread all over the world, the decisions that she had to make were many and difficult. However, she went about her daily tasks with a serenity and peace that could only come from Jesus.

In brief, all she ever wanted to do was God's will. After her death, it was revealed that Blessed Teresa had spent many years in the dark night of the soul. In analyzing her deeds and achievements Pope St. John Paul II answered the question as to where she found the strength and perseverance, to place herself completely at the service of others. His answer was that Blessed Teresa found it in prayer and the silent contemplation of Jesus Christ, His holy face, His Sacred Heart. However, from her letters we have gathered that she experienced severe doubts and struggles over her beliefs which she felt over nearly 50 years. During that time she had very little respite. Her postulator, Reverend Brian Kolodiejchuk, said that Blessed Teresa "felt no presence of God whatsoever, neither in her heart or in the Eucharist. Blessed Teresa herself expressed grave doubts about God's existence and pain over her lack of faith: "Where is my faith? Even deep down … there is nothing but emptiness and darkness… If there be God – please forgive me. When I try to raise my thoughts to Heaven, there is such convicting emptiness that those very thoughts return like sharp knives and hurt my very soul… How painful is this unknown pain – I have no faith. Repulsed, empty, no faith, no love, no zeal… What do I labor for? If there be no God, there can be no soul. If there be no soul then, Jesus, You also are not true."

The supreme paradox is that while she went through this intense dark night of the soul for so many years, her faith that God was working through her calling and mission remained undiminished. The Missionaries of Charity continued to flourish and vocations to her community increased greatly all over the world. While she was deprived of any semblance of closeness to God or assurance that He loved her, she did not question His existence and remained ever faithful to her Eucharistic Adoration and life of continual prayer and service. Many of our Catholic saints have had similar experiences and describe them in their writings. St. Therese of Lisieux termed it a "night of nothingness," which she experienced during the last eighteen months of her life on earth. Blessed Teresa was called by God to love unconditionally, to love in nothingness, even if there were never any response from God. In one of her publicly released letters to Reverend Michael van der Peet, she wrote: "But for me, the silence and the emptiness is so great, that I look and do not see, listen and do not hear. The tongue moves (in prayer) but does not speak… I want you to pray for me that I let Him have a free hand." In her lifetime she always displayed a joy, peace, and trust that could only come from an abiding trust and security in God.

In his first encyclical *Deus caritas est*, Pope Benedict XVI mentioned Blessed Teresa three times to clarify one of his main points of the encyclical: "In the example of Blessed Teresa of Calcutta we have a clear illustration of the fact that time devoted to God in prayer not only does not detract from effective and loving service to our neighbor but is in fact the inexhaustible source of that service." Mother Teresa specified that "it is only by mental prayer and spiritual reading that we can cultivate the gift of prayer."

There are definite similarities between Blessed Teresa and St. Francis of Assisi. Like St. Francis of Assisi, Blessed Teresa served and met Christ in her service of the poor. Her profound love and respect for the poor suggests that Jesus had given her His very own love and devotion for the poor in whose image and likeness they had been created. Like Jesus and St. Francis, Blessed Teresa deemed it an honor and privilege to serve the poor as their servant. They both embraced radical poverty; they both loved and served the poorest of the poor, especially lepers. They both submitted themselves to religious vows of poverty, chastity, and obedience. St. Francis was wedded to Lady Poverty and Blessed Teresa took a fourth vow to serve free the poorest of the poor. They were both outstanding in their submission to Jesus, no matter how challenging the circumstances were. Blessed Teresa was a great admirer of St. Francis. She stipulated that every morning, during thanksgiving after Communion, the Sisters of Charity would recite the Peace Prayer of St. Francis.

In one sentence, this might be a synthesis of the spirituality of Mother Teresa. All she ever wanted to do in life was the will of God. But she knew there was no other way to know what God wanted, every moment of the day, except by asking Him for the grace to know His divine will and then to do it with all her heart. Blessed Mother Teresa, pray for us!

MARIAN SPIRITUALITY

And Mary said: "My soul proclaims the greatness of the Lord; my spirit rejoices in God my savior. For he has looked upon his handmaid's lowliness; behold, from now on will all ages call me blessed. The Mighty One has done great things for me, and holy is his name. His mercy is from age to age to those who fear him."

– Luke 1:46-50

INTRODUCTION:

The Blessed Virgin Mary holds a very special place in the hearts and minds of millions of Catholics all over the world. She has an aura about her that rings true, even though it is hard to describe in words. This mystique has persisted from the first days of the early Church, and will continue till the end of time. The Mother of God is indeed the Mother of God's covenant family. She will love us with the same steadfast devotion as she loved her son. Mary is the new Eve, and in the Hail Holy Queen Prayer, we implore her as 'the poor, banished children of Eve,' knowing that through her son she will obtain for us the blessings and graces of the new and everlasting covenant established by Jesus on the cross. The miracle at the marriage feast of Cana gave us an important clue about her role as our motherly intercessor. The Rosary has become a powerful representation of Mary's intercessory role in our lives. Through her motherly intercession with her son Jesus, many of us have experienced miraculous changes and interventions in our lives. We have an instinctual understanding of the special relationship Mary as mother has with Jesus as her son and the Son of God. Many of us will not go to bed without having prayed the Rosary.   What then explains this umbilical connection between Mary and millions of Catholics, both now and throughout the ages? Why has the Church, through the example of the great saints of the Church, emphasized the need for a special relationship with Mary? Why have the learned Fathers of the Church and countless holy men and women, many of whom had outstanding intellectual and spiritual gifts, given Mary such a central place in their spiritual lives? Why have they seen her as enhancing their relationship with Jesus and through Him with the Father and the Holy Spirit? In this reflection on Mary's spirituality, we will attempt to address these questions.

GOD'S ATTITUDE TOWARD MARY:

The most appropriate way of addressing these questions is to examine the Blessed Trinity's attitude towards Mary. During the Annunciation, the angel's opening statement reveals the depths of the Father's sentiments for her. God has chosen Mary to be the mother of Jesus, Son of God the Father. Mary has been addressed as *"Hail, favored one! The Lord is with you."* A more accurate translation of the Greek *kecharitomene*, would be *Hail, the one having been filled with grace* (the past perfect participle). Mary is the immaculate one, without stain or sin because she is full of grace, who has been chosen to be the mother of Jesus, who is 'God saves.' Jesus' identity and mission are clearly manifested in His name. Accordingly, Mary has been freed from sin in anticipation of her role as the mother of God! The sole purpose of Jesus becoming the son of man by becoming Mary's son is so that we would be restored to grace, to sharing in the fullness of God's divine life! In our restoration through Jesus' sacrifice on the cross, we have been made sons and daughters of God and have the privilege of addressing Him as Our Father. Mary, being full of grace through her Son's death on the cross, is indeed God's daughter!

An important dimension to consider is God's total trust in Mary. God was asking Mary to be the mother of the Savior, Son of the Most High. As one of us and our representative, Jesus would seal the new and everlasting covenant with God through His blood on the cross. To do that Jesus had to become the son of Mary so that He could become the incarnate Son of God. God needed Mary's wholehearted consent in order to carry out His glorious plan of salvation. The Annunciation heralds the fulfillment of God's Plan of Salvation through the birth of Jesus, the Son of God. The appointed time has arrived. The final age has begun. The long awaited time of fulfillment is here. Mary has been chosen to be the mother of the Savior. She is a virgin, betrothed to a man named Joseph. The announcement is a very solemn and awe-filled occasion both for the Trinity and for us. It is now the fullness of time for the revelation of Jesus as Savior of the world! Fittingly therefore, God has commissioned the angel Gabriel as the messenger of these very glad tidings and to receive Mary's response.

MARY'S ATTITUDE TOWARDS GOD:

Mary's response to these effusive encomiums is to be *"deeply troubled by his words,"* and to wonder what the angel's greeting meant! She knew immediately that this was an extraordinary announcement which transcended her life's circumstances. God's eternal designs were now being revealed in time, and she was being invited to be a key player. Nevertheless, her world was being turned topsy-turvy before her very eyes! Mary seemed to sense in her spirit that God was asking her to trust Him and be ready through His grace, to cross every conceivable threshold, beyond anything her mind and logic could bridge. Understandably, she was deeply troubled in her spirit. The angel then reassures her and tells her not to be afraid. She has found favor with God. The angel is reassuring Mary that God's love will definitively trump all her fears and anxieties.

After the angel reassures Mary, he gives her the breath-taking tidings: *"Behold, you will conceive in your womb and bear a son, and you shall name him Jesus. He will be great and will be called Son of the Most High, and the Lord God will give him the throne of David his father, and he will rule over the house of Jacob forever, and of his kingdom there will be no end."* (Luke 1:31-33) The angel offers Mary three awesome truths to ponder for the rest of her life: Jesus, her son to be, is the Son of the Most High. Secondly, Jesus will come from the tribe of David, and will rule over the house of Jacob as Messiah. Thirdly, He will create a new Israel, which will not be an earthly kingdom, and the reign of God in men's hearts as Emmanuel, will last forever. Mary knows that the angel is telling her that the child she will conceive will indeed be the Messiah. Jesus will be His name which means, 'God saves.'

While the angel is trying to reassure Mary, telling her not to be afraid, she is still perplexed, and cannot make sense of how she can be the mother of the *'Son Most High.'* She is grappling with the fact that she is betrothed to Joseph, and is therefore matrimonially bound to him, while not yet being his wife. Mary knows that God is asking her to be pregnant outside of wedlock, raising the terrible specter of death by stoning, as was customary under the Law [Deuteronomy 22]. Once again the angel reassures her: *"The Holy Spirit will come upon you, and the power of the Most High will overshadow you. Therefore the child to be born will be called holy, the Son of God."* (Luke 1:35) Perhaps the most enduring quality of deeply committed disciples is their total obedience to God's intentions, even when God's designs threaten the very fabric of their existence. It is the Holy Spirit who brings about this enduring and steadfast attitude of surrender in them. Trust is the bedrock of their relationship with God. This is especially the case with Mary. Given her response to God's Plan of Salvation, the Church has always seen Mary as the new Eve.

Mary was God's handmaid, always at her Lord's beck and call. She was plunged into a pregnancy outside of wedlock that could have had a life-threatening consequence for her. Knowing that she would be with child by the power of the Holy Spirit stilled her doubts and calmed her anxiety, leading her to proclaim: *"Behold, I am the handmaid of the Lord. May it be done to me according to your word."* (Luke 1:38) When Mary knows clearly what God's designs are, she is totally obedient to God's will. As God's beloved servant-maid, with whom she was in covenant, Mary understood her life to be characterized by obligations to the Most High and not by privileges! From then on, Mary walked steadfastly in the footsteps laid out for her by the Lord. Every divine wish became her command.

Paradoxically, while the Most High addressed her as His highly favored daughter, Mary identified herself as the handmaid of the Lord! There seems to be no more appropriate way of crystallizing Mary's single-minded devotion to her God than by relishing the inspired commendation her cousin Elizabeth gave her at their meeting: *"… Most blessed are you among women, and blessed is the fruit of your womb… For at the moment the sound of your greeting reached my ears, the infant in my womb leaped for joy. Blessed are you who believed that what was spoken to you by the Lord would be fulfilled."* (Luke 1:42, 44-45) Mary was overshadowed by the Most High, and in return enwombed the Son Most High. She became His faithful handmaid and disciple for the rest of her life. She couldn't tell what her future would hold. She had no way of knowing how her relationship with her son and the 'Son of the Most High' would unfold. However, she knew that all was in God's hands, and it was her steadfast conviction to always live her life as 'the handmaid of the Lord.'

MARY, THE PERFECT DISCIPLE:

The angel Gabriel tells her that the Holy Spirit will come upon her and the power of the Most High will overshadow her. Hence the holy offspring to be born of her will be called the Son of God. On the one hand, the news from the angelic ambassador is very reassuring. It is God's mission and who can stop the designs of God? On the other hand, Mary has to deal with the everyday realities of life. How was she going to explain her pregnancy to her parents and to Joseph? How would she cope with the uncertainty and possible opposition that she would experience from her family members to God's designs in her life? Would they really believe that she was walking in the ways of the Lord? Or was her child the result of her waywardness?

After Mary pondered God's intervention in her life, she came to a deep sense of gratitude and exaltation for God's ways and designs. Mary knew all was well, being in God's hands and will, even though her knowledge was accompanied with much uncertainty and anxiety: *"My soul proclaims the greatness of the Lord; my spirit rejoices in God my savior. For he has looked upon his handmaid's lowliness."* (Luke 1:46b-48a) Mary has an attitude of total trust and gratitude towards God. Whatever God chooses to do with her is good because God will always do what is right and good. And so she proclaims, *"The Mighty One has done great things for me, and holy is his name. His mercy is from age to age to those who fear him."* (Luke 1:49-50) God has become first and foremost in all she thinks, says, and does. Mary makes an intimate connection between God's largesse and the spirit of humility or living her life in total dependence and trust in God: *"He has thrown down the rulers from their thrones but lifted up the lowly. The hungry he has filled with good things; the rich he has sent away empty."* (Luke 1:52-53)

Whatever doubts Mary might have had regarding Joseph, they were taken care of by the Holy Spirit. One of the Holy Spirit's actions is to make us see that God's ways are not our ways. Where the human mind conjures up an impossible situation fraught with fear and anxiety, the divine Mind offers hope, peace, and abiding security. When Joseph found out that his betrothed was with child, he was distressed. He was an upright man who was unwilling to expose Mary to the Law or else she would have been stoned to death. So he made the decision to divorce her quietly. Matthew 1:20-21 tells us that *"the angel of the Lord appeared to him in a dream and said, "Joseph, son of David, do not be afraid to take Mary your wife into your home. For it is through the holy Spirit that this child has been conceived in her. She will bear a son and you are to name him Jesus, because he will save his people from their sins."* When Joseph awoke, he did exactly as the angel had directed him and received her into his home as his wife. His doubts were cleared away by the power and reassurance of the Holy Spirit. Henceforth, Joseph was totally committed to his wife, Mary, and their son, Jesus.

MARY'S PARTICIPATION IN HER SON'S KENOSIS:

True to her description of herself, throughout her life Mary was 'the handmaid of the Lord.' The birth of Jesus took place under very unusual and difficult circumstances: *"And she gave birth to her firstborn son. She wrapped him in swaddling clothes and laid him in a manger, because there was no room for them in the inn."* (Luke 2:7) Mary and Joseph accepted this challenge with humility and serenity. Then shepherds came to visit the 'Son of the Most High.' They said that they were visited by an angel who gave them the good news that *"a savior has been born for you who is Messiah and Lord."* (Luke 2:11) This visit was very significant, as the harbinger of good news was an angel. Shepherds had an unsavory reputation in the First Century. God's ways are very different from the ways of human logic: *"And Mary kept all these things, reflecting on them in her heart. Then the shepherds returned, glorifying and praising God for all they had heard and seen, just as it had been told to them."* (Luke 2:19-20)

The Presentation of Jesus in the temple was supposed to be a joyful event for Mary and Joseph. They had come to the temple to fulfill their religious obligations: *"They came to offer the sacrifice of "a pair of turtledoves or two young pigeons," in accordance with the dictate in the law of the Lord."* (Luke 2:24) Simeon had been told by the Holy Spirit that he would not experience death until he had seen the Anointed of the Lord. Accordingly he was led to Mary and Joseph and took the child in his arms, and blessed God for displaying *"a light for revelation to the Gentiles, and glory for your people Israel."* Then he changed the tone of his message: *"Behold, this child is destined for the fall and rise of many in Israel, and to be a sign that will be contradicted (and you yourself a sword will pierce) so that the thoughts of many hearts may be revealed."* (Luke 2:34-35)

One can speculate on the kind of foreboding and uncertainty such a prophecy caused in Mary. As if to fulfill this prophecy as soon as possible, a few days later Herod issued an edict to kill all male children two years old and younger, because he realized that the astrologers had ignored his bidding to let him know about this 'new-born king.' In the dark of night, Mary and Joseph had to make a hasty and desperate retreat from the vicinity of Jerusalem into Egypt: *"The angel of the Lord appeared to Joseph in a dream and said, "Rise, take the child and his mother, flee to Egypt, and stay there until I tell you. Herod is going to search for the child to destroy him."* (Matthew 2:13). In anxious haste and fear, Joseph and Mary made speedy preparations to flee the vicinity of Jerusalem into Egypt so that they could protect their child. In a paradoxical way, Mary experienced the fulfillment of her prayer: *"He has thrown down the rulers from their thrones but lifted up the lowly."* The mighty Herod's plans were thwarted by lowly strangers in his tetrarchy.

A final event relating to Jesus' childhood took place when He was twelve years old. The family had gone to Jerusalem to celebrate the feast of Passover. The child Jesus stayed behind, unknown to His parents who were on their journey home. They traveled for a day thinking that Jesus was among the relatives. When Mary and Joseph realized that Jesus was missing, they returned to Jerusalem in search of Him. When His parents found Him, Jesus was sitting in the midst of the teachers, listening to them and asking them questions. His listeners were all amazed at His intelligence and answers. When His parents questioned Jesus, they were astonished at His answer. *"His mother said to him, 'Son, why have you done this to us? Your father and I have been looking for you with great anxiety.'"* (Luke 2: 48) This is one of many occasions when Jesus' divinity is hidden, and His answer seems strange to human logic. And in this instance, His answer goes beyond the grasp of His parents: *"Why were you looking for me? Did you not know that I must be in my Father's house?"* (Luke 2:49)

The darkness of this kenotic experience is slightly ameliorated by the comment made by Luke in 2:51: *"He went down with them and came to Nazareth, and was obedient to them; and his mother kept all these things in her heart."* How was Jesus to explain to His mother that obedience to His Father's will did supersede obedience to His mother's? That she was the handmaid of the Lord, and would accept the Father's Will, even when she could not comprehend it? Jesus trusted that His mother would accept in faith and trust what did not make sense to her human mind. No matter what, Mary would ponder these events, and choose to be the handmaid of the Lord.

MARY'S PARTICIPATION IN HER SON'S PASSION AND DEATH:

Mary's participation in her Son's kenosis is especially evident during Jesus' passion and death. Except for John who mentions Mary's presence at the foot of the cross, no other evangelist makes mention of her during Jesus' passion and death. John tells us that Mary was present at her son's crucifixion (John 19:25-27). If Mary was present at the foot of the cross witnessing her son's slow and excruciating death, she must have been present all during His passion leading up to His death. It was heart-rending to see how her son was mistreated and made out to be a criminal. The blasphemous cries of the crowd, 'Crucify him,' and 'Give us Barabbas' must have been like sharp barbs piercing her heart. She probably remembered Simeon's prophecy again and again. On the journey to Calvary she was aghast at seeing Him fall repeatedly. She was greatly relieved when Simon of Cyrene helped her son carry His cross. While she did not have any opportunity to speak to her son and console Him along His way to the cross, being the handmaid of the Lord, her heart was in sync with her son's steadfast commitment to His Father's will: to die to sin in our stead so that we could experience new life in Him. Finally they have arrived at Calvary, and Mary beholds the cruel horror of His nailing and hanging on the Cross. Her pain is excruciating beyond words. In silence she communicates with her Son and unites with Him in doing His Father's will for our salvation.

In a final act of love, before He surrendered His life to His Father, Jesus engages in an amazing act of covenant love and union. He bequeaths to His mother a special mission, in fact, the continuation of the same mission that was given to her at the Annunciation: to be the mother of 'the Son of the Most High' in His covenant family, with whom He has become one, and symbolized by John the beloved disciple. And in handing His mother to the safe-keeping of His beloved disciple, Jesus was asking His covenant family to always accord her a special place of honor and reverence in our hearts, similar to the honor and reverence He always had for her. This has been the Church's understanding of the special connection between Mary, Mother of God, and God's Church, also known as God's covenant family. If the Holy Spirit were to offer us a window into their hearts at this moment, we would see how deeply they loved each other, and how truly united they were in mind, heart, and spirit with the will of the Father that the world be saved through His Son and hers, Jesus Christ.

MARY'S PARTICIPATION IN HER SON'S RESURRECTION:

The gospels are silent about Mary's presence during the forty days when the Risen Lord was among His disciples prior to His Ascension and at Pentecost. Similarly, whenever Jesus appeared to His disciples, no explicit mention is made of her. We can presume that if Mary were present at the crucifixion, she was also present with John, her care-taker, and the other disciples of Jesus, when they were assembled in the Upper Room. In 'The Acts of the Apostles', Luke makes mention of the fact that Mary was with the community of disciples as they awaited the outpouring of the Holy Spirit after Jesus' Ascension: *"All these devoted themselves with one accord to prayer, together with some women, and Mary the mother Jesus, and his brothers."* (Acts 1:14) Hence and very fittingly, she was present when her Risen Son appeared in their midst. St. Ignatius of Loyola carries on a long standing Church tradition in the Fourth Week of the Spiritual Exercises that focuses on the Resurrection events. St. Ignatius offers the first apparition of the Risen Jesus as being to His mother. St. Francis of Assisi is of the same mind as St. Ignatius.

In her Risen Son and Lord, Mary finally saw the fulfillment of God's Plan of Salvation, and how all of her life made sense in the divine scheme, and her role as His handmaid was indeed her calling. God had chosen Mary to give birth to His Son, so that through our humanity, Jesus could become the Lamb that was slain for our sins, to wash us white in His blood. Through our humanity, Jesus could become our Savior, and offer us His own body as our food, and His blood as our drink, so that we could become what we receive! Indeed, Mary, the handmaid of the Lord, was chosen by our heavenly Father to play a very significant role in the redemption of humanity through His and her Son, Jesus Christ. She is the Father's daughter, the Son's mother, and the Holy Spirit's bride! She is the new Eve, our worthy representative! She is truly the greatest disciple God could have raised from among us, characterized by total obedience to the Father's will, along with her Son's obedience to His heavenly Father!

THE CHURCH'S APPRECIATION OF MARY:

In her understanding and appreciation of God's perspective on Mary, the Church has always believed in the Assumption of the Blessed Virgin Mary, long before it was declared a dogma of the Church. St. John of Damascus (Born A.D. 676), formulates the tradition of the Church of Jerusalem in this way: *"St. Juvenal, Bishop of Jerusalem, at the Council of Chalcedon (451), made known to the Emperor Marcian and Pulcheria, who wished to possess the body of the Mother of God, that Mary died in the presence of all the Apostles, but that her tomb, when opened, upon the request of St. Thomas, was found empty; wherefrom the Apostles concluded that the body was taken up to heaven."*

By promulgating the Bull, 'Munificentissimus Deus' on November 1, 1950, Pope Pius XII declared infallibly that the Assumption of the Blessed Virgin Mary was a dogma of the Catholic Faith. Very painstakingly Pope Pius XII cites the Fathers of the Church and many saints and bishops who believed in the Assumption of the Blessed Virgin Mary over twenty centuries: *"Various testimonies, indications and signs of this common belief of the Church are evident from remote times down through the course of the centuries; and this same belief becomes more clearly manifest from day to day."* (13) Pope Pius XII also cites examples of holy writers through the centuries who *"employed statements and various images and analogies of Sacred Scripture to illustrate and to confirm the doctrine of the Assumption."* (29) St. Robert Bellarmine, (born 1542, died 1621), was a Jesuit and cardinal. He was one of the most important figures of the Counter-Reformation. He gathered together the testimonies of the Christians of earlier days in the following statement: *"And who, I ask, could believe that the ark of holiness, the dwelling place of the Word of God, the temple of the Holy Spirit, could be reduced to ruin? My soul is filled with horror at the thought that this virginal flesh which had begotten God, had brought him into the world, had nourished and carried him, could have been turned into ashes or given over to be food for worms."* (34) Likewise, the Second Vatican Council taught in the Dogmatic Constitution Lumen Gentium that *"the Immaculate Virgin, preserved free from all stain of original sin, was taken up body and soul into heavenly glory, when her earthly life was over, and exalted by the Lord as Queen over all things."* (59)

Scripture offers compelling evidence for the Assumption of Mary. Luke uses the same word *episkiasei*, when at the Annunciation the angel said that the power of the Most High would descend upon Mary. The same word is used to describe the power of the Most High overshadowing the tent of meeting which held the Ark of the Covenant in the desert: *"Then the cloud covered the tent of meeting, and the glory of the LORD filled the tabernacle."* (Exodus 40: 34) The same word is used as well when Solomon dedicated the temple and God made his abode in it: *"When the priests left the holy place, the cloud filled the house of the LORD so that the priests could no longer minister because of the cloud, since the glory of the LORD had filled the house of the LORD."* (1 Kings 8: 10-11). At the conception of Jesus in Mary's womb, the Father and Holy Spirit are intimately involved in the Trinity's most solemn decision to bring us back into Trinitarian covenant, through Jesus. Mary is then seen as the Ark of the Covenant.

In the Old Testament, Jeremiah the prophet hid the Ark of the Covenant before the temple was destroyed in 587 B.C.: *"The prophet (Jeremiah), in virtue of an oracle, ordered that the tent and the ark should accompany him, and how he went to the very mountain that Moses climbed to behold God's inheritance. When Jeremiah arrived there, he found a chamber in a cave in which he put the tent, the ark, and the altar of incense; then he sealed the entrance. Some of those who followed him came up intending to mark the path, but they could not find it. When Jeremiah heard of this, he reproved them: "The place is to remain unknown until God gathers his people together again and shows them mercy. Then the Lord will disclose these things, and the glory of the Lord and the cloud will be seen, just as they appeared in the time of Moses and of Solomon when he prayed that the place might be greatly sanctified."* (2 Maccabees 2:4-8)

In the Book of Revelation, John talks about the fulfillment of Jeremiah's prophecy. In Revelation 11:19, the last verse of the chapter, John tells us the following: *"Then God's temple in heaven was opened, and the ark of the covenant could be seen in the temple. There were flashes of lightning, rumblings, and peals of thunder, an earthquake, and a violent hailstorm."* This verse concluded the passage on the Seventh Trumpet which proclaims the coming of God's reign after the victory over diabolical powers. The flashes of lightning, rumblings, etc., symbolize the glory of the Lord descending upon the heavenly temple where the Risen Lord upon his ascension, dwells with His Father. To his utter amazement, John discovers the Ark of the Covenant, which had disappeared for more than 600 hundred years.

In Revelation 12, John tells us that the Ark of the Covenant is the woman, clothed with the sun, whose child who is destined to rule the world: *"A great sign appeared in the sky, a woman clothed with the sun, with the moon under her feet, and on her head a crown of twelve stars. She was with child and wailed aloud in pain as she labored to give birth. Then another sign appeared in the sky; it was a huge dragon... Then the dragon stood before the woman about to give birth, to devour her child when she gave birth. She gave birth to a son, a male child, destined to rule all the nations with an iron rod. Her child was caught up to God and his throne."* (Revelation 12:1-5) This is one of the readings during the Liturgy of the Word on the Feast of the Assumption. Mary has been understood to be the woman, and her child is obviously Jesus who has ascended to His Father. In the Assumption, the Church states that Mary is the Ark of the new and everlasting Covenant in Jesus. The Assumption of the Blessed Virgin Mary is a singular participation in her Son's Resurrection and an anticipation of the resurrection of other Christians.

WHAT IS AT THE HEART OF DEVOTION TO MARY?

Through His death on the cross, Jesus established the new and eternal covenant. In doing so, He returned us to His Father. We have become adopted sons and daughters of God. We share Son-ship in the Son, and address Jesus' Father as Our Father. On the cross, just before He died, Jesus gave us the enormous implications of creating His covenant family through a simple and moving gesture. He asked His mother to take John as her son, and requested John to take Mary as his mother (John 19:26-27). Through this gesture Jesus was addressing the identification that He had made with His covenant family. He had become one with it, as represented by John. His mother was to continue to be His mother in His covenant family. Her mission remained the same, given to her at the Annunciation. Only now, she would serve the Son of God in His covenant family. And Jesus commissioned us to love and honor Mary, His mother, in the same way He did.

Over 20 centuries, Mary has appeared to her children in various parts of the world. We are very familiar with her apparitions in Lourdes, Fatima, and Mexico City. In all her apparitions, the message has always been the same: repent of your sins, accept Jesus as your Lord and Savior, believe in the gospel, and pray for the world. Furthermore, in all of these apparitions, the spotlight has always been on Jesus as the Savior of the world. She has remained the handmaid of the Lord.

If you then look at the various Marian devotions, the same emphasis is apparent: Mary is always pointing her children towards Jesus and through Him to the Heavenly Father in the power of the Holy Spirit. The Rosary focuses on the various mysteries of Jesus' life and public ministry. If you have prayed the Rosary consistently, you will have realized how discipleship is best lived out through Mary's own participation and covenant self-offering in the events of her son's life. Like Jesus, Mary was always obedient to the Father's will. Like Jesus, Mary suffered intensely with her son, emptying herself and going through her own passion, in support of her son's mission on earth as Savior and Lord.

Once again, if you examine the 'Hail Mary,' the 'Hail Holy Queen,' and the 'Remember' Prayers, you will notice that we intercede with Mary so that she will bring her intercession on our behalf to her son, through whom alone our prayers can go to the Father. She does for us what she did at the marriage feast at Cana. She does what every mother would do. In loving and caring for us she is caring for and loving Jesus, her son and the Son of God. Incidentally, Jesus as the Lamb of God always does His intercession with the Father on our behalf, surrounded by His covenant family of angels and saints, and Mary is indeed a very distinguished member of His covenant family and ours! Mary, Mother of God, pray for us!

BIBLIOGRAPHY

PRESCRIBED READING:

ANOINT US IN YOUR COVENANT, ABBA-EMMANUEL
THE IMITATION OF CHRIST
THE BIBLE
THE CATECHISM OF THE CATHOLIC CHURCH

RECOMMENDED READINGS:

THE PRAYER OF FAITH BY LEONARD BOASE, S.J.
WHEN THE WELL RUNS DRY BY THOMAS GREEN, S.J.
NEW SEEDS OF CONTEMPLATION BY THOMAS MERTON
JOHN OF THE CROSS FOR TODAY: THE ASCENT BY SUSAN MUTO
JOHN OF THE CROSS FOR TODAY: THE DARK NIGHT BY SUSAN MUTO
FIRE WITHIN BY THOMAS DUBAY, S.M.
THE CLOUD OF UNKNOWING BY ANONYMOUS AUTHOR
THE BOOK OF HER LIFE BY ST. TERESA OF AVILA
THE WAY OF PERFECTION BY ST. TERESA OF AVILA
THE INTERIOR CASTLE BY ST. TERESA OF AVILA
THE ASCENT OF MOUNT CARMEL BY ST. JOHN OF THE CROSS
THE DARK NIGHT BY ST. JOHN OF THE CROSS
THE SPIRITUAL CANTICLE BY ST. JOHN OF THE CROSS
THE LIVING FLAME OF LOVE BY ST. JOHN OF THE CROSS

QUICK REFERENCE GUIDE

Week Thirty: "I know someone in Christ who, fourteen years ago (whether in the body or out of the body I do not know, God knows), was caught up to the third heaven. And I know that this person (whether in the body or out of the body I do not know, God knows) was caught up into paradise and heart ineffable things, which no one may utter." (2 Corinthians 12:2-4)   **385**

SPIRITUAL READINGS INDEX

Made in the USA
Columbia, SC
05 August 2022

64465173R00263